Education 88/89

Editor

Fred Schultz

The University of Akron

Fred Schultz, professor of education at The University of Akron, attended Indiana University to earn a B.S. in social science education in 1962, an M.S. in the history and philosophy of education in 1966, and a Ph.D. in the history and philosophy of education and American studies in 1969. His B.A. in Spanish was conferred from the University of Akron in May 1985. He is actively involved in researching the development and history of American education.

Annual Editions
A Library of Information from the Public Press

Cover illustration by Mike Eagle

The Dushkin Publishing Group, Inc.
Sluice Dock, Guilford, Connecticut 06437

The Annual Editions Series

Annual Editions is a series of over forty volumes designed to provide the reader with convenient, low-cost access to a wide range of current, carefully selected articles from some of the most important magazines, newspapers, and journals published today. Annual Editions are updated on an annual basis through a continuous monitoring of over 200 periodical sources. All Annual Editions have a number of features designed to make them particularly useful, including topic guides, annotated tables of contents, unit overviews, and indexes. For the teacher using Annual Editions in the classroom, an Instructor's Resource Guide with test questions is available for each volume.

VOLUMES AVAILABLE

Africa
Aging
American Government
American History, Pre-Civil War
American History, Post-Civil War
Anthropology
Biology
Business and Management
China
Comparative Politics
Computers in Education
Computers in Business
Computers in Society
Criminal Justice
Drugs, Society, and Behavior
Early Childhood Education
Economics
Educating Exceptional Children
Education
Educational Psychology
Environment
Geography
Global Issues
Health

Human Development
Human Sexuality
Latin America
Macroeconomics
Marketing
Marriage and Family
Middle East and the Islamic World
Nutrition
Personal Growth and Behavior
Psychology
Social Problems
Sociology
Soviet Union and Eastern Europe
State and Local Government
Third World
Urban Society
Western Civilization,
   Pre-Reformation
Western Civilization,
   Post-Reformation
Western Europe
World History, Pre-Modern
World History, Modern
World Politics

Library of Congress Cataloging in Publication Data
Main entry under title: Annual editions: Education.
  1. Education—Addresses, essays, lectures. I. Title: Education.
LB41.A673   370'.5   73-78580
ISBN 0-87967-714-7

Fifteenth Edition

Manufactured by The Banta Company, Harrisonburg, Virginia 22801

Editors/ Advisory Board

EDITOR

Fred Schultz
University of Akron

Members of the Advisory Board are instrumental in the final selection of articles for each edition of Annual Editions. Their review of articles for content, level, currency, and appropriateness provides critical direction to the editor and staff. We think you'll find their careful consideration well reflected in this volume.

ADVISORY BOARD

L. Ross Blythe
Purdue University, North Central

Walter Cass
Southeastern Massachusetts University

Anthony DeFalco
C.W. Post Center,
Long Island University

Lloyd Duck
George Mason University

Robert V. Farrell
Florida International University

William Goetter
Eastern Washington University

Joe Kelly
University of Idaho

Joe L. Kincheloe
Louisiana State University,
Shreveport

Walter H. Klar
Framingham State College

Lawrence Klein
Central Connecticut State University

Gertrude Langsam
Adelphi University

Margaret A. Laughlin
University of Wisconsin,
Green Bay

John McDermott
Moravian College

Joseph Newman
University of South Alabama

James Wm. Noll
University of Maryland,
College Park

Joseph Peyser
Indiana University,
South Bend

Max L. Ruhl
Northwest Missouri State University

Warren Strandberg
Virginia Commonwealth University

STAFF

Rick Connelly, Publisher
Ian A. Nielsen, Program Manager
Celeste Borg, Editor
Addie Kawula, Administrative Editor
Brenda S. Filley, Production Manager
Cheryl Nicholas, Permissions Editor
Charles Vitelli, Designer
Jean Bailey, Graphics Coordinator
Lynn Shannon, Graphics
Libra A. Cusack, Typesetting Coordinator
Diane Barker, Editorial Assistant

To The Reader

In publishing ANNUAL EDITIONS we recognize the enormous role played by the magazines, newspapers, and journals of the *public press* in providing current, first-rate educational information in a broad spectrum of interest areas. Within the articles, the best scientists, practitioners, researchers, and commentators draw issues into new perspective as accepted theories and viewpoints are called into account by new events, recent discoveries change old facts, and fresh debate breaks out over important controversies.

Many of the articles resulting from this enormous editorial effort are appropriate for students, researchers, and professionals seeking accurate, current material to help bridge the gap between principles and theories and the real world. These articles, however, become more useful for study when those of lasting value are carefully *collected, organized, indexed,* and *reproduced* in a *low-cost format*, which provides easy and permanent access when the material is needed. That is the role played by *Annual Editions*. Under the direction of each volume's *Editor*, who is an expert in the subject area, and with the guidance of an *Advisory Board*, we seek each year to provide in each *ANNUAL EDITION* a current, well-balanced, carefully selected collection of the best of the public press for your study and enjoyment. We think you'll find this volume useful, and we hope you'll take a moment to let us know what you think.

The winds of change and redesign are shifting over North America's educational system. This fifteenth edition of *Annual Editions: Education 88/89* reflects on issues facing North American students, families, and professionals at the end of the 1980s. Historic shifts in public and professional priorities regarding the future of schooling and the profession of teaching have occurred in this decade. This edition includes new material which renews the historical context of educational change on this continent in greater detail. Comparative and historical insights share attention with interesting examples of current innovative practice applications of curricula in the schools. The essays selected also consider the concerns of teachers, parents, students, and teacher educators as well as the views of journalists, public policy makers, and the general trade press regarding the state of schools. Other selections reflect the multiplicity of perceptions regarding both the direction and the quality of schooling in North America. Equity agenda issues are examined, and reform in teacher education receives renewed, intensive consideration. The volume continues to address the recommendations of the major reform reports on how the preparation of teachers might be altered. The humanization of teaching and learning is explored in sections which deal with special needs, change, and the future of schooling. The full range of competency recommendations for teachers is again considered in some truly outstanding essays by Michael W. Sedlak, Walter Feinberg, Linda Darling-Hammond, and others. The pressing human resource needs facing the teaching profession at the end of the 1980s are examined. In addition, censorship issues are introduced in the essays on the equity agenda because of renewed efforts by some public interest groups to impact on what is taught or learned in schools. The struggle for freedom to teach and freedom to learn is still with us.

The signs of tension, critical dialogue, and debate are clearly evident all across the continent. The renaissance in the historical reassessment of the North American experience in education, which has been under way since 1960, continues. Never has there been a more exciting or challenging time to be involved in the educational system. Great opportunities, as well as great challenges to human and economic resources, are open to everyone. The revisionist critiques of American history in the field of education continue to develop from different ideological perspectives. The interpretation of the historical bases of the present crises or reform rhetoric in the current literature on education is furthering the development of broader and more accurate perspectives on which to base educational policy decisions. The quality of professional dialogue has been uplifted as educators reassess their goals and values. More balanced, mature, and incisive analyses of how the situation today compares or contrasts with other crises in the educational past contribute valuable information about problems that may stand in the way of progress in educational development.

Every effort is made to stay in touch with movements in educational studies and with the social forces at work in the schools. Members of the Advisory Board contribute valuable insights into this effort, while the production and editorial staff at the Dushkin Publishing Group coordinates it. Through this process we collect a wide range of articles on a variety of topics relevant to education in the United States and Canada.

Each selection must meet basic criteria. An article must address at least one major issue in education which concerns those who work in the educational system or those who are served by the system. In addition, articles in the volume should provide a general overview of the topics which they address. Economic and political forces, forces or pressures in the educational system itself, and government policy makers all affect the formation of the national agenda for debate regarding educational policy issues. The dialogue among those who represent these forces contributes to the depth and intensity of educational debate. All of these factors are considered in determining the relevance of material for inclusion in the volume.

Nine units explore and appraise current controversy regarding the adequacy of goals, policies, and programming in education, the condition of education, the reform movement and the struggle for excellence in education, controversies surrounding commission and individual reports on the quality of schooling, alternatives in educational development, morality in education, discipline problems in schools, equality of opportunity in the field of education, special educational needs, the profession of teaching today, and the future of North American education.

We are always interested in improving the quality of each *Annual Edition*. Let us know your opinions of the book and your views on what can be done to improve it by filling out the article rating form on the last page of the volume. We will sincerely try to respond to your concerns.

Fred Schultz

Fred Schultz

Editor

Contents

Unit 1

Perceptions of Education in America

Five articles examine the present state of education in America. The topics covered include school reform, relationships between families and schools, the future of teaching, and the current public opinion on public schools.

Unit 2

Continuity and Change in Education

Seven selections discuss the effects of technological change, equal opportunity, and the reorganization of school programs on current American education.

To the Reader iv
Topic Guide 2
Overview 4

1. **Schools: Cacophony About Practice, Silence About Purpose,** Patricia Albjerg Graham, *Daedalus,* Fall 1984. 6
   Patricia Albjerg Graham argues that educators must abandon the tired vestiges of **progressive education** and articulate clear purposes for American education. She offers an informative commentary on the evolution of American education since World War II.

2. **Learning from Experience: History and Teacher Education,** Donald Warren, *Educational Researcher,* December 1985. 15
   Donald Warren provides an illuminating overview of the **history of teacher education** in the United States. He poses his argument in the context of the current debate over the **reform of teacher education**.

3. **The Prospect for Children in the United States,** Harold Howe II, *Phi Delta Kappan,* November 1986. 22
   Harold Howe II calls for greater national efforts to meet the needs and interests of **children**—needs that are losing ground to the many issues surrounding adult life. He blames changing national political and economic priorities for the decline in national concern for the educational needs of children and suggests the implementation of a new national coalition of interests to address children's needs.

4. **Professional Credibility Through Wider Links,** David S. Martin, *Educational Horizons,* Winter 1987. 28
   David Martin proposes an agenda for the **reform of** preservice and inservice **teacher education**. He also discusses how teachers might develop deeper and broader links with local communities.

5. **The 19th Annual Gallup Poll of the Public's Attitudes Toward the Public Schools,** Alec M. Gallup and David L. Clark, *Phi Delta Kappan,* September 1987. 32
   The Gallup organization's current survey of American **public opinion** toward American public schools considers several key dilemmas facing the educational system.

Overview 42

6. **An Inside View of Change in Schools,** Eugene Eubanks and Ralph Parish, *Phi Delta Kappan,* April 1987. 44
   Eugene Eubanks and Ralph Parish offer several interesting insights into the process of **inservice professional development** based on their own experiences regarding professional growth and how schools can **change**.

7. **The Business of Talentville,** Gretchen Haight, *Across the Board,* September 1986. 49
   Gretchen Haight describes an exciting way to help children learn important basic **economic concepts**. Marilyn Kourilsky's approach to economic education is an excellent example of how to involve students in classroom activities which lead to development of important attitudes and conceptual understanding.

The concepts in bold italics are developed in the article. For further expansion please refer to the Topic Guide and the Index.

8. **A Good School,** Diane Ravitch, *The American Scholar,* 55
Autumn 1984..

Diane Ravitch gives an in-depth description of efforts to achieve academic *excellence* in all schools. She relates what she observed at the Edward R. Murrow High School in Brooklyn, New York.

9. **Helping Preservice Teachers Learn to Use Teacher** 61
Effectiveness Research, Dorene Doerre Ross and Diane
Wells Kyle, *Journal of Teacher Education,* March/April 1987.

The authors provide their opinion of what *teacher effectiveness training* is about. They also include an excellent list of sources on the topic.

10. **Should Four-Year Education Major Be Ended?** Bernard 66
R. Gifford and Willis D. Hawley, *The Christian Science Monitor,* August 5, 1986.

Bernard R. Gifford and Willis D. Hawley debate the issue of extending the period of *training for prospective teachers*.

11. **Education Reform in China,** Austin D. Swanson and Zhang 68
Zhian, *Phi Delta Kappan,* January 1987.

The authors summarize major *changes* in the organization and governance of *Chinese education*, which is the result of the seventh Five-Year Plan now underway in the People's Republic of China.

12. **Learning About Education from Fifth Graders in Japan,** 74
Rushworth M. Kidder, *The Christian Science Monitor,* April 6, 1987.

This account of the daily rigors of *school life in Japan* provides an interesting contrast to life in American schools.

Overview 76
13. **Changing Our Thinking About Educational Change,** J. 78
Myron Atkin, *The World & I,* March 1986.

J. Myron Atkin assesses the problems concerning *school reform* in the 1980s. He discusses the *economic, political,* and *educational forces* involved in current efforts to improve schools and *teacher education.* He cautions against the implementation of some *reforms* such as *mainstreaming, individualized instruction,* and *bilingual education.*

14. **School Reform: Recent Influences,** Franklin Parker, 84
National Forum, Summer 1987.

Franklin Parker provides a direct, pointed summary of some of the key issues involved in current *reform* efforts in American education.

Unit 3

The Struggle for Excellence: The Drive for Quality and Reform

Four articles discuss the current aims for excellence in American education. Topics include problems concerning school reform, teacher preparation, and competency testing.

The concepts in bold italics are developed in the article. For further expansion please refer to the Topic Guide and the Index.

15. **Tomorrow's Teachers: The Essential Arguments of the Holmes Group Report,** Michael W. Sedlak, *Teachers College Record,* Spring 1987. 86

    Michael W. Sedlak synthesizes the basic recommendations of this important and controversial document. As one of the authors of this report on the **reform of teacher education**, he is able to provide a clear view of the contents and purposes of this report.

16. **The Holmes Group Report and the Professionalization of Teaching,** Walter Feinberg, *Teachers College Record,* Spring 1987. 92

    Walter Feinberg examines the recommendations of the Holmes Group report. His analysis is clear, constructive, and helpful. He addresses the issues involved in efforts to create a new vision of the **teaching profession**, and he situates his arguments in their historical, social, and economic contexts.

Unit 4

Morality and Values in Education

Four articles examine the role of American schools in teaching morality and social values.

Overview 98

17. **Repairing the Public-Private Split: Excellence, Character, and Civic Virtue,** Robert J. Nash and Robert S. Griffin, *Teachers College Record,* Summer 1987. 100

    The authors offer a historically insightful, well-documented, and urbane view of the issues most basic to the development of **civic character and virtue** in a modern nation state. This essay includes a discussion of the relationships between politics and religion in the civic life of North American society.

18. **Moral Education in the United States,** Franklin Parker, *The Education Digest,* April 1986. 108

    Franklin Parker reviews some major turning points in the history of **moral education** in the United States.

19. **Ethics Without Virtue: Moral Education in America,** Christina Hoff Sommers, *The American Scholar,* Summer 1984. 111

    The author examines the controversy over the teaching of **values clarification** and **moral education** in public schools. She critiques the values clarification and Kohlberg approaches to moral education and presents some major issues in the debate over what forms of moral education ought to be permitted in the schools.

20. **The Treatment of Religion in School Textbooks: A Political Analysis and a Modest Proposal,** John W. McDermott Jr., *Religion and Public Education,* Fall 1986. 119

    The author examines the controversy surrounding the issue of how **religion** ought to be considered in text materials and school curricula.

The concepts in bold italics are developed in the article. For further expansion please refer to the Topic Guide and the Index.

Unit 5

Discipline and Schooling

Three articles consider the necessity of judicious and effective discipline in the American classroom today.

Overview   126

21. **Research Evidence of a School Discipline Problem,** Keith Baker, *Phi Delta Kappan,* March 1985.   128

Keith Baker reviews data from federal research projects on the severity of *discipline problems* in American schools. He discusses ways to secure the safety of those who must work and learn in the schools.

22. **Punishment or Guidance?** Dan Gartrell, *Young Children,* March 1987.   135

This essay discusses *guidance* styles of teacher-student interaction which can go a long way toward countering more punitive approaches to *discipline* in classrooms.

23. **Help for the Hot-Tempered Kid,** Michael Petti, *Instructor,* March 1986.   140

Persons who are concerned with learning more about *discipline* or *classroom management* will find that this article summarizes many practical strategies for the management of student anger. It is applicable to day-to-day life in schools.

Unit 6

Equal Opportunity and American Education

Five articles discuss the current state of equality and opportunity in the American educational system. Educational policies, the history of school desegregation, as well as the long-term effects of school desegregation are some of the topics considered.

Overview   142

24. **The Courts and Education,** Thomas R. Ascik, *The World & I,* March 1986.   144

Thomas R. Ascik has synthesized the role of the US Supreme Court in interpreting the constitutionality of selected educational policies from 1833 to the mid-1980s. This is a most valuable contribution to the literature on *equality of opportunity*, the *rights of students*, *academic freedom for teachers*, and *church and state relations* in the field of education.

25. **Are You Sensitive to Interracial Children's Special Identity Needs?** Francis Wardle, *Young Children,* January 1987.   152

Children of interracial background have special identity needs which schools often do not address adequately. They need the opportunity to learn about both of their cultural heritages. The article includes a good list of sources.

The concepts in bold italics are developed in the article. For further expansion please refer to the Topic Guide and the Index.

Unit
7

Serving Special Needs and Humanizing Instruction

Four selections examine some of the important aspects of special educational needs: mainstreaming, self-esteem, child abuse, and drug problems.

26. **The Bilingual Education Battle,** Cynthia Gorney, *The Washington Post National Weekly Edition,* July 29, 1985.   **158**

    Cynthia Gorney takes a comprehensive look at the controversy over *bilingual education*. She traces the origins of bilingual education in the United States and provides in-depth coverage of the problems surrounding its implementation from the perspectives of teachers, parents, and students.

27. **Sexism in the Schoolroom of the '80s,** Myra Sadker and David Sadker, *Psychology Today,* March 1985.   **165**

    The authors discuss the continuing problem of *equality of opportunity* between boys and girls in classrooms. They point out that teachers often tend to pay more attention to boys than to girls and appear to be more helpful to boys than to girls. They call for greater sensitivity in the teaching profession to the importance of this issue.

28. **Censorship in the Public Schools,** Arnold B. Danzig, *Infospective,* Winter 1987.   **168**

    Arnold B. Danzig of the Arizona State Department of Education examines the controversy surrounding *censorship* in the schools and how *academic freedom* issues relating to censorship might be constructively negotiated.

Overview   **174**

29. **"Appropriate" School Programs: Legal vs. Educational Approaches,** Steven Carlson, *The Exceptional Parent,* September 1985.   **176**

    The author draws a distinction between "legally appropriate" and "educationally appropriate" learning environments for exceptional youth. The problems with *mainstreaming* youth who need *special education* programming are surveyed, the issue of educational effectiveness of such programming is addressed, and guidelines for special education are suggested.

30. **Self-Esteem Success Stories,** Patricia Berne, *Instructor,* February 1987.   **180**

    This is a positive article on ways to help young people improve their *self-concepts*. Five case studies are summarized to exemplify and emphasize the author's views on helping children to think well of themselves.

The concepts in bold italics are developed in the article. For further expansion please refer to the Topic Guide and the Index.

31. **Child Abuse and Neglect: Prevention and Reporting,** Barbara J. Meddin and Anita L. Rosen, *Young Children,* May 1986.   **184**
Many teachers express the need for more precise definitions of *abuse* and *neglect* as well as for specific strategies to follow in prevention, identification, and treatment. Specific indicators of neglect or abuse of children are clearly outlined by the authors.

32. **Schoolchildren and Drugs: The Fancy That Has Not Passed,** Richard A. Hawley, *Phi Delta Kappan,* May 1987.   **189**
Richard A. Hawley analyzes the current state of *drug use among American youth*. Chemical abuse among American youth greatly impacts on the day-to-day lives of teachers and students.

Unit 8

The Profession of Teaching Today

Four articles assess the current state of teaching in American schools. Topics include historical background on major teaching issues, teacher education, and what elements make an effective teacher.

Overview   **196**
33. **Our Profession, Our Schools: The Case for Fundamental Reform,** Albert Shanker, *American Educator,* Fall 1986.   **198**
Albert Shanker reviews current *educational reform* efforts in North America. He considers the needs of the teaching profession and the problems of implementing current recommendations.

34. **On Stir-and-Serve Recipes for Teaching,** Susan Ohanian, *Phi Delta Kappan,* June 1985.   **207**
Susan Ohanian discusses the problem with "freeze-dried, ready-made teachers." She describes the possible follies which can occur when evidence of knowledge of educational theory and pedagogical technique are overlooked in the rush to fill job openings in areas where there are critical teacher shortages. She offers some good suggestions to those involved in *teacher education*.

35. **Teaching Knowledge: How Do We Test It?** Linda Darling-Hammond, *American Educator,* Fall 1986.   **213**
Linda Darling-Hammond examines the problems of developing adequate measures of *competence in teaching*. Several important issues are raised, and deficiencies in current tests which attempt to measure teacher competency are highlighted.

36. **Relearning to Teach: Peer Observation as a Means of Professional Development,** Elizabeth Rorschach and Robert Whitney, *American Educator,* Winter 1986.   **217**
The authors explore the possibilities of *peer review* and *observation processes* as important and viable means through which inservice educators can achieve significant *professional growth*.

The concepts in bold italics are developed in the article. For further expansion please refer to the Topic Guide and the Index.

Unit 9

A Look to the Future

Four articles look at the future of education in American schools. Curricula for the future, demographic changes, and educational reform are considered.

Overview   **222**

37. Educating Children for the Coming Century, Edward Cornish, *The Education Digest,* October 1986.   **224**

Edward Cornish, founder and president of the World Future Society, reflects on **possible educational futures** for tomorrow's children. He predicts that we can expect some major shifts in the priorities of educational development in the not-too-distant future.

38. Schools of the Future, Marvin J. Cetron, Barbara Soriano, and Margaret Gayle, *The Futurist,* August 1985.   **226**

The authors fantasize about a school that embodies all or most of the recommendations for **educational reform** which have been suggested in recent studies on how to improve the **quality of schooling**. Demographic and economic factors which will affect the structure, content, and manner of schooling in the very near future are discussed.

39. Curriculum in the Year 2000: Tensions and Possibilities, Michael W. Apple, *Phi Delta Kappan,* January 1983.   **232**

Michael Apple focuses on the content and organization of curriculum and the process of decision making which shapes **curriculum development**. He predicts strong external pressures on the schools to develop curricula which conform to the demands of a changing society.

40. Will the Social Context Allow a Tomorrow for Tomorrow's Teachers? Michael W. Apple, *Teachers College Record,* Spring 1987.   **238**

Michael W. Apple discusses **future educational development** in North America. Responding to the Holmes Group report, he situates the current controversy over the **reform of teacher education** in its social, economic, and ideological contexts.

Index   **242**
Article Rating Form   **245**

The concepts in bold italics are developed in the article. For further expansion please refer to the Topic Guide and the Index.

Topic Guide

This topic guide suggests how the selections in this book relate to topics of traditional concern to education students and professionals. It is very useful in locating articles which relate to each other for reading and research. The guide is arranged alphabetically according to topic. Articles may, of course, treat topics that do not appear in the topic guide. In turn, entries in the topic guide do not necessarily constitute a comprehensive listing of all the contents of each selection.

TOPIC AREA	TREATED AS AN ISSUE IN:	TOPIC AREA	TREATED AS AN ISSUE IN:
Academic Freedom	28. Censorship in the Public Schools	Desegregation	24. The Courts and Education
Alternatives in Education	4. Professional Credibility Through Wider Links		25. Are You Sensitive to Interracial Children's Special Identity Needs?
	6. An Inside View of Change in Schools		26. The Bilingual Education Battle
	7. The Business of Talentville	Discipline in Schools	21. Research Evidence of a School Discipline Problem
	8. A Good School		22. Punishment or Guidance?
	9. Helping Preservice Teachers Learn to Use Teacher Effectiveness Research		23. Help for the Hot-Tempered Kid
	13. Changing Our Thinking About Educational Change	Economic Education	7. The Business of Talentville
Behavior Management	21. Research Evidence of a School Discipline Problem	Effective Teaching	9. Helping Preservice Teachers Learn to Use Teacher Effectiveness Research
	22. Punishment or Guidance?		
	23. Help for the Hot-Tempered Kid	Equality of Opportunity	24. The Courts and Education
Bilingual Education	26. The Bilingual Education Battle		25. Are You Sensitive to Interracial Children's Special Identity Needs?
Censorship	28. Censorship in the Public Schools		26. The Bilingual Education Battle
Child Abuse	31. Child Abuse and Neglect		27. Sexism in the Schoolroom of the '80s
Children's Lives	3. The Prospect for Children in the United States		28. Censorship in the Public Schools
	22. Punishment or Guidance?	Excellence	13. Changing Our Thinking About Educational Change
	23. Help for the Hot-Tempered Kid		14. School Reform
	30. Self-Esteem Success Stories		15. Tomorrow's Teachers
	31. Child Abuse and Neglect		16. The Holmes Group Report and the Professionalization of Teaching
Civic Education	17. Repairing the Public-Private Split	Families and Schools	3. The Prospect for Children in the United States
Collective Bargaining	33. Our Profession, Our Schools		12. Learning About Education from Fifth Graders in Japan
Comparative Education	11. Education Reform in China	Future of Education	37. Educating Children for the Coming Century
	12. Learning About Education from Fifth Graders in Japan		38. Schools of the Future
Competency Testing	35. Teaching Knowledge		39. Curriculum in the Year 2000
Courts and Education	24. The Courts and Education		40. Will the Social Context Allow a Tomorrow for Tomorrow's Teachers?
	26. The Bilingual Education Battle		
Counseling and Discipline	22. Punishment or Guidance?		

TOPIC AREA	TREATED AS AN ISSUE IN:	TOPIC AREA	TREATED AS AN ISSUE IN:
History of Education	1. Schools 2. Learning from Experience 15. Tomorrow's Teachers 16. The Holmes Group Report and the Professionalization of Teaching 20. The Treatment of Religion in School Textbooks	**Reform in Education**	13. Changing Our Thinking About Educational Change 14. School Reform: Recent Influences 15. Tomorrow's Teachers 16. The Holmes Group Report and the Professionalization of Teaching
Holmes Group	15. Tomorrow's Teachers 16. The Holmes Group Report and the Professionalization of Teaching 40. Will the Social Context Allow a Tomorrow for Tomorrow's Teachers?	**Religion and Schools**	20. The Treatment of Religion in School Textbooks
		Self-Esteem	30. Self-Esteem Success Stories
		Special Education	29. "Appropriate" School Programs
Homework	8. A Good School	**Student-Student Interaction**	12. Learning About Education from Fifth Graders in Japan 19. Ethics Without Virtue
Interracial Children	25. Are You Sensitive to Interracial Children's Special Identity Needs?	**Students' Rights**	3. The Prospect for Children in the United States 27. Sexism in the Schoolroom of the '80s 28. Censorship in the Public Schools
Kids and Drugs	32. Schoolchildren and Drugs		
Law and Schools	24. The Courts and Education 26. The Bilingual Education Battle 28. Censorship in the Public Schools		
Mainstreaming	29. "Appropriate" School Programs	**Teacher Education**	9. Helping Preservice Teachers Learn to Use Teacher Effectiveness Research 10. Should Four-Year Education Major Be Ended? 13. Changing Our Thinking About Educational Change 14. School Reform 15. Tomorrow's Teachers 16. The Holmes Group Report and the Professionalization of Teaching 33. Our Profession, Our Schools 34. On Stir-and-Serve Recipes for Teaching 35. Teaching Knowledge 40. Will the Social Context Allow a Tomorrow for Tomorrow's Teachers?
Moral Education	17. Repairing the Public-Private Split 18. Moral Education in the United States 19. Ethics Without Virtue 20. The Treatment of Religion in School Textbooks		
Peer Evaluation	36. Relearning to Teach		
Public Opinion	5. The 19th Annual Gallup Poll of the Public's Attitudes Toward the Public Schools		
Purposes of Education	1. Schools 2. Learning from Experience 13. Changing Our Thinking About Educational Change 40. Will the Social Context Allow a Tomorrow for Tomorrow's Teachers?	**Teaching as a Profession**	33. Our Profession, Our Schools 34. On Stir-and-Serve Recipes for Teaching 35. Teaching Knowledge: How Do We Test It? 36. Relearning to Teach

Perceptions of Education in America

This volume reflects continuing concern over the purposes and direction of the educational system. Ever since the beginning of the public school movement, there has been continuing dialogue among educators, the public, and their representatives in government over public expectations of schools. The perceptions of public and private schools are greatly affected by the evolution of new public demands and the resurrection of older ones. There is a need to place the public's perceptions of the purposes of schooling in the context of historical development. The articles selected for this unit open with two very insightful essays on the historical background of the goals of schools in general and the goals of teacher education in particular.

Perceptions of the content and direction of education run deep in the histories of both Canada and the United States. The formal educational institutions and the professional educators who serve them have been under critical examination at all levels of society. Many factors influence thought and opinion regarding education—individuals' experiences with schools; the economic and social circumstances in which people live; the relative success or failure of persons in their work careers, whether they work or study in or out of the educational system; the political climate of the times and the extent to which persons in government at the local, state, provincial, or federal levels choose to focus on educational issues and public policies affecting education; the impact of the opinions of prestigious private foundations, organizations, and individuals when they make recommendations for improving the quality of schooling or teaching as a profession; and the points of view and the manner of presentation of views on educational issues conveyed by the mass media. The interest of parents, students, teachers, school administrators, and those who must formulate and guide state or provincial educational policy all differ somewhat.

In *The Public and Its Problems* (1927), John Dewey expressed the complexity involved when different social groups in the same community had various interests and opinions regarding education. Today the issues facing schools are even more perplexing than those neglected, sublimated, and, for the most part, ignored in Dewey's time. Since 1983, individuals, commissions, and public and private think tanks have recommended changes in the methods used for preparing young people to become teachers. Other problems in the final years of the twentieth century include a serious and historic decline in the overall rate of secondary school completion in the United States, massive increases in teenage parenthood, and increasing levels of technological job displacement. Demands for more effective performance in meeting the educational requirements of minorities and women are increasing as are demands for overall improvement of the quality of schooling. Although there have been many changes and successes in recent years in the quality and effectiveness of schooling in some areas, the educational system has not always been successful in communicating these changes to the general public.

The primary emphasis of this unit is on the basic differences between myth and reality in public opinion about the schools. According to some writers, signs of qualitative improvement in schooling have been apparent in the last few years. Further, the many national reports and individual analyses of the effectiveness of the nation's schools have sparked intense self-examinations and critical reviews of existing school curricula among the beleaguered incumbents of state and provincial educational systems. Experts look forward to fundamentally significant changes in the content of schooling in the next fifteen years. These changes have already begun to develop in many areas. For instance, concern for a more scientific and technological knowledge base is evident, commitment to teaching basic literacy and computer literacy is strong, and the national certification of teachers in the United States has been adopted by the American Association of Colleges for Teacher Education (AACTE).

However, problems do remain. A national shortage of teachers is developing in many teaching areas. Prestigious research groups such as the Rand Corporation have predicted a major national teacher shortage in the next few years. There is a decrease in the number of persons entering the teaching profession at the same time that most states either already have or are developing plans for competency examinations for teachers. The educational reformers and the various commission and foundation reports on the state of the schools are calling for career ladders for teachers, more traditional subject matter orientations in the process of becoming certified as a teacher, and specific efforts to recruit more intelligent persons into a teaching career (for example, by offering them higher salaries). There is a fundamental tension in all of this. Many teachers believe that the authors of the various commission reports are not aware of the enormity of the problems they face daily in their classrooms. One such problem involves the family. Although it is recognized that the structures of North American families have changed, there are calls for more effective communication between families and schools as well as for a realization of the importance of reinforcing family values in schools.

While it is true that many teachers are discouraged by difficult teaching conditions, others are optimistic about the public's new awareness of the necessity of adequately rewarding good teachers for their efforts and of increasing the social prestige and status of teaching as a profession. Also, there is great hope in the vitality and courage of the young people who are preparing to become teachers. They are embracing the calls for change and reform in the educational system. They are bringing the gifts of idealism and youth to the task of improving the schools. We can take great pride in them.

Looking Ahead: Challenge Questions

Why is there so much talk about practice without sufficient clarification of the purposes of education?

What can we learn from the history of schooling?

What is the difference between myth and reality in American education? Have the public schools done anything right? If so, what? If not, why not?

What are the best ways to get a true portrait of the present state or condition of education?

How can families be more directly involved in the education of their children? What family values ought to be related to the activity of schooling? Is this possible? How could teachers better assist parents or guardians of students in the education of their children?

What are the characteristics and attitudes of future teachers toward educational change?

What are the major crises affecting American teachers today? How can teachers help themselves? How can the public help them?

What are the principal concerns of the general public regarding the quality of schooling today?

What is the functional effect of public opinion on national educational policy development?

What generalizations can you draw from the Gallup Poll data on public perceptions of the public schools?

Schools: Cacophony About Practice, Silence About Purpose

Patricia Albjerg Graham

WHY SHOULD WE EDUCATE? What are the benefits that individuals legitimately should expect from education? What are the benefits that society should expect from an educated citizenry? Are these benefits in conflict or are they mutually reinforcing? How can we achieve them?

Public purposes for education change as the society perceives its needs and priorities differently. Currently our old educational shibboleths have been rejected but new ones have not yet been accepted. The critique of contemporary educational processes is intense, but there is little articulate reformulation of either educational goals or of the means to achieve them.

Writing recently in the *New York Review of Books,* Andrew Hacker commented on the several commission reports and books that have appeared over the last year decrying the state of educational practice in American high schools.

At this point, all we can say with certainty is that no one really knows how far classroom education contributes to the kind of people we ultimately become. But if the schools leave a lot to be desired, the quality of educational commentary has declined even further. We no longer have commanding figures like John Dewey and Robert Hutchins, who, in their different ways, tried to create a vision of an educated citizenry whose members would have some chance at something that could be called the good life. That this goal, however nebulous, is all but absent from current books and reports is far more disconcerting than our lag in teaching algorithms to restless teenagers.[1]

Hacker is correct, I believe, in pointing to the recent dearth of educational commentary comparable to that of Dewey or Hutchins, but there surely has been no shortage of critiques. As Hacker himself observes, "Having been through the mill ourselves, we all feel entitled to expound on education. So, too, we believe that the schools belong to us, and hence we have the right to set them straight."[2]

Indeed, we do have a particularly strong feeling of ownership of our schools, as we should, and many of us who write as part of our way of life feel compelled to write about the schools. Invariably we find them wanting, not providing as good an education for today's youth as we recall they provided for us. That our vision may be skewed either through selective recollection or by the narrowness of our own experience does not trouble us greatly. We often do not remember the fate of others, be they the handicapped child the teacher never called on, the two black kids who were in our first-grade class but somehow were never in another class with us, or the junior-high cut-up who was pumping gas a couple of years later. When some of us attend reunions of our high-school graduating class, we are reminded that the homeroom of the forty who graduated had been three homerooms of forty each in the eighth grade. In short, those of us who "have been through the mill ourselves" and who feel compelled to write about education are likely to be the ones whom the educational system served well. We recall how well it did for us without considering whether it did similarly well for others our age. Judging from what historical evidence we have from reading tests, library usage, and college attendance, it did not serve these others well.

Despite the rose-colored lenses with which successful graduates sometimes view their past education and the clarity with which they point to its deficiencies today, these authors have labored valiantly with their critiques, which are, on balance, beneficial to both the schools and the society. Although the reports do not meet high standards of policy analysis, as Paul Peterson persuasively argues in *The Brookings Review,* what they have done is focus public attention on a matter of urgency, namely, improving the education of our youth.[3]

Schools traditionally have reinforced the advantages that children bring with them as a result of both their genetic and environmental circumstances. In the years since World War II, however, we have said that we expect them to transform their role of reinforcing advantage to one of maximizing the talent available in the population. To do the latter, to maximize talent, schools must undertake revisions in the curriculum and pedagogy so that children who have not mastered the material in the past can master it now. In recent years we have simply assumed that attendance and graduation implied mastery of material. We have learned, to our regret, that such is not the case. To shift the role of the schools from reinforcing advantage to maximizing talent requires both social will and educational expertise. Of the two, social will is more difficult to achieve. What the reports and critiques have done is to begin to mobilize the social will that is essential if educational expertise is to effect a transformation.[4] When Ross Perot takes on the high school athletic establishment in Texas, he may not do so with an elegant policy analysis, but his efforts to modify the priorities in schools may result in real change. Such would be an example of social will.

The reports, then, play an important role in rallying public opinion about the significance of schools and of the importance for children and society to learn in them. This is a necessary function, a prerequisite for the task yet to be accomplished, namely, a forceful discussion of what schools ought to be doing and how they ought to be doing it. That is the commentary that Hacker correctly finds lacking.

As in the days of Hutchins and Dewey—one a lawyer turned university president and the other a philosopher and professor—we expect professional educators to lead such a discussion. Yet today, when derogatory jokes about minorities and even women are considered in bad taste, jokes can still be made with relative impunity about educators. This attitude, coupled with the bad press educators have received in recent years, has had serious consequences.

In the material that follows I will argue that the professional autonomy of educators has been severely eroded and that one effect of that erosion has been silence from them on questions of why we should educate. In the absence of a coherent and audible message about the rationale or purpose of education from today's professional educators, the governing educational philosophy on which practice is implicitly based remains the remnants of progressive education, which was the explicit message of a previous generation of educators. I will argue that the time has come for educators to emerge from this dark night of the soul, to find their voice, to join the discussion, and to argue, as only they can, what they believe that schools ought to do and how they ought to do it.

During the last thirty years, those responsible for schools, their rationale and their practice, have seen their autonomy remarkably diminished. A number of factors have accounted for the demise in the autonomy of educators. A preeminent factor is the success of educators in educating other Americans so that school officials are no longer part of a tiny minority who have successfully navigated the rocks and shoals of the college curriculum. In 1950, only 6 percent of Americans over twenty-five years old had completed college and only one-third had finished high school. In such an environment educators stood apart as experts, unlikely to be challenged in their professional judgments by the majority who had substantially less educational expertise than they. Today such professional educators are victims of their own and their colleagues' success. Currently, 18 percent of educators have finished college, and over 70 percent of adult Americans have completed high school.[5] Within one generation the proportion of college graduates has tripled, and that of high-school graduates more than doubled. Among younger adult Americans, the ones traditionally most likely to be directly interested in educational issues, increases in educational level are even higher. Persons with extensive educational experience themselves are much more likely to challenge professional judgments of educators than those without it. Hence, the previous autonomy of educators is progressively constrained.

Second, the years since World War II have been turbulent ones for educators simply because of the internal problems they have faced within their own institutions. This has been a period of feast and famine, both for enrollments and for funds. For the generation preceding World War II, enrollment levels in public elementary and secondary schools held relatively steady at 26 million. Largely as a consequence of the dramatic increase in the birth rate during and after World War II, and partly as a consequence of increased retention in high schools, enrollments grew to 36 million in academic year 1959-60, to 46 million in 1969-70, peaking at 46.1 million in fall 1971. By the 1979-80 school year, enrollment had fallen to 41.6 million. Current enrollment is just under 40 million.[6]

With these changes in enrollment came commensurate changes in funds. Total public-school revenues in the 1920s and 1930s were around $2 billion annually, but with the enrollment increases after the war they escalated to over $5.4 billion in 1949-50, nearly tripled a decade later to $14.7 billion, jumped to $40 billion in 1969-70, and rose again to $96 billion in 1979-80. The increase, however, masks a decline in purchasing power beginning in 1978 and a decline in adjusted dollars in teachers' salaries over the last decade.[7]

The colleges and universities that trained school personnel prospered as states increased educational requirements for teachers. In 1940, 40 percent of city schoolteachers and 62 percent of rural teachers taught without a bachelor's degree. By 1971, over 97 percent of all teachers had a bachelor's degree, and 27 percent had a master's degree. Teacher training in the colleges grew from just over 36,000 baccalaureate education graduates in 1948, reaching its peak in 1973 when nearly 164,000 received bachelor's degrees in education. By 1979, that number had dropped to just under 108,000 and recent evidence indicates that the decline is continuing. The academic training of administrators has been more extensive than that of teachers. The numbers of doctorates awarded in education grew dramatically, from 470 in 1940 to 1,549 in 1960 to a peak of 7,955 in 1976.[8]

If enrollments grow, so must faculties, facilities, and funds. Thus, educators' concerns focused on problems of expansion: accommodating the many new students, finding the faculty to instruct them, constructing the buildings to house them, finding the funds to support this enterprise. Educators correctly saw many of their immediate problems as solvable by money, and many of their immediate problems were. Such an environment is not one that is conducive to speculation about purposes of education since the practicalities of schooling typically take precedence over such theoretical activity.

The turbulence affecting the educational institutions manifested itself in yet another way: in dissension between students and faculty and in dissension between faculty and administration. Although the issue of students' rights was a troublesome one, likely to involve administrators in even more litigation or the threat of it, it was not as divisive as the spectacle of the split between teachers and administrators in contract negotiations and strikes. The public had assumed, sometimes incorrectly, that teachers and administrators were on the same team, that they had the same goals—the education of children.

No one outside education noticed much when the umbrella organization of elementary and secondary education, the National Education Association, began to splinter. In 1892, it had involved college and university faculty and administrators in formulating the Committee of Ten report on high-school curriculum under the leadership of Charles W. Eliot, then president of Harvard University. By 1937, however, its Department of Superintendence became a separate organization, the American Association of School Administrators, an organization totally separate from the NEA and on some issues completely opposed to it. The only higher education people left in the NEA were a few professors of education; presidents of Harvard or comparable universities did not spend what time they had for elementary and secondary education issues with the NEA.

In 1961, New York City recognized the United Federation of Teachers, an affiliate of the American Federation of Teachers, as the bargaining agent for its public school faculty. Subsequently, during four autumns in the 1960s, New Yorkers and the rest of the nation were exposed to the sight of teachers striking, sometimes joined in opposition to the policies of the Board of Education by the local community and sometimes the reverse. By the late sixties and seventies, teachers' strikes were common throughout the United States. They occurred not just in cities, but in small communities as well, and were led not just by the American Federation of Teachers, which clearly identified itself with the American labor movement, but with considerable frequency by the NEA, that bastion of professionalism of teachers. While such activities undoubtedly led to increases in shamefully low teacher salaries, they also contributed to an adversarial relationship between faculty and administration so that, in the mind of at least much of the public, the united force of educators appeared fractured.

Such factionalism within the profession led to new specializations at colleges and universities that prepared educators. Preeminent among these was management training for school administrators. One of the most popular emerging fields was negotiation strategy. There was no doubt that an administrator needed such skills. Management training was also more compelling to many students than much of the traditional work in the philosophy or history of education, which often suffered from charges of irrelevance in an era when relevance was triumphant. The late-twentieth-century analogue to the history or philosophy of education became policy studies. Here the emphasis was upon analysis, a systematic and careful look at what the policy was and what its effects were. Few such rigorous analysts believed their task extended to considering what the purposes underlying the policy ought to be. Rather, policies were examined for their political feasibility, ease of implementation, consequences for the affected parties. By studying social policy toward education, one encountered some of the issues traditionally considered in studies of history or philosophy but one did so in a much more compelling contemporary context than that of Aristotle, Rousseau, or even John Dewey. One wasn't troubled, except by an example or two, by the arguments of the Federalists that portions of the populace of the new republic be educated. Lessons from the school consolidation movement and the elimination of rural schools could be skipped. Finally, professors of education—often located at universities in which scientific, empirical research was highly valued and who might once have considered normative questions about the purpose of education—found themselves undertaking numerous and often quantitative research projects if they wished to receive either tenure or, particularly, national recognition. The days when outstanding figures in education such as John Dewey, Boyd Bode, George Counts, or Charles Judd, were outspoken about what education *ought* to be, had passed. Now they engaged in meta-analyses of what someone else had found had already happened.

The professional autonomy of educators in formulating what education ought to do was profoundly reduced in the years following World War II as the result of the increased role of the federal government in matters educational. To put the matter simply—too simply, perhaps—the federal government has been primarily concerned about two issues in elementary and secondary schooling since World War II: assuring educational civil rights to groups deemed to be underserved, particularly racial minorities, females, the handicapped, and children of the poor (many of whom overlapped with the above categories); and providing a small, ill-fated attempt to enliven the academic curriculum in mathematics, science, and, to a lesser extent, social studies. In both cases, the federal government believed that its actions were intended as correctives to the efforts of state and local educational authorities that had primary responsibility for the direction, control, and financing of the public schools. Federal funds also went to support vocational education and to provide money for school districts with large concentrations of federal employees, but those programs were protected by powerful political coalitions and largely escaped any serious critical attention from thoughtful professionals.

Neither in the case of civil rights nor the curriculum did the federal government address the fundamental, central issues of public schooling, namely, what ought to be the education provided for the 90 percent of American young people in the public schools? The federal government spoke specifically about failings—about deficiencies—of current educational policy and practice. It disapproved of segregation by race, of lack of access of girls into studies dominated by boys, of isolation of handicapped children from others in classrooms, of the lower performances of children of the poor in academic achievement,

and of old-fashioned science and mathematics curricula that failed to prepare gifted youngsters adequately for professional achievement in those fields. In all cases, federal activity in precollegiate education came from perceived inadequacies of the education currently being conducted under the direction of state and local authorities. The federal strategy was one of intervention when in the minds of federal authorities—minds stimulated by political realities as well as educational ones—the state and local authorities were failing in particular aspects of their assignment to educate the youth of America.

Despite the federal reticence to formulate clear goals and purposes for education in America, the effect of federal activity has been to affect significantly what school people thought and did about education. The influence of the federal government was indirect but powerful. Though government rarely supplied even a tenth of a school system's budget, its impact on decisions in schools dramatically exceeded that relatively minor proportion of the school budget.

The federal impact was great for two principal reasons. To avoid the institutional migraines that would result from a failure to comply with federal procedures, many school officials spent valuable time seeking that exceedingly narrow and obscure path through the forest of federal regulations and community sentiment. Second, the federal regulations and appropriations represented to some extent manifestations of national purpose in education. There was never absolute consensus about educational goals, but, aided by decisions of the Supreme Court, a consensus gradually began to develop regarding the illegality of de jure segregation of the races in public schools and the unequal treatment of women.

At the end of World War II, these matters were not ones that the vast majority of school superintendents, school-board members, professors at prestigious schools of education, or national leaders by themselves would likely have ranked as pressing educational issues. These groups were not composed of minority-group members or women, and many were not deeply concerned about opportunities for these two classes of citizens. The implicit assumption was that educators and national leaders were selected for responsible positions more or less on the basis of their merit. Consequently, if they achieved because of their merit—and others had failed to achieve presumably because of their absence of merit—then society and the educational system that reflected its values were working reasonably well. These educators did not enjoy being first told, and then forced, to change their ways. The federal government found itself in the awkward position of telling those people with the primary responsibility for running schools that they were not doing a good job with certain school populations their institutions were supposed to serve. These school folks had to mend their ways, particularly with staffs who, like themselves, had not always shared either the commitment to the education of these new populations or the expertise to educate them effectively.

For thirty years since the *Brown* v. *Board of Education* decision in 1954, American educators in communities throughout the nation have been attempting to build local support for and find the resources within their own institutions to address the complicated civil rights questions in education that were triggered by federal actions. On the educational level alone they have done reasonably well, particularly with elementary-school students. The society itself has done less well, although the evolution of an expanded minority middle class and diminished occupational segregation for educated women has improved the economic prospects of individuals in those groups substantially.

The argument thus far has been that the autonomy of educators has been substantially reduced in the years since World War II. One caveat must be added, namely, that the federal authorities who so influenced the course of American education by their insistence upon special attention to the needs of the racial minorities, the poor, and the handicapped were not disembodied bureaucrats pursuing some power trip to impose their views on unsuspecting and unsympathetic local educators. Rather, to a very important extent, those notorious "feds" were themselves educators, persons who in their previous employment had served as teachers, principals, school superintendents, professors, or deans of schools of education, and many returned to their former positions or comparable ones following their federal service. During their employment with the federal government, they undertook to achieve through its authority many of the educational reforms in which they had been interested but impotent to implement in their local communities. The dean of the Harvard Graduate School of Education, however concerned he or she might be about the education of the children of the poor, was unlikely to be as effective in getting federal funds authorized and appropriated to provide supplementary instruction in reading and arithmetic for them as was the commissioner of the United States Office of Education. This was a phenomenon that Francis Keppel discovered when he moved from the former position to the latter. Keppel's successor as commissioner, Harold Howe II, was much more effective in bringing about school desegregation, a matter of long concern to him, than he would have been in his previous post as superintendent of schools in Scarsdale, New York. Clearly not all federal officials who were insisting on these new educational arrangements were either as high-minded or highly placed as Keppel or Howe, but the issues on which they tussled with their erstwhile colleagues in the states and localities were ones that were fundamentally important to the nation's vitality.

These issues were vital because in each case the federal initiatives and regulations sought to rescue talent lost both to individuals and to the nation as a result of children not being educated adequately in the schools. What do we mean by "adequacy in schooling"? Adequacy in schooling is a notion like "poverty in America." Its definition is relative and changes regularly, generally escalating. Standards of adequacy in schooling are much higher now than they were in 1935 or 1940. We expect schools to reach a much greater proportion of children for much longer periods of time and to teach them—all of them—much more than we previously did. Similarly, as James Patterson has argued in *America's Struggle Against Poverty, 1900-1980*, we have much higher minimum standards that we believe all persons should meet in diet, housing, plumbing, heating, and clothing now than we did earlier.[9] In both cases we believe that these higher standards are both beneficial to the individual and appropriate or even beneficial to the society. So, too, with adequacy of schooling.

Since World War II, we have repeatedly heard that our schools were inadequate. Parents and groups concerned with special populations (minorities, girls, handicapped, gifted) have persistently and effectively reminded school people that the needs of their individual children were not being met. Their remarks have often been addressed to the federal authorities in an effort for them to intervene on behalf of these children, and to a substantial degree they have done so. The educational protest literature, a prolific genre from the publication of Arthur Bestor's *Educational Wastelands* in 1953 to the National Commission on Excellence's *A Nation at Risk* in 1983, has concentrated upon the general deficiencies of the schools, citing weakened curricular offerings, poorly prepared teachers, and insipid educational goals.[10] The critiques of both the special interest groups and the general protesters have converged to assert that the schools were not accomplishing what the critics believed *ought* to be occurring in the classrooms. Ultimately this was probably the definitive factor limiting the autonomy of the professional educators; the public had lost confidence in the institutions they operated, but the public had not lost confidence in the enterprise they represented, namely, the education of the young. The issue yet to be defined was what that education ought to be.

But who was defining "ought"? What was the source of the reigning wisdom that was intended to govern educational policy and practice in the schools? Given their recent loss of autonomy, professional educators were not providing a definition, and nobody else was either.

To a remarkable degree, practice in schools in the 1980s still owes much to the rhetoric of progressivism in education first popularized in the first half of the twentieth century. No one today would likely describe a comprehensive high school with its variegated curriculum, its movable classroom desks, and its acceptance of the limited authority of the teacher as a school following the canons of progressive education. Nonetheless, the practices of American high schools so much criticized today in the works of John Goodlad, Ernest Boyer, Diane Ravitch, or in the various reports issued in 1983, are embodiments of progressivism in education gone amuck.[11]

The lag time between acceptance of an educational ideal and its widespread acceptance as educational practice is great. When Horace Mann advocated the adoption of a common school movement in Massachusetts in the late 1830s and early 1840s, he was arguing for a notion that did not reach full realization in the nation until the turn of the century. Many midwestern states entered the age of the common school at the end of the nineteenth century, not at the middle of it, as the historiography of the period, dictated by Mann and Henry Barnard's pronouncements, would have it.

The canons of progressivism were introduced to the general public by the turn of the century in the work of the early vocational education (then called manual training) leaders: by Francis Parker with his concern for the centrality of the child in the educational process, and by John Dewey whose work unified concern for the child and the curriculum as well as for the school and the society.[12] Together these educators fought what they believed was the tyranny of the classical or traditional curriculum that dominated school organization and that, in the minds of many of them, forced children into a rigid mold that was not useful for them in later life. Their intentions were honorable in many ways, attempting to right the balance between acquisition of knowledge and attention to children's needs. The excessive formalism of schooling dominated by pedants and characterized by mastery of what many believed to be useless knowledge held sway. The newly recognized concerns for the development of the child received relatively little attention in practice.

Recognition did begin to emerge for schooling that would be appropriate for the children's "probable destinies." Charles William Eliot used this term in an article, "Industrial Education as an Essential Factor in our National Prosperity," in the *National Society for the Promotion of Industrial Education Bulletin* in 1908. As Eliot explained it, "The teachers of the elementary schools ought to sort the pupils and sort them by their evident or probable destinies."[13] This was guidance the emerging group of vocational educators found very congenial and supportive of their cause.

Surely it was reasonable for turn-of-the-century educational reformers to protest a curriculum that was too rigid, that ignored children's individual differences, that failed to engage the majority of the children so that they neither learned the material nor remained in school. The question, however, is the extent to which those recommendations are time-bound and context-bound or the extent to which they are universal. The progressives, Dewey particularly, stressed the necessity for adapting remedies to the needs of the times. Their successors, however, acted as though the principles set forth by the progressives were ultimate ones, not ones conditioned by the circumstances of late-nineteenth-century America.

Following World War I, a new generation of educational reformers, augmented by the continuing presence of John Dewey, preached the doctrine of progressive education. The primary pulpit was Teachers College at Columbia University, where William Heard Kilpatrick, Harold Rugg, and such practitioners as Patty Smith Hill and Otis Caldwell expounded. Their doctrine was child-centeredness, the antithesis of subject-centeredness. They took pride in advocating the centrality of the child in the educational process rather than the subject matter, which in their view had formerly and mistakenly occupied center stage. They stressed needed changes in pedagogy that would make learning more active, less passive, than it traditionally had been in classes dominated by teachers and textbooks. By the 1930s, their colleague at Teachers College, George S. Counts, was encouraging the schools to play a major role in bringing about changes in the society that would reflect collectivist principles, not the capitalist ones on which the society had been based as it tumbled into the depression.[14] Like most of us who advocate a point of view, these educators wrote within the context of their time and their experience. Vocational education, child-centeredness, the rigidity of traditional curriculum, or the viability of capitalism in the 1930s: all were reasonable concerns for educators in the first third of the twentieth century whose educational practice was dominated by reverence for traditional texts that were accessible to only a few students and of interest to only a fraction of those few.

The progressive educators, as they came to be known, expressed their views in the pages of their new journals, particularly *Progressive Education* and *Social Frontier,* at professional meetings of the Progressive Education Association and the National Education Association, and in the classrooms, especially at Teachers College, which was filled with eager teachers seeking to be both professional and progressive. "Professional" and "progressive" came to be nearly synonymous terms for many modern educators in the pre-World-War-II years.

The enunciation of these doctrines and the enthusiastic acceptance of them by many ambitious educators did not, however, immediately transfer their practices into all the schoolrooms of America. Vocational education, which was intended for the poor and those unlikely to remain in school, was introduced to America, Lawrence Cremin tells us in *The Transformation of the School,* in 1876.[15] By World War I, it had made significant inroads in the curriculum of many schools, but even vocational education did not reach widespread audiences until after passage of the Smith-Hughes Act in 1917. Roughly fifty years after the ideas were introduced the practices began to change broadly. So also with some of the other tenets of progressive education, which were argued forcefully in the 1920s. Examples of "progressive practices" could be found in such hot-house environments as New York City private schools (Dalton, Walden, City and Country, Elisabeth Irwin) and some wealthy suburban districts (Winnetka and Bronxville) in the years between the wars. David Tyack, Robert Lowe, and Elisabeth Hansot discuss the belated universality of progressive practices in *Public Schools in Hard Times,* forcefully exemplifying their view with a vignette of a Hamilton, Massachusetts, elementary school serving a predominantly lower-middle-class population in the 1930s.[16]

The widespread acceptance of progressive practices in education probably did not occur until after World War II, by which time the ideology of progressive education was already under attack. Thus, educational practice in the 1970s, much lamented by current critics, owes its philosophic origins to a misinterpretation of the child-centeredness first proposed half a century earlier. Its persistence in schools today is a consequence of two phenomena: the inevitable lag in time between the enunciation of a popular or powerful principle and its widespread acceptance in practice, and the decline in autonomy of professional educators who otherwise might have been expected to reformulate or revise goals and purposes for the schools.

Probably no finer education could be imagined for a child than progressive education at its best. Under those circumstances an intelligent, informed, creative, sympathetic teacher guides children individually and in groups through academic material in ways that trigger their interest and imagination, and lead to their ultimate understanding of the subject, its structure and significance. Most of us would seek such an education for our children. But too often—in fact, most often—progressive education was not at its best, not fully achieved.

Progressive education, partially achieved, was a disaster, and it was disastrous for two reasons. First, it focused upon the child and the perceived needs and interests of the child, thereby galvanizing the iron cloak of race, class, ethnicity, and sex as determinants of the child's future. Second, it minimized mastery of traditional subject matter as insignificant, thereby eliminating the prime educational means by which children could choose a future different from the circumstances into which they had been born.

Certainly focus upon the child should be a component of education, but it must be perceived as a necessary but not sufficient condition for that child's education. When the antithesis of child-centered was adult-centered—that is, schools organized for the benefit of the adults in them, rather than the children—then to strive for a focus on children is clearly appropriate. A child who is hungry cannot learn arithmetic easily; a child who is psychologically troubled will find it difficult to study anything attentively. School people are correct in observing that the children who come to them today to be educated are more difficult to educate than those whom they saw in the past. The reason is relatively simple: they did not see the difficult ones in the past because they dropped, or were pushed, out of school.

To concentrate too narrowly on the child and the child's problems that may be numerous and compelling, however, permits the school to limit its attention to the circumstances of the child's life and to run the risk of accepting the stereotype associated with the child's race, class, ethnicity, and sex. Recognizing individual differences was a hallmark of progressive rhetoric, but too often under the guise of such recognition of individualism was in fact a reinforcement of expectations associated not with the individual child but with the child's external circumstances. Noticing that a child was learning to read slowly, and knowing that the child came from a poor family, was likely to result in placement of that child in the "slow track" where in all likelihood that child would remain, regularly slipping further and further behind his age-mates in school. Such was particularly likely to be the case if the child were a member of a racial minority. It was expected that such children often did not do well in school, and there was plenty of evidence from psychologists and psychometricians documenting the lower scores of blacks and Hispanics on "objective tests." In such circumstances, concern for the child led not to increased learning but to acceptance of expected poor performance.

The explanation was rarely in terms of the inadequacy of the child, for that would have been too damning, but rather in terms of the inadequacy of the child's environment. "Culturally deprived" was the euphemism to describe such matters. Somehow we did not find it as damning to blame a society that permitted people to live in poverty without hope as we did to blame the individual. Fundamentally, we simply did not set expectations as high for some children as for others, and our level of expectations, though ostensibly tied to concern for the child, was, in fact, influenced significantly by the child's race, sex, and socioeconomic circumstances. In such a manner, concern for the welfare of the child, which could have been enormously liberating, became a constriction. Yet as late as 1970, a person as well-established as a Yale professor, Charles A. Reich, provided support for this notion of individuality, apparently oblivious to the social factors that impinge upon educational opportunities. "Each person has his own individuality, not to be compared to that of anyone else. Someone may be a brilliant thinker, but he is not 'better' at thinking than anyone else, he simply possesses his own excellence. A person who thinks very poorly is still excellent in his own way."[17] This became the late-twentieth-century academic rationale for Harvard president Charles William Eliot's 1908 recommendation that schools sort children according to "evident or probable destinies." Such popular expressions as this gave school people confidence that they were not damaging children's opportunities by focusing their attention upon the child.

One of the few canons that progressive educators agreed upon was their antipathy to the tyranny of traditional subject matter. They were "anti–subject-centeredness," as they frequently asserted. Sometimes the antithesis of child-centered was not adult-centered but rather subject-centered. Certainly being child-centered in the school was absolutely consistent with being opposed to being subject-centered. In fact, the former necessitated the latter.

Progressive educators' hostility to academic subject matter was understandable in an age of extensive memorization of miscellaneous and sometimes erroneous information, as much of the late-nineteenth-century curriculum required. By the mid-years of the twentieth century, however, the consensus about what the curriculum ought to include was gone. To continue to be hostile to subject matter was no longer a valid corrective to a narrow view of significant knowledge. Rather, it was an abdication of professional responsibility. Surely, one of a professional educator's primary obligations is to determine what children need to learn in school. As Clifford Adelman has illustrated in his study of high-school transcripts, the academic curriculum for grades nine to twelve has virtually collapsed. It has been replaced in some significant part by "personal service and development courses," some of which are even state-mandated, thereby indicating the complicity of state officials in the disappearance of academic study in the high school.[18]

The demise of the academic curriculum in the high school is due, in part, to the progressive rhetoric that gave approval for study of many things not previously thought justifiable as part of school learning. From the beginning, such "expansions" of the curriculum, as they were frequently called, gave rise to criticism. One Italian immigrant mother quoted by Caroline Ware in her study of Greenwich Village residents in the 1920s shrewdly observed that teaching social adjustment in school was a luxury that could be afforded only by the children of the rich.[19]

During the 1930s, the Progressive Education Association sponsored two major commissions underwritten by funding from the Carnegie Corporation and the General Education Board. The first, the Commission on the Relation of School and College, involved thirty schools, mostly serving college-bound students, and followed their academic records for eight years. The principal finding of this commission, widely heralded in the educational press, was that students who attended progressive schools that had non-traditional curricula did as well in college as did students who had conventional preparation. This conviction was broadly but erroneously conceived to mean that what you studied did not make any difference. The second commission, an outgrowth of the former, developed this line of reasoning further. The Commission on the Secondary School Curriculum, which published its principal work *Reorganizing Secondary Education* in 1939, maintained, in rhetoric typical of the period, that democracy should be inseparable from school life, and that the "needs"—social, economic, and personal—of young people should determine the content of the curriculum.[20] Some of the special reports of the commission on specific fields of study were innovative, interesting, and provocative, and in the hands of the gifted teacher could be very useful and effective in introducing students to science and literature. Those, however, did not become as well known as the commission summary itself.

These reports on the high-school curriculum were based on college-bound students in the depths of the depression. That group constituted about 13 percent of the age group at that time and, it can be safely assumed, over-represented the affluent. These were the children with whom the schools have traditionally been most successful, those for whom the schools reinforced the advantages that the child brought to school. For them, then, the issue of the content of the curriculum was much less important than it was for the child whose home was less likely to nurture him intellectually. The college-bound child of the thirties would likely learn Greek mythology, American history, writing skills, and reading comprehension at home or at college even if the school curriculum did not include it. For the 87 percent who were not college bound, the content of the school curriculum was much more crucial.

Since the commission reports appeared just at the outbreak of World War II, other issues took precedence over high-school curriculum reform in the years immediately following their publication. By the 1950s and 1960s, however, the principles of the reports were accepted by many high-school educators. The educational protest literature of the late fifties testified to the widespread practice of curriculum based on "life-adjustment education," a notion originating with the leader of the earlier vocational education movement, Charles Prosser. Prosser maintained that since only a small minority of high school students were college bound (20 percent) and a comparable proportion able to undertake vocational education, the curriculum for the balance (the majority of 60 percent) should not be academic but rather should consist of instruction in matters that would help them adjust to life as they would likely lead it.[21] This was a revivification of a curriculum to sort children by "evident or probable destiny." Such was the justification for the introduction of courses on marriage and family life (since nearly everybody would be involved in that) and driver's education (since in the new automobile culture everybody would need that skill).

This view underwent a reincarnation under a different term with another former leading progressive educator, Sidney Marland, Jr., who had served with Carleton Washburne in the Winnetka schools when they exemplified the ideal of progressive education. When Marland became United States commissioner of education in the Nixon administration, he argued for a federal initiative to support "career education" that soon became "experience-based career education," a federal program that remained throughout the seventies. Marland's view was that most education should be tied to possible jobs, although he left some room for preparation for college. His chief target was "general education," which he believed, often correctly, was an academic mishmash. His solution, however, was not to invigorate it but to replace it with job-oriented studies.[22] The assumption underlying both was that academic learning, including such fundamentals as literature, mathematics, science, history, and foreign languages, was only intended for an elite. It was unnecessary for the masses who needed job skills. The echo of the Booker T. Washington–W.E.B. DuBois debate over the proper education of blacks at the turn of the century was now extended to whites and lingered on.

Unwittingly, perhaps, the colleges and universities themselves contributed to this diminution of the curriculum by significantly reducing entrance requirements for college freshmen, beginning with the age of relevance of the 1960s and continuing throughout the academic depression of the 1970s. The Ivy League, which had traditionally had the most rigid entrance requirements, began to be much less specific about what a student needed to have studied in high school, and other institutions, which were experiencing serious concern about getting enough students for a freshman class, did not pursue at length just what the content of the high school "communications" course was that had replaced English.

Even more significantly, colleges themselves reduced requirements for mastery of academic disciplines for graduation, thereby eliminating the rationale for high-school disciplinary studies. In the Ivy League in the early 1960s, for example, typical requirements for the AB degree included evidence of satisfactory completion of the intermediate level in two foreign languages, two years of laboratory science, some history, and a respectable level of English composition, not to mention four semesters of physical education. By the end of the decade, one semester of English composition and the physical education requirement remained. Nationally, for example, in a sample of four-year institutions, 85 percent required a foreign language for graduation in 1969, but within seven years that figure had dropped to 54 percent. The typical pattern was one of drastic reduction of general education or distribution requirements for graduation. Students were likely to choose either subjects in their major field or ones closely related to it.[23] In the face of abandonment by the colleges of academic discipline requirements, the high schools, which understood all too well their lower rank in the educational pecking order, were unlikely to insist on those things colleges did not deem necessary.

Insofar as we have had, in recent years, an alternative rationale for education other than the child-centeredness, anti-subject-centeredness of the progressives, that rationale might be equality of opportunity. Certainly much of the rhetoric of the 1960s was filled with that phrase. "Equality of opportunity," however vital a concept, though, does not address the internal pedagogical and organizational questions of schooling. If equality of opportunity means that poor black children and rich white ones can both attend a school in which they take courses that will help them adjust to life according to their probable destinies, then the disparities in genuine educational opportunity remain great.

For equality of opportunity to become real, the content of the curriculum available to all children must enable and encourage them to become *more* than they thought they could be. The essence of opportunity is not "probable destiny" but an increase of the options available to a child. A curriculum that prepares one for one's "evident or probable destiny" does not encourage a child to pursue options that seem unlikely to him or to her. The essence of the curriculum must be to expand children's understanding of the world so that their destinies may be truly chosen, not simply a consequence of their circumstances of birth. Some may choose their "evident or probable destiny," and for them as well as for those who choose an improbable destiny the curriculum will be one that expands their horizons, not limits them.

Such a curriculum is likely to require mastery of English, familiarity and understanding of well written and difficult pieces of literature, mathematical reasoning, principles and practical examples of scientific accomplishments, knowledge of the past, and a foreign language. The pedagogy for accomplishing these demanding requirements will vary greatly among children, but the variance needs to be with the pedagogy, not with the rigor or content of the curriculum.

Historically, when we felt obligated to teach children to whom academic learning did not come easily, we modified the curriculum to make it easier for them to learn, or to make it—as Eliot urged—appropriate for their probable destiny. That tactic needs to be changed. The curriculum needs to remain constant, but the pedagogy of teaching it must be altered. The responsibility needs to shift from the student to the teacher. We have traditionally argued that in a child-centered school, we would have the curriculum modified to fit the child. Now we need to modify the pedagogy, the teacher's task, to meet the child's learning style. The curriculum, filled with the subjects that do endure and do enlighten a child, needs to remain. The means of teaching it to all children will vary.

Discussion about either curriculum or pedagogy is vacuous unless we have some agreement about why we educate. Only then can we have some basis for decision about what the curriculum ought to be and how it should be taught to children. Therefore, we must break the silence about our rationale for education. Vital as it is to improve the curriculum and to modify the pedagogy so that all can learn, thus making equality of opportunity a reality and not a sham, we must also be able to enunciate what our purpose of education is. We especially need to be able to say to schools what their special function is.

The primary responsibility for our schools should be to nurture and to enhance the wit and the character of the young. Both wit and character are vital to this nation and to the individuals who comprise it. In this society, schools have the primary responsibility for stimulating the former, wit, while they have secondary responsibility for molding the latter, character.

"Wit," Webster's unabridged dictionary tell us, is "mind, intellect, understanding, sense." Secondarily, says Webster, wit means "ingenuity, humor." The *Oxford English Dictionary* calls it also "the faculty of thinking and reasoning." Surely those qualities, taken together as wit, provide both a lofty and laudable goal for schooling. By assuming such a goal for schooling we will be accepting the primacy of mind and intellect but also recognizing the crucial additions of understanding, sense, ingenuity, and humor. At its best, and even when not wholly achieved, those qualities are valuable for the young as they advance into maturity. How might high-school seniors today explain how their studies had improved their minds, intellects, understanding, sense, ingenuity, or humor? I fear that the present course of studies followed by many of them would leave those vital faculties singularly unattended. Various non-school experiences—reading, work, family life, friends—can contribute substantially, perhaps in totality even more than schools can, to the enhancement of wit, but no other agency in the society has primary responsibility for assuring that a child's wit is developed. This is not to argue that the school alone can adequately enhance a child's wit. It cannot, but if the school fails to make that its primary *goal*, it will have missed its fundamental calling.

This is not to say that wit alone is sufficient; the experience of the Weimar Republic is enough to demonstrate that. Of the two qualities, wit and character, certainly character is the more important of the two, but the schools' responsibility for forming character is subsidiary to that of the family and perhaps even the community. Nonetheless, any schooling that does not recognize the need for enhancement of character is inadequate. Character, to follow Webster again, means "strength of mind, individuality, independence, moral quality." The *Oxford English Dictionary* succinctly terms it "the sum of the moral and mental qualities which distinguish an individual . . . viewed as a homogeneous whole." These qualities, when combined with wit, are the fundamental qualities of citizenship—informed and enlightened citizenship. We may not always find individuality and independence to our taste or to our political persuasion, and certainly strength of mind is a quality we admire most when it reinforces our own views. Nonetheless, a society that depends upon each member for its governance needs these attributes. Few would be willing to argue against the necessity of moral quality, but as we have seen all too often in our own history, recognition of its virtue has been more common in words than in actions.

Although wit and character are not identical, undoubtedly efforts to stimulate and enhance both cannot be entirely separate. Wit and character are intertwined in the composition of the individual, and doubtless they must also be related in the school curriculum and pedagogy. Nonetheless, the school must recall the primacy of wit in its mission, and its secondary responsibility for character. In the past we have too often stressed the schools' obligations to make society moral (generally an unsuccessful venture) or the schools' use of the democratic process so that youngsters can replicate their school experiences later as adults and citizens in this democratic republic. Our schools have had a penchant for character formation, a hesitancy to tackle wit.

How would our schools change if they were to accept enhancing wit and nurturing character as their primary goals? Some, perhaps a good many, would not change much at all because whether they call it that or not, that is what they are presently doing. Others, and I believe the majority of high schools, would change a great deal because in those institutions the obstacles to taking students' minds seriously are great indeed. For acceptance of these goals to occur, two vital groups must support them: the community and the professional educators. Too often these groups have either been at odds about the schools' fundamental purposes or, more frequently, been in a complicit agreement that the schools can serve as holding pens to keep children out of the job market and, if possible, off the streets and out of trouble. The community and the educators have agreed not to expect the schools to undertake any rigorous education of the young. That complicit agreement needs to be renegotiated, and the new terms should be made explicit and public.

Were the schools to accept their responsibility for the nurturing of wit and character, the curriculum would change, probably dramatically. Not only the curriculum but also the pedagogy would be renovated. In this arena, the expertise of professional educators is essential, and few subjects have been in greater disrepute of late than either curriculum or pedagogy. The research in learning theory is substantial, and the moment is now right for the transition to be made from scholarship to practice. It is possible that here the new work with technology may be helpful.

Traditional instruction in schools has been heavily didactic. When we have moved to "exploration" and less didactic modes, we have too often slipped off the track into a miasma of group discussion, project method, and other ostensible stimulants to creativity. Yet we have known that active learning is preferable to passive learning. We have also known that much adult learning involves not simply rote memorization of texts but cooperative solutions of varied problems. These recognitions have been extraordinarily difficult to translate into effective school pedagogy, but the potentiality that microcomputers offer for new curriculum and for group and individualized learning is immense. That potential has yet to be realized, but it exists.

When we consider the schools' responsibility for character formation, we need to be more imaginative than we traditionally have been about how that can be achieved. Certainly, the simplistic, didactic model has serious limitations. In this case, learning by example is immensely preferable to learning by rote. Study of texts certainly has a role in molding character. Yet a school that delegates to the formal curriculum the obligation to provide cautionary tales about moral development does not respect strength of mind, independence, individuality, and moral quality; furthermore, if the school does not preserve these qualities in its daily routine in all the ways—many of them difficult—that these qualities manifest themselves in school, it will not have fulfilled its obligation to nurture and to enhance character.

Recently Peter Greer, the superintendent of schools in Portland, Maine, has written eloquently about our current educational dilemmas: "Education is an enterprise of the intellect and the spirit. But we have forgotten our mission and are acting like monks in a monastery who are fighting over who is responsible for filling the holy water font."[24] We monks need to be sure that our order includes not only the cloistered educator but also those active in the community. The cooperation of both groups is imperative if we are to be successful in this enterprise of the intellect and the spirit.

When we consider suitable goals for our schools and appropriate means of implementing them, we need also to recognize six cautionary admonitions from our past educational experience. First, even if a statement of educational purpose attracts interest and support, its acceptance in the schools as a guide for educational practice will take a long time. Clearly such new ideas will be accepted in some schools sooner than in others, but the overall pattern of educational practice in America is resistant to change, as Larry Cuban has recently documented in his article in the *Harvard Educational Review*.[25] Such reluctance to accept change is probably, in the last analysis, a good thing, because it has prevented us as a nation from adopting some foolish novelties. We have before us the specter of the People's Republic of China with its radical curriculum revisions shifting with the political winds of the Cultural Revolution and reaction to it.

Paul Mort, a professor of education at Teachers College during the progressive heyday, once observed that educational ideas typically take fifty years to gain acceptance in schools. Probably Mort was not far wrong, for the evidence of the common-school movement, vocational education, and the peculiar progressivism discussed earlier suggests that time period is about right. Recognition of such a lag means that the goals and priorities for the schools require a timeless quality, one not specifically limited to the realities of the period in which the reform is proposed. Such timelessness is difficult to achieve, particularly with the specificity we have sought for educational reform. Aristotle's moral and intellectual virtue has the timelessness but not the specificity.

Second, any statement of an educational desideratum must not depend for its success upon its full and total implementation. The nature of practice is that full achievement of the ideal is rarely, if ever, achieved. Therefore, a worthy goal can not be one that depends for its worth on its full implementation. Rather, it must also be worthy if, as is most likely, it is only partially achieved. That was one fundamental lesson to be learned from progressive education. At its best, which rarely occurred, it was superb; in its partial acceptance, which was much more widespread, it was woefully deficient. Conversely, the classical, traditional curriculum, while offering less opportunity for individuality and creativity for students when taught only in a mediocre manner, nonetheless leaves a child with a residue of knowledge that is beneficial.

Third, as we consider educational goals and purposes we need to be sensitive to the balance between educational aspirations that will primarily benefit the youngster and those that will principally benefit the society. Obviously, in many instances both will benefit, but both must be considered separately. For example, the ardent nationalism of Benjamin Rush expressed itself in urging, "Let our pupil be taught that he does not belong to himself, but that he is public property" and "I consider it possible to convert men into republican machines."[26] That is clearly as excessively societal as the "do-your-own-thing" narcissism of the last decade.

Fourth, all who set goals for the schools need to recognize schools for the limited, though important, institutions that they are. Schools are not fundamental means of reorganizing the society, redistributing income, or even providing the love and care that each child requires. Their function is limited. They ought to be able to instruct children, but the efforts of the school cannot supplant those of a hostile community or family environment. Fortunately, most families and communities are not in violent conflict with the schools, but on those occasions when they are—such as a community's strong commitment to school athletics rather than academic learning—the school will have a difficult time insisting on its priorities against those of the community. That is one reason why it is extremely important for there to be community agreement about the fundamental purposes of schooling, a sentiment that is now rare. Education is a far larger matter than schooling, and those who are professionally responsible for the latter, unlike the broader community that is generally responsible for the former, need clarity and support for the narrower goals of schooling.

Fifth, we now know much more than we previously did about education, and how children learn, and how teachers can be effective in aiding learning. The gains from such research in education, psychology, cognitive science, and the neurosciences are still largely in the monographs, texts, and minds of the researchers. They are not in the practice of the educators, particularly of the school people.

They need to be, for educational expertise that is now available can be of monumental help as new and appropriate demands are made upon school people to assure children's learning. Such transmission of research into practice is difficult and time consuming, but it can and must be done. The wheat of educational research has traditionally suffered from excessive chaff, but kernels are now more numerous and can be utilized.

Sixth, new goals and purposes for education must involve educators. If we have learned one thing from the implementation research of the last two decades, it is that top-down reforms undertaken without the participation of those who must carry them out are doomed to failure. Therefore, revisions of educational purpose that exclude the wisdom of professional educators are likely to meet the same fate as much of the educational protest literature of the 1950s: it will be ignored by the school people. Educators today are in a very different frame of mind than they were in the fifties, and they are, I believe, much more willing and able to participate constructively in discussions about desirable and feasible goals for schools.

We Americans, who are appropriately vociferous in our critiques of education generally and the schools particularly, need to come to fundamental agreement about what we want our schools to do. In reaching that agreement, one group of Americans has a particular responsibility, though not an exclusive one, to participate in that discussion. They are professional educators: teachers, principals, superintendents, professors, college and university administrators. They all need to participate actively in that discussion, bringing the expertise they uniquely have to both the vision of education and the means of implementing that vision.

We must reject the tired vestiges of progressive education that still predominate in much of the educational practice of the schools, particularly the high schools, and we must embrace a new goal for our schools. That goal must be one that helps individuals to become more than they thought they could be, benefits society, and can be accomplished by the schools. We Americans, including the professional educators among us, must accept and move to achieve a clear goal for the schools. Such a goal is nurturing and enhancing the wit and character of the young.

ENDNOTES

I am indebted to Michael Fultz for research assistance in the preparation of this article and to the Spencer Foundation for its support for the larger project, "National Purpose and the Federal Role in Education," of which this essay is a part. I am grateful to Lawrence Cremin, Chester Finn, Harold Howe II, and Jerome Murphy for their comments on an earlier draft of this article.

[1] Andrew Hacker, "The Schools Flunk Out," *The New York Review of Books*, April 12, 1984, p. 40.

[2] Ibid., p. 35.

[3] Paul Peterson, "Did the Education Commissions Say Anything?" *The Brookings Review*, Winter 1983, pp. 3-11.

[4] For a further discussion of this topic, and its links to literacy as a central social purpose of schooling, see Patricia Albjerg Graham, "Whither Equality of Educational Opportunity?" *Daedalus*, Summer 1980, especially pp. 125-131.

[5] *Digest of Education Statistics 1983-84*, Table 8, p. 13.

[6] *Digest of Education Statistics 1983-84*, Tables 20, 21, 22, pp. 26-27, 31.

[7] *Digest of Education Statistics 1983-84*, Table 21, p. 27; C. Emily Feistritzer, *The Condition of Teaching* (New York: The Carnegie Corporation for the Advancement of Teaching, 1983), p. 46.

[8] NEA Research Bulletin, "The Status of the Teaching Profession," 18, no. 2 (March, 1940), p. 57; National Education Association, "Status of the American Public School Teacher, 1980-81," Table 1, p. 21; Charles J. Anderson, *1981-82 Fact Book for Academic Administrators* (Washington, D.C.: American Council on Education, 1981), Chart 173; *Historical Statistics of the United States*, Part 1 (Washington, D.C.: U.S. Bureau of the Census, 1975), p. 388; *Digest of Education Statistics, 1979*, Table 108, p. 113.

[9] James Patterson, *America's Struggle Against Poverty, 1900-1980* (Cambridge: Harvard University Press, 1981).

[10] Arthur Bestor, *Educational Wastelands* (Urbana: University of Illinois Press, 1953); National Commission on Excellence in Education, *A Nation at Risk* (Washington, D.C.: U.S. Department of Education, 1983).

[11] John Goodlad, *A Place Called School* (New York: McGraw-Hill, 1983); Ernest Boyer, *High School: A Report on Secondary Education in America* (New York: Harper and Row, 1983); Diane Ravitch, *The Troubled Crusade: American Education, 1945-1980* (New York: Basic Books, 1983).

[12] See, for example, Calvin M. Woodward, "The Fruits of Manual Training" (1983), in *American Education and Vocationalism*, ed. Marvin Lazerson and W. Norton Grubb (New York: Teachers College Press, 1974), pp. 60-66; Francis W. Parker, *Talks on Pedagogics* (New York: E.L. Kellogg and Co., 1894); John Dewey, *The Child and the Curriculum* and *The School and Society* (1902, 1899; rep. Chicago: University of Chicago Press, 1965).

[13] Eliot quoted in *American Education and Vocationalism*, ed. Lazerson and Grubb, p. 137.

[14] George S. Counts, *Dare the School Build a New Social Order?* (New York: The John Day Co., 1932).

[15] Lawrence A. Cremin, *The Transformation of the School* (New York: Alfred Knopf, 1961).

[16] David Tyack, Robert Lowe and Elisabeth Hansot, *Public Schools in Hard Times* (Cambridge: Harvard University Press, 1984), pp. 1-3, 166.

[17] Charles A. Reich, *The Greening of America* (New York: Random House, 1970), pp. 226-227.

[18] Clifford Adelman, "Devaluation, Diffusion and the College Connection: A Study of High School Transcripts, 1964-1981," unpublished manuscript prepared for National Commission on Excellence in Education, April 1983.

[19] Caroline Ware, *Greenwich Village, 1920-1930* (1934; rep. New York: Octagon Books, 1977), p. 343.

[20] Patricia Albjerg Graham, *Progressive Education: From Arcady to Academe* (New York: Teachers College Press, 1967), pp. 135-138.

[21] For a brief sample of Prosser's views, see his *Secondary Education and Life* (Cambridge: Harvard University Press, 1939).

[22] See, for example, Sidney P. Marland, Jr., *Career Education: A Proposal for Reform* (New York: McGraw-Hill, 1974).

[23] Robert Blackburn, Ellen Armstrong, Clifton Conrad, James Didham and Thomas McKune, *Changing Practices in Undergraduate Education* (New York: The Carnegie Foundation for the Advancement of Teaching, 1976), pp. 33-35.

[24] Peter Greer, "Epilogue: A School Administrator's View," in Chester E. Finn, Jr., Diane Ravitch, and Robert T. Francher, *Against Mediocrity* (New York: Holmes and Meier, 1984), p. 235.

[25] Larry Cuban, "Transforming the Frog into a Prince: Effective Schools Research, Policy, and Practice at the District Level," *Harvard Educational Review*, 54, no. 2 (May, 1984), esp. pp. 138-141.

[26] Benjamin Rush, "Thoughts Upon the Mode of Education Proper in a Republic" (1776), in *Essays on Education in the Early Republic*, ed. Frederick Rudolph (Cambridge: Harvard University Press, 1965), pp. 14, 17.

Learning from Experience:
History and Teacher Education

*ABSTRACT: The inseparable histories of teaching, teachers, and teacher educa-
tion point to social and institutional pressures on the development of teacher preparation in the United States over the past two centuries. Within this enlarged tradition, the forms and directions of teacher preparation appear in sharper focus. The
persistence of basic patterns of influence and policy suggests that the reform of
teacher education requires both programmatic changes and improvements in the
conditions of professional practice.*

DONALD WARREN
University of Maryland

*Donald Warren is Professor and
Department Chair of Education Policy, Planning, and Administration,
University of Maryland, College Park,
MD 20742. His specializations are the
history of U.S. federal education policy and the uses of history in policy
analysis.*

The criticism that focused on
American schools 2 years ago has
come to rest on teacher education.
Given the pattern of educational
reform sentiment that has been
repeated several times since the
mid-1940s, the shift of attention
was predictable. If the pattern
holds, general interest in the ways
teachers prepare for their professional roles will be temporary. The
pressure to make changes quickly is
thus understandable, if not reassur-
ing. The point surely is to improve
teacher education, but some aspects
of the current emphasis weaken
that possibility. In the hands of
traveling in-service trainers, an
important and instructive research
literature is reduced to a "knowledge base" that is optimistically
portrayed as promising more generalized practical applicability than

This article is based on the vice
presidential address for Division F
(History and Historiography), given at
the 1985 AERA Annual Meeting in
Chicago.

social or behavioral science research
can deliver. Overstatement in the
other direction comes from the current round of complaints about
teachers and their professional
preparation. One report announces
that "never before in the nation's
history has the caliber of those entering the teaching profession been
as low as it is today" (Feistritzer,
1983, p. 112). Colorado Governor
Richard Lamm comments, "List
the ten most somnolent courses in
a university, and nine of them will
be teacher courses." That remark
pales in quotability next to Gary
Sykes' characterization of teacher
preparation as "higher education's
dirty little secret." H. Ross Perot,
the Texas industrialist credited with
the recent passage of that state's
school reform bill, likens teacher
education to a fire drill. (Peirce,
1985). The hyperbole borders on
silliness, but it gives historians
something to chew on.

Current proposals offer strategies for raising the quality of those
entering the teaching profession.
Teacher shortages in mathematics
and the sciences are to be reduced,
for example, by appointing retired
people and housewives with appropriate academic degrees to teaching
positions. Others can become teachers by completing an undergraduate
major in a standard discipline and

an extended apprenticeship in the
"real world" of the classroom. People will be encouraged to view
teaching as a temporary commitment, not necessarily a lifelong profession. Formal teacher education
will not be the exclusive province of
schools, colleges, or departments of
education; other academic units will
assume major roles in teacher preparation. Certification will reflect
tested academic achievement and
instructional competence, not an array of education courses. As states
adopt such proposals, they reverse
developments of the past 150 years
that were intended to professional-
ize teaching and teacher education.
Whatever the value or wisdom of
the proposed changes, they are appropriate subjects of historical
investigation.

Earnest and single-minded approaches to the history of teacher
education, however, are apt to miss
some its ironic and truly delightful
developments. As Merle Borrowman (1956) observed almost three
decades ago, this is a history that
has no notable beginning. Put another way, before there was teacher
education—or, from one perspective,
even teachers—there was teaching
or, in Cubberley's (1934) derisive
term, "schoolkeeping." By 1860,
almost 7 million American children
were attending school, all but about

100,000 in what we call today the elementary grades. The vast majority lived in rural areas; even by the turn of the century most students went to schools located in districts and communities of less than 5,000 people. These general demographic characteristics reflected not only the success of the public school in the United States but also the emergence of a pervasive sector of the American labor market: teaching. The existence of new positions in considerable numbers drew people to the job, prepared or not. Given this order of development, it is helpful to understand the history of teacher education experientially, by starting at the beginning, as it were, with sketches of teaching and of those who taught during the period before teacher education became institutionalized or widespread.

Teaching

To call teaching a career in the nineteenth century would be misleading, although some of the young people who entered teaching applied precisely that term to their work. For most, it was a part-time job taken up temporarily. School terms could be measured in weeks, and those who taught tended to move on to other occupations or to marriage after a few years. The job centered on the school, and because the school was essentially a classroom, the most visible assignment was instruction. Throughout most of the nineteenth century, teachers in rural and urban schools alike drilled their students in individual or class recitations with ritualistic precision (Finkelstein, 1970). Learning was thought to have occurred when the child could reiterate the information or emulate the skill. Lucia Downing followed the procedure in her rural Vermont school in 1882, and she had only four students (Hoffman, 1981). She relied on memorization, in part, out of expediency. Lacking textbooks, she created materials for her charges from her own recollections. Here was an example of, and a reason for, teaching as one had been taught. After all, Downing's students had few books at home. Memorization could be as useful to them as it had been to her.

Research by Geraldine Clifford (1978, 1982) and Barbara Finkelstein (1970) and a wealth of primary materials made available through women's studies help us interpret the conflicting testimony about teaching methods during the last century. Surveying the evidence, Larry Cuban (1984) concluded that well into the twentieth century, the American classroom remained essentially teacher-centered. In the role of teacher resided the authority over student learning and deportment. The teacher initiated and was held accountable for whatever classroom educational dynamics occurred. Both forms of school-based behavior—learning and deportment—tended to become routinized. Recent research on the teaching role has shown that such modes of instruction—inflexible pedagogy, preoccupation with classroom order, and commitment to lesson plans—are characteristic of new teachers (Koehler, 1985). Nineteenth-century American communities frequently had only new teachers, year after year. Classroom overseers and disciplinarians abounded, but we can also document inductive pedagogies and sheer wonderment at youthful imagination. Downing recalled "one *big* boy who was *peeved* because I would not allow him the same privilege as the little ones who always wanted to kiss 'Teacher' good night" (quoted in Hoffman, 1981, p. 34). She was 14 years old at the time. Other teachers also recorded the delights and frustrations of their jobs and their efforts to teach well. Such personal accounts do not permit us to generalize about teaching during this early period, but they allow glimpses of a nascent, largely untrained profession thinking about its work.

Qualifications for teaching jobs ranged from nonexistent to formally specified. Many candidates acquired positions through family connections or simply lack of competition. Typically, school committees and local superintendents sought assurances on two fronts: candidates' moral character, and their knowledge of subject matters and of the "theory of teaching." The latter could mean little more than the teacher's resolve to act as disciplinarian. Where candidates

were numerous, their qualifications received greater attention, but faced with few choices, local officials might select the best applicant, hoping if all else failed that new teacher would be an "upright" person. In some cases the best candidate was the one who required the lowest salary. Crude and informal reviews of teaching candidates occurred in all sorts of school districts. Other urban and rural communities, however, employed more formal procedures. Some used structured interviews, but as early as the 1840s candidates qualified for their moral and academic instructional roles by passing written examinations. (See, e.g., the sample questions reprinted in the *Common School Journal of the State of Pennsylvania,* 1844.)

Teaching in the nineteenth century involved more than classroom instruction, as it has ever since. The teacher's community role was visible and presumed to be powerful. Titles were important, as was the way teachers dressed; the younger ones worked at looking older. Classroom discipline brought order to the school and also established the wider authority and social standing of the teacher, who was frequently an outsider within the community. The symbolic realm of teaching—its effective jurisdiction—extended beyond the schoolhouse. When teaching failed, an entire community, not merely the young, was left wanting. Yet Samuel Hall's (1829) complaint remained—and remains—stubbornly true. The job, he observed, offered little more respectability "than manual labor" (p. 16).

On a more mundane level, teaching involved cleaning the school, chopping wood, and making sure the room was warm in the winter—literally, schoolkeeping. Clever teachers managed to delegate the work to their older students, but they could not delegate the responsibility. Teaching contracts could be quite explicit about that. Ventilation and hygiene were practical worries; a backed up flue could empty the school on a cold day. In villages and rural areas especially, teachers worried about their own health. If they became ill overnight, the students would arrive at school the next day regardless, and if a teacher "took sick" during the day, students

16

would have to be dismissed early. Often parents sent young children to school with their older siblings, leaving teachers to cope with 3- and 4-year-olds as best they could. As Clifford (1978, 1982) found, the job included a fair amount of child care. In addition, parents had to be visited, and even in districts that had abandoned the practice of "boarding around," teachers might live with a family during the school term. Justifiably, they felt permanently caught in the public eye. Their interactions with parents and other community adults tended to be immediate and frequent.

Several historians in recent years have stressed the unbureaucratic character of teaching in rural schools and in most nineteenth-century settings (Clifford, 1978; Tyack & Hansot, 1982). However, in curbing a misguided inclination to view all schools from the perspective of twentieth-century experience with urban, bureaucratized schools, we may overlook earlier forms of paperwork required of teachers. After the Civil War period, even those in one-room rural schools probably kept ledgers that enabled them to submit through prescribed channels the complicated average attendance data that eventually appeared in state reports. Teaching, in short, involved conceptualizing, preparing for, and managing more than lessons.

A complex, if diffuse, policy environment filtered and shaped expectations of teaching in the nineteenth century. Positions were relatively plentiful, which allowed interested candidates to shop around among districts and communities. State officials regularly reported shortages. The problem was twofold. Worry about preparation and qualifications was common (Lewis, 1857; Snarr, 1946), but demand for teachers could overwhelm qualms about teachers' "moral and intellectual status." The opening of new schools and the frequent movement of teachers to new jobs or out of teaching altogether combined to create absolute shortages. Thus, the number of teaching positions in Illinois doubled during the 1850s and doubled again in the next decade. During this period, other midwestern states reported average annual

increases in the number of new teaching positions ranging from 150 to 800. These data came from state education officials anxious for additional school funding from their legislatures. We can assume the numbers have been inflated, but there is no denying the demand for teachers was great, especially in the rural areas. The shortages touched every region of the country, far exceeding the number of people prepared in the newly emerging teacher training programs.

Salaries, of course, largely determined who responded to these job opportunities. Downing earned $20 for her 10-week term in rural Vermont and could expect to double that amount in a year by teaching two terms (Hoffman, 1981). Her salary was below average. White teachers in 1870 received an average annual salary of $190. The average income earned by white teachers increased gradually over the years, reaching $1,050 in the early 1930s. Salaries for black teachers were considerably lower. The worry voiced by New Hampshire's superintendent in the 1850s remained well-founded for some time:

The compensation and reputation connected with what are termed the learned professions are strong incitements to effort in aspiring candidates, while a situation in the district school has associated with it none of these motives. The charms of the school are few and dim in the estimation of the talented . . . (quoted in Brown, 1937, p. 19)

The combined effects of available positions and low pay explained why teachers moved from district to district with such frequency. In addition, salaries and working conditions encouraged them to leave teaching for other pursuits. Even though they had few other employment opportunities, the women who were drawn to teaching in increasing numbers could not be counted on to stay put. The tentativeness of their professional commitment was reasonable; it was not surprising that efforts to institutionalize and require professional training failed to attract much response from would-be teachers. Why spend time and money in preparation when the job itself neither required nor rewarded the investment? People pre-

pared for teaching by attending a common school, by self-directed study, or both; they learned how and what to teach from their own teachers. The major incentive for many to become teachers undoubtedly was that they could find no other work to do, at least for the time being.

The grand claims for the importance of teaching voiced by nineteenth-century school reformers must be read with the policy environment firmly in mind. Individual idealists, servants of God and the nation, have left records of their hopes and their labors. However, a mass educational system was arising and few communities or states had the resources or the will to finance their part of it; rural communities, where most teaching occurred, were notoriously cash poor. In this policy environment, teaching positions could be acquired with relative ease, but given the demands and the meager rewards of the job, who would want it?

Teachers

In truth, we know more about teaching in the nineteenth and early twentieth centuries than we know about those who taught. We can be relatively confident only about matters of size and general characteristics. Between 1870 and 1900, the number of teachers grew from 200,000 to 425,000, increasing approximately 80,000 each decade. For the next 30 years the growth per decade was in the neighborhood of 150,000; by 1930 there were close to 800,000 teachers. Most worked in elementary schools, although the proportion of high school teachers rose dramatically after 1910. By 1930, women outnumbered men in the teaching force by more than 5 to 1. From numerous studies of teaching, state reports, and local surveys, we can construct a picture of American teachers during this period. Their formal training was uneven and the total years of schooling they brought to their work remained low. An impression prevailed that as a group they lacked impressive intellectual abilities and academic interests. On all these points, considerable variation existed among regions and within states. The sharpest differences occurred between teachers in large cities and those in farming areas. Urban teachers were better prepared, held their positions longer, and earned higher salaries than their counterparts in villages and rural communities.

David Angus (1983) notes the dearth of historical studies of the social origins of teachers. As he suggests, the topic requires quantitative approaches, and a number of data bases and resource materials invite analyses using contemporary techniques. One difficulty is the unreliability of education-related statistics in early state and U.S. Bureau of Education reports. Some of these weaknesses can be circumvented, however, and there are important reasons for doing so. Needed is the kind of quantitative basis that social class research can provide for examining historically teachers' frames of reference and loyalties.

A tentative beginning of such a project appeared as part of the *National Survey of the Education of Teachers* (Evenden, Gamble, & Blue, 1935) conducted early in the 1930s. Mandated by Congress, the *Survey* was published in six volumes of findings and recommendations in the middle of the decade.[1] It remains the most comprehensive empirical study of the effects, status, and prospects of teacher education in the United States, although by current standards it contains bothersome technical flaws. Oddly enough, the *Survey* did not collect data on teachers' social backgrounds. However, returns on a questionnaire that was distributed to teacher college and liberal arts college students in the midwest permitted the staff to construct general descriptions of the two student populations. The assumption that teacher college students could be safely classified as prospective teachers proved to be wrong. Fewer of these students than liberal arts college students intended to earn degrees. They were more likely to interrupt their studies, usually to take temporary teaching positions, and more of them needed financial assistance. Their parents and siblings were less educated. More of them were born in rural communities and villages, and their families were more likely

to be involved in farming. They were clearer, more precise and fixed, about their vocational goals. They attended colleges closer to their homes. The *Survey* staff was shocked to learn that over 10% of the teacher college students had no plans to become teachers, whereas almost 50% of the liberal arts college students thought they might. The latter were seen as posing a threat to teacher professionalization—they could claim the necessary academic preparation, but they would have missed the education courses needed to help them be effective in the classroom. The "marked provincialism" of teacher college students observed by the *Survey* staff has been noted in studies of active teachers (see, e.g., the review in *Elsbree,* 1939). Tyack and Hansot (1982) found small-town, pietistic backgrounds to be prevalent among nineteenth- and early twentieth-century school administrators and other educational leaders. However, the available data are sketchy and, like those gathered by the *Survey,* tend to be regionally specific. It may also be noted that the *Survey* tells us more about the social class differences of those attending the two types of colleges than about the social class characteristics of prospective teachers.

Sources reviewed by Finkelstein (1970) and Cuban (1984) reflect long-held negative views of teacher effectiveness and instructional styles. Nineteenth-century state superintendents despaired of attracting and holding able, committed teachers in their schools. Their messages to state legislatures regularly reported dissatisfaction with the quality and stability of the teaching force. Rural teachers apparently longed to live and work in cities, whereas teachers in large cities seemed to prefer working in less urban settings. The professional behavior of teachers generally impressed observers as inflexible, unimaginative, insecure, and often uncaring. Such negative assessments were pervasive and consistent—so much so that they inspire doubt. How can we reconcile this portrait of failure and low public regard of teachers with steadily increasing school enroll-

ments? Teachers must have been doing something right, or else parents valued the schooling of their children for reasons other than the perceived quality of teachers.

Susan B. Anthony thought she understood why teaching was held in such low esteem: It was a female job. In her now familiar speech to a gathering of predominantly male educators in Rochester, New York in 1853, she reasoned that because women were viewed as incompetent for any other profession, men choosing to become teachers tacitly admitted they had "no more brains than a woman." Furthermore, they should expect low salaries because they competed "with the cheap labor of women" (quoted in Lerner, 1977, pp. 235-236). The rationales offered for bringing women into teaching in greater numbers stressed economic and pedagogical benefits. Paying women teachers less than men promised absolute savings. In addition, women helped to solve the teacher shortage problem. Finally, they were seen as having natural and special abilities to inculcate morality and to lead the educational development of children. There was a dark side to these explanations as well. Calvin Stowe, who later married Harriet Beecher, thought that bringing women into teaching might deflect feminist urges to speak at public meetings and hold elective office, "notwithstanding the exhortations of Harriet Martineau, Fanny Wright, and some other[s]" (quoted in Knight & Hall, 1951, p. 415). In light of such testimony, the feminization of teaching can be viewed not only as a step toward independence, if not greater social equality, for women, but also as a process of defusing women's quest for larger roles in public affairs. If Anthony was correct, the teaching profession paid a heavy price for the fresh, inexpensive female recruits it gained. Teachers now had to do battle with bias against women as well as against their profession.

Teachers inevitably found themselves thrust into public roles, and several sources have stressed the importance of teachers' relations with the communities in which they worked. Much depended on their ability to fit in. In one study, Clifford (1982) concluded that young female teachers tended to work in districts close to their homes. Elsewhere (1978) she commented on the migratory habits of nineteenth-century teachers generally. We know also of Catharine Beecher's effort to draw eastern women to teaching positions in the West. By mid-century, state superintendents in this region were complaining about the number of "outsiders" teaching in their schools (Snarr, 1946). One could argue that because these states were largely populated by recent settlers, new teachers should have had little difficulty being accepted by their communities. But the influx offended regional sensibilities. A general impression prevailed that the able teachers remained in the East, whereas the unfit and the adventurers moved west. Illinois superintendent David Gregg thought "there would be great advantage in having a body of intelligent teachers educated in our midst, who are well acquainted with western habits, customs, and feelings" (quoted in Snarr, p. 20). The notion that local teachers should be locally trained eventually gained favor among legislators, who invoked it in supporting the establishment of regional state normal schools.

Primary sources confirm Gregg's implied criticism. Teachers in rural areas wrote, often bitterly, of their loneliness, the absence of cultural resources, and the crudeness of local residents. Some remained aloof; others threw themselves into church and community activities. Even those who closed the social and cultural gap might yet confront a more resistant form of alienation by virtue of their roles as teachers. Unlettered parents apparently pushed their children into schooling, however rudimentary; but if the process took hold, strains within the family could follow. Personal reminiscences, from women in particular, tell of family tension and parental resentment over a child's awakened educational aspirations (see, e.g., Lerner, 1977). By simply doing their instructional work well, teachers could set themselves apart from their communities. Loneliness resulting from this sort of alienation would not be erased by locally oriented teacher training.

Teacher Education

The familiar history of teacher education in the United States was a Hegelian account of successive and successful reforms. Moving upward from the founding of the first normal school, this history tended to treat institutions, key leaders, goals, and legislation as a cluster of independent phenomena. It was a history of and for teacher training.

The actual story has been more lively and important. Some colleges and schools provided teacher education unintentionally; others, as Herbst (1980) noted, intended to offer only teacher preparation and found themselves serving students with different destinations in mind. Self-conscious teacher education programs existed early in the nineteenth century, for example, Lancasterian training schools and Mary Lyon's effort at Mount Holyoke (Kaestle, 1972; Green, 1979). Later, some district schools, even in rural areas, offered teacher training for those who would become teachers in the level of schooling they were just completing. Urban high schools added "normal departments." Teacher institutes, financed locally or by the states, attracted large followings. Reformers spoke longingly and frequently of the need for normal schools throughout the century, but those institutions were founded slowly. Toward the end of the century, universities began to establish schools or colleges of pedagogy. The effect of these efforts on the great body of teachers came later. In the meantime, for reasons having little relation to the quality or availability of teacher education, teachers either received no formal training at all, received modest amounts of training after they began teaching, or had recourse to a great variety of sometimes fleeting institutional arrangements. Throughout the nineteenth century, most programs offered high-school level preparation. In the twentieth century we find a steady lengthening and upgrading of teacher education. Four-year degree programs differentiated by teaching specialty became commonplace. This long-term development in teacher training actually occurred—it was no Hegelian fairy tale. It was punctuated by periodic pedagogical reform efforts, just as Cubberley (1934) said. He is as good a source as any for the chronology of isolated developments.

So constructed, the story nevertheless offers little reason for celebration. By 1931, over 65% of white elementary school teachers had preparation ranging from only 6 weeks to 2 years of college work. Even fewer black elementary school teachers received this level of preparation: 22% had only 4 years or less of high school. Black and white high school teachers tended to have 3 to 4 years of college. Rural teachers as a group had less preparation than urban teachers. These general descriptions are based on data collected from teachers in the *Survey* cited previously. Except by level, the questionnaire distributed

The teacher economy continues to function independently of professional judgment about teacher education, as it did in the nineteenth century, and independently of research findings, as it does in our time.

by the *Survey* staff permitted no distinctions among types of institutions. A normal school was assumed to offer college level work.

Conclusions drawn by the *Survey* staff were consistent with the teacher education reform agenda that had been operative for over 75 years. The major objective was to increase the amount of teacher preparation in the now traditional curricular areas of academic studies, professional studies, and practice.

The reform strategy also remained unchanged. If more preparation was assumed to be better preparation, the way to success was enforcement. Minimum age requirements for teachers were necessary. A high school diploma was a prerequisite for admission to teacher education. Certification criteria should specify amounts of preparation required in particular subjects. As the *Survey* staff admitted, however, little convincing evidence available in 1930 showed the quantity of teacher preparation could be correlated with student achievement. The relationship between teacher effectiveness and type of preparatory institution—for example, teacher college, liberal arts college, or university—remained a matter of conjecture. No one could be confident that greater amounts of teacher education, including supervised practice teaching, had a positive impact on teachers' performance in the classroom. Unwilling to end on an uncertain note, the *Survey* staff concluded by calling for more research on teacher education and pressing for preparation programs that would reflect the proven characteristics of effective teaching.

Given nineteenth-century teaching conditions and what we know about the history of teachers, the focus on quantitative reforms of teacher education is understandable. Blaming a defensive professional culture, Church and Sedlak (1976) found that programmatic reforms reflecting enthusiasm for a particular pedagogy or a new teacher education curriculum tended to atrophy over time. In addition, no durable, pervasive institutional structure existed to house pedagogical reforms of teacher education and keep them lively through use and experimentation. In 1930, creating and strengthening the institutional framework of teacher education superseded concern about its quality. In fact, reformers perceived structural growth as qualitative improvement.

In 1985, a mature structure exists. We no longer debate whether its level should be that of higher education or whether preservice preparation should require at minimum a bachelor's degree. A guild of

teacher educators or teachers of teachers, to use Mary Lyon's term, is in place, its work supported by an accumulation of social and behavioral science research. The talk throughout the nineteenth century about a science of education sounds pretentious and quaint compared to twentieth-century confidence and sophistication.

Basic Patterns

In many respects the history of teacher education cannot be read as prologue to the present; it seems so different from current realities as to be irrelevant. Yet, persistence of basic patterns should give us pause. Consider, for example, the following. First, from the early nineteenth century forward, market considerations have driven both the policies and the curricula in teacher education, as both have responded to shortages and surpluses of teachers. The size of the teaching force nationally, the differing pressures it has exerted on the states over time, and the fluctuating demand for teachers have rendered meaningless envious comparisons between teacher education and preparation for other professions, such as law or medicine, that aspired to operate at graduate levels. The teacher economy continues to function independently of professional judgment about teacher education, as it did in the nineteenth century, and independently of research findings, as it does in our time. To be effective, imposed standards in teacher education have required the availability of candidates with restricted employment opportunities or strong altruistic commitments, preferably both.

Second, attempts to clarify responsibility for teacher education reflect a long history of controversy over the separateness of teacher preparation programs. The early advocates of normal schools wanted single-purpose institutions (Learned, Bagley, McMurry, Dearborn, & Strayer, 1920) and complained that students headed for careers other than teaching diluted the professional focus of their schools. Nevertheless, normal schools and, later, teacher colleges served general, nonprofessional educational purposes, one reason being the happy

congruence of a growing demand for accessible higher education and the need of teacher training institutions for students. Harold Rugg (1952) thought the reasons for such contradictory attitudes and policies were fairly obvious. He argued that no college curriculum could be effective unless it was controlled by the faculty responsible for it. Teacher education, like other higher education programs, has felt the effects of academic politics, that is, the faculty's competition for enrollments, budgets, and prestige. Such factors have determined a program's existence, quite apart from its quality; controlling them has been an issue of some consequence for teacher education. Cremin (1965) saw the influence of these factors on relations between Teachers College and Columbia University. Powell (1980) found them at work in conflicts between the Harvard Graduate School of Education faculty and the Arts and Sciences faculty, many of whom argued against education as an appropriate university program while trying to lay claim to education students.

Third, from the outset, teacher education has been viewed as virtually synonymous with instructional preparation. As a result, courses in practice teaching, in professional studies such as history of education and school economy (class management), and in academic studies have received a particular practical slant. This focus has tended to organize and to reinforce a limited conception of teaching as classroom activity. Subtly or overtly, the classroom has been depicted as appropriately teacher-centered, and this view has served to anchor teachers' professional lives. To the extent that the emphasis on methodological practice has prevailed, teacher education ironically has grown increasingly remote from the conditions of teaching and the experience of teachers, neither of which have been confinable to classrooms. Offered in isolation, preparation for instruction has left teachers unprepared for their more difficult responsibilities, which are to conceptualize, innovate, and analyze disparate educational and policy phenomena.

The intrusion of policy on pedagogy in teacher education has left the purposes of teacher education both fixed and fluid. There have not been any unadulterated philosophies at work, and thus temporary passions have mixed with institutional structures and social arrangements in determining how teachers acquire preparation and what they have become prepared to do and to be. Despite changes over the past two centuries, teacher education has seemed to be in perpetual disfavor. The programs were misguided, too short, or superficial; the candidates unpromising. Yet, the persistence of basic patterns of influence and policy suggests that the zeal for improvement has been narrowly focused. Enforced alterations of teacher education programs satisfy an urge for action, but the inseparable histories of teaching, teachers, and teacher education offer resources for more effective strategies. Teachers deserve preparation that conceptualizes and builds upon the broad scope of their actual responsibilities. In addition, assuming reform is the goal, teacher training programs require improvement in the conditions under which teachers work.

Notes

[1]The *National survey of the education of teachers* (Washington, DC: U.S. Government Printing Office) was published in six volumes as follows:

Betts, G.L., Frazier, B.W., & Gamble, G.C. (1932). *Selected bibliography on the education of teachers* (Vol. 1).

Evenden, E.S., Gamble, G.C., & Blue, H.G. (1935). *Teacher personnel in the United States* (Vol. 2).

Rugg, E.U. et al. (1935). *Teacher education curricula* (Vol. 3).

Caliver, A. (1933). *Education of Negro teachers* (Vol. 4).

Frazier, B.W. et al. (1935). *Special survey studies* (Vol. 5).

Evenden, E.S. (1935). *Summary and interpretation* (Vol. 6).

References

Angus, D.L. (1983). The empirical mode: Quantitative history. In J.H. Best (Ed.), *Historical inquiry in education: A research agenda*. Washington, DC: American Educational Research Association.

Borrowman, M.L. (1956). *The liberal and technical in teacher education: A historical survey of American thought*. New York: Bureau of Publications, Teachers College, Columbia University.

Brown, H.A. (1937). *Certain basic teacher-education policies and their development and significance in a selected state* [New Hampshire]. New York: Bureau of Publications, Teachers College, Columbia University.

Church, R.L., & Sedlak, M.W. (1976). *Education in the United States: An interpretive history*. New York: The Free Press.

Clifford, G.J. (1978). Home and school in 19th-century America: Some personal history reports from the United States. *History of Education Quarterly, 18*, 3–34.

Clifford, G.J. (1982). "Marry, stitch, die, or do worse": Educating women for work. In H. Kantor & D.B. Tyack (Eds.), *Youth, work, and schooling: Historical perspectives on vocationalism in American education*. Stanford, CA: Stanford University Press.

Common School Journal of the State of Pennsylvania. (1844). Volume 1 [Entire Volume].

Cremin, L.A. (1965). *The wonderful world of Ellwood Patterson Cubberley: An essay on the historiography of American education*. New York: Bureau of Publications, Teachers College, Columbia University.

Cuban, L. (1984). *How teachers taught: Constancy and change in American classrooms, 1890–1980*. New York: Longman.

Cubberley, E.P. (1934). *Public education in the United States: A study and interpretation of American educational history*. Boston: Houghton Mifflin.

Elsbree, W.S. (1939). *The American teacher: Evolution of a profession in a democracy*. New York: American Book Company.

Evenden, E.S., Gamble, G.C., & Blue, H.G. (1935). Teacher personnel in the United States. In *National survey of the education of teachers* (Vol. 2). Washington, DC: U.S. Government Printing Office.

Feistritzer, C.E. (1983). *The condition of teaching: A state by state analysis*. Princeton, NJ: The Carnegie Foundation for the Advancement of Teaching.

Finkelstein, B.J. (1970). *Governing the young: Teacher behavior in American primary schools, 1820–1880*. Unpublished doctoral dissertation, Teachers College, Columbia University.

Green, E.A. (1979). *Mary Lyon and Mount Holyoke: Opening the gates*. Hanover, NH: University Press of New England.

Hall, S. (1829). *Lectures on schoolkeeping*. Boston: Richardson, Lord & Holbrook.

Herbst, J. (1980). Beyond the debate over revisionism: Three educational pasts writ large. *History of Education Quarterly, 20*, 131–145.

Hoffman, N. (Ed.). (1981). *Woman's "true" profession: Voices from the history of teaching*. Old Westbury, NY: The Feminist Press.

Kaestle, C.F. (Ed.). (1973). *Joseph Lancaster and the monitorial school movement: A documentary history*. New York: Teachers College Press.

Knight, E.W., & Hall, C.L. (Eds.). (1951). *Readings in American educational history*. New York: Greenwood Press.

Koehler, V. (1985). Research on preservice teacher education. *Journal of Teacher Education, 36*, 23–30.

Learned, W.S., Bagley, W.C., McMurry, C.A., Dearborn, N., & Strayer, G.D. (1920). *The professional preparation of teachers for American public schools: A study based upon an examination of tax-supported normal schools in the State of Missouri*. New York: Carnegie Foundation for the Advancement of Teaching.

Lerner, G. (Ed.). (1977). *The female experience*. Indianapolis, IN: Bobbs-Merrill.

Lewis, W.G. (1857). *Biography of Samuel Lewis*. Cincinnati, OH: The Methodist Book Concern.

Peirce, N. (1985, March 26). Putting teachers to the test. *The Philadelphia Inquirer*, p. 9A.

Powell, A.G. (1980). *The uncertain profession: Harvard and the search for educational authority*. Cambridge, MA: Harvard University Press.

Rugg, H. (1952). *The teacher of teachers: Frontiers of theory and practice in teacher education*. New York: Harper & Brothers.

Snarr, O.W. (1946). *The education of teachers in the middle states*. Moorhead, MN: Moorhead State Teachers College.

Tyack, D., & Hansot, E. (1982). *Managers of virtue: Public school leadership in America, 1820–1980*. New York: Basic Books.

The Prospect for Children in the United States

Illustration by Susan Hunt Yule

Children in the U.S. today are losing ground, says Mr. Howe, a former Commissioner of Education. The interests of adults are taking center stage, and the interests of children are being pushed into the wings. Who is the champion for children?

HAROLD HOWE II

HAROLD HOWE II is a senior lecturer at the Graduate School of Education, Harvard University, Cambridge, Mass. This article is based on a speech delivered at the annual convention of the National Association of School Psychologists, April 1986, Hollywood, Fla.

THE OVERWHELMING fact that must be faced regarding children in the U. S. today is that they are losing ground. Efforts to provide children with healthy and rewarding lives are declining even as the needs for such efforts are growing. The self-interest of adults is taking center stage, and the interests of children are being shoved into the wings.

These observations are particularly true of children from poor families, whose numbers are growing, and they are most poignantly true of children

From *Phi Delta Kappan*, November 1986, pp. 190-196. Reprinted by permission of the author.

who, in addition to being poor, are also members of a racial or linguistic minority. In a short time, one-third of the students enrolled in U.S. public schools will fall into these dual categories. But, because of major changes in American family patterns, they are not the only children losing ground today. The growing numbers of single-parent families and of families in which both parents work outside the home are depriving a growing number of middle-class children of adequate adult support.

LOSS OF POLITICAL LEVERAGE

The decline in the fortunes of children stems from a fundamental change in political forces working on their behalf. This shift is best illustrated by the redistribution of voting power in most towns, cities, and states. The proportion of voters with school-age (or younger) children has shrunk, while the proportion of voters without a direct personal interest in schools, in child care, or in the health needs of children has increased. This change was not planned by anyone. It is simply the by-product of a variety of demographic, economic, and social trends. This change has created a powerful political force working in favor of the interests of people who are middle-aged and older in the competition for local, state, and national resources.

Major changes in the structure of the American family and in the work habits of women have combined to create new demands for public services for children and youth at the same time that political leverage on their behalf is declining. The growth in the number of families with two working parents and the parallel growth in the number of single-parent families have created new social needs for large numbers of children — needs for day care, for health services, for special efforts in schools. The complexity and the magnitude of these unmet needs are all too familiar to a great many *Kappan* readers, who work daily with young people whose needs are not being fully met.

The U.S. is the wealthiest nation in the world, but it is rapidly becoming a nation whose political will to provide its children with the necessities for physical, intellectual, emotional, and moral growth is weakening. Look at the national scene, and ask yourself who is the champion for children. Neither the President nor any member of his Cabinet plays such a role. Indeed, the Administration is engaged in the mindless pursuit of military hardware, partly at the expense of the college and job aspirations of children and youth.

A few voices have been raised in Congress, particularly in the House of Representatives, in an effort to slow the erosion of federally provided child services. But no one champions the cause of children in the way that Sen. Claude Pepper (D-Fla.) has for years protected and augmented the fortunes of the elderly. On the whole, Sen. Pepper's success has been admirable, and he has brought dignity and meaning to the lives of a segment of the population that had long been neglected. But where is our sense of balance? Do Americans still care for children, especially poor children, or are we willing to sacrifice them to the political imbalance between the young and the old that now exists in the United States?

When I try to provide my own answers to such frustrating questions, I find myself forced to admit that public money goes where the votes are — and children don't vote. Yet I know this to be a cynical response. Have we really forgotten that the coming generation is the hope on which the future rests? Have we regressed to an amoral condition in which we are willing to neglect the needs of children in favor of the demands of other interest groups that pay higher immediate political dividends? Or might it be possible to put together in this country a political coalition broadly conceived around the needs of children and reflecting Abraham Lincoln's view that "a child is a person who is going to carry on what you have started. . . . He will assume control of your cities, states, and nations. . . . The fate of humanity is in [a child's] hands."

My guess is that such a coalition is possible, but I must acknowledge that constructing it will be no easy task. To start with, we must ask whether a national crusade for children should identify itself with a single political party, or whether it should strive to be a broad bipartisan effort. A few years ago that question would have been difficult to answer, but it's easy now. Considering the views it has expressed and the directions in which it is moving, the Republican party and its national leadership hold no hope for the nation's neediest children. The record is so clear on this matter that there is little need to recite the omissions and commissions of national leadership that support it. At the state and local levels, there are certainly exceptions to the indifference to children that has been exhibited by those in the White House and in the Office of Management and Budget. But these exceptions do not constitute a broad enough base on which to build a nationwide campaign aimed at meeting the needs of the next generation.

If anything with a political identity is to be done in the way of a national children's crusade, it will have to be done by Democrats. This is true partly because they retain some commitment to such endeavors and partly because the recent record of the Republicans in such matters is largely negative. The record of President Reagan and his followers in dealing with the growing problems of

> **T**he overriding circumstance in the lives of children today is our lack of national political will to deal with pressing social issues.

children and youth in a rapidly changing society would earn them a very low score on any fair test of their knowledge of what has *really* happened. They continue to spout the mindless and bombastic assertions that social programs do not work and that they constitute the useless exercise of "throwing money at problems." This worn-out phrase is powerfully denied by convincing evidence. Anyone who cares to spend half an hour with the materials produced by the Children's Defense Fund will gain some understanding of why this assertion is in error; so will anyone willing to examine what we know about the effects of Head Start, of Title I of the Elementary and Secondary Education Act, of the Job Corps, of the food stamps program, and of various other social programs.

CIRCUMSTANCES OF CHILDREN TODAY

Any responsible effort to promote an agenda that meets the needs of children in the United States should not be dominated by squabbles over the record of past programs developed for the same purpose. Instead, such an effort should be concerned with today's circumstances and, to the extent we can predict them, the circumstances of the future. Let me offer a list of six of those circumstances along with some comments on each.

1. *Lack of political will.* The overriding circumstance in the lives of children today is our lack of national political will to deal with pressing social issues. Not only is the national leadership inadequate in bringing these issues to the public, but there is also a numbing sense that we can do nothing about the issues even when we understand them. Our frustration in the face of these issues stems from a combination of worry about the growing national debt, a greedy refusal to consider additional taxes, and the overselling of the needs of the national defense. This leads to a kind of paralysis at the national level that is accompanied by a tendency to thrust domestic social issues out of Washington and into the states and localities, where resources for action on social issues vary widely. The responses that emerge from states and municipalities will almost certainly deny equity to some children who are U.S. citizens and whose life chances should not be left to the political whims of 50 separate jurisdictions.

2. *A negative view of government.* A second circumstance to consider grows out of the efforts of two Presidents to bamboozle us into thinking that our national government is growing and threatening us with excesses of bureaucracy and with a loss of freedom. Jimmy Carter managed to get elected on this theme and didn't do much about it afterward, except to launch some efforts at deregulation. Ronald Reagan used the same theme before his election in 1980 and then proceeded to use government as a tool for reducing protection for civil rights, for enhancing the privileges of the rich at the expense of the poor, and for dumping onto states, localities, and the private sector uncoordinated responsibilities for numerous public needs that transcend local and state boundaries. Against this background, we need a new and better debate on what our national government can and should do in the realm of social issues. Gov. Mario Cuomo of New York offered a thoughtful contribution to that debate in his inaugural message in January 1983. He suggested that there are strong grounds for thinking positively about government as a significant means to develop and enhance freedom.

I might add that most growth in government for the last 20 years has been at the state and local levels, not primarily at the national level.

3. *Demographic trends affecting social strategies.* Today's demographic trends and their implications for the future must be taken into consideration when we think about social strategies. Although these trends were to some extent discernible as early as the 1960s, when the most recent major efforts to use government to help needy people began, they are much clearer today. As I noted above, we know more than we did about changes in the family and in the work habits of women and their impact on children. These changes are sufficiently broad and deep to warrant rethinking all kinds of familiar social programs, including those in the fields of health, education, welfare, and jobs.

But these changes are accompanied by another kind of change that also demands attention. A growing proportion of our population now comes from groups that have suffered discrimination and have, up till now, been least successful economically. Because of their higher birthrates, their younger age distributions, and the rapid immigration of some of these groups, minority Americans who are black, Hispanic, and Asian will soon constitute a majority in many cities. Moreover, the number of white children from homes whose income falls below the poverty level is growing at the same time. If we cannot move rapidly to make such children successful educationally and economically, we will deny ourselves a needed part of our skilled workforce in the years ahead, and we will cast a shadow on the sincerity of our moral commitments as a nation.

Every major national study of education that has appeared in recent years (including the federally sponsored report, *A Nation at Risk*) strongly recommends a significant federal role in addressing the problems of these children. So far, the Reagan Administration's response has been a reduction in the real value of appropriations for that purpose and suggestions that the major program for the schools be turned into a block grant (a proposal that failed) or a voucher plan (a proposal that is likely to fail, as well).

4. *A new interest in children and youth on the part of business.* A fourth circumstance that affects our thinking about children today is the vigorous participation of some of the nation's business leaders in the national debate about

improving the public schools — the largest and most pervasive institution serving children and youth. The emergence of business as a potential ally of education comes partly from the realization that, to be internationally competitive, U.S. business needs better-educated workers. It also stems from the simultaneous realization that the age group now passing through secondary school and college is smaller than it has been in the recent past, thus creating a shortage of workers as these students enter the job market. The private sector will need to dig deeper into each age group to satisfy its needs for skilled employees, and it is seeking ways to help the schools reduce the number of dropouts and enhance learning among poor and minority children.

Business support for improving the schools is welcome, even if it leaves unanswered some nagging questions. Among these is whether the depth and scale of the business commitment will extend to the major needs of public schools for added tax funds, as they struggle with the overwhelming problem of an inadequate supply of able people to fill a rapidly growing number of teaching vacancies. The children of adults who were born in the post-World War II baby boom are just beginning to enter the schools. Over the next 10 years, they will increase school enrollments. At the same time, many of the best teachers are leaving the profession to work at more attractive jobs in the growing service sector of the economy; able women are declaring their independence from teaching and seeking more rewarding professional careers; and the number of people entering teacher training is declining even as the academic ability of those who do enter the profession also declines.

Major changes in teaching conditions, teacher salaries, and teacher preparation will be required if schools are to compete for their share of able people. All these changes will be costly. Although some business leaders seem willing to help with these changes, the jury is still out on any large-scale political support for schools from that quarter. The main activity of business in recent years has been in providing small amounts of aid to individual schools or school systems. This aid is useful, but it is not sufficient to meet the major needs of schools and children. If business ultimately defines its role in this fashion, its requirements for better-prepared workers are unlikely to be met. Moreover, business remains the major contributor to efforts to impose blanket tax limitations on states and localities. Proposition 13 in California and Proposition 2½ in Massachusetts were supported by the business community, and they have deeply

damaged services to children. In Massachusetts, a particularly virulent anti-tax lobby is pressing the state to return surpluses to wealthy taxpayers rather than use them for the needs of children or for other social programs. This lobby is mainly supported by business.

5. *Prospects for children as a result of the school reform movement.* A fifth circumstance of today's national scenario for children is the school reform movement that started in the 1970s and received an added impetus from the publication of numerous reports and studies about the schools in the early 1980s. There has been a massive awakening of educators and citizens generally to the needs and problems of schools. The school reform movement of the 1980s is a multifaceted and complex affair. It consists of initiatives by individual schools, by school districts, and by states. The federal government has played only a minor role in the reform movement. State government has played a major role, particularly through initiatives by governors.

So far, school reform has centered on secondary rather than elementary schools, and its main aims to date have been to raise standards of performance required in schools, to institute testing to measure that performance, and to add course requirements for high school graduation. Similar stipulations typify the actions of states to improve teacher preparation. The reform movement includes other efforts to enhance the instructional roles of school principals, to

tap the creativity of teachers, to motivate teachers by differential salary schemes of various kinds, and to emphasize the substance of what is taught and learned. Within this movement, there has been only a minor emphasis on improving methods of teaching and very limited attention to the needs and nature of children.

My own general assessment of the school reform movement falls into two broad generalizations. On the one hand, this movement has been characterized by the imposition from above of whole new sets of requirements and standards that schools and teachers must meet. These proclamations generally emanate from the state level, and they have rarely been accompanied by adequate resources to help students meet the requirements. They show relatively little awareness of the importance of motivating students and teachers, and they are woefully lacking in any recognition of the extent and nature of educational inequity as it exists in the United States today.

On the other hand, there is a refreshing aspect of the school reform movement that sees schools as places in which teachers, parents, and principals can work together to fashion an education that serves the needs of students. In this view, each school has some freedom to draw on the creativity of those concerned with it, particularly teachers. Some latitude exists for schools to be different from each other, to invent their own futures, and to take pride in their uniqueness. This way of thinking about schools gives public schools some of the freedom that private schools have always had. Beyond this advantage, this aspect of the school reform movement seeks to make learning interesting — to enlist young people in the cause of their own education rather than to allow them to feel that schooling is something that is done *to* them. Children are not seen as receptacles into which learning must be stuffed as they pass through classrooms on an assembly line. Rather, they are viewed as human beings with endless differences from one another but with a shared general need to find in school an atmosphere that welcomes and respects them.

Teenagers who are alienated, rebellious, and sometimes self-destructive can find in this second conception of school reform a chance to bring meaning into their lives. Suggestions that caring adult mentors should help young people with family problems, that school credit should be awarded to stu-

dents who perform tasks valuable to the adult community, and that opportunities should be available to help younger students attain success in school are all parts of this aspect of the school reform movement. Some critics deplore such activities as dilutions of the academic purpose of schools, but my guess is that these activities will promote more academic success and rescue more dropouts than all the new tests, higher standards, and required courses combined.

To the degree that this second set of characteristics prevails, I think that the school reform movement can indeed improve learning. However, it will need a powerful assist from state and national government on behalf of the special needs of poor, minority, and handicapped children. As I've said above, the political will to bring that about is not now in sight.

6. *Economic fortunes of children.* Let me offer a few hard facts about how children will fare if President Reagan's federal budget for fiscal year 1987 is enacted as he presented it to Congress. If Congress resurrects the Gramm-Rudman-Hollings legislation after its debacle in the Supreme Court, the results for children will be even more austere than these examples suggest. Here are some points to consider, all of them taken from *A Children's Defense Budget, An Analysis of the FY 1987 Budget and Children*, developed by the Children's Defense Fund.

1. First, a basic description of child poverty in America:

• Thirteen million children in America are poor.

• More than one in every five children is poor.

• Nearly one out of every four children under 6 is poor.

• Almost two out of every three poor children are white.

• Nearly two out of every five Hispanic children are poor.

• More than half of the children in families headed by females are poor.

2. America leads the world in military spending but ranks 14th in keeping infants alive in the first year of life. A black infant in Chicago is more likely to die in the first year of life than an infant in Cuba or Costa Rica.

3. Under the Reagan budget for fiscal year 1987, poor children and families would lose another $6 billion from programs that have already lost $10 billion a year since 1980. From 1987 to 1991, if the President has his way, children would lose another $33 billion in federal support.

> Americans need to know that they are neglecting their children when their efforts are compared to a number of countries with smaller per-capita resources.

4. The Head Start program now reaches only 18% of the children eligible for its services, and the President proposes to cut the program's budget by $12 million. (The Committee for Economic Development, an organization of major business leaders, has strongly advocated expanding Head Start as the best investment the country can make in its children.)

5. According to Sen. Daniel Patrick Moynihan (D-N.Y.), "The United States in the 1980s may be the first society in history in which children are distinctly worse off than adults."

6. The years 1983 and 1984 saw a small improvement in the poverty rate in the U.S. If that rate of change continues and we assume no more recessions, it would take 30 years to reduce the number of poor children to 1979 levels — levels then regarded as intolerably high.

7. All the figures relating to poverty must be viewed against the background that greater child poverty means worse nutrition, less health care, more homelessness, less education, and greater despair as opportunities and options are foreclosed.

WHAT TO DO?

If these circumstances are a fair reflection of the situation facing the coming generation of children in this country, one cannot help feeling discouraged about their prospects. Most of the forces impinging on children's lives will diminish these prospects. Only two rays of hope shine through. One is the possibility that, to meet its own needs for better-prepared employees, the business community may lend some of its clout to children's causes; the other is

the possibility that child-centered concerns within the school reform movement may overcome some of its less constructive tendencies. Nowhere is there adequate recognition of the pervasive role of federal policies and appropriations on the lives of children and youth.

In such a situation, one can't help wondering whether some major national effort centered on the needs and problems of children in America isn't called for. It is hard for me to predict where the leadership for such an effort might be found, but I have some thoughts about the vanguard that is waiting for that leadership if it ever appears.

An interesting characteristic of education in the United States is the plethora of organizations it has spawned. There is a state and a national organization for every conceivable group connected to schools. Parents, principals, teachers, and teachers of particular subjects join superintendents, school board members, and, for all I know, custodians and bus drivers in this organizational mélange. All these outfits are mainly concerned with their own particular area of the educational scene, and some of them focus narrowly on the interests of their members. Although every one of them asserts an interest in the welfare of children, that interest is often considerably diluted in the programs and activities they promote.

My simplistic notion is that a National Children's Center could be put together through the support and participation of the education organizations. This new entity could develop a children's agenda for consideration by the federal government and a separate agenda for state political authorities to examine. If each membership organization in this country with direct or peripheral interest in the needs and problems of children were to put 1% of its annual membership dues into a national center for policy studies on children, the depth and significance of what we know and think about children's issues would be powerfully augmented. For starters, such an activity could make the American public more aware of the family policies, child health policies, and preschool arrangements of other nations. Americans need to know that they are neglecting their children when compared to a number of countries with smaller per-capita resources.

Whether or not such an agency should become an advocacy group for the interests of children or should remain an information-dispensing agency is a

question for further discussion. I do, however, wish to argue that the small child-advocacy organizations that now exist in the U.S. carry an awesome responsibility, when one considers the limited resources at their disposal. These small, ill-supported agencies, scattered haphazardly across the land, take up their cudgels for children and youth in important ways. They help individual children get their rights under existing laws; they push for more enlightened legislation and regulation on behalf of children; they strive to serve as the conscience of their communities and states in awakening the public to the needs of children.

Since 1978 these agencies have been organized into a National Coalition of Advocates for Students (NCAS), with headquarters in Boston and with a membership of 23 organizations from 20 states. (By far the largest of these organizations is the Children's Defense Fund, located in Washington, D.C.; it operates on both the state and national levels.) The NCAS knows more than anyone else about the day-to-day details of how children are being shortchanged by schools and other agencies that are supposed to serve them. Right now, the NCAS is stretching itself to develop a comprehensive picture of how immigrant children are served by schools and other agencies in the various states and localities in which most immigrants and refugees congregate. This is an important task that ought to have government support, even if it is conducted under private auspices.

There are, of course, social agencies, with programs that emphasize serving families and children. They make a major contribution to the debate about the issues I am raising. Their national organizations are just as relevant to the problems of children as are those of education-related organizations. And the two types of groups do not communicate as effectively as they ought to. In a nation that is now clearly failing its children, getting all these potential sources of interest and support to rally round a national agenda for the interests of children seems to me a worthy goal. Additional resources for such an agency would be found in many university-based programs that are concerned with children and with the issues of public policy that affect their welfare. Paradoxically, the U.S. has done an immense amount of research on child development without ever connecting the research as fully as it might to public programs for serving children.

My argument boils down to two main points. First, we need a national political leader who has an agenda for children along with whatever other agendas he or she may maintain for defense or for the economy or for the well-being of the aged. We have no such leader now, and none is apparent on the horizon. If groups in this country concerned about education can join with others interested in social services or in the needs of families and start looking at national policies with the interests of children in mind, their activity might call forth the required leadership for a children's crusade in a country sorely in need of one.

Second, we need a continuing, independent, and sophisticated capacity to scrutinize the agenda of our national government through the lens of the needs of children and families. We have national independent think tanks that deal with the environment, with foreign policy, and with urban affairs. But we do not have enough similar activity focused on children, families, and family policy. We tend to divide the issues that surround children into separate pieces and discuss such things as the impact of welfare or tax reform or educational initiatives on the prospects of children. We seldom start with *children*. Consider the list of subjects on which our national government maintains programs that directly affect children. Here are the main headings, but there are many more:

- health delivery systems;
- family income maintenance;
- income tax policies;
- food assistance programs;
- low-income housing;
- education, including Head Start;
- youth employment in preparation for work;
- children with special needs;
- the juvenile justice system;
- provision of child care for working parents;
- civil rights of children; and
- research on children's health, mental health, and education.

For years, the President has had a science advisor because the importance of scientific knowledge to our country — and indeed to all the world — is widely recognized. But no President, as far as I know, has even thought about an advisor on the needs of children. I'm glad we don't have one right now because his or her main activity would be to promote prayer and vouchers, two causes that are just as well left to the Secretary of Education. But perhaps at some future time the general notion that the money our national government spends on children and youth is an investment and not an expenditure will again be ascendant. When that time arrives, I hope that you, the readers of this article, will be in the vanguard, along with the millions of others who really care about young people.

Professional Credibility Through Wider Links

Teacher education must be strengthened from the standpoint of its structure, its curriculum, its links with other disciplines, and with society generally.

David S. Martin

DAVID S. MARTIN is dean of the School of Education and Human Services, Gallaudet University, Washington, D.C., and associate professor of education.

Teaching and, by extension, teacher education have struggled through 200 years of history to become established as credible and honorable professions. However, the concept of local control lies deep in the American fabric. There has been resistance to a central authority for the training and payment of teachers, and taxpayers easily vote down levies that would bring teachers' salaries to appropriate levels. The need to move away from local control is being shown by an increasing number of state legislatures which are initiating salary increases for teachers as well as mandates in other areas of education. Indeed, we are witnessing an encouraging trend toward reform. The fact that some of the initiative has come from outside the profession shows that society, for the first time, is aware that an improvement in schools and teaching depends on more than educators.

It is essential now that educators, and teacher educators in particular, recapture the initiative so that the reform movement can be shaped and controlled appropriately. The entire issue of this journal indicates a commitment to the need for professionals to play a strong role in this revitalization.

Let us examine four major domains within which specific action is needed in order to make this revitalization more than a passing fad:
- Changes must be made in the structure of teacher education;
- The content of the teacher education curriculum must be revised;
- Teacher education must be strengthened through links with other disciplines within the university;
- The teaching profession must be improved during both preservice and inservice phases by stronger, innovative links to society.

Changes in the Structure of Teacher Education

Although structural changes in any professional preparation program may at first appear to be purely external and even trivial, certain changes in the structure of teacher education are important and more than cosmetic.

1. *The first fundamental structural change must be raising admission standards for teacher education programs universally.* This idea is no longer new; it is being recognized in university after university as a way to restore positive standing to the teacher education program. It is clear, however, that the move to higher standards is occurring along a broken front and with a great deal of variation. Many fear that by raising standards, candidates may be eliminated and thereby we will reduce the nation's ability to meet the critical teacher shortage, which will deepen into the 1990s. Nevertheless, raising standards has been shown to increase greater academic respectability for the teaching profession on the university campus.

This change in respectability is not limited to students. Their academic advisers, in helping them select a major or a graduate school specialization, automatically begin to have a more healthy respect for teaching if the standards are high. The support of academic advisers is essential in guiding students who are making career decisions. Thus, while the raising of standards for admission appears to be risky, over a period of one or two years, the effect can be positive.

2. *A second structural change must occur in the length of time in which preservice preparation occurs.* Until recently, teacher preparation programs existed at the Bachelor's level within a four-year sequence, or in some cases at the Master's level following an undergraduate major in another field. Today, programs are more diverse. For example, a student who decides to

From *Educational Horizons*, Winter 1987, pp. 54-57. Reprinted with permission of *Educational Horizons*, Bloomington, IN 47401. Published by Pi Lambda Theta, Inc.

become a teacher early in his or her academic career should be able to obtain professional certification in summer sessions alone, or on a part-time basis until the time for practicum. All of these approaches are in current use, and it is time that they be developed and institutionalized. The recent Holmes and Carnegie reports on the reform of teacher education support the notion of alternative paths to professional certification.

It is also time that teacher educators take seriously the concept of mastery learning within teacher education itself. If we believe in the idea of flexible time as it applies to individual needs for children, then we should also apply this concept to the preparation of teachers. The tailoring of teacher education sequences to individual needs would allow teacher education to attract and graduate a diverse population, and also ensure that those receiving the stamp of approval from the institution have indeed mastered the necessary skills.

3. *A third structural change in the teacher education program relates to exit criteria.* As state after state has enacted requirements for the testing of teachers before permitting certification, teacher education institutions have responded by incorporating those same tests as exit criteria. This response is a classic example of reactive change that tends to trivialize the curriculum of teacher education toward only those concepts that can be tested by traditional paper-and-pencil methods. Instead, the profession should take a proactive stance.

If we make significant changes in the content of the teacher education curriculum, then the test items for exit from the program must reflect the same expanded content. The written multiple choice format, used by most states, is not the optimum format for assessing a student's mastery of certain knowledge and skills. If we insist that our future teachers use balanced education methods when they teach, then we as teacher educators should model equally balanced approaches in the testing and evaluating of these future teachers.

Although it would be more expensive, we would be able to obtain a superior profile of the prospective teacher by using a combination of written essay, multiple choice questions, systematic observation by impartial observers, videotaped segments of the candidate in action, and oral interviews. Evaluation is formative as well as summative. It should occur early enough for the results to be used during the learning process. The final exit examination

then becomes an assessment of the candidates after all possible efforts have been expended by the institution to prepare them.

These structural ideas are more than superficial. They will require a commitment beyond the resources and interests of many of today's teacher education programs.

"It is essential that educators, and teacher educators in particular, recapture the initiative so that the reform movement can be shaped and controlled appropriately."

Changes in the Content of the Teacher Education Curriculum

Until recently, the content of the teacher education curriculum had received little challenge. With the exception of a few experimental programs, the standard has been for education students to be involved in foundations courses, some courses in content, courses in pedagogy, and a variety of practicum experiences. With the impending teacher shortage, as well as the now widespread suspicion that not all traditional teacher education courses are worthwhile, the content of the teacher education curriculum is being challenged. The State of New Jersey, for example, has declared that it will not require courses in pedagogy for certification. The abolition of pedagogy, however, truly begs the question of appropriate content, because pedagogy, if properly taught, is far more than methodology.

1. *Pedagogy must be redirected toward incorporating significant*

knowledge of the subject together with the methodology to teach it. For example, "Teaching Social Studies" should emphasize obtaining additional knowledge in political science, anthropology, economics, and sociology. We cannot assume that the teacher candidate has sufficient background in these fields, nor that method will automatically follow content. For example, the social studies methods course instructor should expose students to the field methods of the anthropologist at the same time that the content of other cultures is taught. Then, future teachers of social studies will learn to apply field anthropology methods to their own teaching. Courses can be team taught by one member of the education faculty and one member of the social sciences faculty, thus ensuring the process of connecting content and method. Such teaming would also enhance the image of teacher education as a discipline on the university campus.

2. *Change in content must also come from the infusion of cognitive strategies across all components of the teacher education curriculum.* Teachers will be able to implement cognitive education only to the degree to which they themselves have had cognitive education in the teacher education program. Good teachers have taught thinking skills for centuries. For example, by establishing a laboratory experiment, teachers of science have implicitly fostered an inquiry approach in their students. But this approach is insufficient for teaching students to think with power. We now realize the importance of explicitly teaching thinking and the teaching about thinking (metacognition). A thinking skill such as categorization may be the content of part of a lesson, and the teacher actively focuses student attention on that process. On the other hand, metacognition occurs when the teacher then discusses with the students the various ways in which that particular process is used in subject matter and in life situations.[1]

We now recognize the need to educate prospective teachers cognitively so that they will be able to foster cognitive education in their own pupils. This infusion means that in foundations courses, for example, professors must include some metacognitive opportunities. In methods courses, professors should refer consistently to the cognitive basis of the subject matter and the cognitive consequences of particular methods. In practicum experiences, students should be evaluated on the degree to which they are able to involve children in cognitive activities appropriate to their development.

Changing the content of teacher education to include explicit cognitive education will require retraining teacher education faculty. This responsibility must fall to department chairpersons and administrators to organize faculty development activities and reward teacher education faculty appropriately.

3. *The teaching profession continues to come under attack for its failure to apply the results of empirical research.*[2] One of the true marks of a profession is the building of new skills based on new knowledge. The nature of the classroom with its immediate demands may explain the tendency of many teachers to resist change even when opposing evidence is clear. At least one cause of this conservatism may be the failure of the teacher education program to properly establish the habit of using and doing research.

Teacher education curriculum should infuse regular references to current research within all courses. Trainees must be required to use the literature, critique it, and explain the implications of recent research for practice; then they need to apply that research. Such a change will be more effective if trainees are placed with cooperating teachers who model an inquiring mind.

In addition, the teacher education curriculum should require that trainees develop at least one action research project and carry it out from concept through hypothesis formulation, data collection, analysis, and conclusions. By instilling the research habit in prospective teachers, we can narrow the present gap between research results and application to practice. Of course, these efforts will fail if teachers then take jobs in schools where the administrator insists on a closed-end approach to teaching. That problem is beyond the scope of this article, but the implications for the training of future educational administrators are obvious.

4. *Teacher education curriculum must incorporate regular opportunities for peer evaluation during the training period.* However, for a variety of reasons—not the least of which is the influence of teacher unions—teacher evaluation by peers has not been duly recognized in elementary and secondary education. In fact, teachers often deliberately avoid peer evaluation whenever innovative school site administrators suggest it. Yet, experiences in peer evaluation provide helpful input to a colleague who may need the ''mirror'' of a peer as well as the judgment of a supervisor. In this way, a trainee helps a colleague and

also sees alternative ways of teaching the same lesson.

Peer evaluation at the preservice stage can occur during methods courses by viewing videotapes of other teachers made earlier. Students can critique the teacher on tape; the professor then critiques the critique. Peer evaluation can also occur, under careful guidance, within practicum experiences.

"If we insist that our future teachers use balanced education methods when they teach, then we as teacher educators should model these approaches in the testing and evaluating of these future teachers."

Microteaching (live or videotaped) with anonymous peer critiques is a proven way to protect the objectivity of the evaluator and provide immediate feedback to the person evaluated.

By establishing the habit and credibility of peer evaluation during the formative stages of the individual's professional training, the practice may carry over to the teaching profession at large. With the advent of the ''career ladder'' concept in a number of states, peer evaluation must become part of the school system's core. Who knows better about a teacher's performance than a fellow teacher?

Links with other Disciplines in the University

One of the persistent problems of teacher educators on the university campus is low status in the eyes of academicians in other disciplines. This low status, perceived or real, derives partially from a widespread inferiority complex of educators, condescension by liberal arts faculty toward the practical disciplines, and lower priority for funding support by the university administration. Added to these is the perception that education is not a true

discipline but is instead an amalgam of borrowed concepts from field experience, the social sciences, and a smattering of conventional wisdom that is supported only partially by empirical research. While all of these perceptions may have some basis in reality, teacher educators must also bear some of the guilt for reinforcing this low image by sometimes retreating unto themselves on the campus and not pursuing true integration with the rest of the university. This lack of interaction can and must be changed.

With the emergence of the Holmes Group of research universities in 1985, which are now reexamining their role in teacher education, we may have the basis for a change in status. These universities exhibit, at the highest levels, administrative commitment to the education of future teachers—a responsibility heretofore abdicated by many. Only time will tell whether teacher educators will make the best of this opportunity. In the meantime, several proactive steps are feasible, and necessary, in order to forge links between teacher educators and the rest of the university.

1. *The concept of team teaching between teacher educators and other faculty will immediately enhance the understanding between disciplines and departments.* The history department member will develop an understanding of pedagogical strategies; the education faculty member will understand and develop respect for substantive issues in history. It should be on the immediate agenda of every teacher evaluation program to seek links with at least English, mathematics, social science, and science departments. Problems of faculty workload can be worked out at the administrative level if a strong case can be made for two faculty members working with the same group of students.

2. *The call for improvement in teaching in higher education, particularly at the undergraduate level, is loud and clear. The recent Carnegie report on undergraduate education underscores this need.* Many faculty members in undergraduate departments are criticized for using only the lecture method. The cry for reform presents teacher educators with unique opportunities to model more balanced approaches to pedagogy and assist with improving teaching on the rest of the campus, but deans of education and deans of arts and sciences will need to cooperate to encourage such ventures.

3. *Provide assistance with problem learners in liberal arts.* More and more liberal arts faculty are aware of the

need to balance expertise in their subject area with excellence in teaching. For example, some college students need extensive help to realize their potential. Teacher educators who are experienced school teachers can offer strategies to their colleagues on other faculties. Special government grants may be available for efforts connected with campus developmental education centers staffed by teams of faculty from the liberal arts and education.

4. *For learning problems that seem to defy solution by diagnostic and remedial approaches, joint research projects may be an answer.* Presumably, teacher educators are interested in research and publication. However, they are often required to go outside the university for research subjects. It is appropriate that these faculty carry out their projects on the campus, assisting colleagues in other units with critical problems. The convenience of locally available undergraduate or graduate student subjects is undeniable. The mutual benefit is obvious.

These four avenues for action represent some specific links that will increase the visibility and credibility of teacher education, and also, indirectly or directly, may improve teacher education itself.

Creating Links with the Community

Earlier we discussed the relatively low regard in which society holds the teaching profession. As better relationships within the university campus are established, new forms of interaction with the community can also enhance society's image of teacher education. Some of these links are already in place on a small scale and require expansion; others need to be invented.

1. *To counteract the deepening teacher shortage, imagination is required to attract experienced adults from other fields toward teaching careers.* Recently, Harvard School of Education and several other programs have begun small projects to provide retraining opportunities leading to teacher certificates in mathematics and science for mid-career businessmen and businesswomen. Mid-life career changes are not new, but strong initiatives supported by corporate and other private sources are now essential to stem the impending teacher shortage.

However, this special audience must have individualized and innovative programs. Evenings-only courses and practicum experiences in nontraditional

settings may provide ways to enable the businessperson to make a gradual transition from the higher salary that will be surrendered upon entering the teaching profession.

But, most important is an aggressive recruitment of potential teachers. By working through personnel officers in corporations (who may welcome some turnover of "burned out" employees), these two problems can be solved at the same time. One method to assist in this process is the company's paid leave-of-absence. The employee can visit the university campus, attend several education classes, and observe teaching in at least two school settings in a chosen subject area and level. Cleverly planned experiences of this nature might produce the needed link with untapped sources of teachers.

"[T]he teacher education curriculum should require that trainees develop at least one action research project and carry it out from concept through hypothesis formulation, data collection, analysis, and conclusions."

---

2. *The corporate world has also begun to show interest in partnerships with the schools in ways that have positive implications for teacher education.* Current partnerships involve a pairing of a company with a school or school system in ways that provide the school with both personnel and technical assistance.

But again, a more systematic and national effort is needed to stimulate new kinds of partnerships in every community. The federal government should permit a special corporate tax deduction to businesses that allow up to 20% of their employees to perform voluntary assistance to teachers for short periods at no loss in pay. These assistants could work with students needing extra help, provide special demonstrations on specific topics, and

become mentors for talented students who intend to enter a specific field. For example, a local electronics firm could allow an engineer to assist in a nearby junior high school science program one day each week for a full year. During that day, the engineer might work for one period with a talented student, two periods with students in science who need tutorial assistance, and in a fourth period give a guest lecture to a science class on some aspect of electronics. If this engineer decided to change careers, he or she would already have a true sense of the classroom.

3. *Schools can also profit from the active solicitation and use of volunteers from a broader base.* Now that more families require both parents to work outside the home, and as single parent families increase, fewer parent volunteers can help at school.

Retired persons are an untapped resource which only some schools have utilized. As an example, teacher education institutions in each geographical region could team with at least one large school system to establish a network through the local chapter of the American Association of Retired Persons or Golden Age Groups to identify talent. Orientation workshops, on a smaller scale than those described for businesspersons, can prepare volunteers to assist teachers. In this way, retired persons, teachers, students, and schools of education profit in visible ways and enhance credibility among various publics.

Each of these specific proposals, within the four categories of structure, content, relationship to other disciplines, and relationship with the community, is intended to provide a part of the teacher education agenda for the late 1980s. Courageous risks are necessary, but respect is granted only to those who make the effort.

Is America a nation of materialistic people who will never value education and the teaching professions as do Western European countries and such Asian countries as Japan? The question is often asked in despair by teachers and teacher educators, but it is the wrong question. The proper question is, What specific actions can educators take to foster in America a respect for and interest in education at its most fundamental levels?

1. Arthur L. Costa, "Teaching For, Of, and About Thinking," in *Developing Minds: A Resource Book for Teaching Thinking* (Alexandria, VA: Association for Supervision and Curriculum Development, 1985), 20.

2. "Helping Teachers Use Educational Research," *Research Bulletin*, (Center on Evaluation, Development and Research, 1986).

The *19th* Annual *Gallup Poll*

Of the
Public's Attitudes Toward the Public Schools

*Alec M. Gallup
and David L. Clark*

The 1987 Phi Delta Kappa/Gallup Poll of the Public's Attitudes Toward the Public Schools focuses on educational policies pursued by the Reagan Administration over the past six years. The 19th poll also continues to track trends in opinion on other questions.

Since 1981 federal education policy has changed. For example, federal expenditures for educational programs have been constrained. The report of the National Commission on Excellence in Education, *A Nation at Risk*, called for higher school standards and increased competition among schools and students. Passage of the Education Consolidation and Improvement Act of 1981 reduced categorical program aid to schools and increased the influence of state education agencies by making block grants to states. U.S. Secretary of Education William Bennett chose as the hallmark for his tenure an emphasis on the "three C's": parental *choice, character* education, and the *content* of the curriculum.

As the Reagan Administration nears a close, this survey assesses what the public thinks about the matters the President chose to bring to the country's attention during his years in office.

Perceived Improvement in Local Public Schools

In view of the emphasis on education reform since the publication of *A Nation at Risk*, respondents were asked whether, in the past five years, the public schools in their community had improved, gotten worse, or stayed the same. In general, the public reported sensing very little overall improvement. However, more public school parents (33%) feel that the public schools have improved than that they have grown worse (21%).

The question:

Would you say that the public schools in this community have improved from, say, five years ago, gotten worse, or stayed about the same?

	National Totals %	No Children In School %	Public School Parents %	Nonpublic School Parents %
Improved	25	21	33	26
Gotten worse	22	22	21	23
Stayed about the same	36	36	36	42
Don't know	17	21	10	9

Perceived Improvement in Student Achievement

A plurality of the public believes that, for students of all ability levels, achievement is about the same today as it was five years ago. Public school parents are less likely than nonpublic school parents or respondents with no children in school to believe that student achievement has gotten worse. More public school parents and nonpublic school parents believe that achievement has improved for students of above-average ability than for students of average ability or for students of below-average ability.

From *Phi Delta Kappan*, September 1987, pp. 17-30. © 1987, Phi Delta Kappan, Inc.

The first question:

Compared to five years ago, would you say that student achievement in the local public schools has improved, gotten worse, or stayed about the same for students with *above*-average ability?

	National Totals %	No Children In School %	Public School Parents %	Nonpublic School Parents %
Improved	27	23	34	29
Gotten worse	11	12	10	14
Stayed about the same	41	39	45	38
Don't know	21	26	11	19

The second question:

Compared to five years ago, would you say that student achievement in the local public schools has improved, gotten worse, or stayed about the same for students with *average* ability?

	National Totals %	No Children In School %	Public School Parents %	Nonpublic School Parents %
Improved	19	17	24	29
Gotten worse	14	15	12	15
Stayed about the same	45	42	53	40
Don't know	22	26	11	16

The third question:

Compared to five years ago, would you say that student achievement in the local public schools has improved, gotten worse, or stayed about the same for students with *below*-average ability?

	National Totals %	No Children In School %	Public School Parents %	Nonpublic School Parents %
Improved	20	17	28	23
Gotten worse	22	23	18	26
Stayed about the same	35	32	39	36
Don't know	23	28	15	15

Raising Standards

By stunning margins, the public is confident that raising standards of academic achievement will improve the quality of education. The public feels — by a 7-1 margin — that telling school districts to require higher academic achievement of students will help school quality. Nonpublic school parents are almost unanimous in endorsing this strategy.

The question:

Some school districts have been told that they must require higher academic achievement of their students. Do you think this requirement would help or hurt the quality of the public schools in this community?

	National Totals %	No Children In School %	Public School Parents %	Nonpublic School Parents %
Help quality	76	74	79	89
Hurt quality	11	10	13	6
Don't know	13	16	8	5

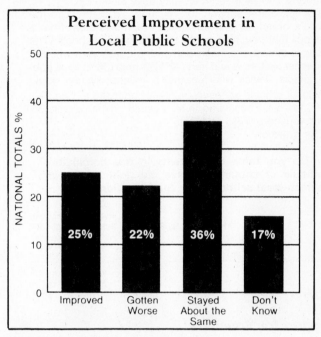

Perceived Improvement in Local Public Schools

Improved	Gotten Worse	Stayed About the Same	Don't Know
25%	22%	36%	17%

Effect on Students from Disadvantaged Backgrounds

One in three respondents (30%) expressed some concern about the effect of increased standards of achievement on students from low-income backgrounds. But a clear majority (52%) said that they think such a move will encourage these students to do better.

The question:

Some people say that raising achievement standards will encourage students from low-income backgrounds to do better in school. Others say that raising the standards will put these students at such a disadvantage that they will become discouraged about school or will even drop out. Do you think that raising achievement standards will encourage students from poor backgrounds to do better in school, or will it cause them to become discouraged or to drop out?

	National Totals %	No Children In School %	Public School Parents %	Nonpublic School Parents %
Yes, encourage	52	52	51	60
No, discourage	30	27	37	28
Don't know	18	21	12	12

Support for Parental Choice

President Reagan and Secretary Bennett have pressed consistently for an expansion of parental choice. Respon-

1. PERCEPTIONS OF EDUCATION IN AMERICA

dents were asked about increasing parental choice with regard to the local schools their children attend. Seven of 10 Americans think that parents should have the right to choose. Asked, more specifically, if they would favor a voucher system to enable parents to choose among public, parochial, or private schools, respondents supported the idea by a narrow margin, as they have since 1981.

The lukewarm support for vouchers, in contrast to the public's broad support for choice, seems to stem from a concern that vouchers might hurt the public schools. The public is almost evenly divided on the question of whether a voucher system would hurt (42%) or help (36%) local public schools. Those who feel that a voucher system would hurt local schools are overwhelmingly opposed to vouchers (81% to 7%). Those who think it would help local schools favor vouchers (73% to 16%).

The question:

Do you think that parents in this community should or should not have the right to choose which local schools their children attend?

	National Totals %	No Children In School %	Public School Parents %	Nonpublic School Parents %
Yes	71	68	76	81
No	20	20	21	15
Don't know	9	12	3	4

Support for Vouchers

The question:

In some nations, the government allots a certain amount of money for each child's education. The parents can then send the child to any public, parochial, or private school they choose. This is called the "voucher system." Would you like to see such an idea adopted in this country?

	National Totals %	No Children In School %	Public School Parents %	Nonpublic School Parents %
Yes	44	42	49	49
No	41	42	40	46
Don't know	15	16	11	5

NATIONAL TOTALS

	1987 %	1986 %	1985 %	1983 %	1981 %	1971 %	1970 %
Favor	44	46	45	51	43	38	43
Oppose	41	41	40	38	41	44	46
Don't know	15	13	15	11	16	18	11

Parental Input on Curriculum, Instructional Materials, and Library Books

No such equivocation exists regarding parental input in setting the curriculum or in the selection of instructional materials and library books. Overwhelmingly, the public feels that parents of public school students should have more (45%) rather than less (8%) to say about the courses that are offered. Thirty-seven percent of respondents feel that parents have about the right amount of say in determining the curriculum.

Despite concerns about censorship, the public also feels that parents should have more, rather than less, influence in the selection of instructional materials (38% to 14%) and in the selection of books placed in school libraries (36% to 16%). Thirty-nine percent feel that the public has about the right amount of say in the selection of instructional materials; 38% feel that the public has the right amount of say in the selection of books for school libraries.

The first question:

Do you feel that parents of public school students should have more say, less say, or do they have about the right amount of say regarding the curriculum, i.e., the courses offered?

	National Totals %	No Children In School %	Public School Parents %	Nonpublic School Parents %
More say	45	40	51	65
Less say	8	10	5	4
Right amount	37	37	41	26
Don't know	10	13	3	5

The second question:

Do you feel that parents of public school students should have more say, less say, or do they have about the right amount of say regarding instructional materials?

	National Totals %	No Children In School %	Public School Parents %	Nonpublic School Parents %
More say	38	36	42	50
Less say	14	15	10	12
Right amount	39	36	46	34
Don't know	9	13	2	4

The third question:

Do you feel that parents of public school students should have more say, less say, or do they have about the right amount of say regarding the books placed in school libraries?

	National Totals %	No Children In School %	Public School Parents %	Nonpublic School Parents %
More say	36	34	40	47
Less say	16	17	11	14
Right amount	38	36	45	33
Don't know	10	13	4	6

Emphasis on the Basics

Few respondents doubt the efficacy of increasing the number of required courses in basic subjects (e.g., math and science), even at the expense of electives. Indeed, three-fourths of the public feel that doing so would improve the quality of the schools. Only 28% of the public feel that elementary schools give enough attention to the three R's. However, nearly half of the public school parents (46%) believe that enough time is given to those subjects in the elementary grades.

For students who plan to attend college, more than 70%

of the respondents would require at least five basic subjects: mathematics, English, history, science, and computer training. More than half would require career education, business education, foreign language, and health education. The 1987 poll revealed an increased desire for required core courses for college-bound students since 1985, when this question was last included in the poll.

The respondents also tended to favor increasing the number of required courses for students who do not plan to go on to college. However, there was less agreement on which courses to require. More than 70% of the public would require mathematics, English, and vocational training. More than half would require history, business education, computer training, career education, and science.

At all grade levels, the public is concerned that every student have adequate exposure to and training in the basics. Moreover, the public does not have great difficulty defining what is basic: English and mathematics are basic for all students at all levels; history, science, and computer training are not far behind; vocational, career, or business education is a basic for the non-college-bound student.

The first question:

Some school districts have been told that they must require students to take more courses in basic subjects, such as math and science, thus reducing the number of elective courses students can take. Do you think this requirement would improve or hurt the quality of the public schools in this community?

	National Totals %	No Children In School %	Public School Parents %	Nonpublic School Parents %
Improve quality	75	74	76	85
Hurt quality	11	9	16	7
Don't know	14	17	8	8

The second question:

Is it your impression that the public elementary schools give enough attention, or not enough attention, to reading, writing, and arithmetic?

	National Totals %	No Children In School %	Public School Parents %	Nonpublic School Parents %
Enough	28	21	46	23
Not enough	58	62	47	67
Right amount*	6	6	5	6
Don't know	8	11	2	4

*Those who said "right amount" volunteered that answer.

Required Core Courses

The first question:

Please look over this card, which lists high school subjects. If you were the one to decide, what subjects would you require every high school student who *plans to go on to college* to take?

For Those Planning to Go to College

	1987 %	1985 %	1984 %	1983 %	1981 %
Mathematics	94	91	96	92	94
English	91	88	94	88	91
History/U.S. government	84	76	84	78	83
Science	83	76	84	76	76
Computer training	72	71	—	—	—
Career education	63	57	—	—	—
Business education	59	59	68	55	60
Foreign language	56	53	57	50	54
Health education	54	48	52	43	47
Physical education	45	40	43	41	44
Vocational training*	31	27	37	32	34
Music	23	24	22	18	26
Art	23	23	24	19	28

*In 1981 this subject was called "industrial arts/homemaking."

The second question:

What about those public high school students who do *not plan to go to college* when they graduate? Which courses would you require them to take?

For Those *Not* Planning to Go to College

	1987 %	1985 %	1984 %	1983 %	1981 %
Mathematics	88	85	92	87	91
English	85	81	90	83	89
Vocational training	78	75	83	74	64
History/U.S. government	69	61	71	63	71
Business education	65	60	76	65	75
Computer training	61	57	—	—	—
Career education	61	57	—	—	—
Science	57	51	61	53	58
Health education	49	43	50	42	46
Physical education	41	40	44	40	43
Foreign language	20	17	19	19	21

Government and the Schools

In the September 1984 *Kappan* President Reagan argued that "we must restore parents and state and local governments to their rightful place in the educational process. . . . Decisions about discipline, curriculum, and academic standards . . . shouldn't be made by people in Washington. They should be made at the local level by parents, teachers, and administrators in their own communities." The public agrees. There is no indication that the American people want to cut *any level* of government out of the educational arena.

However, when it comes to government influence in the schools, the people feel that the closer to home the source of that influence is, the better. Asked whether they favor more or less government influence in the improvement of schools, 37% of the respondents favored more federal influence in school improvement, 55% favored more state influence, and 62% favored more local influence. Only at the federal level did a plurality of respondents favor less influence (39% to 37%); at the local level, more than four times as many respondents favored more government influence than favored less (62% to 14%).

In one instance, the public does not favor vesting authority in local government. Asked who should check to determine whether local schools are conforming to the minimum standards set by the state, the public preferred the state by a 3-2 margin. The concern of the public for minimum standards supersedes its concern for local control.

1. PERCEPTIONS OF EDUCATION IN AMERICA

One special issue surrounding the control of schools is what is termed disestablishment, i.e., dismantling the U.S. Department of Education (ED). ED was established near the end of the Carter Administration. Nearly one-fourth of those queried don't know whether they favor disestablishment. The remainder are divided almost equally on the question: 39% favor dismantling ED; 37% would keep ED intact.

The question:

Would you like the federal government in Washington to have more influence, or less influence, on improving the local public schools? How about the state government? How about the local government?

	Federal Government		State Government		Local Government	
	National Totals %	Public School Parents %	National Totals %	Public School Parents %	National Totals %	Public School Parents %
More	37	41	55	59	62	67
Less	39	42	21	22	15	14
Same amount*	14	10	15	14	15	14
Don't know	10	7	9	5	8	5

*Those who said ''same amount'' volunteered that answer.

Tasks the Federal Government Should Undertake

In a related question, respondents were asked whether or not the federal government should undertake each of 11 different tasks that pertain to public education. Some eight of 10 Americans favored federal involvement in requiring state and local systems to meet minimum standards (84%), advising and encouraging state and local systems to deal with national problems (83%), identifying important national problems (81%), promoting educational programs intended to solve social problems (80%), and funding programs to deal with important national educational problems (78%).

Some seven of 10 Americans would favor federal efforts to recognize the achievement of students, teachers, and schools (76%), to support a national testing program for public school students (74%), to collect and report education statistics (73%), to fund research and development (72%), and to provide financing for fellowships and scholarships for college students (72%).

The question:

This card lists various things that the federal government in Washington might do for education in America. As I read off each item, would you tell me whether it is something that you think that the government should do, or should not do, for American education?

	Yes %	No %	Don't Know %
Require states and local school districts to meet minimum educational standards	84	10	6
Advise and encourage state and local educational systems to deal with important national problems in education, such as illiteracy and poor math achievement	83	10	7
Identify important national problems in education, such as illiteracy and poor math achievement	81	12	7
Promote educational programs intended to help solve such social problems as poverty and unequal opportunities for minorities, women, and the handicapped	80	12	8
Fund programs to deal with important national educational problems, such as illiteracy and poor math achievement	78	15	7
Provide recognition and awards for high achievement by students, teachers, and schools	76	17	7
Support a national testing program for public school students	74	17	9
Collect and report information and statistics that measure the performance of education in the nation	73	18	9
Fund research and development in areas of need, such as the curriculum and teaching methods	72	19	9
Provide financing for scholarships and fellowships for college students	72	20	8
Provide financial aid to the states through block grants that can be used for education or for any other purpose	57	30	13

Character Education in the Schools

Secretary of Education William Bennett has made character education one of his primary emphases. The respondents were asked whether they thought courses on personal values and ethical behavior should be taught in the public schools or left to parents and the churches. Forty-three percent said that such courses should be taught in the schools, and another 13% volunteered that schools, parents, and churches should all be involved.

The question:

It has been proposed that the public schools include courses on ''character education'' to help students develop personal values and ethical behavior. Do you think that courses on values and ethical behavior should be taught in the public schools, or do you think that this should be left to the students' parents and the churches?

	National Totals %	No Children In School %	Public School Parents %	Nonpublic School Parents %
Yes, schools	43	42	45	54
No, parents and churches	36	36	38	31
Both*	13	13	13	11
Don't know	8	9	4	4

*Those who said ''both'' volunteered that answer.

Content of Character Education Courses

All respondents were also asked: 1) whether it would be possible to develop character education courses acceptable to most of the people in their communities, 2) who should have the most to say about the content of such courses, and 3) whether those students who objected to the content of character education courses should be excused from attendance.

Six of 10 Americans (62%) think that it would be possible to develop subject matter for coursework on ethics and values that would be acceptable to most of the residents of their communities. Only about two of 10 (23%) feel that this would not be possible.

By a substantial margin, Americans feel that parents should have the most influence on the content of character education courses. Forty-two percent mentioned parents. The school board, mentioned by 24%, was the next most frequently mentioned group. Relatively far behind are teachers (14%) and administrators (10%). The state and federal governments are at the bottom, named by only 9% and 5% respectively.

By a margin of almost 5-3, respondents favored excusing students from character education classes if their parents object to what is taught.

The first question:

Do you think that it would be possible or not possible to develop subject matter for a character education course that would be acceptable to most of the people in this community?

	National Totals %	No Children In School %	Public School Parents %	Nonpublic School Parents %
Possible	62	59	68	78
Not possible	23	24	22	17
Don't know	15	17	10	5

The second question:

If courses about values and ethical behavior were required in the local public schools, who do you think should have the most to say about the content of the courses? The federal government in Washington, the state government, the local school board, the school administrators, the teachers, or the parents?

	National Totals %	No Children In School %	Public School Parents %	Nonpublic School Parents %
Parents	42	39	49	43
Local school board	24	24	24	30
Teachers	14	14	17	15
School administrators	10	11	8	7
State government	9	9	7	10
Federal government	5	5	5	6
Don't know	12	14	9	6

(Figures add to more than 100% because of multiple answers.)

The third question:

If students or their parents objected to what was taught in these classes, do you think the students should be excused from these classes or not?

	National Totals %	No Children In School %	Public School Parents %	Nonpublic School Parents %
Yes, excused	52	49	57	62
No, not excused	37	37	37	32
Don't know	11	14	6	6

School Prayer

President Reagan has always been unequivocal in his advocacy of school prayer. So has the general public. Seventy-eight percent of the public are aware of the fact that an amendment to the U.S. Constitution has been proposed allowing school prayer. Within that group, 68% favor the amendment, and 26% oppose it. Almost three-fourths of the total sample (71%) feel that only a small percentage of the population would be offended by school prayer.

The first question:

Do you favor or oppose an amendment to the U.S. Constitution that would allow prayer in the public schools?

Asked of those aware of the amendment	National Totals %	No Children In School %	Public School Parents %	Nonpublic School Parents %
Favor	68	68	69	59
Oppose	26	26	26	35
Don't know	6	6	5	6

The second question:

Do you think that a small percentage or a large percentage of the public would be offended if prayer were permitted in the public schools?

	National Totals %	Those Who Favor Prayer %	Those Who Oppose Prayer %
Large percentage	18	12	35
Small percentage	71	78	53
Don't know	11	10	12

Grading the Public Schools

If more people feel that the public schools have improved over the past five years than feel they have gotten worse, that should be reflected in the public's ratings of the local schools. And it is. The percentage of the public who give the schools grades of A or B is up 2% in 1987, and the percentage who give the schools a grade of C or higher is up 4%.

As has been the case in past polls, parents are more likely to give the schools in their communities grades of A or B than are nonparents (56% to 39%). Those Americans who are most likely to give the schools high grades are the best-educated (i.e., college graduates) and those in higher income categories (more than $30,000 a year). Those least likely to award the local public schools high marks tend to be younger (under age 30), less affluent, residents of central cities, and nonwhite.

One troublesome note in these data is the negative correlation between the level of satisfaction with the public schools and already-evident demographic shifts of the next 25 years. That is, the population groups most likely to grow in the coming decades are those that are also most likely to express dissatisfaction with the public schools. This problem is exacerbated by the public's feeling that the reform movement has improved the schools *least* for students of

1. PERCEPTIONS OF EDUCATION IN AMERICA

below-average ability. Barring a change in one of these factors, it is reasonable to predict that the grading of the public schools will decline sometime in the 1990s.

The first question:

Students are often given the grades A,B,C,D, and FAIL to denote the quality of their work. Suppose the *public* schools themselves, in this community, were graded in the same way. What grade would you give the public schools here — A,B,C,D, or FAIL?

	National Totals %	No Children In School %	Public School Parents %	Nonpublic School Parents %
A + B	43	39	56	25
A	12	9	19	7
B	31	30	37	18
C	30	29	30	45
D	9	9	9	15
FAIL	4	4	3	8
Don't know	14	19	2	7

	A + B %	A %	B %	C %	D %	FAIL %	Don't Know %
NATIONAL TOTALS	43	12	31	30	9	4	14
Sex							
Men	42	12	30	34	9	3	12
Women	43	11	32	27	10	5	15
Race							
White	43	11	32	30	9	4	14
Nonwhite	35	14	21	34	11	8	12
Age							
18 - 29 years	36	8	28	34	12	4	14
30 - 49 years	44	13	31	33	10	5	8
50 and over	46	13	33	25	6	4	19
Community Size							
1 million and over	35	10	25	29	13	7	16
500,000 - 999,999	42	12	30	37	7	3	11
50,000 - 499,999	44	12	32	34	7	4	11
2,500 - 49,999	45	15	30	26	7	3	19
Under 2,500	53	13	40	28	7	2	10
Central city	28	7	21	39	14	6	13
Education							
College	46	11	35	30	10	3	11
Graduate	49	12	37	26	11	3	11
Incomplete	42	9	33	33	10	4	11
High school	40	11	29	32	9	5	14
Graduate	43	12	31	33	10	3	11
Incomplete	35	9	26	30	7	8	20
Grade school	40	19	21	22	6	6	26
Income							
$40,000 and over	48	13	35	29	10	4	9
$30,000 - $39,999	47	13	34	31	10	3	9
$20,000 - $29,999	45	12	33	31	7	5	12
$10,000 - $19,999	35	8	27	32	9	4	20
Under $10,000	45	16	29	24	10	3	18
Region							
East	39	11	28	29	11	6	15
Midwest	45	13	32	29	7	4	15
South	47	12	35	30	7	4	12
West	36	10	26	34	13	4	13

Respondents were also asked to grade separately the high schools and the elementary schools in their communities. High schools received markedly lower ratings than elementary schools. Forty percent of the public at large and 51% of respondents with children in the public schools awarded the high schools in their community a grade of A

or B. The elementary schools received an A or B from 52% of the public at large and from a remarkable 70% of public school parents.

The second question:

How about the public *high schools* in this community? What grade would you give them?

	National Totals %	No Children In School %	Public School Parents %	Nonpublic School Parents %
A + B	40	37	51	30
A	11	10	17	10
B	29	27	34	20
C	26	26	24	29
D	9	9	9	16
FAIL	4	4	3	10
Don't know	21	24	13	15

The third question:

How about the public *elementary schools* in this community? What grade would you give them?

	National Totals %	No Children In School %	Public School Parents %	Nonpublic School Parents %
A + B	52	46	70	45
A	16	12	28	11
B	36	34	42	34
C	22	22	19	36
D	4	4	5	5
FAIL	3	2	1	6
Don't know	19	26	5	8

Grading School Personnel

Teachers in local public schools receive high grades; 49% of the public give teachers a grade of A or B, as they have in previous polls. Public school parents rate teachers even higher; nearly two-thirds (64%) give them grades of A or B.

For the second year in a row, the ratings given administrators lagged behind those given teachers; 43% of the public award public school administrators a grade of A or B. However, public school parents rated principals and other administrators much higher than they were rated by respondents with no children in school or by nonpublic school parents. Six of 10 public school parents graded principals A or B, while only about four of 10 other respondents did so.

Not surprisingly, the public grades the personnel in elementary schools more favorably than the personnel in high schools, just as it grades the elementary schools higher than the secondary schools. When respondents were asked to grade local teachers, the grades were lower for high school teachers (43% gave them grades of A or B) than for elementary school teachers (53% gave them grades of A or B). Similarly, the grades given high school principals were lower (38% A or B) than those given elementary school principals (47% A or B).

The first question:

What grade would you give the teachers in the public schools in this community — A,B,C,D, or FAIL?

	National Totals %	No Children In School %	Public School Parents %	Nonpublic School Parents %
A + B	49	44	64	44
A	15	12	24	12
B	34	32	40	32
C	25	25	25	31
D	6	5	7	9
FAIL	3	3	2	5
Don't know	17	23	2	11

The second question:

What grade would you give the principals and administrators in the public schools in this community?

	National Totals %	No Children In School %	Public School Parents %	Nonpublic School Parents %
A + B	43	37	59	37
A	14	10	23	11
B	29	27	36	26
C	27	27	25	29
D	9	8	8	13
FAIL	3	3	4	8
Don't know	18	25	4	13

High School vs. Elementary School

The first question:

How about the local public *high school* teachers?

	National Totals %	No Children In School %	Public School Parents %	Nonpublic School Parents %
A + B	43	40	51	39
A	12	10	17	11
B	31	30	34	28
C	24	24	24	26
D	8	8	8	14
FAIL	3	3	2	4
Don't know	22	25	15	17

The second question:

How about the local *elementary school* teachers?

	National Totals %	No Children In School %	Public School Parents %	Nonpublic School Parents %
A + B	53	47	71	51
A	18	14	30	14
B	35	33	41	37
C	21	21	17	29
D	4	4	5	8
FAIL	2	2	1	3
Don't know	20	26	6	9

The third question:

How about the local public *high school* principals and administrators?

	National Totals %	No Children In School %	Public School Parents %	Nonpublic School Parents %
A + B	38	36	46	33
A	11	10	15	9
B	27	26	31	24
C	24	24	22	28
D	9	8	11	15
FAIL	5	5	4	8
Don't know	24	27	17	16

The fourth question:

How about the local *elementary school* principals and administrators?

	National Totals %	No Children In School %	Public School Parents %	Nonpublic School Parents %
A + B	47	40	63	46
A	15	11	26	14
B	32	29	37	32
C	23	24	21	32
D	6	5	6	7
FAIL	2	2	2	4
Don't know	22	29	8	11

Liberal Arts Degrees for Teachers

Despite the relatively high grades given to teachers by the American public, the 1987 survey still shows a demand for higher standards and requirements for teaching personnel. In the 1986 poll, 85% of the public favored requiring experienced teachers to pass a statewide test of basic competence in their subject areas. Three previous education polls showed across-the-board support for teacher competency testing.

This year the public was asked whether or not a prospective teacher should be required to have a four-year liberal arts degree with a *subject-matter major* before entering a teacher training program. This requirement, which has been advocated by two major reform groups in teacher education (the Carnegie Forum on Teaching and the Holmes Group), is favored by 72% of the public. Only 17% oppose it.

The question:

A recommendation has been made that anyone who wants to become a public school teacher must have a four-year liberal arts degree with a major in some subject before he or she can enter any teacher training program. Do you favor or oppose this recommendation?

	National Totals %	No Children In School %	Public School Parents %	Nonpublic School Parents %
Favor	72	70	76	75
Oppose	17	16	19	19
Don't know	11	14	5	6

Support for Sex Education

Although the results of the 1987 Gallup/Phi Delta Kappa survey show no statistically significant increase over the past two years in support for sex education, a substantial increase in the percentage of those favoring sex education has been recorded since the question was first asked in 1981. In that year, the inclusion of sex education in the public school curriculum was favored by a substantial majority (70%) for high school students and by less than a majority (45%) for elementary students. Today, 76% of the public favor sex education for high school students, and 55% support sex education in elementary school.

The first question:

Do you feel that the public high schools should or should not include sex education in their instructional program?

	National Totals %	No Children In School %	Public School Parents %	Nonpublic School Parents %
Should	76	73	82	81
Should not	16	16	14	18
Don't know	8	11	4	1

The second question:

Do you feel that the public elementary schools should or should not include sex education in grades 4 through 8?

	National Totals %	No Children In School %	Public School Parents %	Nonpublic School Parents %
Should	55	52	60	69
Should not	37	38	35	29
Don't know	8	10	5	2

Topics to Be Covered in Sex Education

As for specific topics that should be covered in sex education, somewhat more liberal attitudes appear to prevail in 1987 than was the case in 1981. Approximately 4% more of the public find coverage of the seven topics selected for evaluation acceptable today than in 1981 — both for high school students and for elementary students.

Large differences emerge between those topics that are acceptable in high school and those that are acceptable in elementary school. The two exceptions to this rule are the biology of reproduction and teenage pregnancy, which more than eight of 10 Americans feel should be covered in both the elementary schools and the high schools. Eight of 10 Americans think venereal disease, AIDS, and birth control should be covered in high school classes, but only about half would include these topics in the elementary school curriculum. A distinct minority would include the topics of homosexuality, premarital sex, abortion, and the nature of sexual intercourse at the elementary level — a figure that has not increased since 1981.

The question:

Which of the following topics, if any, listed on this card should be included in sex education in high school? In elementary school?

	Topics That Should Be Included In High School			In Elementary School		
	1987 %	1985 %	1981 %	1987 %	1985 %	1981 %
AIDS*	84	—	—	58	—	—
Birth control	83	85	79	49	48	45
Venereal disease	86	84	84	59	49	52
Biology of reproduction	80	82	77	82	89	83
Premarital sex	66	62	60	37	34	40
Nature of sexual intercourse	61	61	53	41	45	36
Abortion	60	60	54	28	28	26
Homosexuality	56	48	45	30	28	33
Teen pregnancy*	84	—	—	87	—	—

*These topics were not included in the earlier surveys.
(Figures add to more than 100% because of multiple answers.)

Most Important Problems Facing Local Public Schools in 1987

In 1986, for the first time, the public identified drug use (or abuse) as the most important problem facing the public schools. This year, drug use was again the number-one concern, and the percentage of the public mentioning it increased from 28% to 30%. Four other problems increased by 3% each in frequency from 1986 to 1987: lack of proper financial support, 11% to 14%; difficulty in getting good teachers, 6% to 9%; large schools/overcrowding, 5% to 8%; and pupils' lack of interest/truancy, 3% to 6%.

Lack of discipline was cited by 22% of the respondents and remained the number-two problem with which Americans feel the public schools must deal.

The question:

What do you think are the biggest problems with which the public schools in this community must deal?

	National Totals %	No Children In School %	Public School Parents %	Nonpublic School Parents %
Use of drugs	30	31	29	27
Lack of discipline	22	22	20	28
Lack of proper financial support	14	12	18	14
Difficulty in getting good teachers	9	9	10	9
Poor curriculum/poor standards	8	7	10	9
Large schools/ overcrowding	8	7	10	5
Moral standards	7	7	6	9
Parents' lack of interest	6	6	6	11
Pupils' lack of interest/truancy	6	7	5	4
Drinking/alcoholism	6	6	7	4
Teachers' lack of interest	5	4	7	12
Low teacher pay	5	4	5	9
Lack of respect for teachers/other students	4	4	5	8
Integration/busing	4	4	4	3
Crime/vandalism	3	4	2	5
Problems with administration	2	2	3	7
Lack of needed teachers	2	2	3	1

	National Totals %	No Children In School %	Public School Parents %	Nonpublic School Parents %
Lack of proper facilities	2	2	1	3
Transportation	1	1	2	*
Fighting	1	1	1	*
Too much emphasis on sports	1	1	1	*
Communication problems	1	1	1	*
Peer pressure	1	1	1	1
Mismanagement of funds/programs	1	1	1	1
Parents' involvement in school activities	1	1	*	*
School board politics	1	1	1	*
Too many schools/ declining enrollment	1	1	1	1
There are no problems	2	2	4	1
Miscellaneous	7	6	11	6
Don't know	14	17	7	8

*Less than one-half of 1%.
(Figures add to more than 100% because of multiple answers.)

The Public's Knowledge of Issues in Education

Few policy issues in education are likely to force their way onto the front pages of newspapers. When 13 education issues were presented to public school parents who were then asked if they had heard or read *something* about them, only six issues were checked by more than half of the respondents.

Some items considered critical by the makers of education policy are barely visible to the general public. For example, only one in five people had heard about the introduction of character education courses in the public schools; only about one in four knew of the national achievement awards programs for students and schools or about voucher plans; roughly four of 10 had heard about efforts to transfer authority from the federal government to the states, to increase the number of required courses in school, to teach about the role of religion in this country and the world, or to foster parental choice of the schools their children attend. On the other end of the scale, three-fourths of the public school parents had heard about sex education and about efforts to introduce organized prayer in the schools.

What the people have heard about and what they are concerned about are not always the same. People are concerned about sex education (27%) and prayer in the schools (25%). But they are also concerned about voucher plans (24%), the transfer of authority to the states (19%), and parental choice of children's schools (23%) — all issues about which the majority claims to have heard or read nothing.

The question:

This card lists various issues related to public education in this country that have been discussed in the news recently. Would you read off, by letter, all of those issues, if any, that you have heard or read something about?
Which of these issues worry or concern you?

	Public School Parents	
	Heard or Read About %	Worried or Concerned About %
Requiring sex education in the public schools	76	27
Permitting organized prayer in public schools	73	25
Requiring higher standards in the public schools	60	14
Recent efforts by the state government to improve public school education	59	15
Recent efforts by the federal government to improve public school education	53	14
Requiring higher achievement of public school students	52	14
Increasing the number of required courses in school and reducing the number of electives	40	14
Permitting parents more say about which local school their children attend	40	23
Teaching about the role played by religion in the history of this country and the world	38	17
Transferring the authority and responsibility for public education from the federal government to the state governments	36	19
Establishing national awards for high-performing public schools and for high-achieving public school students	28	11
Proposals to provide school vouchers to public school parents that could be used for any public, private, or church-related school	27	24
Introducing required courses in character education to develop personal values and ethical behavior	19	17

Research Procedure

The Sample. The sample used in this survey embraced a total of 1,571 adults (18 years of age and older). It is described as a modified probability sample of the U.S. population. Personal, in-home interviewing was conducted in all areas of the nation and in all types of communities. A description of the sample and sample design is available from Phi Delta Kappa.

Time of Interviewing. The fieldwork for this study was carried out during the period of 10-13 April 1987.

The Report. The heading "Nonpublic School Parents" consists of parents of students who attend parochial schools and parents of students who attend private or independent schools.

Due allowance must be made for statistical variation, especially in the case of findings for groups consisting of relatively few respondents, e.g., nonpublic school parents.

The findings of this report apply only to the U.S. as a whole and not to individual communities. Local surveys, using the same questions, can be conducted to determine how local areas compare with the national norm.

Continuity and Change in Education

Continuity in an educational system necessarily implies the reevaluation of cherished traditions. Change necessarily implies questions such as: What change, if any? Change in what direction? For what purposes should educational systems be changed? And, among others, if change in a certain direction, for a certain purpose, is desirable, then what ought the specific curricular or programmatic dimension of such change be? What needs to stay the same in educational goals, theory, and practice? What needs to change?

The above questions are the core concerns of this unit, and certainly of later units to follow, especially units 3, 4, and 9. The essays in this unit reflect concern over innovation in both structural arrangements and day-to-day practice. There are essays on the dynamics of systemic change as well as on the day-to-day practice of teaching and learning. The issue of whether the four-year program in teacher education should or should not be retained is debated. Two brief commentaries are included which compare other educational systems with that of the United States. Concerns regarding more effective ways to link the public and private sectors in schooling are discussed. Readers are also introduced to "teacher effectiveness training."

In every decade of the past century, we have witnessed concern over the need for a sense of continuity in social traditions and the role of the nation's schools in providing that sense of continuity. This concern has been counterbalanced by equally fervent awareness that continued change in the technological bases and economic structures of North American society places additional pressure for change in the content and manner of schooling. Continuity and change are twin forces in a historic polarity in dialogue as to the best directions educational systems might take in the future. The tension between the concepts of continuity and change and how these concepts are defined in each generation rests on the answers to the following questions: What is best about what has been thought and said and done that ought to remain in school curricula? What new development in each generation must receive placement in formal curricular content? In each decade of the past one hundred years, these two questions have been reviewed and debated by British, Canadian, and American educators.

The 1980s have been no exception in terms of continuing dialogue among educational conservatives and liberal and radical interpreters of the nature and functions of continuity and change in schooling. What things should be retained in school curricula and what new skills and new bodies of knowledge ought to be added to educational studies? What humane interests should govern or at least be part of the formal education of all youth? What new scientific or technological content and skills must be implemented? This dilemma between continuity and change in the advancement of human knowledge bases and technological sophistication was essentially debated by Thomas Huxley, Matthew Arnold, and Herbert Spencer in the 1870s and 1880s.

The displacement of hundreds of North American workers in recent years and the continued overdependence on the manufacturing and technological capabilities of Asian and European nations leads to one inevitable question: Should education in North America focus on educating youth to be functionally competitive in technological and scientific skills with their counterparts in Europe and Asia? The present curriculum has proven to be an ineffective and non-competitive mythic model for national educational development (witness the complete disutility in today's marketplace of the American general high school diploma). Should more time be spent examining how others educate their youth in comparison to the way the United States has chosen to do so? Does America wish to be an industrially and technologically independent force in the world or a dependent one?

In the late 1960s and early 1970s, the search for and development of alternative schools and alternative methods of educating persons in non-school environments dominated the literature in education. Intense dialogue continues regarding how to develop quality alternative learning experiences in the wake of recent reports on the state of schooling in America. Qualitative reconstruction of educational programming is a subject of great interest and debate in both public and private schools and among those interested in continued exploration of how to educate people in non-traditional educational environments. The search continues for a way to preserve the best and noblest of traditions in education while creating more effective learning alternatives to serve the interests of those who desire a choice.

There is growing professional distrust of outside experts who seek to tell educators their own art. The resultant "fortress mentality" impedes the development of constructive dialogue among those who work in and out of formal educational settings. There are also those who severely criticize the manner in which school systems appear to follow so closely the needs of business and industry. They mistrust the motivations of the proposed innovations in schooling, while others defend a strong linkage between the development of high technology in industry and its rapid introduction into schooling. Parents seek a greater liaison with schools, industries, libraries, and museums. These various "publics" in and out of the profession must strive to reduce feelings of distrust in order to foster the ideal expressed so well by Matthew Arnold, that education should be "the best that has been thought and said." There is a place for the old and new in education. Our youth deserve the best and most effective means of attaining mastery over what they try to learn.

The articles in this unit reflect the whole spectrum of the concerns outlined above. They all address some significant issues related to the problem of how to retain the best of what is known about effective schooling while providing reasonable choices as well. They deal with topics that, in one way or another, are concerned with the relationship between political and economic changes in society and changes or continuity in the educational process. Although there is no unified North American consensus on either the aims of education or on the issue of chance, most agree that it is necessary to seek ways to broaden the educational alternatives of persons in a rapidly changing high-tech society.

Looking Ahead: Challenge Questions

If it is true that there should be a common curriculum at the primary and middle grade levels, should there also be a common curriculum at the secondary level?

Whether public or private, should there be different types of North American secondary schools with different curricula and different instructional missions? What

would be the relative advantages or disadvantages of such a policy?

What, if anything, can teachers in the public schools learn from teachers in private schools?

To what extent can schooling be restructured to most effectively emphasize academic achievement as well as intangible but important factors such as character and initiative?

Are there more political and economic pressures on educators than they can be reasonably expected to manage? Is this sort of pressure avoidable? If so, how? If not, why not?

What is a good school? What is your personal view of a sound balance between old and new in school curricula? What should be learned by everyone, and to what level of proficiency? What are your criteria for evaluating a school program?

Can schools become something other than what they are now? What are your reasons for your views?

Can the theory and practice of other nations' educational systems help the United States?

An Inside View of Change in Schools

A dean and a professor abandon the ivory tower to serve as an assistant superintendent and a principal. Here are the lessons they learned about administration and bringing about change in organizations.

EUGENE EUBANKS AND
RALPH PARISH

EUGENE EUBANKS is dean of the School of Education at the University of Missouri-Kansas City, where RALPH PARISH (University of Missouri/Kansas City Chapter) is an assistant professor in the Department of Educational Administration.

EVERYONE knows that professors of educational administration come from backgrounds as practitioners in the field. Indeed, some administrators probably look on a professorship as a gainfully employed retirement from the day-to-day tribulations of school administration. After all, having left the trenches, not many professors choose to go back, even temporarily.

We are now back at the University of Missouri-Kansas City, after extended stints of service as administrators in the public schools. Eugene Eubanks served a year as assistant to the superintendent and the board of education and a second year as a deputy superintendent in the Kansas City Schools. Ralph Parish spent a year as principal of a high school in a suburb of Kansas City.

In both cases, the leaders and policy makers of the school community had decided that a change in school organization was needed. Our university vig-

orously pursues a policy of contributing service to the community, so it supported our efforts and generously granted us community-service leaves. All parties involved assumed that, as professors of educational administration who were not seeking permanent employment, we could bring fresh ideas concerning administrative and instructional practice to the public schools. Because of our previous work, we were also expected to know something about organizational change and the ways to bring it about.

School boards, top public school administrators, university administrators, and community leaders were all very supportive of the efforts to place university people in the public school culture. They remained supportive and helpful during the period of our work. The school board members with whom we worked were intelligent people, dedicated to providing the highest quality education for all the students in their district. They spent many hours working through the maze of local politics to provide the best for the students.

During our period of work in the public schools and after our return to the university, many public school practitioners and many of our university colleagues asked us what we learned from our experience. (Some of our questioners seemed to feel that we had a lot to learn.) Of course, we have been asking ourselves that same question. And there were times during our experience in the public schools when we might have answered, "Who has time to learn anything? The war started an hour ago."

Upon reflection, however, it seems funny to assume that people from a university setting would actually know how to bring about change. If we could change things, why haven't we been able to change the university or our school of education? Undergraduate teacher education and professional training for existing and future administrators ought to provide plenty of chal-

From *Phi Delta Kappan*, April 1987, pp. 610-615. Reprinted by permission of the author.

lenge to those who are concerned with institutional change and improvement. So one thing that we have certainly learned is never to forget the importance of the saying, "Physician, heal thyself."

For example, both of us understood that it might take from three to five years to make substantive changes in a suburban high school and perhaps as many as from five to seven years in an urban school district. So what did we think we were going to accomplish in a single year? Well, we would never find out if we didn't try, and suddenly we were working in real time on real problems. We began our year's effort full of energy and plans, determined to make a difference.

Almost immediately, we had to modify our expectations. Both of us made lists. Eubanks made lists at the office, and he hung others on his bedroom wall. Parish was satisfied with an office list and made only occasional notations to himself at his coffee table at home. The end of a week when nothing is crossed off the list and five new things are added is frustrating indeed. You feel you're on a treadmill and can never catch up. On the other hand, when three or four things are crossed off in a single day and nothing is added, the sense of exhilaration can overwhelm your critical faculties. There is a foolish but temporary belief that maybe you can make real changes after all.

More than ever we are convinced that a leader must be able to establish systems to take care of normal activities and to delegate the responsibility for supervising these operations to capable assistants. Both of us encountered situations in which there was no established system for handling something except that "the boss" could delegate and explain what was needed. If building a school culture and establishing a school vision are important functions — and we found them to be — then energy must be devoted to them. And if a school leader is to have any time or energy left, then he or she had better do some delegating.

Some examples of the kind of routine affairs we are talking about are: orderly processing of purchase orders and business affairs; routine personnel matters; checking to be sure that memos and other communications have been proofread for typographical and syntactical errors. (Teachers dearly love to pick apart errors in communications from the principal or central office. Finding errors just proves what they want to believe about administrators anyway, and no

> ## IF A LEADER IS TO HAVE ANY TIME OR ENERGY LEFT, THEN HE OR SHE HAD BETTER DO SOME DELEGATING.

one believes that the errors are in the processing or that being rushed caused a dumb mistake. Still, we ought to reduce the incidence of such errors.)

If a principal or superintendent has to double-check everything personally, then valuable time is wasted. Yet in the school organizations in which we worked, no structures promoted independent work by subordinates in the course of normal operations. No one felt free to change the work of the "bosses." Even when others had vital information or knew that something wouldn't work, they would often continue working in nonproductive ways, rather than inform their superiors that a problem existed or seek a solution on their own. The people in these school organizations clearly believed that the messenger would be held accountable for the message.

To our surprise, we found that we could not assume that structures existed for doing routine things well. Establishing structures for carrying out routine tasks was one of the changes we made. Each of us found that sometimes we had to choose between paying attention to some important change efforts or stopping to follow up a routine matter. In almost every case, we chose the change effort and hoped that our subordinates were following through on the nuts and bolts of school operations. In almost every case, we paid for our choice with a minor — though always time-consuming — foul-up.

H OW MUCH fundamental change can be accomplished in one year? Our experience suggests that you can help people become aware of a new direction and even begin to help them look down

a very different road. You can set up some structures to support that new awareness and hope that those who follow will not revert to old, unsuccessful ways. If you can accomplish that much in a year, that is all that can be expected. In the literature, this quality of leadership is called "culture-building." We found culture-building to be an essential aspect of change.

As school administrators, each of us gained some insight into our own strengths and weaknesses. We learned that we could perform well in the jobs we had filled. We were both invited to stay on: Eubanks as a superintendent and Parish as a principal, with substantial financial inducements. (School districts pay much better than universities. It was something of a shock to discover that school administrators — and even some teachers — make several thousand dollars more per year than the average professor with a Ph.D. in our university.) Nevertheless, each of us declined.

Our public school colleagues could not understand why we chose to return to the university for less money. We couldn't understand why they thought there was enough money in the world to pay for the madness, stress, limited independence, and lack of success that public school administrators must endure.

For example, our average work week as public school administrators was between 60 and 70 hours, with a few 80- to 90-hour weeks thrown in. In Parish's case, the high school sponsored 38 activities, most of which were scheduled after school or at night — and often more than one activity was going on at the same time. A principal or one of the vice-principals had to attend most of these activities. This meant that every Saturday and parts of some Sundays had to be spent catching up on paperwork and reports. A high school principal is lucky to spend one night during the week at home. Once in a great while, a working day would be as short as 10 hours.

In the superintendent's role, Eubanks had to attend board meetings, public and community meetings, meetings with staff members at all levels who were trying to carry the load of running the schools, and meetings with attorneys involved in a major desegregation case for which he was the architect and which has led to additional resources exceeding $300 million over a six-year period for 36,000 students. They needed direction and support. The deputy superintendent's role averaged between

70 and 80 hours a week, including Saturdays and Sundays.

Each of us tried to create some new structures to help take care of routine matters and also provide some support for our change efforts. Eubanks appointed some elementary and secondary directors to assist principals with the nuts and bolts of running a school and, at the same time, to promote site-based planning for change. He established a special projects office for school-level projects, such as effective schools projects, schools-within-a-school in high schools, and the College Board's Degrees of Reading Power in junior high schools and in ninth grade. In addition, he restructured a staff development office and implemented a regular Wednesday afternoon inservice training program that grew out of site-based plans, with only limited support by the central staff.

At the high school, Parish established three committees: policy, curriculum and instruction, and staff development. A high school administrator and a central office administrator were members of each of these committees; the remainder of the members were elected by the faculty. A teacher was elected as the head of each committee. These were functioning committees, not advisory bodies. They took care of such routine matters as approving faculty requests for professional leave, establishing a mission statement, designing a new schedule that included an optional before-school hour, and so on. The committees also began to seek out new programs to introduce into the schools.

We intended to build collaborative systems that would support change, to give those systems a chance to handle some real problems, and to provide continuing support for the new structures. From our knowledge of the literature on organizational change and from our own experience, we concluded that participative structures are essential if a school organization is to be able to plan and direct its own change. Creating a new culture that supports change requires these new structures.

But the difficulty of changing the public schools isn't merely a matter of the time involved. Both of us are accustomed to working 50 or more hours per week. However, we have considerable control over our university work. We can choose to do things that challenge us intellectually. We can get involved with colleagues, discuss ideas, or attempt to be creative. We can take a few hours or even an entire day off. No

THE PUBLIC EXPECTS SCHOOLS TO PRODUCE EXCELLENT OUTCOMES AT BARGAIN BASEMENT RATES. IT WON'T HAPPEN.

matter how well we organized our public school work, it was largely controlled by the needs of others — a schedule, a season of the year, the political context, and always the unexpected crisis. During our time in the public schools, we used to daydream about having an afternoon with nothing to do but think. Perhaps we would read and review research — perhaps even write a little. That afternoon never came.

WE HOPE WE have not created the impression that all is "rosy" in higher education, especially in colleges of education. This is certainly not the case. We face such problems as trying to reform teacher education programs so that they reflect common sense, effective practice, and research; inadequate resources and lower status than a number of other professional schools; faculty members who sometimes seem immutable; and the problem of attracting to teacher education minorities and able students from all backgrounds. These issues in higher education are important, and we suggest that our colleagues in K-12 education might spend a year with us and experience these problems firsthand.

When we embarked on our new "careers" as public school administrators, the people in the schools expected us to behave in certain ways, and they spent considerable time trying to teach us to conform to their expectations. Therefore, we had to spend time teaching them that we had different ideas. Each of us has occasionally had the recurring nightmare that we might become the

kind of person that those who worked in these school organizations thought we would be.

We think of the kind of behaviors that people expected of us under such headings as "That's the Boss' Job" or "Send for the Enforcer." For example, there is the story of the principal who announces during a planned staff development program at her school that the film she had planned to use for the session did not arrive and that she has no alternative plan other than to have the teachers sit quietly in their chairs during the hour and a half of staff development time. (If such a thing should occur during a very trying day, the temptation to throw something against the wall could become very great.) Then there is the story of the teacher on cafeteria duty, who walks all the way across the cafeteria to tell the principal that a student in her area has a sign on her shirt that is inappropriate (it has the word *bitch* on it). Asked what she did about it, the teacher replied, "I came to get you."

Each day, at least one (and usually more) of these little incidents occurred. Some seemed almost intentionally designed to keep us occupied with "bossing and enforcing." Some people seemed to think that this was a better use of our time than having us wander the halls and visit classrooms or get involved in the life of a school or of a school district.

Those we worked with in the high school and in the school district office seemed determined not to decide things that the boss could be tricked into deciding, even when those seeking a decision already had the best information about a situation. After we had asked them appropriate questions, obtained good information, and suggested a possible course of action, our petitioners would often say something like, "Well that's what we thought too, but we just thought we'd better find out what you wanted." If they already had a perfectly good solution to a specific problem and they were willing to follow through on it, why were they asking us? Why weren't they doing something? Was this some kind of test to see if the boss could guess the right answer?

WE HAVE come to realize that people in schools are very vulnerable to criticism both from those within and from those outside the school organization. School administrators and teachers learn the truth of the statement, "No matter what you do, they're going to burn you. But you don't have to carry the wood for them." We believe that, if you want to have a fire, someone has the carry the wood and that it's better if we all carry our fair share.

Many of the administrators and teachers with whom we worked firmly believe that covering yourself, just in case, is the wisest course of action (or inaction). Suppose, for example, that some staff members are assigned jobs that they know will mean making changes that those with whom they must work will not wish to make. Individually, they begin sending memos at a furious pace, with copies to everyone in sight. Sometimes as many as 40 or 50 people (always including the superintendent and the assistant superintendent) will receive memos. Even as they are circulating these memos, they know that others are doing the same and that the likelihood that all memos will be read is remote. Meanwhile, if anything bad should happen, the paper trail can prove, as more than one person told us, "I did my job."

The high school in which Parish served as principal had a history of adversary relations between teachers and administrators. Teachers insisted on having everything in writing and properly witnessed. Whenever possible, they seemed bent on creating issues on which people could take sides. This created a we/they situation that not only wasted time but insured that problems were not solved. There may have been a time when the teachers needed to band together, for good reason, to protect themselves from arbitrary and capricious management. But such structures impede change and create a culture of mistrust and suspicion. Both of us found it difficult to convince people that they must discard their nonproductive habits and create new relationships that do not depend for their success on how well you cover your rear.

At the university, public arguments and disagreements over ideas, policy, and decisions are expected. A reputation for independent action is worn like a badge of honor. "Collegial" means that no one, including deans, is better or has more authority than anyone else. If a dean asks a faculty member to do something, it will be done in that person's own special way. If a faculty member is asked for an opinion or an idea, more often than not it will be given without regard for the position of the person asking.

It is very hard to get used to the idea that others are watching you in order to determine how things are going or to get a clue about what they are supposed to think. A raised eyebrow, a frown, a laugh, a scream (there was a conference room in the high school that, with the door shut, allowed one to let out a good loud yell) may mean one thing to a leader, but others take action based on their reading of these signs. If the boss is tired and a little irritable one day, the rumor is about that "something is up," and imaginative guesses abound about what that something is.

Schools and other organizations are full of myths and legends about change: top-down change is bad, bottom-up change is good, the pendulum of change always swings back, incremental change will produce substantive change over time, fundamental change must be carried out ruthlessly, and so on. We have learned that while there may be some small truth to these sayings, they are actually myths that continue to exist in schools and school organizations for a reason. And that reason is to promote change efforts that guarantee that the changes will stay within acceptable ranges of existing practice or will be done in such a way that the changes are doomed to fail because of the process employed. This failure is rationalized by such statements as, "It was a good idea, but the way they did it was wrong."

The fact is that the amount of time, energy, and resources needed just to keep a school running is so enormous that precious little is left over to expend on changing things. Moreover, the culture of schooling is such that those who will be implementing school reforms (teachers and principals) must be meaningfully involved with the planning, selection, and design of the change efforts if they are to have any chance of success.

Pulling people from school sites into central offices and giving them full- or part-time responsibilities for these change efforts produces modest results at best — even when the people are very capable. Pulling top-quality people from schools for 25 to 30 days during the school year probably does not provide enough time to accomplish substantive changes, and taking good people out of classrooms and schools for that many days can seriously damage the instructional program of a school. Workshops held periodically either before school or after school and workshops held during days set aside for inservice training can result in some improvement of existing practice. But these measures — even if the workshops are of the highest quality — will not guarantee substantive change or improvement.

Traditional approaches to school change, such as those outlined above, allow teachers and principals to maintain control of the day-to-day life of their schools and classrooms even as they appear to respond to political pressures for change and improvement. However, these traditional approaches can at best maintain and support a change effort already under way. Serious efforts to bring about reform require, among other things, regular time set aside during the work week to permit teachers and administrators to plan and implement effective change.

We often felt, during our time as public school administrators, that somewhere a plot was being hatched to block all efforts to improve things. But who were the plotters? The people we worked with were running as fast as they could and working as hard as they could. We are convinced that what people in the schools need is help to work smarter, not harder. Someone in the schools always seems to be saying, "If everyone just works and tries a little harder, things will get better." But working harder on something that doesn't work probably will not make it work any better. Working smarter just might. Working smarter means thinking, planning, developing productive organizational structures that create a "learning organizational culture," and making rational use of all the talent available within an organization.

However, we need to make it very clear that many people out there in the schools are doing outstanding jobs. We chose to leave because our personal levels of tolerance for ambivalence are too low to make school administration a long-term career (though we do return from time to time).

But there are those who are hanging in there, "planting seeds," as one of them puts it. This remarkable person goes around at the beginning of the school year taking care of such problems in her program as students who haven't been properly scheduled, or staff members who haven't been trained, or counselors and principals who act as if they've never heard of the program even though it has been in operation in their schools for four years. What keeps this person coming back and starting over year after year can only be the fact that the students in her program average two years' growth in reading comprehension. If administrators were working smart, such people would not have to start over every year. Starting over every year means never getting very far.

There are teachers who return each year brimming with enthusiasm and bringing excitement and creativity to their classrooms. Although conditions are often far from ideal, they do not let the organized anarchy of schools deter them from doing their jobs; they insist, as one teacher described it, on "making sure that every one of my students is learning something."

There are also some principals and central office personnel who are able to deflect much of the madness that surrounds public schooling and thus keep their organizations focused on learning and the success of the students. These administrators have a high tolerance for ambivalence, a willingness to be slightly insubordinate at times, a passion for work, low ego needs, a family that loves them even when they rarely see them, and, most important, an understanding that resources and authority must be structured to support change.

Teachers and administrators such as these hold the schools together. We need more of these people. School districts and schools of education need to know how to find and support them. We need to find ways to train administrators to create organizational conditions that are hospitable to these types of educators. But we are not likely to do so without massive expenditures of energy and resources.

OUR EXPERIENCE in the public schools taught us that professional development activities, even when planned and carried out by practitioners, can at best share good existing practices. They do not appear to foster substantive change. And this seems to be true of teachers and administrators alike, unless staff development is an integral part of the work day and week.

If our aim is substantive change, an-other feasible option may be extensive professional work during the summer. But this option will require teachers, principals, and district personnel to be paid professional salaries to work on real problems. We must help both the public and some schoolpeople understand that this type of work is just as important as teaching. Universities and schools of education might be a part of this summer effort, although the structure must differ from that of traditional summer school classes.

Time is available in the summer for significant professional development activities. During the school year, ongoing professional development can then be designed to follow up on the summer efforts. Such a design, which would allow school staffs to spend periods of two or three weeks — not two or three days — looking at their working relationships so that they can consider and plan together, might lead to the kind of school reform and improvement all of us know is vitally needed. The talent to help schools and school districts make such a program work is already there — if we have the imagination to throw away our old history and build a new one together.

It is not uncommon for those in higher education to criticize those in the public schools for not using research, or for not using good theory, or for not changing unsuccessful practices. And there is certainly a considerable body of knowledge that can instruct us in ways to change schools. Nevertheless, as many observers have pointed out, schools have remained relatively unchanged for decades.

It is now clear to us that the communities for which we worked could not provide the resources — both fiscal and human — that would have enabled those in the schools to make the kinds of changes needed to create excellent schools for everyone. Indeed, many people wondered how they could continue to maintain current levels of support for schooling. Others wondered if the schools would know how to spend additional money to produce desired changes even if they had it.

Those in the private sector know very well what it takes to make fundamental changes in an organization. It may take between 10% and 15% of an organization's resources to make substantive changes, and in some cases that figure can soar above 20%. Schools seldom have as much as 1% of their budgets earmarked for change efforts, and professional staff members are often expected to donate their time. Small wonder, then, that professional development in the schools is so often ineffectual. It's amazing that anything is ever improved.

If the people of this nation — or at least those in Missouri, where we worked — want excellent schools, then they are going to have to pay for them. We have not seen a commitment of the resources required to move us toward this goal. The public expects excellent outcomes at bargain basement rates. It won't happen.

Our experiences in the "real world" (what world do practitioners think *we* live in?) have given us a better understanding of our colleagues in the schools, as well as greater credibility with them. We also have a much greater appreciation of our university work and of its value.

Would we agree to work as school administrators again? Yes, given the right circumstances. We certainly wouldn't want to have to repeat the same experiences again, mistakes and all. But if we were given a chance to act on what we've learned? Maybe.

Should others try what we did? We wouldn't presume to say that they should; that must remain an individual decision. Should universities and schools of education find ways to involve schoolpeople in teacher education, administrator preparation, and ongoing professional development for all? Unquestionably! It is just as important for practitioners, with their considerable experience and knowledge, to be involved in changes in schools of education as it is for schools of education to be involved in changes in schooling.

THE BUSINESS OF TALENTVILLE

Gretchen Haight

Gretchen Haight, former managing editor of *Across the Board*, is now a writer in Los Angeles.

Once upon a time in the Land of Knowledge, a young entrepreneur convinced the few business owners in the fledgling economy that they could improve their advertising and increase sales by having logos designed for their companies. He set up a small business to design the logos, and soon had several customers. But when the logos were delivered, the customers found them awful and canceled their orders.

the country, with such names as the Land of Knowledge, Karate Kids Land, and Gigglesville.

The Mini-Society is an innovative method of teaching the basics of business and economics to elementary-school children. At a time when parents worry almost as much about children's economics intelligence as where the kids are at night, schools are experimenting with ways to give students a headstart in business. Mini-Societies let children learn by doing.

Created by Dr. Marilyn L. Kourilsky, dean for teacher education at UCLA's Graduate School of

Then an artist came to the entrepreneur and offered to do all of the designing for him. The arrangement worked well, until the entrepreneur began saying that the artist wasn't worth the money he was paying her. Angry at the way she was being treated and seeing that the demand for logos was growing, the artist set up her own logo-designing business. Not a particularly entrepreneurial person by nature, she nonetheless had learned enough about business and economics to be confident that she could make it on her own.

The Land of Knowledge is not a parable on corporate excellence, business ethics, or the success of the entrepreneurial woman. It tells of real events in a "Mini-Society" set up in a third-grade classroom. This one happened to be in Southern California, but there are more than 100,000 Mini-Societies in classrooms in 40 states across

Education, the Mini-Society program is both a reflection of its creator's enterprising personality and a product of the times. More than half of the states in the country now require economics courses for high-school graduation, including Kourilsky's home state, California, which passed such a bill in January.

Kourilsky has worked extensively with the Joint Council on Economic Education, which works with councils in all 50 states to improve economic education in schools and colleges, and with the Economic Literacy Council of California. Her success in combating economic illiteracy is impressive. She and her team of researchers have given true-false tests in economic principles to hundreds of Mini-Society graduates and to college sophomores in their first year of basic economics. They score in the same range.

Kourilsky is a champion of entrepreneurship,

These days Dick and Jane are learning
the ABC's of business and economics in primary
school. The Mini-Society program created by UCLA's
Marilyn Kourilsky is unleashing an army
of baby-entrepreneurs.

and her thinking about it is fundamental to the Mini-Society. Her research shows that 25 percent of kindergarten children demonstrate entrepreneurial talent—that is, they consistently show qualities usually identified with business success, such as risk-taking and the need for achievement. By high school, however, only about 3 percent of the students do. Something happens during the educational process, Kourilsky maintains, that suppresses these qualities.

Although she is interested in nurturing the talent of the 25 percent who may go on to be the entrepreneurs of the next generation, Kourilsky

create the type of society they live in—with resources either communally or privately owned. Mini-Societies replicate that learning process in the classroom.

Kourilsky's system is designed for children in grades three to six. Elementary-school pupils are at a perfect age to understand economic concepts and values, she believes: young enough to be imaginative in questioning values, old enough to perceive themselves as a group. (Kindergartners still see themselves only as individuals.)

The Mini-Society program runs for a minimum of 10 weeks, with three 45-minute periods

Illustrations from *Mini-Society* by Marilyn L. Kourilsky.
Copyright © 1983 by Addison-Wesley Publishing Company

is more concerned with helping all students to experiment, find out what their talents are, and learn to use problem-solving strategies.

Although economics for grade-school children is a comparatively new idea, Kourilsky's approach goes back to John Dewey, who emphasized that people learn more from experience than from being lectured or told what to do. The first inspiration for the Mini-Society, however, came not from an educator or an economist but from a physicist, Jacob Bronowski. Kourilsky saw the description of agrarian societies in Bronowski's book *The Ascent of Man* as the cornerstone of an economics-education program. Primitive societies develop economic values only when they face scarcity. Their traditional values about sharing and individual initiative, applied to scarcity,

each week. First of all, the teacher establishes a scarcity of an item needed in school, such as felt-tip pens or erasers. He or she may even move some desks out of the room. Once the children are aware of the problem—they are trying to function in the classroom and keep running into the problem of the shortage—the teacher leads a discussion (called a debriefing) about ways of coping with the shortage. The class must decide who gets to use the erasers or pens, and why.

The pupils typically try many different ways of solving the problem. For example, they may start by trying "first come, first served." But someone further down the line claims to need a felt-tip pen more than the person who got there first. They may then decide to let the teacher allocate the pens on the basis of need, but they may not agree with the choices. (A teacher may deliberately make a bad choice in order to illustrate the risks in leaving the decision in one person's hands.) They may then try a lottery, but usually end up asking why a pen should go to someone who hasn't earned it.

Economic concepts very quickly lead to a consideration of values. The notion that the use of scarce commodities must be earned leads to further issues: If one child cleans out the rabbit cage to earn the right to use a pen, and someone else washes the blackboards for the same reason, who gets to use it first? Do they get to use it for the same length of time?

These considerations eventually lead to the creation of a currency to facilitate the exchange of goods and services. It doesn't always happen at the teacher's suggestion, Kourilsky says. Instead, through trial and error, the children are drawn to almost inevitable solutions to the classroom problem—such as establishing a currency.

Out of the initial solution to the problem of scarcity, an economy grows. In no time at all, deals are made, businesses are set up, and workers are hired. The first enterprise is frequently one that produces billfolds in which the youngsters can keep their "quibblings," or whatever they've named their money. Services spring into existence—for a fee, of course. Banks quickly come into being.

Government decisions may come about as a result of a debriefing. In one Mini-Society, for instance, the kids insisted that the lemonade at a student's stand had been watered down. They had to protect themselves as consumers, so, acting as the government, they instituted quality control. They might have reached a different solution: setting up a competing business that would produce a better product. "We want them to think in terms of trade-offs, of opportunity costs," Kourilsky says.

Through debriefing, they also learn the economic names for the situations they have experienced: scarcity; opportunity costs; supply and demand; price ceilings; price floors; inflation. Once they have learned an economic concept such as scarcity and learned its name, the children read more about it in the form of an imaginative, sometimes witty fable from the teachers' training workbooks, written by Kourilsky. At the end of each story are questions about the economic problem at hand and its solution, and questions relating the fable to the real world and to the Mini-Society.

In "The Kingdom of Rumtumtum," for instance, there was an infinite supply of clothes, food, everything, thanks to the great magician Flim Flam. But when Flim Flam walked off the job, King Fiddlestick and his kingdom were left with inevitable shortages of everything.

In "The Biteable Bonanza Fable," a little girl, Kirsten, drifts off to sleep, dreaming about a parade of gooey sweets. But in the dream there is a limited supply of sugar, so the bakers ask her whether she wants chocolate cake, a creamy custard pie, or oatmeal cookies. She recognizes that her opportunity cost is her second favorite dessert, which is what she has to give up.

"The Curse of Inflate-Shun" recounts the tale of Ms. Inflate, who dies and wills everyone in the town of Same-O Same-O equal amounts of her money. The townspeople fight over what they want to buy, pushing the prices up. They then demand higher wages, prices go up again, and Judge Shun pleads with them to not ask for more money. They run him out of town, hoping to get rid of Inflate-Shun once and for all.

Fanciful as all of this seems, the children actually make serious decisions and choices that they will have to live with. In order to encourage learning by experience and risk-taking, the children do not get grades in a Mini-Society, and the teacher functions not as the usual authority but as a guide. Sometimes a teacher acts as a paid consultant, although even a handsome salary of quibblings won't buy much outside of school.

The key to the success of the program, of course, is the teacher. "The Mini-Society is not restricted to gifted students," Kourilsky says, "but it *is* for gifted teachers." Some teachers have difficulty relinquishing the tight control they are used to exerting. When one teacher set herself up as the government, the children went to their parents for help; they felt that the ground rules of the Mini-Society were being violated. The parents supported them, and the children threw the teacher out of government. Later they wanted her back, but only if she would share the lawmaking role with four of the pupils. They also agreed that only one person would carry out the law, but that it would not be the teacher.

These kinds of considerations come up during debriefing, which is concerned as much with economic and social values as with economic concepts. If 20 quibblings are stolen from the bank, for example, the teacher might guide a discussion of various ways of getting money: earning it, stealing it, borrowing it, or receiving it as a gift. When the person from whom the money was stolen talks about what he had to do to earn the money, the class sees the theft in terms of the victim's feelings, the hours of work he has lost, and the bills that he is unable to pay.

Robbery debriefings have had varying outcomes. Sometimes the money has been secretly put back in the till, but at other times the thieves have let it be known that they don't like the victim or care how hard he worked. In most instances, however, the robbers don't steal again, according to Kourilsky. In one Mini-Society that had had three bank robberies, the class decided that they themselves had created an atmosphere in which this could happen. They agreed to all be taxed and to return the money to the bank.

Many groups try to solve the problem of scarcity through communal ownership. Usually

> **"We want them to think in terms of trade-offs, of opportunity costs," says Kourilsky.**

Wrong division: A sample problem from the Mini-Society teacher workbook, showing the importance of issuing currency in various denominations.

there are so many arguments over who owns what and how they're going to use it that the group moves toward private ownership. Only about 8 percent of Mini-Societies across the country have maintained a socialist system beyond the initial arguments, Kourilsky says.

The question of what types of societies emerge from these classroom exercises is of great interest to Kourilsky. There are still many questions about the effects of culture and of a child's stage of development. "I would be interested in trying out the Mini-Society in an environment very socialist in nature," she says. "We have tried it on Indian reservations, and they have ended up more market-oriented than socialistic. But we haven't gone to a country where there is no competing value structure.

"Most Mini-Societies have a lot of what you'd call socialistic institutions, some sort of welfare system," she continues, "but it's different from ours. For instance, the students might say that they should help someone who has tried hard to start a business three times and failed, or a new person just coming into the class. Often if a student leaves school, he or she wills his money not to a best friend, but to someone new in the class, or someone just starting a business. We have found that legislating charity [imposing taxes to provide assistance] doesn't work, but that when it's not forced, the children will frequently

The children study fables with such names as "The Curse of Inflate-Shun" and "The Biteable Bonanza."

decide on a charitable solution to a problem in their society."

Kourilsky believes that individuals try to better themselves no matter what system they are in. "The difference between people who want a Marxist system and those who want a free-enterprise system is the difference between whether they'd rather depend on the whim of the buyers or the whim of the planners. If you're a fantastic musician, and you don't feel that the market will ever realize how good you are, you might want to be at the whim of the planners. I think Elvis Presley would rather have been at the whim of the buyers.

"You can give two youngsters clothes to choose from and an expert to help out in choosing. One will say, 'I don't care if he's an expert, I want to wear the crewneck shirt, not the turtleneck.' The other one wants the planner to tell him what he looks good in.

"If there's one main point to the Mini-Society, it's to increase one's self-concept, but it doesn't work if it isn't based in reality. When a mother convinces her daughter she's beautiful, and then she has a few experiences that prove that's not the case, it's not so good. There's nothing wrong with the kid who would like to have a planner pick out his shirts for him, but it will help him to know that's what he's comfortable with."

What about girls in the Mini-Society? Are

How The Mini-Society Works

Talentville is now in session" is how Doris Stevenson opens her Mini-Society class in Wilmington, Delaware. For Stevenson, one of the first teachers trained by Marilyn Kourilsky, the Mini-Society has been a showcase of her own talents. She was named "teacher of the year" for 1986 by the state of Delaware.

Last semester, Stevenson's second-grade students named their community Talentville (naming is the first task of every Mini-Society) and their currency "tigers."

Each day, after the class is called to order, the students go to wherever they've stored their products, set them up, and begin buying and selling. "They don't always sell products," Stevenson says. "One girl set up a fortune-telling business. If a student can't think of an idea, I'll offer to sell him or her a few ideas"—an admirable opportunity for a discussion of consulting firms.

Consistent with Mini-Society practice, students learn economic concepts as they arise naturally out of their trading activities. For example, the class learned about economic competition when one student wanted to make wallets. He made a few simple billfolds for his classmates to keep their tigers in, sold them, and produced some more. He was excited about his growing enterprise. Then, the next day, someone else wanted to do the same thing. "That's not fair," the entrepreneur told his classmate. "It was my idea."

This was an opening for Stevenson to guide a discussion of competition. What are some examples of competition in the real world?

Take fast-food places, she suggested. What are the children's favorites? Why do they go to McDonald's? The students might then talk about quality, about keeping prices low. About what would happen if there were only McDonald's—no Burger King, no Wendy's. And so on.

A lesson in market saturation came about this way: A boy began selling "god's eyes"—ornaments made of yarn and popsicle sticks. They sold well, and eventually he had his whole family making them at home for him. But so many children had bought them that he couldn't sell any more, and he wasn't too happy about it.

Stevenson held a debriefing about market saturation and what the boy's choices were. Lower his prices? Create a gimmick to sell more? Go out of business?

He finally decided to make mobiles, on which people could hang the god's eyes. It was not a haphazard decision, however. He surveyed the students to find out what price they'd be willing to pay for the mobiles, and worked up a price-and-demand schedule.

Incidentally, Stevenson also has the children keep profit-and-loss statements, which they update each day.

Kourilsky says that there are about 20 economic problems, such as competition and market saturation, that will inevitably arise in a Mini-Society. Part of the teacher training is learning what they are, how to recognize them, and how to turn them into lessons.

—**G.H.**

they as entrepreneurial as boys? "The program is valuable for girls," Kourilsky says, "but what happens in the classroom is overestimated by observers. They say, 'I went into a class and there's absolutely no sexism whatsoever. You should have seen all of the girls in business and the amount of wealth they owned.' These observers are coming in late. The girls don't start out being entrepreneurial."

Most Mini-Societies follow a similar evolution: The girls start out working for the boys; then there is a fight, and the girls go off, set up competitive businesses, and become role models for the other girls. "And there's something else I've noticed," Kourilsky says. "The girls will almost always need the support system of a partner when they set up a business. The boys are much more likely to go it alone. I'm a strong woman and I don't like to see these differences, but I do see them. I think they're social—defi-

Kourilsky believes that the educational process tends to suppress entrepreneurial qualities.

nitely not inherent—and I think they start young.

"The boys may figure out that all they have to do is be nice and they can get the girls to do all their work, but the girls learn from the same program that they don't have to do all of this work for the boys. They can work for themselves."

Economists who have worked with Kourilsky praise her program. "The children learn economics as a logical deductive system," says Daniel Blake, an economics professor who has taught in the workshops. "The children also learn to make personal decisions—as consumers, voters, workers, and business people—and group decisions about where the society is going," says Blake, professor of economics at California State University at Northridge and director of the school's Center for Economic Research and Education.

"They know why their parents go to work, why there are stores, and why there is specialization. They become insightful about business. They realize it has to serve customers, but that to survive, it has to be good for the workers and the owners as well. Many of my college students, by contrast, think business has a stranglehold on the customer. They think it doesn't need to do anything to survive."

Not all teachers are able to master the Mini-Society program. Some have trouble with the economic concepts; others find it difficult to abdicate their position of authority. One teacher encouraged monopoly when she told two children that they couldn't set up a bank because there already was one in the class. In another instance a teacher reprimanded a child for charging a fee for borrowing money, inadvertently eliminating a lesson on interest rates. Kourilsky was shocked to visit one program and find a sign over the door to the cloakroom reading "Debtors' Prison." The teacher explained proudly that anyone who didn't pay back a debt was put in the cloakroom and didn't go out at recess.

But these stories are extremes. The majority of teachers may make some mistakes, but chalk up new approaches and insights as a result. In Delaware, the Mini-Society program has become an integral part of training for elementary-school teachers, and the state has now trained about 300. About 10 years ago, Kourilsky and Dr. James O'Neill, director of the Center for Economic Education at the University of Delaware, taught the Mini-Society program to 10 key teachers; they, in turn, have trained all the rest.

Not surprisingly, O'Neill has plenty of good things to say about the program, but he is candid in acknowledging that not all teachers are good at teaching it, and that some have not been adequately trained. They may not have even attended a workshop.

This leads to another criticism, which is that the Mini-Society is, in Kourilsky's words, "teacher-intensive." A school setting up a Mini-Society has to pay for teachers to attend workshops. It can't just show a film.

"The girls start out working for the boys; then there's a fight."

There is criticism among economists, too, according to O'Neill. "No, it's not so much criticism as skepticism," he decides. "They are so used to thinking of economics as a complex, abstract subject that they can't imagine teaching it to children. But they've never thought about how to break down the abstraction. Once they have a child in the program, or some other reason to see how it works, they're all for it."

The success of Mini-Societies may go beyond a better understanding of economics. The program has worked well in schools in disadvantaged areas. A number of Detroit teachers underwent the workshop training, used the Mini-Society in their curriculums, and reported in follow-up workshops that truancy and dropout rates for kids in a Mini-Society program were lower than for the rest of the school's population, for which such rates were high. Kourilsky says the reason is that verbal ability is minimized. "A youngster who is a whiz at learning the economics may be less successful at running a business. He may have no street smarts. An IQ never taps this angle. And the class entrepreneur, on the other hand, may have to hire a kid with A's in math to be his auditor."

Kourilsky and others have wasted no time in testing the program, and the results live up to expectations. Many teachers have done before-and-after tests of students participating in a Mini-Society. Among the psychological benefits: a more positive attitude toward school, increased assertiveness, greater control over actions, and a greater willingness to take risks.

Most revealing of all are children's drawings. When asked, before becoming involved in a Mini-Society, to draw "a successful business person," most of them draw the stereotypically disgusting businessman: a fat face with sweat dripping from it and a big cigar stuck in his mouth. After participation in the program, their drawings of business people show all of the normal variation of kids' drawings of men and women. What's more, many of them look remarkably like themselves.

A Good School

Diane Ravitch

Diane Ravitch, adjunct professor of history and education at Teachers College, Columbia University, is the author of, most recently, The Troubled Crusade: American Education, 1945-1980. *A collection of her essays,* The Schools We Deserve, *was published in the spring of 1985 by Basic Books.*

In the not distant past, when attitudes toward public education were strongly positive, it rarely occurred to anyone to seek out examples of "effective schools." The evident assumption was that most schools were good, and that the ineffectual school was an aberration. The first annual Gallup poll about public schools in 1969 showed a strikingly high regard for schools and the teaching profession; three out of four persons responded that they would like to see their children take up teaching as a career. The level of public esteem for the schools at that time was even more remarkable in light of the overwhelmingly negative tone of the popular literature on schools in the mid-1960s.

After a decade of strident attacks on the schools, a decade in which public confidence waned, a small number of educational writers and researchers started looking for examples of good schools. There had long been a tradition of writing about a particular school as a way of trumpeting certain values that the school embodied, but the climate of the times tended to define the "good school." In the Progressive Era, certain schools were singled out because of their anti-traditional features, such as their combination of work and play or their engagement in the social life of the surrounding community. In the 1960s, certain schools were lauded for their political activism or their success in "liberating" children from bourgeois values.

By the late 1970s and early 1980s, an "effective school" came to be identified with the characteristics set out in the writings of the late Ron Edmonds of the Harvard Graduate School of Education. Perhaps because Edmonds was black, he was able to assert values that would have sounded disturbingly traditional to the educational establishment if

voiced by a white. Edmonds identified schools where academic achievement seemed to be independent of pupils' social class, and he concluded that such schools had an outstanding principal, high expectations for all children, an orderly atmosphere, a regular testing program, and an emphasis on academic learning.

Edmonds's conclusions may have seemed like a series of commonplace observations to most people, but they were received as stunning insights in the arcane world of educational policy. (Outsiders are repeatedly astonished by what passes for revelation in the education field; for instance, one of the great discoveries of recent years—though still not universally accepted—is that student achievement may be positively related to something called "time on task." In other words, what one learns is determined in part by the time spent learning it.) Happily, Edmonds was not alone in his interest in learning as the major measurement of school quality. Other studies reinforced his view that student achievement could be raised by sound educational practices. To appreciate the importance of this change in orientation, one must recall the many years in which academic achievement was treated with disdain in comparison with non-academic goals.

Writing about a single school is also a good way for a writer to test his own educational ideals and to display them for public inspection. Now, in the interest of candor, I confess that I instinctually hew to John Dewey's admonition: "What the best and wisest parent wants for his own child, that must the community want for all of its children. Any other ideal for our schools is narrow and unlovely." The best and wisest parents, I expect, want their child to read and write fluently; to speak articulately; to listen carefully; to learn to participate in the give-and-take of group discussion; to learn self-discipline and to develop the capacity for deferred gratification; to read and appreciate good literature; to have a strong knowledge of history, both of our own nation and of others; to appreciate the values of a free, democratic society; to understand science, mathematics, technology, and the natural world; to become engaged in the arts, both as a participant and as one capable of appreciating aesthetic excellence. I expect such parents would also want a good program of physical education and perhaps even competence in a foreign language. Presumably, these mythical best and wisest parents want their child to have some sense of possible occupation or profession, but it seems doubtful that they would want their child to use school time for vocational training, at least in the pre-collegiate years.

That our public schools have long operated on contrary assumptions should be obvious. The program I have described is usually called the academic track, and not more than 35 to 38 percent of American secondary students were recieving this kind of well-balanced preparation in the early 1980s. Acting not *in loco parentis* but on behalf of the state, educators have sorted children into vocational or general tracks, the former to prepare for a specific job, the latter being neither academic nor vocational. For reasons that are rooted largely in misplaced compassion—not in meanness or ignorance—our educational philosophy has dictated that academic learning is not for everyone; that it is too demanding for the average student; that its apparent inutility limits its value to the average student; that too much of it will cause students to drop out of high school in droves; and that such students should take courses that provide job skills, life skills, practical know-how, and immediate relevance to their own lives.

In public schools, curricular tracking has become a common practice. By tracking, I refer to the academic/vocational/general trichotomy, not to ability grouping. Ability grouping permits students to take different amounts of time to reach roughly similar goals; tracking offers students vastly different kinds of educational programs. The practice of tracking raises all sorts of questions: Who decides which students go into the academic track? At what ages does the tracking begin? To what extent is the decision to funnel a student into a non-academic track a response to his parents' occupations and social class? Should the public school—supported by taxes from all citizens—have the right to determine that some students will receive an education of high quality while others will get a denatured version?

To such questions, which go to the core of our democratic ideology, the defender of the present system might well respond: "Such naiveté! Dreams of perfection! In a perfect world, where all children have the same genetic and cultural inheritance, such a scheme of high-quality education for all might make sense. But in reality, children differ dramatically. Some come to school already knowing how to read, others can barely decipher words after six years of trying. Some are brilliant, others struggle to master the rudiments of learning. The smart ones are clearly college-bound and should have an academic curriculum. The others should have courses where the level of challenge is not too high, where they can have a feeling of success.

And more than subject matter, what the majority needs most is vocational training to get them ready for the workplace. That is what they want, and they should get it. Let us not forget that the great achievement of modern educational research has been the recognition that the curriculum must be adjusted to meet the differing needs of children."

For years, such views have represented the conventional wisdom in public education. The school that I have selected as an example of an effective school—the Edward R. Murrow High School of Brooklyn, New York—explicitly rejects these views. Its principal, Saul Bruckner, is a product of the public schools as well as a twenty-seven-year veteran of the New York City public school system. I learned a great deal by spending time in his school; I changed some of the ideas I brought with me. I am not sure that I agree with every practice and program in the school, but I deeply admire its tone and its high academic aspirations for all its pupils. I think what Bruckner is doing deserves attention, not because it is the only way or even the best way, but because it is one succesful way of wedding traditional goals with non-traditional means.

Murrow was opened in 1974 and officially designated an experimental school by the New York City Board of Education. Its 3,000 students are drawn from the borough of Brooklyn. Half of the students are white, and half are members of minority groups. One of the many unusual features of the school is that it treats all of its pupils as college-bound. No one is tracked into a vocational or "general" program. Yet the school is purposely composed of children with a broad range of abilities. By board of education mandate, at least 25 percent of Murrow's entering students read below grade level; no more than 25 percent read above grade level; and the remaining 50 percent read at grade level. There is no entrance examination, but competition for admission is vigorous; last year, there were some 9,500 applicants for 800 places in the entering class. Critics complain that special schools like Murrow "cream away" the best students from other public high schools, but about one-fourth of Murrow's enrollment consists of students from parochial and independent schools whose parents had previously rejected the public schools. Student morale is undoubtedly lifted by awareness of the difficulty of gaining entry into Murrow. The very process of applying makes every student a committed participant in his own education and eliminates the handful of unwilling students who otherwise make school life an ordeal for teachers and other students. Since Murrow has the luxury of not admitting those who have a well-established record of truancy, disruptive behavior, or criminal activity, it occasionally gets pilloried by detractors as "atypical," but the school may instead demonstrate that mixing those who want to learn with those who don't want to learn is no favor to either group.

Even though the students at Murrow represent a wide ability range, all are expected and required to take a strong academic program in order to graduate—that is, a minimum of five academic courses throughout the school year. The academically gifted take more than five, and there are advanced placement courses in every subject area. The New York City school system requires one year of a foreign language, but most students at Murrow take three or four (the school offers Spanish, French, Latin, Hebrew, and

Italian). Similarly, most students take more than the required two years of science and mathematics. Advanced science students may enroll in a sequence that includes six years of science; weak science students may take astronomy or horticulture instead of the rigorous course in physics. All must take at least four years of English, including a year of writing instruction, and three-and-a-half years of social studies. This level of academic engagement stands in stark contrast to the figures reported by national surveys. For example, only about 15 percent of American secondary students study *any* foreign language; only 6 percent of the nation's students finish a third year of foreign language study, but at Murrow at least 65 percent do. When compared to national enrollment rates in subjects like algebra, geometry, and the natural sciences, Murrow looks like a private school instead of a public school made up of a broad cross section of pupils.

The students who read two or more years below grade level receive intensive remedial instruction in reading and writing while still enrolled in regular courses. The school does not exclude average or below-average students from any of its uppper-level courses, as many schools do. Consequently, even advanced placement courses in English, social studies, mathematics, and science contain a diverse range of students, and occasionally teachers complain about students in their advanced placement class or the calculus class "who don't belong there." But the school's philosophy is that no student should be discouraged from taking on an academic challenge. Unlike many other public schools, Murrow does not practice grade inflation (20 percent of all its grades last year were "no credit," the equivalent of not passing the course) or social promotion (no one graduates until all of the academic requirements are met, and some students take longer than four years to finish).

The academic results of the Murrow program have been impressive. The annual dropout rate is only 4 percent, compared to a citywide rate of 11 percent. Daily attendance averages 88 percent, far above that of other urban high schools. Nearly 90 percent of its graduates continue either a four-year or a two-year college program. The school urges even those who intend to be secretaries to take a degree at a community college in order to enhance their occupational mobility later. The chairman of the social studies department, Mary Butz, explained to me on my first visit to the school, "The climate of the school is middle-class Jewish. These kids all believe that education will help them get ahead, move up into college and good jobs. They have bought the whole package. They believe in themselves, and they believe in us."

How can Murrow get away with its ambitious program? Well, for one thing, its students have been persuaded that Murrow is a very special school and that they are very special students. The school year and the day are organized somewhat differently than they are at a more traditional school. Instead of two semesters, there are four cycles of ten weeks each. The principal believes that the advantage of four ten-week courses is that students are encouraged to take risks, knowing that they won't be stuck for an entire year (or semester) with a bad choice. Instead of every subject meeting daily, the time is divided into four weekly meetings; this gives the students some blocks of optional time that they can use as they wish, either to study, do homework, or socialize with friends. Unlike the students at most other schools, students at Murrow are permitted to cluster in the halls during their optional time, and affinity groups have claimed different territories (none based on race, however). "Over there are my theater groupies," says Bruckner. "And those kids are the science groupies." As we walk through the hall, he sees a Hispanic girl curled up on the tile floor, deeply engrossed in a paperback book. "What's that you're reading?" She holds up the book, and he reads: "Richard II." In the English "resource center" (like a study hall), a group of youngsters works together on a project. In an otherwise empty classroom, half-a-dozen boys are setting up a videotape camera, part of a project for their literature course, "Detective Story." In the computer center, two or three students share a single machine, figuring out problems together, teaching each other.

Murrow represents an ingenious answer to the question: How do you enlist students' interest in their education without giving them control of the curriculum? Murrow does it by setting high requirements for graduation, but the school permits students to meet those requirements by choosing among a carefully designed mix of required and elective courses. The required sophomore course in American literature, for example, focuses on textual analysis of major poems, novels, and plays. Whether required or elective, all academic courses include homework and writing exercises. The many ten-week elective courses have jazzy titles, but fairly traditional readings; for example, students in "Youth and Identity" read Salinger's *The Catcher in the Rye*, Carson McCullers's *A Member of the Wedding*, Paul Zindel's *The Pigman*, and Elie Wiesel's *Night*. Students in "Novel into Film" read *The Great Gatsby* and *Great Expectations*. Many electives are unabashedly classical, like the Shakespeare class that reads *Romeo and Juliet*, *Richard II*, and *Othello*, or the advanced placement course that reads the works of Milton, John Donne, Ben Jonson, Jane Austen, and other great English writers.

In reviewing the literary offerings available to Murrow students, I could not help but contrast them to my own public school education in Texas. Although it is customary to lament the decline of public education, I believe that Murrow is a far better school than my alma mater in Houston. The literature curriculum of San Jacinto High School was uniform and limited. I recall a year of British fiction that never moved beyond *Silas Marner* and *Julius Caesar*. I have no idea why this selection was inviolate for so long, especially since I believe that such books as *Pride and Prejudice* or *Emma* or *Great Expectations* are wonderfully appealing to adolescents, while few adolescents have the maturity to appreciate George Eliot's complex prose.

Wisely administered, electives enable a school to provide what I would call the illusion of choice. Students do, in fact, make choices, but "wisely administered" means that they should not be permitted to make bad choices, like junk courses without academic merit ("Bachelor Living" or "Personal Grooming"). The illusion of choice can be readily adapted to the English sequence because the traditional English I through English VIII (which I took in my four years of public education) can easily be rearranged and attractively packaged. Thus, a course called "The Woman Writer" appeals to the modern sensibility, but is a fine setting in which to teach the works of Jane Austen, George Eliot, and Charlotte Brontë, and "The Literature of Social

Protest" turns out to be a good marketing tool for the works of writers such as Orwell and Dickens.

Where the repackaging can work neatly for the English curriculum, it has proved to be nearly a disaster in the undisciplined realm of "social studies." This field—once dominated by history—is now rootless and very nearly formless. Among social studies educators, the phrase "chronological history" is frequently used as a term of derision. Even courses entitled "American History" are likely to eschew the traditional narrative of events, leaders, ideas, and institutions in favor of themes, topics, and trends. A significant portion of the Murrow social studies curriculum reflects the political and social fragmentation of the past generation, as well as the disorganization of the social studies as a field. There is a required course in American government, concentrating on political institutions, and a reqired course on American diplomatic history, presenting the history of America's foreign policy, but most other courses are either specialized excursions into some thematic "experience" (the word "history" is usually avoided) or overly broad, like "the global experience." While history is in retreat, psychology, economics, and law studies are thriving: a student, for example, may choose from among eight different psychology courses (for instance, Social Psychology, Abnormal Psychology, Developmental Psychology, the Psychology of Aging).

Despite my reservations, the social studies program at Murrow is far stronger than at most schools. For one thing, there are no contentless courses in "values clarification," "process skills," or "decision making"; second, while the catalogue contains the feminist "Herstory" and "The Black Experience," there is otherwise no further ethnic or group fragmentation of the curriculum. Perhaps most important, the department includes some gifted teachers, who have before them at all times the example of their principal, Saul Bruckner, himself a master teacher of American history. He is frequently in classrooms, observing, prodding, and instructing other members of the staff to enliven their presentations and teaching styles. Under his critical gaze, the course"Origins of Western Civilization" really is a treatment of Western civilization from ancient Rome to the Renaissance, and the "Isms" course turns out to be a history of eighteenth- and nineteenth-century Europe.

I ought to explain how I happened to learn about this school. I was involved in sponsoring a conference in Minneapolis in the spring of 1984, on behalf of the National Endowment for the Humanities, on improving the teaching of the humanities in the high schools. The opening speaker was a distinguished social historian, who discussed the problem of integrating ethnic diversity into the common culture. It has been my experience that public discussions of ethnicity, especially among educators, invariably are pervaded by a sanctimonious tone. Everyone speaks reverentially of the nobility and struggles of oppressed minority groups, and the air becomes heavy with guilt and piety.

During the coffee break, a young teacher grabbed me by the arm to tell me, in an unmistakably Brooklyn accent, that an American Indian woman—known in current bureaucratic language as a Native American person—had just assailed her in scatological language. "What?" I said. "What? How can this be?" "Well," she said, "this Indian woman asked me if she could use the bathroom, and I told

her that the bathroom was reserved for conference participants. So, she used the bathroom anyway. When she came out a few moments later, she jabbed her finger in my chest, called me by an odious term, and warned, 'White woman, don't mess with me anymore.' "

Her name card said, "Mary Butz, Edward R. Murrow High School, Brooklyn, New York." Charmed by her indifference to the demands of ethnic piety, I asked her to tell me about her school. She said, with what I later learned was characteristic candor, that it was the best school in New York City, because it had the best principal and "the greatest kids." I was startled, because over the years, I have met so many embittered teachers in the New York City school system, people who recall or have heard of the school system's reputation in another era, an era when the New York City public schools were widely recognized as pioneers and when their students were pressing hard for future greatness as literati or scientists.

Naturally, I wanted to see the best school in New York City, the best principal, and the greatest kids, particularly because I had been in so many high schools that seemed like armed camps and in so many subway cars at the end of the school day when high school students used their raw energy to intimidate everyone else. So not many days later, I trekked out to the Midwood section of Brooklyn to find an undistinguished, nearly windowless modern brick building, set in the midst of a pleasant middle-class neighborhood. An example of incredibly stupid planning, the Murrow building abuts elevated subway tracks (the noise of passing trains regularly disrupts classes) and has no surrounding campus, although the students are able to use another school's athletic field across the street.

As it happened, on the day that I arrived, Bruckner was teaching an advanced placement section of American history. There were about thirty youngsters in the class, and the question for the day was: "Was it moral for the U.S. to drop the atomic bomb on Japan?" Something inside me warned that I was in for a session of moralistic Truman-bashing, but I was wrong. The students (some of whom were Oriental) had read the textbook description of the war. When I entered, the class was discussing the incidence of cancer in Hiroshima and Nagasaki. Then Mr. Bruckner used an overhead projector to display contemporary news stories from the *New York Times* and the *Herald Tribune*. One headline told the human cost of caturing Okinawa: forty-five thousand American casualties, ninety thousand Japanese casualties. How many lives might be lost in an invasion of the mainland? A mimeographed handout discussed Japanese kamikaze raids and brutality toward American prisoners, which gave the students a flavor of Japanese and American wartime attitudes. A fair conclusion, which did not involve prejudice toward our Japanese adversaries, was that they would fight ferociously to the end. Lest anyone jump to the easy conclusion that the decision to drop the bomb was moral, the teacher also displayed comments by generals and revisionist historians who felt that dropping the bomb was not necessary to end the war.

The lesson was taught in a Socratic manner. Mr. Bruckner did not lecture. He asked questions and kept up a rapid-fire dialogue among the students. "Why?" "How do you know?" "What does this mean?" "Do you really think so ?" Sometimes he called on students who were desperately waving their arms, other times he solicited the views of those who were sitting quietly. By the time the class was finished, the students had covered a great deal of material about American foreign and domestic policies during World War II; they had argued heatedly; most of them had tried out different points of view, seeing the problem from different angles. It was a good lesson: it was well planned, utilizing a variety of materials and media; and the students were alert and responsive.

Bruckner's lesson was at odds with the usual characterization of American teaching. In the past year or two, most critics of the schools have complained about the quality of teaching. Educators like John Goodlad of UCLA and Theodore Sizer, a former headmaster of Andover Academy, have asserted that there is too much "teacher telling," too much student passivity, and little if any thought-provoking activity in the typical classroom. A major study prepared for the National Institute of Education a few years ago contended that teaching in American schools has remained unchanged—that is, boring and teacher-dominated—throughout the century. Well, I thought to myself, I have seen one great teacher; what happens in the other classrooms?

I visited many classrooms and observed teachers in every subject area. I saw some outstanding teaching, some passably good classes, and a few that failed, but in no instance did I see a teacher droning on to a class of bored students. The teaching style in the building was remarkably consistent, and every teacher used materials and experiences that were outside the textbook. In the best classes, the focus of the lesson was on the intellectual exchange sparked by the teacher and kept alive by student participation. In one literature class, the students debated O. Henry's use of language to establish the tone of a story; in a chemistry class, thirty-five students jointly figured out the answer to the question, "how does a battery operate?"

I later learned that Bruckner requires all his teachers to use what is called the "developmental lesson" or the "socialized recitation." If they do not know how to teach this way when they are assigned to Murrow, they are taught the method by their department chairman. At its best, it works magnificently: students listen, speak out, think, disagree with each other, change their minds, make judgments. For this method to work, two things are necessary: first, the teacher has to be well prepared, having planned out the lesson in advance with an "aim" or problem to be solved, with pivotal questions to provoke student discussion, and with materials (a political cartoon, a newspaper headline, a quotation from a participant or critic, or an excerpt from a book) to stimulate the new lines of inquiry; second, the students must bring something to the class in the way of reading or homework, so that they can respond to the teacher's questions with ideas and insights of their own. If the teacher does not prepare well and if the students are uninformed, the developmental lesson can dwindle into a vapid exchange of uninformed opinion, of less value than a traditional didactic lecture.

Bruckner's biggest problem is building a good teaching staff. Within the context of the public school bureaucracy, this requires consummate skill. When Bruckner opened Murrow in 1974, he was officially permitted to select only 35 percent of his staff. Because he was a veteran of "the system," he was able to play the teacher-selection game

like a Stradivarius, and he ended up with a staff in which about 70 percent of the teachers were of his choosing. He might encourage a skilled teacher to apply to join his staff, who would then not be counted as one of his "picks." Since the school opened in the midst of the city's fiscal crisis, Bruckner was able to hire many talented young teachers who had been laid off by other schools. Among the 30 percent or so that he did not choose were, inevitably, some lemons. It is possible, but not easy, to fire a probationary teacher (one who has taught for less than three years); it is nearly impossible to oust a tenured teacher. "A principal can't fire a teacher simply because he is boring or incompetent or even when you know that he treats the kids like dirt," Bruckner says. "He must be grossly negligent, persistently late for class, drunk in class, something like that."

What a principal can do, however, is lay off staff, but only in order of seniority. One principal, Bruckner says, wiped out most of his English department to get rid of a teacher with fifteen years of seniority; seven able young teachers were laid off in order to drop a bad senior teacher. Bruckner closed down his guidance department in order to remove the person assigned to Murrow. Eventually the Brooklyn superintendent for high schools ordered him to hire guidance counselors, and he continued to hire and lay off until he got the people he wanted. Usually it is easier to lay off personnel than to go through the procedure of ousting them. Not only is it time-consuming, but if the principal wins, the teacher is stripped of his license. It is akin to having a lawyer disbarred, with this exception: the teacher can get a licence in another area. For example, Bruckner had the licenses revoked from two probationary teachers, one who taught the handicapped (special education), another who taught social studies. Before long, both were reinstated. The ex-special education teacher had become an elementary teacher, and the ex-social studies teacher had moved into special education. "Well," Bruckner says with resignation, "I didn't get them out of the system, but I got them out of this school."

Bruckner speaks with passion about how the structure of public education contributes to the "infantilization" of teachers. "Teachers," he complains, "have little responsibility for the conditions of their working lives. We call teaching a profession, but if so, it is the only profession in which there is no opportunity for growth while remaining in the profession." The teacher has lost a great deal of authority to make decisions, not only to supervisors, but also to their own organizations and to federal, state, and local mandates. "For most of the important things in their day," Bruckner says, "teachers depend on someone else. Someone else assigns them a room, someone else gives them a daily schedule, someone else writes their lesson plan." Yet in the classroom they have total control, and no matter what the offcial course of study says, the teacher defines the curriculum every day. Outside the classroom, however, the teachers "are like students: they have very limited say over their lives, and that creates bitterness and hostility." To break through this "infantilization," Bruckner encourages teachers to design their own courses and to take more responsibility for school affairs. Perhaps the most promising innovation has sprung from the science department, where teachers visit one another's classrooms and discuss content and methodology; their professional critiques of one another take the place of an official observation by a supervisor. Bruckner hopes that other departments will follow suit: "Doctors observe each other practice and learn from one another; so do lawyers. Why shouldn't teachers?"

Like other big-city high schools in the 1980s, Murrow is constantly threatened by financial pressures. Average class size is now up to thirty-four in the city's high schools, the largest in many years. The library is funded at only one dollar per year per student; half of the library budget pays for the *New York Times* on microfilm and its index, leaving only $1,500 for books and magazine subscriptions. At today's prices, $1,500 does not buy much of either. In order to continue using a diversity of materials and media in the classroom, which is integral to the lively approach that Bruckner advocates, the school has heavy expenses for equipment, supplies, and repairs. Occasionally, he has traded in a teaching position (valued at $33,000) in order to maintain the school's Xerox machines, mimeograph machines, computers, overhead projectors, and audiovisual equipment.

The school has a climate that is relaxed and tension-free. Teachers and students alike know that they are in a good school, and this sense of being special contributes to high morale. Yet the tenuousness of the authority structure of a big school was revealed to me one morning when the principal was away at a conference mandated by the board of education. Word spread through the building that the police bomb squad had closed off part of the second and third floors, and it was true. Students milled in the corridors, elaborating on the rumor. An assistant principal announced on the public address system, "Everyone return to your classroom. There is no danger at the present moment." Since the police had sealed off a major portion of the building, most students had no classroom to return to. In the absence of sensible adult instruction, nearly half of the students went home. The surprising thing, Mary Butz observed, was not that so many left, but that so many stayed, because the bomb scare had effectively ended the school day.

Schools cannot function as they once did. Teachers cannot presume to have the respect of the students. They have to win it in the classroom. Many New York City school teachers have found it difficult to adjust to the loss of authority over the past generation and the change in the pupil demography from predominantly white to predominantly black and Hispanic. Some professionals in the New York City public schools labor with a sense of nostalgia for a lost golden age, a time when student motivation could be taken for granted and when teachers were respected figures in the community. This image of a lost golden age is a mixture of truth, misty memories, and historical accident. The Great Depression was a time when many over-educated teachers entered the school system because there were no jobs in higher education or the professions; when there was an unusual number of second- and third-generation Jewish students who were eager to use their education to get ahead; and when the less-motivated students dropped out to work as elevator operators or messengers or in some other low-skill job.

Life was hard for most people during the Depression, but in many ways it was not as complicated for school people as it is today. Many of the children at Murrow, who come from a broad mix of racial, religious, and ethnic backgrounds, bear the scars of social dissolution. While trying to educate them, the school cannot ignore the family crises, the broken homes, the child abuse, the parental negligence that cuts across all socio-economic lines. In other urban schools, the wounds that families inflict on their children are far worse. Sometimes the best that a school can do is to provide a sympathetic adult who will listen.

Bruckner knows that the school competes for the child's attention with the pathology outside its doors, with the lure of television, drugs, sex, and the adolescent culture. He has not created a social service program; the school is not a social work agency. What he has tried to do is to make it a place where adolescents feel at home, a place that they might want to come to even if they didn't have to. He has done this, not by turning the school into a playing field with low hurdles, but by harnessing non-traditional means to traditional academic goals. The smart kids have no ceiling on their ambitions; they can go as far and as fast as their brains will take them. Not many public schools in the nation can match Murrow's advanced courses in science and mathematics. But this richness for the bright students is not achieved by pushing the average ones into nursing and automobile mechanics. All of them have available a strong basic curriculum and a diversity of learning opportunities that enable them to learn at their own pace, and all are accorded equal respect as students.

There are many different kinds of effective schools. Some of them, like Murrow's neighbor in Brooklyn, Midwood High School, are highly structured and traditional. Visiting Midwood is like stepping into a school in the early 1950s; it is quiet and orderly, and the students seem serious and purposeful. What effective schools have in common should be available to all American students: a strong academic curriculum, a principal with a vision and the courage to work for it, dedicated teachers, a commitment to learning, a mix of students from different backgrounds, and high expectations for all children.

Helping Preservice Teachers Learn to Use Teacher Effectiveness Research

Dorene Doerre Ross

Diane Wells Kyle

Ross is Associate Professor, College of Education, University of Florida; Kyle is Associate Professor, School of Education, University of Louisville.

Ross and Kyle provide teacher educators with a way of presenting and discussing teacher effectiveness research in the context of the teacher education curriculum. The authors argue that it is imperative that preservice teachers develop an ability to use and reflect on conflicting research findings. The reading research and direct instruction studies serve as paradigmatic cases.

What do beginning teachers need to know and be able to do? Educational reform efforts in a number of states have focused attention on this question and, in hopes of assuring increased teacher competence, have adopted induction programs based on teacher effectiveness research. Teacher educators responsible for the preparation of those who face this scrutiny as teacher interns must find ways of helping students understand the teacher effectiveness literature and of developing the skills of direct instruction assessed in the programs.

However, the exclusive focus on the findings from the teacher effectiveness research as the basis for the evaluation of beginning teachers might suggest to neophytes that direct instruction is the most effective teaching strategy. Such an inference is too sweeping. Teacher educators working with preservice teachers bear a particular responsibility to help them learn the appropriate applications of these research findings and to make deliberative judgments in selecting appropriate instructional strategies. By presenting the teacher effectiveness research within the context of related research about the teaching of reading,[1] this article can help teacher educators guide preservice teachers in elementary education toward a more comprehensive understanding of the implications of the effectiveness literature.

Characteristics of Direct Instruction

Much of the teacher effectiveness research centers on identifying management and instructional strategies that will enable teachers to help low ability, low SES students to score higher than expected scores on standardized tests of achievement in reading and mathematics. The management strategies suggested by the teacher effectiveness literature are consistent with a wide variety of instructional styles and strategies, but this is not necessarily the case with the findings related to effective instruction. In fact, direct instruction, the approach found to be most effective for teaching explicit concepts and skills to low achieving students, seems in direct contradiction to strategies such as those associated with cooperative learning, student experimentation, and problem solving. Because many faculty in colleges of education advocate the use of such strategies, students faced with the powerful body of research supporting the effectiveness of direct instruction may have difficulty determining the appropriate application of the research. For this reason, this article focuses on the findings and applications of research concerning the effectiveness of direct instruction. What is direct instruction? According to Rosenshine (1986), "The major components include teaching in small steps with student practice after each step, guiding students during initial practice, and providing all students with a high level of successful practice" (p. 62). These characteristics have been supported repeatedly in the research literature (Anderson, Hiebert, Scott, and Wilkinson, 1985; Berliner, 1984; Brophy, 1979; Gage, 1978; George, 1983; Good, 1979; Good and Grouws, 1979; Harris, 1979; Powell, 1979; Rosenshine, 1976; Rupley and Blair, 1978).

Effective teaching practices, as perceived by advocates of direct instruction, increase the amount of time students engage in and experience success on activities related to the skills tested on outcome measures of achievement. Consequently, teachers are expected to use whole group instruction to maximize direct supervision of each student; use lecture, demonstration, drill and practice to teach skills and concepts; use low cognitive level questioning to assure fast-paced lessons of high student involvement; provide immediate teacher feedback; and monitor student engagement and success rates during teacher-directed lessons and during independent practice.

States such as Florida and Kentucky now base their evaluation of beginning teachers on the demonstration of the teaching behaviors outlined above. Responsible teacher educators face the task of presenting the literature supporting these behaviors and of working to ensure that prospective teachers can demonstrate their use. However, many would argue that no one set of teaching behaviors will ensure effectiveness; the limits on the appropriate use of the teacher effectiveness research must be understood by prospective teachers. Several of these limits are addressed in the following sections.

Appropriate Use of Teacher Effectiveness Research

Those associated with teacher effec-

tiveness research as well as their critics have indicated several limitations that should be understood and considered by anyone making instructional decisions. For example, the research is most applicable for teaching low cognitive level skills in reading and math to low achieving, low SES students (Soar and Soar, 1983). Key factors, then, concern *what* is to be taught and *who* is to be taught.

Many researchers have noted that for high cognitive level learning, less direct and controlled instruction seems more beneficial (McFaul, 1983; Peterson, 1979; Rosenshine, 1986; Soar, Medley, and Coker, 1983). In fact, Soar and Soar (1972, 1975) found that high levels of teacher control reduced high cognitive level learning by students.

Additionally, lower control over learning tasks seems important for many other aims of education. For instance, researchers have found that the high level of teacher structure and control of learning activities suggested in the teacher effectiveness research may have a negative impact on students' problem-solving abilities (Corno, 1979); anxiety level and self-esteem (Soar and Soar, 1975); and creativity, attitudes toward school and teacher, and independence and curiosity (Peterson, 1979).

The learning task, then, becomes an important consideration, as do the learners themselves. High ability, highly motivated, low anxiety students, and those with an internal locus of control, have demonstrated higher scores on achievement measures when the classroom is less structured and controlled than recommended by the teacher effectiveness research (McFaul, 1983; Peterson, 1979; Soar and Soar, 1983). This suggests that teachers must vary lesson format and control based on their goals, and it supports the idea that the most important teacher behavior is the flexibility and judgment necessary to select the appropriate strategy for the particular goal and student involved.

As teachers attempt to make these complex judgments about when and how to use the findings of the teacher effectiveness research, related theory and research can be helpful. This can be illustrated more fully by examining research on reading and the implications for instructional strategies.

Research on Reading Instruction

Although basal reader programs

with their accompanying emphasis on low cognitive level decoding skills dominate reading instruction in elementary classrooms (Anderson et al., 1985; Strange, 1978; Durkin, 1981), many reading researchers argue that learning to read is, in fact, a complex process requiring high cognitive level skills (Olshavsky, 1977; Gutknecht and Keenan, 1978; McNeil, 1984). In their views, children's experiences with reading must include looking at reading material, selecting relevant cues, making inferences and predictions about the text, and then making judgments about the accuracy of their predictions. Anderson et al. (1985) summarize the current position about the nature of the task of reading.

> Based on what we now know, it is incorrect to suppose that there is a simple or single step which, if taken correctly, will immediately allow a child to read. Becoming a skilled reader is a journey that involves many steps. Similarly, it's unrealistic to anticipate that some one critical feature of instruction will be discovered which, if in place, will assure rapid progress in reading. Quality instruction involves many elements. Strengthening any one element yields small gains. For large gains many elements must be in place. (p. 4)

This perspective calls into question the applicability of direct instruction as the dominant strategy for reading instruction, in spite of the fact that such instruction will help children learn the low cognitive level skills necessary to score better on achievement tests. According to McNeil (1984), these tests assess comprehension skills that can be measured objectively, but this conveys a limited notion of what can be comprehended in a text.

Reading researchers express concern that the aim of improving test scores will result in a disproportionate amount of classroom time being spent on easily tested, low cognitive level skills, at the expense of the more complex reading skills which cannot be measured objectively. Researchers such as Anderson et al. (1985) encourage teachers to spend less time on drill using worksheets and dittos and more time on children's reading and writing; however, these recommended tasks do not fit the lecture, demonstration, drill and practice model suggested by the teacher effectiveness research.

The appropriate recommendation here is for teachers to use multiple methods to teach reading. During low level primary skill lessons, direct instruction seems applicable and effective. During reading comprehension and writing sessions, direct instruction seems less applicable. Because less structured outcomes are desired, less structured methods are required. (For specific suggestions of methods in the area of reading see Anderson et al., 1985; Bussis, 1982; Durkin, 1978; Taylor, 1977; Roser and Jensen, 1978.) Confirmation of the importance of focusing on higher cognitive elements during reading instruction comes from studies of good and poor readers and from research on language learning.

Research on Good and Poor Readers

Consideration of the research on the difference between good and poor readers is important, because our ultimate goal for low achievers is not higher scores on tests but performance more like high achievers. One recurrent finding from these studies is that the two groups of children approach learning tasks differently. For example, research shows that good readers demonstrate more flexibility in their thinking and reasoning, in their selection of an appropriate reading strategy, and in their application of skills appropriate to the task (Smith, 1967; Kavale and Schreiner, 1979). Poor readers, on the other hand, "perceive reading as an exercise in decoding" (Winograd and Greenlee, 1986, p. 19).

High achieving students monitor their learning efforts; that is, they expect that learning will make sense, monitor their progress, and seek help when necessary. In contrast, several studies have documented that poor readers lack a demand for meaning (Taylor, 1977; Allington, 1983; Davey, 1983; Anderson et al., 1985). According to Winograd and Greenlee (1986), "Good readers know when they are making sense out of text and when they are not. Poor readers, in contrast, seem to have particular trouble with this aspect of fluent reading" (p. 18). And, perhaps because they lack an expectation that text will make sense, low achievers do not monitor their reading efforts (Allington, 1983; Kavale and Schreiner, 1979; Smith, 1967; Davey, 1983; Fitzgerald, 1983; Holmes, 1983; Anderson et al., 1985). Furthermore, once a student has determined that a learning task does not make sense, he or she must be able to remedy the problem, an additional skill lacking in low achieving students.

According to advocates of direct instruction, teachers should monitor students' success and provide immediate feedback about correct responses. Although this may enable students to acquire certain low level skills, a high level of teacher monitoring may impede students' acquisition of other important learning strategies such as the ability to determine independently whether the text makes sense and, thus, to develop necessary skills of self-monitoring (Allington, 1983; Doyle, 1978).

At issue is not whether teachers should provide assistance but the degree to which they should assume responsibility for determining when that assistance is needed. Nelson-LeGall (1985) suggests that the most beneficial help is given in response to a student-expressed need rather than when the teacher perceives help is warranted.

According to Nelson-LeGall (1985), self-help skills are more likely to develop when students are taught in small group settings, when they have some autonomy in the selection of learning tasks, when learning tasks are challenging but not too difficult, and when help is offered in response to student-expressed need. These strategies are inconsistent with the recommendations of the teacher effectiveness research. Again, this suggests that, while direct instruction is an appropriate and necessary instructional tool for skills that can be directly taught, other teaching strategies are equally important to the development of students' competence in more complex, higher cognitive level tasks.

Research on Language Learning

Researchers of language learning have found that young children are proficient language learners. From a complex array of oral, gestural, and social cues, children construct their language system (Donaldson, 1978). All children, except those with severe handicaps, accomplish this complex task of pattern detection, hypothesis generation, and confirmation. Furthermore, the language learning environments of high and low SES children are similar, except that higher SES parents speak more responsively with their children (Schachter et al., 1979). According to Schachter and Strage (1982), this responsive interaction may be a critical

factor in children's development as autonomous language users.

While some reading researchers believe that reading should be taught in small sequential steps, many others believe that reading, like oral language, must be presented as an integrated whole rather than simplified into steps and taught formally. Studies of the learning processes and skills of children who learn to read without instruction suggest that over-simplification of reading may impede children's progress at mastering reading in the broader sense (Douglass, 1978; Goodman, 1978; Hoskisson, 1979; Smith, 1977). Thus, these researchers conclude that reading must be constructed by the child in ways similar to the way in which the young child constructs and applies the rules of grammar while learning to communicate with speech. In their view, formal instruction in skills disrupts the process of learning to read, just as instruction in elocution and syntax would impede a young child's ability to communicate orally.

The perspective offered by researchers of language learning is supported by the work of cognitive psychologists who state that children construct meaning from their experiences in the environment (Elkind, 1979; Piaget, 1969; Siegel, 1984: Vygotsky, 1978) and of brain researchers who note that the human brain constructs thoughts, concepts, and perceptions and must be challenged (Bussis, 1982; Levy, 1983; Tipps, 1981).

What does this body of knowledge suggest as implications for instruction? Researchers studying how children learn would encourage teachers to coordinate direct instruction with other approaches that stress the overall complexity of basic skills and to use individual and small group strategies that enable the teacher to interact responsively with children. They also would suggest that guided problem solving, where children develop hypotheses and test them in order to construct their own learning, is an important aspect of basic skill learning and should not be omitted.

Summary and Implications

The findings of teacher effectiveness and other research on learning suggest the need for teachers to have a varied repertoire of teaching strategies. For teaching low cognitive skills, low achieving students, and drill and practice lessons, direct instruction is effective. For helping students develop higher cognitive skills, problem-solving abilities, creativity, a demand for meaning, self-monitoring skills, and self-help skills, other teaching strategies become more important.

This literature suggests that the most competent teacher, like the most competent learner, must use his or her skills with flexibility and intelligence. Consequently, teacher educators must assist their students in examining research findings critically and in developing an informed basis for making judgments about teaching. How might teacher educators accomplish this? While there are no proven answers to this question, several suggestions emerge based on our efforts to help students develop this knowledge and judgment.

1. Present the teacher effectiveness research to students early in their teacher education programs and give it a position of prominence in the program. In many programs this research is presented in bits and pieces throughout a student's program instead of as an integrated whole. When this happens, students are less likely to develop a clear understanding of the tenets of good direct instruction and may gain their first comprehensive view of the implications of the research during inservice or a beginning teacher program. Without adequate knowledge of the research, graduates may accept it without reservation and may reject other, seemingly contradictory, teachings from their teacher education programs as "not relevant in the real world."

2. Present the teacher effectiveness research (along with other research), such as that discussed in this article, in order to help students understand its benefits and limitations. In the PROTEACH program at the University of Florida, students are introduced to the extant research in a course entitled, Research in Elementary Education, taken during their second semester in the program. Students in this course read many of the articles discussed here. The initial focus in the course is on the development of a comprehensive understanding of the teacher effectiveness research. They learn the tenets of good direct instruction. They learn to use the instructional organization and management sections of the Florida Performance Measurement System, and they practice observing the behaviors of direct instruction on videotape and in classrooms. During the second part of the course, students read critiques of teacher effectiveness research, syntheses of reading and mathematics research that suggest the importance of alternative practices, and articles that discuss the appropriate use of research in developing implications for practice. In this way, students become critical consumers of research who learn to base their decisions about the applicability of particular studies and findings upon their chosen aims for education and knowledge about the students in their classrooms. Further, they learn to articulate the reasons for selecting one instructional strategy over another, making it more likely that they will be able to defend the validity of their professional judgments as they move into the classroom.

3. Help students develop performance competence in the behaviors associated with effective direct instruction. In states such as Florida and Kentucky, the competence of beginning teachers is determined, in part, by their ability to demonstrate competent direct instruction. Competence in this aspect of instruction may help students develop the confidence necessary to make judgments about teaching and adapt practice to educational aims. Further, unless students, as beginning teachers, have the skills necessary to demonstrate competence to their evaluators, they will not be given the freedom necessary for the development and exercise of professional judgment.

4. Help students develop performance competence in additional teaching skills, such as guiding cooperative learning and conducting problem solving activities. Knowledge about the importance of alternatives to direct instruction is of limited utility unless a teacher knows how to conduct other types of lessons.

These suggestions provide a way of presenting the implications of the teacher effectiveness research within the context of other research that counters the notion that direct instruction is the primary teaching strategy. If this is done, preservice teachers may acquire a clearer understanding that teaching is a complex process requiring creativity, intuition, and the ability to improvise and perform (Gage, 1985).

Reference Note

[1]In developing the ideas for this article, we have focused primarily on research related to reading instruction. Others may want to analyze research in another field in order to explore further the ideas we have raised.

References

Allington, R. L. (1983). The reading instruction provided readers of differing reading abilities. *Elementary School Journal, 83,* 548-559.

Anderson, R. C., Hiebert, E. H., Scott, J. A., & Wilkinson, I. A. (1985). *Becoming a nation of readers.* Washington, DC: National Institute of Education.

Berliner, D. C. (1984). The half-full glass: A review of research on teaching. In P. L. Hosford (Ed.), *Using what we know about teaching* (pp. 51-77). Alexandria, VA: Association for Supervision and Curriculum Development.

Brophy, J. E. (1979). Teacher behavior and student learning. *Educational Leadership, 37,* 33-38.

Bussis, A. M. (1982). "Burn it at the casket": Research, reading instruction and children's learning of the first R. *Phi Delta Kappan, 64,* 237-241.

Corno, L. (1979). A hierarchical analysis of selected naturally occurring aptitude-treatment interactions in the third grade. *American Educational Research Journal, 16,* 391-409.

Davey, B. (1983). Think aloud — modeling the cognitive process of reading comprehension. *Journal of Reading, 27,* 44-47.

Donaldson, M. (1978). *Children's minds.* New York: Norton.

Douglass, M. P. (1978). On reading: The great American debate. In E. W. Eisner (Ed.), *Reading, the arts and the creation of meaning* (pp. 89-109). Reston, VA: National Art Association.

Doyle, W. (1978, March). *Student mediating responses in teaching effectiveness: An interim report.* Paper presented at the annual meeting of the American Educational Research Association, Toronto.

Durkin, D. (1978). Pre-first grade starts in reading: Where do we stand? *Educational Leadership, 35,* 174-177.

Durkin, D. (1981). Reading comprehension in five basal readers. *Reading Research Quarterly, 16,* 515-544.

Elkind, D. (1979). Beginning reading: A stage structure analysis. *Childhood Education, 55,* 248-252.

Fitzgerald, J. (1983). Helping readers gain self-control over reading comprehension. *Reading Teachers, 37,* 249-253.

Gage, N. L. (1978). The yield of research on teaching. *Phi Delta Kappan, 61,* 229-238.

Gage, N. L. (1985). *Hard gains in the soft sciences: The case of pedagogy.* Bloomington, IN: Phi Delta Kappa Center on Evaluation, Development and Research.

George, P. S. (1983). Instruction: Ten tarnished truths. *Educational Forum, 48,* 34, 36-42.

Good, T. L. (1979). Teacher effectiveness in the elementary school. *Journal of Teacher Education, 30* (2), 52-64.

Good, T. L., & Grouws, D. A. (1979). Teaching and mathematics learning. *Educational Leadership, 37,* 39-45.

Goodman, K. S. (1978). What is basic about reading? In E. W. Eisner (Ed.), *Reading, the arts and the creation of meaning* (pp. 55-69). Reston, VA: National Art Association.

Gutknecht, B., & Keenan, D. (1978). Basic skills: Not which but why, and an enlightened how. *Reading Teacher, 31,* 668-674.

Harris, A. J. (1979). The effective teacher of reading, revisited. *Reading Teacher, 33,* 135-140.

Holmes, B. C. (1983). A confirmation strategy for improving poor readers' ability to answer inferential questions. *Reading Teacher, 37,* 144-148.

Hoskisson, K. (1979). Learning to read naturally. *Language Arts, 56,* 489-96.

Kavale, K., & Schreiner, R. (1979). The reading processes of above average and average readers: A comparison of the use of reasoning strategies in responding to standardized comprehension measures. *Reading Research Quarterly, 15,* 102-128.

Lanier, J. E., & Little, J. W. (1986). Research on teacher education. In M. C. Wittrock (Ed.), *Handbook of research on teaching* (3rd ed.) (pp. 527-569). New York: Macmillan.

Levy, J. (1983). Research synthesis on right and left hemispheres: We think with both sides of the brain. *Educational Leadership, 40,* Issue 4, 66-71.

McFaul, S. A. (1983). An examination of direct instruction. *Educational Leadership, 40* (7), 67-69.

McNeil, J. (1984). *Reading comprehension.* Glenview, IL: Scott, Foresman.

Nelson-LeGall, S. (1985). Help seeking behavior in learning. In E. W. Gordon (Ed.), *Review of Research in Education* (Vol. 12, pp. 55-90). Washington, DC: American Educational Research Association.

Olshavsky, J. E. (1977). Reading as problem solving: An investigation of strategies. *Reading Research Quarterly, 12,* 654-674.

Peterson, P. L. (1979). Direct instruction: Effective for what and for whom? *Educational Leadership, 37,* 46-48.

Piaget, J. (1969). *Science of education and the psychology of the child* (D. Coltman, Trans.). New York: Viking Press.

Powell, M. (1979). New evidence for old truths. *Educational Leadership, 37,* 46-48.

Rosenshine, B. (1976). Recent research on teaching behaviors and student achievement. *Journal of Teacher Education, 27,* 61-64.

Rosenshine, B. (1986). Synthesis of research on explicit teaching. *Educational Leadership, 43,* 60-69.

Roser, N. L., & Jensen, J. M. (1978). Real communication: Key to early reading and writing. *Childhood Education, 55,* 90-93.

Rupley, W. H., & Blair, T. R. (1978). Characteristics of effective reading instruction. *Educational Leadership, 36,* 171-173.

Schachter, F. F., Marquis, R. E., Shore, E., Bundy, C. L., & McNair, J. H. (1979). *Everyday mother talk to toddlers: Early intervention.* New York: Academic Press.

Schachter, F. F., & Strage, A. A. (1982). Adults' talk and children's language development. In S. G. Moore & C. R. Cooper (Eds.), *The Young Child: Reviews of Research* (Vol. 3, pp. 79-95). Washington, DC: The National Association for the Education of Young Children.

Siegel, I. E. (1984). A constructivist perspective for teaching thinking. *Educational Leadership, 42* (3), 18-21.

Smith, F. (1977). Making sense of reading and of reading instruction. *Harvard Educational Review, 47,* 386-395.

Smith, H. K. (1967). The responses of good and poor readers when asked to read for different purposes. *Reading Research Quarterly, 3,* 53-83.

Soar, R. S., Medley, D. M., & Coker, H. (1983). Teacher evaluation: A critique of currently used methods. *Phi Delta Kappan, 65,* 239-246.

Soar, R. S., & Soar, R. M. (1972). An empirical analysis of selected Follow Through programs: An example of a process approach to evaluation. In I. J. Gordon (Ed.), *Early Childhood Education* (pp. 229-260). Chicago: National Society for the Study of Education.

Soar, R. S., & Soar, R. M. (1975). Classroom behavior, pupil characteristics, and pupil growth for the school year and the summer. *Journal Supplement Abstract Service Catalog of Selected Documents in Psychology, 5,* 200. (Ms. No. 873).

Soar, R. S., & Soar, R. M. (1983). Context effects in the teaching learning process. In D. C. Smith (Ed.), *Essential knowledge for beginning educators* (pp. 65-75). Washington, DC: American Association of Colleges for Teacher Education.

Strange, M. C. (1978). Considerations for evaluating reading instruction. *Educational Leadership, 36,* 178-181.

Taylor, J. (1977). Making sense: The basic skill in reading. *Language Arts, 54,* 668-672.

Tipps, S. (1981). Play and the brain: Relationships and reciprocity. *Journal of Research and Development in Education, 14* (3), 19-29.

Vygotsky, L. S. (1978). *Mind in society.* Cambridge, MA: Harvard University Press.

Winograd, P., & Greenlee, M. (1986). Students need a balanced reading program. *Educational Leadership, 43* (7), 16-21.

SHOULD FOUR-YEAR EDUCATION MAJOR BE ENDED?

Yes—these programs don't attract top students
No—five-year requirement carries hidden costs

Bernard R. Gifford
Special to *The Christian Science Monitor*

Bernard Gifford is dean of the school of education at the University of California at Berkeley.

Two recent reports on the need for reform in teacher-education programs, and in the nature of teaching itself, have called for the abolition of the undergraduate education degree. I agree with this recommendation.

If we are going to build the kind of teaching profession envisioned in these two pathbreaking reports—one that encourages, supports, and rewards reflective and effective instruction—we must take a hard look at the quality of undergraduate teacher-education programs:

• It is difficult to conceive of a four-year undergraduate program that could provide aspiring teachers with an appropriate level of subject-matter expertise while providing high-level course work in instructional sciences. The almost-universal requirement that undergraduate education students complete up to a year in student teaching virtually guarantees that none will be given the proper academic preparation.

• Education programs have always had a difficult time competing with other fields of study for students who have demonstrated high levels of academic achievement. Given the career preferences of college-bound high school seniors—which is the strongest influence on enrollment patterns—it is nearly impossible to mount and sustain excellence in undergraduate education programs because the pool is simply too small.

Because of this unpleasant fact, education programs on too many campuses are second-rate, designed for second-rate students.

Ironically, many states have compounded the problem by assigning major responsibility for teacher education to low-prestige, underfinanced state colleges with low admission standards. The message is unmistakable: Programs in educational studies are for students with low ability and poor self-esteem, who warrant less support than better students. That we do attract some highly talented students into undergraduate education programs is no small miracle.

• The existence of undergraduate education programs discourages many bright students from careers in education—especially those who enjoy the pleasures of studying a subject in depth.

Students who make an early decision to pursue education studies as an undergraduate (vertical recruits) tend to be less able students than those who make the decision to go into teaching later (lateral recruits). Lateral recruits will rarely accept a diet of undergraduate education courses on top of their regular academic course load. So long as this is a prerequisite to a teaching credential, the supply of lateral recruits will remain minuscule.

• Undergraduate education programs serve to relieve other departments of their responsibilities for the education of teachers. This is inimical to the cause of real school reform. Few academic departments live up to their responsibilities to think systematically about the relationship between the accumulation of knowledge and the transmission of knowledge from one generation to the next. On many campuses, there is no recognition that this relationship is worthy of investigation. Faculty members serve as sidewalk superintendents of the education programs, smugly contemptuous of education majors.

• Because we have permitted faculty in letters and science departments to avoid their responsibility to think systematically about instruction and play a greater role in teacher education, we have virtually guaranteed that teacher-education programs will be characterized by a lack of fit between subject-matter content and the instructional sciences. I can think of few errors as counter-productive as the separation of these two.

A teacher must know something about what he or she is going to teach. A strong undergraduate major, supplemented by a solid course of studies in letters and sciences, strikes me as being the appropriate minimum requirement for entry into a teacher education program.

In turn, a strong teacher-education program should make students knowledgeable about developments in the instructional sciences (i.e., development and instructional psychology, reading instruction, general curriculum theory, test and measurement protocols, computer-based tutoring systems, etc.) and how this knowledge can best be applied.

Willis D. Hawley
Special to *The Christian Science Monitor*

Willis Hawley is dean of the school of education at Vanderbilt University.

If there is a bandwagon in the teacher-education reform parade, it carries the banner "Only those with five years of college need apply."

But the ride on this bandwagon is an expensive one for the public and prospective teachers; it is not clear how many college students will play the tune, and there is no evidence whatever that it will get to its destination. Moreover, there are less-expensive vehicles for improving teacher education and, while they make less noise, their design is more streamlined, and they promise better mileage per taxpayer dollar.

Five-year teacher preparation programs increase the taxpayers' share of annual instructional costs of higher education by 10 to 15 percent. And, because students in five-year programs must not only pay tuition and loan fees, as well as forgo earnings for a full extra year, the costs of becoming a teacher will double. If we were to place a $20,000 tax on becoming a teacher—which is what five-year programs will do—would we expect the quality and quantity of new teachers to improve? So, if we are to have such extended programs *and* improve teacher quality, we will have to subsidize the graduate education of teachers. Such subsidies, plus the cost to taxpayers of paying for additional college instruction, could cost as much as $4 billion to $5 billion a year.

The advocates of five-year programs argue that longer teacher education will result in increased teacher status and salaries. But the link between teacher status and education obtained is tenuous, at best. Half of the nation's career teachers now have the equivalent of a master's degree. In Japan, teachers enjoy considerable prestige, even though less than 3 percent of the teachers have advanced degrees. A teacher in the United States with a master's earns only about 6 percent more than those with bachelor's in most school districts, hardly a good investment.

The evidence we now have about five-year programs ought to raise serious questions about the wisdom of extending preservice teacher preparation. For example, California has prohibited teacher certification following undergraduate education for many years. In California, teacher candidates rank near the bottom of the occupational distribution of scores on college entrance examinations. Moreover, because of the limited supply of candidates, almost half of the newly appointed teachers have only a bachelor's degree. And there is—despite relatively large class sizes—a teacher shortage.

This does not mean that reform is not necessary. But it does mean that we should aggressively pursue alternatives to five-year programs. Two steps are fundamental to improve the quality and status of teacher preparation, and the success of neither is improved by extending teacher education:

• We must ensure that teacher education is intellectually rigorous and enhances the ability to use theory and systematic inquiry to solve complex problems. There is no reason to believe that this will be easier if students are a year older. And the faculty will be the same.

• We must provide better ways to induct new teachers into the profession. Too many bright, idealistic teachers are discouraged by an unsuccessful first year on their own. There is growing agreement that we need what are being called professional development schools, in which practical teaching skills can be learned.

Establishing professional development schools would be a costly innovation, but it makes little sense to improve curricula—in four- or five-year programs—without improving teacher induction. Professional development schools will also free time in the undergraduate curriculum, where further opportunities are needed for students to explore how the key ideas of the subjects they will teach can be learned. Such learning can best be achieved in the context of a liberal arts-based undergraduate curriculum rather than in stand-alone professional schools.

Of course, teachers should be encouraged to pursue graduate study. But such study could be built into a career path as a privilege to be earned, if taxpayers are expected to provide support.

While reform of teacher education is essential, the costs of five-year programs are high and the outcomes are uncertain.

Education Reform In China

After stagnating during the Cultural Revolution, education is playing a crucial role in the modernization of the People's Republic of China. Its highly centralized structure is rapidly being dismantled; indeed, headlong decentralization is the key to Chinese reforms, say the authors.

AUSTIN D. SWANSON

AND ZHANG ZHIAN

AUSTIN D. SWANSON (Columbia University Chapter) is a professor in the Department of Educational Organization, Administration, and Policy at the State University of New York at Buffalo, where ZHANG ZHIAN, an assistant to the president of Beijing Teachers College, Beijing, China, is a doctoral student.

THE SEVENTH Five-Year Plan to guide the economic and social development of the People's Republic of China was approved on 12 April 1986 by the Fourth Session of the Sixth National People's Congress. This plan is the product of two years of deliberation involving the Communist party and the national government. Documents resulting from this process clearly indicate that education, both formal and informal, will play an important role in the strategies leading toward China's Four Modernizations.[1] The importance of education was clearly spelled out in the guidelines for the plan, proposed by the Central Committee of the Communist party and adopted

From *Phi Delta Kappan*, January 1987, pp. 373-378. Reprinted by permission of the authors.

in September 1985 by the party's National Conference.

Economic construction, social development, and scientific and technological progress all depend on the intellectual development of the Chinese nation, an increased number of trained personnel, and further growth of education based on economic development. During the period of the plan we must attach as much importance to education as we do to economic development and, orienting our work to the needs of modernization, the world, and the future, strive to bring about a new situation in education.[2]

This position differs markedly from official policy during the period of the Cultural Revolution (1966-76), when the intelligentsia were held in suspicion and contempt, when colleges and universities were closed and faculty members were dispersed throughout the countryside "to learn from the people," and when lack of discipline among students and low academic expectations among faculties characterized the primary and secondary schools. Part of the price of these policies is the acute shortage today of academics, engineers, teachers, technicians, and skilled workers of all kinds.

Recognizing that there may still be a residue of anti-intellectualism, the party's guidelines further state:

We must work harder to eliminate prejudice against knowledge and skilled people, to promote a social climate of respect for knowledge, teachers, and other educated people and enable China's intellectuals to play an important role in the socialist modernization programme. We should continue to take effective measures to gradually enhance the competence, raise the social status, and increase the material benefits of scientists, engineers, teachers, and other specialized personnel and to provide them with better working, studying, and living conditions.[3]

This Seventh Five-Year Plan does not represent a change in direction, but rather a reaffirmation of the changes that started after the death of Mao Zedong in 1976 and the subsequent arrest and imprisonment of the "Gang of Four." Similar principles can be found in the Sixth Five-Year Plan (1981-85), but they are stated more clearly and with much greater confidence in the newer documents. The changes that be-

*T*he National Education Commission has been assigned jurisdiction over all educational programs except for military education.

gan haltingly in 1976 are now sweeping through the People's Republic. Among these many changes, Li Shenzhi, vice chairman of the Chinese Academy of Social Sciences, has identified 10 ideological shifts.

The party's central focus has shifted:

1. from class struggle to economic construction;
2. from proletarian dictatorship to democracy;
3. from looking down on intellectuals to respecting educated people;
4. from treating knowledge and culture as foreign and antiquated to stressing their importance for maintaining a wholesome spiritual civilization while modernizing society;
5. from a closed-door policy to an open-door policy, which is considered essential to the success of Chinese modernization;
6. from using public ownership as a criterion of social progress to permitting a degree of private and collective ownership with the aim of increasing productive forces and improving living standards;
7. from comprehensive economic planning to a blending of market economic forces with noncomprehensive economic planning;
8. from embodying the government in the party to separating the party from government;
9. from endeavoring to promote a worldwide socialist revolution to striving to maintain world peace; and
10. from seeking truth through ideology to seeking truth through practice.[4]

NATIONAL EDUCATION COMMISSION

The new prominence of education became apparent with the replacement

of the Ministry of Education with the National Education Commission on 18 June 1985. Vice Premier Li Peng, an engineer with a broad knowledge of the economy, was appointed the commission's first chairman. As a comprehensive department of the State Council, the new commission now shares a rank equal to that of the State Planning Commission and the State Economic Commission.

Formerly, the Ministry of Education was responsible for primary and general secondary schools and for teacher training institutions. It directly administered 36 of the nearly 300 institutions of higher education sponsored by the national government, and it coordinated the activities of the 500 provincial institutions.[5] The 206 institutions that were not under the control of the Ministry of Education had highly specialized curricula, as in the Soviet model. These institutions were controlled by other ministries, although the Ministry of Education held some responsibility for coordination of nontechnical curricula.

Indeed, most of China's more than 90 ministries, commissions, and bureaus at the national level are involved in educational activities of some sort.[6] The Ministry of Education was responsible for the formulation of overall education policy and for the general direction of education, but its authority outside this clearly circumscribed jurisdiction was very limited. The National Education Commission has been assigned jurisdiction over all educational programs in China except for military education. With its high standing in the national government, the commission can give direction to all educational programs in all ministries and in every province.

Vice Premier Li Peng, chairman of the National Education Commission, has said that the commission was established because

education is something related to every walk of life. It will affect every section of society. Education reform will involve not only elementary, secondary, and higher education, but also vocational and technical schools and adult education. Education reform requires not only the initiatives and enthusiasm of the education department, but also the initiatives and enthusiasm of other departments, of other areas, of other walks of life. But past practice proved that it was very hard for the Ministry of Education to play the role of making overall planning for education.[7]

In addition to the chairman, the commission has eight vice chairmen (only two of whom are from the original Ministry of Education, including the former minister, He Dongchang). Six of the vice chairmen are from basic units, such as universities and provincial governments. The commission will meet quarterly. In order to enlarge its power, the commission invites five vice ministers – from the State Planning Commission, the State Economic Commission, the State Scientific and Technology Commission, the Ministry of Finance, and the Ministry of Labor and Personnel – to be members.

The missions of the commission are to implement the decisions of the party's Central Committee on education reform, to draw up a series of laws and regulations governing education, to give greater freedom to institutions of higher education, and to encourage the whole society to launch education projects. The decision to establish similar education commissions at the local level will be left to local governments, which can best take into account their specific practical conditions.[8]

DECENTRALIZING MANAGEMENT AND FINANCE

While setting policy for education has become more centralized at the national level, the implementation and financing of that policy have been decentralized. Before 1977 all public support for education (more than 90% of the total) was provided by the national government.[9] Since 1980 the national government has provided no direct support to primary and secondary schooling – with the exception of subsidies for secondary schools in rural areas with below-average wealth, for vocational education, and for teacher education.

However, the Ministry of Finance does set quotas to be included in the annual budgets for primary and secondary education within the 21 provinces, three municipalities, and five autonomous regions. These quotas may be stated as a specific amount per pupil or as a more general target. The functions of bureaus of education at this level correspond roughly to those of state boards of education and state education departments in the United States. Nearly 300 tertiary institutions are funded directly by the national government, while some 500 institutions are supported by the provinces, municipalities, or autonomous regions. The central government also directly supports some nonformal education, such as the TV University.

There appears to be little effort to equalize differences among districts' ability to support educational services.

But most nonformal education is supported by local governments and enterprises.[10]

With the exception of "key" schools, the operating unit of primary and secondary schools is the county (or, within municipalities, the district). The more than 2,000 bureaus of education at the county/district level function in much the same way as a large school district in the U.S. This level of school governance can supplement the financial appropriation provided by the province, municipality, or autonomous region.

In the Haideian District of Beijing, for example, the average annual expenditure per pupil is 60 yuan (about $20). Of this, the amount specified by the National Finance Minister to be included in the municipal budget of Beijing is 30 yuan. The district provides an additional 15.60 yuan from its own resources – 3.60 yuan from profits of district-owned enterprises after levies paid to municipal and central governments and 12 yuan from levies by the district on enterprises owned by central and municipal governments. Another six yuan come from profits made by enterprises operated directly by the schools. Finally, parents pay certain charges, including tuition (2.50 yuan per semester for primary schools and five yuan per semester for middle schools), purchase of textbooks (approximately three yuan), and supplies and workbooks (between three and five yuan).[11] Rural schools might also receive support from brigades, units smaller than a county.[12] Such funds may be used to pay for school lunches, school construction, and *minban* teachers (teachers who have no formal teacher training).

This rather complex financial scheme makes it easier to finance innovations that cannot be supported on a broader scale. It runs the risk, however, of permitting great disparity to exist among

districts as to the level and quality of educational services provided. There appears to be little effort to equalize these differences among districts' financial ability to support educational services.

THE DECISION ON EDUCATION REFORM

Other reforms strike at the curriculum and management of schools, colleges, and universities. These reforms were promulgated in *The Decision on the Reform of the Education System*, released by the party's Central Committee on 29 May 1985.[13] This document listed the major problems of education in the People's Republic as weak elementary education, a shortage of schools and qualified teachers, and retarded development of vocational and technical education. Textbooks were criticized as outdated and overspecialized in certain fields. Strict government control over schools – and especially over institutions of higher learning – was seen as stunting their vigor. This comprehensive document will probably guide the design and operation of educational institutions in the People's Republic for years to come.

Duration of education. Five to six years of primary education are now almost universally available in the People's Republic, with 94% of the appropriate age group in school.[14] Two-thirds of primary school graduates continue their studies for three years in junior middle schools. Twenty-seven percent of those who graduate from junior middle schools will be admitted to senior middle schools (where they will remain for two to three years), and approximately 10% of these students will ultimately be admitted to tertiary institutions. Progress from one level to the next is determined primarily by examination.[15]

The proportions of young people attending school at each level vary considerably from region to region, but the *Reform Decision* targets improvement for all regions. In large and middle-sized cities, in the coastal areas, and in a few inland regions the local economy and educational systems are already comparatively well developed. In these areas, universal education through junior middle school is expected to become reality by 1990. By the turn of the century, many of these cities and regions are expected to have universal education through the senior middle school. About 250 million people (one-quarter of China's population) reside in these places, and they form a solid intellectual foundation for the rest of the nation.

For the rural towns and villages, where half of China's population resides and where development is not as advanced, the immediate target is to make primary education universal. Universal middle schooling is not expected to be realized until at least 1995. In economically backward areas, where the remaining one-quarter of the population resides, universal literacy is the main challenge, along with an expansion of elementary education in whatever forms and to whatever extent possible. By the turn of the century the *Reform Decision* envisions a China in which one-quarter of the population will be receiving schooling through the senior middle level (12 years), half through the junior middle level (nine years), and one-quarter through at least a basic elementary education.

Quality of schooling. Determining the quality of schooling is a very complex issue. Following the Cultural Revolution, the national government realized that it did not have the human or economic resources to educate all students who were enrolled in school. Rather than provide a uniformly poor program to all students, the government instituted the concept of "key schools" — schools assigned the best-qualified teachers and larger appropriations for facilities, equipment, and instructional supplies. Students assigned to key schools are those who have scored highest on entrance examinations.

The concept of key schools is now being challenged as elitism, incompatible with socialist ideology. Critics feel that focusing on key schools has led to the neglect of ordinary schools, in which 80% to 90% of China's students are enrolled. Under this system a child's future may be determined by age 6 or 7, since entering a key primary school leads to a progression through other key schools and finally to a university.[16]

The examination system that governs access to China's schools has been criticized both in concept and in construct. Some critics charge that this system contributes to an overemphasis on book learning and develops respect for authority to the detriment of creativity, inquisitiveness, and an enterprising spirit. The impact of the examination system is doubled by the fact that examination results are used not only to evaluate the students, but also to evaluate their teachers and schools. Moreover, the results affect teacher pay.[17] As secondary schooling becomes universal and if

> *F*or the rural towns and villages, where half of the population resides, the immediate target is to make primary education universal.

key schools are abolished, the examination system will come into play only in determining admission to tertiary institutions.

The examination system has also been criticized for being too narrow. The examinations test achievement only in Chinese and mathematics. Furthermore, reliance on a test score alone to determine academic advancement ignores other important indicators of academic success, such as academic record and an assessment of character. In an attempt to deal with the latter criticism, beginning in 1985, a very limited number of students were advanced to a higher level of schooling solely on the recommendation of their school principals. If this experiment produces positive results, the practice may be expanded.

The important issue of improving the qualifications of teachers is being dealt with through ambitious inservice training programs and through an increase in the number and size of teachers colleges, which are financed and administered primarily by provincial, municipal, and autonomous regional governments. Inservice training is provided primarily by county/district bureaus of education.

Vocational education. During the Cultural Revolution, all vocational and agricultural secondary schools were closed, as were work-study programs. No new enrollment was permitted in institutions of higher learning and in other specialized secondary schools. As a result, it is estimated that at least one million people who, under normal circumstances, would have been trained as engineers, as academic specialists, and for the professions remained untrained;

perhaps as many as two million technicians never received appropriate schooling.

Those who were already trained were not permitted to practice their specializations or to maintain contact with their academic colleagues for nearly a decade. Consequently, with normalization in 1976, those responsible for preparing scientists and technicians were themselves grossly out of touch with developments in their fields. All of this has created a critical shortage of people capable of providing leadership in scientific and technological undertakings.[18] Although an ideal ratio between engineers, technicians, and skilled workers might be 1:4:12, in China today that ratio stands at 1:0.67:4. This suggests that the most acute shortages are at the levels of technician and skilled worker.[19]

Since 1976 vocational courses have been added to ordinary middle school curricula, and beginning in 1981 vocational schools were opened. But by 1984, though 45.5 million students were enrolled in ordinary middle schools, only 3.7 million vocational and technical school students were enrolled — a mere 7.5% of the total. While graduates of vocational schools are in great demand, graduates of ordinary middle schools in such major cities as Shanghai still suffer unemployment.[20]

To overcome these shortages of vocational and technical school graduates, the *Reform Decision* proposes (and the Seventh Five-Year Plan provides) that all expansion at the level of senior middle schools be in vocational and technical schools and that some ordinary schools be converted to these purposes. The goal is to increase the proportion of vocational and technical school graduates to 50% of the student population within five years. Furthermore, private enterprises and individuals are being encouraged to establish additional schools of this type. Graduates of vocational and technical schools will be given priority in job assignments; other job-seekers will have to take tests to demonstrate their technical competence.

Higher education. During the Seventh Five-Year Plan, 2.6 million people are expected to graduate from institutions of higher education — an increase of 70% over the previous five years. A fourfold increase is expected at the postgraduate level, involving 200,000 persons. To accomplish this, the guidelines of the plan state: "We must . . . encourage [institutions of higher learning] to meet the needs of economic, scientific, technological, and social development on their own initiative."[21] The *Reform Decision* spells out how this is to be accomplished.

Under the "Presidential Responsibility System," presidents of institutions of higher education are to be given much greater authority. Currently, presidents are primarily managers, not policy makers. Any important matter of policy must be referred for a decision to the college's Party Committee. The sponsoring Ministry of Higher Education also exercises rigid controls. Under the new proposals, however, presidential powers will include:

• deciding on teaching plans and curricula and compiling teaching materials;

• accepting projects from, or in cooperation with, other social establishments for scientific research and technological development, as well as setting up project teams involving teaching, scientific research, and production;

• suggesting appointments and dismissals of vice presidents and officials at various levels;

• disposing of funds allocated by the state for capital construction and investment; and

• using college funds to develop international exchanges.[22]

A number of institutions are already functioning under the new Presidential Responsibility System, and similar reforms are being tried in the primary and secondary schools.

Considerable slack already exists in the staffing of China's colleges and universities. They are currently functioning with a student/teacher ratio of 4:1. The World Bank has been highly critical of this practice and has encouraged a gradual increase to 10:1.[23] The reform of presidential powers will give presidents a great deal of flexibility in increasing this ratio (presumably through expanding enrollments rather than decreasing staff).

Beginning in 1983, the requirement that all students must live in dormitories was relaxed. Today students may live at home and commute, or they may arrange their own accommodations near the campus. This has removed a major constraint on increasing enrollments.

Now enterprises will be able to enter into contracts directly with tertiary institutions to provide graduates with specific skills and knowledge, instead of petitioning the central government. This will provide a new source of students and a new source of funds, while insuring a better match between college programs and the personnel needs of industry.

> *China's top priority is clearly economic expansion, and there can be no doubt that its economic and educational development are linked.*

Colleges and universities will continue to enroll students according to national quotas, but they will also be able to admit students sponsored by enterprises and students who pay for their own expenses. All students will have to pass nationally developed entrance examinations, however.

To pay for this greater flexibility, tuition will be charged — except for students at teachers colleges and for those who are likely to work under very difficult conditions after graduation. (Modest tuition charges are already assessed at the primary and secondary levels.) Scholarships will be provided for those qualified students who cannot afford to pay. Dormitory charges will also be instituted, and students will continue to pay for their board and books.

In the past, the government has assigned jobs to graduates of colleges and universities, but, with students supported through a number of funding sources, this procedure is being relaxed. Students admitted under the state plan will indicate to their college or university a preference for employment. That institution will then nominate a group of interested and qualified students to a prospective employer, which will offer jobs (up to the limit of its quota under the state plan) to those it prefers. A student is not obliged to accept any offer, nor is an enterprise obliged to employ any nominee. Students sponsored by a work unit (enterprise) will be assigned jobs by that unit; self-supporting students will seek jobs on their own. Enterprises may hire such persons to meet their employment needs beyond those recognized under the state plan.

A FOREIGN observer — especially one from the United States, where the education system is among the most decentralized in the world and where both the dangers and the advantages of decentralization have become apparent — can only be amazed at the rapidity with which the highly centralized structure of control in China is being dismantled. The centralized system was inflexible and stultifying, but it was relatively equitable. It undoubtedly needed to be reformed, but the present race toward decentralization seems to be taking place without an appreciation of the magnitude of the inequities that are likely to result.

Decentralizing both the financing and the administration of education compounds the danger. The quality of educational services in a given area will now be a function of both the wealth of the area and the attitude of its local leaders toward education. In those areas that are relatively wealthy and that have leaders who hold education in high regard, educational services will expand and improve. In poverty-stricken areas, however, and in areas in which the leadership places a higher priority on other government services, the educational services will suffer.

Maintaining a tolerable balance between rich and poor areas and between committed and noncommitted local leaders can be achieved only through the activity of the national government. In terms of finance, this national presence must be expressed in some sort of equalization aid that will permit the national wealth to supplement local resources. In terms of local commitment, the national government must provide some minimum standards and regulations.

What may appear on the surface to be a lack of commitment may actually be a lack of knowledge. When all orders were issued from a single central authority, local administrators needed little sophisticated managerial expertise. As responsibility is shifted to the lower levels, however, the policy-making and managerial skills in some areas and regions may not be sufficient to handle the new responsibility. China freely admits its lack of managerial skills, and this is especially true in education, a field in which administration is not even a recognized course of study.

China's top priority is clearly economic expansion, and there can be no doubt that its economic and educational development are linked. Unlike many socialist states, however, China sees those links as being "loosely" rather than "tightly" coupled. The education reforms that are under way have been guided by this view.

China also recognizes that development will be uneven. But this is viewed with a sense of optimism. In a recent interview, Deng Xiaoping said, "There will be differences when different regions and people become prosperous. Some people will become prosperous first, and others later."[24] However, Deng remains confident that, as long as public ownership plays a dominant role, China will be able to avoid the polarization of the rich and the poor. He looks for the regions that prosper to help those that have not prospered. His theory will be put to a stern test during the next five years.

1. China's four modernizations are in industry, agriculture, national defense, and science/technology.

2. Central Committee of the Chinese Communist Party, "Proposal for the Seventh Five-Year Plan for National Economic and Social Development," *Beijing Review*, vol. 28, 1985, p. xv.

3. Ibid., p. xvi.

4. Li Shenzhi, "The Guiding Ideology Changes in China," Zhang Zhian, trans., paper presented to the New York State Joint Conference on Asia, Africa, and the Americas, Rochester Institute of Technology, 5 October 1985.

5. World Bank, *China, Socialist Economic Development, Vol. III, The Social Sectors: Population, Health, Nutrition, and Education* (Washington, D.C.: World Bank, 1983), p. 161.

6. Ibid., p. 177.

7. Yang Jiangyie, "Work at Education as Important as Work on Economy: Interview with Mr. Li Peng, Vice Premier and Chairman of the State Education Commission," *Chinese Education Daily*, 16 July 1985, p. 1.

8. Chen Guanfeng, "Education Commission Gets Greater Power," *China Daily*, 26 June 1985, p. 1.

9. Interview with Wang Jinhan, deputy director, Beijing Municipal Bureau of Education, 3 June 1985.

10. Interview with vice director, Planning and Finance Department, Ministry of Education, 5 June 1985.

11. Interview with Wang Jia-jun, director, Haideian District Education Bureau, Beijing, 6 June 1985.

12. The reform of the contract system in the countryside has led to substantial economic gains among peasants, especially those living near urban areas and having access to a free market. There is good evidence that some of those gains are being used to enhance educational opportunities in rural areas.

13. Central Committee of the Chinese Communist Party, *The Decision on the Reform of the Education System* (Beijing: People's Press, 1985).

14. National Statistics Bureau, *Brilliant Thirty-Five Years: 1949-1984* (Beijing: Chinese Statistics Press, 1984), p. 134.

15. Jan-Ingvar Löfstedt, "Educational Planning and Administration in China," *Comparative Education*, vol. 20, 1984, p. 58.

16. "Key Schools May Be Abolished," *China Daily*, 13 April 1985, p. 3.

17. Liang Baiping, "Exam System 'Merely Tests Memory'," *China Daily*, 24 May 1985.

18. China Handbook Series, *Education and Science* (Beijing: Foreign Languages Press, 1983), p. 22.

19. Liu Zhanshan, "Why We Should Devote Major Effort to Develop Vocational Education," *Chinese Education Daily*, 9 July 1985, p. 2.

20. World Bank, p. 188.

21. "Proposal for the Seventh Five-Year Plan . . . ," p. xv.

22. "Upgrading Education Through Reform," *Beijing Review*, vol. 28, 1985, p. 16.

23. World Bank, p. 193.

24. Deng Xiaoping, quoted in *Time*, 4 November 1985, p. 39.

Learning about education from 5th-graders in Japan

Rushworth M. Kidder
Staff writer of The Christian Science Monitor

Tokyo

Ten-year-old Riei Fuse, gripping her pencil, works quickly down the 20-question worksheet, multiplying and dividing fractions and reducing the answers.

Mr. Sakai has given her fifth-grade class here at the Bancho Primary School five minutes to finish. No one questions his authority: Except for the noise from younger children on the playground below the third-floor windows, there isn't a sound in the classroom of 45 students.

Riei finishes ahead of her deskmate, a boy in a plaid shirt and denim shorts with the words "Tom Sawyer" on the back pocket. When Sakai calls for answers—singling out his students by last name from a sea of raised hands—she is relieved to see that she has missed only one question.

Riei may not know it, but she is probably getting one of the finest public elementary educations in the world.

That, at least, is the view of an increasing number of educators from other nations who, concerned about educational reform, are looking to see whether Japan might have some answers.

What they are finding is a nation that ranks at the very top of international math tests—and which, as Harvard researcher Merry White notes in her new book "The Japanese Educational Challenge," has an illiteracy rate of only 0.7 percent (compared to 20 percent in the United States).

That doesn't mean that all is well with Japanese education. Prime Minister Yashuhiro Nakasone has made education reform, along with reforms in government and taxation, one of the three goals of his administration.

And recent Monitor interviews with leading educators in Tokyo, Kyoto, and Hiroshima reveal deep undercurrents of concern—especially about the poor state of Japanese higher education, the intense pressure put on students competing for university admission, and the activities of the private cram schools, or *juku*, that prepare students for this so-called examination hell.

But on one point these educators agree: that of all the links in Japan's education chain, primary school is the strongest.

All that, of course, may not be noticeable to Riei. True, her 45-minute arithmetic class is an exercise in concentration: Short attention spans, it seems, are not tolerated here. But like fifth-graders everywhere, Riei is poised between the world of friends and the challenges of learning—a pretty girl dressed in an apricot-colored sweatshirt, gray wool skirt, green socks, and (when indoors) regulation red-and-white slippers.

Shy with visitors, speaking through an interpreter, she says she likes arts and crafts but has difficulty with science—which has centered on astronomy.

On the back of her sweatshirt, embroidered in a fine hand below a picture of a girl with a dog, are several sentences in English. "Walking with my dog in every morning. Then I go to school with my friends. It's my happy days." In fact, she confesses, she doesn't have a dog. But she does walk to school each morning.

And that's clearly an advantage—especially when at the end of her walk is the 115-year-old Bancho Primary School. Located in Tokyo's exclusive Bancho and Kojimachi area, it has a sterling reputation. Despite Japan's success at equalizing the quality of education across the nation, parents still move to this part of the city in part because of this school—or, if they live elsewhere, deluge the school with applications for their children.

Once here, they discover who the best teachers are. One of them, clearly, is Kunimitsu Sakai.

One might not think so just from looking at Mr. Sakai's classroom. Like most Japanese schoolrooms, it has little physical appeal.

The cracked plaster walls were once painted military grey. The institutional-green doors are scratched and battered, and the naked fluorescent tubes overhead shine down on the worn wooden tops of the desks. Even the sunlight flooding the floor makes its way through venetian blinds that could well belong to an aging army barrack.

All that, however, is part of a Japanese educational ethos which holds that students should not be distracted by their surroundings and should be taught to endure discomfort. Here at Bancho, says principal Yasuji Kusano, that ethos is sometimes hard to maintain: He worries that his 700 students are "spoiled" and that they "can't take too much suffering."

To the visitor, however, it hardly seems as though Sakai is bent on making his students suffer. A veteran of 18 years in the system, he moves easily through the government-established curriculum that calls for him to teach his fifth-graders arithmetic, Japanese language, Japanese geography, science, physical education, and home economics—including sewing and cooking. "I'm a good cook," he says with a laugh. Music and art, also part of the curriculum, are taught by others. Like his fellow teachers at this particular school, Sakai dresses well. Today he's wearing a three-piece gray suit, white shirt, and tie—although in place of slippers (which even visitors must don), he wears running shoes. On his bulletin boards are a few announcements decorated with his students' designs. On the ledge near the large television set at the front is a vase containing fresh tulips. At the rear near the sink bubbles an aquarium of green water-plants.

Nor are his students suffering under a fear-inspiring regimen—insofar as such things can be judged by visitors whose very presence has probably shifted the ground-rules for the classroom, causing curious sidelong stares from the students. Sakai teaches with gentleness and good humor, occasionally eliciting laughter and never needing to raise his voice. Calling for answers, he is greeted by a chorus of voices chanting out the numbers as he writes them on the board with a typically Japanese "Ohhh!" of appreciation.

To be sure, his students are polite and obedient—bowing to the visitors, standing to answer his questions, writing carefully in their notebooks. But they are clearly not cowed: When one boy, without feeling the need to ask permission, comes to the back of the room to use the electric pencil sharpener near the visitors' seats, he draws no rebuke for starting a run among his peers who suddenly discover a need for sharper pencils. Nor is absolute silence a rule: Much of the time there is a low murmur of voices as deskmates chatter with each other even while copying from the blackboard.

An exceptional classroom? Perhaps. But a visitor can easily see why the recent report of the US Department of Education, "Japanese Education Today," speaks so highly of this island nation's elementary schools.

"While Japanese classes are larger than American ones, Japanese classrooms are more orderly," the report's authors write. "Students are more attentive and better behaved, and transitions between activities are more rapid and orderly.

"The net result is significant: Japanese students spend about one-third more time during a typical class period engaged in learning than American students do during a typical class period."

They also, however, spend time studying outside the classroom. Riei says she spends an hour a night. Sakai says she is probably under-reporting, not wanting to be thought a bookworm by fellow-students who crowd around during her brief interview.

And that, in the view of educators here, hints at the dark side of the Japanese system. Even now, at age 10, Riei attends a *juku* after school, where, says Sakai, she reviews her in-school work in preparation for the day, seven years away, when she will take her university entrance exams.

For now, however, Riei's schooling seems orderly and effective. Sitting in the sunlight of Sakai's Class 5-1, her pencil-box before her and her friends around her, she divides five-ninths by six and then by five—accurately, quickly, and unaware that the eyes of the world are watching to see just how she does it.

The Struggle for Excellence: The Drive for Quality and Reform

No conscientious educator would want to acknowledge, or at least would not wish to publicly affirm, that some sort of commitment to excellence in teaching or learning was *not* at the core of his or her professional practice. The issue surrounding excellence, and arguments over it in general educational debate and debate over the specific purposes of schooling, is derived from the very different conceptions of the meaning of this term. Since there are many different purposes for educational systems in the more complex technological social orders such as the United States and Canada, should schooling become more specifically focused on varying sets of these purposes after the elementary grades? If specific specialization in programs is necessary at the secondary school level, then should the United States and Canada offer more than one type of secondary educational experience by creating specialized high schools to meet different educational purposes, as is done on the continent of Europe? Or, are the American, Canadian, and British comprehensive secondary schools meeting the task of providing different educational experiences at the secondary level?

If the answer to the last question above is "yes, they are meeting the task," what changes are called for to make them more effective in doing this? If the answer is "no, they are not meeting the task," then how do we find equitable ways to decide who takes part in what sort of secondary educational experiences? Will Americans ever adopt the "streaming" or "tracking" models of secondary student placement so unpopular in the United States since the late 1960s? Will any structural changes in the organization and content of curricula and types of schools facilitate or hinder the qualitative improvement of schooling? Are we willing to pay the social costs of such policy changes? Will North Americans really accept any serious structural realignments in the conduct of schooling? Are such structural realignments unnecessary; if so, for what reasons? These are core questions in discussions about change and continuity in formal education. They imply gravely important social as well as academic concerns.

Should social or academic goals control the nature, content, and direction of educational change in North America? Or, is this a false dichotomy with the real issue surrounding simply the complex links and interrelationships between not only social and academic goals as such, but the manifest (explicit) and latent (real but implicit) effects which will follow from any particular set or combination of such goals? How do we assess fairly what we have in terms of what we need? Can there ever be sufficient national consensus regarding America's educational needs to assure a just and effective resolution of this dilemma?

In the past three decades, criticism of schooling has made many North American educators dubious of the rhetoric of blue ribbon panels regarding excellence, however it is defined, and dubious as to the motivations of reform rhetoric. The goal of excellence is not controverted. Some of the suggestions for achieving it are controverted. Indeed, J. Myron Atkin is accurate when he refers to educators as gun shy of some of the new reform efforts. Before North American citizens can decide on what new changes to make in school curricula, they need to be made aware of the excellent aspects that already exist. In the dozens of individual, group, and commission reports on excellence, there is a disturbing and academically conservative and limiting commonality in the language of the reports. Most of the reports essentially say the same things, make the same recommendations, and avoid recommendations for basic structural changes in programming of North American elementary and secondary schools. Instead there is an almost unified appeal for a return to a basic curriculum.

Does an industrial high-tech social order have to diversify the types of educational programming it offers to its young? All other industrialized nations answer in the affirmative. Can it be that the United States, where individuality is purported to prevail, is the only industrialized nation where a common set of behavioral objectives is to be mastered by all of its young, whatever their unique gifts or burdens? For the United States, the answers to these questions hinge on whether a common basic academic program is necessary to meet foreign economic competition or basic domestic needs.

Part of what must be considered regarding excellence in education and the new reform rhetoric is whether or not more basic changes are needed in the content and purpose of elementary and secondary education than those recommended in the report. Should excellence imply one thing, such as a common basic academic programming based on traditional classical curricula, or should excellence be multidimensional, with more than one meaning and different types of schools to deal with the different meanings of the concept? The reform reports have all failed to grapple honestly with these questions. They also avoid dealing with the question of why other industrialized nations in Asia and Europe have always championed both traditional academic and technically oriented conceptions of excellence. The reports want changes in the present structure of schooling. Would they be willing to consider, or should they consider, basic changes in the structure of schooling itself? Calls for longer school days and years and more homework are

typical of scholastic band aids on a seriously ill (and technologically displaced) patient.

Where do teachers, school principals, teacher educators, and counselors fit into the construction of reform rhetoric? Why aren't their views as highly regarded as the opinions of others? What alternative structures should or should not be considered by the educational system? The essays in this unit were selected to provide penetrating insights into the issues at stake in the current debate over excellence. They require careful consideration.

This unit may be used in courses that deal primarily with the social context of schooling and the issues facing educators. The essays could relate to those parts of the course that highlight either curriculum issues or the history of education. They can also be discussed in conjunction with equality of educational opportunity discussed in Unit 6. The nation faces many problems as it strives for higher achievement. Popular concern regarding the subject makes the articles in this unit relevant to all discussions of the social context of education.

Looking Ahead: Challenge Questions

Examine the controversy surrounding how best to achieve excellence in education. What are the differences in the interests of members of blue ribbon commissions and the interests of teachers and school administrators? What might be the primary concerns of teachers when they consider the topic of educational reform?

What changes in society and its schools have created such intensive interest in striving for excellence in education?

What can be learned from recent reports on the state of American education? What are your views on the recommendations being offered to improve the quality of schooling?

How could school curricula and instructional practices be modified to encourage excellence in teaching and learning?

What are the minimum academic standards that all high school graduates should have achieved?

What are the most significant issues to be addressed in the development and use of minimum competency testing?

Is there anything new in the struggle for excellence? What can be learned from the history of efforts to reform education?

Changing Our Thinking About Educational Change

J. Myron Atkin

The education reform fervor triggered in early 1983 by the report of the National Commission on Excellence in Education, *A Nation at Risk,*[1] was greeted with trepidation by teachers and school administrators. Given its indictment of the quality of public education and its focus on the "rising tide of mediocrity" in the nation's schools, it was not clear whether the report was a prelude to educational improvement or the beginning of a new wave of attacks on schools and teachers. Judging from the polls, the public seemed to be in a mood to take constructive steps to improve the quality of public education, but teachers and school administrators had become gun-shy over a period of three decades as a result of previous reform efforts that assigned blame recklessly, raised expectations unrealistically, and led to legislative and other initiatives that sometimes had effects on teaching exactly the opposite of what had been intended.

As reports continued to be issued on the state of American secondary education in the months following *A Nation at Risk,* it became clear that an extraordinary phenomenon in the history of American education was taking place. Each new statement —Ernest Boyer's,[2] John Goodlad's,[3] Mortimer Adler's,[4] the College Board's,[5] the Twentieth Century Fund's,[6] the National Science Foundation's[7]—captured front-page attention, editorial comment (usually favorable), and even significant time on the television network evening news. Public interest in the quality of education clearly was deep. The mood for change was strong. It even began to appear that legislators were willing to appropriate more money for education if they could be convinced that the additional funds would produce higher quality.

The theme of the reports, taken as a group, was that the school curriculum had become soft, particularly for children with strong academic ability; that standards were poorly defined and low; that the quality of teachers seemed to be declining; that teacher education programs were weak; and that schools were not meeting the needs of business and industry as well as they should. Most of the recommendations for improving schools were couched in general terms, but the reports converged on the remedy that a common curriculum for all children should be reinstated and that clear goals and expectations for pupils in the subjects of English, history, science, and mathematics should be formulated. Teachers at the secondary school level should major in the subjects they were to teach. Some of the reports suggested that schools should be less preoccupied with training youngsters for specific occupations than with making sure they possess basic skills, especially in written communication.

The suggested educational reforms may not have seemed particularly startling, even if the public appetite for them was; but in addition to the extraordinary publicity attendant to release of the reports, the lineup of those who were pressing for change in the educational system was different and noteworthy. In the period immediately after the launching of Sputnik I, in 1957, those who exerted maximum influence on the tone and substance of education reform were university professors who were experts in the subjects taught in secondary and elementary schools. They provided the driving force and conceptual leadership for new programs in the teaching of biology, physics, mathematics, social science, and language. It was a major feature of the education reform scene ushered in in 1983 that for the first time in recent memory major business leaders were identifying education as a key national problem and priority. Chief executive officers of some of the country's major corporations began to involve themselves in coalitions to improve public education, giving of both their time and their influence. The country's productivity and trade position were seen as threatened, and the cure lay in part, the public was told, in producing a more efficient work force. The California Business Roundtable consisted of several-score corporation presidents (not their public affairs officers), who devoted significant energy and intelligence to learning about the state's educational problems and what might be done about them.

Just as significant, state-level politicians from coast to coast rediscovered the issue of education. Through most of the 1970s, education committees in the state capitols represented virtually the last choice for freshman legislators with verve and ambition. Governors, too, preferred to focus on social welfare programs, prisons, environmental issues, agriculture, and industrial expansion—anything, it seemed, but education. Before 1983, most politicians saw little advantage

 From *The World & I,* March 1986, pp. 635-646. Taken from CHALLENGE TO AMERICAN SCHOOLS: THE CASE FOR STANDARDS AND VALUES, edited by John H. Bunzel.

and considerable risk in emphasizing issues associated with educational improvement. Schools were being closed in every state because of the decline in the numbers of children. Money was tight. People feel passionately about their schools, particularly those who send their children to them, and politicians saw little to be gained by becoming associated with the unpopular decisions necessary to shrink a huge enterprise with a strong emotional foothold in virtually every community, while dealing with a powerful, large, and increasingly assertive union. Suddenly, it seemed in 1983, politicians were featuring education improvement in their major speeches and in their election platforms. Even those with national political aspirations, such as Gov. James Hunt of North Carolina, were asking to be judged on the basis of their records in education.

While the renewed interest in education seemed encouraging to many teachers and school administrators, there was still apprehension and skepticism. Would the nation hear once again that the problems in the schools are caused by teachers who are too child centered, or insufficiently informed about their subjects, or too preoccupied with raising their own salaries? Would there be a tendency to find scapegoats or to blame the victims? Just as much a cause of concern among informed school people, would there be initiatives by an awakening public that might actually impair the ability of schools to improve educational quality, however well motivated those initiatives might be? If so, it would not be the first time that the best of public intentions became associated with changes in schools that did not have the desired effects, and in fact were counterproductive. Educational change is tricky business. How does one balance the imperative of political will and the advantages of informed professional latitude? Which changes are best planned by state education departments and which by teachers and administrators in local districts? How does one best influence a "system" of about three million teachers who work for 16,000 different employers?

When Americans look for solutions to problems in the field of education, as in most areas of public concern,

they usually begin by examining the possibility of writing new laws. School codes—laws and accompanying regulations—now run to tens of thousands of pages in many states. Children do not read well? Pass a law that requires the demonstration of reading ability at a certain level before the child may be moved to the next grade or awarded a high school diploma. Concerned that handicapped children are not receiving instruction geared to their distinctive needs? Pass a law that requires an "individualized education plan" for each child; in addition, require that the plan be negotiated by the teacher with the parents to give those with the most at stake a chance to participate in the process. How better to assure accountability? Legislative responses to serious problems seem deeply satisfying. The laws often have a direct appeal and an apparently compelling logic. They are usually preceded by considerable study and debate. Those responsible for the initiatives work hard for them. The prime movers feel a sense of concrete accomplishment.

Examine the results of each piece of legislation designed to improve educational outcomes, however, and you begin to note results that do not always correspond to the intent of those who wrote the laws. With the passage of "minimum competency" laws, for example, test scores, at least for some children, go down, not up. Pass a law requiring an individualized education plan for each child, and service to handicapped children declines rather than expands. How come?

At one level, new laws are symbolic expressions of shifting public attention and priority. They reflect a new focus of public interest and sometimes crystallize consensus: we had better take the plight of handicapped children and their parents more seriously; our school system is not doing well enough for youngsters who need basic reading skills; non-English-speaking children need special attention. Insofar as such declarations represent a new resolve by the public to attend to a matter whose priority is elevated, little harm is done. Public schools are public institutions. Politics is an expression of the public will. Schools have always been subjected to intense political pressures. Howev-

er, when legislators move beyond an affirmation of intentions to frame laws governing specific educational practices, to be followed by regulations that prescribe the details of how teachers are to work with children and which tests are to be administered for which purpose, the results become unpredictable and often seemingly perverse. This is the situation in much of the United States today.

For example, with respect to the minimum competency legislation, the intention and the message to teachers and school administrators are clear enough. We have a large population of youngsters in school who are not learning basic skills associated with reading and computation. The situation is undesirable and perhaps intolerable. The law directs renewed attention to the educational needs of this population. Unless the examinations are passed, the child does not advance in the educational system or does not receive a diploma.

As intended, after such laws are introduced, reading scores do go up for youngsters who before the law was enacted did not possess the skills required to pass the examination. Children who did not read and compute are now reading and computing. But success is not that simple (though accomplishment is seldom acknowledged). It is noticed, too, that scores for the most able children begin to decline at the same time. What is happening?

Determining causality is always a difficult issue in understanding social phenomena, but it seems reasonable to conclude that without an increase in resources, which typically is the case when new demands to serve the educational needs of a large population of youngsters are imposed, the other children receive less time from teachers. Here is one way it happens: because of new test requirements, a school superintendent or a principal is expected to raise the skill levels of a significant number of youngsters in the school quickly, as many as 20 or 30 percent of the children in some instances. The administrator examines the resources available to meet the educational needs of all the youngsters in the school and decides to give priority to those policies that use available resources to serve the most children. The decision is made to close small classes and reassign their teachers. The principle seems reasonable, fair, uniform in applications, and easy to explain: concentrate the available teaching force in classes that enroll the largest number of children.

It turns out, however, that the large classes are the introductory courses in a subject or the remedial courses intended to teach the minimally required skills. The small classes are often those in advanced biology, or calculus, or the third year of a foreign language. The minimum competency movement, so reasonable in intent, seems to lower the educational accomplishments of a district's most able students because it deprives them of a chance to do advanced work, an outcome no one intended and few people predicted.

Minimum competency laws are passed at the state level. The Education of All Handicapped Children Act is a federal law. It is unusual for the federal government to become involved in matters of education. The Tenth Amendment to the Constitution reserves to the states those functions not explicitly assigned to the federal government, and education is not mentioned in the Constitution. In areas of clear federal responsibility, such as strengthening the national defense and assuring equal protection for all citizens, the Congress has a role. The Education of All Handicapped Children Act was passed in 1975. It flowed directly from principles that were enunciated in the 1960s and early 1970s as part of the civil rights movement. Handicapped children were seen in the minds of those who lobbied for them and of those in the Congress as a minority group, like blacks or Hispanics. They were entitled to the education received by everyone else. The law called for handicapped children to be put in the "least restrictive environment" in every school. This action led to the "mainstreaming" of handicapped children—that is, to their placement insofar as possible in regular, not special, cases.

In many instances such placements prove effective for the handicapped child, though not always. Many handicapping conditions require almost constant adult supervision. Mainstreaming has sometimes resulted in a reduction of service to the afflicted child. Putting that outcome aside, however, we can say that the placement of handicapped children in regular classrooms almost always requires a level of attention from the teacher that is disproportionate to the attention given other children. The regular teacher is often illprepared to work with youngsters who are mentally retarded, emotionally disturbed, orthopedically disabled, or visually impaired. The impulse to mainstream is humane. Often, though not always, it is in the best interest of the handicapped child. But there is a trade-off. The disproportionate amount of time that the teacher must work with handicapped youngsters is time taken from the other children.

Advocates of new social policy initiatives attempt to support their policy preferences with research whenever possible. When the new laws affecting the education of handicapped children were passed, there was indeed a considerable amount of education research indicating that the educational achievement of children with handicapping conditions was often improved by their being required to meet the standards held for other children, and in the same settings. However, about 90 percent of the studies that had been done on mainstreaming at that time addressed only the issue of how such a practice affects the children to be mainstreamed. Only a few studies gave any attention to the effect that such a practice has on the teacher or on the other children.[9]

In the same Education of All Handicapped Children Act, and as if to give another example of how laws about the details of teaching practice can be mischievous, the Congress incorporated a requirement that an "individualized education plan" be developed for each child, to be negotiated between teacher and parent. Such a plan was advocated by specialists in the education of handicapped children. Representatives and senators were also impressed by the effectiveness of such a practice in serving the needs of handicapped children in many districts. It seemed to represent sound practice where it was used, and it provided an uncommon degree of accountability. Impressed, the legislators wrote the requirement into law.

Soon afterward, it was noticed that in order to develop the new plans for each child, teachers began to spend an increasing share of their time in conference with parents and in providing the written documentation that the law and subsequent regulation required. The written document —the individualized plan—became the instrument for monitoring compliance with the law. Administrators, parents, and the education auditors took the plans seriously. The result: teachers spent less time with the children. They were busier conferring with parents and keeping the written records that the law demanded. Since new teachers usually were not hired, direct service to handicapped children actually declined. To a degree, the preparation of the written document became a surrogate for personal service to youngsters.

Global definitions of educational problems tend to breed global solutions. Most legislators have a penchant for translating good ideas into legal requirements. It is the only tool at their disposal. They aren't stupid, of course, or mean. But the public expects them to act on problems, not necessarily with much thought about which problems are most amenable to legal redress and which to other methods.

Laws are blunt instruments. There is little understanding or appreciation of the fact that the provision of a personal service, such as teaching a child to understand the binomial theorem, often requires a degree of sensitiviy and accommodation at the site where the service is provided that enables the person providing the service to adjust his or her approach depending on circumstances. Out of frustration with what we see as poor service, we attempt to assure at least a minimum level of accomplishment and accountability, but such attempts almost invariably lead to a standardization of practice. There frequently is some elevation in minimum accomplishment as a result, but there is usually a leveling down as well.

This argument is not meant to

minimize the importance of accountability on the part of teachers and school administrators. The issue, rather, is one of how to achieve a balance between the initiatives best taken by the public's elected representatives and those attempts at enhancing quality that are best left to the professionals who operate the system. The tension is not new in American education, but the momentum in recent years has been clearly in the direction of greater political assertiveness and reduced professional discretion.

To strike the most effective balance between politicians and teacher, it would be helpful to have a clearer picture of the kind of teacher the country wants. If teaching is something like plumbing, then it is appropriate for the public through various laws and codes to specify in considerable detail the standards to be applied in judging adequacy. Those who practice the craft must understand the requirements, but there is not much latitude associated with how an individual task is to be accomplished. If teaching third-grade arithmetic is like soldering a joint, then some individual discretion is required, as in any craft, but not much. The emphasis is on skill. On the other hand, if teaching mathematics requires that the teacher make adjustments based on the motivational level of different children in the class, on his or her understanding of the intellectual level at which different children are functioning, and on a comprehension of the subject matter sufficient to know which of the children's questions have intellectual mileage and which do not (and which should therefore dominate in classroom discussions), then considerable latitude is necessary at the level of classroom instruction. It makes little sense to try very much prescription of practice from afar.

Moving to a different issue associated with the current legally rooted strategies for educational change, we note that a partial result of the recent pattern of problem identification, leg-

islation, and regulation in education is that the public identifies one troublesome matter at a time, then directs virtually all attention to it. There is concern about gifted children and the space race in the late 1950s, and a massive attempt is made to improve the quality of the curriculum in science and mathematics. It turns out that the schools respond positively. America is first on the moon. High technology thrives. But the country does not seem to notice. In the time it takes to respond discernably to the identified problem, the public has shifted its attention to a different criticism of the schools, this time the distressing achievement levels of the poor. The nation and the schools redirect energy toward that population, again with success. Within a decade, test scores go up for those who used to do least well. But again the achievement does not seem to register with the public. Instead, there is a new outpouring of publicity about declining test sores for the brightest children and America's diminishing position in world trade. Priorities in education change with unpredictable frequency and intensity. The schools are told to work on one feature of the system with little understanding of what is as a result happening to others. And there is little acknowledgement of the volatile and impermanent nature of the public attention span.

One of the most troublesome aspects of the American inclination to change priorities quickly is that teachers become demoralized. As a group, those who staff the schools want to serve youngsters and please the public. Very few people enter the field because of the financial rewards or, these days, the job security. Teachers and school administrators are no more or no less conscientious than others. When the nation says it wants to train scientists and mathematicians, the schools respond; and they succeed. Similarly, monumental progress is made on teaching basic skills when the public sends the message to schools that this is the outcome it wants. However, when the accomplishments of the schools in response to each new declaration of urgency are ignored, discouragement sets in. It is understandable that priorities shift. They do in almost every enterprise. But, some-

how, in the field of education teachers seldom receive a message conveying a sense of appreciation for work that has been done well.

The argument advanced here is not that the country should diminish attempts to improve educational quality for a range of children in the schools through the political process. It should not diminish them. Rather, the intent is to question how such a goal is to be achieved without weakening the capacity of schools to provide education, and in particular without discouraging those who must play a major role in doing what the public wants. A possibly fatal flaw in attempts to improve programs primarily through legislative remedies is that expectations at the level of school and classroom are lowered for developing creative responses to problems. When it is reiterated in the various cycles of educational reform that problems and their resolution are universal and that legislators will develop the "solutions," the local inclination to be responsive is diminished. After a while, the expectation is created that problems will be solved primarily by somebody else.

For example, transcript analyses of California high school students reveal that there is considerable consistency in the courses taken by the top 20 percent of students. Putting aside the issue of what actually happens in Algebra I when the door is shut, the titles of the courses taken by the top-ability group are similar as one moves from one youngster to the next. They are probably guided in their choices by college requirements. Similarly, there is consistency in course titles for youngsters in the poorest achieving 20 percent. They probably know what courses they must take to prepare for the minimum competency examinations. However, there is little pattern in course taking for the middle 60 percent.

Are there too many electives? Are the youngsters preparing for a large number of different occupations? Is there a broad range of ability in the middle group? Is there considerable pressure from the community to offer a variety of courses? The "solution" to the "problem" of patternlessness depends in significant measure on the diagnosis. If the pattern reflects an outdated or no-longer-supported view about choice or a casual response to apparent interests, then a well-defined core curriculum may be indicated. On the other hand, if the population served is enormously varied and if the school has a community-supported approach to help different children reach clearly defensible goals, then a plan to institute a core program might be misdirected. Legislatures do not make these distinctions.

Another example: a school district is having great difficulty teaching youngsters in the first grade whose first language is not English. This problem indeed exists in thousands of school districts across the country. Assume that those who recognize and must deal with the issues understand the limitations of solely legislative remedies. What strategies for educational change make sense?

One approach is to assemble experts: linguists, authorities on language acquisition, successful teachers, sociologists, psychologists, and others. Ask the group to develop a course of study based on the soundest research and most reasonable theories to teach English to six-year-old youngsters in American schools who speak it poorly and who were raised in a different tongue. Millions of dollars might be invested in course development by a determined nation. The task is then to "disseminate" the program devised by the experts to school districts around the country.

This method of curricular development and educational change was prevalent during the 1960s, when school programs were being modified at the urging of the National Science Foundation to develop a cadre of young people with strong education in science and mathematics. Outstanding scientists were assembled. They worked with teachers, psychologists, and other educational experts to prepare new courses. Although these efforts of the 1960s had many beneficial effects, the courses of study developed during that period were seldom used as designed. More traditional texts continued to predominate (though they began to include topics suggested by the reformers). Where the new texts were used as written, however, the programs rarely met the expectations of the developers. Physics texts, for example, were prepared to help children understand how scientific lines of argument are developed—that is, how scientists think about the issues they work on. The children were often expected to engage in independent inquiry so that they would begin to have firsthand experience with scientific thinking.

When the curriculum developers observed in classrooms where the new texts had been adopted, however, they were sometimes shocked by what they saw. Children were often taking turns reading from the new books. They would then be asked by the teacher to repeat what they had just read. The method of teaching was directly counter to the spirit intended by the course developers. Although books had been written to stimulate original inquiry, reading and occasional lecture, followed by recitation, were still the primary methods of instruction. Somehow the guiding impetus for the new courses did not seem to be captured by teachers, at least not by large numbers of them.

On the other hand, modern topics in science and mathematics were introduced as a result of the curricular reform movement. Texts became more accurate as well. Furthermore, teachers were motivated at a high level because outstanding scientists and mathematicians, by redirecting their own activities toward issues of precollege education, were underscoring the importance of secondary school teaching to the country. In addition, considerable amounts of money were devoted to new programs of in-service teacher education, often during the summer months, in which teachers were subsidized to learn about the new topics. There were thus many beneficial effects, but large-scale teaching in the spirit of the course developers was not one of them.

The implementation of new educational programs is a difficult and sensitive matter. Teachers vary enormously in their training, their interests, and their tastes. So do children. So do individual communities.

Different high schools have different expectations of their children and teachers that are complex and special —and uncomprehended in a policy-making body far from the school. A text-writing team has as much difficulty as a state legislature in designing courses and teaching approaches that they can expect to be instituted with fidelity.

Is there an approach to fostering educational change that holds more promise of success than those typically employed do, or are the current strategies for change in schools the only ones available? The answer is that there are indeed other methods, but they are relatively untried on a systematic basis, and there are weaknesses associated with them, too. To stay with the same example, if one wants to improve the teaching of English to youngsters in the first grade who speak it poorly and and for whom it is not the first language, it might at the outset be noted that because the problem is widespread in the United States there already are thousands of classrooms where teachers are wrestling with the issue. While there may not be a single, ideal approach in evidence anywhere, some teachers are clearly more effective than others. Furthermore, most observers would agree about which programs are best. One strategy for educational change that capitalizes upon rather than ignores the natural variation already existing within the system is to identify the teachers who do relatively well. What particular combination of teaching technique, site leadership, student population, community support, and school organization seems to be operating to have established a praiseworthy program? Instead of solely designing a completely new approach to the problem, those who want to improve schools might search as well for factors that seem responsible for existing high-quality programs. By analyzing their characteristics, one begins to understand how programs in other locations that seem similar in essential points like level of teachers' competence, demographics, and financial support might be improved. The main theme of this line of argument, of course, is the age-old admonition "Build on strength." Do not devote all energies to redressing weaknesses. An inclination to recognize and capitalize on strength is not only an acknowledgement of success that has arisen within the system; it also provides proven direction for educational change.

n approach broadly along the lines outlined here would place a greater premium than commonly exists on understanding the origins of current practice. Teachers and school administrators are no more capricious, stupid, or perverse than legislators, politicians, businessmen, or professors. As in every field, some are well motivated, some are more able, some are more intelligent than others; but, as a profession, teachers and school administrators strive as conscientiously as anyone else to meet the varying demands on their time and skills, probably more so because they are in the eye of the public continually. School boards, more than 16,000 of them across the country, are monitoring, setting policy, and providing direction. So are state departments of education. So are politicians. So are journalists. If a program for teaching reading, science, or mathematics exists in a school district, it has obviously met the usual impediments to innovation successfully. It becomes important, then, to understand how a new practice has taken root, how inertia was overcome, how competing interests have been accommodated, and how the resources were identified to establish the program. Instead of continual remediation, policymakers might begin to look at what's right and try to understand it.

The imagery employed here is that of biological evolution. Natural variation exists in a system as large as American education. Some of the variation is adaptive. The strategic task becomes one of finding out how the particular niche for the program was created and of reproducing or tailoring it to new settings.

Among the advantages of such an approach to educational change is the fact that the new school programs thus identified are credible to teachers and administrators. If practices exist, then those who currently teach

have reason to believe people already staffing the schools have the capacity to make improvements. Strategies for educational change that build on strength also have the advantage of raising the self-esteem of teachers, a significant goal in today's climate of criticism and crisis.

Strategies for changing schools are centered almost exclusively on the system of public education. More than independent schools, of course, public schools are regulated by and legally accountable to political bodies. Despite the extraordinary attention to the deficiencies of tax-supported education, there has been very little public interest in or movement toward non-public schools, at least so far. In 1976, 10.5 percent of the children in elementary and secondary schools were in non-public institutions, including parochial schools. That figure climbed to 10.9 percent in 1980. (In 1960, the figure was 13.3. percent.)[10]

It could be otherwise. In the national concern about and impatience with the educational system, one might expect attempts to seek an alternative. Such a possibility is highlighted by periodic attempts to introduce tuition tax credits and school voucher plans. Such initiatives may yet prevail. So far, however, despite the personal support given these two measures by the President of the United States, other politicians, business leaders, and the general public seem to be rejecting the private school option.

While there are many reasons for continued attention to the improvement of public education, and while it would be difficult to predict how long the emphasis will last, one explanatory factor may well be associated with our urgent search for national identity and purpose. Americans as a group have seemed disappointed with themselves through much of the 1960s and 1970s. There has been little celebration of accomplishment. As the country searches for institutions that have the potential to help establish a sense of nationhood, the schools stand out. There probably is a significant cultural memory that helps people appreciate the role of the public schools in helping to unify an extraordinarily varied population in the past. The common schools were an American invention of the nineteenth century. The public was persuaded that

they were created to pursue the common good. They are widely credited with helping an emerging people develop a sense of unity and purpose. There is an unarticulated hope, perhaps, that these institutions will be a major force once again in helping the country ascend to its next phase of accomplishment and pride.

Yet the potential of well-intended reform to cripple the system is real. In its impatience for change and in the national preoccupation with faults, the country runs the risk of weakening the very institutions it is trying to strengthen. Schools are more vulnerable than many people seem to think. If changes are imposed that lower morale or have other pronounced negative effects, even if unintended, the system is significantly damaged. It becomes a target for fresh criticism, and a downward spiral can be the result. For this reason, strategies for educational change should be examined with as much care and sensitivity as can be mustered—with a special eye on unintended side effects—even if such a posture means blunting some apparently irresistible reforms. Better to institute changes piecemeal and steadily than to risk large numbers of untested but mammoth perturbations to the system that as a result of unanticipated and undesirable consequences breed counterreaction and overcorrection. No system is infinitely resilient. It is time in American education to consider more conservative and realistic approaches to educational reform, even if they mean reassessment of the goals for public education and somewhat lowered expectations.

[1] National Commission on Excellence in Education, *A Nation at Risk: The Imperative for Educational Reform* (Washington, D.C.: Government Printing Office, 1983).

[2] Ernest L. Boyer, *High School: A Report on Secondary Education in America* (New York: Harper & Row, 1983).

[3] John I. Goodlad, *A Place Called School: Prospects for the Future* (New York: McGraw-Hill, 1983).

[4] Mortimer Jerome Adler, *The Paideia Proposal* (New York: Macmillan, 1982).

[5] College Entrance Examination Board, *Academic Preparation for College: What Students Need to Know and Be Able to Do* (New York: College Board, 1983).

[6] *Report of the Twentieth Century Fund Task Force on Federal Elementary and Secondary Education Policy* (New York: Twentieth Century Fund, 1983).

[7] National Science Board Commission on Precollege Education in Mathematics, Science and Technology, *Educating Americans for the 21st Century* (Washington, D.C.: Government Printing Office, 1983).

[8] Conrad Carlberg and Kenneth Kavale, "The Efficacy of Special versus Regular Class Placement for Exceptional Children: A Metaanalysis," *Journal of Special Education*, 14 (Fall 1980), pp. 295-309.

School Reform: Recent Influences

Franklin Parker

FRANKLIN PARKER *is distinguished professor, Center for Excellence in Education, Northern Arizona University, Flagstaff, AZ.*

Our schools are being "eroded by a rising tide of mediocrity that threatens our very future," begins *A Nation at Risk.* If an enemy had imposed on us the "mediocre educational performance that exists," we would see "it as an act of war." "Unthinkingly," we imposed mediocrity on ourselves, implied the report, by dismantling post-Sputnik basic education gains, thus weakening our schools, disarming ourselves, mortgaging our future, and causing job losses at home, foreign trade imbalance, and military weakness in the face of U.S.S.R. strength.

The implied culprits responsible for schools' "rising tide of mediocrity" must have been advocates of the open classroom movement (1965–75); the Elementary and Secondary Education Act of 1965, with its massive federal aid to poor school districts; the 1964 Jobs Corps and Project Headstart; school integration after 1954; the child-centered Progressive Education Movement of the 1930s; and earlier liberal–progressive school movements.

Grave school faults were cited: 13 percent of all seventeen-year-olds, 40 percent of minority youths, plus twenty-three million adults are functionally illiterate; Scholastic Aptitude Test (SAT) scores dropped during the years 1963–80, with consistent declines in English, math, and science; and complaints are made about costly remedial programs required in colleges, industry, and the military. Reforms needed, said the *A Nation at Risk* writers, are to reinstate basic education; lengthen the school day and year; hold educators and officials accountable for all students mastering four years of high school English; and require three years each of math, science, and social studies, one-half year of computer science, and, for the college bound, two years of a foreign language.

A Nation at Risk stimulated the national debate about school reform, kept President Reagan from abolishing the President Carter–National Education Association (NEA)-backed cabinet-level Education Department, and moved public schools further toward the center of national politics.

After *A Nation at Risk* set the tone for current school reform, forty-three states raised high school graduation requirements, thirty-seven states assessed student achievement, thirty states raised teacher certification requirements (many included teacher competency tests), and three hundred state-level education study groups adopted key national report recommendations, with more recommendations of their own. High school curricula stressed English, math, and science; electives, personal development, and entertainment courses dropped; SAT and American College Testing (ACT) scores rose.

Taken for granted in good times, schools are frequently blamed for bad times. Reform becomes politically fashionable. Schools are highly visible, touch

> *"Taken for granted in good times, schools are frequently blamed for bad times. Reform becomes politically fashionable."*

many lives, involve many people, and are central to our way of life. The optimistic belief is: reform schools and you reform society.

Teacher education was the major concern in the 1986 second wave of school reform reports, which recommended replacing the undergraduate education degree with an arts or science major, adding a graduate education degree, and creating a professional teacher career ladder. This recommendation was made in *Tomorrow's Teachers,* by the Holmes Group of prestigious research university deans of education, and in *A Nation Prepared: Teachers for the 21st Century,* by the Carnegie Forum on Education and the Economy. The Carnegie Forum proposed a National Board of Professional Teaching Standards (now at work) specifically to plan a graduate teachers' career ladder, starting licensed teachers at $15,000 for ten months, paying more for experienced certified teachers, paying still more for advanced certified teachers, and finally paying "lead" teachers $72,000 for twelve months to direct other teachers and to run schools.

Dire reasons for school reform in the 1986 reports included: United States loss of world markets; low-skilled jobs going abroad; and increased numbers of dropouts, functional illiterates, and other unemployable youths. The reports urged more academic rigor, discipline, motivation, and achievement. The forceful National Governors' Association (NGA) report, *Time for Results,* endorsed Holmes Group and Carnegie Forum recommendations; dramatically asked states to take over "bankrupt" school districts that fail to meet standards; and justified this drastic step because America is losing jobs to Japan, Korea, and other countries whose children go to school more, learn more, are more literate, and later outproduce our workers. The NGA challenge was clear: our future depends on schools giving the many the same high quality of education historically reserved for the fortunate few.

Said NGA chairman, Tennessee's then-Governor Lamar Alexander: "We need better jobs in the South. . . . To get those jobs we need better schools." His education improvement plan paid off in General Motors' $5 billion Saturn auto plant at Spring Hill, Tennessee, a site chosen over one thousand others considered in thirty states. One reason for the choice, a General Motors spokesman said, was Tennessee's commitment to "excellence in education," referring to its pioneer Teachers Career Ladder program which, through merit pay, raised top teachers' salaries to $45,000 a year.

The new initiative is from governors and legislators concerned with state job losses and from corporate industry needing trained manpower to improve the domestic economy, overcome foreign trade deficits, and pay for a costly arms race. These new interests now lead such traditional school reform initiators as professional educators, parents, the public, and the federal government. Federal aid to education, lowest in twenty years, fell during the Reagan years 1980–86 from 9 percent to 6.5 percent of total public school funding.

Business interest in school reform, heralded in the Committee for Economic De-

Reprinted with permission from *National Forum: The Phi Kappa Phi Journal,* Summer 1987, pp. 32-33.

velopment report *Investing in Our Children: Business and the Public Schools* (September 1985), was best expressed by American Can Company executive William S. Woodside. He urged business people to visit schools, "get a sense of how many demands are made on the time of a teacher or an administrator." The corporate world, he said, needs to focus "on the political arena, because it is where the major decisions are going to be made about the funds, priorities and programs that will be so critical to the future of our system of public education." Critical of Education Secretary William J. Bennett's proposed vouchers for low-income children to use private schools, Woodside told businessmen instead to elect officials who will provide "public funds for *public* education."

To reform or upgrade schools is not a new rallying cry. Many hoped that schools would help solve economic problems in the Depression and would strengthen national defense after Sputnik. Schools alone could work no miracles. American educational history is full of uncertain reform attempts from colonial America to the present.

If we consider just the most recent pressures to reform public schools, most of them admittedly short-lived, the list is rather long:

○ Americanization, and health and hygiene, increasingly after the Civil War;
○ social reconstruction, advocated by Counts, Rugg, and others in the 1930s;
○ essential subjects after 1938, called "basic education" since the late 1950s;
○ patriotism, loyalty, discipline, religious and moral values, usual since colonial times, heavily endorsed in the 1980s;
○ area studies: Asia, Africa, Latin America, especially after World War II;
○ inquiry learning, urged by psychologist Jerome Bruner and other new-math, new-physics, new-biology, and new-chemistry advocates, after 1950 when National Science Foundation grants became available;
○ Black studies, women's studies, since the 1960s and '70s;
○ the open classroom, by neoprogressives, 1965–75;
○ alternative schools, first by progressive liberals in the 1960s and '70s, then private academies, by white parents to avoid integrated schools in the '70s and by fundamentalists to include religious studies in the '80s;
○ behavioral objectives, urged by B.F. Skinner and others;
○ accountability, urged by fiscal and other administrative conservatives;
○ vouchers, tuition tax credits, and school prayer, favored by President Reagan and other conservatives;
○ equal time for "creation science," by

fundamentalists to counter the teaching of evolution;
○ and many others.

Skeptics ask: What happened to teachers' centers, prominent under the Carter administration; career education, popular under Education Commissioner Sidney Marland, Jr.; team teaching, part of the open classroom; home teaching by concerned parents, advocated a few years ago by John Holt and others? In times of national crisis many so-called school reforms burst forth to light the sky but fail to solve fundamental problems and are often short-lived.

Skeptics about the success of 1980s school reform view the barrage of critical reports as a massive media blitz. They doubt that the new coalition of state politicians and industry can ever possibly coordinate a reform effort that combines the many competing interest groups who make up and affect United States public schools. They point to some thirteen thousand diverse school districts in fifty economically unequal states and the thousands of competing, self-serving professional education groups (subject area and administrative groups, universities and colleges, teacher unions, and others). The inertia seems too great, and the shibboleth about changing a curriculum being as difficult as moving a graveyard seems too true.

Skeptics say that even if massive efforts to upgrade school standards partially succeed, they will mainly affect and only slightly enlarge the limited pool of the brightest few. Not many more of average ability and fewer of those of below-average ability will be able to meet raised standards. The bell curve will hold. As standards rise, dropouts will increase, especially among minorities and other disadvantaged. In 1940 (the good old days of traditionally tough school standards), the high school dropout rate was 76 percent. A dropout now is far worse off than one was in 1940. The highly motivated and academically bright succeed with or without school reform. Forced academic feeding hurts the low-ability and low-income majority. Vast funds that massive reform will require ought not to be wasted but ought to be used to remediate those on the bottom, say skeptics.

Obstacles are indeed formidable: take the teacher shortage and teacher quality, for instance. United States public schools will need 1.1 million new teachers in the next seven years, or 23 percent of each college graduating class well into the 1990s. But only 4.5 percent of college students in 1985 said they planned to become teachers. Also, the college talent pool is limited: no profession, let alone education, can bid successfully for the brightest 25 percent of college graduates—not medicine or industry or law or the

military. What's to be done, then?

Graveyards are moved; curricula do change; revolutions do happen. By every yardstick, current school reform seems deep, wide, and powerfully urged. The reform reports are not attacks by enemies but by friends, potential allies, people who care about public schools. No major report recommended tuition-tax credits or vouchers; all accept public education as the main delivery system by which to raise new generations. School reform has lasted and mounted in intensity for some years; course requirements have stiffened, and teacher salaries and state school budgets are up—some significantly.

Medical education was in a sorry state and the medical profession much less respected seventy-six years ago. The Flexner report of 1910, Carnegie-sponsored and prepared by a nonphysician, helped transform once-scandalous medical schools, create rigorous programs with a substantial knowledge and clinical base, raise entrance standards, and establish self-policing state medical certification boards. Authority, autonomy, responsibility, and respect followed.

Hard choices and creative solutions can do the same for teachers. Other professions have shortages but find ways to serve without sacrificing standards. One way is to give no emergency or temporary teacher certificates to the ill-prepared, despite the shortage, just as no emergency medical or law credentials go to ill-prepared doctors or lawyers. Just as some qualified teachers now volunteer to coach students, so might qualified teachers be asked to teach one additional period after school for extra pay, as one way out of the coming teacher shortage. Increasing class size, lengthening the school day, tapping the altruism of qualified teachers (with extra pay) are better solutions for some years than putting a generation of children into the hands of unqualified teachers. Such temporary expediencies would provide time for the creation by Holmes Group, Carnegie Forum, and other leaders of a sound national teacher board certification process, a truly reconstructed teaching profession, consisting of certified teachers as highly paid professionals, assisted by interns and instructors and computer lab technicians, aided by paraprofessionals and clerical and administrative staff, helped by tutors and volunteers.

The best of the reform reports hold up this vision, and some very bright people are working on ways to achieve it, including AFT President Albert Shanker, who said, "We have before us the great possibility of forever transforming the lives of teachers and students in America." Americans may be ready to accept Henry Brooks Adams' wise comment, "Teachers affect eternity. They can never tell where their influence stops."

Tomorrow's Teachers:
The Essential Arguments of the Holmes Group Report

Michael W. Sedlak

Michigan State University

This abbreviated version of the Holmes Group Report, written by one of the original co-authors of *Tomorrow's Teachers*, provides an overview of the proposals for the reform of teacher education that the contributors of this symposium are reacting to.

The Holmes Group is a consortium of education deans and chief academic officers from the major research universities in each of the fifty states. It was named for Henry W. Holmes, dean of the Harvard Graduate School of Education during the 1920s, who sought to raise the quality and professional status of teacher education. The nucleus of the Holmes Group gathered initially in the autumn of 1983 to consider generally the issues confronting teaching and teacher education. The group has evolved into its present form over the past several years through a series of occasionally painful deliberations on the strengths and weaknesses of teacher education and the profession of teaching in the United States.

The first public report of the Holmes Group, *Tomorrow's Teachers*, which is the object of this symposium, consists of three related sections: an essay outlining the problems with the status, rewards, and work associated with teaching that jeopardize the recruitment and preparation of qualified teachers; a series of essays introducing and addressing a number of potential obstacles to improving the quality and preparation of the teaching force; and a detailed set of proposals for reform of teaching and teacher education. This article will reconstruct the report's essential arguments for those who have not yet had the opportunity to read the full report. Interested readers are invited to examine the final report's extensive discussions of teaching practice and professional knowledge, central topics of which are only introduced here.

The Holmes Group differs from its predecessors committed to improving the professional preparation of teachers in its recognition that teacher education is largely a creature of teaching itself: its career opportunities, reward structure, traditions of recruitment, working conditions, and authority relations in schools. Without substantial changes in the career

of teaching, improvements in the selection and training of teachers will inevitably wither and evaporate. Without addressing the impact of labor-market and working conditions in teaching, schools of education will not be able to attract the clientele they desire, nor will they be able to convince prospective teachers to invest in or endure the sort of extended academic study, professional education, and clinical experience that the Holmes leaders agree is needed. The teaching profession itself must be changed in order to reinforce and protect changes in the level, content, and standards of teacher education. Holmes leaders understand, in other words, that teacher education cannot be reformed significantly without fashioning a market that preferentially rewards graduates of improved programs.

The Holmes Group also differs from most of its predecessors in its appreciation of the necessity of engaging talented teachers and committed administrators in the reform process. The group's leaders are aware of the limited and often unintended results of top-down reform. Just as they recognize that teacher education cannot be improved in isolation, they understand that reforms cannot be arrogantly directed from political offices or academic departments.

These differences in the perspective of the Holmes leadership, coupled with the group's locus in institutions of teacher education, shape the complex, multifront campaign outlined in *Tomorrow's Teachers*. As will become evident from the following discussion of the goals and assumptions presented in the report, the Holmes Group is dedicated not just to the improvement of teacher education but to the construction of a genuine profession of teaching. Briefly, the group's five goals or proposals for action are:

1. To make the education of teachers more intellectually sound; to make prospective teachers thoughtful students of teaching and its improvement. This will require reform of instruction in the preprofessional undergraduate liberal arts and sciences; of subject matter professional pedagogy instruc-

The author would like to express his appreciation to the other authors of Tomorrow's Teachers, *particularly Judith Lanier, David Cohen, Richard Elmore, and Richard Prawat, whose contributions have also been drawn upon in the preparation of this abbreviated version of the Holmes Group Report. It is printed with the permission of the Holmes Group. The author is additionally grateful to Jonas Soltis and Janet Johnson for their insightful recommendations.*

tion; and of the clinical experiences in teacher education. Expanding the general education and subject matter exposure of prospective teachers will also require shifting professional academic and clinical studies from the undergraduate to the graduate level.

2. To recognize differences in teachers' knowledge, skill, and commitment, and in their education, certification, work, and career opportunities by distinguishing among novices, competent professional teachers, and high-level professional leaders. The Holmes Group labels these distinctive practitioners Instructors, Professional Teachers, and Career Professionals. This will require differentiated staffing or role responsibilities in schools as well as differentiated professional education and credentials.

3. To create standards of entry to the profession—examinations and educational requirements—that are professionally relevant and intellectually defensible. This will require imaginative assessments and evaluations.

4. To connect institutions of higher and professional education with schools in order to make better use of expert teachers in the professional education and induction of other teachers and in research on teaching, and to build demonstration sites where new career opportunities, working conditions, and administrative arrangements can be developed and refined. This will require the establishment of new institutional relationships.

5. To make schools better places for teachers to work and for students to learn by altering the professional roles and responsibilities of teachers. This will require changes in the authority relationships in schools and in the nature and scope of autonomy for professional teachers.

Attaining these ambitious goals will obviously depend on the collaboration of individuals associated with a variety of institutions sharing responsibility for shaping the educational enterprise: university academic departments, professional schools of education, school districts, and state houses. In developing these goals and their corollary proposals for action, the Holmes Group anticipated struggles over their implementation and attempted to address many of the most serious concerns that such a broad agenda would inevitably raise in those who will have to change in order to improve our schools and programs of teacher education.

There are far easier ways of getting through the next decade than beginning to implement the Holmes Group proposals. Teacher education programs, for example, could do nothing and get rich as the demand for teachers swells their enrollments. Many faculty members in the academic departments would probably prefer to be left alone to allow the reward structures of their disciplines to shape what is allowed to pass as undergraduate education. The Holmes Group leaders recognize, however, that demographic and social trends have conspired to leave us faced in the next decade with the task of staffing classrooms with the teachers who will remain in schools well into the twenty-first century. To allow this opportunity—which might not return for forty years—to slip away would be foolish and destructive.

Careers

The traditions of recruitment, norms of preparation, and conditions of work in schools have severely hindered efforts to improve the quality of teaching. This unfortunate legacy was created by the youthful, transient, and large work force needed to staff our schools as the United States attempted to achieve universal education. During the perennial shortages that have plagued teaching during the past century or more, the nation relied on the generous subsidy of those whose opportunities were limited by prejudice and civic customs in employment, particularly women and minorities. Shortages were handled with emergency certificates and inordinately weak credentials. Such deceptive remedies created the illusion that all was well by masking the crucial distinction between covering classes and providing effective teaching. These norms and traditions contributed to a flat career pattern, roundly condemned as teaching's "careerlessness," where ambition and accomplishment went unrewarded both in terms of expanded responsibilities and autonomy, and higher salaries.

The Holmes Group recognizes that teaching's traditional career structure, increasingly dysfunctional in the face of changed social and demographic realities, must be changed if the quality of teaching and teacher education is to be improved. Employment options for women and minorities have expanded dramatically over the past twenty years. Coupled with increasing stress on the job and a decline in real purchasing power, such opportunities accelerated the defection of competent teachers from the profession and discouraged many promising prospective teachers from ever entering it. The imminent shortage of qualified teachers makes our response to the problems of recruitment, preparation, induction, and retention more critical than at any point in our nation's history. For the first time, the desirability of a teaching career will be tested in an open labor market. If we respond as we have in the past by relying on emergency certificates and spurious credentials, unprecedented numbers of incompetent teachers will be hired. Circumstances will keep them in the classroom. Their abilities and posture toward professional responsibility will shape the norms and effects of teaching for years to come.

Based on this understanding of the problems associated with the prevailing career structure in teaching, the Holmes Group endorses the concept of differentiated staffing in order to improve the quality, engagement, and commitment of the teaching force. To attract, prepare, and retain a truly competent teaching force, intellectually capable adults must have more flexible access to the classroom. We must counteract the confining role definition for teachers that discourages many effective practitioners from remaining in their classrooms. Improving teaching's attraction and retention powers requires a differentiated professional teaching force able to respond to the opportunities provided by a staged career that would make and reward formal distinctions about responsibilities and degrees of autonomy.

Differentiating the teaching career would be advantageous to individuals, public schools, and professional schools of education. It would make it possible for districts to go beyond limited financial incentives and to challenge and reward commitment. This is essential to encourage teachers to reinvest in their work, and earn rewards while remaining in their classrooms; it would also counterbalance the defection of talented, committed teachers into administration. Some occupational mobility and choice, so absent today, would help to ease the frustrations that drive talented teachers from their classrooms.

Differentiated staffing would make it possible for communities to respond to disequilibrium in the supply of and demand for teachers. Instead of lowering standards and awarding full professional status to individuals with questionable preparation, differentiated staffing would permit responsible expansion and contraction of a pool of teachers, while protecting the integrity of the teaching force. A hierarchy of levels of responsibility corresponding to degrees of professional education, experience, and performance evaluations would make it possible to adjust to spot shortages in specific fields, or to more generalized shortages, by adding, subtracting, or shifting personnel resources in a fashion far more rational than is customary today. It would be possible to limit the autonomy of certain teachers who would work under supervision, thereby avoiding the traditional practice of bestowing full professional prerogatives on everyone brought into the classroom, regardless of their credentials or demonstrated abilities.

Finally, since the Holmes Group understands the reciprocity between teaching and teacher education, differentiating the career would enhance professional schools of education. Expanding career opportunities and rewards in teaching would create a market for professionally trained teachers with advanced graduate credentials.

A differentiated profession would be built on the distinctive contributions of three groups of practitioners. The first group, which the Holmes Group calls *Instructors,* would be bright, well-educated adults interested in teaching a specific subject without making a career commitment to teaching. They might be undecided about a vocation, or prefer to teach children as secondary work. Because of their limited exposure to professional knowledge, Instructors would have their lessions structured and supervised. They would not set school policy, determine curricula, or evaluate personnel or programs. They would possess limited rights, responsibilities, and benefits. They would not have tenure, nor autonomy and the obligations afforded fully professional teachers. The Instructors' contribution to education, despite their limited investment in a teaching career, would be invaluable to the schools.

Obviously the teaching force should not consist entirely of individuals who participate on a temporary or limited basis. Capable college graduates must also be encouraged to invest fully in a teaching career. Such *Professional Teachers,* constituting the profession's backbone, deserve working conditions that support sustained success, and they need alternatives in schools to accommodate their different aspirations. Unlike Instructors, Professional Teachers would be certified as fully autonomous practitioners, entitled to exercise their classroom duties without supervision. They would be specialists in both subject matter and pedagogy. They would understand the core ideas in the subjects they teach, the probable learning problems children encounter at different ages, and the multiple ways by which teachers can overcome these problems. They would not only be effective instructors, but would also be better prepared to function as child advocates to ensure that schools and communities served, in the broadest sense, the educational needs of their children. Many teachers thrive on this intensely focused role in school. They find their success in instruction rewarding, and their training, creativity, and commitment are best directed toward their classrooms. Nothing should undermine their effective instruction in the

subjects and grade levels for which they have demonstrated competence.

Other teachers, however, would appreciate and benefit from alternatives to their work directly with children. Interested more broadly in educational policy and improvement, they would like to collaborate with other adults on problems related to school effectiveness. Providing opportunities for these *Career Professionals* would improve the educational effectiveness of other adults in schools. Presumably they would participate in teacher education (guiding Instructors, for example, or providing staff development opportunities), curriculum improvement, and testing and measurement, or conduct action research. Although they would constitute perhaps 20 percent of a school's staff, Career Professionals would play a key role in revitalizing the teaching profession.

Some occupations have used differentiated staffing to make artificial and counterproductive distinctions in the workplace, to fabricate hierarchies in order to claim higher status and autonomy. Holmes Group leaders are aware of such problems and caution against their replication in teaching. Large, complex organization, nevertheless, do become hierarchical: Educational institutions have been so for more than a century. The problem lies not with differentiation and hierarchy, but with illegitimate, irrational, and spurious distinctions. Rational, differentiated staffing based on defensible differences in training, authority, and responsibilities will make it possible to respond fairly to the complexities of teaching and learning in large, diverse institutions. The question is not whether hierarchies will persist in educational organizations. The question is whether they will be based on defensible, rational distinctions, or on the flight from teaching and traditions of sexism, as they ordinarily are in schools today.

Teaching

To change the preparation of teachers and the nature of instructional work in schools, the Holmes Group recognizes that it is essential to challenge prevailing views of teaching that oversimplify the knowledge, skills, and dispositions essential to effective and equitable practice. Many people, for example, hold an inaccurate, excessively simple "bright-person" model of teaching. They have been convinced that teaching is a one-way process of delivery, of crafting a lesson and presenting it to a group of prospective learners. In their view, the onus of learning rests entirely on the students. To them the characteristics of the classroom group, and the individuals in it, influence the lesson and mode of delivery only modestly. The teachers' responsibility basically ends when they have told students what they must remember to know and do. If effective teaching actually consisted of such behavior, most individuals who knew something of a subject could easily teach it. But this view blithely overlooks critical aspects of quality teaching—particularly the extent to which lessons are appropriate only for the specific students for whom a teacher is responsible and for whom the lesson should be crafted.

Unfortunately, simple and naive models of teaching are often most attractive to bright, studious individuals who took major responsibility for their own learning as students. Reasoning that what worked for them will work for others, they believe that everyone else can just as easily survive a teacher intent on just presenting the material. Such a belief can too easily ignore or disparage professional knowledge because it assumes that teachers' lessons can have quality independent of student learning.

The Holmes Group challenges such naive linear definitions of teaching. It offers in contrast a vision of teaching and learning that is fundamentally interactive. The professional knowledge that competent teachers possess goes beyond a strong, coherent liberal education. It is not merely common sense, nor is it learned only through trial-and-error teaching or the experience of being a student. Rather, it includes academic and clinical learning that prepares one to manage both mastery of content and the complex social relations of the classroom in a way that fosters student learning as well as an attachment to learning. Because of this shared interactive view of the learning process, Holmes leaders are convinced that the knowledge, skills, and dispositions essential to effective teaching are acquired through extended professional education.

Liberal Education

Aggravating the problems of the bright-person model is the reality of learning in the arts and sciences at the undergraduate level. Improving the education of any prospective teacher is impossible without the concomitant reform of the nonprofessional components of the undergraduate curriculum. Students pursuing their professional studies must arrive already equipped with a sound command of the undergirding disciplines and have developed the qualities of engaged, inquiring learners. As a number of scathing reports have recently demonstrated, it is difficult for undergraduates, regardless of whether they intend to teach, to develop such skills. The prevailing pattern of fragmented, excessively specialized, and prematurely vocationalized curricula, coupled with uninspired pedagogy, does not provide appropriate models of intellectual coherency and engagement.

At best, the contemporary academic major is largely a preparation for graduate study in a disciplinary field. This limited vision and focus often fails to elaborate the structure of the discipline, its origins and goals, and ignores criteria that would allow learners to distinguish between issues meriting deep study and other more trivial topics. Traditional baccalaureate study fails teachers who, at all levels, must find and present the most powerful and generative ideas in a way that both preserves the integrity of disciplinary knowledge and leads students to understand a subject. It is too easy for critics of teacher education to say that prospective teachers need simply to take more courses in the arts and sciences. The disarray of knowledge in the disciplines has been well documented.

Holmes Group leaders understand how hard it is to change the curricula and pedagogy of the disciplines, and how costly it is to confront the prevailing reward structures of most academic departments. Improving the quality of teaching, nevertheless, depends on changing the course selection patterns, class content, and existing pedagogy encountered by prospective teachers during their preprofessional studies. Such reform would not only benefit prospective teachers, however, but would strengthen the higher education of all college students.

Professional Education

Reforming the education of teachers depends on engaging in the complex work of identifying the knowledge base for competent teaching, and developing the content and strategies whereby it can be effectively mastered. Although specialized professional knowledge has been under development for some time—and dramatic strides have been made during the past two decades—an amalgam of intuition, unreflective reactions, and personal dispositions still seems to ground the right to teach.

Basically a "nonprogram" at present, professional studies are rarely interrelated or coherent. The curriculum is seldom reviewed for its comprehensiveness, its redundancy, or its responsiveness to research and analysis. Advisement is too often ineffective, leaving students to wander about rather than progressing systematically in a cohort through their programs.

Building on an increasingly mature body of scholarship and empirical research, a program of professional studies in education must integrate at least five components to qualify as a comprehensive plan for teacher preparation. The first is the study of teaching and schooling as an academic field. This would provide a description and explanation of the phenomenon of schooling itself—its development, its purpose, and the macro and micro mechanisms that make schooling possible and sustain it. The second is knowledge of the pedagogy of subject matter. This would consist of the ability to reformulate content knowledge so as to engage a variety of pupils and to strengthen the critical acumen necessary to judge the value of available curricula for particular settings and goals. Such pedagogical expertise is essential to bridge personal understanding and the capacity to teach. A related third component is comprised of the skills and understandings implicit in classroom teaching—creating a communal setting where students of varying ability have the opportunity to develop and learn. Building such an environment requires values, dispositions, and a sense of ethical responsibility: the fourth component of a comprehensive program of professional education for teaching.

The academic pedagogical studies common to most colleges of education routinely fail to develop such essential professional knowledge, skills, and dispositions in the teachers they prepare. As it is customarily encountered, the clinical, or fifth, component of the pedagogical studies program similarly fails to strengthen the professional qualities needed to ensure effective classroom instruction. Virtually every evaluator of teacher education concludes that program graduates attribute their success to their student teaching and early induction experiences. Many reformers recommend that the entire teacher education program be infused with such clinical opportunities.

The Holmes Group, however, is skeptical about widely held claims for the benefits of the traditional clinical experience. Although students value it most highly, as do their counterparts in all professional preparation programs, the prospective teacher's field experience is neither broad nor deep. Cooperating teachers are usually arbitrarily assigned and too often lack essential professional knowledge and skills needed to strengthen the learning of prospective teachers. University supervision is infrequent. It is common for the experience to be limited to a single school, classroom, and teacher, and it rarely builds on the general principles and theories emphasized in earlier university study. Everyone does well. Yet most students quickly conform to the expectations and practices of their single supervising teacher, and rarely put novel techniques into practice or risk failure. They succeed so easily because they relinquish the norms of professional colleges of education without a struggle. The experience emphasizes imitation of and subservience to the supervising teacher, not investigation, reflection, and problem solving.

Holmes Group leaders believe that university faculty and selected clinical staff from cooperating schools need to reexamine contemporary professional pedagogical offerings to produce an articulate, coherent curriculum with intellectual integrity. Similarly, they endorse clinical experiences in multiple sites with youngsters of diverse ability, motivation, and cultural background.

Professional Development Schools

Recognizing the interdependence of teaching and teacher education suggests a promising alternative to traditional sites for preparing teachers. Professional development schools, the analogue to medical education's teaching hospitals, would bring practicing teachers and administrators together with university faculty in partnerships that improve teaching and learning on the part of their respective students. Such schools would largely overcome many of the problems with traditional academic clinical and pedagogical studies by providing opportunities for teachers and administrators to influence the development of their profession, and for university faculty to increase the professional relevance of their work. These institutions assume that improving teaching ultimately depends on providing teachers with opportunities to contribute to the development of professional knowledge and practice, to form collegial relationships beyond their immediate working environment, and to mature intellectually as they expand the range of their responsibilities. Such collaborative sites would help university-based research and instruction to strengthen its professional roots in practice and to maintain the professional schools' vitality and credibility.

In addition to improving teacher education, professional development schools would expand opportunities for strengthening knowledge and practice: to test different instructional arrangements under different working and administrative conditions. Innovative professional practice would be developed, demonstrated, and critically evaluated at these exemplary sites before being disseminated elsewhere.

Finally, professional development schools would strengthen the profession by serving as models of promising and productive structural relations among Instructors, Professional Teachers, Career Professionals, and administrators. Improving these relations, expanding opportunities and responsibilities, would make working conditions attractive enough to entice talented novices and to retain dedicated, competent teachers. Such a program would provide an optimally balanced plan of study and experience for the neophyte under the tutelage of teacher educators and teachers working in the vanguard of practice. It would offer talented teachers who love their work and want to improve it a means of advancing without leaving the classroom, physically or psychologically.

Credentials

Recommending that the status of teaching be elevated by raising standards, improving career opportunities through differentiated staffing, and reforming both professional education and instruction in the liberal arts and sciences has its potential pitfalls. Because the undertaking would be costly to individuals and institutions alike, it is essential to anticipate and overcome the unintended, undesirable consequences of such ambitious proposals. Earlier initiatives in education and other occupations, shaped by similar dedication to tougher standards and professionalism, have shown that good intentions alone cannot prevent several predictable problems. New credentials themselves, for example, are easily abused. Individuals unfamiliar with the examination and certification processes, most commonly minorities, are too often excluded. By misrepresenting what practitioners can actually do, credentialing can ultimately erode the public's trust in the quality of a profession. Problems with credentials can lead individuals to squander money, time, and energy, and can cause institutions to waste resources. Even worse, problems with the integrity of credentials can lead to outright quackery: providing services that actually harm clients.

Schools have a special relation to the public. Because education is compulsory for all citizens, teaching and teacher education have a unique obligation to avoid the pitfalls of credentialism. Education must resist the temptation to enrich itself as other occupations have done, by offering mediocre performance behind a facade of higher credentials. We cannot pretend that raising credential standards for teachers is the same as improving teaching.

Teaching can improve its professional status only by improving its effectiveness—by raising the level of children's achievement and deepening their engagement with learning. Similarly, teacher education's professional status can be improved only be bestowing genuine credentials that reflect the highest standards and the most rigorous preparation possible.

There are several forms of irresponsible credentialism of which teaching and teacher education must be particularly aware, particularly the trap of *pseudo-credentialism*: bestowing credentials regardless of demonstrated ability. Pseudo-credentialism does not require professional schools to raise their standards or to improve the quality of the education they offer. It allows them to continue what they have been doing by awarding a different credential. Pseudo-credentialism takes different forms in different occupations. Teachers, for example, are paid according to the number of credits earned beyond the bachelor's degree, regardless of whether additional graduate education improved their teaching. State-imposed continuing certification requirements routinely benefit teachers and teacher educators financially, with little regard to the substance or rigor of the advanced credentials invested in or awarded. Teacher educators must not simply add on course requirements, endorse standardized examinations, or demand a fifth year of training without rethinking the value of such changes. Regardless of the form that is takes, pseudo-credentialism is a powerful weapon in the arsenal of opportunistic professionalization and must be challenged.

The potential abuse of credentials, however, should not lead us to reject professional education and certification, and to replace them with the assumption that those who know something can automatically teach. Opening the entitlement to teach to the open market—one response to the disenchantment with the abuse of existing credentials—would not solve the problem of teacher quality. Indeed, as noted above, *deregulation,* as this strategy is called, would aggravate the learning difficulties of many children.

The Holmes Group recognizes that rejecting professional education in favor of allowing college graduates from the academic disciplines to assume full responsibility for classroom instruction only substitutes one form of pseudo-credentialism for another. In one case the credential consists of doing whatever is necessary to complete a traditional teacher education program (ordinarily maintaining a minimum grade-point average and passing specified courses in order to accumulate credits). In the other case, the credential consists of doing whatever is necessary to earn a bachelor's degree in one of the disciplines (by similarly accumulating course credits and maintaining a specified grade-point average). Course grades and the accumulation of credits constitute the coinage of both credentials. In neither case is real teaching ability being required, recognized, or developed. Neither case necessarily produces good teachers. Neither approach is likely to help us respond effectively to the situation we face.

Just as there is a role for higher education to play in building maturity and disciplinary knowledge, there is a role for professional education to play in strengthening prospective teachers' understanding of responsibility, developing their ability to engage students, and cooperatively guiding their induction into the classroom. The Holmes Group proposes an alternative of legitimate professional education and certification to the forms of irresponsible credentialism outlined above. Endorsing professional education does not imply that

real performance evaluations will not be made, or that the credentials will be accepted in lieu of on-the-job assessments of teaching ability. The issue is how to prepare the pool of teachers who are to be allowed to be evaluated. The problem is how to prepare the pool of teachers who will earn the highest assessments for their instructional effectiveness.

Conclusion

Struggling to address these potential obstacles to improving teaching and teacher education, and anticipating and answering the vital questions that they raise, has strengthened the Holmes Group leaders' understanding of the reform process and their appreciation of the opportunities that will open over the ensuing decade. As the Holmes agenda is implemented, there will inevitably be many mistakes, false starts, and unanticipated problems. Solutions that work in one setting may require adaptation to work in another. Because the group recognizes the necessity of adaptation as the strengths and weaknesses of its vision and proposals are exposed, Holmes leaders are committed to responding imaginatively with a variety of alternatives and to sharing the wisdom of experience with all Holmes institutions and with the other individuals and organizations whose cooperation is essential to improving teaching and teacher education in the United States.

The Holmes Group Report and the Professionalization of Teaching

Walter Feinberg
The University of Illinois, Urbana

Critical of the economic orientation and assumptions of the Carnegie report, Feinberg finds the Holmes Group report less problematic. Nevertheless, he raises questions about liberal and professional studies, secondary and primary teachers, professional hierarchy, similarities to medical education, and the relation of schooling to social-economic problems.

It is not difficult to be excited about the Holmes Group report and to admire its bold attempt to restructure teacher education. In response to criticism from outside of the profession, the Holmes Group proposes to abolish undergraduate teacher education programs, to require that all future teachers have a liberal arts major, and to reestablish teacher education as a graduate program. In response to criticism from within the university, it points to the importance of a broad, liberal education for all teachers while expressing concern that the quality of instruction in the liberal arts needs to be improved. In its response to recent criticisms of the teaching profession, the Holmes report also attempts to provide a rationale for the different components of teacher education. For example, to counter the view that anyone who knows a subject well can teach it, the report points to the special needs of high-risk populations of students and argues that proficiency in the theory and skills of pedagogy are necessary components of teacher education. In its recommendation for the establishment of professional development schools, the analogue of medical education's teaching hospitals, the Holmes Group provides a potentially sound way to ground these different components of teacher education in a sustained and controlled teaching environment.

Perhaps even more important than its specific recommendations, the Holmes Group offers a renewed image of the teacher, an image that serves as a strong response to much of the recent criticism of teaching. Professional teachers are to be active agents in the teaching process and not simply conduits transmitting skills, behaviors, or attitudes to a group of children through the use of prescribed materials. Rather, Professional Teachers, when properly trained, will be able to evaluate and pass judgment on the transmission process. They will be able to challenge the advice of "experts" and knowledgeably advance the cause of individual students. Moreover, they will be able to do this out of the sense of confidence that comes from a clear understanding of a child's needs and of the effective ways in which to meet them.

HOLMES AND CARNEGIE

In evaluating the Holmes report, it is important to distinguish it from another proposal for reform issued at about the same time—the Carnegie Forum's Task Force on Education and the Economy, entitled *A Nation Prepared*. The two reports make a number of similar recommendations that are worth serious consideration, but there are also important differences. As its title indicates, the Carnegie report is intended as a response to the earlier report of the President's Commission on Excellence in Education, entitled *A Nation at Risk*. As such, it follows that earlier document by focusing on what it claims to be the link between education and the economy. While the report gestures to other functions of schooling, such as developing an informed citizenry and assuring equal opportunity, its primary focus is on the importance of a renewed teaching profession in helping the nation to meet the economic challenges it describes. Thus whereas the Holmes Group has provided a report about the educational needs of the teaching profession and the structural changes that must be made to meet them, the Carnegie Forum has provided a statement about the competitive position of the United States in the international market and has elaborated the educational changes that improving this position would entail.

This is an important difference and raises certain ques-

Reprinted by permission of the publisher from Walter Feinberg, "The Holmes Group and the Professionalization of Teaching" in Jonas F. Soltis, ed., REFORMING TEACHER EDUCATION: THE IMPACT OF THE HOLMES GROUP REPORT, pp. 56-67 (originally published as *Teachers College Record*, Vol. 88, No. 3, Spring 1987, pp. 366-377). New York: Teachers College Press.

tions about the content of the Carnegie report that need not be raised about the Holmes document. For example, the basic point of the Carnegie report is that dull, routine, repetitive work is moving to other areas of the world because American workers are no longer willing to do such work for the wages that workers in other countries are willing to accept. This means that if American labor is to be competitive in the years ahead, it will have to engage in highly technical activity requiring a good deal of intellectual training. Hence schools, which once were content to teach by drill and routine and to develop habits appropriate to the assembly line, now need to be teaching more abstract skills and more flexible patterns of behavior. More than ever, the report tells us, students will be required to think rather than simply to follow the directions of others. The plausibility of the Carnegie recommendations therefore depends on the accuracy of its assessment of the future economic needs of the country. However, the fact that it fails to address research showing that a substantial number of jobs will continue to require rather routine skills significantly detracts from the case it is trying to make.[1]

An even more serious problem with the Carnegie report is the way in which it describes the movement of labor. American labor is pictured as simply unwilling to work for the low wages that foreign workers are eager to accept. The reader is told of Korean workers who produce video recorders for the American market working seven days a week, twelve hours a day, for $3,000 a year and is warned that as long as "produces and services can be produced by people with low skills who are willing to work hard for relatively low wages, the technology and capital will move to their doorstep" (p.12). What the Carnegie report does not mention is that it is very difficult to tell whether Koreans are willing to work for $.67 an hour because the organizations through which their voices could be expressed, such as unions, are essentially illegal. It also neglects to mention that one important reason serious union activity is banned is because, should Korean workers demand too much in the way of wages, capital could flow again to other countries where wages are lower, unions are outlawed, and standards for pollution control and worker safety are nonexistent. Moreover, much of the capital that flows to Korea and other nations is American, West European, and Japanese capital. Korean industrialists, whether they work on consignment from foreign firms or whether they simply manage firms that are owned by U.S. or Japanese companies, must always look over their shoulders at the prevailing wage scales in other areas of the world. These are the conditions whereby workers are "willing" to work for $.67 an hour.

The important point, however, is that neither capital nor wages flow to these areas as water might flow down a stream. They are directed by the policies and choices of many individuals. A well-functioning American educational system would help students to understand this process and it would also help them to reinterpret such practices in ways that did not remove from them the factors of deliberation and responsible action. Contrary to the Carnegie report, such an education might not always be good for business, at least as it is presently constituted.

What is most interesting and most disturbing about the Carnegie report, then, is that it is able to appropriate a criticism that has been made of American educational policy—

that it has often been designed to prepare some students for lower-level, routine positions—and then deflect this criticism by legitimizing that very same policy on the international level. In other words, if it is now important for American schools to teach children how to think, then one must wonder about the proper task for Korean schools.

The tone set by the economic analysis of the Carnegie Task Force is unfortunate because the report contains many worthwhile pedagogical recommendations, ones that are similar to those in the Holmes report. However, because the Holmes Group avoids the kinds of problems mentioned above, it is easier to take their document seriously as a report about education. Unfortunately, because of the timing of the two reports and the fact that a number of the recommendations are similar, the two have been linked together in the public mind. Moreover, perhaps because of the political influence of the Carnegie Corporation, the members of the Holmes Group have not seemed inclined to discourage the association.

PROFESSIONAL TRAINING AND LIBERAL EDUCATION

In any case, the Holmes report will generate considerable controversy of its own. For example, one of the concerns about the Holmes report that will need to be addressed is the effect it will have on institutions that are not research universities. I am especially concerned about the fate of education programs in the smaller liberal arts colleges, some of which already serve as centers of instructional excellence. Although graduates of these colleges would be allowed to enter teaching on a temporary basis as Instructors and could, of course, enter graduate programs to prepare to become Professional Teachers, there would be no special incentive to take courses in education since the rank of Instructor would be open to anyone with a liberal arts degree. Since some of the education programs in these colleges have been especially imaginative and creative, a program aimed at improving the standards of the profession should be cautious about taking any steps that could seriously weaken them.

Nevertheless, there are a number of good arguments that can be used to support the spirit of the Holmes proposal. A liberal education should provide the foundation, although not serve as a substitute, for the professional education of teachers. To advance these arguments it is useful to make a distinction between liberal and professional studies. Liberal studies are intended to provide many of the skills that a person requires to become an intelligent participant in public discussions while professional studies aim to provide the theoretical knowledge required for participation in a market through the development of higher-level skills. If one of the essential functions of a university is to maintain and improve the quality of public participation, then the Holmes Group recommendation that a liberal arts major be required makes sense not only for future teachers, but for any student seeking a professional university degree.

Consider, for example, the vocational pressure that the recent growth of business and engineering programs on the undergraduate level has placed on the undergraduate curriculum. If there is one lesson universities could learn from the recent tragedy of the space shuttle it is that we need to worry as much about the poorly educated engineer or manager as we do about the poorly trained one. While the latter may not be able to spot a dangerous flaw in the rocket, the former continues to manufacture the rocket after the flaw has been noticed. Thus, in insisting on a strong, liberal basis for teacher education, the Holmes Group has addressed an important area for undergraduate professional education in general. A professionally trained person is not necessarily synonymous with a well-educated one. In this respect, the Holmes Group is on the right track. A university has a responsibility to ask more of its professional school students than it presently does. Having said this, however, there still are some questions that will need to be answered about the practical workings of the Holmes proposal before a full appraisal can be made.

First, consider the Holmes Group requirement that teachers be restricted to instructing only in those areas in which they have a liberal arts major or minor. It is important that teachers be competent in their subject matter areas. This is the only way in which the teacher can help students guard against the slanted presentations that often appear in textbooks. For example, a few years ago I was reading my daughter's history textbook. It presented the Vietnam war as a well-intended attempt on the part of our national leaders to save democracy in Vietnam, an attempt that was flawed only by the distance of Vietnam from the United States and the lack of a democratic tradition among its population. Good history teachers should help students to develop alternative interpretations. However, in order to do so, they would need to know much about their subject. In this instance, a teacher would need to know about the efforts of the United States to halt a scheduled election between North and South Vietnam in the 1950s as well as about the undemocratic character of the various regimes that were able to obtain the support of the American government. The teacher would also need to know something about the activity leading up to the Gulf of Tonkin Resolution and the treatment of Vietnamese villagers by the "pacification" movement. If Professional Teachers are to teach students how to question the received point of view, they will need to be able to exert judgment on the texts that are used in the classroom. The Holmes report is certainly correct in arguing that more than a narrow technical training is required for the Professional Teacher.

Nevertheless, the report is unclear about how its proposal to restrict a teacher's field of instruction to his or her major and minor fields is to be translated on the primary level of instruction. The implication of this proposal would seem to be that the self-contained classroom will need to be abandoned even in the primary grades. Yet given the nurturing function of the school, especially on the primary level, and the problem that many children might have in moving from the personal environment of the home to a more functional, subject-centered school environment, one must wonder about the appropriateness of this proposal on the primary level. The Holmes Group seems to recognize this problem because its recommendation for primary school teachers does differ somewhat from its proposal for secondary teachers. However, its recommendation that these teachers have the equivalent of a minor in each of the subjects they will teach is not a satisfactory solution. It entails too much

material and too little depth. One suspects that if the education of primary school teachers is to be addressed in a satisfactory way some of the traditional distinctions between education courses and liberal arts courses will have to be reexamined.

Moreover, restricting teachers to instructing only in their subject matter major seems to inhibit the establishment of experimental, interdisciplinary programs by reinforcing departmental boundaries and legitimizing the view that the lines between subject matter areas are fixed by some unbending law of nature. Thus caution is needed in order to avoid one of the more subtle yet persistent problems in schools—the sense of fragmentation and intellectual isolation that a strongly compartmentalized curriculum often develops.

PROFESSIONAL HIERARCHY

A second concern is the Holmes report recommendation that the teaching profession be divided into a three-tiered structure. The initial rank of Instructor will not carry tenure and the license will be restricted to a five-year, nonrenewable term. The other two ranks, those of Professional Teacher and Career Professional, carry permanent tenure, with the latter having significant responsibility. Some will find this ranking objectionable because of the elitism that it seems to reflect. They will perceive this arrangement to be similar to proposals for merit pay and will be concerned that it will introduce a divisive element into the schools. While I believe that their concerns are quite warranted with respect to merit pay, the principle behind this proposal—functional differentiation and rewards—is in fact more defensible. Indeed, one of the weaknesses of merit pay proposals is that by allowing an administrative staff to make judgments about quality, professional decisions are located outside of the teaching profession. The proposal offered by the Holmes Group is different in that it offers differential rewards for differential functions.

One of the factors that makes the proposal unique is the implied relationship between the Instructor rank, which requires some supervision, and the rank of the Career Professional, which carries with it supervisory responsibilities. The provision for including as a part of the teaching force a nontenurable rank occupied by a temporary staff for no more than five years provides a way for the profession to control market factors during periods of both rapidly advancing enrollments and rapidly declining ones. Hence it adds a degree of stability to the profession that has been absent in recent years. If the proposal were to work, schools could meet the need for more instruction without oversaturating the market with more tenured teachers.

The provision for establishing a rank with considerable supervisory authority, including the supervision of instructors, and schoolwide responsibility adds credibility to the claims to professional status made by teachers. The important thing about the role of the Career Professional is that it makes a statement about the kind of knowledge base that is needed to support the profession of teaching. The fact that there is to be pedagogical specialization within this rank, as the Holmes Group suggests, is a statement that the body of knowledge required for teaching is too large for any single individual to be expected to learn in a relatively short period of time. An indirect implication of this claim is that if accepted, it will require that market factors be controlled by professional concerns. However, the more direct implication is that many years of study and practice are required to develop the expertise that effective teaching demands and that much of this expertise must be developed outside of the practical, everyday work of the classroom. Hence both Professional Teacher and especially Career Professional status require graduate work.

The key question, then, is whether the proposal is likely to work to achieve both the market control and the professional status that the Holmes Group seeks. The question of supervision is key here because were Instructors allowed to practice on their own, it would be difficult to argue that teaching requires a level of knowledge and advanced training that cannot be acquired on the job. While it is clear that the Holmes Group believes some supervision will be required, the question of how much and for how long remains unaddressed. The report speaks of "beginning Instructors" licensed to teach under the direct supervision of a fully certified professional. It is not clear, however, whether "beginning" refers to an individual instructor who is just starting to teach or whether it refers to Instructors as a group who, because of their status, are always to be thought of as beginners. If the former were the case, then of course there would be a serious chink in the professional armor since it would be difficult to find an acceptable reason to dismiss people who, having performed satisfactorily for five years, are not permitted to continue simply because they have entered the sixth year. While one might expect that during periods of teacher surplus, the six-year rule will be honored, it is less likely to hold during periods of shortage.

I have been told[2] that it is the intent of the Holmes Group to provide Instructors with continuous supervision over the five years of their non-renewable contract. Hence, even though the language is not clear in the report, the idea is that Instructors are really not fully qualified teachers who can work on their own. From the point of view of maintaining the integrity of the profession, this would seem to be the more prudent course of action. However, there are still problems with the proposal. After all, if a school can afford to supervise an Instructor for five years, and assuming, because of greater experience, that the amount of supervision required would be reduced each year, then would it not be more efficient to allow Instructors to stay on as long as they are needed rather than hire a new one at the end of the five-year rotation? The document is also unclear about the nature and extent of the supervision that will be required. If a great deal is required, then questions of efficiency will inevitably arise. If very little is required, then the claims for the legitimacy of the different professional ranks may itself be challenged on the basis of actual practice. I want to join the Holmes Group in arguing the need for a professional group of teachers, but I do find the problem raised above to be a difficult one to resolve.

PROFESSIONAL TRAINING PROGRAM

One of the more disappointing aspects of the Holmes Group report is the surprisingly limited treatment given to the professional components of a proposed teacher train-

ing program. While it would be unrealistic to expect a detailed course of study, one would expect more than the scant list provided. Indeed, other than the notion that teachers should be knowledgeable about at-risk populations, there is very little in the list of components that allows the reader to grasp the vision of the new, professional teacher that has guided the proposal's development. The proposal to develop demonstration sites is an attractive idea, but the Holmes Group has not really provided enough description of the work that would go on in them to warrant the likely expense. Indeed, many medical school training hospitals, on which these demonstration sites are modeled, are themselves becoming a serious financial burden and proposals have been made to sell them. Clearly, the value of such sites in developing professional attitudes and skills should not be dismissed, but I suspect that before a more expensive arrangement will be acceptable to the public, a clearer conception of its superior value will have to be developed.

Perhaps the most disappointing aspect of the Holmes Group proposal is its rather sketchy and narrow conception of the professional components of the curriculum. Its focus is almost exclusively on classroom practice. For example, it lists five required components: the academic study of teaching and schooling, knowledge of pedagogy of specific subject areas, skills and values implicit in classroom teaching, values and ethics of teaching, and clinical experience. Given the group's concern to develop teachers who are broadly educated, it is striking that there is nothing in this list that explicitly relates education to the context of the larger society. Of course it would be possible to interpret the academic study of teaching and schooling and the area of ethics broadly enough to include the social and philosophical context of education. Yet still missing is the understanding that schools are but one of the sites in which learning and education occur. It would be unfortunate if this aspect of many existing teacher education programs were to be neglected in future designs. If teachers are to be more than simply classroom technicians, they will need to develop the interpretive and normative skills required in order to understand the larger social context of their own work.

It is interesting in this regard to observe the changes that are occurring today in medical education. After decades in which most nonclinical and biological studies were excluded from the curriculum, many medical schools are beginning to see that it is necessary for physicians to understand the social context of their practice. Teacher education has long recognized the significance of this. It would be sadly ironical if teacher education, as it attempted to become accepted as a professional field, were to neglect this important area. While Professional Teachers certainly do need the skills required to effectively carry out their assigned tasks, they also need the ability to join the public debate about the tasks that are most appropriate for the schools to assume.

INFLUENCE

Because the Holmes Group represents but one constituency within education, the probable influence of its proposals is uncertain. One would expect, for example, that many smaller state universities that define their mission more in terms of undergraduate teaching than of graduate training and research will not greet the report enthusiastically.[3] Nevertheless, even assuming that most of the Holmes Group recommendations can be implemented, one still needs to ask whether we can expect an improvement in the quality of public education. To put it another way, can we assume that by improving the stability and status of the teaching profession, a corresponding improvement will result in the education of children in the public schools?

If the development of professional medical education is to serve as a model for teacher education, as many leaders in the profession wish, then the answer to this question is not obvious. After the publication of the Flexner Report on the improvement of medical education in 1910,[4] there was a significant improvement in the status and income of doctors. Moreover, there was a steady decline in infant mortality rates and an increase in longevity, which many attributed to the more rigorous standards of professional selection and training. Yet the connection between the increased status of the physician and the improvement in health was not as clear-cut as it seemed. Many advances were under way before Flexner's study was undertaken. Improved sanitation, diet, and immunization accounted for a good deal of the improvement that occurred. Moreover, the Flexner model has not proven to be universally benign. There are still many Third World countries where Western models of health care fail to address very basic problems. For example, we sometimes find countries where very large segments of the population die of amebic dysentery yet where the health sector spends its funds on highly technical medicine such as open-heart surgical units.

Increasing the stability and rewards of an occupational group by enhancing its professional status may help improve the services provided to a potential client population, but there are no guarantees. In order to get a sense of the possible effects on public school children of reforming teacher education, we need to take a closer look at the nature of the problem. When some of the recent reports on schools speak of a crisis in education, they are really referring to two related, but different problems. The first involves the perceived failure of the schools to produce the skilled people needed to develop and maintain the higher levels of technology in today's post-industrial society. The second involves correcting the high levels of illiteracy and stemming the tide of school dropouts. It is not at all clear that these problems require the same kind of solution. Nor is it clear that a teacher, trained to address the one, will be equally equipped to handle the other.

I am rather skeptical about the seriousness of the first of these problems, and have not been convinced that the difficulties experienced by our economy are related to the failure of schools.[5] Because this seems to be a minority opinion, some explanation is required. As I already mentioned, one of the problems with the Carnegie report is that it accepts the view that there is a direct and linear relationship between the quality of schooling and the strength of the economy. (A Nation at Risk also adds that a similar connection exists between the quality of schooling and the strength of the military.) The implication is that problems in the economy can be traced to problems in schools, and that problems in schools can be documented by the fact that standardized test scores have fallen over the last twenty years. Similarly, it is believed that the problem in the schools is caused by a decline in the quality of prospective teachers, who have consistently scored lower on college entrance examinations than students intending to enter other fields.

The Carnegie report continues this line of reasoning with an elaborate display of charts of the differences in test scores among different nations. Nevertheless, no convincing evidence is shown to support the link between test scores and economic growth or between test scores and a person's ability to teach. For example, the Carnegie report presents one chart that shows that out of fifteen countries, eighth-grade students in the United States score below students from all other countries except New Zealand and Sweden. The commentary alongside the chart tells us that "at a time when economic growth is increasingly dependent on mastery of science and technology, U.S. eighth graders' knowledge and understanding is below that of most of their counterparts in other industrialized countries" (p. 16). Yet given the countries listed above the United States, only one of them—Japan—has had a significantly more robust economy while those of many of the others have been decidedly more sluggish. If one were to take seriously the relationship between test scores and economic competition, then Israel should be a significant economic threat. For obvious reasons, however, Israel is not even listed on the chart. Education does have some relation to economic growth, but it is not a simple linear one, and in the present climate of international trade, those who are worried about economic growth would do better to look at such things as government investment policies and military budgets.

When it comes to the other perception of the crisis, the high illiteracy rate and the large number of dropouts, we see a situation where schools may have a more direct impact. Here, however, the implication of many reports that the intellectual quality of the teaching profession is inadequate to the task needs a very close examination. We simply do not know whether high SAT scores are indicative of good teachers. It may be that there is a strong correlation between doing well on tests and being a good teacher. It may also be that the relationship is other than linear. On the one hand, we might find that middle-level test scorers are too rule bound and therefore make only mediocre teachers. On the other hand, we might find that those who score high are impatient with slower learners and less able to detect the kinds of problems that they have in assimilating certain material. We might also find that the tests actually measure very few of the qualities required to deal with school dropouts or to handle problems of illiteracy. Indeed, in some areas where job prospects for high school graduates are slim, or where teenage pregnancy rates are high, the capacity to understand and articulate the concerns of the local community may be much more important than the skills that are measured by the SAT. Again, there is an analogy in medicine. By taking the highest test scorers, medical schools have chosen those students who are most likely to specialize in a highly technical area and have indirectly contributed to the decline in primary care and to the inequitable distribution of health services. The fact is that a lot of assumptions are being made about the relationship between test scores and teacher performance that have not been substantiated by research.

To its credit, the Holmes Group report has not rested

its case on these assumptions. It has simply provided a sketch of the kind of knowledge that a Professional Teacher needs to have. Yet the question remains: How will this training improve the quality of education? I think there are two answers to the question. The first speaks to the classroom itself and the second speaks to the national system of education.

To expect a well-trained teacher to improve the inequities that exist in the educational system would be much like expecting a well-trained physician to improve the inequities that exist in health care. The distribution of health and educational services is a system problem and needs to be addressed on a system level. We expect a well-trained doctor to be able to diagnose accurately and treat well the illness that she or he encounters in the office. We should expect the well-trained teacher to be able to do the same with the ignorance that is encountered in the classroom. This is a minimum requirement, but it is an important one and speaks for better training programs than we now have.

Yet just as most of the conditions for health are found outside of the physician's office, many of the conditions for learning exist outside of the classroom. When these conditions do not allow good teaching to result in good learning, they must be addressed with the force of enlightened understanding. When these conditions are maintained by structures that are too powerful for a single individual to change, then a collective voice, with significant respect in the community, is required. A well-informed, skillfully trained teaching profession is a first step. However, as we can see from the frequent failure of the American Medical Association to support a progressive agenda, it is only a *first* step.

The actual influence of the Holmes Group report will not be known for some time. However, by opening up a new area for debate, by addressing the role of the liberal arts in teacher education, and by advocating a renewed vision of the teaching profession, it has performed an important service.

NOTES

1. Henry M. Levin and Russell W. Rumberger, *The Educational Implications of Higher Technology* (Stanford: Institute for Research on Educational Finance and Governance, 1983); and Russell W. Rumberger, "The Growing Imbalance Between Education and Work," *Phi Delta Kappan*, January 1984, pp. 342-50.

2. This point was clarified by Nancy S. Cole, who served on the group.

3. A similar conflict is presently under way in nursing education between four-year, university-based nursing programs and two- and three-year hospital-based programs.

4. Abraham Flexner, *Medical Education in the United States and Canada: A Report to the Carnegie Foundation for the Advancement of Teaching* (New York: Carnegie Foundation for the Advancement of Teaching, Bulletin no. 4, 1910).

5. See Walter Feinberg, "Fixing the Schools: The Ideological Turn," *Issues in Education* 3, no. 2 (Fall 1985): 113-38.

Morality and Values in Education

There are people in North American society who have firm beliefs of what it means to be a moral person, and they think that their concept is what should be taught in the public schools. However, we are one of the most culturally and ideologically pluralistic continents on earth. Great constitutional issues are at stake in this controversy over moral education which have to do with whether or not religious or naturalistic conceptions of morality should persevere in public institutions. Some major court cases have been handed down involving evolution vs. creationism. Other court cases and institutional settings have had to deal with the ethical issues surrounding freedom of speech and the press. Concern for the moral and civic virtue of North American youth is deeply rooted in our colonial and early national pasts. Schools, to some extent, have always been expected to prepare the virtuous and responsible citizen.

There has always been widespread interest in the subject of moral education. Since Socrates (and before), schools have been encouraged to teach certain civic values in order to develop more socially responsible citizens. However, civic education has taken many forms over the past ten decades. Several religious groups and secular organizations have called for the effective development of courses and curricula which will teach elementary school, secondary school, and university students the basic skills needed to reason through ethical issues. They are still divided, however, over the type of curricula that would achieve such an educational ideal. There is also a stand-off between religious groups who would like to see their cherished core values taught in the schools and others who believe in the strictest possible separation of church and state in the public schools.

Today the United States and Canada are amidst the controversy regarding what ethical decision-making skills and what content formats are most important for the moral education of youth. Conservatives do not wish the public schools to be involved in any form of moral instruction; they believe that this is a responsibility of the home and other institutions, e.g. churches or temples. Others believe that the school *cannot* avoid teaching certain values and moral standards by virtue of the fact that teachers apply some ethical standards in the process of instruction. Some believe that teachers cannot hide their own values entirely; they can only learn how to deal with students justly in terms of fairness and respect for students as persons with their own moral standards. The debate is fierce. Some, like Socrates, say values cannot be taught; others disagree and want the chance to do it.

Do the schools have a responsibility to inform students of shared civic values? Democratic societies do not generally wish to see only indoctrination of common cherished values. Democratic countries have to help their citizens learn how to make moral decisions. Any attempt to teach ethical principles of human conduct must confront questions concerning how to do this in a just manner and what substantive moral values to include. Where a plurality of divergent moral systems coexist in a society, the schools must reflect a due regard for fair and compassionate approaches to the topic of moral education. Moral education of the young requires clarification as to what precisely constitutes morality. When advocates of competing moral standards demand that their views be represented in schools, the schools must find just ways to respect the interests of students and also to teach the highest standards of reasoned moral action. Before the question of whether or not moral education belongs in public schools is resolved, a clearer understanding of what moral education means must be developed.

Schools in all nations have always been called upon to encourage responsible student conduct and to teach those shared standards of civic duty which prevail in particular societies. American and Canadian schools have been called upon to do this since the seventeenth century. The issue cannot be avoided by schools, but it can be simplified by defining exactly what ethical principles all students should learn. Although there is no overall agreement regarding how moral education should be approached in North America, there is an emerging consensus in the United States and Canada as to those civic values which the vast majority of citizens share, such as belief in equality before the law, respect for life, the right to safety, the right to one's own convictions, and the value of participation as equals in society. The key is to teach methods of ethical decision making by encouraging virtuous and just behavior in pluralistic nations, such as the United States and Canada, in a manner in which students will retain their freedom to choose substantive standards of value. On the one hand, educators should not teach students merely superficial methods of choosing in the absence of any instruction as to what specific standards of virtue and moral behavior are available to

them. On the other hand, educators must avoid indoctrinating students with their own values.

The essays in this unit represent a comprehensive overview of this topic, with considerable historical and textual interpretation of it. Some positions are examined very critically. As a unit, the articles present an interesting synopsis of the controversy surrounding the topic in North America. The authors consider this controversy in the context of current national debates on these issues.

This unit can be used in courses dealing with the historical or the philosophical foundations of education. The articles also relate well to issues confronting teachers, public pressures on schools, the rights of minorities, and the social responsibilities of schools.

Looking Ahead: Challenge Questions

What is private and what is public regarding the debate over moral education? Or, can such a distinction be made?

What are the differences in the issues surrounding moral education in public and private schools?

Are there consensus values on which most North Americans can agree? Should they be taught in schools?

Should local communities have total autonomy over the content of moral instruction in local schools as they did in the nineteenth century? What are the best lines of argument either for or against this?

What is moral education? What is your understanding of what it means? Why do so many people today wish to see some form of moral education in the schools?

What are some of the problems with the manner in which ethics and ethical decision-making skills have been taught in the schools? For what reasons is there continuing controversy regarding this topic?

What is civic education? How do states encourage civic education in the schools?

Should schools be involved in teaching people to reason about moral questions? Why or why not? If not, who should do it? Why?

What ethical principles should prevail in teaching about morals and ethics in schools?

What is the difference between indoctrination and instruction?

Should ethics be taught in the absence of studying different conceptions of virtue?

Is there a national consensus concerning what specific form of moral education should be taught in schools? Is such a consensus likely if it does not now exist?

What attitudes and skills are most appropriate for learning responsible approaches to moral decision making?

REPAIRING THE PUBLIC-PRIVATE SPLIT: EXCELLENCE, CHARACTER, AND CIVIC VIRTUE

Robert J. Nash, Robert S. Griffin

University of Vermont, Burlington

Currently, a group of writers on schooling in America advocates the importance of education for excellence and character.[1] While it is true that some of this writing has its hyperbolic and polemical tendencies, its main emphases are far too significant to the dialogue about schooling to be dismissed cavalierly by critics as merely "neo-conservative," or "reactionary." While throughout the history of American schooling theorists have advocated the need for such "basics" as general education, high standards of academic excellence, and a virtuous citizenry, today the advocacy is more insistent, and more cogent, than in the past, at least at the conceptual and educational-policy levels.

Excellence advocates stress a drastic paring down of schooling's traditional functions and purposes to the teaching of a common core of subjects—writing, science, mathematics, the liberal arts, and even computer literacy—as a necessary step toward fostering the skills of analysis, historical understanding, and critical reasoning. While there are many versions of excellence education—some, in contrast to those just characterized, emphasize mastery learning, or the raising of test scores, or the development of what are called "effective" schools—we are primarily referring to that group of writers who believe that excellence in education denotes the cultivation of mind, imagination, and intellect through a lengthy and probing study within the liberal arts tradition of the best ideas and creations the Western world has yet produced.[2] By and large, these excellence advocates believe that the insights contained in the Western cultural heritage ought to be allowed to speak for themselves. Thus, they avoid imposition and indoctrination in the hope that this cultural wisdom alone will lead to the living of a life consistent with the intellectual ideals embodied in Western civilization's greatest cultural treasures.

Character writers' emphases are somewhat different as they stress the retrieval of certain desirable moral characteristics from the great traditions of the American experience. Some within this movement call openly for the teaching of what to them are preferred moral characteristics such as honesty, decency, respect for property and the law, diligence, fairness, civility, self-discipline, love of country, and respect for legitimate authority. Most character educators contend that the schools should foster a kind of decorum in students that respects the traditional conventions of the formal educational experience, and instills a sense of allegiance in students to those prevailing social and cultural norms that advance the values of fairness, generosity, and tolerance.[3]

Some critics of these two movements worry that excellence and character education are merely symptomatic of the more general fundamentalist and reactionary tendencies in the culture at large. They see both movements as motivated in part by an uncritical nostalgia for a golden age in which moral virtues were fixed and absolute. They are concerned, too, that school people might rush to embrace a culturally prescribed code of conduct that promises magically to relieve the seemingly intolerable ambiguity and anxiety of living in this pluralistic and relativistic society. These critics also point out that excellence/character education is excessively deferential in its respect for the white, middle-class, Western cultural heritage, and deplore what appears to them to be an insensitivity to the value of non-Western ethnic and racial heritages throughout the world.[4]

These accurate criticisms notwithstanding, the excellence/character movement is raising important questions at all educational levels for Americans to consider. It is acutely sensitive to the absence of any sense of coherent moral purpose among recent educational innovations. From Sputnik to the war on poverty, the schools have been so overburdened with conflicting mandates—to teach intellectual skills, transmit social values, nurture creativity and imagination, encourage self-esteem, promote good health, provide vocational preparation, prepare for life and leisure, develop moral integrity, and sort and sift the college-bound from the work-bound—that issues of moral purpose have been submerged.

In reaction to this confusion of objectives, excellence/ character writers openly advocate an education of virtue, defined as the systematic moral cultivation of responsible human beings dedicated to the advancement of what George Will calls "social cohesion"—"a sense of community rooted in a substantial range of shared values and aims."[5] Excellence/character writers, despite their individual differences in emphasis and tone, are attempting rightly to restore some sense of purpose to the almost tragic fragmentation of educational mandates like those listed above. They sense correctly that such mandates are a contradictory, often expedient, stew of private and public interests, too often guided by limited vision. Few of these mandates are truly calculated to advance individual human dignity or benefit society as a whole.

Almost absent in the United States today is a sense of what the founders of the American republic called "public happiness"—a state whereby trust and civic friendship make public life something to be valued, enjoyed, and respected, rather than avoided, perfunctorily undertaken, or ridiculed. Some excellence/character writers are justly troubled that the price of extreme diversity and pluralism in this country seems to be too little agreement as to what might constitute a common good. They are aware that trust in a democracy must be based in a sense of shared values and a shared fate. They concur with Santayana that "a soul is but the last bubble of a long fermentation in the world."[6]

The main value of much current discussion about excellence and character in the schools is that no longer is concern about these perennial topics relegated to the realm of private educational anxiety. The inner debate has become to a heartening degree public discourse about what in our view are arguably *the* most fundamental educational questions of all: What kind of human being should the schools cultivate? What should an educated person know? What kind of citizens should students become? And perhaps the most timely of all sets of questions today: How can the schools best dispose persons to consider public as well as private interests? How can the schools best balance a heightened concern for individual autonomy and dignity with a growing commitment to civic virtue?

As part of the answer to these questions, we hold that at this time educational advocates of excellence and character need to depend and extend their perspective to include an ideal that we will explore for the remainder of this article—civic virtue. Civic virtue is a concept that attempts to balance private good with public commitment. Few excellence/character writers appear to be sufficiently attentive to the tensions that have existed in this country between the ideals of liberal individualism and those of the common good.

LIBERAL INDIVIDUALISM AND CIVIC AND RELIGIOUS TRADITIONS

Historically, the ideals of liberal individualism are rooted in the seventeenth-century thinking of Thomas Hobbes and John Locke, who held that the ultimate source of value in society is individual preference and will. The individual in this conception exists outside of—is prior to—social relationships, and human values are actually manifestations of the power to control. Hobbes and Locke saw individuals as self-interested egoists, driven essentially by their passions. Social relationships were important only insofar as they provided a context for an individual to advance his own interests.

It was Immanuel Kant who countered this rather depressing view of individualism by constructing a rational defense for the autonomy of the individual governed by nonutilitarian rules. Kant posited a set of universal moral principles grounded in the dignity and respect owed to human beings as ends in themselves. What Kant succeeded in doing, however, in addition to advancing a conception of the individual as inherently valuable, was to legitimize via Christian principles the Hobbesian/Lockean view of the political realm as an embattled arena in which struggles of self-interested passions were bound to occur. In the United States today, politics is experienced mainly as a procedural system of regulating behavior, as a way to keep the fight fair. The Lockean social contract idea, so attractive to the key political figures in early America, is a moral ideal designed to foster social peace as self-interested private individuals do battle within the constraints of a public world.

At the same time, however, there is embedded in American culture today two powerful, indeed complementary, antidotes to the excesses of liberal individualism. One is the omnipresent undercurrent of Jewish and Christian religious traditions; the other is a civic republican tradition originating in the cities of classical Greece and Rome and expressed in the civic humanism of late medieval and early modern Europe, and in the formation of modern Western democracies.[7] Both of these antidotes presuppose that the citizens of a republic are motivated by a civic virtue as well as by self-interest. Both view public involvement as essentially a form of moral endeavor whose purposes are the attainment of social justice, personal autonomy, and the public good.

What excellence/character writing needs at this time is this conception of citizenship, calling for an education that cultivates moral human beings who can contribute to such a polity. The ultimate purpose of an education rooted in standards of intellectual excellence and high moral character ought to be grounded in Enlightenment traditions of individual dignity and human rights and the biblical and civic ideals of committed, informed, and unselfish public engagement. As writers we value greatly the individualistic traditions in American life. It is at the same time true that Americans too seldom realize that their individuality, justly cherished, exists not outside or prior to social relationships. To be an individual is not simply to assert control over, and to achieve success in, the worlds of family and career. Rather, to be an individual in the most evolved, mature sense includes the capacity to realize a responsible selfhood through cooperative civic and community projects. Human dignity itself depends on the moral/ethical dimensions of social relationships, which in turn are ultimately public and political concerns. We hold that a conception of civic virtue—understood as shared initiative and responsibility among persons committed to mutual care and responsibility—in a democracy logically extends and supports the kind of education that excellence/character enthusiasts prize: the formation of the habits of intellectual excellence, self-restraint, and, we would add, the quality of public-spiritedness.

THE IDEAL OF CIVIC VIRTUE

There is presently a growing body of interdisciplinary literature relevant to the concept of civic virtue authored by scholars outside the field of education.[8] Much of this scholarship has been published during the current decade. These thinkers develop a number of concepts that could greatly benefit excellence/character advocates as they attempt to recover the insights of the older biblical and civic republican traditions for the theory and practice of education today. What these authors have to say about seven admittedly archaic-sounding topics—virtue, telos, moral consensus, public good, community, tradition, and transcendence—can go a long way toward helping educators repair the split between private and public good in America today. Also, these topics can increase educators' understanding of the meaning of civic virtue for contemporary Americans, as these seven together comprise the larger concept of civic virtue. What follows then is a brief analysis and application of these seven dominant concepts drawn from the work of selected authors outside the field of education with suggestions for the further development of the notion of civic virtue.

Virtue
There are at least three very different conceptions of virtue in the writings mentioned above. A Homeric virtue is the quality that enables an individual to discharge his social role selflessly. An Aristotelian virtue, in contrast, is the quality that enables an individual to move toward the achievement of a natural or supernatural telos or end. A utilitarian virtue is a quality that contributes to the achievement of earthly and heavenly success. What these three conceptions have in common is the awareness that there is an essential correspondence between the character of a citizen and the welfare of the polis. Too often today in the United States individual welfare is perceived mainly in terms of such abstractions as liberty, rights, and entitlements, each the important democratic legacy of the Enlightenment. For Aristotle, however, it is the quality of an individual's life—excellence of character, and not self-interestedness—that is of ultimate political significance. In his view, there were objectively desirable states of character that every rational being had reason to acquire—wisdom, prudence, courage, and justice. Only the virtuous person, the person who possessed these states of character, could be truly happy. In the end, for Aristotle, there is only one ideal, the harmonious state, where these true virtues flourish, and where each person is encouraged to pursue his special excellence, in accordance with one central principle—that the improvement of citizens is the crucial social undertaking.[9]

Where much writing on character education today is particularly salient is in its concern that schooling be a kind of moral undertaking: Education at its best leads to the emancipation of the individual from the hegemony of his passions. The virtuous person is one who knows that he cannot live optimally except in accordance with certain moral principles such as self-denial, moderation, civility, and self-restraint. Character educators are aware that there can be no public dialogue around such values as fairness, compassion, service, and justice unless the aforementioned moral principles are respected. Not stressed enough, though, by the character advocates, is the truth that a proper education in the virtues teaches that a person's good as a human being is one with the good of the human community. For the ancients, there is simply no way of pursuing a good that is not shared by others. Aristotle's conception of friendship, the ideal form of human relationship, is always drawn in terms of shared virtues. Hence, any kind of education that views the person as an egoist, seeking fortune apart from others, is gravely mistaken about where ultimate human good lies. For Aristotle, and Cicero and Plato as well, there can be no genuine human happiness in a society where the intimate connection between human perfectibility and the political order is sundered.

Thus, whenever character education emphasizes civic virtue as obligation to others, it correctly reflects that ancient system of morality which has been profoundly influential in the shaping of modern political and moral thought. But is this enough in a modern democratic society such as ours? What must be explored further by character educators is the extent to which the exercise of virtue, based on a life lived in common, makes any sense in diverse, post-industrial, pluralistic societies. Since it is almost impossible to agree on ultimate goods and preferred civic virtues, short of totalitarian imposition, all that is realistically left for Americans is a set of procedural rules and negative injunctions, what some political philosophers call a "thin consensus." Practical reason may have worked for Aristotle when persons in the Greek city state, reflecting on a shared life, were able to agree on an ultimate good and on those virtues necessary to achieve that good. Now, however, each person is left for the most part to pursue the good in the privacy of the interior self.

In the absence of any real sense of a unified individual moral life that is one with a unified public life, it would be unwise if educators were to be content merely with exhorting youth to develop a sense of patriotism, acquire a respect for private property, and become more self-disciplined and less hedonistic in their private lives.[10] Whether these characteristics can ever alone soften an acquisitive, individualistic, essentially free market economy in a way that personal freedom and social justice are guaranteed is highly unlikely. It may be true that a moral culture centering on virtue is superior in some ways to one based on simple procedural rules of justice. If the alarming current tendency to perceive virtue as a grab-bag of desirable personality qualities meant to maintain a factitious social harmony persists, however, then civic republicanism will have been sabotaged as a way to achieve both social justice and individual freedom.

Telos
A telos is a specific set of aims and goods toward which human beings move by nature. As understood by the ancients, and later by Christians, a telos constitutes a transcendent vision of the good of a whole human life. For Aristotle, human life is a unity that moves toward *eudai-*

monia, a kind of blessedness, happiness, and well-being. For Christians, to identify a telos with money, honor, or pleasure is to frustrate the cultivation of the theological virtues—faith, hope, and charity—which lead to an ultimate supernatural good. Much of the current writing on character and excellence assumes but does not spell out a set of aims and goals toward which people ought to move.

In the literature on excellence,[11] there is general agreement that such teleological questions as those raised by Charles Frankel in 1981 are the essential ones:

> What images of human possibility will American society put before its members? What standards will it suggest to them as befitting the dignity of the human spirit? What decent balance among human employments will it exhibit? What cues will be given to our citizens . . . that will indicate to them the values authoritative institutions of our nation . . . regard as of transcendent importance?[12]

The consensus among excellence educators with a strong liberal arts bent seems to be that although human beings have a natural drive toward the contemplative life, they still have to be persuaded anew in each generation that knowledge of history and of literature has intrinsic worth. Like friendship, love, beauty, or music, any contemplative activity must be assiduously cultivated, not only by the scions of the privileged but by every citizen in a democratic society. This is the case because without the morality, wisdom, and shared understanding embodied in the humanities, society becomes unbalanced and segmented. Excellence educators fear that "images of human possibility" are ever in danger of being usurped by technocratic despots who have little sense of a collective past or any truly humane vision of a worthwhile future.

Unfortunately, in this pluralistic society Americans inhabit, there is major disagreement on a definitive answer to Aristotle's question: "What is the good life for human beings?" Different answers, of course, send individuals in different and often incompatible directions. Without an overriding conception of the telos of a whole human life, conceived as a unity, it is almost impossible to assess the relative worth of a good such as justice. How justly people are living in giving others their proper due is virtually unanswerable in a society where no good can ever be posited as a superior good because this would warrant putting others' goods in a subordinate place. In education, curricular revision in this country has been consistently compromised by political self-seeking, mere expediency, and unnecessary compromise.[13] Rarely have curricular reforms been the outcome of principled dispute about the moral superiority of one subject matter or philosophy of education over another. As is the case in moral argument generally in this country, educators also believe that there can be no valid, rational justification for any claims that objective and impersonal standards exist for the preferred ordering of subject matter in a curriculum. Thus, it is often left to curricular "experts" to work out political compromises regarding a school's and a community's preference for one kind of educational excellence over another.

Prescinding from the question of whether objective and impersonal standards can *ever* exist in a democracy, we hold that excellence/character authors need to reassert continually the truth of the classical view that the human telos (whatever it may be) is grounded in a *social* vision of human nature. Because it is a fact that outside a community of shared practices and values there can never be human beings, in one sense, the sociopolitical community must always be ontologically prior to the individual. It is the polis that creates human beings, and it is therefore in an association characterized by justice and fellowship that human nature most fully expresses itself. When excellence advocates emphasize the exploration of America's national identity— its telos?—through its common literature, music, and art, they are rightly attempting to promote a political vision focused on what is common to us amidst our diversity.[14] For it is through this cultural legacy that the central symbols of the citizen and the commonwealth—justice, mutual support, individual dignity—can best be reaffirmed by all people, social class and ideology notwithstanding. The difficult task in the period ahead will be to avoid a narrowly conceived, exclusionary, grade-driven conception of educational excellence that merely sustains the status quo of a somewhat misguided and divided public whose goods and burdens are unjustly distributed.[15]

Moral Consensus

Emile Durkheim once observed that society was above all a moral community whose solidarity is maintained by a widely shared, continuing consensus. Whenever that consensus breaks down, coercion must take its place. In the Western world, because secularization has weakened or dissolved many traditional religious meanings, it is crucial to ask which institutions in modern society are capable of providing a shared and plausible morality: the family? the church? the school? the state? Some current educational literature assumes that there is already a moral consensus (albeit latent) present in the United States, and that educators should seize the opportunity to generate a new consensus that, while it may not include everyone, might incorporate that "vital center" on which democracy depends.[16] In theory, a telos takes the metaphysical high road of laying out a specific set of transcendent ends toward which all human beings ought to move. A moral consensus, in contrast, takes the sociological low road of clarifying which moral interests individuals hold in common, how they understand those interests, and how social institutions mediate them. One is normative, the other descriptive.[17]

Despite their theoretical differences, the two concepts, teleological and sociological, imply the need for appropriate mediating institutions whose role is to construct a common culture rooted in common moral goods. For some writers, the family ought to be the primary mediating institution of such ideals as privacy, autonomy, empowerment, rights, and community.[18] Others believe that the church ought to be the major mediator of meaning in the social sphere by advocating divine purpose, justice, peace, and equality, all the while challenging secularist dogmas.[19] Still others hold that government ought to be the institution to provide answers to the questions of how people should live. This view maintains that legislation is always moral legislation because it shapes the public's conception of right and wrong not only in law, but in broad spheres in life.[20]

In order to foster civic virtue, is it ever appropriate to take the view that the *school* should seize the lead toward forging a new moral consensus? A few contemporary educators believe that the forging of a radical egalitarian consensus should be the proper function of the school.[21] In theory, of course, most educational institutions, like the church, the government, and the family, are far too entangled in the current Kulturkampf to take such leadership. At the same time, it is mainly in the school where changes in the moral climate of a society are channeled, however diffusely. It is over the course of their many years in school that large segments of a society acquire a vision of human nature and morality. It is in school, at the most rudimentary existential level, that people daily experience success and failure, the mystery of awe and terror, and where they initially attempt to resolve the tension between a life of private and public virtue. What matters most to people in their everyday lives does not take place in the political arena, but in the mediating structures of their personal existence. As long as political structures continue down the path of moral delegitimation, it will be the dynamic of education that holds the only real promise of binding together a nation in a way that may more nearly approximate civitas. This entails, of course, that the schools resist the degeneration of learning into the solipsisms of the moment: self-fulfillment and high-tech careerism. The institution in the years ahead that will have the greatest public influence in building a moral consensus will be that institution which best shapes moral judgments about how the world is and how it ought to be.

Public Good

Telos and moral consensus lead ineluctably to the concept of the public good. What the excellence/character literature needs at this time is an assertion of a public philosophy in the face of moral fragmentation: one that advocates the cultivation of a community of morally responsible, mutually concerned citizens, and that challenges a social contractarian notion of a state as mainly a political arrangement of conflicting individual interests. In the nineteenth century, Alexis de Tocqueville took two volumes to delineate how a desirable balance could be struck between individual autonomy and the common good in this democracy. For him, the public good was reached when the right of each person to a moral existence was affirmed, and, when in "mutual interdependency," citizens took part in common discussion about how they should live together.[22]

The search for an adequate vision of the public good in this country reaches back to the beginnings of the republic. Jefferson, Paine, Hamilton, and Madison were all agreed that a government could survive only if animated by a spirit of virtue and a concept of the public good. The virtuous citizen was the one who identified his own good with the common good, who understood that personal welfare is dependent on the general welfare. The ideal political leader was one who could place the public good above his own region's special interests. As Americans turned more and more to private advancement and local economic growth during the nineteenth and twentieth centuries, the life of the local community was decisively subordinated to the nationwide development of capital. Bellah et al. have shown how various visions of the public good in the United States—from populism to neocapitalism, from welfare liberalism to economic democracy—have never truly mitigated the tension between private and public interest in this society. Today, it sometimes seems that the United

States is a society shattered into as many special interests as there are individuals.[23]

An education in civic virtue realizes that all citizens in a democracy must participate in governance, and that full participation depends on moral awareness, prudential judgment, and knowledge. The way that a free society solves its problems depends not only on its economic and administrative resources, but on its political vision. The survival of a free people depends on an informed and active citizenry. Democratic citizenship requires the sensitivity and sensibility to assess, weigh, and reach conclusions about public and private issues related to the common good. Where but in the nation's schools should these skills be learned? A conception of the public good assumes the existence of at least a roughly agreed upon moral consensus in America. But do Americans believe that there exists a public good that they can pursue together? Where but in the public schools can students come to grips with a common heritage and a common set of ideals? Further, there is a basic incompatibility between an unbridled free market economy and a virtuous citizenry. Where but in the schools can students learn best how to balance these competing values? And in the struggle between the forces for equal access and excellence that still persists in some sections of the United States, the question for educators is how to ensure that *full* citizen participation in democratic life will continue regardless of social class, racial, and sexual distinctions.

Todd Gitlin, in speaking about media's responsibility in a democracy to contribute to the seeking of a public good, also speaks by implication to the nation's schools:

> Yet if we are serious about living in a democracy, the fundamental responsibility of the media should be to help people better pursue their rights and obligations as citizens, not to sell goods, or serve as an amplification system for politicians, or shore up the prestige of the privileged, or sprinkle flakes of celebrity otherwise dedicated to private gain. Democracy requires an active, engaged citizenry committed to determining and seeking the public good.[24]

Community

Contemporary thinking about the public good presupposes, and eventuates in, a concept of community. In the nineteenth century, de Tocqueville saw the isolation from community to which Americans were especially prone because of their immersion in private economic pursuits. These endeavors pulled citizens away from civic organizations in which they played a role in shaping public life through debate and public initiative. For de Tocqueville, associational life was seen to be the major bulwark against the condition he feared most: being easy prey to a political despotism.[25] Today, many urban and suburban Americans rarely think of themselves as belonging to a bona fide community—that is, a social organization that attempts to be an inclusive whole that celebrates the interdependence of public and private life. Neither do most Americans generally see themselves as participating with each other in protracted discussion and decision making in order to define the commonweal. The deterioration of town meeting forums throughout the country to narrower and narrower (and more technical) economic agendas is a sad indication of how far Americans have departed from the original ideal: to define and create more responsible and cooperative communities through vigorous discussion and decision making in *all* areas of community life.

Rather, most communities today are what Bellah et al. call "life-style enclaves," where people share only certain features of their private lives: appearance, consumption, and leisure activities. People are not interdependent, do not participate politically, and do not share a history. Life-style enclaves are an outgrowth of industrialization and the national market, and are most clearly evident in the affluent sectors of American life.[26] To their credit, in a radically individualized society, life-style enclaves do provide at least some form of collective support.

In the long run, though, the life-style enclave is a fragile and shallow substitute for community. Today Americans are experiencing increasing anxiety and uncertainty about achieving more important and enduring relationships than are possible in a life-style enclave. Therapists and pastoral counselors are aware of these fears and are encouraging their clients to get involved with groups. People are seeking to join churches, or "support groups," or to become involved in political activity in order to "reconnect" with others. It is the moral content of community that fulfills the human needs for objectified standards of right and wrong, and for a common commitment to the good. In spite of its inherent authoritarianisms—for example, traditional ethnic and religious conventions that can be oppressive at times to those who are experimenting with new forms of self-awareness—a community can provide common understandings so that a rough consensus is possible. Not everything is up in the air all the time. Traditional needs to relate in certain ways—familial, religious, civic—persist stubbornly in a pluralistic and mobile United States, as does the search for sharing common moral understandings, even in the face of the contention that such needs are impossible to satisfy.

An education grounded in a sense of civic virtue challenges those on both the Left and the Right who understand social relations to be primarily contracts entered into by individuals seeking personal security and gain. The notion that reciprocity and mutual aid result exclusively when individuals pursue their own self-interests must be exposed as mythical by those educators who refuse to accept family, friendship, and religious associations as necessarily reactionary, or atavistic. The political view that an expansive capitalism and a utilitarian individualism best ensure equal access and emancipation for all is becoming less convincing as a moral argument for maintaining the liberal state.[27] The rediscovery of civic virtue could add a moral dimension to current educational writing on excellence and character: the realization that the personal quest for intellectual potency and a worthwhile life is bound up with interdependency and so with a collective form of power.

For better or for worse, the tie to community binds people together in times of crisis and bestows new forms of power on them. It would be a mistake to think of all forms of patriotism, for example, as a blind nationalism rooted in blood and soil. Rather, the underlying conception that historically has animated some expressions of patriotism in America has essentially been a moral one: that individuals ought to be committed to each other in a bond of fundamental trust, and ought to come to each other's aid when that covenant is dangerously and unfairly threatened by enemies. Augustine, Aquinas, and later contemporary thinkers incorporated this insight into their defenses of just war theory.[28]

Tradition

A community is an "empty shrine" when there are no traditions to sustain it. If individuals are only what they choose to be, if they can detach themselves from social and historical roles at will, if they can ignore their embeddedness in those traditions from which they derive identity, and if there is no telos to give life direction and purpose, then society is little more than a collection of strangers, bereft of community and tradition, each pursuing private interests with no restraints or sense of transcendence. We believe that this is the sum and substance of a life without a sense of civic virtue. Diane Ravitch, an educational historian, believes that knowledge of a culture's traditions, including art, literature, philosophy, law, architecture, language, government, economics, and social life, establishes a context of human life in a particular time and place. Ravitch believes that history, taught well, infuses students with an intimate understanding of their culture's special traditions from which they can draw for the rest of their lives.[29] Each individual, whether he or she likes it or not, inherits a specific past, a number of significant traditions, which is always present to some degree in the here and now.

Traditions create a bond of shared expectations among individuals. In fact, the achievement of ideals such as justice, autonomy, and community can take place only in a society where the spirit of social continuity is dominant. It can be inferred that Ravitch would teach history in a way that keeps alive the spirit of social continuity by illuminating rich traditions of biblical and civic republicanism in the United States. Chief among the insights gained from a historical understanding is the learning that citizenship in this country is rooted in a moral tradition, beginning in the ancient paideia, and extending to the contemporary ideal of a more humane and just commonwealth.[30] Historically, it has been the principles of justice and mutual support grounded in civic covenant that best embody the ideal of human dignity in the United States.

Educators must still resolve several questions regarding the American tradition. Is it desirable to retain civic republican and biblical traditions that may have flourished in very different times under extremely different conditions? How can educators avoid simply hanging on to the nostalgic practices of a distant past, today only thinly remembered but desperately yearned for? How can proponents of excellence and character successfully reappropriate tradition—that is, find sustenance in civic and biblical virtues by applying them actively and creatively to present realities? Not all traditions in the United States are calculated to advance civic virtue today. Some traditions are mean and petty; others are simply irrelevant. If this is true, how can educators avoid choosing those traditions that continue to reinforce private aspirations at the cost of cooperative endeavors? When education becomes primarily an instrument for individual careerism, self-actualization, or mastery of a technology, then it is powerless to provide either authentic personal meaning or civic culture.

Transcendence

Following the lead of Durkheim, several of the noneducational writers referenced in the notes below hold that there must be some ultimate value or truth, some transcendent telos, that gives a final sanction to human rights and civic obligations. For them, transcendent symbols function to synthesize a people's ethos, their moral and world view, and provide a "sacred canopy" under which individuals dream their dreams and attempt to sort out the anomalies of their troubled lives. A recent survey of religious attitudes in the United States found that adherents of organized religious institutions are going well beyond required minimum standards of church membership to explore the transcendent meaning of their faith. Individuals seem to want not only to be part of their church; they want to "be" the church by identifying with their religious heritage. According to this survey, a belief in transcendence (as ultimate supernatural value or truth) remains the top factor in guiding individual lives.[31]

From its earliest years, this country had religious meaning to the colonists. Indeed, a pattern of establishment existed in America's colonies throughout their history. Over time the sheer diversity of religious groups, the presence of dissenters, deists, and rationalists in the colonies, and the overall impact of the Enlightenment thought on American liberalism finally resulted in the disestablishment of religion, and its consignment to the private sphere of life. Religion did not stop being concerned about moral order, but now it began to emphasize individual self-control and voluntary association. The privatization of religion after disestablishment shifted the focus away from biblical traditions and ex cathedra theological pronouncements to a kind of generalized benevolence and personal uplift. Thus was the secular world reinforced rather than challenged.[32]

In spite of the deterioration of authoritarian religion, however, churches have continuously exerted influence on public life right up to the present time. Many of what are called the "mainline" churches in America have tried to relate biblical faith and practice to the whole of contemporary life. The great contribution to society that many of the mainline churches make today is the emphasis they place on the complementarity of individuals and the social order. The churches remind Americans that absolute independence is a false ideal; it delivers not autonomy but loneliness and vulnerability.

There is an ironic truth in the literature on civic virtue and biblical traditions that loyalty to the civitas can safely be nurtured only if the civitas is *not* the object of highest loyalty. Politics itself derives its directions and legitimacy from the dynamic of religious values, whether these values are called a Judeo-Christian ethic, a moral consensus, a civil religion, or a telos. It is the dynamic of religion that binds a nation together in a way that most closely approximates a community. In fact, politics itself poses a great threat to a nation in which there is no transcendent reference to check or keep it within limits. Without transcendence there is the stark possibility of political hubris. In the wishful words of the Lutheran minister Richard Neuhaus, "Americans can consent to a claim that is infinite. They can consent to the civitas because they know it is not their ultimate home."[33]

What then are the implications for those excellence/character educators who are concerned about transcendence in the classroom? Does it make any sense to look to the mainline liberal churches in America as the major mediators of transcendent meaning when there is so much self-doubt about their true mission? American churches are in a bind: On the whole, they are antiecumenical, beset on all sides by evangelicals, facing dropouts, and delicately allied with the secular society, which wants religion confined to the private sphere. However, if in the tradition of civic virtue, politics is the cultivation of a community of morally responsible persons, then the churches should have much to say. As a collective force in the life of Americans, however, the churches advance neither the common good nor private interests very well. Too often they have aligned themselves with the view of politics as the individualistic contest of passions, tempered only by a crude cost-benefit calculation based on a need to survive. Neither can transcendence be successfully confined to ther personal sphere: Steven Tipton has shown how a personal mysticism lacks an effective social discipline, makes too many compromises with the world, and is too much one with the therapeutic quest for self-actualization and personal enlightenment.[34]

Educators must continually remind students that in the absence of a transcendent warrant, politics is forced back on itself. Politics must become self-legitimating, a game played only for its own sake. Contrary to its secular critics, however, religion has neither disappeared nor been completely confined to the private spheres of life. In fact, the cultural legacy—literature, philosophy, history, psychology, art, theater, and music—derives, in great measure, its values and visions from deep-seated religious traditions in this culture. How can students claim to be educated if they do not know how Americans have tried to achieve a sense of transcendence, how Americans throughout their history have developed a variety of religious responses to fundamental questions about the meaning of existence?

The revival of interest in transcendence and civic virtue today is not merely a "neoconservative" phenomenon. Such a revival speaks to the anxieties of all Americans who have been shaken by the fragility of the social bond. A centuries-old constitutional polity based on individualism and self-interest has simply not been adequate to protect the rights of the most vulnerable groups in the United States, including the middle class. A resurgence of interest in the work of the Protestant theologian Reinhold Niebuhr testifies to the contemporary need for a transcendent view of the world amidst the "poverty of affluence" in this country. For Niebuhr, belief in God was not like feeling warm inside. He was put off by easy belief, angered by cost-free piety. Rather, religious faith was meant to detect "a mystery of Grace . . . beyond the conscious design and contrivances of men." His lifelong task was to weld together the tragic sense of life and the pursuit of justice.[35] Excellence/character educators would do well to heed the eloquent words of Niebuhr's biographer: "For all his doubts about the power of mind, Niebuhr was sure that men and women were called to enact justice, make their own history, in full awareness of the pride and foolishness that would plague their efforts. All the while they could shake their heads in wonder at the spectacle of life that was forever 'full of grace and grief.' "[36]

Niebuhr's tragic vision is neither conservative nor liberal in the strict sense. It seeks instead to combine self-interest, social commitment, and ultimate concern in a way that recognizes the finite character of life but also seeks to transform the world. In the years ahead, it will be the responsibility of excellence/character educators to learn from the concepts mentioned in this article in order to determine whether Niebuhr's vision is enough. Is a cultural transformation possible without also confronting the need for fundamental political and institutional reform? How is it possible to change the culture of individualism without simultaneously challenging the logic of the capitalistic system? Is a rehabilitation of the ideal of civic virtue alone sufficient to produce equity and social justice for all people? Indeed, is the ideal of a "moral" community so far-reaching that narrower concepts of equity and social justice could be overlooked or devalued?[37] The various writers included in this article have provided one kind of critical exploration of these important questions. It is time now for all educators to debate the question of which visions and practices will best sustain community and democracy in the years ahead. The dialogue around character and excellence, enhanced by a concern for civic virtue, is an important beginning.

NOTES

1. For example, see theme issues, "Excellence School by School," *Educational Leadership* 42, no. 6, March 1985; also, "The School's Role in Developing Character," *Educational Leadership* 43, no. 4, December 1985/January 1986.

2. See Chester E. Finn, Diane Ravitch, and Robert T. Fancha, ed., *Against Mediocrity: The Humanities in America's High Schools* (New York: Holmes & Meier, 1984); Diane Ravitch, *The Troubled Crusade: American Education 1945-1980* (New York: Basic Books, 1983); Mortimer J. Adler, *The Paideia Proposal: An Educational Manifesto* (New York: Macmillan, 1982); and Eva T.H. Brann, *Paradoxes of Education in a Republic* (Chicago: University of Chicago Press, 1979).

3. See Edward A. Wynne, *Looking at Schools* (Lexington, Mass.: Heath Lexington, 1980); also idem and Herbert J. Walbert, eds., *Developing Character: Transmitting Knowledge* (Posen, Ill.: ARL, 1985).

4. For example, see Michael W. Kirst, *Who Controls Our Schools?* (New York: W.H. Freeman, 1984); and Marvin Lazerson et al., *An Education of Value: The Purposes and Practices of Schools* (Cambridge: Cambridge University Press, 1985).

5. George F. Will, *Statecraft as Soulcraft: What Government Does* (New York: Simon and Schuster, 1983), p. 150.

6. Quoted in ibid., p. 164.

7. See Robert N. Bellah et al., *Habits of the Heart: Individualism and Commitment in American Life* (Berkeley: University of California Press, 1985). See also our essay review of this book, "Balancing the Private and Public," *Harvard Educational Review* 56, no. 2 (May 1986): 171-82.

8. See, for example, Brigitte Berger and Peter L. Berger, *The War over the Family: Capturing the Middle Ground* (New York: Anchor Books, 1984); Sara M. Evans and Harry C. Boyte, *Free Spaces: The Sources of Democratic Change in America* (New York: Harper & Row, 1985); Bellah et al., *Habits of the Heart*; Alasdair MacIntyre, *After Virtue: A Study in Moral Theory*, 2nd ed. (Notre Dame: University of Notre Dame Press, 1984); Richard John Neuhaus, *The Naked Public Square: Religion and Democracy in America* (Grand Rapids, Mich.: Wm. B. Eerdmans Publishing, 1984); Michael Novak, *The Spirit of Democratic Capitalism* (New York: Simon and Schuster, 1982); Edward Shils, *Tradition* (Chicago: The University of Chicago Press, 1981); William M. Sullivan, *Reconstructing Public Philosophy* (Berkeley: University of California Press, 1982); Steven M. Tipton, *Getting Saved from the Sixties: Moral Meaning in Conversion and Cultural Change* (Berkeley: University of California Press, 1982); Will, *Statecraft as Soulcraft*; and Bernard Williams, *Ethics and the Limits of Philosophy* Cambridge: Harvard University Press, 1985).

9. MacIntyre, *After Virtue*, pp. 184-85.

10. See materials available from American Institute for Character Education, Box 12617, San Antonio, Texas.

11. See John H. Bunzel, ed., *Challenge to American Schools: The Case for Standards and Values* (New York: Oxford University Press, 1985); also Chester E. Finn, Jr., Diane Ravitch, and R. Holley Roberts, ed., *Challenge to Humanities* (New York: Holmes and Meier, 1985).

12. Quoted in Chester E. Finn, Jr., and Diane Ravitch, "Conclusions and Recommendations: High Expectations and Disciplined Effort" in *Against Mediocrity*, p. 261.

13. Despite its laudable advocacy of liberal studies, universal cultural literacy, and an enlightened citizenry, the report of the National Commission on Excellence in Education, *A Nation at Risk: The Imperative for Educational Reform* (Washington, D.C.: Government Printing Office, 1983), shows the dilutive effects of political and economic compromise. See Robert J. Nash and Edward R. Ducharme, "Where There Is No Vision, the People Perish: A Nation at Risk," *Journal of Teacher Education* 34, no. 4, (July-August 1983): 38-46.

14. See, for example, the essays on teaching the humanities in the classroom in *Challenge to the Humanities*. See also Neil Postman, *Teaching as a Conserving Activity* (New York: Delta, 1980), ch. 7.

15. See Joseph Adelson, "Four Surprises, or Why the Schools May Not Improve Much," in *Challenge to American Schools*, pp. 17-28, for hints of a narrowly conceived presentation of excellence. See especially entire theme issue, "Excellence," *Educational Leadership*, March 1985, as an example of the current concern with the *implementation* of excellence programs, rather than with the preferred *content* of such programs.

16. For example, see Kirst, *Who Controls Our Schools?*; also, Lazerson et al., *An Education of Value*.

17. See Berger and Berger, *The War over the Family*, pp. 196-98.

18. For example, ibid.

19. For example, Neuhaus, *The Naked Public Square*.

20. For example, Will, *Statecraft as Soulcraft*; also, idem, *The Pursuit of Virtue and Other Tory Notions* (New York: Simon and Schuster, 1982).

21. See especially Philip A. Cusick, *The Egalitarian Ideal and the American High School: Studies of Three Schools* (New York: Longmans, 1983); for two radical statements see Ira Shaw, *Culture Wars: School and Society in the Conservative Restoration 1964-1984* (Boston: Routledge & Kegan Paul, 1986); and Henry A. Giroux, *Theory and Resistence in Education: A Pedagogy for the Opposition* (South Hadley, Mass.: Bergin & Garvey, 1985).

22. Alexis de Tocqueville, *Democracy in America*, trans. George Lawrence, ed. J.P. Mayer (New York: Doubleday, Anchor Books, 1969).

23. Bellah et al., *Habits of the Heart*, pp. 250-71.

24. See Todd Gitlin, *Inside Prime Time* (New York: Pantheon Books, 1985), p. 334.

25. de Tocqueville, *Democracy in America*, pp. 506-10.

26. Bellah et al., *Habits of the Heart*, pp. 71-75.

27. See Christopher Lasch, *The Minimal Self: Psychic Survival in Troubled Times* (New York: W.W. Norton, 1985).

28. See Sullivan, *Reconstructing Public Philosophy*, pp. 160-61; see also Robert N. Bellah, *The Broken Covenant: American Civil Religion in Time of Travail* (New York: Seabury Press, 1975).

29. Diane Ravitch, "From History to Social Studies: Dilemmas and Problems," in *Challenges to the Humanities*, pp. 80-95.

30. See John P. Diggins, *The Lost Soul of American Politics: Virtue, Self-Interest, and the Foundations of Liberalism* (New York: Basic Books, 1985).

31. Kenneth A. Briggs, "Religious Feeling Seen Strong in U.S.," *The New York Times*, December 9, 1984, p. 30.

32. See Martin E. Marty, *Pilgrims in Their Own Land: 500 Years of Religion in America* (New York: Penguin Books, 1985).

33. Neuhaus, *The Naked Public Square*, pp. 77.

34. Tipton, *Getting Saved from the Sixties*.

35. See Reinhold Niebuhr, *The Irony of American History* (New York: Pantheon Books, 1985), pp. 297-98.

36. Richard Fox, *Reinhold Niebuhr: A Biography* (New York: Pantheon Books, 1985), pp. 297-98.

37. See two useful critiques of tradition, community, and liberal notions of cultural change: Daniel Callahan, "Tradition and the Moral Life," *The Hastings Center Report* 12, no. 6 (December, 1982): 23-30; and Gar Alpherovitz, "The Coming Break in Liberal Consciousness," *Christianity and Crisis* 46, no. 3 (March 3, 1986): 59-65.

Moral Education in the United States

FRANKLIN PARKER

Franklin Parker was Benedum Professor of Education, West Virginia University, Morgantown. In the fall of 1986, he became Distinguished Professor, Center for Excellence in Education, Northern Arizona University, Flagstaff.

AMERICA began as a country in search of religious freedom. Religion for salvation and good behavior, begun in colonial schools, lasted in modified form well into the nineteenth century. Fear of a single dominant religion led to adoption of the First Amendment to the United States Constitution, separating church and state. Yet Horace Mann and other public school founders favored and promoted the general Protestant moral ethic that pervaded American schools.

In a college curriculum dominated by Latin classics, theology, and some mathematics, the moral philosophy course taught by the president to seniors was the unifying capstone, stressing character in those soon-to-be leaders. This moral philosophy course, which had originated in the medieval university's seven liberal arts, was the incubator of subjects soon to spring from it and replace it: the social, natural, and physical sciences.

Many changes led to the lessening of this strong moralistic atmosphere, particularly by the 1890s, a decade historians say marked the nation's shift from rural-agrarian simplicity to urban-industrial complexity. Sectarian religious battles, fueled in part by new immigrants' religious beliefs or lack of them, tended to reduce religion-based ethics in lower and higher schools.

Science, with its reliance on testable facts, began to raise questions about and challenge ethical beliefs and value judgments. The moral philosophy course faded and higher education's unit was fragmented under the onslaught of new subjects, electives, subject-department dominance, and undergraduate and graduate specialization.

What declined was idealism, introspection, intuition, unity, and undergraduate ethical and moral concerns. Scholars in new subjects, wanting to imitate science, embraced its methods and tried to make new discoveries and so enhance their reputations. With the coming of Freudian and behavioristic psychology, psychological adjustment tended to replace ethical choice.

Curriculum unity and the ethical and moral atmosphere it fostered also declined in the lower schools, swamped at the turn of the century by numbers, duties, and courses. The restructuring of schooling into elementary, junior high, and senior high schools may have helped house students better and hold mass enrollments, but by isolating younger from older students, it lessened older children's ethical influence.

Besides restructuring, a new philosophy of adjustment entered public schools—pragmatic, progressive, experimental, child-centered, activity-oriented. Its spokesman was John Dewey; observers did not at first grasp that his concern was to integrate and reconcile what educationally had always been kept separate: interest *and* effort, school *and* society, individualism *and* the group, the child *and* the curriculum.

Progressive methods added to the new tasks imposed on public schools, which were already Americanizing immigrants' children, socializing the young, caring for their health, and equipping them for work. The progressive movement also changed course content. Civics and American history gave way to broader-based social studies, and some criticized progressive education for fostering broader social ethics at the expense of individual ethics. Inevitably weakened was the ethical content of the old courses and the moral atmosphere of the old schools.

The Great Depression led higher educators to try to recapture the ethical unity of the old moral philosophy course by reviving the liberal arts. World War II also shocked educators into a renewed search for curriculum unity and moral uplift. Then Sputnik, in 1957, shocked Americans into vast curriculum revision for bright students; the academic scene was tilted toward the gifted, isolating the average and below-average student.

Cracks had already appeared in that student generation, and writers and artists, such as J. D. Salinger and James Dean, had already tried to mirror the somber mood of troubled youth. This modern anxiety came to a boil in the social turmoil of the 1960s and early 1970s—civil rights, freedom riders, free speech, student protests, Vietnam, Watergate, women's liberation, the energy crunch—all aggravated by the recession and job losses of the early 1980s. These dislocations, plus rising crime and drug use, showed a discontent, anger, and drive for

From *The Education Digest*, April 1986, pp. 22-25. Originally from and reprinted with permission from *The College Board Review*, No. 137, Fall 1985, copyright © 1985 by College Entrance Examination Board, New York.

Moral education as a facet of the educational program in American schools, has, over the years, been eroded by First Amendment decisions, social dislocation, and the redefinition of traditional family values. Today the school system is at a crossroads and has an opportunity to play an increasing role in America's moral foundation. This child is faced with a system that may or may not allow him to develop a positive set of values.

self-destruction that are still incomprehensible. Violent acts are television events shown daily, and a 1983 study reported American drug use as the highest in any industrialized nation.

To rising crime and drug use add a 50 percent divorce rate. Add the pain, anger, guilt, and confusion of child custody fights and property division. Add the new crime of child snatching by divorced parents. Add the many one-parent homes, latchkey children, runaway children, etc. One is hard put to explain the profound and sudden shift in American mores and to account for the drive for self-destruction among so many young Americans, though some have tried: The pollster Daniel Yankelovich, for example, has argued that the trauma of national limitations in the era of the 1973 oil embargo, coming after the affluence of the 1960s and early 1970s, has put us in a new stage, seeking community, commitment, and connectedness, and has restored ethical and moral anchors.

Signs of New Life

An overview of the moral education revival in lower schools includes:

1. Released time (since 1913) sent public school children to nearby churches and synagogues for religious instruction or offered such instruction near or in public schools. In 1947, two million children were so taught. In 1948, the Supreme Court declared such instruction unconstitutional when given on school grounds during school time (in 1952 it approved such instruction *off* school grounds). Released time has since dwindled because of First Amendment challenges.

2. Prayer in public schools was also declared unconstitutional by the Supreme Court (in 1961); despite challenges, the ruling seems likely to stand.

3. Humanistic education (since the early 1960s), including affective learning, emphasized concern for others and valuing human relations, and stressed feeling, sympathy, altruism, helpfulness. Humanistic education has a growing literature but few formal programs.

4. With values clarification, the idea is to clarify dilemmas from a subjective point of view, choose from alternatives, and act on that choice; it is said to be popular in classrooms and successful in book sales. However, values clarification has also been called superficial, ineffective, and possibly dangerous because of its public disclosures, subjectivity, and moral relativism.

5. Moral development or moral reasoning has a large following, literature, measuring scales, curricular programs, and prestigious leaders, such as Jean Piaget and Lawrence Kohlberg.

The California legislature and state board of education a few years ago did recommend moral education for kindergarten through grade 12. Yet one surveyor of California public high schools found that nearly half of the high schools did not have a moral education syllabus, course, or program; 80 percent of high schools did not have a list of moral education materials available for their teachers; and over 80 percent of schools reported very little school district urging for moral education. The investigator pointed out correctly that moral education must first be taught to future teachers before it can be effective in schools and that, as yet, California teacher education institutions have shown little interest in it.

6. Private Christian academies spread rapidly in the last decade. They emphasize religion, morality, and basic skills. Many were begun to circumvent racial integration. Though many have small enrollments and do not survive, they reflect a strong national concern for moral education and are backed by the new evangelical Right and by President Reagan.

College Ethics Courses

But it is in higher education that ethics courses have really grown. A 1977-78 survey by the Hastings Center, in New York, shows that out of 2,270 higher education catalogs, 623 list 2,757 ethics courses. Fifty percent of these courses were applied ethics: bioethics, business ethics, secretarial ethics, legal ethics, medical ethics, etc. The surveyors estimate that up to 12,000 courses are now offered in United States undergraduate colleges; that most of them began in the last 10 years; and that most of them tend to be interdisciplinary, elective, and oriented to such specific issues as euthanasia, bribery, atomic power, and the reporting of misdeeds.

The survey identified these concerns: the qualifications of ethics teachers; what department should administer ethics courses; disputes over course goals, methods, and content, and student evaluation; and whether ethics should be a course on its own or part of other courses. Surveyors found ethics teachers feeling somewhat isolated from their colleagues and fearful that the ethics phenomenon is a fad rather than something of lasting interest.

Do Soviet schools teach moral values any better than we do? Their moral education ideas were pioneered by Anton S. Makarenko, who, from 1920, successfully salvaged war-orphaned delinquents by appealing to their group spirit, cooperativeness, and loyalties. Attitudes are shaped by exhortation, banners, posters, textbooks, teachers, and quotations from Lenin, Makarenko, and others. Children are exposed to exemplary models of revolutionary heroes, workers, peasants, soldiers—all showing courage, effort, and victory in adversity. Soviet youth groups are well organized, staffed, and financed. The Soviets use open indoctrination, a method most Americans abhor. While comparable statistics may not be available, observers say that Soviet crime, juvenile delinquency, alcoholism, divorce, and other evidence of immorality are not negligible.

Change and dislocation have been the pattern of our time. Consequently, blows have fallen on family, home, marriage, children, church, state, school, and nation. Yet each persists and is resilient. School especially needs to be a place set aside to transmit and improve the culture. If, as most Americans believe, moral education and ethics courses have healing power, if they help our better natures and highest hopes, then we ought to support and nurture them.

Ethics Without Virtue

Moral Education in America

CHRISTINA HOFF SOMMERS

Christina Hoff Sommers, assistant professor of philosophy at Clark University, is the editor of an anthology, Vice and Virtue in Everyday Life *(Harcourt Brace Jovanovich).*

What do students in our nation's schools do all day? Most of them are clearly not spending their time reading the classics, learning math, or studying the physical sciences. It is likely that, along with photography workshops, keeping journals, and perhaps learning about computers, students spend part of their day in moral education classes. But these classes are not, as one might expect, designed to acquaint students with the Western moral tradition. Professional theorists in schools of education have found that tradition wanting and have devised an alternative, one they have marketed in public schools with notable success.

A reform of moral education is not a task to be undertaken lightly. The sincerity and personal integrity of the theorist-reformers is not at issue, but their qualifications as moral educators is a legitimate subject of concern. The leaders of reform do not worry about credentials. They are convinced that traditional middle-class morality is at best useless and at worst pernicious, and they have confidence in the new morality that is to replace the old and in the novel techniques to be applied to this end. In 1970 Theodore Sizer, then dean of the Harvard School of Education, co-edited with his wife Nancy a book entitled *Moral Education.* The preface set the tone by condemning the morality of "the Christian gentleman," "the American prairie," the McGuffey *Reader,* and the hypocrisy of teachers who tolerate a grading system that is "the terror of the young." According to the Sizers, all of the authors in the anthology agree that "the 'old morality' can and should be scrapped."

The movement to reform moral education has its seat in the most prestigious institutions of education. Its theories are seldom contested, and its practice is spreading. Students who have received the new moral instruction have been turning up in freshman college classes in increasing numbers. While giving college ethics courses during the past six years, I have become convinced that the need for a critical appraisal of the claims and assumptions of the movement is urgent. My experience is that the students who received the new teaching have been ill served by their mentors.

One gains some idea of the new moral educators from the terminology they use. Courses in ethics are called "values clarification" or "cognitive moral development"; teachers are "values processors," "values facilitators," or "reflective-active listeners"; lessons in moral reasoning are "sensitivity modules"; volunteer work in the community is an "action module"; and teachers "dialogue" with students to help them discover their own systems of values. In these dialogues the teacher avoids discussing "old bags of virtues," such as wisdom, courage, compassion, and "proper" behavior, because any attempt to instill these would be to indoctrinate the student. Some leaders of the new reform movement advise teachers that effective moral education cannot take place in the "authoritarian" atmosphere of the average American high school. The teacher ought to democratize the classroom, turning it into a "just community" where the student and teacher have an equal say. Furthermore, the student who takes a normative ethics course in college will likely encounter a professor who also has a principled aversion to the inculcation of moral precepts and who will confine classroom discussion to such issues of social concern as the Karen Ann Quinlan case, recombinant DNA research, or the moral responsibilities of corporations.

The result is a system of moral education that is silent about virtue.

The teaching of virtue is not viewed as a legitimate aim of a moral curriculum, but there is no dearth of alternative approaches. From the time the values education movement began in the late nineteen sixties, its theorists have produced an enormous number of articles, books, films, manuals, and doctoral dissertations; there are now journals, advanced degree programs, and entire institutes dedicated exclusively to moral pedagogy; and for the past several years, teachers, counselors, and education specialists have been attending conferences, seminars, workshops, and retreats to improve their skills in values-processing. At present, two opposing ideologies dominate moral education: the values clarification movement, whose best-known proponent is Sidney Simon of the University of Massachusetts School of Education; and the cognitive moral development movement, whose chief spokesman is Lawrence Kohlberg, a professor of psychology and education, and director of the Center for Moral Education at Harvard.

Values clarification, according to Sidney Simon, is "based on the premise that none of us has the 'right' set of values to pass on to other people's children." Its methods are meant to help students to get at "their own feelings, their own ideas, their own beliefs, so that the choices and decisions they make are conscious and deliberate, based on their own value system." The success of the values clarification movement has been phenomenal. In 1975 a study from the Hoover Institute referred to "hundreds perhaps thousands of school programs that employ the clarification methodology" and reported that ten states have officially adopted values clarification as a model for their moral education programs. Proponents of values clarification consider it inappropriate for a teacher to encourage students, however subtly or indirectly, to adopt the values of the teacher or the community. In their book, *Readings in Values Clarification*, Simon and his colleague Howard Kirschenbaum write:

We call this approach "moralizing," although it has also been known as inculcation, imposition, indoctrination, and in its most extreme form brainwashing. Moralizing is the direct or indirect transfer of a set of values from one person or group to another person or group.

The student of values clarification is taught awareness of his preferences and his right to their satisfaction in a democratic society. To help students discover what it is that they genuinely value, they are asked to respond to questionnaires called "strategies." Some typical questions are: Which animal would you rather be: an ant, a beaver, or a donkey? Which season do you like best? Do you prefer hiking, swimming, or watching television? In one strategy called "Values Geography," the student is helped to discover his geographical preferences; other lessons solicit his reaction to seat belts, messy handwriting, hiking, wall-to-wall carpeting, cheating, abortion, hit-and-run drivers, and a mother who severely beats a two-year-old child.

Western literature and history are two traditional alienating influences that the values clarification movement is on guard against. Simon has written that he has ceased to find meaning "in the history of war or the structure of a sonnet, and more meaning in the search to find value in life." He and his colleagues believe that exposure to one's cultural heritage is not likely to be morally beneficial to the "average student."

Because values are complex and because man's thoughts and accomplishments are both abundant and complicated, it is difficult to recommend that the average student rely on this approach. It takes substantial mental stamina and ability and much time and energy to travel this road. While the study of our cultural heritage can be defended on other grounds, we would not expect it to be sufficient for value education.

The values clarification theorist does not believe that moral sensibility and social conscience are, in significant measure, learned by reading and discussing the classics. Instead Simon speaks of the precious legacy we can leave to "generations of young people if we teach them to set their priorities and rank order the marvelous items in life's cafeteria."

As a college teacher coping with the motley ideologies of high school graduates, I find this alarming. Young people today, many of whom are in a complete moral stupor, need to be shown that there is an important distinction between moral and nonmoral decisions. Values clarification blurs the distinction. Children are queried about their views on home-made Christmas gifts, people who wear wigs, and whether or not they approve of abortion or would turn in a hit-and-run driver as if no significant differences existed among these issues.

It is not surprising that teachers trained in neutrality and the principled avoidance of "moralizing" sometimes find themselves in bizarre classroom situations. In a junior high school in Newton, Massachusetts, a teacher put on the blackboard a poster of a Hell's Angel wearing a swastika. The students were asked to react. "He's honest, anyway. He's living out his own feelings," answered one. "He's not fooling," said another. When the students seemed to react favorably to the Hell's Angel, the teacher ventured to suggest that "an alienated person might not be happy."

The following conversation took place between a values clarification teacher and her students:

STUDENT: Does this mean that we can decide for ourselves whether to be honest on tests here?

TEACHER: No, that means that you can decide on the value. I personally value honesty; and although you may choose to be dishonest, I shall insist that we be honest in our tests. In other areas of your life, you may have more freedom to be dishonest.

AND ANOTHER TEACHER: My class deals with morality and right and wrong quite a bit. I don't expect them all to agree with me; each has to satisfy himself according to his own conviction, as long as he is sincere, and thinks he is pursuing what is right. I often discuss cheating this way, but I always get defeated because they will argue that cheating is all right. After you accept the idea that kids have the right to build a position with logical arguments, you have to accept what they come up with.

The student has values; the values clarification teacher is merely "facilitating" the student's access to them. Thus, no values are taught. The emphasis is on *learning how*, not on *learning that*. The student does not learn *that* acts of stealing are wrong; he learns how to respond to such acts.

The values clarification course is, in this sense, contentless. As if to make up for this, it is methodologically rich. It is to be expected that an advocate of values clarification emphasizes method over content in other areas of education, and indeed he does. Many handbooks, strategies, board games, and kits have been developed to help teachers adapt the methods of values clarification to such subjects as English, history, science, math, and even home economics and Spanish. Values clarification guides for girl scout troops and Sunday school classes are also available, as well as manuals to assist parents in clarifying values at the dinner table.

Simon and his colleagues explain that it is useless and anachronistic to teach the student at a "facts level." In a history lesson on the Constitution, for example, the teacher is advised not to waste too much time on such questions as where and when the Constitution was drawn up. Undue attention should also not be given to the "concepts level," where, for example, the teacher discusses the moral origins of the Bill of Rights. When the learning of subject matter is unavoidable, Simon and his colleagues recommend that it be lifted to a higher and more urgent level where students are asked "you-centered" questions, such as, "What rights do you have in your family?" Or, "Many student governments are really token governments controlled by the 'mother country,' i.e., the administration. Is this true in your school? What can you do about it?" And, "When was the last time you signed a petition?"

The classical moral tradition will not be revived by the practitioners of values clarification. Indeed, it is, in their eyes, an alien tradition that is insensitive to the needs and rights of the contemporary student.

II

Lawrence Kohlberg, the leader of the second major movement in moral education, shares with values clarification educators a low opinion of traditional morality. In his contribution to Theodore and Nancy Sizer's anthology, *Moral Education*, he writes, "Far from knowing whether it can be taught, I have no idea what virtue really is." Kohlberg's disclaimer is not a Socratic confession of ignorance; he considers the teaching of traditional virtues to be at best a waste of time and at worst coercive. Like Sidney Simon, he, too, uses the language of conspiracy to characterize the American educational system. He refers often to the "hidden curriculum" and insists that the teacher must not be "an agent of the state, the church, or the social system, [but] rather . . . a free moral agent dealing with children who are free moral agents." Kohlberg cites as an example of covert indoctrination a teacher who yelled at some boys for not returning their books to the proper place. "The teacher would have been surprised to know that her concerns with classroom management defined for her children what she and her school thought were basic values, or that she was engaged in indoctrination." Kohlberg and his disciples are currently busy transforming some of the best school systems in the country into "just communities" where no such indoctrination takes place.

Kohlberg's authority derives from his cognitive developmental approach to moral education. Following John Dewey, Kohlberg distinguishes three main stages of moral development (each of which is partitioned into a higher and lower stage, making six in all). The first stage is called the premoral or preconventional reward/punishment level. In the second stage morals are conventional but unreflective. In the third stage moral principles are autonomously chosen on rational grounds. Kohlberg's research applies Piaget's idea that the child possesses certain cognitive structures that come successively into play as the child develops. According to Kohlberg, the latent structures are a cross-cultural fact of cognitive psychology. Kohlberg's more specific thesis on the unfolding of the child's innate moral propensities has received a great deal of deserved attention. The literature on Kohlberg is controversial, and it is far too early to say whether his ideas are sound enough for eventual use in the classroom. Kohlberg himself has urged and already put into practice pedagogical applications of his ideas.

From the assumption of innateness, it is but a short step to the belief that the appropriate external circumstances will promote the full moral development of the child. It then becomes the job of the educator to provide those circumstances "facilitating" the child to his moral maturity. The innate structures are essentially contentless, and Kohlberg and his followers do not think it is the job of the moral educator to develop a virtuous person by supplying the content—that is, the traditional virtues. To do that would be, in Kohlberg's contemptuous phrase, to impose on the child an "old bag of virtues." Kohlberg and his associate Moshe Blatt remark in the *Journal of Moral Education*:

Moral education is best conceived as a natural process of dialogue among peers, rather than as a process of didactic instruction or preaching. The teacher and the curriculum are best conceived as facilitators of this dialogue.

If moral education is to be a dialogue among peers, the relation between teacher and student must be radically transformed. Fully prepared to accept these consequences, Kohlberg, in 1974, founded the Cluster School in Cambridge, Massachusetts. It consisted of thirty students, six teachers, dozens of consultants, and Kohlberg—all of whom had an equal voice in running the school. According to Kohlberg, "The only way school can help graduating students become persons who can make society a just community is to let them try experimentally to make the school themselves." As he soon learned, these student-citizens were forever stealing from one another and using drugs during school hours. These transgressions provoked a long series of democratically conducted "town meetings" that to an outsider look very much like EST encounter groups. The students were frequently taken on retreats (Kohlberg and his associates share with the values clarification people a penchant for retreats), where many of them broke the rules against sex and drugs. This provoked more democratic confrontations where, Kohlberg was proud to report, it was usually decided that for the sake of the group the students would police one another on subsequent retreats and turn in the names of the transgressors. Commenting on the rash of thefts at the Cluster School, Kohlberg said, "At the moment there is clearly a norm in the Cluster School of maintaining trust around property issues. But there is uncertainty about whether the norm has [fully] developed." Since the Cluster School lasted only five years, this uncertainty will never be resolved.

In turning to the just communities, Kohlberg has consciously abandoned his earlier goal of developing individual students to the highest stages of moral development. The most he now hopes for is development to stage four, where students learn to respect the new just social order. His reasons are revealing. In 1980 in an anthology edited by Ralph Mosher, *Moral Education: A First Generation of Research and Development*, Kohlberg writes, "Perhaps all stage six persons of the 1960's had been wiped out, perhaps they had regressed, or maybe it was all my imagination in the first place."

The Cluster School has been the subject of a great many articles and doctoral theses. Careers have been advanced just by praising it. In Mosher's anthology one critic writes about the school:

Cluster School . . . in my judgment, is a unique secondary school environment, characterized by a respect and caring for persons and a determination to make the governance structure one in which students can experience the roles necessary for full participation in democracy.

From these remarks—and similar ones by others who visited Cluster School—you would never guess that the school was in shambles and just about to close. The school was racially divided; drugs, sex, and theft were rampant; and Kohlberg was fighting bitterly with the teachers. Here was a school —with thirty students and six exceptionally trained and dedicated teachers—that by any objective standard must be counted a failure. Yet in American professional education nothing succeeds like failure. Having scored their failure at the Cluster School, the Kohlbergians have put their ideas to work in more established schools. (For example, they now exercise a significant influence in such diverse public school systems as Pittsburgh, Pennsylvania; Salt Lake City, Utah; Scarsdale, New York; and Brookline, Massachusetts.)

Brookline High School in Massachusetts

provides a particularly sad example of the way the new ideologies can penetrate a fine high school. The school administration has been taken over by Kohlbergians who, with the help of federal funds, are trying to turn it into a "just community." To this end the governance of the school has been given over to the entire school community—students, teachers, administrators, secretaries, and janitorial staff. To make the process work smoothly, not all students are invited to the weekly "town meetings," just their representatives. But, because many of the two thousand or so students are indifferent, many student representatives are self-appointed. And a big problem is that most of the teachers do not attend (nor, of course, do tired secretaries and maintenance workers).

I attended one meeting with thirty students, five teachers, two student visitors from Scarsdale who are working with Kohlberg and studying the Brookline program in hopes of using it in New York, and two observers from the Carnegie-Mellon Foundation, who were there to investigate the possibility of making a film about the Brookline experiment for public television. The kids who participated in the meeting were charming and articulate, and the Carnegie-Mellon people were clearly pleased, and they will make their film. Like many educational experts who admire the Brookline town meetings, these observers are probably unaware that many of the teachers feel harassed and manipulated by the Kohlberg administration. So far, the participants in the town meetings—who are mostly teenagers exercising more power than they will ever be granted in college or graduate school—have voted to rescind a rule against Walkman radios on campus, to prohibit homework assignments for vacation periods, to disallow surprise quizzes, and they have instituted a procedure for bringing teachers who give tests or assignments that are too demanding before a "Fairness Committee." One teacher told me that the students had never asked for the powers they now enjoy. According to the teacher, the school authorities handed these powers over to students "for their own good." Just communities are Kohlberg's answer to the oppression exercised by established authority. Evidently, Kohlberg sees no need to question his assumption that established authority is intrinsically suspect. In any event, it is ironic that now, when teachers with authority are so rare, educational theorists like Kohlberg are proposing that authority itself is the evil to be combated.

Ralph Mosher, a Harvard-trained Kohlbergian, is the chief educational consultant to the Brookline High School. In his anthology he writes the following about the standards that had been in place:

Moral education, all the more powerful because it is "hidden," is embedded in the tacit values of the curriculum and the school. For example, the most worthy/valued student in Brookline High School is the one who achieves early admission to Harvard on a full scholarship. How few can accomplish this is obvious. Yet teachers, counselors, and parents put great, albeit subtle, pressure on the many to do likewise.... What the research [in moral education] has attempted to do is to make some schooling more just.

Mosher's attitude is instructive. Ideals, it seems, are not goals to aim for. They must be attainable by the majority of students. If any goals are set up, they must be ones to which most students can realistically aspire. For Mosher, vigilance against superimposing a hidden agenda with elitist bias is the order of the day.

Kohlberg's ideas have taken hold in the better schools, where one can still find a fair number of parents who can afford to hold attitudes against elitism. Should the public schools of Brookline, Cambridge, or Scarsdale fail to provide the education necessary for admission to the best colleges, those parents have recourse to some fine private schools in the neighborhood. In the meantime they can indulge the unexceptionable concept of a just community, whose egalitarian character is welcomed by those who find themselves uncomfortably well-fixed, particularly after the radical views they held in the halcyon sixties.

The values clarification and cognitive development reformers are well aware that they are riding a wave of public concern about the need for an effective system of moral education. Thus Mosher writes:

[A] high proportion of Americans (four of five in recent Gallup Polls) support moral education in the public schools. What the respondents mean by moral education is, of course, moot. Probably the teaching of virtues such as honesty, respect for adults, moderation in the use of alcohol/drugs, sexual restraint and so on.... Educators would have to exceed Caesar's wife not to capitalize on an idea whose time appeared to have come.

This last remark about capitalizing on the parent's desire for higher moral standards is disarmingly cynical. Naturally the public wants its "old bag of virtues," but educational theorists such as Mosher are convinced that giving the public what it wants is ineffective and unjust. The traditional moralists have failed (witness Watergate), so now it's their turn. Mosher's attitude to the benighted parents is condescending. No doubt for Mosher and Kohlberg, the morally confident leaders of the reform movement, theirs is the right kind of elitism.

The deprecation of moralizing common to values clarification and cognitive development theory has been effective even in those schools where the reforms have not yet penetrated. Increasingly nowadays, few teachers have the temerity to praise any middle-class virtues. The exception is the virtue of tolerance. But, when tolerance is the sole virtue, students' capacity for moral indignation, so important for moral development, is severely inhibited. The result is moral passivity and confusion and a shift of moral focus from the individual to society.

III

The student entering college today shows the effects of an educational system that has kept its distance from the traditional virtues. Unencumbered by the "old bag of virtues," the student arrives toting a ragbag of another stripe whose contents may be roughly itemized as follows: psychological egoism (the belief that the primary motive for action is selfishness), moral relativism (the doctrine that what is praiseworthy or contemptible is a matter of cultural conditioning), and radical tolerance (the doctrine that to be culturally and socially aware is to understand and excuse the putative wrongdoer). Another item in the bag is the conviction that the seat of moral responsibility is found in society and its institutions, not in individuals.

The half-baked relativism of the college student tends to undermine his common sense. In a term paper that is far from atypical, one of my students wrote that Jonathan Swift's "modest proposal" for solving the problem of hunger in Ireland by harvesting Irish babies for food was "good for Swift's society, but not for ours." All too often one comes up against a grotesquely distorted perspective that common sense has little power to set right. In one discussion in my introductory philosophy class, several students were convinced that the death of one person and the death of ten thousand is equally bad. When a sophomore was asked whether she saw Nagasaki as the moral equivalent of a traffic accident, she replied, "From a moral point of view, yes." Teachers of moral philosophy who are not themselves moral agnostics trade such stories for dark amusement. But it appears that teachers in other disciplines are also struck by the moral perversity of their students. Richard M. Hunt, a professor of government at Harvard University, gave a course on the Holocaust to one hundred Harvard undergraduates. In the course he was disturbed to find that a majority of students adopted the view that the rise of Hitler and the Nazis was inevitable, that no one could have resisted it, and that in the end no one was responsible for what happened. Hunt's teaching assistant remarked to him, "You know, I think if some of our students were sitting as judges at the Nuremberg trials, they would probably acquit—or at least pardon—most of the Nazi defendants." Professor Hunt has dubbed his students' forgiving attitude toward the past "no-fault history."

It is fair to say that many college students are thoroughly confused about morality. What they sorely need are some straightforward courses in moral philosophy and a sound and unabashed introduction to the Western moral tradition—something they may never have had before. But few teachers will use that tradition as a source of moral instruction: the fear of indoctrination is even stronger in the colleges than it is at primary and secondary schools. In a recent study of the teaching of ethics prepared by the Hastings Center, a well-respected institute for the study of ethical questions, the authors write:

A major concern about the teaching of ethics has been whether and to what extent it is appropriate to teach courses on ethics in a pluralistic society, and whether it is possible to teach such courses without engaging in unacceptable indoctrination.

And elsewhere in the same report:

No teacher of ethics can assume that he or she has a solid grasp on the nature of morality as to pretend to know what finally counts as good moral conduct. No society can assume that it has any better grasp of what so counts as to empower teachers to propagate it in colleges and universities. Perhaps most importantly, the premise of higher education is that students are at an age where they have to begin coming to their own conclusions and shaping their own view of the world.

It would, however, be altogether incorrect to say that the colleges are ignoring moral instruction. The spread of moral agnosticism has been accompanied by an extraordinary increase in courses of applied ethics. Philosophy departments, isolated and marginal for many years, are now attracting unprecedented numbers of students to their courses in medical ethics, business ethics, ethics for everyday life, ethics for engineers, nurses, social workers, and lawyers. Today there are dozens of journals and conferences, hundreds of books and articles, and—according to the Hastings Center—eleven thousand college courses in applied ethics.

The new interest in applied ethics is itself a

phenomenon to be welcomed. Public discussions of controversial issues will surely benefit from the contributions of philosophers, and the literature of applied ethics should be read by anyone who seeks a responsible understanding of topical issues. In reading the anthologies of applied ethics, a student encounters arguments of philosophers who take strong stands on important social questions. These arguments often shake a student's confidence in moral relativism. Nevertheless, the literature of applied ethics, like the literature of values clarification and cognitive moral development, has little or nothing to say about matters of individual virtue. The resurgence of moral education in the college thus reinforces the shift away from personal morals to an almost exclusive preoccupation with the morality of institutional policies. After all, most students are not likely to be involved personally in administering the death penalty or selecting candidates for kidney dialysis; and, since most will never do recombinant DNA research, or even have abortions, the purpose of the courses in applied ethics is to teach students how to form responsible opinions on questions of social policy. A strong ethical curriculum is a good thing, but a curriculum of ethics without virtue is a cause for concern.

The applied ethics movement in the universities started in the late nineteen sixties when philosophers became interested once again in normative ethics. Between 1940 and 1968 ethics had been theoretical and methodologically self-conscious, to the relative neglect of practical ethics. A large number of philosophers emerged from the sixties eager to contribute to national moral debates. But like Simon, Kohlberg, and their followers, these philosophers were suspicious and distrustful of moralizing and deeply averse to indoctrination. It is no small feat to launch a powerful and influential movement in normative ethics without recourse to the language of vice and virtue and a strong notion of personal responsibility, but that is exactly what is being attempted. The new university moralists, uncomfortable and ideologically at odds with the discredited middle-class ethic, are making their reform movement succeed by addressing themselves, not to the vices and virtues of individuals, but to the moral character of our nation's institutions. Take a look at almost any text used today in college ethics courses—for example, *Ethics for Modern Life*, edited by R. Abelson and M. Friquegnon, *Today's Moral Problems*, edited by R. Wasserstrom, or *Moral Problems* by J. Rachels—and you will find that almost all of the articles consist of philosophical evaluations of the conduct and poli-

cies of schools, hospitals, courts, corporations, and the United States government.

Inevitably the student forms the idea that applying ethics to modern life is mainly a question of learning how to be for or against social and institutional policies. Appropriately enough, many of the articles sound like briefs written for a judge or legislator. In that sort of ethical climate, a student soon loses sight of himself as a moral agent and begins to see himself as a moral spectator or a protojurist. This is not to deny that many of the issues have an immediate personal dimension. They do, but the primary emphasis is not on what one is to do as a person but on what one is to believe as a member of society—in other words, on ideology and doctrine rather than on personal responsibility and practical decency.

The move to issue-oriented courses is hailed as a move back to the days when moral instruction played a significant role in education. Nothing could be further from the truth. Where Aristotle, Aquinas, Mill, and Kant are telling us how to behave, the contemporary university moralist is concerned with what we are to advocate, vote for, protest against, and endorse. Michael Walzer has compared the applied ethics movement to the scholarly activities of the Greek Academicians, the Talmudists, and the medieval Casuists. The comparison is inept, for those earlier moralists were working in a tradition in which it was assumed that the practical end of all moral theory was the virtuous individual. The ancient sophist, with his expertise in rhetoric and politics, is a more convincing analogue to the teachers of issue-oriented ethics, who find little time for the history of ethical theory with its traditional emphasis on the good and virtuous life. One may therefore be wary of the widespread enthusiasm for the "exciting new developments" in the teaching of ethics. Especially misleading is the frequent observation that the revival of interest in practical ethics is a great advance over the earlier preoccupation with evaluative language (meta-ethics). Admittedly the preoccupation with meta-ethics that characterized the teaching of ethics a decade ago left the student undernourished by neglecting normative ethics. But, in all fairness, neither students nor teachers were under any illusion that meta-ethics was the whole of ethics. Today the student is learning that normative ethics is primarily social policy. This being so, moral action should be politically directed; the individual's task is to bring the right civic institutions (the true moral agents) into place. The student tacitly assumes that ethics is not a daily affair, that it is a matter for specialists, and that its practical benefits are deferred until the time of institutional reform.

The result of identifying normative ethics with public policy is justification for and reinforcement of moral passivity in the student. Even problems that call for large-scale political solutions have their immediate private dimension, but a student trained in a practical ethics that has avoided or de-emphasized individual responsibility is simply unprepared for any demand that is not politically or ideologically formulated. The student is placed in the undemanding role of the indignant moral spectator who needs not face the comparatively minor corruptions in his own life.

How, finally, is one to account for the ethics-without-virtue phenomenon? A fully adequate answer is beyond me, but clearly there is a great deal more to the story than the national disenchantment with a system of education that "failed to prevent" moral lapses such as Watergate. A historian of ideas would probably take us back to romantics like Rousseau and to realists like Marx. George Steiner has written of this theme in Rousseau:

In the Rousseauist mythology of conduct, a man could commit a crime either because his education had not taught him how to distinguish good and evil, or because he had been corrupted by society. Responsibility lay with his school or environment for evil cannot be native to the soul. And because the individual is not wholly responsible he cannot be wholly damned.

The values clarification theorists can find little to disagree with in this description.

For social-minded reformers, justice is the principal virtue, and social policy is where ethics is really "at." The assumption is that there is an implicit conflict between the just society and the repressive morality of its undemocratic predecessors. An extreme version of this theme is presented in a little book edited by Trotsky, *Their Morals and Ours,* with it searing attack on the "conservative banalities of bourgeois morality." For Trotsky, of course, social reform requires revolution, but his indictment of the hypocrisies and "brutalities" of "their morals" must sound familiar to the Kohlbergians. The fate of those societies that have actually succeeded in replacing personal morality with social policy is the going price for ignoring the admonition of Max Weber: "He who seeks salvation of the soul—of his own and others—should not seek it along the avenue of politics."

An essay on contemporary trends in moral education would be incomplete without mention of the Moral Majority. I have refrained from discussing this movement partly because it receives a great deal of public attention compared to the relative neglect of the movements inspired by the New England professors of education. But I suspect another reason for my silence is my own dismay that at this moment the Moral Majority constitutes the only vocal and self-confident alternative to the ethics-without-virtue movement.

The Treatment of Religion in School Textbooks: A Political Analysis and A Modest Proposal

John W. McDermott, Jr.

Professor of Education, Moravian College (PA).

Surveys consistently show that teachers rely upon textbooks or other common resources for most of their course material. Because the textbook has always been such a staple of instruction, individuals and groups in every generation since the advent of the Republic have taken considerable interest in its content. Generally, they expect that their perspectives will be fully represented, and they object to the expression of ideas with which they disagree. As Edward Jenkinson has shown, this is a game that any number can play, and the points of view have been varied and frequently conflicting.[1]

Few issues have been more contested in the history of American public education than the role that religion should play in shaping the curriculum and the moral agenda of the schools. In the theology of public education, Horace Mann's attempt to establish a pan-Christian framework in nineteenth century schools yielded to the naturalism of the twentieth century progressives. In the past twenty years, the Supreme Court's attempts to resolve the issue on constitutional grounds have refueled the controversy over the intentions of the Founding Fathers concerning the role of religion in American public life. Whatever the particular ideological temper of the times, the schools have undoubtedly reflected the religious predispositions of their community sponsors. Because of this contentiousness, the public schools and the publishers who cater to them have become cautious about religious content and practice in the program.

Too cautious, some would say. Religious critics of the public school have responded in a wide variety of ways. Some have tried to strike compromises, urging such policies as shared time during which students may leave the school to attend religious classes. Some have persuaded Congress to support equal access for students and teachers who wish to hold self-initiated religious meetings on school premises. Some have sought to restore prayer and Bible reading, despite the Court's clear injunction against it. A number of these critics have sought to restore a commitment to the country's "Judeo-Christian heritage" to the public schools, or failing that, to establish a public policy that would eliminate the "state school monopoly" in favor or institutional pluralism and parental choice. A few have argued that the public schools and the books that support them are in fact religious and embody the doctrine of "secular humanism." Endorsement of the doctrine, critics claim, violates the spirit, if not the letter, of the First Amendment's establishment clause.

As the polemical tone of the criticism has increased, others less freighted with ideological baggage have been hard pressed to show how the importance of religion in American life can be appropriately included in the public school curriculum within the framework established by the Court. Unfortunately, the more doctrinaire religious critics do not appear to have the patience for such an undertaking, preferring instead to create a bogeyman out of "secular humanism" as a way to rally support for their entire political agenda, of which the school issue is only a part.[2]

TEXTBOOK STUDIES

Recently, however, several studies of the treatment of religion in public school textbooks have at least begun to define the problem in a way that can be addressed by scholars and teachers of different religious perspectives. Two of these studies—by Robert Bryan and Paul Vitz—have clear neoconservative or evangelical leanings, but that does not diminish their value or importance in calling attention to the problems of balance and perspective in the treatment of religion in school textbooks. Although others may well object to the stated and implicit assumptions of these two studies, leaping to the barricades will not help to resolve the issues that they raise. In fact, as we will see, a study supported by Americans United for the Separation of Church and State (Americans United), an organization with a long history of guarding against religious practices in public schools, has reached a similar conclusion concerning the treatment of religion in the curriculum, as has People for the American Way, an organization formed in response to Jerry Falwell and his Moral Majority. Clearly, the time has come to marshal the considerable knowledge that we already have about

From *Religion & Public Education*, Vol. 13, No. 4, Fall 1986, pp. 62-77. Reprinted with permission of the author and *Religion & Public Education*, the Journal of the National Council on Religion and Public Education.

119

the historical and contemporary place of religion in American life and show how textbook writers and curriculum developers can represent that knowledge in meaningful and appropriate ways.

Bryan, a Washington D.C. writer with a doctorate in ecclesiastical history from the University of London, conducted the first of these studies. In it he evaluated the treatment of religion in the secondary school social studies textbooks approved for use in Montgomery County, Maryland, a large and prestigious school district, affluent, suburban, and generally progressive.[3] His report, a slender, sixteen-page document, was published by LEARN, Inc., an education studies group whose officers, directors, and statement of principles reflect a clear, neoconservative bent.

Bryan concludes that all but one of the more than twenty textbooks surveyed must be "judged incompetent" in their treatment of religion "under even the most rudimentary standards of historical scholarship." Students who rely on these textbooks must conclude that Christianity has had no historical presence in America since 1700, Bryan asserts. He found no mention of revivalism or the cultural impact of the Great Awakening; no discussion of the role of religion in the Revolution, or in the anti-slavery, women's suffrage, or temperance movements; no discussion of anti-Catholicism or of the Catholic impact on politics and labor; and no discussion of the religious dimensions of immigration, including the persecution of non-Christians. Only the impact of Puritanism in colonial America is consistently discussed, Bryan observes, and that treatment typically takes on a critical cast. Underneath all this, Bryan detects a pervasive historiographic theme: the impact of religion in American history has been negligible, but to the extent that it has had any influence at all, that influence has been negative. The texts implicitly propound the thesis that America was settled to promote religious freedom, which, Bryan concludes, "means the absence of religion." Once the settlements are established and independence declared, he says, the texts suggest that "religion ceased to have any impact because the settlers escaped from it."[4]

Bryan concludes that even the modest attention given to religion is marred by oversimplification, anachronism, and discontinuity. Although textbooks tend to oversimplify most complex issues, anachronism and discontinuity particularly flaw the textbook treatment of religion. Bryan finds that textbook writers fail to interpret historical events in their contemporary context, but rather attribute to the past the attitudes, opinions, and prejudices of the present. Religious concepts such as Puritanism are identified with a particular historical period, but there is little recognition of their transformation and persistence throughout American history. The result, Bryan concludes, is a "that-was-then-this-is-now sense of history in which inappropriate judgments are made about the past from an inappropriate contemporary frame of reference, yielding an anachronistic view of the past which is often smugly judgemental." The students who read the textbooks are "drawn into a kind of conspiracy with the authors against the past" and leave their reading with a complacent contempt for their heritage rather than a heightened understanding of it. "With a knowing wink,

the textbooks draw [the students] to despise the past, and to mock it, as they [the authors] mock it." "Adolescents love to scoff at their elders," Bryan asserts. "These books invite them to indulge themselves."[5]

Not surprisingly, Bryan's conclusions are consistent with the conservative principles of his sponsors: He dwells on the textbooks' preoccupation with Roger Williams and Anne Hutchinson as martyrs in the cause of religious freedom. In so doing, he implies that the textbook writers have overemphasized religious freedom at the expense of settled beliefs, thus propounding a radical rather than a conservative view of history.

Bryan's analysis cannot be lightly dismissed as yet another ideological tract, however. Although his report is too brief to suggest in any detail how the religious dimensions of American history *should* be represented to secondary school students, it is clear that students of American religion must work to correct the problems of anachronism and discontinuity that Bryan identifies. Clarity and accuracy are particularly important in the study of religion, which is so easily distorted to serve special interests.

The second (and by now better known) analysis of religion in public school textbooks confirms Bryan's general findings and goes well beyond them. Working under a grant from the National Institute of Education, Paul Vitz, a professor of psychology at New York University, set out to observe how religion, religious values, the family, and family values are presented in public school social studies textbooks and basal readers. Clues to Vitz's frame of reference can be found in his earlier book, *Psychology as Religion: The Cult of Self-Worship,* in which Vitz presents a conservative, Christian critique of humanistic psychology and the "self-theorists"—Erich Fromm, Carl Rogers, Abraham Maslov, and Rollo May. Vitz assails their concepts and principles—which emphasize growth, autonomy, and change—as unscientific, socially destructive, and subversive of values such as duty, patience, self-sacrifice, and personal commitment.[6]

Since a summary of Vitz's report also appears in this issue of *Religion & Public Education* as well as in a recent issue of *The Public Interest,* I will only refer to the salient points here.[7] Like Bryan in his more modest study, Vitz tells a tale of neglect and distortion. Like Bryan, Vitz finds that the historical references to religion, to Puritanism for example, convey the sense that religion is old fashioned. The few contemporary references are slanted toward minority religions. Although textbooks acknowledge religion to be important in other cultures, its importance in our own is neglected. Children's readers typically neglect religion, Vitz finds, except for passing references in the context of Black or Native American life. All of this, he concludes, adds up to "the obvious censorship of religion":

> Those responsible for these books appear to have a deep seated fear of any form of active contemporary Christianity, especially serious, committed Protestantism. This fear has led the authors to deny and repress the importance of this kind of religion in American life. That is, for those responsible for these books, active Protestantism is threatening and hence taboo.[8]

When religious references "break through the secular censorship process," Vitz concludes, they reflect the principle of "distancing" by treating less controversial, minority religions rather than more threatening fundamentalist/evangelical Protestantism. Distancing involves emphasizing groups and practices long past, confining examples to distant cultures and places, and "washing out" religious references to people and events by neglecting to explore their religious significance.[9]

The questions that Vitz asks about the textbook's treatment of family values, sex roles, and politics reflect his conservative, Christian perspective. From this perspective, he finds the texts, for the most part, unacceptable. Although families play an important part in the texts for the primary grades, the texts appear to sanction the demise of the traditional family and of the "basic values" that Christian evangelicals and fundamentalists in particular have set out to affirm. Indeed, Vitz observes, the textbooks emphasize many types of families—some with single parents, some childless—with the implicit message that all are equally legitimate. He objects that "there is not one text reference to marriage as the foundation of the family."[10] Although he found "countless references to mothers and other women working outside of the home in occupations such as medicine, transportation, and politics," he could find "not one citation indicating that the occupation of a mother or housewife represents an important job, one with integrity and providing satisfactions." He objects to a tendency of the sixth-grade world cultures texts to project "a feminist emphasis" into the distant past. The readers also include articles about prominent women's rights advocates; but these, Vitz concludes, are at least "honest and straightforward in their purpose."[11]

On these and other matters, Vitz asserts, the texts and readers reflect "a clear partisan political character of a liberal bent." The historical and contemporary figures selected as political role models, he believes, are overwhelmingly identified with liberal politics and social reform:

> Examples of people never selected are: Robert A. Taft, Barry Goldwater, William Buckley, Jesse Helms, Jack Kemp; no neoconservatives, e.g. Irving Kristol; not one of the youthful breed of business entrepreneurs behind today's high tech business, Silicon Valley for example, was ever featured; indeed not a businessman (or woman) active since World War II was selected as a role model. Such conservative women as Nellie Gray, Phyllis Schafly, or Jeane Kirkpatrick were ever represented. And, of course, Billy Graham and Jerry Falwell were omitted.[12]

If the texts are to be believed, Vitz concludes, the nation's political agenda is limited to minority rights, feminism, and ecological and environmental issues. In particular, "there was no mention of the anti-ERA movement; the pro-life movement; or the tax revolt." In all of the children's readers he studied, Vitz was able to find only five stories "with any patriotic theme," and most of those were more feminist than patriotic.[13]

Finally, Vitz concludes, the tendency of textbook writers to underrepresent "our entrepreneurial business spirit" and the value of work is further evidence of their "liberal bent." There are no positive stories about business achievers, although, to be sure, there are no stories about labor or labor unions either. Despite his enthusiasm for entrepreneurship and the youthful denizens of Silicon Valley, Vitz objects to the association of work with money and status, an association that he finds running through the textbooks. What is lost, he asserts, is the spirit of voluntarism, "working out of concern for others or because of the intrinsic value of certain kinds of work." Clearly he has the "basic family values" in mind again and, in particular, the traditional roles of the housewife and mother.[14]

Although it is not a major theme in his analysis, Vitz further associates the textbooks' "liberal bent" with opposition to the concept of educational choice through tuition tax credits or educational vouchers. He notes that despite the emphasis on religious toleration and freedom elsewhere in the American history texts, the rise of Catholic and Protestant alternative schools is not mentioned. He attributes this neglect in part to a lingering anti-Catholic prejudice but mainly to the influence of "the present public school monopoly" and its fear of competition from the new Protestant schools.[15] Associating the church-related school movement with religious freedom would dignify the principal opposition to the monopolistic state schools. The fact that the textbooks neglect the alternative religious schools allows Vitz to build his case for the various parental choice initiatives. They are part of his call for Christian political action, including "the quiet but persistent, immediate but long-term withdrawal of support for the anti-Christian activities of the modern state," including public education.[16]

Clearly this is research for a purpose, and his conclusions have not gone unnoticed. Vitz, himself, has proposed a program for parents that links his NIE report to the call for Christian action outlined in *Psychology as Religion*. In a signed article in *Christianity Today* he asserts that "the minds of many children are being coerced against the will of their parents" by textbooks that "exclude the history, heritage, beliefs, and values of millions of Americans." He calls upon parents, PTA's, and others to demand that the textbooks be changed "to present a more truthful picture of America's past and present." Parents should "challenge Christian publishers to produce such books, and not only for Christian schools, but for public schools as well." But even this is not enough. Parents should have "greater freedom to choose their child's schools," Vitz asserts; "It would also support new publishers and more varied textbooks. We must finally recognize that the very pluralism of American life requires pluralism in American schools."[17] Vitz's proposed campaign to reform the religious content of public school textbooks is clearly an extension of his broader challenge to Christians to engage in a political response to institutionalized "selfist humanism" in American life, including but not limited to withdrawal of personal and financial support of "government-sponsored hostility to Christianity."[18]

Whatever one's view of Bryan's and Vitz's religious and ideological perspectives, their general conclusion that school textbooks neglect, obscure, and misrepresent the importance of religion in history and in contemporary life seems irrefutable. Vitz's religious frame of reference clearly draws him to certain themes in the textbooks and basal readers, but another frame of reference would probably not reveal a much more substantive and informed representation of religion. In fact, the study sponsored by Americans United—by Charles Haynes—of religious liberty in public school social studies texts has concluded that "the concept of religious freedom is largely ignored in the curriculum of our nation's public schools." Like Vitz, Haynes found that American history textbooks largely ignore the historic relationship between religion and education, the religious dimensions of American immigration, the significant religious awakenings, the emergence of new religious groups, the church-state debates, and other issues in American religious history. Although the sponsor of the Haynes study, the Research Foundation of Americans United, is unlikely to march behind the banner that Vitz unfurled in his *Christianity Today* article, the organization apparently takes little comfort in the textbooks' neglect of religion.

Although Haynes attributes the inadequate representation of religious freedom to neglect, Bryan and Vitz regard it as purposeful, that says more about their different perspectives than it says about the textbooks. All who examine the textbooks find them flawed.[9]

As Haynes' review indicates, religious conservatives are not alone in their concern about the representation of religion in school textbooks. Even more remarkable is the conclusion recently drawn by People for the American Way in its own review of history textbooks. Although the PAW study was not intended to evaluate the treatment of religion, the study team decided to go back over their research with this issue in mind. Anthony Podesta's introductory comment on their findings is strikingly similar to the conclusions of Vitz, Bryan, and Haynes:

> Religion is simply not treated as a significant element in American life—it is not portrayed as an integrated part of the American value system or as something that is important to individual Americans. The two themes which have been in tension since the earliest times—religious intolerance and religious idealism—are not recognized as essential to an understanding of the American character.[20]

THE DEPARTMENT OF EDUCATION'S INTEREST IN TEXTBOOKS

Textbook treatment of religion promises to be a major political issue for some time. It is no surprise that the Reagan Administration's Department of Education has taken a keen interest in the question. In the same issue of *Christianity Today*, the Secretary of Education, William Bennett, affirms that students cannot grasp our political and moral culture without understanding the important place of religious beliefs in the development of American society. Although he acknowledges limitations imposed upon the Department in the setting of curriculum, Bennett asserts the Department's obligation "to call attention to possible deficiencies." Perhaps with Bryan or Vitz's study in mind, he concludes:

> Its a problem when our textbooks do not acknowledge the central place of religion in the lives of Americans. Can one understand important American figures like Abraham Lin-

coln or Martin Luther King without understanding how their religious traditions influenced them?[21]

It seems clear then that Bennett's Department of Education intends to persuade others to redress what it regards as an ultraliberal bias in public school textbooks, particularly as it is reflected in the treatment of traditional values and the role of religion in American public life. Representatives of the Department have already encountered vigorous opposition. When Secretary Bennett and Under Secretary Gary Bauer appeared before the Education Appropriations Subcommittee of the U.S. Senate in April, 1986, Senator Lowell P. Weicker, the subcommittee chairman, was not persuaded by Bennett's distinction between setting curriculum and identifying deficiencies. In a heated exchange, with Vitz's study as a backdrop, Weicker charged the Department with violating a law which prohibits the Department from exercising "direction, supervision, or control" over school textbooks. This, of course, Bennett and Bauer denied (and, indeed, there is precedent for Department of Education interest in balance and perspective in the public school curriculum, in the studies of race and sex stereotyping in textbooks undertaken under the Women's Education Equity Act Program in the 1970s). The point to be made is that there are good reasons why the role of the Department of Education in curriculum shaping should be circumscribed, but there is equally good reason to address the issues raised on their own merits, putting aside the partisan clamor.[22]

CHANGING TEXTBOOK CONTENT— ALWAYS A CHALLENGE

If thoughtful observers, reflecting different views and commitments, now agree that religion is inappropriately excluded from the public school curriculum despite clear support from the Supreme Court's acknowledgement that such study in no way offends the separation of church and state, it should be possible to correct the neglect.

Therein lies the challenge. Vitz's study in particular takes aim at values education programs loosely related to the various schools of humanistic psychology popular in the 60s and 70s, the "self-theorists" that Vitz rejects in his book. Opinion has become so polarized on the subject, with the specter of "secular humanism" on one side and fears of theocracy on the other, that defining a place to stand between secularism and sectarianism has become increasingly difficult. Those who endorse objective, non-confessional, and analytic study about religions in the public schools risk offending those who object to having their deeply held commitments subjected to critical scrutiny and weighed against other views with which they so profoundly disagree. On the other hand, those who contend that the moral education of children cannot be separated from religious affirmation arouse the objection of those who guard the line between teaching religion and teaching about religions. Any attempt to remedy the neglect of religion in the public school curriculum must work to expand the presently limited room to maneuver between these positions.

Also at issue are differences over how the school curriculum should reflect the concept of pluralism. The conflict is often represented as arraying those who embrace the school as "a marketplace of ideas" against those who affirm that truth, confidently transmitted, is the key to personal freedom. In the first instance, pluralism is reflected in the right of children to experience diverse opinions and ideas and to fashion a personal set of values and commitments. In the second, a commitment to pluralism requires that parents have a reasonable chance to affirm and transmit their values to their children free from the coercive scrutiny of state-directed and approved curricula and without having to pay for alternative schooling. Vitz's appraisal and his subsequent comments clearly support the latter view.

Given the intensity of the controversy, it is easy to speculate on why publishers have neglected the role of religion in world affairs generally and in American public life in particular. There is at least anecdotal evidence to suggest that publishers engage in considerable self-censorship and go out of their way to avoid controversial issues that might limit their share of the market.[23] Vitz goes further and suggests that the neglect of religion reflects denial and repression, masking overt hostility to religion; but that may be more of an explanation than we need. On the other hand, Vitz's examples of the textbooks' treatment of gender and the family, even allowing for his selective vision, show that publishers will respond to social and political trends once their direction has become clear. By now there can be no question that textbook writers and curriculum developers have worked hard to reconcile their materials with the changing status of women and racial and ethnic minorities. Senator Weicker's criticism of the Bennett Department of Education reflects the concerns of many educators and liberal politicians that if religious conservatives and their political allies are able to rally support behind a conservative moral agenda, those who market textbooks in adoption states will once again respond.

Those who urge that textbooks be revised to acknowledge the importance of religion in history and public affairs have several problems to resolve. First, they must show textbook writers and publishers how such a revision can be done within the constitutional limits affirmed by the Supreme Court. Second, they must create an informed constituency among teachers, curriculum coordinators, school board members, and others who influence decisions at the state and local levels. Without this constituency, attempts to influence the publishers will be futile. Third, they must, or should, strive for changes that do not add to the problems of discontinuity, fragmentation, and revisionism in our textbooks.

While Vitz has not proposed a textbook rating system based on the text's treatment of religion and traditional values, his charge to textbook publishers in *Christianity Today* coupled with his tendency to characterize texts as "completely unacceptable," "slightly better," or "by far the best of those analyzed" could present an irresistible temptation for others to translate his findings into a selection list. Indeed, the use of rating systems by interest groups in adoption states has drawn considerable attention across the ideological spectrum. While such groups have every right to do so, the proliferation of rating systems, many of them conflicting, will do little to improve the coherence and quality of textbooks and will only make them even more like straws in the winds of political change.

LOCATING COMMON GROUND

If there really is a commitment to promote an understanding of the historical and contemporary role of religion in American life and in the world generally, ways will have to be found to transcend theological and ideological differences and define some common ground for textbook writers to explore. Certainly there is no lack of informed and accessible literature on the American religious experience upon which both liberals and conservatives can compare. Sydney Ahlstrom's *A Religious History of the American People* and Winthrop Hudson's *Religion in America* detail the events and themes in American religious history within the broader contexts of American social and intellectual history. Martins Marty's *Pilgrims in Their Own Land: 500 Years of Religion in America* is a superb interpretive synthesis, full of personal profiles and vignettes of the sort that lend life and humanity to the typically abstract and bloodless recitations of secondary school history. Marty's bibliography is also a useful guide to other such sources. A. James Reichley's *Religion in American Public Life,* written recently for the Brookings Institution, addresses the mounting tension between liberals and conservatives in its historical and philosophical context. Although there is room to challenge his interpretation of the 1st Amendment and the intentions of the Founding Fathers, reading the appraisal in the context provided by Ahlstrom, Hudson, Marty, and others should suggest countless ways to incorporate the role of religion into the most conventional American history or "American culture" textbooks.[24]

We might begin by taking seriously Robert Bryan's point about the discontinuity and anachronism that characterize most textbook references to religion. We need to recognize that our current differences over the role of religion in American public life generally and in American education in particular have their origins in the biblical and Enlightenment traditions in which our institutions are rooted. Indeed, the current controversy over the content of public school textbooks in Tennessee and elsewhere cannot be understood apart from that historical context, as Kenneth Strike has recently shown.[25] As Vitz, Bryan, Haynes, and others have noted, religion did not cease to be a factor in American life after the revolution: quite the contrary, as even a cursory consideration of immigration, anti-slavery, urban social reform, foreign policy, public education, religious revivalism, and the civil rights movement reveals. In coming to terms with the concept of religious liberty as Charles Haynes would have us do, we must also acknowledge the darker side of religion manifested at one time or another in anti-Catholicism, anti-Semitism, insensitivity to religious minorities and, yes, in a tendency to label rather than to respect the conscientious objections of those who want to protect their children either from the temptations and moral ambiguities of a secular society or from those who would impose their own theological stamp upon American public institutions. None of this is particularly new or particularly mysterious if we take some time to review the role that religion has played in American history.

Locating this common ground does require that we find ways to bring informed people together from different religious perspectives to explore areas of agreement and to clarify that upon which we disagree. Once again, there are precedents. The fury that followed the Schempp and Murray decision in 1963 caused informed and conscientious students of religion to organize and develop materials illustrating the legitimate study of religion in public education. Although the Public Education Research Studies Center (PERSC) at Wright State University ceased its operation some years ago, the National Council on Religion and Public Education (NCRPE) has preserved interest in public school religion studies and is presently working to revise and update some of the PERSC materials to make them available to teachers. Although the active membership in NCRPE is not particularly large, it continues to involve many of those who initiated the curriculum work of the 1960s and 70s. It is one of relatively few organizations that might serve as a focus for this reassessment.

The National Council for the Social Studies (NCSS) is another such organization with a much larger membership and greater visibility among publishers and curriculum developers. On at least two occasions, in 1969 and 1981, the NCSS journal *Social Education* devoted a special section to teaching about religion in the public school social studies program. It is interesting to look at these two sections again in light of the recent appraisals by Bryan, Vitz, and the others. Despite the quality of work on comparative or world religions and even on the Bible as literature, there is little on the American religious experience. The NCSS position on public school religion study is, at the moment, schizophrenic. For a number of years, NCSS has maintained a Committee on Religion in the Schools to advise its Board of Directors on policy and to remind teachers and administrators what the Supreme Court rulings prohibit and what they permit and encourage. In 1984, the Committee devised a Policy Statement and Guidelines which have become NCSS policy. NCSS also supports a Special Interest Group on Religion in the Schools which provides a focal point for teachers and curriculum developers with an interest in study about religion. On the other hand, as Charles Haynes has recently noted, the NCSS professional staff has thus far been reluctant to promote the development of materials on the study of religion as part of its own publication program. Like the textbook publishers, the NCSS staff needs to be persuaded that such a project can be undertaken without fragmenting the broad, national membership of NCSS. This act of persuasion might well be a task for the Committee and the Special Interest Group to undertake.

Over the last two years, NCRPE and the NCSS groups have rediscovered each other. Actually, the rediscovery was simply a recognition of their common purpose and, in many cases, overlapping membership. In 1985 the NCRPE annual meeting was held in conjunction with the NCSS annual meeting; and a similar, somewhat expanded joint effort is planned for 1986. Out of these joint meetings an active correspondence and the beginnings of some joint projects have grown. If a consensus in support of a more visible and informed study of the role of religion is to be built, such collaborative efforts will have to be fostered and others initiated.

Despite these hopeful developments, serious problems remain. Many of those who criticize the absence of religion studies in the public school program are in fact building a support for the endorsement of religiously oriented alternative schools and for a public policy that supports them through educational vouchers or tuition tax credits. These critics are unlikely to be satisfied with mere curriculum changes. Such changes, in the critics' view, should be only a part of a more extensive program that includes the restoration of school prayer and the recognition of Bible study and devotional groups as legitimate activities to be accommodated in school facilities and on school time. This agenda is vigorously opposed by those who affirm that religious liberty requires the separation of church and state. They would also resist an approach that exclusively affirms the Judeo-Christian roots of the American experience and inscribes a particularly conservative version of that legacy upon American institutions and public policy. If the textbook debate is nothing more than a metaphor in the struggle for political power, there is little hope that it can be resolved on its own merits.

On the other hand, we have these intimations of an alternative to arming the battlements and repelling invaders. We should support and be grateful for the efforts already undertaken by NCRPE and NCSS, and we should work to identify other organizations that may be inclined to support the effort. Sponsorship might be found for a small group of informed students of religion in America from a range of theological perspectives to build on the reports by Haynes, Vitz, and Bryan and show how we might address the glaring deficiencies in the materials that we have. There is a tendency for liberals to reach for their guns whenever a pronouncement comes down from the Bennett Department of Education, but the fact remains that Bennett and others have raised important questions about the moral and substantive drift of American public education, questions that deserve a thoughtful response. Although the Department must stick to its statutory knitting, it is also in a position to support reasonable attempts to address the ignorance and misinformation that Bryan, Vitz, Haynes, and others have helped to describe. Some will find the undertaking inadequate, and others will warn that it is the camel's snout under the tent of religious freedom, but perhaps the time is right to take the chance.

NOTES

1. Edward B. Jenkinson, "Schoolbook Skirmishes Leave Longlasting Scars," *Religion & Public Education*, 13 (Winter 1986): 18-28. Also Jenkinson's *The Schoolbook Protest Movement* (Bloomington: Phi Delta Kappa, 1986).

2. Three of many possible examples: Tim LaHaye, *The Battle for the Public Schools* (Old Tappan, NJ: Fleming H. Revell, 1983). Barbara M. Morris, *Change Agents in the School* (Upland, CA: Barbara M. Morris Report, 1979). Jon Barton and John Whitehead, *Schools on Fire* (Wheaton, IL: Tyndale House, 1980).

3. Robert Bryan, *History, Pseudo-History, Anti-History: How Public-School Textbooks Treat Religion* (Washington: LEARN, Inc., 1985). LEARN Inc., 655 Fifteenth St. N.W., Suite 310, Washington, D.C. 20005.

4. Ibid., 12.

5. Ibid., 7.

6. Paul C. Vitz, *Psychology as Religion: The Cult of Self-Worship* (Grand Rapids, MI: William Eerdmans, 1977).

7. Paul C. Vitz, "Equity in Values Education: Do the Values Education Aspects of Public School Curricula Deal Fairly With Diverse Belief Systems?" NIE Grant: NIE-G-84-0012 (Project No. 2-0099) Final Report. July 15, 1985, 1-4. Paul C. Vitz, "Religion and Traditional Values in Public School Textbooks," *The Public Interest* 84 (Summer 1986); 79-90.

8. Ibid., 13.

9. Ibid., 13.

10. Ibid., 35-38.

11. Ibid., 66-70.

12. Ibid., 66-70.

13. Ibid., 39, 66-70.

14. Ibid., 42.

15. Ibid., 29.

16. Vitz, *Psychology as Religion*, 112.

17. "Textbooks Flunk Exam," *Christianity Today* 30 (March 7, 1986): 15.

18. Vitz, *Psychology as Religion*, 106-114.

19. "Interview: Education Secretary Bennett: Redirecting a 200-Year Debate," *Christianity Today* 30 (March 7, 1986): 46.

20. "Senators Irked as Bennett and Aide Defend Textbook Reviews," *Chronicle of Higher Education* 32 (April 16, 1986): 13, 24.

21. Jim Buie, "Forgetting Religious Freedom," *Church and State* 39 (April 1986): 8-10. Charles C. Haynes, "Teaching About RELIGIOUS LIBERTY in American Secondary Schools," Typescript. Americans United Research Foundation Religious Liberty Education Project Study I. December 15, 1985.

22. O.L. Davis, Jr., et al., *Looking at History: A Review of Major U.S. History Textbooks* (Washington, DC: People for the American Way, 1986): 3.

23. Barbara Cohen details Harcourt Brace Jovanovich's attempt to delete religious references in her *Molly's Pilgrim* before including it in a third grade reader. Not an easy task in a story about the origin of Thanksgiving in the Jewish celebration of Sukkos. "Censoring the Sources," *School Library Journal* 32 (March 1986): 97-99.

24. Sydney E. Ahlstrom, *A Religious History of the American People* (New Haven: Yale University Press, 1972). Winthrop S. Hudson, *Religion in America* Third Edition (New York: Charles Scribner's Sons, 1981). Martin E. marty, *Pilgrims in Their Own Land* (Boston: Little, Brown, 1984). A. James Reichley, *Religion in American Public Life* (Washington: The Brookings Institution, 1985).

25. Kenneth A. Strike, "A Field Guide of Censors: Toward a Concept of Censorship in Public Schools," *Teacher's College Record* 87 (Winter 1985): 239-258.

Discipline and Schooling

Probably nothing creates more anxiety for preservice teachers than the issue of behavioral problems in public schools. Professors in teacher education programs must devote considerable time to the discussion of strategies or ethical behavioral management plans for use in public schools. While the need to control classes is unfortunate, it is a very real dimension of public schooling. Findings from federal research projects indicate that serious discipline problems still exist in schools today. The lead article of this unit details some of that research. Few problems influence the morale of teachers more than the issue of managing student behavior in the elementary and secondary schools. School discipline involves many moral, legal, and ethical questions. It is a highly value-laden topic on which there is a great diversity of opinion over what techniques of behavior management are effective and desirable. The essays in this unit respond to some of the concerns of inservice as well as preservice teachers on this issue.

Teachers' core ethical principles come into play in their efforts to decide what constitutes both defensible and desirable standards of teacher-student relations. As in medicine, realistic preventive techniques and humane but clear principles of procedure in dealing with issues seem to be effective approaches toward good student behavior. Teachers need to realize that before they control behavior they must identify what student behaviors they desire in their classrooms. They need to reflect, as well, on what emotional tone and what ethical principles are implied by their own behaviors. In order to optimize their chances for achieving the classroom learning atmosphere they wish to have, teachers must strive for emotional balance within themselves; they must learn to be accurate observers; they must learn the skills involved in hearing and/or seeing clearly what goes on in their classrooms; and they must build just, fair strategies of intervention for constructing the conditions for students to learn self-control and behavior management. A good teacher is a good model of courtesy, respect, tact, and discretion. Children learn from how they see other persons behave as well as from how they are told to behave.

Recent studies point out some effective preventive measures to minimize the incidence of serious discipline problems in the classroom. Researchers examine why disobedience and disrespect toward teachers are common in some settings but rare in others. They explore ways to reduce the level of hostility, violence, and disobedience in the more troubled school settings. Experts study teacher behaviors that may trigger or encourage disobedience. Some suggest that teachers would be able to control student behavior more effectively and humanely if they had more control over conditions and situations that often incite or anger students. In the interest of creating genuine and humane conditions of learning, educators are engaged in a critical reexamination of all dimensions of this issue. These dimensions cross socio-economic lines throughout the country; it is not just an urban issue.

Teachers are demanding the respect to which they believe all working people are entitled. They want safety, peace, security, a sense of pride, and the opportunity to practice their art in environments where that effort is appreciated. Nothing less than this is satisfactory. Nothing less should be. The National Education Association (NEA) and the American Federation of Teachers (AFT) are calling for public support of teachers in order to improve the quality of teaching and learning in the schools. Teachers must be treated with respect. This would indeed be a major turning point in American education. It is a goal worth seeking.

This unit can be used in conjunction with several sectors of basic foundations courses. The selections can be related to classroom management issues, teacher leadership skills, the legal foundations of education, and the rights and responsibilities of teachers and students. In addition, the articles could also be discussed in portions

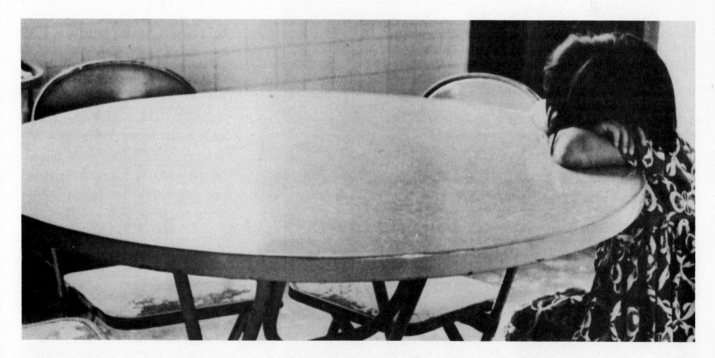

of the course involving curriculum and instruction or individualized approaches to testing. The unit falls between the units on moral education and equal opportunity because it can be directly related to either or both of them.

Looking Ahead: Challenge Questions

What reliable information is available on the extent and severity of school discipline problems in North America? What sources contain such information?

What are some of the best means for preventing or minimizing serious misbehavior in school settings?

What types of punishment are defensible in teaching?

What ethical issues may be raised in the management of student behavior in school settings? What specific authority should a teacher have?

What are some of the best techniques for helping someone to learn self-control?

What civil rights do students have? Do public schools have fewer rights for controlling student behavior problems than do private schools? Why or why not?

Do any coercive approaches to behavioral management in schools work better than noncoercive ones?

Does corporal punishment have a place in disciplining students? What are your reasons for being for or against it?

What are the rights of a teacher in managing student behavior?

Research Evidence of A School Discipline Problem

Illustration by: Joe LaMantia

Keith Baker

KEITH BAKER is a social science analyst in the Office of the Deputy Undersecretary for Planning, Budget, and Evaluation in the U.S. Department of Education. He helped prepare the Cabinet Council Report, Disorder in Our Public Schools, *and the congressional testimony that provided material for this article.*

Research indicates that the discipline problem in U.S. public schools is severe enough that it should concern educators, says Mr. Baker. The education community must face the problem squarely and take steps to improve conditions in the schools.

IF WE ARE TO improve discipline in our schools, we must first agree that a problem exists. Considerable research evidence indicates that the discipline problem in U.S. public schools is severe enough that it should concern educators for a number of reasons.

Crime and violence in the schools merit attention because they are socially undesirable. In a statistical sense, murder in the schools is not a big problem, because it does not happen very often. In a moral sense, however, even one murder is unacceptable. Crime and violence of any kind in the schools must always be a concern of educators. Even where the school crime rate is zero, educators must make sure it stays that way.

Schools in which the crime rate is high probably experience high rates of other, less serious discipline problems as well. Therefore, we can probably use the findings of studies of school crime to help us solve other discipline problems. For example, one of the major conclusions to emerge from the most extensive study of school crime and violence yet conducted is that school safety depends on clearly stated and fairly enforced rules of behavior. That is generally good advice, and its value is not limited to crime prevention.

Finally, educators must be concerned about the lack of discipline in the schools because an educational environment depends on good discipline. A study of inner-city schools in London used data collected over a number of years to show that, when children move from primary school (ages 5 to 11) to secondary school, their behavior and achievement are affected by school characteristics.[1] Students who transferred from behaviorally "bad" elementary schools to "good" secondary schools became good students and vice versa.

The relationship between good behavior and academic performance is shown in Table 1, which displays data from a nationally representative sample of 30,000 high school sophomores. For all types of misbehavior, there was a clear association between poor grades and misbehavior. For example, a student whose grades were mostly D's was nine times as likely as a student whose grades were mostly A's to have had trouble with the law, 24 times less likely to have done homework assignments, and about three times more likely to have cut classes.[2]

Drug abuse and drinking, which must also be numbered among a school's discipline problems, both have a debilitating effect on learning and are generally illegal — at least for young people. A reviewer of the literature on adolescent drug abuse concluded that problem drinking among teenagers is generally related to poor school performance, participation in antisocial activities, and lack of supervision.[3] A study of 367 high school students found that regular consumption of alcohol was associated with lower grades.[4]

A good climate for learning is a climate with good discipline. Fundamental to improving the quality of the schools is the maintenance of a degree of civil behavior sufficient to allow educational improvements to have a chance to succeed.

THE EXTENT OF THE PROBLEM

Eight years ago, the National Institute of Education (NIE) surveyed a nationally representative sample of principals, teachers, and students in secondary schools on the extent of criminal activity in U.S. schools.[5] Because many crimes are not reported to the police, a survey of the population of potential victims of crime provides better statistics on the scope of the problem than do court records or records

of police arrests. In fact, the NIE study, commonly referred to as the "Safe School Study," found that only about one in every 58 crimes that occurred in the schools was reported to the police.

According to the Safe School Study, the scope of criminal activity *each month* in America's secondary schools in 1976 was as follows:

- 282,000 students were physically attacked;
- 112,000 students were robbed through force, weapons, or threat;
- 2.4 million students had their personal property stolen;
- 800,000 students stayed home from school because they were afraid to attend;
- 6,000 teachers were robbed;
- 1,000 teachers were assaulted seriously enough to require medical attention;
- 125,000 teachers were threatened with physical harm;
- more than 125,000 teachers encountered at least one situation in which they were afraid to confront misbehaving students;
- one out of two teachers was on the receiving end of an insult or obscene gesture;
- 2,400 fires were set in schools;
- 13,000 thefts of school property occurred;
- 24,000 incidents of vandalism occurred; and
- 42,000 cases of damage to school property occurred.

These figures reflect what happened during a *typical* month in U.S. secondary schools. Over the course of the 1976 school year, there was more than one theft for every secondary school student and teacher in the United States.

Students as victims. As the NIE study showed, students are the most frequent victims of crime in the schools. In addition to the obvious undesirability of being

> Educators must be concerned about the lack of discipline in the schools because an educational environment depends on good discipline.

a victim of a crime, the crime rate in schools has an indirect, but perhaps even more serious, effect on students: crime in school teaches students to fear school.

A study of 1,200 families in Philadelphia found that 27% of the adolescents feared school grounds, 28% feared school hallways, and 22% feared their classrooms.[6] In a study of the Dade County, Florida, public schools, one-fifth of the secondary school students said that their ability to learn in the classroom was adversely affected by fear of other students.[7]

A detailed analysis of data from the Safe School Study found that in 1976 there were about 3.7 million fearful students in public high schools.[8] Almost 800,000 secondary students (8%) reported staying home from school for at least one day a month because they were afraid to go to school. Students who were afraid received lower grades and were more likely to rate themselves below average in reading ability. These students viewed schools as hostile places offering little promise of academic reward or personal safety. They

Table 1. Grades and Behavior of a Sample Of High School Sophomores

Type of Misbehavior	Grades			
	Mostly A's	Mostly B's	Mostly C's	Mostly D's
Average days absent per semester	2.28	2.99	4.20	7.87
Average days late per semester	2.05	3.12	4.41	6.44
Percentage of sample not doing assigned homework	1.10	2.73	6.27	24.72
Percentage of sample who cut a class during the school year	28.73	43.39	58.15	67.21
Percentage of sample who have been in serious trouble with the law	1.62	2.93	7.37	14.06

*Source: Thomas DiPrete, Chandra Muller, and Nora Shaeffer, *Discipline and Order in American High Schools* (Washington, D.C.: National Center for Education Statistics, 1981).

were more likely than nonfearful students to think that teachers were unable to maintain order or to hold students' interest. Apprehensive students were more likely to dislike their schools, their teachers, and their fellow students. The authors of the study pointed out that fear among students reduces their ability to concentrate on schoolwork, creates an atmosphere of hostility and mistrust in school, undermines morale, and teaches that the staff is not in control — that "student disorder is more powerful than the adult call for order."

The Safe School Study found that students from minority groups were generally much more likely to be victims of crime than were white students. Consistent with this finding, in 1982 the Gallup Poll found that members of minority groups were more concerned about school crime than whites were. While 68% of white respondents thought that the discipline problem in the schools was very serious or fairly serious, 81% of nonwhite respondents believed this to be the case.[9]

Students can victimize themselves, too. Alcohol and drug abuse are examples of so-called victimless crimes, in which the victim is the perpetrator. Students' abuse of alcohol and drugs is widespread. As the Third Special Report to the U.S. Congress on Alcohol and Health noted:

A national survey of students in grades 7 through 12 found 74% of the teenagers were drinkers . . . [and] nearly 19% of the students were problem drinkers — 23% of the boys and 15% of the girls.

Approximately two-thirds of high school seniors report ever having used any illicit drug — 60% marijuana, 39% an illicit drug other than marijuana. Six in 10 have used marijuana at least once; one in two use it daily.[10]

Teachers as victims. For many teachers, school has become a hazardous environment and a place to fear. Many teachers face situations in which self-preservation, not teaching, becomes their major concern. For example, a teacher in New Orleans watched while two boys threw a smaller student off a second-floor balcony. The teacher chose not to intervene, lest she, too, be attacked. Other teachers are not so lucky. In Los Angeles, high school girls who were angry about their grades tossed lighted matches into their teacher's hair, setting it on fire. Subsequently, the teacher suffered an emotional collapse.

But criminal acts are only part of the problem that confronts teachers daily in their classrooms. Generally uncivil behavior by students is one of the major causes of teacher burnout. In one survey, 58% of the teachers polled reported that "individual students who continually mis-

---

Table 2. Number of Teachers Who Would Not Go into Teaching Again, by Experience with Discipline Problems

Discipline Problem	Number of Teachers Who Would Not Go into Teaching Again for Every 100 Who Would
Had students with six or more chronic behavior problems	146
Misbehavior interfered with teaching to a great extent	183
School's disciplinary policy not clear	132
School's disciplinary policy not strict enough	131
Personal property damaged or stolen	192
Attacked by a student	184

Source: National Education Association, *Teacher Opinion Poll* (Washington, D.C.: NEA, 1980).

---

behave" are the primary cause of job-related stress.[11]

Teacher burnout is a major problem in U.S. schools. More than 90% of 1,282 teachers surveyed in one study had experienced feelings of burnout, and 85% of 7,000 teachers surveyed in another study felt that there were chronic health problems related to teaching. Nearly half (40%) of the teachers responding said that they took prescription drugs to treat job-related illness. In another study of 5,000 Chicago teachers, more than half reported having had some job-related illness.[12]

The stress of teaching led one psychiatrist to compare teaching to war, calling teacher burnout a type of "combat neurosis." In another study, Alfred Bloch and Ruth Bloch reported having treated 575 teachers psychiatrically over a seven-year span.[13] All the treated teachers shared two characteristics: they reported that school was an extremely stressful environment and that violence at school was out of control.

Job-related stress drives teachers out of teaching. *Learning* magazine surveyed more than 1,000 teachers, almost one-quarter of whom said that they were planning to leave teaching because of burnout.[14] The National Education Association (NEA) asked active teachers if they would go into teaching again if they had the chance to begin anew.[15] Table 2 shows that teachers who would not go into teaching again were much more likely to have experienced discipline problems than were teachers who would go into teaching again.

Elementary school teachers in the NEA poll reported just as much on-the-job stress as did high school teachers. This finding raises an important point that is often overlooked in the public debate over the lack of discipline in the schools: the

problem is not confined to urban high schools. In fact, the NEA teacher poll found that elementary school teachers generally reported *more* interference with their teaching from student misbehavior than did high school teachers. Half of all elementary school teachers in the U.S. reported that student misbehavior interfered with their teaching to a moderate or great extent. Very few (7.7%) elementary teachers reported having no problems with student misbehavior.

Of course, there are obvious differences in the types of misbehavior encountered in the high schools and in the elementary schools. High school teachers are more likely to encounter criminal acts. However, an impromptu game of tag in a second-grade classroom can more seriously disrupt learning for an entire class than a single act of violence on the school grounds.

The NEA poll suggests that student misbehavior interferes more with teaching in the elementary schools than in the high schools. Yet more serious misbehavior — especially criminal acts — occurs in the secondary schools.

Is this a contradiction? Probably not. In many high school classrooms teachers and students have worked out a compromise, a tacit understanding that allows them to coexist in a state of truce. The teacher "agrees" to let troublesome students sit in the back of the room, read comic books, and ignore the lesson. In return, these students tacitly agree not to disrupt the class — at least not too often. The teacher then addresses the lesson only to those students who want to pay attention and ignores the others.

Elementary school teachers do not do this. They are more likely to insist that all students pay attention to the lesson. Consequently, elementary teachers face a

Criminal acts are only part of the problem. Generally uncivil behavior by students is one of the major causes of teacher burnout.

more persistent battle with disruptive students.

Taxpayers as victims. Although teachers and students are the most direct victims of classroom disorder, taxpayers are also victimized. The Safe School Study found that each month there were 2,400 acts of arson, 13,000 thefts of school property, 24,000 incidents of vandalism, and 42,000 cases of damage to school property. The National Parent/Teacher Association (PTA) has observed that the annual cost of vandalism — probably in excess of $600 million — exceeds the nation's total spending for textbooks.[16]

TRENDS OVER TIME

As I pointed out above, the most comprehensive data on the extent of school crime come from the Safe School Study and were collected in 1976. Since then, many schools have undertaken programs to reduce school crime and to improve discipline. What has happened during the past eight years?

Deciding whether the problem is getting better or worse is difficult because so few trend data exist. Here I will review two kinds of data: 1) trend data from those few areas for which such data exist and 2) the most recently available data, which, though not nationally representative, provide a picture of the current situation in various parts of the U.S.

Oliver Moles analyzed two sets of data that permit national trends to be established over several years.[17] Using the NEA teacher poll, Moles examined teachers who were victims of assault and property damage between 1972 and 1983 and teachers who were victims of theft between 1978 and 1983. He reported that there were more attacks on teachers during the period from 1979 through 1983 than in the period from 1972 to 1978. Property damage held more or less constant during the same period, except for peaks in 1972

and 1979. Except for a peak in 1979, theft held fairly constant.

Moles used the Department of Justice's crime victimization surveys to study crimes against students and argued that these surveys do not give accurate estimates of the *level* of school crime. However, they can be used to assess trends, since the bias in the data should be the same each year. The crime victimization surveys contain data from 1973 through 1980 on both completed and attempted assaults, thefts, and robberies. Moles concluded that completed assaults rose between 1973 and 1978, dipped in 1979, and then returned to the 1978 level. Attempted assaults were stable over the eight-year period. Theft, the crime most frequently reported by students, declined steadily over the period. The number of reported robberies in several years was too small to permit meaningful analysis.

A comparison of data from 1976 with Moles's data from 1980 shows that assaults on teachers increased by 59% and theft of teachers' property increased by 46%. Completed assaults against students rose by 13%, but attempted assaults declined by 17%. Completed thefts against students dropped by 60%, and attempted thefts fell by 43%.

Another source of information on the changing pattern of school discipline problems is a question from the NEA teacher poll that asked the extent to which teachers find that student misbehavior interferes with their ability to teach. From 1980 through 1983 this question was asked in the same way. The results, displayed in Table 3, suggest some decline in the proportion of teachers complaining of moderate to great interference and a corresponding increase in the proportion of teachers saying that student misbehavior interfered with their teaching to a small extent. The proportion of teachers who reported no behavior problems remained roughly constant at about 10% of all teachers.

From these studies, what can we conclude about the trends in discipline prob-

lems since 1976? The picture is confusing. There have been increases in the incidence of some crimes — most notably crimes against teachers — and declines in the incidence of other crimes — most notably thefts against students.

On balance, the data suggest a slight overall improvement. However, it must also be noted that considerable year-to-year variations exist in many of these statistics and that, with the exception of thefts against students from 1973 to 1980, there are no clear-cut trends. On the one hand, it is encouraging to see any indication of improvement. On the other hand, it is discouraging to see that the improvement is so small, especially in light of the extensive efforts of many schools to cope with the problem.

A second way to update the data from the Safe School Study is to examine the most recent data available from school districts and states to see if they are currently experiencing problems. In 1983 the *Detroit Free Press* conducted a survey of teachers across Michigan and found that, during the last school year, 46% of all teachers in the state had been threatened with violence — including 23% who had been threatened by parents of their students.[18] One out of five teachers (19%) had been hit by a student, while 3% had been hit by an intruder and 3% had been hit by a parent. Two out of three teachers said that unmotivated and undisciplined students were a serious problem in their classrooms. One middle school teacher included a can of Mace among her basic teaching supplies.

A study of California schools over a five-month period in 1981 found 100,000 incidents of violence, with an average of 24 teachers and 215 students assaulted every day. Property damage during the five months was $10 million.[19]

The National School Boards Association reported on a 1983 study of crime in seven school districts across the U.S.[20] More than 10% of the students in four of the seven districts admitted breaking windows in school buildings. From 6.6% to

Table 3. Extent to Which Student Misbehavior Interferes with Teaching

Degree of Interference	1979 %	1980 %	1981 %	1982 %	1983 %
Great	16.8	20.9	23.2	17.0	14.5
Moderate	23.1	32.9	28.9	29.8	30.4
Small	33.9	37.7	37.5	42.9	46.0
None	26.2*	8.5	10.4	10.2	9.1
N	1,768	1,731	1,257	1,310	1,467

*In 1979 this response category was "little, if at all."
Source: National Education Association, *Teacher Opinion Poll* (Washington, D.C.: NEA, 1979, 1980, 1981, 1982, 1983).

5. DISCIPLINE AND SCHOOLING

> Teachers who function as baby sitters or police officers are not teaching. Students whose teachers do not teach cannot learn.

21.7% of the students in the districts admitted stealing from other students' desks. The proportion of students in each district who reported that they had been victims of such thefts ranged from a low of 42.6% to a high of 72.2%. Between 5.5% and 19.5% of the students reported being victims of physical attacks. A total of 16.4% of the teachers in the seven districts reported that students verbally abused them and swore at them. In one city, 80% of the teachers reported being the victims of verbal abuse.

Boston established a Safe Schools Commission that interviewed 495 high school students from four Boston high schools and found a "disturbingly large amount of victimization"[21] — including the fact that 38% of all Boston high school students had been victims of robbery, assault, or larceny during the previous school year and that incidents occurred at the rate of 63 per 100 students. This is one of the few studies to have differentiated victimization rates (the number of victims during some specified period) from rates of incidence (the number of crimes committed). The difference between the two shows that a large proportion of victims were victimized more than once.

Half of the students reported racial harassment. More than one in four students (28%) said that they were fearful at school on occasion, and 36% said that they avoided some places at school from fear for their personal safety. Twenty-eight percent of Boston high school students admitted carrying weapons to school.

Another study for the Boston Safe Schools Commission surveyed a representative sample of 874 Boston public school teachers and found that half of them had been victimized at least once on school property during the previous year; 11.6% had been victimized five or more times.[22] One out of three Boston teachers (32%) claimed to be afraid or extremely

afraid while at school. Theft and vandalism were considered to be very widespread by 19% of the teachers, and 12% said that drug use was very widespread.

For the 1982-83 school year, the Los Angeles Unified School District reported 13,154 violations of the law (down 4% from the year before) and property losses totaling $5,824,784 (down 11% from the year before).[23]

Nationally, the 1983 NEA teacher poll reported that during the preceding school year 28% of all teachers had personal property stolen or damaged at school. During the same period, 4.2% had been attacked by students.

To repeat an important point, crime statistics are the best available data, but they represent only part of the problem. Noncriminal misbehavior probably has a far more serious negative impact on the educational process. In the 1983 NEA teacher poll, very few teachers (less than 10%) reported *no* deleterious effects on their teaching from student misbehavior. By contrast, 14.5% reported that misbehavior interfered with their ability to teach to a great extent, 30.4% reported moderate problems, and 46% reported interference to a small extent.

In Boston, 28% of the teachers thought discipline was a very severe or an extremely severe problem in their schools; this figure includes 17% of elementary teachers and 36% of middle school teachers.[24] Thirty percent of the Boston teachers thought that persistent disruption of classes was very widespread, and 23% said that verbal abuse was very widespread. Elementary and high school teachers classified 8% of their students as severe discipline problems, while middle school teachers reported that 15% of their students were severe discipline problems. More than half of the teachers (53%) disagreed or strongly disagreed with the statement that "student troublemakers are kept in line."

From this brief rundown of studies that can be used to update the findings of the Safe School Study, we can conclude that lack of discipline continues to be a

serious problem in U.S. schools. Even if there has been some modest improvement since 1976, the current level of discipline problems — especially the level of disruptive behavior in the classroom — is a major problem for public education.

LEARNING IS THE MOST IMPORTANT VICTIM

From an educational perspective, the most important victim of student misbehavior is learning. Students in a drunken or drugged stupor cannot learn. Fighting students cannot learn. Students playing tag or being generally boisterous in the classroom cannot learn. Imagine what happens to the time spent on learning tasks when teachers spend between 30% and 80% of their time addressing discipline problems.[25]

In most cases, the educational consequences of student misbehavior go beyond the effects on the individual misbehaving student. When a third-grade teacher has to interrupt a reading lesson to stop an impromptu game of tag involving only two students, the education of the entire class suffers. When teacher burnout resulting from the stress of coping with ill-mannered students reduces a teacher's classroom effectiveness or drives a good teacher out of teaching, every one of that teacher's students suffers. When crime and violence create an atmosphere of fear and hostility at school, the efficiency of the education of all students is impaired. Teachers who function as baby sitters or police officers are not teaching. Students whose teachers do not teach cannot learn.

In the study of Boston teachers, teachers were asked their opinion of students. Teachers who had been victims of violence were much more likely than nonvictims to have negative attitudes toward *all* students in their classrooms. Victimized teachers were more likely to think that their students had severe behavior problems, were underachievers, or had minor behavior problems. Victimized teachers thought their students were less interested in school, less likely to have high ability,

Table 4. Percentage of Students Inclined Toward Unethical Behavior, by Victimization by School Crime

If You Could Get Away with It, Would You:	Attack		Robbery	
	Victims	Nonvictims	Victims	Nonvictims
Cheat on a test?	23	19	25	19
Spray-paint school walls?	10	4	11	4
Take money from other students?	9	4	9	4
Skip school?	28	24	27	24

Source: National Institute of Education, *Violent Schools, Safe Schools: The Safe School Study Report to the Congress, Vol. 1* (Washington, D.C.: NIE, 1978).

and more likely to have low ability. The research literature has demonstrated that teachers' expectations of students are related to students' performance. Therefore, victimizing a teacher may indirectly affect the learning of all of that teacher's students.

Children also learn from the misbehavior of others. They learn that authority cannot or will not protect them. They learn to be afraid of school. They learn that adults fear children. They learn that crime does indeed pay, as every day they see other students who rob, steal, talk back, fight, or refuse to do homework — yet are not punished. In such a climate, it should not be surprising that ethical standards of students suffer. The Safe School Study showed that victims of attacks or robberies in high schools were more inclined toward unethical behavior than were nonvictims (Table 4).

THE SCHOOLS' RESPONSE

The data reviewed above and the continuing public concern over school discipline suggest that the response of the schools to the discipline problem has been inadequate. This conclusion is supported by other data. For example, in the 1982 NEA teacher poll, three out of five teachers who had been physically attacked by students felt that the response of school officials was inadequate. In almost half of the cases, no significant disciplinary action was taken.

In addition to surveying students and teachers to determine the actual incidence of crime in schools, the Safe School Study also asked principals about the existence of crime in the schools. The contrast between the views of students and teachers and the views of principals is sobering. While teachers and students reported being victims of more than three million crimes a month, 75% of the principals claimed that crime was either not a problem or only a small problem in their schools. Principals acknowledged only 157,000 crimes and said that two-thirds of these were never reported to the police.

In Boston, 57% of the teachers disagreed or strongly disagreed that their principals were effective disciplinarians, 53% disagreed or strongly disagreed that student troublemakers were kept in line, and 43% felt that the school board was not at all responsive to teachers' concerns about their safety. Among elementary school teachers, 59% thought that suspensions were not used often enough.[26]

When students who commit *criminal* acts go unpunished, the merely unruly or disorderly students know that they have even less to fear. School administrators should pay heed to the National PTA's recommendation: "Students should be punished by the law when they are involved in assaults or violence."[27]

Why are school officials so reluctant to face the discipline problem? First, principals may be motivated to ignore or play down the problem out of fear of appearing incompetent and unable to control their schools. Before the problem can be solved, however, school officials must admit that it exists.

Second, many schools have failed to establish even minimal procedures for dealing with the discipline problem. In many cases, school officials do not know what is happening. Corrective action cannot begin until school officials know the extent and nature of the problem.

Third, many disciplinary actions are ineffective because they are inappropriate. For example, in one school, 45% of all suspensions were for tardiness or skipping classes. It seems obvious that suspending a student who has clearly indicated that he or she does not wish to attend school is more a reward than a punishment. In such cases, a Saturday detention might be more effective than a three-day suspension. Take another example. Many schools still use corporal punishment, though some research indicates that corporal punishment is relatively ineffective.[28] Schools must find more creative solutions to the discipline problem.

Fourth, a number of recent court decisions may have had a chilling effect on the willingness of school officials to enforce disciplinary standards.[29] It is not clear from the literature whether or not school officials have actually been hampered in their enforcement efforts by the actions of the courts or whether some school officials fail to act because they believe the courts have blocked them from acting. In any case, too many of them fail to act.

Fifth, laws and regulations have unintended consequences. To some degree, laws restricting the age at which students can leave school only exacerbate the problem of school discipline. Young people who are kept in school against their will probably create more discipline problems than other students. The U.S. Office for Civil Rights collects information on suspensions and expulsions and analyzes it for patterns of discrimination. Requiring disciplinary actions to be reported may also discourage school officials from taking action against misbehaving minority students (whose victims are also likely to be minority students). As a result, minority students may inadvertently become the victims of violation of their right to a safe school.

The American Association of School Administrators listed the following reasons for administrators and teachers to be reluctant to report crimes in school.[30] The list for administrators includes:

- to avoid bad publicity;
- to avoid blame;
- to avoid litigation;
- because they find some offenses too trivial to report;
- because they prefer to take care of the problems themselves;
- because they suspect that the police and the courts will not work with them; and
- to avoid appearing ineffective.

The list for teachers includes:

- to avoid blame;
- to avoid legal action;
- from fear of retaliation;
- because they are not sure who was to blame; and
- to avoid stigmatizing young people as criminals.

School crime and disorder pose major challenges to America's schools. An effective school system must maintain a level of civil behavior sufficient to allow learning to take place. The available evidence, though not complete, suggests that in far too many of our schools uncivil and even criminal behavior disrupts the learning process.

Although many schools have taken steps to improve their disciplinary climate, one continuing cause of the persistence of discipline problems remains: the failure of many educators and administrators to face the problem squarely, to recognize its importance, and to take steps to improve conditions in the schools.

1. Michael Rutter et al., *Fifteen Thousand Hours: Secondary Schools and Their Effects on Children* (Cambridge, Mass.: Harvard University Press, 1979).

2. Thomas DiPrete, Chandra Muller, and Nora Shaeffer, *Discipline and Order in American High Schools* (Washington, D.C.: National Center for Education Statistics, 1981).

3. M. T. Schmidt and L. D. Hankoff, "Adolescent Alcohol Abuse and Its Prevention," *Public Health Review*, vol. 8, 1979, pp. 107-53.

4. T. Bradley, "High School Drinking Habits Among Illinois Students," *Journal of Alcohol and Drug Abuse Education*, vol. 28, 1982, pp. 59-65.

5. National Institute of Education, *Violent Schools, Safe Schools: The Safe School Study Report to the Congress, Vol. 1* (Washington, D.C.: NIE, 1978).

6. Michael Lalli and Leonard D. Savitz, "The Fear of Crime in the School Enterprise and Its Consequences," *Education and Urban Society*, vol. 8, 1976.

7. Dade County Public Schools, *Experiences of Teachers and Students with Disruptive Behavior in the Dade Public Schools* (Miami, Fla.: Dade County Public Schools, 1976).

8. Ivor Wayne and Robert J. Rubel, "Student Fear in Secondary Schools," *Urban Review*, vol. 14, 1982, pp. 197-237.

9. George H. Gallup, "The 14th Annual Gallup Poll of the Public's Attitudes Toward the Public Schools," *Phi Delta Kappan*, September 1982, pp. 37-50.

10. Ernest P. Noble, ed., *Third Special Report to the U.S. Congress on Alcohol and Health* (Rockville, Md.: National Institute of Alcohol Abuse and Alcoholism, 1978).

11. Fred Feitler and Edward Tokar, "Getting a Handle on Teacher Stress," *Educational Leadership*, March 1982, pp. 456-57.

5. DISCIPLINE AND SCHOOLING

12. R. C. Newell, "Learning to Survive in the Classroom," *American Teacher*, February 1981.

13. Alfred M. Bloch, "Combat Neurosis in Inner-City Schools," *American Journal of Psychiatry*, vol. 135, 1978, pp. 1189-92; and Alfred M. Bloch and Ruth Bloch, "Teachers: A New Endangered Species," in Robert Rubel and Keith Baker, eds., *Violence and Crime in Schools* (Lexington, Mass.: D. C. Heath, 1980), pp. 81-90.

14. "Readers Report on the Tragedy of Burnout," *Learning*, April 1979, pp. 76-77.

15. National Education Association, *Teacher Opinion Poll* (Washington, D.C.: NEA, 1980, 1982, 1983).

16. James McPartland and Edward McDill, eds., *Violence in Schools* (Lexington, Mass.: D. C. Heath, 1977).

17. Oliver C. Moles, "Trends in Interpersonal Crimes in Schools," paper presented at the annual meeting of the American Educational Research Association, Montreal, April 1983.

18. Glen Macnow, "Violence Casts Pall over Teachers' Lives," *Detroit Free Press*, 19 September 1983, p. 1-A.

19. Kimberly Sawyer, "The Right to Safe Schools: A Newly Recognized Inalienable Right," *Pacific Law Journal*, vol. 14, 1983, pp. 1309-41.

20. National School Boards Association, *Toward Better and Safer Schools* (Alexandria, Va.: NSBA, 1984).

21. James S. Fox, *Violence, Victimization, and Discipline in Four Boston Public High Schools* (Boston: Safe Schools Commission, 1983).

22. Karen S. Seashore, *Boston Teachers' Views About Problems of Violence and Discipline in the Public Schools* (Boston: Safe Schools Commission, 1983).

23. Los Angeles Unified School District, *Statistical Digest (1982-83)* (Los Angeles: Office of Administrative Services, Security Section, n.d.).

24. Seashore, *Boston Teachers' Views*. . . .

25. Debbie Walsh, quoted in, "Our Schools Come to Order," *American Teacher*, November 1983, p. 14.

26. Seashore, *Boston Teachers' Views*. . . .

27. McPartland and McDill, *Violence in Schools*, p. 104.

28. J. H. Meier, "Corporal Punishment in the Schools," *Childhood Education*, vol. 58, 1982, pp. 235-37; and Irwin A. Hyman et al., "Discipline in the High School: Organizational Factors and Roles for the School Psychologist," *School Psychology Review*, vol. 11, 1982, pp. 409-16.

29. Julius Menacker, "The Supreme Court Smorgasbord of Educational Policy Choices," *Planning and Changing*, vol. 13, 1982, pp. 92-103; William Hazard, "Court Intervention in Pupil Discipline," *American Behavioral Scientist*, vol. 23, 1979, pp. 169-205; Edward A. Wynne, "What Are the Courts Doing to Our Children?," *Public Interest*, Summer 1981, pp. 3-18; and Larry Eberlein, "The Teacher in the Courtroom: New Role Expectations?," *Clearing House*, vol. 53, 1980, pp. 287-91.

30. American Association of School Administrators, *Reporting: Violence, Vandalism, and Other Incidents in Schools* (Arlington, Va.: AASA, 1981).

Punishment or Guidance?

Dan Gartrell

Dan Gartrell, Ed.D., is a professor of early childhood at Bemidji State University in northern Minnesota. He has been involved in CDA training since 1973.

When a problem situation arises with children, adults sometimes blur the distinction between punishment and discipline, and often do not think of *guidance* at all. *Punishment* implies the infliction of pain, loss, or suffering for a crime or wrongdoing. It connotes retribution rather than correction.

Punishment usually stops the unwanted behavior, but tends to have negative side effects. The child may harbor resentment that is shown in aggressive acts, "sneaky" behaviors, refusing to learn, or in other ways. The boy or girl may come to feel like a "problem child" and live up to that label—the self-fulfilling prophecy. Even if the child is more submissive after punishment, the "good" behavior may be the result of fear rather than of understanding what it is adults want done, combined with a decision to *do* it. The purpose of punishment appears to be to show children they are wrong. While punishment *is* a form of discipline, *discipline* suggests intent to establish habits of self-control. Punishment is not the most effective form of discipline because it does not guide children toward behaviors the adult considers *right,* and does not ensure that children *understand* what they are to do and how it is to be done.

Child guidance is another form of discipline (also termed *positive discipline, a self-concept approach to discipline*). Child guidance is a *process,* the process of assisting children to understand and use constructive behaviors. The goal of *child guidance* is to guide the child *by means of positive helping interactions* toward *self*-discipline, which has self-acceptance as well as self-control as its dynamic. The goal of child guidance is to help children develop positive self-concepts and healthy functioning consciences. This is the only way we can hope for responsible, caring, and creative adults. We want young people, as they develop, to say no, not because they might get caught, but because they have decided that to say yes is wrong. Such actions take faith in one's self, nurtured by caring adults.

Positive group management is a form of child guidance involving the adult and a *group* of children. The adult attempts to help each child feel that she or he is a worthy part of the group who *wants* to cooperate with it. The group's dynamics are used to this end.

Child guidance and positive group management require high level social skills of empathy and openness. These processes take commitment and practice. They deal with the young child's need to feel safe and secure, through personal acceptance, sensible limits, gentle correction, and genuine encouragement. They address behavior that needs addressing but respect the feelings of the child: This is the essence of a positive approach. A vast body of experience, research, and written material discussing positive discipline has been generated during the many decades since specialists began to focus on child development. By establishing the habit of regularly reading books and articles on childrearing and early childhood classroom practice (as the author has done) and of applying and practicing sensible ideas in our work with children, each of us can develop a positive discipline philosophy and an accompanying collection of approaches to implement it. Increasingly, early childhood educators prefer adult intervention that is guidance rather than punishment oriented.

Unless handled positively, discipline of *any* kind may be perceived by the child as punishment. Children of 3 to 8 years are still just beginning to learn the advanced skills of seeing things from another person's perspective, and even, sometimes, empathizing with other people's feelings. What may seem a *logical consequence* disciplinary action to an adult may be seen by the child as a personal rebuke. For example, to an adult, it is logical to have a child remove markings she or he put on furniture or a wall. In making the request, however, our tone may be accusatory and the primary learning on the part of the child may be shame.

The more the consequence is logical *from the child's point of view*, the closer we are to child guidance and the farther from a form of discipline that has the effect of punishment. Probably the child should wash off the markings, but maybe we should make the request after our temper has cooled. Or, perhaps, we can give start-up help, thus showing the child that we are still on her or his side. These actions make the consequence more like guidance and less like punishment. They correct but they also protect self-concept.

Be alert, use preventive techniques

Use foresight. Prevent potential problems. Good planning eliminates many discipline situations before they arise.

Structure activities and schedules so children can be active learners, and will not be bored into disruptive behavior. Effective teachers avoid prolonged adult-directed lessons or other nonactive "activities" that put children in a passive position.

Observe, head off trouble before it starts. A preventive approach means reinforcing effort and productive behavior rather than playing up what you dislike. It means offering encouragement and praise in ways children can accept and understand, and thinking twice about who needs reinforcement the most. As Jean Illsley Clark (1978) writes in *Self Esteem: A Family Affair,* "what you stroke is what you get."

Be a professional, not a technician. When teachers use preventive techniques, they are functioning as professionals, not as technicians. They make hypotheses about situations and children, try a course of action, learn from the results, and, if necessary, try another approach. These are things that technicians, working primarily by rote from fixed policy, find difficult to do. Effective teachers see themselves as professionals.

Build a relationship with each child. Use the relationship to help the child get through touch-and-go situations and potential crises. Obviously this step—building a friendship with each child—is the basis of sound discipline.

Use other preventive techniques as suitable.
- Recognize who will need extra orientation or encouragement in order to fully participate.
- Change activities when children seem bored.
- Reduce empty waiting times during transitions.
- Consider starting restless children in activities first.
- Use other adults in the classroom to reach children who are easily frustrated or distracted.
- Place children strategically when you really need to, but in low-key, matter-of-fact ways.

Seek to understand the individual child

In an attempt to understand children, adults must take into account ages, needs, and family situations of the individuals in their care:

Ages. Sharing, losing, waiting for turns, sitting for long periods—these are behaviors that are difficult for all 3s, most 4s and 5s, even some 6s and 7s. On such matters, the adult should try to adjust expectations to the child's development.

Needs. Children have similar basic needs, although they perceive and meet these needs in individual ways. Even if a child expresses a need in an extreme fashion, the need is real and is being communicated in the only way the child can express it at that time. Sometimes it is difficult to fully meet a need for security or affection, but this should *not* serve as an excuse for failing to *attempt* to meet the need. It is important to see the child behind the behavior.

Family situations. Though a child is in our care for many hours, she or he is in the family environment a good deal more. Family strains and crises do occur and they do affect children's behavior—sometimes in quite profound ways. As Jeannette Galambos Stone (1973) states in *What About Discipline?,* continued serious misbehavior almost always is the result of trouble in the child's life that goes beyond the immediate problem in the classroom.

The adult also works to recognize the "level" of the child's mistaken behavior.

Three levels of mistaken behavior

In seeking to understand the individual child, it is helpful to consider three different levels of mistaken behavior. For example, a behavior like swearing can have different meanings for children.

Usually the mildest form of mistaken behavior is the

experimentation level. At this level the child is trying things out to learn how they work and how the environment will respond. You walk by a child who is sitting alone saying to herself: "Ship, no; sip, no . . ." She comes upon the right pronunciation of the "no-no" word and smiles. If the child does not notice your presence, keep on walking. There is no sense needlessly stifling curiosity, problem-solving skills, and developing phonetic abilities. If the child looks at you, smiles, and says the word, respond matter-of-factly, "You've discovered a word. Some words we don't use at school, Mary. There are lots of other words you can use instead." Be kindly here and try to hide your smile.

The second level of mistaken behavior is the *social habit* level. Here children learn and use a behavior because they erroneously think it appropriate, because it has a peer payoff, or because in another context it *was* appropriate (it was common usage). On the first morning of Head Start, a teacher in a new community was shocked when three different children told her, "I got to shit, Teacher." After thinking for a moment, the teacher realized that these children were merely using the word that was used elsewhere in their lives to describe a bodily function. It was not a swearword. Level two mistaken behavior calls for good teaching. The child should be taught what else can be said, not simply punished for saying the wrong thing.

The third level of mistaken behavior is the *deep emotional needs* level. As mentioned, children at this level have trouble in their lives and are reacting to stress. Level three mistaken behavior often takes extreme forms of expression. We all have level three experiences once in a while. If extreme behavior continues, however, it is time for collective staff concern. For example, whenever Paul faces what seems to you a relatively minor frustration, he becomes furious and uses a string of expletives that would make a seasoned hand blush. This pattern continues. Adults should try to understand the *real* focus of anger, rather than concentrating on the swearwords.

Think of a child in your program who often has problems. What might be some reasons for the mistaken behavior? What can you say about the child that addresses her or his *strengths?* How can you improve your relationship with this child? What can you do to help?

At all three levels of mistaken behavior, it is important that the adult seek to understand the child. To the extent possible, we should try to do so before we intervene. Our most important learning, however, often comes from reflection after the intervention we have tried. The more serious the pattern of mistaken behavior, the harder we need to work to understand the child.

Strive to understand the situation

Frequently teachers have to enter a group of chil-

dren not knowing what is happening, just that there is an incident occurring. No one can instantly grasp all aspects of the event, nonetheless the adult must try to determine what happened. Is it an accident (spilled milk)? Is it partially justified (the child had a right to be upset)? Is it something the children can work out by themselves (who will push and who will ride)? Is it getting on only the *teacher's* nerves (that kid always has an answer)? Inevitably, there are reasons for children's behaviors, which the concerned adult seeks to understand. When was the last time you were blamed for something unjustly? How did you feel when accused?

Child guidance or group management?

In attempting to understand the situation, the teacher should decide between child guidance responses and group management responses. If the situation is mainly the result of one or a few children's behavior, a *child guidance* approach is indicated. The adult's response should be as private as possible to avoid the punishment of public embarrassment. Going public with a child's relatively personal problem is a control technique teachers often use. Yet, many a person can remember the exact words of humiliation uttered by an adult as long as 60 years ago! For many, public embarrassment is the longest lasting negative side effect of all, far outweighing any logical lesson the adult was attempting to instill.

If we wish to avoid the effects of embarrassment, then *group management* responses also must avoid calling attention to individuals. Generalized comments, worded positively, are the goal. To illustrate, the adult might avoid saying, "Henry and Sylvia, please sit like everyone else, on your bottoms." Instead, the teacher might say, "I like the way you all are sitting today, just like pretzels and looking right at me." Or, "I like the way many of you are sitting. As soon as we're all ready, we can get back to the story." These group management reminders protect the dignity of individual children yet, with practice, get the job done. Seeking to understand the situation is an important step in a positive approach to discipline.

A solution orientation

Approach discipline problems with a *solution orientation.* Help children find solutions to conflict situations, do not just "discipline" them for having conflicts. A solution orientation means providing information so that next time children will know what to do instead, rather than just letting them know what not to do. Teachers set understandable limits with children, and reinforce them, but not with put-downs, threats, or physical punishment. Rather, diversion, alternatives, requests for cooperation, shared jokes, or "I" statements are used. Alone to a child, an adult may say,

"Billy, I am a little overloaded with the noise. Your 'radio' is so loud. You may sit with us and listen to the story or you may do puzzles at the table, but keep the volume down, OK?" The goal is to help children solve problems.

A solution orientation means the adult will selectively ignore borderline behavior that does not greatly affect the group. It may mean asking a child who reports a grievance to attempt to solve it on her or his own. The adult may pay attention to the innocent victim first; this gives attention where it's due and helps the other child think things over.

When two children are having a disagreement, you may not always want to jump in too quickly because children can solve many problems among themselves, and the more opportunities they have to practice social problem-solving skills, the better they become at using them. Moreover, if *children* are working through a problem, you know their thoughts are at their mental level—are understood by them. However, when adults step in, inserting thoughts at an *adult* mental level, misunderstandings are likely to occur.

The teacher with a solution orientation realizes that children are still learning to get along in the world beyond home. Social responsiveness and openness take years to develop and are even hard for adults.

A visitor to a class of young children was once astonished, then enlightened: A very upset child said, "Damn it to hell."

The teacher responded, "Good for you, Arthur," and went over to talk to him.

When she returned, the teacher smiled at the visitor and said, "Until last week whenever Arthur got upset, he would hit or kick. We've been trying to get him to use words instead, and he did."

Sometimes progress takes a while or comes in little steps. A solution orientation maximizes chances of success.

Address the situation, do not judge the child

This is important because diminished self-esteem leads to insecurity, even hostility. Assess for yourself which statement is more supportive of the child's self-concept:

Oh, clumsy Carl, wipe up your spill again.	It's OK, we all spill, the wipe rag is in the bucket.
Paul, you are being rowdy; no throwing sand.	I am upset. Sand is for playing, not throwing.
Don't try and get out of things. You used the blocks, you put them away.	All who used the blocks need to help put them back. As soon as they're away we can go out.

Part of the learning process for children is feedback about their behavior. Child guidance statements that don't label but do reinforce limits are: "This upsets me. What can you do to fix it?" "Nancy didn't like it when her house was knocked over." "Hitting hurts, Billy." "You may be part of our group activity, or you may read books by yourself; you choose." "I know how hard you are trying, Darcie, and I really appreciate it." Statements such as these are generally used on an *individual* basis.

When managing a *group*, comments that address situations but protect self-concepts might be these: "The puzzles are still on the floor." "I am waiting for just a few now, we're almost ready to start." "You worked so hard today, I am proud of you."

If praise is meant to recognize the individual rather than control the group, then it, like individual criticism, is often better given in private. Praise that describes and appreciates *efforts*, not character or personality, tends to be the most honest and effective.

Respond clearly in problem situations

When possible, it is better for the child's self-esteem—and the group atmosphere—not to give ultimatums that force power struggles. Effective teachers adjust the use of authority to the degree of mildness, moderateness, or severity of the situation through inviting, requesting, or if necessary commanding cooperation:

Inviting: "I need some strong helpers who can pick up the blocks and put the tables and chairs back in place."

Requesting: "If you are going to work together, you will need to keep the noise down, and show me you are getting a lot done."

Commanding: "Rodney, you choose: Cooperate with the small group, or do the activity on your own. Which will it be?"

This use of authority, permissive in some situations and authoritative in others, still leaves the responsibility of choice with the child, and grants the child humanness.

As a last resort: Remove or restrain

Sometimes words won't work and actions are called for, notably when there is danger of physical harm or a child is too upset to talk or listen. For the good of the child and group, teachers must act firmly. Removal from the situation or restraining the child are accepted measures of last resort, coming after words have failed.

The usual method of *removal* in the preschool and primary years is having a child sit in a specifically designated "timeout chair," though there may be some advantages to expecting the child to use any quiet part of the room. Isolation outside the room is generally not recommended for younger children, nor are prolonged periods away from the group. The intent of a "cooling down time" is to help the child get calm enough to understand the reason for removal. When the main feelings created in the child are shame and doubt, removal has lapsed into punishment.

Restraining entails use of the nonviolent bear hug. The teacher restrains a child only when he is emotionally out of control. The adult quietly holds the child on a lap until the tantrum has subsided. Though it may not seem so to the dismayed adult, after the child realizes he won't be let go, he is gradually calmed by the security of the physical closeness and the understanding that if *he* can't control himself he is still safe because a sensible adult will take charge.

Repeated use of restraining or removal indicates that there is trouble in the child's life, and more understanding of both situation and child is needed. Decisions to remove or restrain are among the most difficult teachers must make. We may fear that physical intervention might give way to punishment, either *by* or *to* us. We worry that cooperative attitudes we have worked to establish in the class may be undermined and that the child being disciplined may dislike us. It is important, of course, to recognize the difference between firmness and harshness. Appropriate firmness must be seen as the test and measure of the positive system of classroom operations that we believe in. Harshness, whether physical or psychological, is a frailty in humanness, with which the teacher must learn to cope.

Reconciliation

When using either of the actions of last resort noted, the adult needs to recognize that the episode is not over until the child is reunited with the group and reconciled with the teacher. It is the teacher's responsibility to follow through with the reconciliation process. Some suggestions for this important assistance are:

1. After the child (and the teacher) have cooled down, the two should talk about the situation. The discussion should use a child guidance perspective and be based on facts more than on morality. The discussion may be before or after the child has been helped to rejoin the activity.

2. If a cooling down time is used, the adult can tell the child that he may rejoin the group when ready.

3. A kitchen timer can be set for a few minutes—not more than five. The young child can listen for the timer and then return on her or his own initiative.

4. Children often need assistance to rejoin the group. A quiet welcome by the teacher helps: "Here are some magic markers, Carol; we're making pictures of what each child likes to do in the fall. It can be anything you'd like."

5. Children should not be forced to say they're sorry if they're not ready. Think about the last time you were upset at someone; how long was it before you were ready to make up? Give children time to work things through. Invite reconciliation only if you think it will help, and in a low-key way. Moods change quickly in children; they may have already reconciled and only need our acknowledgement.

Recognize your humanness

We must accept that we teachers are human too. In the National Association for the Education of Young Children booklet *Caring: Supporting Children's Growth,* Rita Warren (1977) discusses the human side of teaching. One important comment by Warren is that we cannot expect to love every child. In many classrooms there are one or two children that the teacher has a hard time accepting. In such situations it is important to make efforts to understand more about that child's life. Have a co-teacher work more closely with the child. Look for the child's strengths and accomplishments. Discuss the situation with staff, parents, and other appropriate professionals.

Our goal need not be to love each child, but it should be to accept each as a person of worth and as a welcome member of the group.

Finally, we need to recognize that we all get angry sometimes. (See Ginott, 1971, p. 71.) We all have difficult days. We all have trouble forgiving, accepting, or communicating with some children (and adults). This, again, is the *frailty* side of our humanness. Perhaps a first step in learning to recover from a bad episode is to recognize our feelings and forgive *ourselves.* Only then can we figure out how to make the best of the situation and to forgive the other. Thoughts in the middle of the night may be part of this healing process and talks with others important to us certainly are. Children are forgiving and sometimes *need* us to be firm. If the undercurrent of our firmness is appreciation of the worth of each individual child, reconciliation offers the possibility of fuller understanding and more productive relationships. As Ginott (1971) suggests in *Teacher and Child,* true reconciliation means change. For professional teachers who care about young children, change means learning and growing.

References

Clark, J. I. (1978). *Self esteem: A family affair.* Minneapolis: Winston.

Ginott, H. G. (1971). *Teacher and child.* New York: Macmillan.

Stone, J. G. (1973). *What about discipline?* Cambridge, MA: Education Development Center.

Warren, R. (1977). *Caring: Supporting children's growth.* Washington, DC: NAEYC.

Help for the Hot-Tempered Kid

How to encourage children to recognize their boiling points

Michael Petti

Michael Petti is school psychologist for Woodbridge Township, New Jersey's largest suburban school district.

At the water fountain fifth grader Scott punches Carlos in the stomach because Carlos cut in front of his buddy Eric. Meanwhile in the lunchroom third grader Paula screams out a few choice words because the aide reminded her to remain seated while eating.

Temper flare-ups like these occur unexpectedly and at any time at school. Often, teachers are forced to use external control at the time, leaving the lesson—how to control a temper—left unlearned.

There are certain daily strategies that can be used to help students to learn self-control. And if a quick-tempered student, such as Scott, is helped to deal with his anger, it is certainly an important lesson for him as well as his future acquaintances.

Show a child it is possible to change. Some children believe that being a hothead is part of their nature. Take Paula, for instance, who thinks she is "just like Mom" in that they both tend to blow off steam easily. Just as you can convince pupils that they are able to learn, you can

convince someone like this child that she can change her explosive behavior. Pep talks and rap sessions are useful tools. In an academic sense, you probably use this technique all the time. When a student is stuck on a new math concept, you remind him or her that just three weeks earlier, he or she was unable to do one-digit multiplication and now has mastered the technique. Then you tell him or her that in all probability, he or she will be able to do the two-digit multiplication easily three weeks from now. With Paula, you can cite previous examples of her success with self-control: "Paula, I know you can control your temper. Yesterday, you did not explode when James accidentally knocked over your books."

In calm situations remind a pupil, such as Paula, that all people get mad and want to explode with anger. The difference, however, is that they don't. In a quiet and friendly moment with Paula, point out how someone else in the class, perhaps her best friend, Becca, was able to control her temper when she couldn't find her sneakers for gym class. Here, too, you can remind Paula that losing control will not solve the problem. Her friend did not yell or curse because things did not go exactly as planned. Instead, Becca looked under her desk,

checked her locker, and finally noticed her sneakers under her book bag. You might ask Paula how long it might have taken Becca to find the lost sneakers if she had wasted her time by flying into a rage.

Discourage pupils from thinking they are Judge Wapner of "People's Court." This strategy applies to Scott, a child quick to correct an injustice. When he thought Carlos cut in front of Eric, he felt justified in punching Carlos for "punishment." You can tell Judge Scott that people who drive cars do not make rash judgments about, or retaliations for, the actions of other drivers. Even if the other driver was obviously wrong, responsible adults don't pull up at the next stoplight and curse him or her out. In a calm atmosphere, explain to Scott that he will always be agitated if he feels he has to correct everyone and everything that he perceives as wrong in this world.

Another student, Jay, needs a little help, too. What starts out as a little discussion about which toy company makes the best transformers turns into a nasty argument. Sensing that he is losing, Jay calls the other student's mother a foul name.

When both students have calmed down, point out to them that they both may be right to a degree. While one toy is more graphic and may be the better of the two artistically, the other toy might convert more easily into a robot, thereby being the better of the two toys mechanically.

Explain that a person can lose a dispute without losing self-respect. Tell Jay that by "going off the wall," he is throwing his self-respect right out the window. Adults and children do not admire sore losers. Suggest to Jay that he back away from arguments. Explain that some people can never be won over. Throughout the year, you might need to build up his self-esteem by having him be your helper. In this way, he can still feel good about himself, even when he has lost an argument.

The next strategy could apply to George, the boy whom Jay has argued with. *Discourage kids like George from talking down to others.* Some people, such as Jay, may lash out if they are backed into a corner. George can be discouraged from this behavior through role reversal. Through the use of play or a puppet show, you can imitate his one-upmanship and let him take the part of the student being talked down to. George will then have an idea of how his remarks make others feel.

Try to get a student to understand someone else's feelings. For instance, Jane yells at her peers when they do not play exactly by her rules. Pretend to be Jane playing a game with another student. Every time she makes a mistake in the game, complain and say that she's doing it all wrong. Afterwards, ask her how she feels about

---

> *"Some kids think of themselves as Judge Wapner. They're quick to punish perceived injustices."*

---

being picked on. Then explain to the child that she does not make her friends feel very good when she con-

stantly tells them how to play. People do not like it when someone is always trying to be the boss.

Get the student to ask for clarifications before confronting another person angrily. Because Meagan often misinterprets comments, she's often on the defensive and miffed with people. Just as students can learn to memorize their multiplication tables, students like Meagan can learn to memorize and repeat verbatim in many situations: "I think you are saying. . . ." The intent is for the child to make a sincere effort to find out what the other person really means.

Discourage students from being jealous. When Shinita breaks Amy's crayons because Amy receives a better grade on her spelling paper, she is probably envious. Explain to Shinita that she is only putting herself down when she acts jealous. Help her to see herself in a better light by reviewing her past accomplishments. List them on a special index card for her to keep.

Help children to recognize their own boiling point. When Scott feels dumped on, he becomes tense. Paula may feel her temple throbbing, and Shinita may feel a sudden burst of energy. Discuss with the students how they feel right before they explode with anger. Once they are able to recognize clues that their bodies are sending them, they may be able to learn how to remain calm. Suggest thinking about something else—a favorite TV show, a fun activity. Slowly counting to 10 might help.

Teach the child to recognize the boiling point of others. If someone is getting angry, students should learn to hold off arguing with him or her. Kids can jot down all possible tip-offs that a certain person may be getting mad (a red face, tapping a pencil).

Encourage students to talk over concerns when both parties are calm. Discourage kids from bottling up annoying things to the point that they become preoccupied with them and then display a burst of anger. Have them practice assertive responses to neutral situations that include talking to others about petty matters.

Karen has learned how to do this. When her teacher praises Karen's

friends but not Karen for the castle built for social studies, she feels hurt and angry. Instead of showing her teacher how furious she is, Karen remembers that the teacher she had last year encouraged her to discuss her concerns. Karen then calmly and courteously explains that she also worked on the project.

Help the pupil see the public image that he or she presents when incensed. You do not need video equipment. A mirror will be very effective. You might also want to have a tape recorder handy. When the dust has settled in a day or two, replay the ranting and raving. If a child sees or hears the spectacle that he or she makes, he or she may finally realize how intense his or her anger becomes.

Teach students to release pent-up anger and frustrations. Suggest that they engage in a physical activity, such as bike riding, bouncing a ball, or running, to work off anger. Another way to ease tension is to discuss the matter with a close friend.

Get the student to ask: "Is this really worth getting upset about?" Present hypothetical situations and have the student judge whether the matter is worth getting angry over. If he or she feels that it is, ask why. Are there other solutions to the situation that would not involve getting hot under the collar? If students become defensive or their minds are blank, remind them that the goal of this exercise is to use their imaginations.

Just as it is difficult for a dieter to give up certain foods, it is hard for some people to stop being hotheads. *Encourage kids to give themselves a pat on the back for any incident wherein they were able to successfully control their tempers.*

Learning to defuse a short temper takes practice and there will be setbacks. Progress is not as evident as when a student is able to master a list of spelling words in a week. *When a student demonstrates control as a result of your help and encouragement, give yourself a pat on the back.* This strategy will help *you* from losing your cool later when new situations heat up.

Equal Opportunity and American Education

What constitutes the civil rights of students and teachers in schools has been a question often raised before state and federal courts. The equal treatment of students under national constitutional guidelines is of great importance. Decisions made by courts on issues affecting the lives of students and teachers concern the study of religion in schools, prayer and scripture reading in schools, the racial desegregation of schools, bilingual education, and academic freedom for teachers and students. The federal judiciary in the United States has established important precedents in all of the above

areas. In both Canada and the United States, there is great importance attached to the development of workable opportunity structures in national educational systems. The interpretation of what these opportunity structures are has evolved over many years, and the evolution of lines of argument in the courts on these matters continues.

The just balance of the equality interests of citizens of democratic societies is based on the belief that in any free society a plurality of interests must be protected. In addition, so must the dignity and opportunity of each individual citizen to optimize his or her possibilities as a human being. The unjust limitation of freedom of expression or the limitation of an opportunity to attain an adequate education are not tolerable possibilities in any democracy.

Few matters are more basic to the maintenance of democratic social institutions than the establishment of just principles for guiding the education of the young. From preschool to post-graduate school fellowships, issues of equality must be considered by those who seek an education. The vast and complex cultural pluralism that people enjoy in North America is a priceless treasure and the source of the need for guarantees under the law for equality in education.

Americans have witnessed one of the greatest struggles for equality before the law in all of human history. That struggle is well known to educators, especially. More than thirty years ago, the Supreme Court of the United States gave the first of what was to be a long chain of decisions affecting majority-minority relations in American schools. The famous 1954 decision of the United States Supreme Court in *Brown v. Board of Education of Topeka,* expanded the equality agenda for education to include equality of educational opportunity for women, linguistic minorities, cultural minorities, the aged, and the defenseless. This struggle to achieve the full implementation of the American constitutional promise of equality of opportunity in the field of education has been a triumphant testimony to the possibility of social justice under the law. Future generations of Americans and other free peoples will forever look with awe at the struggle for civil rights in American schools from 1954 to the closing years of the present century. Rarely have free peoples asserted their rights under the law as forcefully and effectively as the American people have on the question of equality of educational opportunity.

Determined to uphold constitutional promises, and inspired by the knowledge that significant progress has been made on this issue, the closing years of this century can be approached with renewed hope and confidence. A vast body of research and opinion on this issue has evolved from the many federal court decisions since 1954. Problems of equity in the schools have been well documented and the nation is developing increased sophistication and effectiveness in the development of solutions to these problems. The desegregation of American

schools has been forcefully initiated over the nation, and progress is continuing in majority-minority relations in the schools. It is not only the cultural minorities who have benefitted from the federal school desegregation cases, however. Affirmative action in employment and admission to professional schools, the students' rights issue, and the rights of women and the aged have been based on the same constitutional arguments and precedents established in the major school desegregation cases and the Civil Rights Act of 1964. Likewise, the rights of linguistic minorities to learn the English language in public schools have been based on these same constitutional principles. Every American has benefitted either directly or indirectly from this triumph of constitutional law over racist tradition.

The essays in this unit provide solid background on these matters. The first article reviews major United States Supreme Court cases involving religion, prayer, and Bible reading in schools, the recent precedents regarding tuition tax credits, school desegregation, and academic freedom.

The articles in this unit consider many important dimensions of the civil rights movement in American education. The legal context of the struggle for equality of educational opportunity is clearly developed in some of the selections, while other selections explore factors such as discrimination on the basis of sex. Sensitive human issues related to the topic are dealt with, along with problems of freedom of the press and expression.

Looking Ahead: Challenge Questions

What have been the most important legal precedents affecting freedom of belief in American schools?

What were the constitutional precedents for the school desegregation cases?

What academic freedoms should every teacher and student have?

What are the issues in the controversy over bilingual education?

What are the remaining gender issues facing North American schools?

What are the legal issues involved in the controversy over tuition tax credits?

What are the educational issues which teachers of interracial children should understand?

What are the issues surrounding censorship in school settings?

The Courts and Education

Thomas R. Ascik

Thomas R. Ascik, a lawyer and former teacher, is a Senior Research Assistant in the Law and Public Management Division of the National Institute of Education, U.S. Department of Education.

The Supreme Court said in 1960 that "the vigilant protection of constitutional freedoms is nowhere more vital than in the community of American schools."[1] Starting with the cases of *Everson v. Board of Education* (1947) and *Brown v. Board of Education* (1954), and continuing with one precedent-shattering case after another, the Supreme Court has applied the concept of constitutional rights to nearly every aspect of American education. Although the United States has been flooded by studies and reports severely critical of the nation's public schools,[2] the historic changes in education wrought by the Supreme Court over the past four decades have hardly been mentioned.

Most critical are those rulings in which the Supreme Court has applied the Constitution to education without prior precedent. These have particularly affected public aid to nonpublic schools, prayer and spiritual values in public schools, racial segregation, and teacher and student rights. In these four areas, the Court, on its own initiative, has broken with the rest and established comprehensive national educational policies.

PUBLIC AID TO NONPUBLIC SCHOOLS

The authority of any branch of the federal government to intervene in state public policies regarding religion traditionally has been governed by the doctrine of the 1833 case of *Barron v. Baltimore.*[3] In this case, concerning city damage to private property, Chief Justice John Marshall, speaking for a unanimous Supreme Court, ruled that the Court had no jurisdiction over the case because the Bill of Rights placed no restrictions on the actions of city or state governments. The framers of the Bill of Rights had not "intended them to be limitations on the powers of the state governments,"[4] explained Marshall.

In the 1920s and 1930s, however, the Court abandoned *Barron v. Baltimore* and began developing perhaps the most important judicial doctrine of this century: the "incorporation" of the Bill of Rights into the Fourteenth Amendment. That amendment, ratified in 1868, made federal citizenship preeminent over state citizenship and declared in its most important parts that "no state shall...deprive any person of life, liberty, or prosperity, without due process of law; nor deny to any person within its jurisdiction the equal protection of the laws."

By incorporating the various rights guaranteed by the Bill of Rights into these Fourteenth Amendment guarantees, the Court gave itself power to overturn state law dealing with almost all areas covered by the ten amendments of the Bill of Rights.

The Court ruled in the 1947 case of *Everson v. Board of Education,*[5] for instance, that the First Amendment's clause prohibiting laws "respecting an establishment of religion" was binding on the states. In this most important Supreme Court education case, except for *Brown v. Board of Education* (1954), the Court was construing the Establishment Clause for the first time. At stake was the constitutionality of a New Jersey statute requiring local school boards to provide free transportation, along established routes, to children attending nonprofit, private (including religiously affiliated) schools.

More significant than the specific ruling in the case was the Court's construction of the First Amendment's Establishment Clause. Declared the Court:

The "establishment of religion" clause of the First Amendment means at least this: Neither a state nor the Federal Government can set up a church. Neither can it pass laws which aid one religion,

 From *The World & I*, March 1986, pp. 661-675. Reprinted from Eileen M. Gardner, ed., A NEW AGENDA FOR EDUCATION. Washington, D.C.: The Heritage Foundation, 1985.

aid all religions, or prefer one religion over another. Neither can it force nor influence a person to go to or to remain away from a church against his will or force him to profess a belief or disbelief in any religion. No person can be punished for entertaining or professing religious beliefs or disbeliefs, for church attendance or nonattendance. No tax in any amount, large or small, can be levied to support any religious activities or institutions, whatever they may be called, or whatever form they may adopt to teach or practice religion. Neither a state nor the Federal Government can, openly or secretly, participate in the affairs of any religious organizations or groups and vice versa. In the words of Jefferson, the clause against establishment of religion by law was intended to erect "a wall of separation between Church and State."... That Amendment requires the state to be neutral in its relations with groups of religious believers and nonbelievers.[6]

Until this declaration, the most widely held view of the meaning of the Establishment Clause was that it prohibited government preference of one religion over another. When the Supreme Court concluded that states cannot "pass laws which aid one religion, aid all religions, or prefer one religion over another," it introduced for the first time the notion that the Establishment Clause forbade not only government preference of one religion over another but also government preference of religion over nonreligion.

More than twenty years passed before the Court heard its next significant case concerning government aid to religious schools, *Board of Education v. Allen.*[7] In *Allen,* the Court examined a challenge to a New York statute that required local school boards to purchase textbooks (in secular subjects only) and loan them, without charge, to all children enrolled in grades seven through

twelve of public or private schools. The books were not limited to those actually in use in the public schools but could include those "designated for use" in the public schools or otherwise approved by the local board of education.

The Court applied *Everson* to the case and decided that the provision of textbooks, like transportation, was permissible means to the accomplishment of the legitimate state objective of secular education of all children. Religious schools participated in the public interest because "they pursue two goals, religious instruction and secular education."[8] Parochial schools, the Court said, "are performing, in addition to their sectarian function, the task of secular education."[9] This was the birth of the "secular-sectarian" distinction that has defined religious schools as partly serving the public good (the secular subjects in the curriculum) and partly not (religious instruction).

Various cases followed that further defined the principles laid down in *Everson,* including a case dealing with the question of reimbursement to nonpublic schools for their expenditures on teachers of secular subjects and secular institutional materials (*Lemon v. Kurtzman* [1971][10]). In *Lemon,* the Court ruled the reimbursements unconstitutional because of the danger a teacher under religious control could pose to the separation of the religious from the secular. In *Committee for Public Education and Liberty v. Nyquist* (1973),[11] maintenance and repair grants to nonpublic schools were judged to have the primary effect of advancing religion because the buildings maintained and repaired were not restricted to secular purposes. Also in this case, tuition reimbursements and tuition tax deductions were rejected by the Court as being effectively indistinguishable from aid to the schools themselves: "The effect of the aid is unmistakably to provide desired financial support for nonpublic sectarian institutions."[12] Furthermore, said the Court, states could not "encourage or reward"[13] parents for sending their children to religious schools because this advances religion. Finally, the plan failed the "politically divisive" test because it had the "grave potential" of stimulating "continuing political strife over religion."[14]

Separate strong dissents were filed by Chief Justice Warren Burger and by Justices William Rehnquist and Byron White. Burger thought that there was a definitive difference between government aid to individuals and direct aid to religious institutions. He wrote: "The private individual makes the decision that may indirectly benefit church-sponsored schools; to that extent the state involvement with religion is substantially attenuated."[15] Rehnquist argued that, if the Court could uphold the constitutionality of exempting churches from taxation, then it should similarly uphold the constitutionality of exempting parents from taxation for certain educational expenses. White contended that the Court was ruling as unconstitutional schemes that had "any effect"[16] of advancing religion, whereas the test was properly one of "primary effect."

The Thirty-Years War between the Supreme Court and those states seeking to give public aid to their private schools may have ended with the Supreme Court's 1983 decision in *Mueller v. Allen.*[17] In an opinion written by Justice Rehnquist, a majority of the Court upheld a Minnesota law allowing a deduction on state income taxes for tuition, textbooks, and transportation expenses incurred in the education of students in elementary or secondary schools—public or nonpublic.

Rehnquist decided that the deduction had a secular purpose of "ensuring that the state's citizenry is well-educated"[18] regardless of the type of schools attended. Minnesota also had "a strong public interest"[19] in assuring the survival of religious and nonreligious private schools because such schools relieve the public schools of the financial burden of educating a certain percentage of the youth population and because private schools provide "a wholesome competition"[20] for public schools. Furthermore, the primary effect of the law was not the advancement of religion, Rehnquist concluded, in the most important part of his opinion.

Minnesota's plan was distinguished from the tax deductions in *Nyquist* because "the deduction is available for educational expenses incurred by all parents, including those whose children attend public schools and those whose children attend nonsectarian private schools or sectarian private schools."[21] Rehnquist cited the Court's 1981 decision in the *Widmar v. Vincent*[22] ruling that if a state university makes its facilities available for use by student groups, it must allow student religious groups to use the facilities on an equal basis. In keeping with the *Widmar* decision, Minnesota was here providing benefits on an equal basis to a "broad spectrum of citizens,"[23] and this nondiscriminatory breadth was "an important index of secular effect."[24]

Having thus distinguished *Nyquist*, the Court was then able to say that there is a significant difference, in terms of the Establishment Clause, between providing aid to parents and providing it directly to schools despite the reality that "financial assistance provided to parents ultimately has an economic effect comparable to that of aid given directly to the schools attended by their children."[25] Religious schools received public funds "only as a result of numerous, private choices of individual parents of school-age children,"[26] and this exercise of parental choice caused the financial benefits flowing to religious schools to be much "attenuated."[27]

Implications

The *Mueller* decision and the *Widmar* decision requiring state universities to give "equal access" to student religious groups may signal an emerging Supreme Court view of the relationship of church to state and a possible end to the struggle between the states and the Court over public aid for nonpublic education. In *Mueller*, the Court accepted the principle that parents whose children attended religious schools could receive benefits so long as public school parents were equally eligible for benefits. This principle, allowing a state to accommodate its citizens with religious purposes on an equal basis with those pursuing secular purposes, received strong bipartisan support in Congress in 1984. By significant majorities, both Houses passed the

"equal access" bill requiring elementary and secondary schools to allow student religious clubs to use their facilities on an equal basis with other student clubs. This was nothing more than the extension of *Widmar* to elementary and secondary schools.

In the United States, religion has always been the major motivation for the formation and continuation of private schools. Without the *Everson* doctrine, therefore, there would be many more U.S. private schools.

SPIRITUAL VALUES IN PUBLIC SCHOOLS

The Supreme Court addressed prayer in schools in the 1962 case of *Engle v. Vital*,[28] a constitutional challenge to the mandated daily recitation of a nondenominational prayer in a New York State school district that said:

> Almighty God, we acknowledge our dependence upon Thee, and we beg Thy blessings upon us, our parents, our teachers, and our country.

The prayer had been carefully crafted in consultation with a wide range of Jewish and Christian leaders and officially recommended (in 1951 and 1955) to the state's school districts by the New York State Board of Regents as part of its "Statement on Moral and Spritual Training in the Schools." In the lower state courts and the New York Court of Appeals (the highest court of New York), the constitutional challenge to the prayer had been rejected with the caveat that no student could be compelled to recite the prayer. Twenty-three other states joined New York in its petition to have the Supreme Court uphold the constitutionality of the prayer. This, however, the Court did not do.

In what might have been unique for such an important case, Justice Hugo Black, writing for the Court, referred to no previous Supreme Court decision as precedent. Instead, he explained the decision by means of an essay on the history of the separation of church and state. Significantly, almost all of the history considered was preconstitutional—the history of religion in England and the writings of various men, especially Madison

and Jefferson, at the time of the ratification of the Constitution and of the Bill of Rights. Justice Potter Stewart, the sole dissenter, argued that the case brought the Free Exercise Clause into consideration in two ways.[29] First, the lack of compulsion meant that the state was not interfering with the free exercise of anyone's religion. Second, the children who wanted to pray were denied the free exercise of their religion, Stewart contended, and they were denied the "opportunity of sharing the spiritual heritage of our Nation."[30] History is relevant, Stewart argued, but not "the history of an established church in sixteenth century England or in eighteenth century America."[31] Instead, the relevant history was the "history of the religious traditions of our people, reflected in countless practices of the institutions and officials of our government."[32]

A year later in the companion cases of *Abington v. Schempp* and *Murray v. Curlett*,[33] the Court struck down state laws requiring the reading of the Bible in public schools. In *Schempp*, the Unitarian plaintiffs challenged a Pennsylvania state law, passed in 1949, requiring the reading of ten verses from the Bible, without comment or interpretation, in the public schools at the beginning of each day. Upon written request, parents could excuse their children from the readings. The plaintiffs had bypassed the Pennsylvania Supreme Court and sued in federal district court, where the law was struck down in a decision based primarily on the *Everson* decision.

In *Murray*, militant atheist Madlyn Murray and her son challenged a 50-year-old rule of the Baltimore School Board requiring the reading of the Lord's Prayer each day in the city's public schools. As in Pennsylvania, parents could excuse their children from the practice. Murray did not request that her son be excused but brought the suit claiming that the rule violated religious liberty by "placing a premium on belief as against nonbelief."[34] The Maryland Supreme Court appealed to the U.S. Supreme Court, and eighteen other states joined Maryland's defense of its customs.

The Supreme Court ruled in favor of Murray. *Engle* and especially *Everson* formed the basis of the decision.

The Court quoted the *Everson* statement that neither the states nor the federal government "can pass laws which aid one religion, aid all religions, or prefer one religion over another." Once more the Supreme Court was ruling that the influence of religion must be absolutely segregated from the affairs of state. Finally, the Court invented a test for the establishment of religion: a law is constitutional only if it has "a secular legislative purpose and a primary effect that neither advances nor inhibits religion."[35] According to these principles, the practices in these cases were unconstitutional because they were indisputably exercises of which both purpose and effect were religious. The Court denied that its decision advanced what amounted to a religion of secularism but gave no reason for its denial.

I n *Epperson v. Arkansas* (1968),[36] the Supreme Court added a new wrinkle to its judicial attitude toward religion: a law may be unconstitutional, stated the Court, if the legislative motive for passing the law was religious. Since 1928, an Arkansas law prohibited the teaching of evolution in its public schools. The law had never been enforced. In 1965, however, a high school biology teacher, confronted with newly adopted biology textbooks that taught evolution, maintained that she was caught between opposing duties and sued to have the law declared void. In a two-sentence opinion, the Arkansas Supreme Court turned back the challenge by concluding that the law was a "valid exercise of the state's power to specify the curriculum in its public schools."[37]

In addition to the question of religious influence in public schools, at least four other profound issues were involved here: the content of the school curriculum, the authority of states over their public schools, the authority and ability of the federal judiciary to prescribe or proscribe parts of the curriculum, and the growing legal movement to have the federal courts promulgate some First Amendment-based rights of academic freedom. In its resolution of the *Epperson* case, the Supreme Court confined itself to two rationales. The first and more important rationale for the decision was the principle of the *Everson*, *Engle*, and *Schempp* cases. There was no relationship between church and state, the Court said; instead there was a wall. Such a statute clearly violated the "purpose" of the *Schempp* two-part test. The purpose of the statute was clearly religious, and the state did not have the right to make its decisions about school curricula "based upon reasons that violate the First Amendment."[38] In its strongest statement yet about the *Everson* neutrality principle, the Court emphasized that government must treat religion and nonreligion equally, for "the First Amendment mandates government neutrality between religion and religion, and between religion and nonreligion."[39]

As its second rationale, the Court quoted the statement in *Shelton v. Tucker*, that "the vigilant protection of constitutional freedoms is nowhere more vital than in the community of American schools," and the statement in *Keyishian v. Board of Regents* that the First Amendment will not tolerate "a pall of orthodoxy over the classroom."

Through *Epperson v. Arkansas*, the Court brought the results of constitutional litigation affecting higher education to elementary and secondary schools. To Arkansas's claim that it had constitutional power over its public schools, the Supreme Court declared that the Bill of Rights is applicable everywhere, and constitutional powers are not superior to constitutional rights. Said the Court: "Fundamental values of freedom of speech and inquiry and of belief"[40] are at stake here. Quoting *Keyishian*, "It is much too late to argue that the State may impose upon the teachers in its schools any conditions that it chooses, however restrictive they may be of constitutional guarantees."[41] With this concern for the academic freedom (free speech) of teachers, the Court invented independent rights for teachers to control the curriculum of public schools.

Implications

No court has ever doubted the authority of the states to prescribe moral and spiritual instruction in their public schools. The New York State Board of Regents was exercising that authority when it composed the prayer that became the issue in *Engle*. Today there is a growing consensus that more character training is needed in public schools. Historically, almost all systematic codes of Western morality or developed notions of character have been based on religion.

The effect of these Supreme Court decisions has been to prevent religion from influencing the education of those attending public schools. These decisions have forced those who believe that education cannot be separated from religion and who cannot afford private schools to attend institutions whose governing values are antagonistic to their own. In his concurrence in *Epperson*, Justice Black strongly implied that, if the wall of separation meant that nonreligion may influence the curriculum of public schools but religion may not, then the wall might very well be interfering with the free exercise of religion of some of those in attendance. This is, of course, a step beyond governmental neutrality between religion and nonreligion. Under governmental neutrality, the schools are merely indifferent to the values of religious people.

If any statement about the relationship of religion to education is itself a religious statement, then public education that does not discriminate against anyone is impossible under a system of absolute separation of church and state. The only alternative is the opportunity for individuals to exempt themselves at those times when the values presented or implied are antagonistic to their own. But the Court has rejected this principle of voluntariness. So the dilemma grows.

In his dissent in *Schempp*, Justice Stewart said government and religion must necessarily interact. Until *Everson*, they had at least been interacting throughout American history without any of the persecution that the court said it was trying to prevent with the *Engle* decision. In fact, it was *Everson* that launched an unprecedented era of church-state conflict in the U.S., chiefly in the context of education. American history before *Everson* dealt with interaction; since *Everson* it has been the history of conflict. It may be that neutrality is impossible.

DESEGREGATION

An abundance of writing has traced the development of the Supreme Court's doctrine regarding the desegregation of public schools. Three questions place the controversy in perspective: (1) When did the Supreme Court decide that desegregation was incompatible with the American tradition of neighborhood schools? (2) How did the Court come to endorse busing as a remedy for segregation? (3) What has been the attitude of the Court toward education—teaching and learning—in the midst of the desegregation issue?

The fundamental ruling in *Brown v. Board of Education (Brown I)*,[42] the most important education case and probably the most important Supreme Court ruling except for *Marbury v. Madison* (1801), was that school systems are forbidden intentionally to segregate the races by law or practice. Yet the Court's basis for this ruling and the full meaning of the ruling have been enigmatic and the cause of much disagreement. Legally, the Court addressed two questions: Does the Constitution forbid segregation; and, if it does, how can the Court get past its own 1896 ruling in *Plessy v. Ferguson*[43] that as long as public policy treated the races "equally," it could require them to be "separate?"

Addressing the "separate but equal" doctrine of *Plessy*, the Court was faced with a situation in which there were "findings...that the Negro and white schools involved have been equalized, or are being equalized, with respect to buildings, curricula, qualifications and salaries of teachers, and other 'tangible' factors."[44] With no deprivation of equality in measurable educational factors, the Court decided to consider whether there was equality of "intangible" factors. It decided that there was not and that the definitive inequality was the separateness itself.

The effect on blacks of racial segregation was "a feeling of inferiority as to their status in the community that may affect their hearts and minds in a way unlikely ever to be undone."[45] In its now-famous Footnote Eleven, the Court justified this psychological interpretation and inaugurated a new area of American law by citing the research of various social scientists. "Separate educational facilities are inherently unequal,"[46] the Court concluded. Thus, with this combination of the "separate" with the "equal," the Court effectively overturned *Plessy* in *Brown I* by declaring that modern social science had proved that separate equality was impossible in education.

In reaching this momentous decision, the Court did not address the enormous problem of how to require the dismantling of dual school systems until the following year in the second installment of the same case, *Brown II*.[47] Here, the Court refrained from attempting to declare a universal remedy applicable to every discriminating school system, but concluded, instead, that "because of their proximity to local conditions and the possible need for further hearings, the courts that originally heard those cases can best"[48] fashion specific remedies and, in each case, decide upon the best means to "effectuate a transition to a racially nondiscriminatory school system."[49] This was the beginning of the now commonplace judicial supervision of school systems.

Because the Court in *Brown II* put the burden on school authorities, federal district courts in the South spent the next thirteen years ruling on the constitutionality of various schemes that these authorities fashioned to carry out the mandate of *Brown I*. Only a few cases of significance reached the Supreme Court over this period. In truth, *Brown II* was not much more specific than *Brown I*. Until the Supreme Court's decision in *Green v. New Kent County* (1968), neither the lower federal courts nor the school systems knew whether the *Brown* mandate contained a prescription as well as a proscription.

In *Green v. New Kent County*, the Supreme Court announced that it was going to demand more than simply dropping laws requiring segregation. The case concerned the school board of the Virginia county of New Kent, a county with complete racial segregation between its only two schools, which initiated a "freedom-of-choice" plan whereby black and white students could choose which school they wanted to attend. Students not exercising this choice were reassigned to the school they had attended the previous year.

The effect of this plan was to offer to every student, black or white, the opportunity to attend either school, the traditionally all-black school or the traditionally all-white school, while not disturbing the segregated status quo if few or no students made the choice. This plan presented the Court with the question whether its *Brown* decision required the changing of the old laws requiring segregation, that is, de jure segregation, or the changing of the results of the old laws, that is, de facto segregation.

The school board, in effect, was asking the Court to rule on this distinction between de jure and de facto segregation. In reply, the Court said that it had already done so in *Brown II*: "The Board attempts to cast the issue in its broadest form by arguing that its 'freedom-of-choice' plan may be faulted only by reading the Fourteenth Amendment as universally requiring 'compulsory integration,' a reading it insists the wording of the Amendment will not support. But that argument ignores the thrust of *Brown II*."[50] This "thrust" was the requirement of the "abolition of the system of segregation and its effects,"[51] the Court explained.

The Court here was introducing the notion that segregation had continuing legal effects after the policy of segregation itself was ended. In telling the New Kent School Board that it was not merely freedom or lack of coercion but a certain social result that it was seeking, the Court said that the continuing effects of segregation (what one may have thought was an aspect of de facto segregation) were part of de jure segregation. In other words, it maintained that it was very unlikely that there could be legally acceptable de facto segregation in any district that had a history of de jure segregation. A plan was to be measured by its "effectiveness...in achieving desegregation."[52] Eliminating segregation was not enough; desegregation must be achieved.

After *Green*, it was only logical for

the Court to endorse busing and racial balance in *Swann v. Charlotte-Mecklenburg Board of Education* (1971).[53] If the prime evidence of the continuing efforts of a defunct policy of segregation was, as the Court said in *Green*, schools that remained heavily one race, and if a legally enforceable freedom to transfer was ineffective in achieving the redistribution of the two races, then the races must be specifically reassigned to achieve that goal. In *Swann* the Court endorsed three means of reassigning students: racial balances and quotas, busing, and the redrawing of school attendance zones. The Court's rationale for the acceptability of all three was the same: They all worked—that is, they were indisputably "effective" in achieving racial redistribution. *Swann* was the specific application of *Green*.

In summary, the *Brown* decision declared that the problem was that the races were legally required to be separate—not the inequality of facilities, curricula, or staff between black and white schools. The Court ruled that separation was itself an inequality (a psychological inequality) and was unconstitutional. In *Green*, the Court found that the continuing effect of segregation was the continuing separation of the races, and this finding was used to justify race-conscious student reassignment in *Swann*.

In *Milliken v. Bradley* (1977) (*Milliken II*),[54] however, the Court concluded what, on its face, seemed to be a contradiction not only of *Green* but also of *Brown*. The main issue of the case was "the question whether federal courts can order remedial education programs as part of a school desegregation decree."[55]

In *Milliken II*, the defendant Detroit school system charged that the district court's remedy of requiring the system to undertake the retraining of teachers and provide remedial reading and testing and counseling services to black children was not based on the nature of the constitutional violation; and that "the Court's

decree must be limited to remedying unlawful pupil assignments."[56] In rejecting this argument, the Court answered that a federal court's power to fashion remedies was "broad and flexible."[57]

What the Court really did in *Milliken II* was extend the "continuing effects" of *Green* and while doing away with the "separation" basis for *Brown* and *Green*. "Discriminatory student assignment policies can themselves manifest and breed other inequalities built into a dual system based on racial discrimination....Pupil assignment also does not automatically remedy the impact of previous, unlawful educational isolation,"[58] the Court concluded. For the first time, the Court was saying that there was a justifiable "impact" of racial separation beyond the separation itself.

Implications

In many cities where the question of busing has become moot because blacks have come to comprise the majority of the enrollment, the courts are more interested today in educational remedies than in busing and other remedies of mandatory student reassignment. This often becomes quite detailed, with the judge prescribing not only specific remedial programs but also the books to be used in such programs. Thus judges have taken over educational duties.

The *Brown* decision, the Civil Rights Act of 1964, the Voting Rights Act, and other laws have helped to change black political impotence to power. The full participation of blacks in government policy making may allow judges to permit the revival of local control of schools. If the courts are convinced that there are no impediments to black equality of political opportunity, they may be willing to give back control of the schools to communities, parents, and educators. This would allow the courts to avoid the problem of judicial prescription of the school curriculum. And it may be a necessity for the educational and social welfare of the children.

Contemporary research in education suggests that community and parent involvement and a shared sense of purpose are central to an effective school.[59] A federal district court recently endorsed these conclusions in the desegregation case in-

volving the school system of Norfolk, Virginia. Faced with the obvious failure of busing,[60] the dubious status of the "self-image" social psychology incorporated into *Brown*,[61] and the difficulties of judicial supervision of the curriculum, the courts may have to turn to other means to guarantee equality of educational opportunity for all children.

THE RIGHTS OF TEACHERS AND STUDENTS

The first important case applying the constitutional principle of free speech to the field of education was *Shelton v. Tucker* (1960).[62] One of the most important First Amendment cases, it was decided by a narrow five to four margin. An Arkansas statute required prospective teachers at public schools or colleges to disclose every organization to which he or she had belonged or contributed regularly in the preceding five years. Some teachers who refused to do so, challenged the statute as a deprivation of their "rights to personal association, and academic liberty, protected by the Due Process Clause of the Fourteenth Amendment from invasion by state action."[63]

In overruling the Arkansas Supreme Court, which had upheld the statute, The Supreme Court said that this case differed from that group of First Amendment cases[64] in which the Court had invalidated state statutes because the statutes did not really serve a legitimate governmental purpose. Here, there was "no question of the relevance of a State's inquiry into the fitness and competence of its teachers."[65] Nevertheless, without any discussion at all, the Court immediately reached two definitive conclusions:

1. It declared that teachers had "a right of free association, a right closely allied to freedom of speech and a right which, like free speech, lies at the foundation of a free society."[66]

2. Rather than consider the issue of the permissible qualifications that a state may place on public employment, or the question of the uniqueness of teachers as public employees, the Court asserted that a constitutionally protected "personal freedom"[67] of teachers was at stake here. At stake were "freedom of speech....freedom of inquiry....free-

dom of association....the free spirit of teachers....the free play of the spirit....the free[dom] to inquire, to study, and to evaluate."[68] Consequently, "the vigilant protection of constitutional freedoms is nowhere more vital than in the community of American schools."[69] This last statement and the two conclusions upon which it is based have presaged most of the substance of other key cases.

The Court found that a teacher could have many associations that would have no bearing upon the teacher's competence or fitness. Therefore, "The statute's comprehensive interference with associational freedom goes far beyond what might be justified in the exercise of the State's legitimate inquiry into the fitness and competency of its teachers."[70] The four dissenters all joined two separate dissents written by Justices John Harlan and Felix Frankfurter. Their similar arguments had two main points. First, there was no evidence that the information collected had ever been abused or used in a discriminatory manner. Secondly, this was a reasonable and not excessive way for the state to exercise its conceded right to inquire into the fitness of its teachers.

That a major change had been effected in the attitude of the federal judiciary to the situation of teachers in government-operated schools was made evident in *Keyishian v. Board of Regents of New York* (1967).[71] In *Keyishian* the Court overturned the same New York "loyalty oath" law that it had sustained fifteen years earlier in *Adler v. Board of Education*.[72] The law excluded anyone from public employment who advocated the overthrow of the government by force or violence. Pursuant to the law, the Board of Regents of the state university system had required university employees to certify that they were not members of the Communist party or, if they were, that they had communicated the fact to the president of the university. Keyishian and three other faculty members refused to certify themselves and challenged the constitutionality of the law and its application.

In *Adler*, the Court had turned back such a challenge and declared:

A teacher works in a sensitive area in a classroom. There he shapes the attitude of young minds toward the society in which they live. In this, the state has a vital concern. It must preserve the integrity of the schools. That the school authorities have the right and the duty to screen the officials, teachers, and employees as to their fitness to maintain the integrity of the schools as a part of ordered society, cannot be doubted.[73]

But in *Keyishian*, the Court decided that the New York law was unconstitutional. Declared the Court:

There can be no doubt of the legitimacy of New York's interest in protecting its education system from subversion. But "even though the governmental purpose be legitimate and substantial, that purpose cannot be pursued by means that broadly stifle fundamental personal liberties when the end can be more narrowly achieved." *Shelton v. Tucker*...."The vigilant protection of constitutional freedoms is nowhere more vital than in the community of American schools." *Shelton v. Tucker*."[74]

In *Adler*, the Court had said that teachers "may work for the school system upon the reasonable terms laid down by the proper authorities of New York. If they do not choose to work on such terms, they are at liberty to retain their beliefs and association and go elsewhere."[75] But throughout the *Keyishian* opinion, the Court cited numerous cases that it had decided in the area of the First Amendment since 1952. What had happened between 1952 and 1967 was that the reach of the First Amendment had been dramatically extended by the Court.

In the 1968 case of *Pickering v. Board of Education*,[76] the *Shelton* and *Keyishian* rationales for freedom of association for teachers were applied by the Supreme Court to freedom of speech for teachers. A county board of education in Illinois had dismissed a teacher, after a public hearing, for publishing a letter in a newspaper criticizing the board's performance in the area of school finance. The board found that numerous statements in the letter were false and that the publication of the statements unjusti-

fiably impugned the board and the school administration.

The Supreme Court found that the teacher's right to free speech prevented his dismissal:

To the extent that the Illinois Supreme Court's opinion may be read to suggest that teachers may constitutionally be compelled to relinquish the First Amendment rights they would otherwise enjoy as citizens to comment on matters of public interest in connection with the operation of the public schools in which they work, it proceeds on a premise that has been unequivocally rejected in numerous prior decisons of this Court....*Shelton v. Tucker*....*Keyishian v. Board of Regents*...."The theory that public employment which may be denied altogether may be subjected to any conditions, regardless of how unreasonable, has been uniformly rejected." *Keyishian v. Board of Regents*....the threat of dismissal from public employment is nonetheless a potent means of inhibiting speech.[77]

In *Tinker v. Des Moines* (1969),[78] the rights established in *Shelton* and *Keyishian* were extended to students:

First Amendment rights, applied in light of the special characteristics of the school environment, are available to teachers and students. It can hardly be argued that either students or teachers shed their constitutional rights to freedom of speech or expression at the schoolhouse gate.[79]

The case stemmed from the deliberate defiance of a school system's rule prohibiting the wearing of armbands —in this instance protesting the Vietnam War. "Our problem," the Court said, "lies in the area where students in the exercise of First Amendment rights collide with the rules of the school authorities."[80] Wearing of armbands was akin to "pure speech" and implicated "direct, primary First Amendment rights."[81] The students' expression of their political views by wearing armbands had caused no disorder or disturbance in the schools, had not interfered with schools' work, and had not intruded upon the rights of other students. Furthermore, the mere fear of a disturbance was not reason enough to justify this curtailment of speech, the Court decided, because "our Constitution says we must take this risk."[82] With this ruling, the Court established a new presumption in American education. "In the absence of a specific showing of constitutionally valid reasons to regulate their speech, students are entitled to freedom of expression of their views."[83]

In a scorching dissent, Justice Black, a lifelong First Amendment advocate, asserted that the Court had launched a "new revolutionary era of permissiveness in this country fostered by the judiciary"[84] by arrogating to itself "rather than to the State's elected officals charged with running the schools, the decision as to which school disciplinary regulations are 'reasonable'."[85] Although he did not explicitly deny that students have free speech rights, Black may have argued so in effect, writing: "Nor are public school students sent to the schools at public expense to broadcast political or any other views to educate and inform the public...taxpayers send children to school on the premise that at their age they need to learn, not teach."[86]

With its decision, the Court reversed what had been the unquestioned social agreement that school authorities were to be obeyed always and that only in the rarest and most extraordinary cases, where a student had been seriously wronged, could a redress of grievances be pursued. Now, with regard to speech in schools, the reasons for student obedience must be demonstrable beforehand.

Implications

The issue of the *Brown* case was student assignment; in *Everson* and its progeny, the Supreme Court was intervening to prevent religion from influencing education. In both areas, the Court rearranged traditional ways of doing things in American education. However, when it applied the constitutional principles of freedom of speech and freedom of association to education, the Court added to the educational enterprise. To the business of teaching and learning were added "direct, primary First Amendment rights" of teachers and students, that is to say, personal liberties, independent of educational purposes but applied to education, enforceable in a court of law.

Schools have a purpose other than that for which they were established, the Supreme Court has said. This purpose is often called "academic freedom," and as the Supreme Court has outlined, it is protected by courts even when not desired by those who founded, and continue to fund, the public schools. For students, it means that they have a legally enforceable right to do other things than learn at school. And for teachers, it means that they have a legally enforceable right to be employed at schools, regardless of whether the school authorities want them there, and a legally enforceable right to say things other than what the school hired them to say. These rights, especially with the powerful presumptions that they carry with them, have fundamentally altered the school board-teacher and teacher-student relationships.

Notes

1 *Shelton v. Tucker* 364 U.S. 479 at 487 (1960).
2 Mortimer Adler, *The Paideia Proposal*; U.S. Department of Education, *A Nation at Risk*; Ernest L. Boyer, *A Report on Secondary Education in America*; Twentieth Century Fund, *Report of the Twentieth Century Fund Task Force on Federal Elementary and Secondary Education Policy*; John Goodlad, *A Place Called School: Prospects for the Future.*

3 This Just Compensation Clause prohibits the federal government from condemning anyone's property without paying him a just compensation for his loss at 249.
4 330 U.S. 1.
5 *Ibid.* at 15-16.
6 392 U.S. 236.
7 *Ibid.* at 243.
8 *Ibid.* at 248.
10 403 U.S. 602 (1971)—together with *Early v. DiCenso.*
11 413 U.S. 756.
12 *Ibid.* at 783.
13 *Ibid.* at 791.
14 *Ibid.* at 795.
15 *Ibid.* at 802.
16 *Ibid.* at 823.
17 103 S. Ct. 3062.
18 *Ibid.* at 3067.
19 *Ibid.*
20 *Ibid.*, quoting Justice Powell in *Wolman v. Walter*, 433 U.S. 229 (1977) at 262.
21 *Ibid.* at 3068.
22 454 U.S. 263.
23 *Mueller* at 3069.
24 *Ibid.* at 3068.
25 *Ibid.* at 3069.
26 *Ibid.*
27 *Ibid.*
28 370 U.S. 421.
29 *Ibid.* at 430.

30 *Ibid.* at 445.
31 *Ibid.* at 446.
32 *Ibid.*
33 374 U.S. 203.
34 *Ibid.* at 212.
35 *Ibid.* at 222.
36 393 U.S. 97.
37 242 Ark. 922, 416 S.W. 2d 322 (1967).
38 *Epperson* at 107.
39 *Ibid.* at 104.
40 *Ibid.*
41 *Ibid.* at 107.
42 347 U.S. 483.
43 163 U.S. 537.
44 *Brown* at 493.
45 *Ibid.* at 492.
46 *Ibid.* at 494.
47 349 U.S. 294 (1955).
48 391 U.S. 563.
49 *Ibid.* at 568, 574.
50 393 U.S. 503.
51 *Ibid.* at 506.
52 *Ibid.* at 339.
53 402 U.S. 1.
54 433 U.S. 267.
55 *Ibid.* at 279.
56 *Ibid.* at 270.
57 *Ibid.* at 281.
58 *Ibid.* at 283, 287-88.
59 See: Thomas Ascik, "Looking at Some Research on What Makes An Effective School," in *Blueprint for Educational Reform*, The Free Congress Foundation, Summer 1984. Also, inter alia: Richard Murnane, "Interpreting the Evidence on School Effectiveness," *Teachers College Record*, Fall 1981; Thomas Corcoran and Barbara Hansen, "The Quest for Excellence: Making Public Schools More Effective," The New Jersey School Boards Association, 1983; Gilbert Austin, "Ex-

emplary Schools and the Search for Effectiveness," *Educational Leadership*, October 1979; and Edgar Epps, "Towards Effective Desegregated Schools," paper commissioned by the National Institute of Education, 1983.
60 David Armor, "The Evidence on Busing," *The Public Interest*, 28, 1972; and James Coleman, "Recent Trends in School Integration," *Educational Researcher*, July-August 1975; Dennis Cuddy, "The Problem of Forced Busing and a Possible Solution," *Phi Delta Kappan*, September 1984.
61 "School Desegregation, The Social Science Role," *American Psychologist*, 38, 8, August 1983; Walter G. Stephan, "Blacks and Brown: The Effects of School Desegregation on Black Students," *School Desegregation and Black Achievement*, National Institute of Education, 1984.
62 364 U.S. 484.
63 *Ibid.* at 485.
64 E.g., *NAACP v. Alabama*, 357 U.S. 449 (1958).
65 *Shelton* at 485.
66 *Ibid.* at 486.
67 *Ibid.*
68 *Ibid.* at 487.
69 *Ibid.*
70 *Ibid.* at 490.
71 385 U.S. 589.
342 U.S. 485.
Ibid. at 493.
Keyishian at 602-03.
Adler at 492.
Keyishian at 605-06.
77 *Ibid.* at 300.
78 *Ibid.*
79 *Green* at 437.
80 *Ibid.* at 440.
81 *Ibid.* at 507.
82 *Ibid.* at 508.
83 *Ibid.* at 509.
84 *Ibid.* at 511.
85 *Ibid.* at 518.

Are You Sensitive to Interracial Children's Special Identity Needs?

Francis Wardle

Francis Wardle, Ph.D., is Director of the Adams County Head Start and Adams County Day Care in Denver, Colorado.

Early childhood educators continually adjust to changes in the children and families they serve. Educators must provide for children not living with their natural parents, children from abusive families, children who rarely see their parents, and children from single-parent homes. Early childhood educators are becoming increasingly aware of children living in single-father families (Briggs & Walters, 1985), as well as single-mother families. Now these professionals have an additional challenge: to be sensitive and supportive of the unique needs of interracial children and their families.

The number of interracial marriages has increased to more than 100,000 in the past decade. The 1983 census cites 632,000 interracial marriages in the United States; 125,000 are Black/White unions. These figures reflect only current interracial marriages; they do not include divorced parents or interracial unions not resulting in marriage (Shackford, 1984). Although

there are no data on the number of interracial children in our society, because census forms do not include an *interracial* or *mixed* category, it is clearly increasing and posing new challenges to all involved in raising children (Wardle, 1981). These new challenges include the interracial child with one Black and one White parent, and all other combinations of one parent of color and one White, including Asian American/White, Native American/White, and so on.

Conflicting information

Although there is an increasing need for early childhood educators to address the needs of interracial children and their families, this is difficult to do because of the lack of information about this growing population. There has been little interest in this area by professionals, and a resistance by interracial couples to be studied (Poussaint, 1984). One reason we know so little is because professionals (educators, researchers, sociologists, and psychologists) have accepted —and often perpetuated—the culturally accepted notion that the interracial child must select the identity of one parent, usually the parent of color. Studies that do exist on interracial families are

often contradictory (Aldridge, 1978), and our historic fixation on skin color and the inferiorities associated with individuals of darker skin have made objective analysis difficult (Baptiste, 1983).

Interracial families

In 1967, the United States Supreme Court struck down existing state laws against interracial marriages. That decision, along with the 1954 Supreme Court decision on school desegregation (*Brown v. Topeka*), the Civil Rights Movement, and the greater frequency of minorities and Whites living in the same neighborhoods and attending the same schools and colleges, has led to the increase of Black/White interracial families—other interracial marriages of one person of color and one White have also increased. American servicemen who fought in World War II, the Korean War, and the Vietnam War have had great impact on this increase, as have servicemen and servicewomen who choose spouses from the various countries where U.S. bases exist. Historically, soldiers have married citizens of the countries they have conquered or protected. Although data about interracial marriages are contradictory (Aldridge, 1978), and a lot of commonly held myths about these rela-

From *Young Children*, Vol. 42, No. 2 (January 1987), pp. 53-58.

Rick Reinhard

Parents and teachers of interracial children need to examine their values and provide environments in which open discussion of racial identity is encouraged.

tionships are just that—myths (Poussaint, 1984), some general descriptors can be suggested:

1) Public approval of interracial marriage has changed with 20% approving in 1968 to 43% in 1983 (Gallup Poll Report, 1983, cited in Baptiste, 1985).

2) More public interaction between the races will result in a growing number of interracial unions (Aldridge, 1978).

3) Contemporary interracial marriages are more likely to involve spouses from the same social class than was formerly the case (Aldridge, 1978).

4) Urban inhabitants are more likely to engage in cross-race marriage than rural people (Aldridge, 1978).

5) Stationing of U.S. military personnel throughout the world continues to affect the number of interracial unions.

6) People who marry across racial and ethnic lines tend to be less devout religiously, and also tend to marry across religious barriers.

7) On the average, both spouses in an interracial marriage marry at a later age than other married people.

8) Interracial relationships are as stable as other marriages (Monahan, 1973; Pavela, 1964).

Studies of interracial marriage have been fairly unanimous in their assessment of outstanding problems encountered—housing, occupation, and relationships with families and peers (Aldridge, 1978). "However, the tendency to look for ulterior motives in interracial marriages—a popular notion—is not supported by research. Perhaps [this notion] says more about the individual making these interpretations and about the society we live in than about the couple who intermarry" (Aldridge, 1978, p. 359). When this individual's profession (teacher, psychologist, psychoanalyst) gives status to these intepretations, the confusion is magnified.

Interracial children

There are various viewpoints about the terminology used to describe interracial children: *Interracial, biracial, mixed, brown,* and *rainbow* have all been suggested. The term *interracial* is used here because it is inclusive of families with a variety of heritages: African, European, Asian, Native American, Hispanic, and so on (Shackford, 1984).

Additionally, there is a considerable debate about how interracial children's identities should be developed and supported. A range of approaches is being used by parents of interracial children, which is understandable in a society that is totally illogical about racial identity (Shackford, 1984). This debate is particularly intense because of the general recognition that identity development is a critical element of overall early development (Moore, 1985).

According to Ladner (1984), parents of interracial children tend to deal with the racial and ethnic identity of their children in one of three ways: Some parents say their child is a human above all else—color is totally irrelevant; other parents teach their children to have a Black identity or the identity of the parent of color and to learn minority survival skills; the third group teaches its children that they are interracial and should have an interracial identity. Many researchers stress that it is important for interracial children to learn to cope as Black people or people of color, because society ultimately is going to categorize them as such (Ladner, 1984; Shackford, 1984).

Chen (1984) notes that the 3.5 million Asian-Americans in this country comprise eight distinct ethnic groups. "We are a diverse group—some born and acculturated in Asia; many first, second, or third generation Americans—born knowing no language other than English" (p. 11). Yet most Americans see Asian-Americans as Asian first.

Poussaint reports that all the interracial college students he interviewed for a study identified themselves as Black. "Blackness, therefore, is very strong stuff—one drop makes you Black" (Poussaint, 1984, p. 9).

However, today many parents are teaching their children to accept both cultural backgrounds and to define a truly bicultural and interracial identity (Baptiste, 1985; Wardle, 1981, 1983). Contemporary interracial families are choosing a different path to follow. They are emphasizing the dual cultural heritage of their children. This important change reflects a different kind of society than that of 30, 20, or even 10 years ago (Baptiste, 1985).

Baptiste comes to this conclusion by comparing the results of Porterfield's study (1978) with those of Baptiste, Campbell, and Matthews (Baptiste, 1985). The comparison shows that both Black and White communities are becoming more receptive to interracial families, and that both White and Black extended families are more accepting of interracial couples and their families.

During the last 20 years there has also been a great increase in the self-determination of interracial families (Baptiste, 1985; Wardle, 1984). Parents of this new generation of interracial children are products of the 1960s who believe

Black? White? Human above all else?

in the equality of all people and who want their children to have the richness of both parents' heritages. The White parent in the relationship is no longer willing to give up her or his heritage. These couples truly believe their children are stronger and better equipped to meet the challenges of society (Baptiste, 1985). These parents serve as strong role models and believe that the cultural heritage of both parents is an integral part of their child's self-esteem. The number of support groups (see list of interracial family organizations) and the interest in conferences on interracial issues seems to support this affirmation of the contemporary interracial family.

Chen (1984) tells about his son's identity. "I hear my 6-year-old son respond to the recurrent question of 'Where are you from?' with the reply that he is from New York City, and that he is both Chinese and American" (p. 11). The trend is to raise Asian-American/White children so they have positive contact with both sides of the family and frequent exposure to other Asian-American/White children.

The contemporary interracial child has, from birth, been intimately exposed to different life styles, speech patterns, mannerisms, and cultural norms (Baptiste, 1985). Children can pull the best from both backgrounds and use this doubly rich heritage to society's advantage. They are closer to being citizens of the world than are most children. Interracial children have the survival skills to function in many cultural environments (Wardle, 1984).

The role of early childhood educators

Teachers, social workers, and psychologists often believe that problems interracial children experience stem from the fact of being interracial (Shackford, 1984). These professionals may believe popular myths about interracial families, including the tendency to marry for ulterior motives (Aldridge, 1978), or may see interracial children as the result of a union they dislike (Wardle, 1981). Parents and in-laws may also view all problems as race-related, when in fact they may be the result of developmental stages or other stresses that cause the child difficulty (Shackford, 1984).

Because a child's identity is so dependent on setting, and it is in early childhood that the interracial child is exposed to the social pressure of being different, teachers must provide a supportive environment. While almost nothing has been written about this issue (Baptiste, 1983), and there is still considerable debate as to the best approach to take, general indicators for professionals working with

Francis Wardle

Young children are surprisingly aware of race. Adults should help them engage in positive interactions on the subject.

young interracial children can be suggested (Baptiste, 1983; Jacobs, 1978; Phillips & Wardle, 1984; Wardle, 1981).

1) Teachers should fully examine their feelings regarding interracial marriage and the fundamental issues of race and ethnicity to discover whether personal values prevent them from working effectively with interracial children and their parents. (McGoldrick, Pearce, and Giordano, 1982 recommend that therapists of interracial children do this too.)

2) Parents of interracial children should be treated as *sincere* parents who are concerned about their children and who want the best educational program for them.

3) Recognize that interracial children are different from each *other,* just as all children are. No child should be stereotyped.

4) Meet with the parents before each school year and then regularly. During these meetings, discuss, along with issues that affect all parents and children, what the *parents* consider their child's cultural and ethnic heritage to be, how

Teachers should consult parents about the child's heritage and how to handle it.

they support that heritage at home (including celebrations), and how they would like to see the heritage supported in the classroom. Find out how parents tell their children to handle derogatory comments from other children.

5) Love, support, and accept the child.

6) Provide an open atmosphere where racial issues can be discussed, where children can freely talk about questions of physical differences, feelings, and negative reactions they may have experienced. Do not gloss over the child's physical differences and the fact that her or his parents are different. Other children—of all racial and ethnic backgrounds—are very aware of these differences. Talk about them. Also point out to the interracial child that many people are uncomfortable with differences, and therefore will stare, but also stress the richness and beauty of being different, and the many, many ways other than racially that people are different, one from the other. Talk, too, about ways all people are the same: All people have heads, eat, breathe, and so on.

7) Support interracial children in handling difficult situations—with children and adults. Give them skills and confidence to protect themselves from verbal and physical abuse. Some parents even give their children wise words to say in such situations.

8) Provide curricula and materials that support both of the child's parents, and support the child's positive identification with both parents.

9) Provide ongoing experiences for all children in multicultural, multiracial environments where many heritages are celebrated, and where the interplay of heritages is stressed. Include in the curriculum people of interracial and multiracial backgrounds who are prominent in sports, history, and the arts (see list of books for interracial families). Visual materials—posters, pictures, books, collage materials—should include adults and children who are interracial.

10) Avoid always breaking the populations of the world into specific categories defined by color and physical attributes; rather, describe people with national and

other common descriptors. Examine whether you are breaking study units into racial or ethnic labels like "studying Indians." Art, music, dance, literature, and science transcend racial and ethnic boundaries.

11) Avoid automatically labeling a person or child of color as a member of a specific ethnic category. Avoid attributing racial stereotypes to that category. Chen (1984) describes this incident: "I recall the discomfort of my New York born and raised daughter, who has never learned Chinese, when her teacher asked her to write some Chinese characters on the board" (1984, p. 11).

12) Be sensitive to the child's need to define her or his identity. An interracial child may play with a White doll, a Black doll, or both. The child may paint faces brown, black, or pink. The child may have confusing arguments with other children about her or his racial heritage. And she or he may comment, as one child did during a group reading of a story about a Black family, "Where's the father? He should be White—not Black like the mother" (Wardle, 1981, p. 8).

13) Reinforce the parent's method of identifying the child. If a parent considers the child biracial or interracial, use that label to show the child she or he has an identity group.

14) Through stories, role playing, films, and other activities, illustrate that many people in this country effectively mix religions; national heritages; and ethnic, racial, and political backgrounds through marriage. Use a child with English/Polish parents, or one with Italian/Swedish parents, to work into the issue of parents who are a combination of White and a minority.

15) Encourage interracial children to act out their family situations. View this as an affirmation of the child's parentage. Also view it as a positive contribution to the classroom climate.

Mary Harrison

Teachers and parents can work sensitively to feature cultural customs of both races represented in each interracial child, as well as create ongoing experiences for all children in which multicultural diversity is celebrated.

16) Encourage parents who indicate interest in joining a local support group (see list of interracial family organizations), or starting their own. Be open to parents searching for the best way to raise their interracial children. Many parents of young interracial children are struggling with their *own* sense of their child's identity. Be supportive of these parents.

17) Realize that parents of interracial children are often particularly sensitive to racism. While all families of young children are under pressure, interracial couples feel additional kinds of pressures. Few days go by without each parent hearing a negative comment about

the other parent's race. Many have lost emotional and economic support of *their* parents and grandparents. They see their children suffer from choices they made. There is the tendency to blame all their problems on the interracial status. Parents may seem supertouchy about anything construed as racism.

18) Be aware of the negative effects of government and other agencies' requirements to break down children's enrollment into neat, ethnic categories. Many forms do not provide a category for the interracial child. This author spent 40 minutes arguing with an official about his child's identity. Finally,

the official wrote: race unknown. This attitude is very frustrating to interracial parents. Encourage officials and form designers to include a *combination,* or *mixed,* category.

Biologically interracial children are a mixture of two racial and ethnic backgrounds and traditions of both parents. Teachers of these children—and other cross-race and cross-ethnic children—must not go along with society's attempt to classify by the parent of color, but must teach them they are culturally members of both races. Positive models of both races must be apparent to children during these early years. Access to the respective races' cultural customs and practices should be provided. And support for the parents' struggle to develop a strong family unit where positive interracial identification can take place must be given. Young children's programs need to work with parents to help develop this strong, new American child.

References

Aldridge, D. (1978). Interracial marriage: Empirical and theoretical considerations. *Journal of Black Studies, 8*(3), 355–368.

Baptiste, P. (1983, December). Rearing the interracial child. *Communique,* pp. 4–5.

Baptiste, P. (1984, September). Multiculturalism: A support for the interracial family. *Communique,* pp. 1–8.

Baptiste, P. (1985, April). The contemporary interracial child. *Communique,* pp. 1–7.

Briggs, B. A., & Walters, C. M. (1985). Single-father families: Implications for early childhood education. *Young Children, 40*(3), 23–27.

Chen, C. L. (1984). Growing up with an Asian American heritage. *Interracial Books for Children Bulletin, 15*(6), 11–12.

Gordon, A. (1964). *Intermarriage.* Westport, CT: Greenwood.

Jacobs, J. (1978). Black/White interracial families: Marital process and identity development in young children. *Dissertation Abstracts International, 38*(10-B), 5023.

Ladner, J. (1984). Providing a healthy environment for interracial children. *Interracial Books for Children Bulletin, 15*(6), 7–8.

Long, M. (1984). The interracial family in children's literature. *Interracial Books for Children Bulletin, 15*(6), 13–15.

Matthews, S. (1983, December). Interracial marriage on the increase. *Communique,* p. 2.

McGoldrick, M., Pearce, J., & Giordano, J. (Eds.). (1982). *Ethnicity and family therapy.* New York: Guilford Press.

Monahan, T. P. (1973). Marriage across racial lines in Indiana. *Journal of Marriage and Family, 35,* 632–640.

Moore, E. G. J. (1985). Ethnicity as a variable in child development. In M. B. Spencer, G. Brookins, & W. Allen (Eds.), *Beginnings: The social and affective development of Black children.* Hillsdale, NJ: Erlbaum.

Pavela, T. H. (1964). An exploratory study of Negro-White inter-marriage in Indiana. *Marriage and Family Living, 26*(6), 209–211.

Phillips, P., & Wardle, F. (1984). What do biracial children need? Suggestions for parents and teachers. *Interracial Books for Children Bulletin, 15*(6), 8.

Porterfield, E. (1978). *Black and White mixed marriage: An ethnographic study.* Chicago: Nelson-Hall.

Poussaint, A. F. (1984). Study of interracial children presents positive picture. *Interracial Books for Children Bulletin, 15*(6), 9–10.

Shackford, K. (1984). Interracial children: Growing up healthy in an unhealthy society. *Interracial Books for Children Bulletin, 15*(6), 4–6.

Wardle, F. (1983, October). Biracial children—rich in heritage. *Rocky Mountain News.*

Wardle, F. (1984, September). Please check one: White, Black, Other—Mixed. *Communique,* pp. 2–3.

Wardle, F. (1985, Fall). Mummy's Black, Daddy's White, and I'm Brown. *Communique,* 4–7.

The Bilingual Education Battle

Cynthia Gorney
Washington Post Staff Writer

They were a mystery to Barbara Ruel, these exuberant Spanish-speaking children in Redwood City, Calif., whose faces went empty every time she opened a reader and began to write English vocabulary on the blackboard. Even the most recent of the Central American immigrants understood some English, and Ruel was a veteran reading teacher, but every word she gave them seemed gone by the next week. They would stare at their readers, and Ruel could see them struggling, as though the shapes had blurred before them.

What was she doing wrong?

Then in 1976, intrigued by a controversial idea that was gaining momentum among a few teachers, Ruel decided to try something so different that she was not certain the school administration would even allow it. Working in secret, she and her Spanish-speaking aide sat down together and wrote an entire first-grade reading primer in Spanish.

Ten words a week, Ruel told the aide—two characters, a boy and a girl, admiring spring. *Mariposa.* Butterfly. *El pajaro vuele.* The bird flies. Ruel ran the pages off on the school mimeograph, the aide watched the door to make sure no one was coming, and with no advance warning Ruel presented her Spanish-speaking first-graders one day with a small stapled volume written entirely in their own language.

All at once, Ruel says now, she had a roomful of voracious readers. She had children who ran to her at the end of each day to ask what stories or new sentences they might take home that night. "We could not keep up with them," she said recently. "I thought, 'God, it's fabulous, it's just fabulous.' They started to read like normal first-graders read."

And as Barbara Ruel sat back in the nearly deserted lunchroom at Hoover Elementary and remembered those children, a single glimpse through the open classroom doors nearby might have hinted at the breadth of the change in the decade since Ruel stapled together her primers. The school district's hard-bound Spanish readers lay in fat stacks on the bookshelves, wall-length dual alphabet charts displayed the Spanish *ll* and *ch*, and a bright construction-paper leprechaun smoked a pipe under the large bulletin board letters that identified him: *El Duende.*

Ten years ago, spurred by a Supreme Court decision arguably as significant for non-English-speaking students as *Brown v. Board of Education* was for black students, the U.S. Office of Education began an effort of which the premise was unprecedented in American education. The scope was massive, affecting school districts from southern Florida to the Alaskan bush. Although their drive did not carry the force of law, the officials, wielding educational research and the Supreme Court ruling, declared that in the American public school system, every non-English-speaking child below high school age had a right to be taught in his own language—to learn basic subjects from a bilingual teacher so the child might develop self-confidence, sharpen his thinking skills and keep from falling behind in school while he was mastering English.

It was called "bilingual education," and the clamor it raised was tremendous, from the legislative battles to the heated school board meetings to the teachers who stopped speaking to each other in faculty lunchrooms. In the modern history of this nation's public schools, nothing except racial desegregation has so thoroughly entangled the classroom

From *The Washington Post National Weekly Edition*, July 29, 1985, pp. 6-10. © The Washington Post.

with intense feelings about ethnicity, politics and the meaning of becoming an American.

And although the outcry has quieted since the the early 1980s, the dilemmas of bilingual education have not. If you set out this year on a random tour of American classrooms, you would find, amid teachers still deeply divided about the idea, half a million children enrolled in widely varying programs that their schools classify as bilingual education—an effort that is costing local school boards and the federal government about $500 million a year.

You would find young Boston Haitians learning culture in Creole, and Mississippi Indians learning to read in Choctaw, and children of Michigan immigrants learning history in Albanian and Arabic. You would find math workbooks in Spanish, Italian reading primers, Chinese vocabulary cards, Navajo storybooks, an Earth sciences text in Lao, a U.S. history text in Vietnamese, and color and shape charts written in the Filipino dialect Tagalog.

In Houston or San Francisco, you would visit classrooms that take another approach, in which non-English-speaking students are immersed in English as a Second Language courses—they hear and read nothing but English.

You would visit a Spanish bilingual class whose teacher speaks no Spanish; a bilingual Cambodian class whose teacher speaks no Khmer; a bilingual Chinese class whose teacher has no intention of learning Chinese and believes most dual-language education has no place in the taxpayer-funded schools of an English-speaking society.

You would visit Oakland, where on March 1, nine years after state officials began requiring bilingual education for children who speak another language more fluently than they speak English, the California State Education Code finally caught up with Franklin Elementary School.

Spurred by an Oakland parents' lawsuit demanding improved bilingual classes citywide, a judge ordered the city's schools into compliance with the state guidelines that map out the largest bilingual education effort in the nation. In California, if an elementary school has one grade with at least 10 limited-English students from a particular language group, the school has to offer a bilingual class just for them.

Inside Franklin, which sits in the midst of inexpensive rental housing that attracts new immigrants, 14 languages are spoken in the course of a normal school day. According to state regulations, the school was supposed to offer bilingual classes in Cantonese, Spanish, Vietnamese, Lao, Khmer and the Ethiopian language Tigrinya.

Priscilla McClendon, a fifth-grade teacher who jokes that she finds challenge aplenty in just mastering English, was assigned a group of fourth- and fifth-grade Cambodians and told to promise in writing that she would learn Khmer.

Francesca Ferrari was assigned a collection of first- to third-grade Ethiopians and told to promise in writing that she would learn Tigrinya. Since state law requires at least one-third of the children in a bilingual class to be native English speakers, she got some of those, too—eight black American children and one Hispanic girl whose mother had just pulled her out of a Spanish bilingual class because she thought her daughter wasn't learning enough English.

Pat Eimerl lost her Cambodian-Vietnamese-Ethiopian-Thai-Hispanic sixth grade, which on the books had been labeled a Cambodian bilingual class, since Eimerl had earlier promised in writing to learn Khmer. Her new students, all of whom filed in one afternoon carrying the contents of their former desks, are Cantonese-speaking Vietnamese. Eimerl was told to promise she would learn Cantonese, since this was now supposed to be a Chinese bilingual class, but for weeks she refused to sign the promise.

"See, with Cambodian I'm safe, because there aren't any classes," Eimerl said, referring to language classes for teachers. She was so angry her voice shook, "But there are Chinese classes. I've got three kids. I'm 40 years old. I'm not about to go try to learn Chinese."

A Disappointing Decade

When federal officials began the push for bilingual education, grand hopes and promising research armed them against their critics. High school dropout rates for Hispanics were far higher than those for white students, they observed; here, they argued, was a possible remedy. Theory and their own convictions convinced them that students who learned at least part-time in their native language had a much better chance in the schools: They would keep up academically, they would maintain their self-esteem, and they might in the end become literate and articulate in two languages.

A decade later, much of the whole enterprise has dismayed both its longtime critics and some of the people who most ardently believe in bilingual education. National Hispanic high school dropout rates, although not reliably monitored, are as high as ever: just under 40 percent, according to estimates by the Washington-based National Hispanic Policy Development Project. Teachers from San Francisco to Providence can be heard complaining that bilingual classes hold students back or keep them away from English. A U.S. Department of Education study, published in 1983 to vehement criticism from many bilingual educators, found "no consistent evidence" that dual-language instruction improved students' academic progress.

And bilingual advocates say schools are slapping the "bilingual" label on classes that have almost nothing to do with dual-language teaching. They also say that because some states don't require bilingual education and some schools ignore their own state requirements, more than three-quarters of the limited-English-speaking children in this country are receiving no dual-language instruction at all.

"What's going on in 90 percent of the classrooms in this country is a joke in respect to what bilingual education ought to be," says Duane Campbell, a Spanish-English bilingual teacher who now works in the bilingual teacher training program at California State University at Sacramento. "And if you're going to tell me that doesn't work, I'll agree with you. It doesn't work."

The term "bilingual education" covers such vast territory—gifted teachers and dreadful teachers, imaginative new workshops and rote learning in overcrowded classrooms—that it defies the kind of generalizations people seem to want when such a controversial idea is proposed as public policy. So complex is the argument that critics and advocates cannot even agree on how many children in this country come to school with what the jargon calls "limited English proficiency;" the estimates range from 1.5 million to 3.5 million.

But a look at the problems in this massive undertaking, the business of helping immigrant schoolchildren in their own language, might begin at Franklin Elementary, or Franklin Year-Round, as the school is officially named: Its side-by-side buildings now hold children in a schedule that has eliminated the summer break. Down the long hallways, the bulletin boards all a-color with spring tulips and construction paper Humpty-Dumptys, doorways frame bright classrooms crowded desk to desk with the children of the new immigration. *Phumpuang Phaisan, Khadijah Muhammed, Phonevil Pomsouvanh, Kai-Phong Mack, Alejandro Esparza.* The names, in careful block lettering, fill pink and green class lists on the desk of Franklin's harried bilingual coordinator, and next to each name the numerical code for the language the child brought to school: Khmer, Tigrinya, Lao, Cantonese, Spanish.

"If you figure just the amount of time, money and education disruption . . . the fact that English speakers have zero rights . . . this has been costly as hell," says Martha Muller, the coordinator who for the last three months has been shuffling and reshuffling names into lists that will comply with California state education laws. "The law is not meant for this kind of school. It is meant for a nice, neat, orderly, Spanish-English population, or a Chinese-English population, or something. But it's not meant for a multilanguage school."

"Now that we're in compliance, it's just as ridiculous as when we were out of compliance," says Michael Phillips, who teaches his combined fourth- and fifth-grade class in both English and the Vietnamese he learned in preparation for a year's military assignment in Vietnam. "So all my English-speaking kids have to sit there and wait while I'm translating for the Vietnamese. Now who's being served there?"

As chaotic as it is at this school, with nearly every morning bringing new immigrants to the front office to enroll their children, bilingual education at Franklin is in some of the same trouble that has plagued schools across the country for the past decade. It begins with California state law—a law, similar to those in some of the 22 states that mandate or permit bilingual classes, that lays out the number of speakers of any single language that is supposed to trigger a bilingual class.

It was violations of that requirement, among many other complaints, that moved a group of Oakland parents last fall to bring what turned into a bitterly argued lawsuit that accused the city school board of causing "irreparable injury" to thousands of students by failing to offer them bilingual classes. The documentation listed Franklin as one of the worst offenders: The school was missing teachers or aides in five languages, including Lao and Tigrinya. How does a school find candidates for a job like that?

School officials actually interviewed a few people, Franklin principal Jay Cleckner says, although lawyers for the parents' group insisted Oakland had done far too little recruiting and hiring. But almost nobody qualified as an American classroom teacher, Cleckner says. And if a few spoke English well enough to work as classroom aides, he says, he could not keep them in part-time jobs that paid about $5 an hour and offered no benefits. "I have interviewed for aides and for teachers, people who are very qualified," Clecker says. "But they can go back to work for four times what I can pay them, and I tell them, 'Go. Take care of yourself.' "

Where Do You Find a Teacher Who Speaks Hmong?

The national shortage of qualified teachers has for some years been one of bilingual education's major problems. There is not a single Khmer- or Hmong-speaking credentialed teacher in California, which has the nation's highest numbers of refugees from Cambodia and the part of Laos that was home to the Hmong people. Even qualified teachers who speak fluent Spanish are in short supply in many states; when Houston bilingual administrator Delia Pompa was presented this year with the revised Texas mandates for bilingual education through fifth grade, she calculated that even with extensive recruiting and $1,500 bonuses for the mostly Spanish-speaking dual-language teachers, conventional teaching patterns were going to leave the district short 400 teachers qualified to work in two languages.

"Before, when Hispanics went to college, they went into teaching," says Pompa, who plans to accommodate the short-

age by classroom rearrangements such as teacher pairing. "Hispanics are starting to go into other professions . . . Teaching, and education in general, is going through a low period. Teaching isn't looked at as a real respected profession. You're looking at a lot of problems."

Hardly anybody seriously expects schoolteachers such as the ones at Franklin to learn Khmer or Lao in their spare time. But one of the ways many areas have adapted to the shortage is by asking teachers to sign up for courses in languages that seem more manageable to learn. In California, state figures show that fully half the "bilingual" teachers are regular teachers who have pledged to learn dual-language teaching methods and become fluent in a second language (usually Spanish, but occasionally English) while a bilingual aide helps them with the children.

That leads to a whole new set of problems. How well those teachers are actually learning both the language and the complicated business of dual-language teaching varies from school to school, particularly since many principals are dubious about the idea to begin with. One elementary school will house an after-hours class for teachers who are genuinely committed to learning Spanish, and usually doing so on their own time. A second will sign up "bilingual" teachers who plainly have little interest in ever learning more than a few words of the language. Even when they do try, bilingual advocates sometimes wonder what comes of their efforts: A Hispanic attorney tells of the newly trained Texas teacher who stood before a parents' group and began, "*Damas y caballos,*" which is a salutation of sorts; it means "Ladies and horses."

And the proceedings inside the dual-language class are only as effective as the teacher who runs it. In visits this spring to more than 20 bilingual classrooms, a reporter watched one bilingual teacher review long division in English scarcely intelligible through his Spanish accent, and another teacher who spoke no Spanish and left all the Spanish business to an aide she clearly distrusted: "I don't even think she's graduated from high school," the teacher confided.

Here were teachers translating right through history and arithmetic lessons, despite linguists' warnings that simultaneous translation is the least effective bilingual teaching method because it lets the student listen to the language he knows best. Here were teachers frustrated by school systems that hurried children into full-time English so fast that, as the teachers saw it, some of the point of bilingual education was being lost—the idea that children's English work will be stronger and more confident if they are allowed to develop fully and work in their own language at least part time for more than a year or two.

Here were teachers so tired of the whole bilingual effort—of juggling multiple two-language reading groups, battling supervisors and watching children's confusion when a school offered them dual-language classes at one grade but then abruptly not at another—that the teachers had finally bailed out. "You go crazy—that's why a lot of bilingual teachers go out of the program, because they can't handle it," says Erlinda Griffin, a quadrilingual Filipina who left bilingual teaching seven years ago for a school supervisory job in the central California farm city of Fresno. Griffin believes bilingual education theory, and she has seen programs that seem to her to use it successfully. "But unfortunately, they were in the minority—there were so few of them."

And here, too, were teachers, nearly all of them monolingual English speakers, convinced that the bilingual classes they had seen were in large part misguided efforts that held a lot of children back. An Arizona teacher remembered Geme, her Navajo student who had sat through five years of bilingual classes before somebody realized the boy was having trouble because he had spoken scarcely a word of Navajo before he came to school. A suburban San Francisco teacher remembered Spanish-speaking children who never seemed to make the promised transition into English. A Rhode Island counselor remembered the Puerto Rican boy, bewildered by his referral to bilingual classes, who told the counselor in flawless English that he had grown up and gone to school in Lawrence, Mass.

"This is the stuff that goes on all the time," the counselor said. "I think a lot of kids are kept in those programs simply to build up the numbers and justify the programs. We've got kids in those programs who are fluent in English."

Remedial Instruction vs. Linguistic Enrichment

If anybody does belong in bilingual classes, who is it? Some states reserve bilingual classes for children who speak Spanish or some other language, prompting complaints about ethnic and linguistic segregation. California requires them whenever possible to be in classes with native English speakers so the children won't be segregated and will have role models to help them learn the language.

But that doesn't satisfy everybody either. Because most bilingual classes are designed as remedial programs, aimed at moving children into English as rapidly as possible, English-speaking parents have often been disappointed when they allow their children into bilingual classes in the hope that they will learn Spanish. And in towns such as Fillmore, a heavily Hispanic southern California farming community where the expansion of bilingual classes set off an angry Anglo protest this spring, English-speaking parents say their children waste time in a class taught partly in another language.

"Who's going to meet *my* daughter's needs?" demands Judy Collins, a Fillmore parent whose husband recently proposed a controversial city council-adopted resolution making English the "official language" of Fillmore. "The amount of time that teacher is speaking Spanish is time that my child is not getting English instruction," Collins says.

Complaints like these have complicated the response to a generally unenthusiastic 1983 bilingual-education report by two U.S. Department of Education researchers. At the request of a White House policy review group, the researchers examined several hundred studies on bilingual education, many of which concluded that the classes had improved students' academic performance, and found only 39 to be "methodologically acceptable." After analyzing those 39 studies, the researchers reported bilingual education producing only mixed results.

"Sometimes kids did better," says Department of Education analyst Keith Baker, the report's coauthor. "Sometimes it had no effect. And sometimes it had negative effects."

Baker and his partner, who have been criticized for their own methodology, suggested in the report that although limited-English-speaking children clearly needed some special attention, education officials might rethink their reliance on classes using native languages—that full-time intensive English programs, for example, might be more effective in some cases.

Would Franklin Elementary's Francesca Ferrari, facing her tiny Ellis Island of a classroom earlier this year, have done any of her students a greater service by using their own language?

"This I do not know," she says. "I do not know what I really think about bilingual education."

When the Oakland parents' lawsuit was settled in May, with school officials committing themselves to a considerable expansion of the bilingual staff, the central office finally found some qualified teachers' aides for Franklin; a Tigrinya-speaking Ethiopian man now helps in Ferrari's classroom for 80 minutes a day. And she welcomes his presence, she says. He makes things easier for her. In June they were working on *sq* words, and Ferrari did not have to go into contortions or bring lemons into class to explain *squirt* and *squint* and *squid.*

These are ideas the children would have grasped without translation, Ferrari says. Demonstrations, in her experience, are sometimes even more vivid than translation. But she is happy to have the aide anyway—"grateful," Ferrari says. "I think it's a sense of security for the children to have him there, I really do."

Her class no longer includes the Spanish-speaking child; it is now all Ethiopian and native English-speaking children, and in March, as a welcoming gesture, Ferrari put up an Ethiopian market poster and wrote the Tigrinya words for "How are you?" in big bright letters on a poster she taped to the classroom door: *Camilla ha.*

Some weeks later, in discreet messages conveyed through the principal's office, Ferrari was told that this had distressed the Ethiopian families. Parents of all but three of her Ethiopian students indicated on signed forms that they wished their children taught exclusively in English, so Ferrari need no longer abide by her implausible promise to learn Tigrinya.

"They don't want their culture brought in," Ferrari says. "They feel they can take care of that at home." She took the poster down and pulled *Camilla ha* off the classroom door.

Immersion: An Aid or a Threat to Bilingual Education?

In a San Francisco classroom bright with wall decorations, a line of raggedly cut paper pandas stretched overhead, Liana Szeto sat cross-legged on the floor and explained the morning game to the children around her. She would start with five plastic cubes and a milk carton with the top cut off, and they were to close their eyes while she hid some of the cubes under the milk carton. Then they could count the remaining cubes and figure out how many she had hidden.

Szeto suggested Sparky might make the next guess.

Jesse (Sparky) Manger, a small blond boy in standard-issue kindergarten blue jeans and sneakers, squeezed his eyes shut and covered them with his hands. "Sparky," Szeto said, *"Gu yahp bihn yauh gei do go?"*

Just as she had all morning—just as she does for every full school day in a class made up of white children, black children, Chinese-American children and a Chinese-Hispanic child—Szeto was speaking straight Cantonese.

Sparky, whisking his hands away and gazing at the single cube left atop the milk carton, contemplated her question: Yes, he could guess how many she had left inside. *"Sei,"* he said. Szeto lifted the carton and clapped her hands in approval. Four, of course, was right.

Szeto, a 27-year-old Hong Kong immigrant who coaxes and performs her way through each day with a vigor that is almost exhausting to watch, speaks excellent English; she learned it in Hong Kong schools and in the junior high schools she attended when her family arrived in San Francisco. But many of her students don't realize she speaks any English. From the first day of school last September, confronted with 24 kindergarten children who by and large spoke not a word of Cantonese, Szeto has never used English in her classroom. She uses posters, gestures, games, songs, repetition, theatrics, picture books, field trips and anything else she imagines might help her teach, but whenever she speaks—from "Please take out your pencils" to "Let's tell the story of the five foolish fishermen!"—she speaks in Cantonese.

And Sparky Manger's mother Judy, an airline ticket agent who has cringed at most Americans' inability to manage other languages, is delighted. "With China becoming a world power, in his lifetime, it's really going to be beneficial for him to learn Chinese," she says. "I thought he was going to come home and say, 'Mom, what have you done to me?' And he's never once said anything to me about that. He loves it . . . Now he tells me his name is Jesse Wong sometimes."

There is a label in educationalese for the work Szeto is doing with these children, all of whom were sent to West Portal School because their parents wanted to experiment with a teaching method now being tried in at least 18 public school districts around the country. It is called language immersion, and although the methods vary, the principle is the same: English-speaking children, principally from homes where nothing but English is spoken, spend part or all of their days in classes conducted entirely in another language.

In Baton Rouge, La., fourth-graders last month were discussing the tax system, studying the Louisiana government and answering written test questions about layers of the atmosphere—all in French. In Culver City, Calif., fifth-graders were working long-division problems and reading aloud stories about construction workers and shy cats—all in Spanish.

There is Spanish immersion in Tulsa, French immersion in Montgomery County, Md., German immersion in Milwaukee and Cincinnati. San Francisco school officials, already immersing students in Spanish and Cantonese, are thinking of adding Mandarin.

And although some of the programs, like San Francisco's, are too new for any serious evaluation, many administrators have reported results comparable to those out of Canada, where for 20 years public schools have been offering French immersion that University of Southern California linguistics professor Stephen D. Krashen has written "may be the most successful program ever recorded in the professional language-teaching literature."

In the vast new array of efforts at teaching in two languages, no approach has been so carefully monitored, so widely praised for its effectiveness—and, in one of the more complicated ironies of this whole controversial field, so disturbing to advocates of the more familiar theories of bilingual education, which insist that a child should learn to read and think first in his native language.

The vision of these immersion classes, of American-born children learning math and reading from teachers who never address them in English, has prompted opponents of public bilingual education to ask the obvious question: If you can drop an English-speaking child into a special all-Spanish classroom and get him working and thinking in Spanish with no damage to his psyche or test scores, why can't you do the same thing in reverse? Isn't this a natural way to accustom Spanish speakers to English without having to teach them reading and basic skills in Spanish?

School districts in several states already are trying special all-English programs for Spanish-speakers, and the federal government, in U.S. Department of Education reports and in increased availability of special funds, has troubled bilingual-education advocates by showing considerable interest in the idea. And the heat this argument has generated—some teachers and language experts use words like "a crock" and "a crime" to describe the practice of immersing Spanish-speakers into special all-English classes—is part of the national debate about America's attitude toward non-English languages, about the role of language in an immigrant society, about the ties between language and the human spirit.

'If I Can Speak Spanish, I Can Do Anything'

It was show-and-tell time in an afternoon kindergarten and first-grade class in Culver City's El Rincon School, just outside Los Angeles. Irma Wright, her black hair curled and a carnation pinned to her lapel, summoned around her a noisy collection of children and announced who would begin.

"Tu no eres primera," she admonished a small blond girl who had clamored to be first. "Cheryl es primera."

The child nodded, resigned to the primacy of Cheryl, and said in English, "Can I be second?"

Thus it went, the children—nearly every one of them from an English-speaking home—looking entirely unconcerned that their teacher spoke to them only in rapid, native Spanish. Cheryl showed off a stuffed gray bear that she said belonged to her mother, and Wright asked, "Quien le dio eso a tu madre?" Nobody had given it to her mother, Cheryl answered. "She saw it and she got it in a store."

"Que tiene este oso en la nariz?" Wright asked, wondering what was appliqued on the bear's nose. The children knew a heart when they saw one: "Un corazon!" they cried.

Irma Wright, a Hispanic woman who grew up in El Paso, has been teaching the kindergarten immersion class since 1971, when the Culver City schools opened the first U.S. version of the program that was generating so much interest in Canada. A school outside Montreal, now in its 20th year, had set off the whole experiment when a group of English-speaking parents asked for a dramatic and effective way to teach their children French; by last year, according to an article in the Canadian magazine Language and Society, 115,000 Canadian children were studying in one of the French immersion programs now offered in every province.

Culver City administrators, under the supervision of linguists at the University of California at Los Angeles, followed almost precisely the Quebec model: no English at all for the first two years (although the children are free to speak English, and the teacher must be bilingual so that she or he can understand and answer); an hour a day of English reading and language arts in second and third grades; and then a steady increase of English teaching time, until by the fifth grade students are doing more than a third of their classwork in English. "When they leave the elementary school, they are functionally bilingual," says Eugene Ziff, the principal at El Rincon. "They can understand, read, write and speak Spanish in a functional manner, and they have done this without losing any of their basic skills in English."

As he has done for dozens of uncertain parents, Ziff pulls out the mimeographed sheet listing El Rincon's most recent scores on the California Test of Basic Skills, which is administered in both English and Spanish to students in the immersion classes. In 1983 the sixth-grade students were testing out at eighth-grade level on English vocabulary and comprehension. Language mechanics and expression, math concepts and computation—all showed above-average scores, and in the case of language expression, far above average. Only English spelling fell slightly short.

As for their Spanish skills, the Spanish reading test scores are not quite up to averages for native language speakers, but a visit to Mary Nabours' fourth- and fifth-grade classroom, for example, is startling: Children with names like Jennifer Feingold and Pentti Monkkonen read easily from their Spanish texts, or talk in Spanish about characters in the story they have just finished, or work in longhand on their definitions.

Their accents range from good to nearly native; Nabours, who is American but lived in Mexico while studying Spanish, speaks with almost no trace of an American accent. They discuss words like *supongo*, suppose, and *interes*, as in bank interest, and if their grammar is often not quite right, they plow cheerfully through what they are trying to say. A lively red-haired girl, asked to escort a visitor to the kindergarten, is asked in Spanish whether she found the two languages difficult to manage, and she says in slightly ungrammatical but entirely unselfconscious Spanish, "No, because I'm used to it."

"They don't have any trouble getting across what they want to say," Nabours says. "The program encourages creativity in a certain way, but the main thing it encourages—this is my opinion; I can't prove it, but I feel it in every cell in my body—is this feeling of, 'I can' . . . . 'If I can speak Spanish, I can do anything. I can do math. I can do science. I can do anything.' "

So why shouldn't it work in reverse? Why shouldn't Spanish speakers learn English the same way? To answer that, teachers like Nabours believe, you must think about English and Spanish and the social roles they play here. The linguists who designed immersion programs like Culver City's have insisted the programs be used only for children who speak English, children who will go straight into an English middle school, children whose families have sought out the second language and who will never, as long as they live in North America, risk losing the language they grew up with.

One six-school program in San Diego is using the Culver City model on both English and Spanish speakers, immersing them all into Spanish and then gradually working English into half the school day, but its goal is the same as Culver City's—to encourage bilingualism, and to celebrate the learning and reading of two languages rather than one.

That very notion, the idea that schools should promote bilingualism and should have advanced classes in both languages, has been thoroughly attacked during public debates over dual-language education for Hispanics. There is still a strong feeling among many teachers and parents' groups that American schools ought to be teaching in English, that offering special classes for bilingual children amounts to catering to certain ethnic groups.

When Spanish speakers are immersed in English, as several Texas school districts are doing in a state-sponsored pilot program, no one imagines that they will gradually have Spanish worked back in to take over half their school day. The point is simply to teach them English, using techniques that have worked for Anglophones in places like Culver City: Speak nothing but English to the children, but let them use Spanish when they wish; use vocabulary and phrasing aimed at children just learning the language; fill the gaps with posters and pantomime and things the children can touch.

English as a Second Language, Houston-Style

Teacher Rachel Echavarry smiles as she traverses the rows of quiet children, holding up small picture cards and waiting for each response.

"Jesus, what's this?"

"It's a cat."

"What's this?"

"It's a cow."

"Where is the cow?" Hesitation.

Then, tentatively: "The cow—is in—the barn."

There is nothing unique about a class like this; it is standard English as a Second Language (ESL) teaching, offered as part of many public schools' bilingual programs. The difference, at Gregory-Lincoln Education Center in Houston and the other Texas schools trying similar approaches, is that Jesus and his classmates are immersed in English all day. They are never supposed to hear Spanish from their teachers. Indeed, many of

From Chinatown to The Supreme Court

SAN FRANCISCO—Even as Edward Steinman pushed his lawsuit, working his way through the courts with an argument that would help spread bilingual education through the American public school system, his aunts invoked the memory of his late father—the child of immigrants from Russia, speaking nothing but Yiddish, who was thrown into American public schools and made to learn English on his own.

And the elder Steinman did learn English, fluently enough to spend his life as a journalist. "I think there are many, like my father, who did it without bilingual education," Steinman says. "But the studies show there are hundreds of thousands of people who without bilingual education are not going to learn English."

Steinman was barely out of law school, a long-haired 25-year-old working in 1970 out of a cramped basement office in San Francisco's Chinatown. Some of his Chinese clients would come to him for other reasons, then end up complaining that their children were not following what went on in school, like the woman who visited him to talk about a problem with her landlord. Then, as Steinman remembers it, she hesitantly began answering his questions about her 6-year-old son.

The boy, Steinman says she told him, spoke only Chinese. The teachers spoke only English. The woman's name was Kam Wai Lau, and within a year the name of her son, Kinney, led the long list of plaintiffs in a lawsuit that eventually reached the U.S. Supreme Court. Confronted with evidence that fewer than half of San Francisco's Chinese-speaking students were receiving any language help, the court declared that schools must offer language-minority children some special attention. And that attention, a federal panel concluded in 1975 in a controversial set of guidelines, was to be dual-language education. Although bilingual education was not a new idea, this was different because the government was demanding it.

As for the young Lau, who now goes by the name of Kenny and is a 21-year-old part-time computer programming student at San Francisco's City College, the whole case is a memory so dim that he had to be reminded in an interview who Steinman was. "I think the only reason I lost out is because I was lazy—that's all there is to it," he says. "It's nothing to do with understanding what an instructor's saying."

Might Chinese language instruction have helped him do better in school?

"I don't know," he says. "Well, maybe—yeah, it might have made a difference—let's say if I didn't understand something, maybe I could hear a different version of it in Chinese. I don't know. Never happened to me."

—Cynthia Gorney

the teachers at Gregory-Lincoln do not speak Spanish or any of the Indochinese languages that nearly a quarter of the students arrive with; instead, in Saturday workshops and in-class training, they have studied ESL teaching techniques.

How well it works—whether these Texas children are having an easier time learning English while keeping up in their other classes—is still in some dispute.

"Thank God for the English immersion," says Linda Hunter, a fourth-grade teacher now in her 10th year at Gregory-Lincoln, which used to offer an hour a day of Spanish-language instruction. Her colleague Sherilyn Kozodoy, a third-grade teacher whose class includes two Spanish-speaking children, agrees. "I had students in [my former school] who had been going to the bilingual classes for three or four years and still had difficulty with the English language," Kozodoy says. "They learn it much more slowly."

Some teachers are similarly enthusiastic in Texas cities such as McAllen, which has attracted national attention for its English immersion pilot; and in Virginia's Fairfax County, which for seven years has insisted on intensive English instead of dual-language instruction. But preliminary Texas data indicate so far that the immersion classes there, experimentally begun four years ago in cities that also offered bilingual programs, are producing English test scores no higher than those from the bilingual classes, and there are misgivings about the experiment even among some administrators in charge of it.

"I had one teacher start crying and saying, 'Look, I can't do this, it's not fair to the kids,' " says Pompa, Houston's bilingual education administrator. "There were others, to be perfectly fair, who thought it was a good option . . . . I'll be honest. I would prefer a dual language program, because I don't know what kind of cognitive deficits [the immersion children] are going to have four or five years later. And I think there are going to be some."

Wallace Lambert, the social psychologist and language expert who developed the first French immersion programs in Quebec, has argued for more than a decade that to use these techniques on language-minority children is, as he wrote in a 1984 California Department of Education volume, "not only wrong but dangerous." The danger, he argues, lies in what he calls "subtractive bilingualism"—the elimination in school of the language the child first used to think, to conceive ideas and accept who he is.

"We are not removing their language from school," counters Sally Clyburn, acting instructional supervisor for the Houston schools. "We are removing the language from instruction . . . the students *are* using their native language. They can be seen walking to the school cafeteria, to and from the playground, using their native language."

"The child is basically being told, 'Your language is not worth anything,' " says William Prather, who teaches in Spanish to English speakers at Rock Creek Elementary School's Spanish immersion program in Chevy Chase, Md., and who thinks the approach is entirely wrong for non-English speakers. Teachers like Prather and Mary Nabours believe a child whose language is kept out of the classroom will probably lose much of it, if his is not the language of society at large, and that public schools do children a great disservice that way.

The argument over language immersion is not really about the merits of the few programs now trying in some formal and monitored way to place non-English speaking children in special all-English classes. There are not very many of those programs—most are either small experiments or are aimed at children like the Indochinese, who often have no bilingual teachers available—and it is highly unlikely that in the near future they could replace bilingual classes. Federal funds that can be used for special English immersion programs are limited to less than 10 percent of the $139 million budgeted for bilingual education this year.

The battle over that funding was fierce, though, with bilingual education critics wanting much more of the budgeted money to be available to English immersion-type experiments. Bilingual education advocates fought back, some of them declaring that these special immersion classes were simply a convoluted path back to the days when schools openly sent Spanish and Chinese-speaking children to fend for themselves in standard all-English classes—the kind of approach the Supreme Court prohibited 11 years ago.

So the argument is really about the value and meaning of native language in a child's schooling, and that makes it much bigger and more complicated than the proceedings inside a few public school classrooms.

"I think the issue becomes an emotional issue, and people stop looking at what kids need, and what works for kids," says Houston's Delia Pompa. "It becomes in some ways a threat, and sometimes 'I-made-it-why-can't-they,' and sometimes people bring political baggage and emotional baggage to it. I think sometimes people miss the point."

Sexism in the Schoolroom of the '80s

*THINGS HAVEN'T CHANGED.
BOYS STILL GET MORE ATTENTION, ENCOURAGEMENT
AND AIRTIME THAN GIRLS DO.*

MYRA AND DAVID SADKER

Myra and David Sadker are professors of education at American University, Washington, D.C.

I f a boy calls out in class, he gets teacher attention, especially intellectual attention. If a girl calls out in class, she is told to raise her hand before speaking. Teachers praise boys more than girls, give boys more academic help and are more likely to accept boys' comments during classroom discussions. These are only a few examples of how teachers favor boys. Through this advantage boys increase their chances for better education and possibly higher pay and quicker promotions. Although many believe that classroom sexism disappeared in the early '70s, it hasn't.

Education is not a spectator sport. Numerous researchers, most recently John Goodlad, former dean of education at the University of California at Los Angeles and author of *A Place Called School*, have shown that when students participate in classroom discussion they hold more positive atti-

tudes toward school, and that positive attitudes enhance learning. It is no coincidence that girls are more passive in the classroom and score lower than boys on SAT's.

Most teachers claim that girls participate and are called on in class as often as boys. But a three-year study we recently completed found that this is not true; vocally, boys clearly dominate the classroom. When we showed teachers and administrators a film of a classroom discussion and asked who was talking more, the teachers overwhelmingly said the girls were. But in reality, the boys in the film were out-talking the girls at a ratio of three to one. Even educators who are active in feminist issues were unable to spot the sex bias until they counted and coded who was talking and who was just watching. Stereotypes of garrulous and gossipy women are so strong that teachers fail to see this communi-

cations gender gap even when it is right before their eyes.

Field researchers in our study observed students in more than a hundred fourth-, sixth- and eighth-grade classes in four states and the District of Columbia. The teachers and students were male and female, black and white, from urban, suburban and rural communities. Half of the classrooms covered language arts and English—subjects in which girls traditionally have excelled; the other half covered math and science—traditionally male domains.

We found that at all grade levels, in all communities and in all subject areas, boys dominated classroom communication. They participated in more interactions than girls did and their participation became greater as the year went on.

Our research contradicted the traditional assumption that girls dominate classroom discussion in reading while boys are dominant in math. We found that whether the subject was language arts and English or math and science, boys got more than their fair share of teacher attention.

Some critics claim that if teachers talk more to male students, it is simply because boys are more assertive in grabbing their attention—a classic case of the squeaky wheel getting the educational oil. In fact, our research shows that boys are more assertive in the classroom. While girls sit patiently with their hands raised, boys literally grab teacher attention. They are eight times more likely than girls to call out answers. However, male assertiveness is not the whole answer.

Teachers behave differently, depending on whether boys or girls call out answers during discussions. When boys call out comments without raising their hands, teachers accept their answers. However, when girls call out, teachers reprimand this "inappropriate" behavior with messages such as, "In this class we don't shout out answers, we raise our hands." The message is subtle but powerful: Boys should be academically assertive and grab teacher attention; girls should act like ladies and keep quiet.

Teachers in our study revealed an interaction pattern that we called a "mind sex." After calling on a student, they tended to keep calling on students of the same sex. While this pattern applied to both sexes, it was far more pronounced among boys and allowed them more than their fair share of airtime.

It may be that when teachers call on someone, they continue thinking of that sex. Another explanation may be found in the seating patterns of elementary, secondary and even postsecondary classrooms. In approximately half of the classrooms in our study, male and female students sat in separate parts of the room. Sometimes the teacher created this segregation, but more often, the students segregated themselves. A teacher's tendency to interact with same-sex students may be a simple matter of where each sex sits. For example, a teacher calls on a female student, looks around the same area and then continues questioning the students around this girl, all of whom are female. When the teacher refocuses to a section of the classroom where boys are seated, boys receive the series of questions. And because

WHILE GIRLS SIT PATIENTLY WITH THEIR HANDS RAISED, BOYS LITERALLY GRAB TEACHER ATTENTION.

boys are more assertive, the teacher may interact with their section longer.

Girls are often shortchanged in quality as well as in quantity of teacher attention. In 1975 psychologists Lisa Serbin and K. Daniel O'Leary, then at the State University of New York at Stony Brook, studied classroom interaction at the preschool level and found that teachers gave boys more attention, praised them more often and were at least twice as likely to have extended conversations with them. Serbin and O'Leary also found that teachers were twice as likely to give male students detailed instructions on how to do things for themselves. With female students, teachers were more likely to do it for them instead. The result was that boys learned to become independent, girls learned to become dependent.

Instructors at the other end of the educational spectrum also exhibit this same "let me do it for you" behavior toward female students. Constantina Safilios-Rothschild, a sociologist with the Population Council in New York, studied sex desegregation at the Coast Guard Academy and found that the instructors were giving detailed instructions on how to accomplish tasks to male students, but were doing the jobs and operating the equipment for the female students.

Years of experience have shown that the best way to learn something is to do it yourself; classroom chivalry is not only misplaced, it is detrimental. It is also important to give students specific and direct feedback about the quality of their work and answers. During classroom discussion, teachers in our study reacted to boys' answers with dynamic, precise and effective re-

sponses, while they often gave girls bland and diffuse reactions.

Teachers' reactions were classified in four categories: praise ("Good answer"); criticism ("That answer is wrong"); help and remediation ("Try again—but check your long division"); or acceptance without any evaluation or assistance ("OK" "Uh-huh").

Despite caricatures of school as a harsh and punitive place, fewer than 5 percent of the teachers' reactions were criticisms, even of the mildest sort. But praise didn't happen often either; it made up slightly more than 10 percent of teachers' reactions. More than 50 percent of teachers' responses fell into the "OK" category.

Teachers distributed these four reactions differently among boys than among girls. Here are some of the typical patterns.

Teacher: "What's the capital of Maryland? Joel?"

Joel: "Baltimore."

Teacher: "What's the largest city in Maryland, Joel?"

Joel: "Baltimore."

Teacher: "That's good. But Baltimore isn't the capital. The capital is also the location of the U.S. Naval Academy. Joel, do you want to try again?"

Joel: "Annapolis."

Teacher: "Excellent. Anne, what's the capital of Maine?"

Anne: "Portland."

Teacher: "Judy, do you want to try?"

Judy: "Augusta."

Teacher: "OK."

In this snapshot of a classroom discussion, Joel was told when his answer was wrong (criticism); was helped to discover the correct answer (remediation); and was praised when he offered the correct response. When Anne was wrong, the teacher, rather than staying with her, moved to Judy, who received only simple acceptance for her correct answer. Joel received the more specific teacher reaction and benefited from a longer, more precise and intense educational interaction.

Too often, girls remain in the dark about the quality of their answers. Teachers rarely tell them if their answers are excellent, need to be improved or are just plain wrong. Unfortunately, acceptance, the imprecise response packing the least educational punch, gets the most equitable sex distribution in classrooms. Active students receiving precise feedback are more likely to achieve academically. And they are more likely to be boys. Consider the following:

☐ Although girls start school ahead of boys in reading and basic computation, by the time they graduate from high school, boys have higher SAT scores in both areas.

☐ By high school, some girls become less committed to careers, although their grades and achievement-test scores may be as good as boys'. Many girls' interests turn to marriage or stereotypically female jobs. Part of the reason may be that some women feel that men disapprove of their using their intelligence.

☐ Girls are less likely to take math and science courses and to participate in special or gifted programs in these subjects, even if they have a talent for them. They are also more likely to believe that they are incapable of pursuing math and science in college and to avoid the subjects.

☐ Girls are more likely to attribute failure to internal factors, such as ability, rather than to external factors, such as luck.

The sexist communication game is played at work, as well as at school. As reported in numerous studies it goes like this:

☐ Men speak more often and frequently interrupt women.

☐ Listeners recall more from male speakers than from female speakers, even when both use a similar speaking style and cover identical content.

☐ Women participate less actively in conversation. They do more smiling and gazing; they are more often the passive bystanders in professional and social conversations among peers.

☐ Women often transform declarative statements into tentative comments. This is accomplished by using qualifiers ("kind of " or "I guess") and by adding tag questions ("This is a good movie, isn't it?"). These tentative patterns weaken impact and signal a lack of power and influence.

Sexist treatment in the classroom encourages formation of patterns such as these, which give men more dominance and power than women in the working world. But there is a light at the end of the educational tunnel. Classroom biases are not etched in stone, and training can eliminate these patterns. Sixty teachers in our study received four days of training to establish equity in classroom interactions. These trained teachers succeeded in eliminating classroom bias. Although our training focused on equality, it improved overall teaching effectiveness as well. Classes taught by these trained teachers had a higher level of intellectual discussion and contained more effective and precise teacher responses for all students.

There is an urgent need to remove sexism from the classroom and give women the same educational encouragement and support that men receive. When women are treated equally in the classroom, they will be more likely to achieve equality in the workplace.

CENSORSHIP IN THE PUBLIC SCHOOLS

Arnold B. Danzig, Ph.D.

Dr. Danzig is Director of the Educational Information Center at the Arizona Department of Education.

- *"Officials pull books from library."*
- *"Board lifts ban on two stations but not Pratt."*
- *"Schools will keep 'Mockingbird' in classes despite NAACP attack."*

Censorship is alive and well in Arizona's public schools. The Arizona newspaper headlines listed above are samples of some of the efforts to control what students hear, see, and read on the way to school and in the classroom. According to a recent report (Attacks on the Freedom to Learn, 1986) censorship is on the upswing nationally—up 35 percent from last year and up 117 percent from four years ago. Perhaps more surprising is the fact that almost 60 percent of censorship instances were attempts to censor ideas, information and teaching methods.

The purpose of this information brief is to familiarize teachers, administrators, parents and school board members of some of the arguments involved in the censorship debate. This will be followed by a discussion of censorship issues in school textbook adoptions and consideration of the drama of school censorship. Finally, practical steps will be given for members of the education community to use in dealing with censorship.

Defining Censorship

Historically, censorship was the work of an appointed official given the specific task of reviewing material for its potential objectionable quality. According to Webster's Third New International Dictionary (1976), censor means: "1: one of two magistrates of early Rome who acted as census takers, assessors and inspectors of moral conduct;

2a: an official empowered to examine written or printed matter (as manuscripts of books or plays) in order to forbid publication, circulation, or representation if it contains anything objectionable."

Using these definitions, censorship refers to materials that have already been selected and are then subject to public scrutiny. Any parent or interested party may take objection to school materials. Since the private citizen cannot remove anything from the school or classroom, this is not considered censorship. It is the removal of already selected material by a school teacher, a school librarian, an administrator or school board which may qualify as censorship. And, it is because these people hold *public positions*, that their actions may be regarded as "censorship."

The Encyclopedia of Education (1976) defines censorship as "the efforts of individuals or organizations to remove certain intellectual or creative expressions, because of their alleged deleterious effects, from the sight or hearing of others" (volume 5, p. 168). This definition places censorship in opposition to intellectual freedom and supports the view of censorship as the act of *removing* information, methods or materials from the classroom, library or school.

Efforts to Remove Methods and Materials

The classic example of censorship is removing books. A book was brought to the attention of school administrators in Mayer Junior High School after a school board member complained that the book his son brought home from school contained "questionable language and encouraged students to

From *Infospective*, Winter 1987, pp. 1-6. Reprinted by permission of the author.

rebel against their families" (*Prescott Courier*, 2-14-86). The school board voted unanimously to ban seven books identified as containing "subversive ideas" or "foul language." A committee was then formed to screen all texts coming into the district.

Using Audiovisuals

Another case which may be considered censorship involves the use of audiovisual equipment. In Davis v. Page (1974), a federal district ruled on an objection to using audiovisual equipment (filmstrips, films, overheads) in the elementary school curriculum. Apostolic Lutheran parents claimed that A-V use infringed on their sincerely held religious beliefs. The court ruled that the use of audiovisual materials for educational purposes did not violate the establishment clause; however, whenever such equipment is to be used for entertainment purposes, the students must be excused.

Listening to Certain Radio Stations on School Buses

According to another headline (*Mesa Tribune*, 12-12-86), the Apache Junction Unified School District recently lifted its ban on listening to two radio stations on school buses but continued to prohibit the airing of a local disc jockey. Parents complained to district administrators about objectionable insinuations and lyrics heard on the two radio stations. The school board asked the superintendent to form an advisory committee to help the board create a policy for school bus radio usage.

Reading Selected Novels

School board members in Casa Grande (*Arizona Republic*, 12-11-85) voted unanimously in the past year to retain the Pulitzer prize winning novel *To Kill a Mockingbird*. A parent complained that the book contained characters and the use of derogatory terms for blacks. Although there was no attempt to remove the book from the library shelves, the parent, president of the county branch of the National Association for the Advancement of Colored People, claimed that it was inappropriate for a junior high school reading list. This claim was supported by at least one teacher in the district. However, the school district determined not to remove the book from the reading list.

The examples suggest the difficulty faced by school districts in determining what books, materials, curriculum and instructional methods are to be used. It is possible for parents to find offense in many areas. It is the nature of the public school as a common good that forces its mission to be constantly kept under scrutiny by parents interested in the education of their children. However, criteria must be developed by which school officials may make intelligent and fairly based decisions on when to remove, restrain, or withdraw materials.

The Case Against Censorship

The case against censorship begins with the first amendment which guarantees freedom of speech and press and implies the freedom to hear and to read. The anticensorship view is that it is inconsistent with a democratic society to restrict information or ideas. Censorship is seen as imposition of one particular view of the world by eliminating opposing or controversial views. The marketplace or student interest should determine what is read and what is purchased.

The anticensorship view does not argue that the schools should be neutral since it is obvious that all positions take on a value base. It argues that all value positions have a place in the schools and that it is the obligation of the school to help children understand the vested interests and the underlying rationale of these positions.

Instead of using education then to indoctrinate and impose, the anticensorship view is that the purpose of education is to reveal and expose both overt and covert bias, vested interests, and the unconscious bias of tradition.

The way to avoid imposition and indoctrination is reliance upon the pupils' intelligence. This implies that growth, both intellectual and social, should be developed by every child. The end result of this growth is yet to be determined. The method of growth is seen as democratic participation in the public school (Sorenson, 1985). If the schools are to promote reliance on the pupils' intelligence, they must reveal rather than conceal sources of information. People need access to information in order to intelligently decide on how to act. The method is one of gathering information, sorting and reaching one's own conclusion, seeing the roots of one's own beliefs. This is the way to prevent indoctrination.

The Case for Censorship: Sheltering Childhood

The case for censorship revolves around the view that adults have a right and obligation to make choices about what is appropriate material for children. This position is used to restrict the rights of children in any number of areas including alcoholic beverages, driving, accepting certain types of employment and attending school. Professionals make decisions which involve choices over the selection of materials, curriculum, library books, literature and information. The question is not whether there should be principles by which professional judgment is exercised but rather, what are the principles by which professional judgment is exercised.

Wynne (1985) suggests a number of criteria and qualifications which could be examined in determining how to restrict access of information to young people. He argues that children and adolescents are unique. A properly structured learning environment should eliminate certain aspects from the life of a child in the attempt to present an orderly exposure of information and material to the child. Some materials are more appropriate for older children than for younger children. Secondly, even though restrictions may be imperfect, this is not a reason to ignore or eliminate them. The important thing about restrictions is not eliminating all opportunity for young people to purchase or possess these materials. Rather, it is to say that adults judge these materials as inappropriate. This, in fact, affects the behavior of young people.

While making restriction decisions, Wynne argues that certain objectionable material, when placed in context, may be less objectionable. Great literature, for example may have bias. Its inclusion in the curriculum may reveal the changes that the nation has gone through.

Child advocates have argued that childhood should be a garden to be nurtured. Adult judgment of choices and, to a certain extent restrictions, are a perfectly valid way to view the case for censorship. What may be good for adults may not necessarily be good for unknowing children. It is interesting that the report on the *Commission on Obscenity and Pornography* (1970) also promotes the view that restriction to young people, in spite of little substantive research on the subject, is permissible. However, the *Commission* referred to pictorial material only rather than textual materials in its conclusion.

Censorship and Precensorship

Precensorship refers to the problem that selectors of curriculum and instructional materials may limit their selections to avoid controversy and litigation. This may result in removing controversial material and the so-called "dumbing-down" of textbooks.

The California State Board of Education recently rejected all mathematics books proposed for kindergarten through eighth grades based on the view that the books did not help students to learn to reason and think through problems. A recent *New York Times* article (6-3-86) entitled "Religion Lack in Texts Cited" points to criticism of school texts from both sides of the spectrum. The argument is that textbook publishers, fearing loss of sales, attempt to offend the fewest number possible. Honest treatment of religion in history texts is often equated with advocacy of a particular religious position. A recent study of textbooks by Paul Vitz (1985), a New York University psychology professor, claims that a liberal bias in the publishing industry results in the active

removal of religious themes from American textbooks.

Censorship in Curriculum and Textbook Adoptions

Censorship has traditionally involved arguments to remove certain materials. Recently, the stage has changed to include debate over which materials will be selected or adopted in the first place. This is in large part due to the U.S. Supreme Court's ruling in Board of Education, Island Trees Union Free School District No. 26 v. Pico (1982). The Supreme Court, in a split decision, ruled against parents trying to remove textbooks that the parents felt were objectionable. The ruling, however, left great discretion within the local community and school board to establish and apply the school curriculum (Epley and Moore, 1985).

Since *Pico*, the forum for censorship debates has included curriculum and textbook adoptions. In Alabama, 640 fundamentalist parents sued to rid "secular humanism" from the curriculum. In Tennessee, seven fundamentalists won the right to "opt out" of a reading program designed to enhance appreciation of cultural pluralism and religious diversity. In Louisiana, educators challenged a law requiring schools to teach creationism along with evolution.

Clearly, the selection process is a many faceted problem. On the one hand, textbooks are criticized for being undercritical because strong positions will limit sales. Others argue that school textbooks and curriculum have a vested interest in value neutrality and "secular humanism" is itself a "religion." These are some of the issues to be resolved.

The Drama of School Censorship: Legislation and Litigation

Clignet (1986) argues that it is the drama of school censorship cases which should be studied in order to assess the deeper movements and underlying themes shaping education. Just as an audience in a play often needs a program to understand what is going on, Clignet argues that it is helpful to understand who the players are in the censorship debate. Questions that come to mind include: Who are the claimants? Who are the opponents? Which public authorities are involved? What tactics are being used? What types of proof are needed? What is the setting?

Sorenson (1985) points out that the debate over curriculum materials and instructional methods is taking place in the social and political arena and the courts, rather than in the scholarly books and journals as has been the case in past decades. She says "this may be a sign of a broader public awareness, concern, and involvement in the education of children in the present decade" (p.80).

The report, *Attacks on the Freedom to Learn* (1986), suggests that censorship advocates are becoming more sophisticated and that their increased efforts are largely due to increased backing from national organizations. Four organizations are mentioned: The Eagle Forum headed by Phyllis Schlafly, Freedom Council headed by the Reverend Pat Robertson, Concerned Women for America headed by Beverly LaHayes and the National Association of Christian Educators with its component Citizens for Excellence in Education.

The report argues that the new right has taken to legislation and litigation in order to further its claims. Phyllis Schlafly reportedly sent a letter to 250,000 parents urging them to use the "Hatch amendment regulations to prevent the schools from adopting certain materials and methods." Two years ago, the U.S. Senate approved a bill that included a provision barring federally funded magnet schools from the teaching of "secular humanism." The so-called "Hatch amendment" applied only to federal funds. In Arizona, a state version of the Hatch amendment was introduced and passed by both houses of the legislature in 1985-86, but was vetoed by Governor Bruce Babbitt. In 1985, Congress dropped its "Hatch Amendment" prohibition (*Education Weekly*, 10-15-86).

Phyllis Schlafly, President of the Eagle Forum, suggests that her group's efforts are not censorship but rather the assertion of parental rights. She says that the 130 incidents documented "are a nothing" in a country with 15,000 school districts and 300,000 libraries (*Education Daily*, 8-29-86).

In order to understand the drama of school censorship cases, two court cases will be discussed in detail. A more complete discussion is presented in Zirkel and Gluckman (1986).

Case #1—Grove v. Mead (1985)

Cassie G. was assigned to read the book *The Learning Tree* in her sophomore literature class. The book is an autobiographical portrayal of a poor black adolescent's painful coming of age. The purpose of the book and its effect is to expose students to the attitudes and outlooks of American blacks. Some passages in the book cast various fundamentalist Christian beliefs, such as the power of prayer and the benevolence of God, in a bad light.

Cassie read part of the book and, finding it offensive, showed it to her mother, who read the book and agreed with her daughter. They voiced their objections to the teacher, who assigned Cassie a different book to read and also gave Cassie permission to leave the classroom during the discussion of *The Learning Tree*, although she chose to remain.

The parent filed a formal complaint about the book with the superintendent who referred the mother to an evaluation committee. The committee concluded that the book was an appropriate element of the curriculum. Cassie's parents appealed to the school board which, after a hearing, denied that the book be removed from the curriculum.

The parents filed suit in federal court contending that the use of the book violated the free exercise of establishment clauses of the first amendment. The district court ruled in favor of the school district's motion for a summary judgment, a pretrial ruling in which the judge concluded that there is no genuine issue with regard to material facts of the case and that the moving party is entitled to judgment as a matter of law.

The Ninth Circuit Court of Appeals affirmed the summary judgment for the school district and pointed to the school system's excusal option for the pupil. The court found a "lack of coercion," which is an essential element to the free exercise claim. Further, the court reasoned that the required discontinuance of *The Learning Tree* for nonobjecting students would impede the state's interest in providing a well-rounded public education (Zirkel and Gluckman, 1986, pp. 99-101).

Case #2—Mozert v. Hawkins County Pub. Schools (1985)

Plaintiffs, supported by Beverly LaHaye's organization Concerned Women for America, charged that a Holt, Rinehart and Winston, K-8 reading series violated their religious beliefs. A group of fundamentalist Christian parents and their children requested an "opt out" or excusal option under which they would read some other state-approved reading texts. The parents claimed that the Holt texts were offensive to their religious beliefs based on various alleged teachings in the books. The plaintiffs cited a letter in one of the teacher's editions of the series which states that whereas the previous reading series "emphasized a Judeo-Christian value system" the new series emphasized the need "to understand and to be mindful of the richness of our diversity" (Zirkel and Gluckman, 1986, pp. 100).

The school district argued that the Holt series was instructive, attractive and effective in enhancing the reading skills of students. The superintendent suspended the students who refused to participate in the regular reading program. The district argued that if these children were allowed to have their own separate reading classes, there would be no control over the management and skill sequence, and the future learning process would become completely unmanageable.

On appeal, the Sixth Circuit Court of Appeals overturned a lower court ruling in favor of the school district and remanded the lower court's decision for further proceedings. The Appellate Court concluded that there was a genuine issue with respect to whether the school district infringed on the plaintiffs' sincere religious beliefs or whether the plaintiffs' request for an accommodation would infringe on the district's governmental responsibilities.

In December 1986, U.S. District Judge Thomas G. Hull awarded more than $50,000 to the seven fundamentalist Christian families who paid to send their children to private schools. The district promised to appeal.

Why the different outcomes? There may be a number of reasons for the different outcomes in these two cases. The issue of coercion seems to come into play. The first case allowed the child to be excused while the second case prevented an "opt out" possibility. The second issue in the two cases was the district's making an issue of the sincerity of the parents' religious beliefs. The eventual outcome of the two cases is far from over however and it may be that the final judgments will be different for both cases.

The drama of censorship cases then has changed. Whereas censorship cases traditionally involved removing books from the shelves, new cases are involving the selection of appropriate materials and methods for schools. In addition, the setting for the drama is no longer scholarly journals but the legislature and the courthouse.

How Educators Might Respond

Pupils, teachers, administrators, school board members, and the State Board of Education all have important parts in the decision of what goes on in the classroom. This last section of the paper examines what these members of the education community can do to deal with some of the issues raised earlier.

Pupils—The quality of reading material and curriculum selections is ultimately judged by the users of the material. Students, especially in high school grades, may be the best judge of what materials are appropriate and at the very least which materials are popular. Pupils have an obligation to take responsibility for the atmosphere and quality of the learning environment in which they participate. Boredom in schools is at least partially a responsibility of the learner. Pupils need to more aggressively communicate to parents and teachers both satisfactions and dissatisfactions with texts, materials and instruction. In addition, it is appropriate for older pupils to become involved in district efforts to choose and to handle challenges to instructional materials.

Teachers and Textbook Adoptions—Teachers, increasingly, will be asked to rate textbooks before they are selected for adoption. Teachers must be given time and money to do this properly. Teachers must lobby their boards for a mandate or criteria from which they will be able to make informed decisions as to which texts are appropriate. They further must lobby for time and scheduling so that in spite of their full-time jobs and tight schedules, the possibility to review books will be made available. Teachers must also reject the view that a new text is adopted one day and used in the classroom the next. Once texts are adopted, funds need to be provided for teachers to become familiar with the new books and the accompanying teacher's manuals. Master or mentor teachers could play a part in the role of text orientation.

Without specifying a specific content, teachers need guidelines to rate textbooks. The criteria may include assessment of: (1) *content*—accuracy, up-to-dateness, comprehensiveness; (2) *instructional design*—match of content and objectives, match of content and test items, appropriate alerting and reviewing of material; (3) *classroom use*—teacher's guides and workbooks assist in learning, material compatibility with instructional methodology; (4) *presentation*—appropriateness of materials for grade level, writing style, engagement of students through format and illustrations. These are some of the issues and criteria to be addressed by teachers in developing ways by which textbooks can be rated prior to adoption.

School Officials—The most important step for school officials to take is to have in place a school material selection policy. According to Richard Morrow, Superintendent of the Island Trees Union Free School District (of *Pico* fame), this policy should be clearly written and well publicized and endorsed by each new school board. The policy might include a statement on objectives of the selection process and define lines of authority for making selections. A clearly defined procedure for challenging materials is also necessary. Morrow recommends that parental involvement in developing these policies is important as is publicity announcing how materials are selected and where they may be viewed (Epley and Moore, 1985).

No matter how diligently these suggestions are followed, there may be cases of materials being objected to by community members. Stahlschmidt (1982) suggests a "workable strategy for dealing with censorship" in which written policies for selection and for handling of challenged materials are developed. She points to the Iowa plan in which an 11-member standing committee made up of a teacher, librarian, central office administrator, five community members, and three high school students, meets monthly to consider written requests for reconsideration of materials. Based on the committee's recommendations, materials are retained, reclassified, or withdrawn. According to

Stahlschmidt and Morrow, the existence of such committees is a determining factor in reducing the extent and duration of conflict over school textbooks.

State Board of Education—Finally, the State Board of Education plays a major role in censorship cases through its textbook adoption policies. Michael Kirst, former president of the California State Board of Education, says that board members need to be aware of a number of issues involved in textbook adoptions. Board members must address issues concerning textbook content. This involves appointing members to serve on curriculum review committees; it also involves questions of alignment between curriculum, textbooks and testing procedures. Finally, alignment of the cycles of textbook adoption between the state and local school districts is critically important, especially in Arizona where the cycles are out of sequence for most school districts.

Kirst says board members need training in key issues, concepts and criteria for selecting textbooks in each subject field. Board members need to be made aware of the tendency for education policy to be cyclical. When public policy focused on the bottom third of student populations, textbooks ignored the top third. Conversely, as policy is focused on "quality indicators" textbook needs of disadvantaged students may be neglected. Overall, board members need to consider the various policy and alignment issues involved in textbook selection and adoption. It is the role of state board members to inform themselves and provide leadership from which local decisions can occur.

Conclusion

The purpose of this information brief was to inform interested parties about the debate over curriculum, instructional materials including textbooks and the delivery of these materials. The paper covers seven major issues in the censorship debate. Censorship is defined and examples are given. The case for and against censorship is briefly described. The issue of precensorship is discussed and applied to school textbook adoptions. This is followed by an examination of the drama of censorship cases and how this might reveal deeper currents in American political and social thought. Finally, there is discussion of what the pupils, teachers, administrators, school boards and the State Board of Education can do to address the issues involved in censorship.

Reference List

Arons, S. (1981, November). The crusade to ban books. *The Education Digest*, pp. 2-5.

Associated Press. (1986, December 16). Court awards $50,000 in textbook suit. *Tempe Daily News*, p. A5.

Board of Education, Island Trees Union Free School District No. 26 v. Pico, 457 U.S. 853 at 857, 102 S. Ct. 2799 at 2803 (1982).

Christianson, B. (1986, December 12). Board lifts ban on 2 stations, but not Pratt. *Mesa Tribune*, pp. B1, B7.

Clignet, R. (1986). On obscenity, censorship, and schools: a sociological perspective. *Issues in Education, 4*, 74-82.

Davis v. Page, 385 F. Supp. 1078 (D.N.H. 1974).

Epley, B.G. & Moore, K.M. (1985, December). Censorship in the schools: The responsibilities of courts, boards, and administrators. *NASSP Bulletin*, pp. 54-60.

Gove, P.B. (Editor in Chief). (1976) *Webster's third new international dictionary*. Springfield, MA: G. & C. Merriam.

Grove v. Mead, 753 F.2d 1528 (Ninth Cir. 1985).

Kirst, M.W. (1984, Summer). Choosing textbooks. *American Educator*, pp. 18-23.

Lowe, S. (1986, February 14). Officials pull books from library. *Prescott Courier*.

Merritt, L.C. (1975). Libraries, intellectual freedom in. In L.C. Deighton (Ed.), *The Encyclopedia of Education* (Vol. 5, pp. 569-574). New York, NY: MacMillan Company and Free Press.

Mirga, T. & Reeves, M.S. (1986, October 15). On trial: Secular humanism in the schools. *Education Weekly*, pp. 1, 12-14.

Mozert v. Hawkins County Public Schools, 765 F.2d (Sixth Cir. 1985).

National Commission on Obscenity and Pornography (1970). *Report*. Washington, DC: U.S. Government Printing Office.

People for the American Way. (1986). *Attacks on the Freedom to Learn* (1985-1986 Report). Washington, DC.

Shaffer, M. (1985, December 11). Schools will keep 'Mockingbird' in classes despite NAACP attack. *Arizona Republic*.

Shaw, C. (1986, November 3). Textbook evaluation stirs little controversy in Dade. *Miami Herald*, p. B1.

Sorenson, G.P. (1985). Indoctrination and the purposes of American education: A 1930s debate. *Issues in Education, 3*, 79-98.

Stahlschmidt, A. (1982, October). A workable strategy for dealing with censorship. *Phi Delta Kappan*, pp. 99-101.

Vitz criticizes schools for lacking Religious Training. (1986, April 28). *Education Daily*, p.10.

Vitz, P.C. (1985). *Religion and traditional values in public school textbooks: An empirical study* (NIE-G-84-0012). New York, NY: New York University, Department of Psychology. (ERIC Document Reproduction Service No. ED 260 019).

Werner, L.M. (1986, June 3). Religion lack in texts cited. *New York Times*, p. C1, C8.

Wynne, E.A. (1985). The case for censorship to protect the young. *Issues in Education, 3*, 171-184.

Yoder, E.M., Jr. (1986, December 16). A true oxymoron: creation science. *Miami Herald*, p. 21A.

Zirkel, P.A. & Gluckman, I.B. (1986, March). Objection to curricular materials on religious grounds. *NASSP Bulletin*, pp. 99-103.

Serving Special Needs and Humanizing Instruction

We are all human beings sharing the same universe and the common heritage of our species, and yet, marvelously, each of us is exceptional in some way. Each of us has special gifts and special limitations. The ancient Greeks believed every person could be educated to the optimum extent in order to perfect his or her excellent qualities as a person. To a certain extent, we can also be educated to compensate for disabilities. Children are born into many special circumstances and different social atmospheres. Some must struggle to survive and fight to maintain their sense of dignity and self-worth. What con-

stitutes the most appropriate learning atmosphere for each student has become a serious legal and moral question in recent years.

All individuals are special, unique human beings who have different levels of abilities and needs in certain areas. Often these special needs and abilities are called exceptionalities. Exceptionalities of certain kinds, whether they be physical or cognitive (mental) sometimes require special intervention or treatment skills. How can education address those unique needs, interests, abilities, and exceptionalities of students? How can teachers best serve needs for attention and intellectual stimulation, demonstrate concern for the students, and also meet regular instructional responsibilities? Many children do not have sufficient opportunities to become aware of their special needs and potentialities. School systems must find ways to help students discover their academic and social capabilities. They must create conditions whereby students and teachers can optimize their chances for effective academic and social progress.

The Education of All Handicapped Children Act of 1975 (PL 94-142) was passed by Congress to address the special needs of handicapped learners by placing them in least restrictive learning environments. However, exceptionality does not just refer to handicaps. Gifted persons are exceptional, too, and their least restrictive learning environments can indeed call for special intervention strategies. Herein lies one of the dilemmas of special education as a sector of teacher education. There are many special and exceptional students and they all need carefully worked out strategies for optimizing their chances for a quality education. In addition to diagnosed exceptionalities, children sometimes develop special needs for carefully individualized attention from their teachers due to injuries or mistreatment. The nation's schools are called upon to address a range of special needs that is so vast, the schools are financially and professionally stressed to their limits.

Since the passage of Public Law 94-142, there has been increased sensitivity to the educational requirements of exceptional children and youth. What might be a liberating classroom learning climate for one student, however, may be a stifling and boring one for another student.

Helping children adjust to the demands of school and providing them with opportunities for fulfilling their own unique learning potential challenges the talent of any teacher. Mainstreaming is the educational policy response to the federal legislation passed in 1975 to aid handicapped students by placing them in individually prescribed, least restrictive learning environments. However, there is a big gap between the hopes and expectations for mainstreaming and the policy realities of efforts to implement it. The attempt to develop individualized diagnostic and teaching strategies that classroom teachers can use with their students is part of the national effort to respond constructively to the needs of exceptional children. As a result, the tension created by trying to attain equality and quality in schools is raising new educational issues. Some of these issues are concerned with how to provide en-

riched learning experiences for gifted students while providing least restrictive learning environments for cognitively (intellectually) handicapped students. Other issues relate to the demand placed on teachers' time and the difficulties involved in the total effort to individualize instructional programs for students. There are shortages of resources of both diagnosis and treatment.

The unit opens with an account of the serious problems encountered in correctly implementing the educational approaches to mainstreaming. "Legal" compliance is not the same as "educational" compliance. Many school districts achieve legal compliance with mainstreaming but at the expense of the intent of the federal and state laws which were passed to guarantee the rights of exceptional children. Other essays in this unit deal with student self-esteem, child abuse, and chemical abuse among young people.

Each year this anthology addresses some professional concerns that are usually not included in traditional textbooks on curriculum and instruction, but are issues of real interest to all teachers. Over the years, the selections in this unit have not always fallen under the typical definitions of social foundations of education, methods of teaching, or curriculum and instruction. However, some of the articles are directly related to those areas, and most of the selections work well in courses about the methods of teaching curriculum and instruction, the equity agenda, equality of opportunity, and the general social foundations of education.

Looking Ahead: Challenge Questions

How could a mainstreaming program in a school be legal but not educational?

What is meant by least restrictive placement? What would be an example of such placement for children with various handicaps? What might such a placement be for a gifted exceptional child?

What can school systems and teachers do to assist students living in single-parent homes?

What can teachers do to identify child abuse and neglect? How can abused or neglected children be helped?

Are professional situations of elementary and secondary teachers different when it comes to individualizing instruction? If so, in what specific ways? If not, why not?

What is meant by individualization? How can it be accomplished?

What is the present state of drug use or chemical dependency in the United States?

"Appropriate" School Programs:

Legal vs. Educational Approaches

Steven Carlson
Steven Carlson teaches in the Department of Educational
Psychology in the Special Education Program at Rutgers
University.

With the passage of Public Law 94-142, the Education for All Handicapped Children Act, disabled children and youth were guaranteed a free, appropriate public education. Unfortunately, a *legally* appropriate education may be very different from an *educationally* appropriate education. I hope to explain the important difference between them. Parents need to understand both the legal and the educational issues. While all parents are not going to be legal experts, all parents can evaluate the quality and educational appropriateness of programs for disabled children and youth, with the help of some clear guidelines.

The Legal Definition of Appropriateness

The courts have struggled with the meaning of appropriateness and a legal definition has slowly emerged. This legal definition currently rests on three "legs."

The first leg examines how well proper procedures were followed in protecting the rights of children and parents. The law requires that
- Notification of parents about the evaluation and placement of their children in special education.
- Parental permission before these actions can be taken.
- Parental participation in initial decisions and in any subsequent changes in a child's program.
- Specific guidelines for evaluation and specific means for appeal.

A legally appropriate program is, according to this first leg, one in which these parental rights have been respected.

The second "leg" investigates the degree to which the recommended program of services and studies was followed. If the recommendations of the multidisciplinary team, to which the parent has agreed, are followed, the program may be considered legally appropriate. For example, the recommendation is for two hours of physical therapy each week. Legally, the question is: Has the recommendation been followed or not? How

closely the recommendation must be followed has not yet been legally determined.

The final "leg" of this legal triad examines the actual progress a student makes in school. Movement through school grades is considered the final confirmation of the legal appropriateness of the program.

It may be legal, but is it educationally appropriate?

While these three areas of legal concern provide some assurance of attention to the educational problems faced by disabled children and youth, they fail to address the issue very much on the mind of most parents: *educational effectiveness*. It is possible for a child to be properly evaluated, properly placed, and progress through the grades, yet learn less than might be hoped or expected. For example, grade progress may be due to lowered standards and teacher expectations rather than to increased quality of teaching or level of student learning.

Standards for Educationally Appropriate Special Programs

The issue of quality must be addressed by parents and concerned educators. At the present time, educational appropriateness is itself not a legal issue. The following guidelines are provided to assist concerned parents and educators to evaluate program appropriateness *where quality of learning is the central concern*. These guidelines are general in nature and care must be taken to remember that they are suggestions, not legal requirements.

Uniqueness

To be educationally appropriate, a program should be a new and unique learning experience. This means that whatever the reason for placing a child in special education, the services provided should differ from those which were previously provided. The greater the similarity between

Originally appeared in *The Exceptional Parent*, September 1985, pp. 23, 25-26, 28-30. Reprinted with permission of THE EXCEPTIONAL PARENT magazine, 605 Commonwealth Ave., Boston, MA 02215.

regular and special programs, the weaker the case for educational appropriateness. Repeating, in a different classroom, what has already been shown not to work makes little sense. Additionally, if special programs are not truly unique, it is possible that the negative consequences of labeling and/or removing a child from a less restrictive setting will outweigh the positive benefits of the special program. Recent research makes it quite clear that special education sometimes fails to be truly different.

Parents can help guard against this possibility by understanding the purpose of student evaluation and by raising questions during the Individual Education Program (IEP) meeting. One part of this evaluation is to determine whether a student is eligible for special education services; another part is to determine what should be taught and the best way to teach it. This second part of the evaluation process determines the potential effectiveness of instruction. Educational evaluation should uncover what specific skills must be learned as well as the adequacy of teaching techniques and materials used in the past. Parents can ask evaluators to discuss what was done in the past, what is being recommended for the future, the differences between these approaches, and the reasons why current suggestions will be more effective.

A child's IEP should specifically state *what* to teach and *how* to teach. Moreover, practices previously shown to be ineffective should be discontinued and those with promise should be the focus of future instruction. Often, a child's IEP describes the special education curriculum but provides neither the parent nor the teacher with the most important information: the way that the curriculum will be translated into learning.

Recent research makes it quite clear that special education sometimes fails to be truly different.

Long Range Benefit

An educationally appropriate program is one in which instructional goals and objectives lead toward the long range goal of independence. If a child differs from his or her peers to such an extent that a special program of studies is necessary, emphasis should be placed on reducing the size of this difference. It is important for school planning teams and parents to anticipate future school and life demands. This means that a good program will strive to alter the child's impaired approach to learning, social functioning, or dealing with his or her environment.

For example, a child is placed in a special program due to an emotional or behavioral disability. Success in the regular classroom, in the social environment of the school, or in future adult life may depend upon the child behaving in a more acceptable way. Instructional emphasis, therefore, should be on behavioral change. If the special setting serves only to control the behavior and to teach traditional skills, the child's underlying problem will not be addressed or solved. In this case, the child will not be able to function well in non-special settings in the future. The standard of long range independence is equally true for programs for children with learning, physical, and sensory disabilities.

Parents might ask school planning teams whether they have considered future requirements for independent functioning, and how proposed instruction can be expected to reduce the need for future special services. Hopefully, parents will feel free to raise such concerns and to work with school personnel to assure that they are addressed. Once instruction begins, progress toward a greater degree of independent functioning should be as apparent outside of the special class as it is inside. Additional effort should be made to make sure that children, even those who succeed in special classrooms, can apply this learning in other school and life situations.

Attention to the long range benefit of special education is very important. Parents and teachers who are primarily concerned with academic performance must remember that a diploma is of little value to a student who is unprepared to function independently in life, to find employment at the level of his or her true potential, or to take advantage of academic or technical training beyond high school.

High Expectations

An educationally appropriate program is one where expectations for student performance are high. Learning activities and requirements for independence should be challenging. The lives of disabled children and youth are often filled with frustrations and failures. As a result, teachers and parents frequently strive to reduce the probability, or even possibility, of failure. Although such attitudes and practices are well intended, all too often they result in an unnecessary lowering of standards and expectations.

It has long been known that, whenever possible, children will live up or down to the expectations held for them by teachers and parents. This is the main reason for maintaining reasonable yet challenging expectations. Hesitating to challenge children may result in increased dependence since the teacher or parent must do for the child what the child could be taught to do for him or herself. It is important to remember that these children, many of whom lag behind their peers in some significant way, will not "catch up" by going even more slowly, being asked to do less, and having more provided for them. It may well be that disabled children need to work harder than their non-disabled peers. It may also be that teachers and/or parents who lower their expectations may be making it harder for disabled children to adjust to the consequences of their disabilities.

One sign of a program with high expectations is often the confidence of the special teacher that "with hard work we can do it."

Classroom instruction should generally be intensive and briskly paced with little time wasted in nonproductive discussion or fun activities that have marginal instructional value. A teacher with high expectations will find ways to make challenging and productive learning activities enjoyable.

When it is necessary to lower performance standards, instruction should be designed to help children attain standards that are ever more demanding. Whether special materials are used or regular materials are modified, children can still be taught how to cope with the idea of "standards." Future employers are not likely to modify the workplace or alter work materials. Once out of school, the child will be expected to meet many, if not all, the same demands as his or her peers.

An educationally appropriate, quality program is one which addresses this harsh reality, which maintains high performance standards, and which helps children and youth learn to meet the expectations which will be imposed on them throughout life.

Instruction is Powerful

An educationally appropriate program is one where the special teacher uses those techniques and principles which have proven to lead to greater student progress. There is a great deal of research with both disabled and non-disabled children which assesses the effectiveness of various teaching styles. Since teachers make choices about their teaching techniques, they should choose those that work best.

Although independent seat work has an important place in teaching and learning, it should comprise only a portion of a child's learning time. The teacher can constantly call upon students to answer questions and demonstrate developing skills. When errors are made. children should receive immediate and specific feedback on the nature of their error, including direct instruction about how to avoid such errors in the future.

Children can be engaged in learning a high percentage of time. Then, there is little "down time" spent waiting for the teacher or locating materials. Lessons should move quickly, activities should be varied, and positive comments should be offered to show students that their efforts are both valuable and valued. Time should be spent reviewing previously learned skills so that important information is not forgotten. Learning activities should be challenging and designed so that, with effort, the student can be successful.

Disabled children have more to lose than their peers if the initial approach to instruction is wrong and left uncorrected throughout the school year.

Moving Toward Goals

In an educationally appropriate program, instruction either leads toward specific goals or general change. Disabled children often present teachers with complex instructional problems which must be solved. It is unreasonable to believe that any teacher can be 100% successful in helping children if the goals which have been established are truly challenging.

It is not unreasonable, however, to expect teachers to be aware of a child's progress toward goal attainment. When students are initially placed in special education programs, information collected during the evaluation serves as the basis for educated guesses about what the child needs to learn and how the child will learn best. As with any guess, error is a possibility.

Disabled children have more to lose than their peers if the initial approach to instruction is wrong and left uncorrected throughout the school year. Not only should highly specific performance information be routinely collected, but this data should be used to modify instruction if the child's progress slowed or stalled.

If progress is less than desired, a program may still be appropriate if the teacher is using information about a student's performance to discard techniques that do not work, and substitute other techniques, gradually finding the necessary formula for maximizing student progress. Many people believe that it is this fine tuning which distinguishes special from traditional education.

Parents can ask to review specific information on their child's progress. Examples would be asking about the percentage of words read correctly and incorrectly at the start of instruction and at the present time, or how much the independent mobility of a physically disabled child has changed from week to week.

Specific information about how a child learns is far more useful for fine tuning instruction than test scores. In most cases, even testing experts would maintain that scores, especially those which express grade level performance, are relatively useless for purposes of instruction. If progress is limited, parents should ask the teacher to explain how instruction has been changed to lead toward progress in the future.

Teacher Training

In an educationally appropriate program, teaching is done by individuals who have formal training or recognized expertise. Few would disagree that a teacher should know how to teach the skills and behaviors which are called for in a child's IEP. In elementary school resource rooms, or part day programs, where basic skill instruction (reading, spelling, etc.) is often the emphasis, teacher training is generally adequate because these skills are a standard of special education training.

Self-contained, or full day classroom programs, require teachers to teach not only essential basic skills, but such subjects as science, health, and social studies. It is quite possible that the special education teachers who deliver such instruction have received little or no training in how to do so. If they do teach such material, they may not be effective. Even worse, if they feel unprepared to teach a certain subject, they may fail to teach it at all.

This deficiency may also exist in the secondary grades when a special educator either tutors a student in a particular area or actually provides all the instruction and academic credit in subjects like government, biology, or history. Even when teachers are trained, they should be familiar with a variety of approaches and materials, capable of analyzing errors and providing proper correction, and able to teach students the reasoning which leads to the correct answer.

Parents must feel free to ask the planning team whether any standard material is not part of the program, why it is omitted, and whether the child's teacher has had training in the areas selected as

learning goals. No teacher can be expected to be expert in everything. Quality programs may require students to receive instruction from more than one special educator or be creative in modifying other standard practices.

Consistency of Goals and Instruction

An educationally appropriate program is one where instruction and classroom activities always correspond to the child's IEP. Legal guidelines require that IEP goals be taught but say little about how consistent the plan and the practice must be. It is unreasonable to expect that pre-defined goals will be attained if they are not being emphasized in instruction. Ideally, there should be few instances where instruction is not directly related to these goals.

Parents can try to visit their child's classroom occasionally and, at a convenient time, discuss with the teacher what is being taught and its relationship to the IEP goals. It is not uncommon for teachers to discover that children have more pressing needs than those formally documented on the IEP. It is important, however, that parents and team members be consulted before significant changes are made. Occasionally, teachers claim that they are unaware of what goals specific children are expected to meet. In these cases, appropriateness is questionable, and parents need to take an active interest in the content of instruction.

Conclusion

Providing educationally appropriate, quality programs to disabled children is a relatively new phenomenon in education. It must be assumed that this undertaking, like any other important and complex new effort, will have problems. When quality of instruction is the immediate concern, there appears to be little help available from the courts. The surest way to improve quality appears to be true cooperation between parents and educators.

Such cooperation may take time and effort to develop. It is important to recognize that all parties are interested in the well-being of the child. Differences are often not in values but in approach. The guidelines which I have offered are intended as a general yardstick for parents and educators to evaluate program appropriateness from the perspective of quality. I hope they will lead toward improvements in the education of disabled children by helping all parties to recognize that real change takes time and depends upon mutual respect and trust.

Self-esteem success stories

Kids can overcome low self-esteem. Here are strategies one educator used to help five students recognize their self-worth. Use these techniques to help children you know resolve self-image crises.

Patricia Berne

Patricia Berne, a former elementary diagnostic tutor, is now a clinical psychologist in private practice in Washington, D.C. She is coauthor of *Building Self-Esteem in Children* (Continuum Publishers, New York, 1981).

Part of the work of childhood is building a healthy self-image. This happens as children sense themselves in relation to other kids, explore their potential, and recognize their value. Children who possess strong self-images volunteer their ideas, express their points of view, and are able to show disappointment as well as delight. They manage adolescence successfully and step into adult life with a sense of freedom.

But children who feel poorly about themselves have little regard for their own point of view—everyone else's needs to come first. If their feelings run contrary to someone else's, their perceptions must have been incorrect. A negative cycle begins as each failure deepens their lack of belief in themselves. Over the years, these kids become withdrawn, depressed, or angry.

Feelings of inadequacy and confusion make children with low self-esteem hard to work with—and sometimes hard to like. Their problems often include a difficulty making friends and feeling liked; fear of facing new situations; inability to stand up for oneself; a facade of bragging and bullying; a view of oneself as not valuable or lovable; need for constant approval; and little sense of whom to trust, how to trust, or when to trust.

Your role is a powerful one. The earlier you intervene, the easier it is for kids to build lasting self-confidence and rid themselves of these handicaps. The following are five case studies of children who were sent to me for extra help. Their names and some details have been changed. Here are their stories, along with some simple and successful techniques.

*B*illy feared new situations

Being thrust into a new classroom, even for part of the day, can provoke an array of frightening feelings for a child with self-esteem problems. While kids with high self-esteem realistically assess what is expected of them and develop reasonable expectations for themselves, low-self-esteem children are often overwhelmed by the risks they perceive.

Billy's teacher asked that he be tutored in reading, and she let me know he would be a bit wary of this new situation. After all, I was a strange teacher taking him to a strange room. So I started off with a safe question, "Where do you live?" He looked up blushing and speechless. His fear of the situation caused his mind to go blank.

Billy needed to know that our time together wouldn't be threatening. I put out a few objects I thought might interest him—a prism, magnifying glass, kaleidoscope, and a magic box that made a penny disappear and reappear. I had brought these to school especially to share with him, and I told him so. We looked at them together, and while he played, I talked about whom I was and why he was with me.

As the weeks went by, Billy felt increasingly comfortable and successful. I encouraged him to try new things and applauded his accomplishments. A few months passed and Billy's class decided to put on a play. Billy volunteered and was given a small part. What a milestone! Just a little while ago, this would have been terrifying to him. Now it seemed do-able, interesting, fun. He was well on his way.

Suggestions: When working with children who are overly fearful in new situations, make the situation as comfortable, interesting, and fun as possible. The initiative has to be yours—children are too busy coping with fears of new expectations. Your ongoing recognition of how well they're doing will help kids realize they *can* tackle new tasks and situations. And as you remind them of their new history of successes, suggest that there are more to look forward to.

*A*lice couldn't make friends

It's not easy to make friends—or to be a friend—when you're not feeling good about yourself. Some low-self-esteem children become shy; others brag and are aggressive. Alice was the latter. She was bossy with everyone and never seemed comfortable unless she was in control—and still things didn't go smoothly. Because she lacked the appropriate social skills, she usually ended up alone.

Alice needed to use her natural tendency to take charge in ways that built friendships rather than blocked them. The visiting art teacher's birthday provided the opportunity. Alice's teacher and I encouraged her to help organize a surprise birthday party. This way, Alice could begin to develop a positive, working rapport with her teacher and classmates—and have a healthy outlet for her leadership abilities.

Together we planned the party. It was a huge success—and a begin-

ning for Alice. Teachers and classmates began to see her in a new light, and so did Alice. Her esteem grew.

Alice's mother also recognized her daughter's problem and, in an effort to help, invited a group of classmates over after school. But because there were no organized activities, Alice knew no other way to relate than to boss everyone around. No one had a good time.

Alice, and later her mother, shared this experience with me. I suggested that, next time, Alice's mother invite fewer kids and plan something specific for them to do, like bake brownies together. Alice's mom and I agreed that she would not leave the scene or turn control over to Alice. It worked. The kids had direction and ended up enjoying one another's company.

Additional structured situations helped Alice see herself in a new light, helped others be more welcoming of her, and helped the two of us discuss her growing good feelings.

Suggestions: When working with low-self-esteem children who have difficulty making friends, create situations where friendship can flourish. Try to do this by building on the natural strengths and talents of the child. Plan structured situations for a scheduled time, with a successful outcome assured. Keep control of the situation until you see that it's working well.

*C*indy ignored her own rights

Cindy was always nice. She was the first to defend someone, give something away, and listen to someone else's opinion. Her self-esteem was so low and her self-image so poor that she felt she always had to be nice—or she'd lose what little self-esteem she had. When her friend Ellen's parents were getting a divorce and the other kids were tired

of Ellen's depression, Cindy reminded them, "Ellen has a right to feel badly. Her home is breaking up." Cindy could stand up for Ellen's rights, but when it came to defending her own, she drew a blank.

One morning Cindy hadn't completed her assignment. She explained that the time she had allotted to work on it was taken up substituting as a patrol guard. Maria, a girl in Cindy's class, had slept late, so couldn't make it to her guard station on time. This happened often, and rather than give up her position as a guard, Maria made a habit of calling Cindy to take her place. It was an easy out—Cindy never refused her.

We discussed the situation. No, Cindy didn't think it was fair. She felt resentful and taken advantage of but didn't know how to say no. What would Maria think of her? What would she tell the other kids? Besides, it was fun to be a patrol guard, even if she didn't get to go to meetings or on special field trips.

I asked her what her advice would be if Ellen were in her place. Her strong feelings that Ellen should confront Maria and discuss the problem helped Cindy see that she should, too. We role-played the situation.

The next time Maria called, by chance, Cindy had also woken up late. There was no way she could get ready in time. She told Maria and added that it wasn't fair to always count on her. If Maria wanted to be a member of the patrol, it seemed like she had ought to start doing her job. Maria confessed that she didn't really like being on the safety patrol. And at that point, Cindy volunteered to take her place!

Cindy was growing in self-esteem but still had difficulties expressing her opinion. She felt she had nothing worthwhile to say. I commented on the many things she said that were helpful and asked her to note classmates who expressed ideas, offered opinions, and stood up for their rights. Together we formulated ways for Cindy to express her ideas and opinions in class. Cindy was learning to pay attention to her feelings and act on them.

Suggestions: To help children who can't seem to stand up for their own rights, look for opportunities where the child is subtly expressing a want or an opinion and encourage its clear and direct expression. The opinion may not always be agreeable, but these children need to learn to get their ideas and feelings out. If possible, find examples when the child did stand up for someone else's rights. Ask, "Isn't this your right, too?" Whenever possible, point out how the child's expression of a right, need, opinion, or idea has been helpful to others. Your modeling and reinforcement will help.

*L*amont didn't feel liked or accepted

Kids who have difficulty feeling liked and fitting in often become the kids no one notices. They resist any behavior that would call attention to themselves. And because they don't expect to be liked, these children often miss the overtures and invitations that do come their way. They remember only those times they weren't chosen, weren't asked their opinion, and were left to sit alone.

Lamont entered the fourth grade in a new school. He and his family were spending a year in our area. Surrounded by strangers, Lamont became shy, scared, and withdrawn. Not only was he afraid the kids at his new school wouldn't like him, he was worried that his old friends would forget him.

As part of Lamont's tutoring, we talked about him writing to his old classmates to show that *he* hadn't forgotten *them*. I suggested to Lamont's mother that she write to his old school and request that his class be in touch with Lamont, just to let him know that they were looking forward to his return.

Lamont and I also talked about him leaving in a year and noted that he and I would not forget each other.

*G*inny has to be perfect

Ginny seems fine to you. Her work is satisfactory and consistently handed in on time. She has every reason to feel comfortable at school. But Ginny doesn't agree. As far as she's concerned, her work isn't perfect and that means she's failing her personal standards. Third-grader Ginny has such high expectations of herself that she's constantly apologizing for her inadequacy and feels incapable of success.

For her, praise seems to come only when her performance is outstanding, so she has never learned to measure herself in degrees. To Ginny, there is always a hidden message: Less than perfect has no value.

How to recognize kids like Ginny? Public performances generate high levels of anxiety. If asked to expand on an answer, these kids presume their answer wasn't good enough—and in a panic their minds go blank. Criticism is an unbearable attack. Negative comments loom so large that positive ones go unnoticed.

When something goes well for Ginny the first time around, she's hesitant to try again. What if it was beginner's luck? In reality, her fears and inhibitions hadn't had time to impede her natural abilities. If she were to try again, there's a good chance her fears would act as paralyzers.

You can help children like Ginny learn to make realistic self-evaluations. Take care to first establish a trusting relationship, because from this bond comes respect. Children will let themselves believe what you say and look to you for honest opinions. Give more than a judgement on performance and behavior. Talk about special things a child does, appreciates, notices. These kids need to hear that your appraisal of their behavior is separate from your regard for them as people.

Acknowledge that there are things you don't know or can't do, and things you are working to improve at. Model accepting your own imperfections, while still loving and respecting yourself.

Remember, kids like Ginny live by extremes—good-bad, win-lose, succeed-fail. Help them to evaluate where they are in the process of mastery, to realistically define what they should accept as good, and to view themselves and their performances fairly. These skills and your support will help them grow into young men and women who have a realistic sense of their own worth and talents.

I assured him that I would continue to like him and was counting on him to still like me even after he went back home.

But, of course, this wasn't the only issue. We had to get on with Lamont's life in the present. We discussed which of the children in his new classroom he liked and which ones he thought liked him. Perhaps these possible "likes" could be used to build friendships. I suggested that Lamont take the first step and start a conversation—talk to a potential friend while telling himself inside that the child liked him. Or he could ask someone to join him in a game or a puzzle. We even practiced.

Over the next few weeks, I asked Lamont to share his successes with me, no matter how small. Had he been included in a conversation? Had he been asked to play a game?

As he shared each triumph, I pointed out the growth in his relationships with classmates. We both enjoyed the progress—the warmth and excitement of watching friendships and esteem grow.

Suggestions: When children have difficulty feeling liked and fitting in, encourage them to relate to others in positive ways, as if they are well-liked already. You may need to model that behavior. Ask kids to share successes or to keep a private record. Don't forget to express the qualities you find likable about them. Help these kids to see that they are inviting and valuable people.

Are there kids like Billy, Alice, Cindy, and Lamont in your class? Children who don't relate to others, won't cooperate, and can't seem to fit in? No matter how deep their downward spiral of deteriorating self-esteem, each child has an innate drive to see the self as meaningful, valuable, capable, and lovable. You can count on that drive for help.

Child Abuse and Neglect

Cleo Freelance Photo

Prevention and Reporting

Barbara J. Meddin
Anita L. Rosen

Barbara J. Meddin, Ph.D., is a child protection specialist and human services consultant in Carbondale, Illinois.

Anita L. Rosen, Ph.D., is a private consultant in Silver Spring, Maryland.

Each year nearly 1.2 million children in the United States are reported to be abused or neglected. Even more alarming is the possibility that more than 2 million other cases are not reported to the agencies whose responsibility it is to protect children from further abuse (U.S. Department of Health and Human Services, 1981).

Most of these situations are treatable, however, and a great deal of harm to children is preventable (Kempe & Helfer, 1972). Because teachers are often the only adults who regularly see the child outside of the immediate family, teachers are often the first to observe children who have been or are at risk for abuse and/or neglect (McCaffrey & Tewey, 1978).

Teachers of young children are an essential part of the professional team that can prevent abuse and neglect. What steps can you as a teacher take to be alert to potential abuse or neglect? If indeed you believe a child has been harmed or is at risk of harm, how should it be reported?

What is child abuse and/or neglect?

Child abuse and/or neglect is any action or inaction that results in the harm or potential risk of harm to a child. Includes

- physical abuse (cuts, welts, bruises, burns);
- sexual abuse (molestation, exploitation, intercourse);
- physical neglect (medical or educational neglect, and inadequate supervision, food, clothing, or shelter);
- emotional abuse (actions that result in significant harm to the child's intellectual, emotional, or social development or functioning); and
- emotional neglect (inaction by the adult to meet the child's needs for nurture and support).

Reprinted by permission from *Young Children*, Vol. 41, No. 4 (May 1986), pp. 26-30. Copyright © 1984, National Association for the Education of Young Children, 1834 Connecticut Ave., N.W., Washington, DC 20009.

Every state mandates that *suspected* cases of child abuse be reported by professionals such as teachers (Education Commission of the States, 1976). In Illinois, for example, professionals who do not report are subject to loss of their license to practice the profession. Those who report suspected cases are protected by law from any personal or civil liability growing out of that report (Illinois Public Law, 1979).

Teachers are not expected to know for sure whether a child has been harmed as a result of abuse and/or neglect. It is up to the child welfare or child protection agency to confirm the existence of abuse or neglect. Neither is the teacher expected to take custody of the child. The child protection agency or the police decide what action needs to be taken to protect the child.

Only about 13% of all child abuse reports are made by teachers or other school personnel (The American Humane Association, 1983). It appears that teachers are reluctant to report suspected cases, especially when physical neglect or emotional abuse and neglect are involved. Some teachers may feel they should not interfere with family relationships or childrearing techniques, and thus do not report cases where children are at risk (Underhill, 1974). However, it is both a legal and ethical responsibility for teachers to combine their knowledge of child development and their observation skills to identify children in need of protection.

Indicators of abuse and neglect

Physical manifestations, child or adult behaviors, and environmental situations may indicate a child has or may be at risk of abuse or neglect. The factors that most often can be observed by teachers will be discussed here.

Child characteristics

Many of the characteristics described here occur in contexts other than abusive situations. Rarely does the presence or absence of a single factor signal child abuse. A pattern of these factors and behaviors will more likely indicate harm or risk to the child.

Teachers of young children often observe bruises or wounds on children that are in various stages of healing. This indicates the injuries occurred at different times, and may have been inflicted on a regular basis. Physical abuse can be suspected, for example, if injuries appear a day or so after a holiday or long weekend (bruises take a day to show up). Injuries that occur on multiple planes of the body or that leave a mark that looks like a hand or tool should also be considered nonaccidental.

Children naturally use their hands to protect themselves. Usually when a child falls, the hands go out to stop the fall and protect the face. Children's hands, knees, or foreheads are usually injured when they attempt to break their fall. If children report their injuries were caused by a fall, but the injuries do not include these areas, you should be suspicious.

When children fall, they also are most likely to fall on one side or plane of the body. Therefore, multiple injuries, such as a head injury coupled with a bruise to the ribs or buttocks, should be considered suspicious because more than one plane of the body is involved.

For example, a first grade teacher noticed that a child in her class returned from the Christmas holiday with bruises on the right side of her face and on the back of her left arm. Although the child said she had fallen, the teacher contacted the state child welfare agency. The child's mother initially contended the girl had been roughhousing with her brothers. Further investigation revealed that she had been hit twice by her grandfather who had been visiting and allegedly could not tolerate the girl's loud noises.

Burns often leave clues as to their origin. Oval burns may be caused by a cigarette. Stocking or doughnut-shaped burns may indicate that the child was put into a hot substance. Any burn that leaves an imprint of an item, such as an electric stove burner on a child's hand, may indicate that the injury was not accidental. The natural response of children is to withdraw when a body part comes in contact with a hot object; thus only a small section of skin is usually burned if the burn is accidental.

School-age children who come to school early and leave late may be indicating they have a reason not to go home. Likewise, young children who say they have been harmed should be believed. Rarely do children make up reports of abuse.

Older children may also discuss harmful events with classmates. Help children feel comfortable enough to confide in you because of your shared concern for a child. Susan, age 8, told a friend she had been molested by her father. The classmate confided in the teacher, who made a report. Susan had indeed been molested. Through counseling for the family, the molestation was stopped.

Children who take food from others may be suffering from neglect. One agency investigated a case where a preschool child constantly took food from other children's lunches. The child was receiving one-half of a peanut butter sandwich a day at home and needed the additional food for survival.

Another common sign of neglect is children who come to school inappropriately dressed for the weather. The child who wears sandals in the winter or who doesn't wear a coat on a cold snowy day meets the definition of neglect and can be seen as at risk of harm.

Young children cannot be expected to sit still for long periods. However, some children who have trouble sitting may be experiencing discomfort in their genital areas as a result of sexual abuse. Children whose knowledge of the sexual act is much more sophisticated than that of peers or for their level of development may also be indicating they have been sexually abused. For example, a child might engage in inappropriate sex play with dolls or with other children in the dramatic play area or at recess.

Radical behavior changes in children, or regressive behavior, should be viewed as a possible indicator of abuse or neglect. For example, children who suddenly become extremely hostile or withdrawn should be considered to be possible victims of abuse or neglect. Regression often indicates that children are attempting to protect themselves or to cope with the situation. Typical of such a behavior change might be the 5-year-old child who develops toileting problems. Likewise, the child who strives to do everything exactly right, or fears doing anything wrong, may be trying to avoid incurring the anger of adults.

Another behavior that is a possible clue to abuse or neglect is the child who always stays in the background of activities. This child usually watches intently to see what adults are doing—possibly to keep out of the way of adults in order to prevent being harmed.

Children who are abused frequently expect such abuse

from all adults. Do you know children who cower when you lift your hand in the air? Are there children in your group who hide broken crayons rather than asking for tape to repair them? Discussion, stories written by the children, drawings, or sharing time may also reveal episodes of abuse and neglect.

It is important to stress that teachers should be alert to a *pattern* of characteristics and behaviors that indicate child abuse or neglect.

Indicators of child abuse

Child

- bruises or wounds in various stages of healing
- injuries on two or more planes of the body
- injuries reported to be caused by falling but which do not include hands, knees, or forehead
- oval, immersion, doughnut-shaped, or imprint burns
- reluctance to leave school
- inappropriate dress for the weather
- discomfort when sitting
- sophisticated sexual knowledge or play
- radical behavior changes or regressive behavior
- child withdraws or watches adults
- child seems to expect abuse
- revealing discussion, stories, or drawings

Adult

- unrealistic expectations for child
- reliance on child to meet social or emotional needs
- lack of basic childrearing knowledge or skills
- substance abuse

Stress

- positive or negative changes—moving, new baby, unemployment, divorce

---

Adult characteristics

Parent (or other prime caregiver) behavior may also give clues that children are at risk of harm. Most preschool program staff see parents twice a day, and occasionally during parent conferences or home visits as well. Teachers of primary-age children have fewer occasions to observe parents, but can still be aware of parent behaviors through responses to notes, questionnaires, or phone calls.

There are a number of indicators of an adult's inability or unwillingness to care for and protect children. The parent who has unrealistic expectations for the child can be seen as placing the child at risk. For example, a parent may believe a 6-month-old child can be toilet trained, or that a 5-year-old

---

Watch for a *pattern* of characteristics and behaviors that indicate child abuse or neglect.

---

should be able to read, or that an 8-year-old should always act like a lady.

Adults who look to their children to meet some of their own social or emotional needs can also be seen as a high-risk parent. The teenager who keeps her baby to have someone to love her is likely to be very disappointed!

Whenever possible, observe the parent and child interacting with one another. Parents who lack basic childrearing knowledge or skills place children at risk. For instance, a parent who doesn't know about nutrition or health care, or who has a serious physical illness, may be unable to adequately care for a child. Parents who are substance abusers—either drugs or alcohol—place their children at risk. Because most parents don't deliberately harm their children, all the parents with these types of problems need support to help them function in healthier ways with their children.

At the same time, when teachers observe parenting styles, they must be aware of and sensitive to social and cultural differences. Child protection services are not designed to impose middle-class parenting standards on everyone, but are aimed at insuring a *minimum* standard of care for all children so they are free from harm.

While none of the above factors automatically indicate child abuse, the presence of any of them, along with other clues or patterns of suspected abuse, may indicate harm or potential harm for children.

Stress in the environment

Adult stress can often be the cause of one-time or chronic harm to children. Therefore, whenever a family is under stress, the likelihood that abuse or neglect may occur is increased. The source of stress can be either positive or negative—a move, the birth of a new baby, unemployment, death, inadequate housing, divorce. Any stressor can affect parents' ability to care for their children and to maintain their own self-control.

Once again, however, stress should be considered as just one indicator that may produce a potentially dangerous situation for children.

Preventing abuse and neglect

Teachers of young children have many opportunities to aid in the prevention of child abuse and neglect. Certainly each teacher is a role model for parents. Many of your actions, such as your way of greeting children when they return from an illness or vacation, your methods for handling misbehavior, and your expectations for children, can help parents see positive ways to guide children.

For teachers who are not in contact with children's parents every day, it is more difficult to serve as a role model. However, you can talk with parents often by phone, hold discussion groups about common concerns such as discipline or early reading, and encourage parents to visit your classroom.

Once you are familiar with the clues that indicate children and families may be at risk, you can spot potential problems early. If a family is going to move, for example, you can talk with them about how to make a more comfortable transition for their children into their new school (Jalongo, 1985).

If you sense a potential danger to the child, you can help the family link up with appropriate supports, such as counseling services or material assistance, before their need becomes overwhelming and children are harmed.

What happens when a report is made?

In most states, one child welfare agency receives and investigates reports of suspected child abuse or neglect. The main purpose of the agency is to protect children from harm or from further harm, not to punish parents. These agencies work on the assumption that the best context for childrearing is in the child's own home (Kadushin, 1978).

Teachers are role models for parents.

When abuse or neglect is a reality, children will not necessarily be removed from their parents. The agency will strive to take the appropriate action to protect the child at home in the short run, while working with the parents to solve the problem for the future. All services are aimed at enhancing the parents' ability to care for and protect their children.

Before calling your local child protection agency, review the policy and procedures established for your program or school. These policies may help you determine when it is best to report, may support you in making the report, and may stipulate channels for reporting. The report should always be made in accordance with those policies and procedures, and should be done factually and without emotion.

Depending upon the state, a report is made either to a central or a local field office of the child welfare agency. That agency must begin its investigation by contact with the child, the child's family, and the alleged perpetrator of the harm. This contact is usually initiated within 24 hours, but can begin immediately if it appears the child is currently in danger.

While the family will not be told who initiated action, the agency may ask for your name, address, and phone number when you make the report. This identification is necessary in case the agency needs to get back to you for further information.

Program directors and principals should offer in-service training to teachers to keep them abreast of the state's reporting law, the specific practices of the state child welfare agency, and the school's policy and procedures. Familiarity with the procedure, and the implicit support for reporting suspected abuse, can help teachers to follow through with their responsibility.

Filing a report of suspected child abuse begins a process through which the child welfare agency determines whether or not the child has actually been harmed or is at risk of harm from abuse or neglect. When harm has occurred, then the agency works to protect the child and help the family protect the child. The emphasis is always on treatment, not punishment. Teachers are an important part of a multidisciplinary team to help prevent and treat victims of abuse and neglect.

While teachers may hesitate to report suspected cases of abuse or neglect for fear of straining the parent-teacher relationship, that fear is often unfounded (Jirsa, 1981). Most parents love their children and are concerned about their welfare. Abuse and neglect rarely occur as a result of deliberate intent to harm a child. Rather, it occurs when a parent temporarily lacks control or judgment, or lacks the knowledge or resources to adequately care for the child. After their initial and appropriate anger at the intervention of the agency, most parents feel a sense of relief that the problems has been identified, and they are usually very willing to work toward a solution.

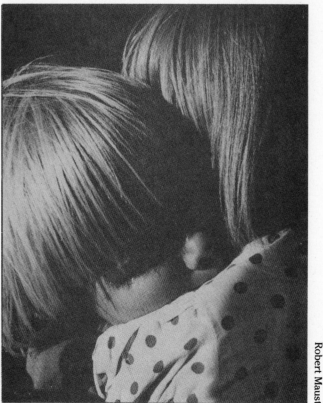

Robert Maust

All services are aimed at enhancing the parents' ability to care for and protect their children.

In cases where only the potential for abuse or neglect exists, the link with the child welfare agency can provide parents with the resources or referrals needed to create a more effective home environment.

Like teachers, child welfare professionals' first allegiance is to the child. Teachers of young children are in a unique position to both report and help prevent child abuse and neglect through their daily contact with children and families.

When in doubt, report. Only then can we all work together to intervene on behalf of the child, work toward solutions, and enhance the quality of life for children and families.

References

American Humane Association. (1983). *Highlights of official child neglect and abuse reporting.* Denver, CO: Author.

Education Commission of the States. (1976, March). *A comparison of the states' child abuse statutes* (Report No. 84). Denver, CO: Author.

Kempe, H., & Helfer, R. (Eds.). (1972). *Helping the battered child and his family.* Philadelphia: Lippincott.

Jalongo, M. R. (1985, September). When young children move. *Young Children, 40*(6), 51–57.

Jirsa, J. (1981). Planning a child abuse referral system. *Social Work in Education, 3*(2), p. 10.

Kadushin, A. (1978). *Child welfare strategy in the coming years.* Washington, DC: National Association of Social Workers.

Illinois Public Law. (1979, November). *The abused and neglected child reporting act* (Public Act 81-1077).

McCaffrey, M., & Tewey, S. (1978, October). Preparing educators to participate in the community response to child abuse and neglect. *Exceptional Children, 45*(2), p. 115.

Underhill, E. (1974). The strange silence of teachers, doctors, and social workers in the face of cruelty to children. *International Child Welfare Review,* (21), 16–21.

U.S. Department of Health and Human Services. (1981). *Study findings: National study of the incidence and severity of child abuse and neglect.* Washington, DC: Superintendent of Documents.

The authors wish to thank Leigh Bartlett of the Department of Community Services in Perth, Australia for her help in developing case examples provided here.

Schoolchildren and Drugs:

The Fancy That Has Not Passed

RICHARD A. HAWLEY

Richard A. Hawley is director of the Upper School at University School/Hunting Valley Campus, Chagrin Falls, Ohio. He has written frequently on drug-related issues. His latest book is Drugs and Society: Responding to an Epidemic *(Walker).*

I. BACKGROUND

COME NOW, haven't we schoolpeople heard *enough* about drugs? The question is more than fair. Stories about drugs in the print media — big busts, latest threats to health, controversial testing programs, involvement of celebrities — are so ubiquitous that each new one raises little more interest than the daily weather report. And most televiewers would agree that, if Geraldo Rivera made only one documentary on the subject, it would be one too many.

But while drug-related journalism may have lost the power to engage us, the issue of school-age children altering the course of development of their central nervous systems with toxic chemicals continues to command our immediate attention. However inured to it we have become, the "drug problem" has not gone away. In many regions and in whole school systems, student drug use is virulent. Nationwide it continues to be — and this is the technically correct word — epidemic.

According to the best and most far-reaching survey, Lloyd Johnston, Patrick O'Malley, and Jerald Bachman's *Drugs and the Nation's High School Students*, more than nine out of 10 members of the high school class of 1985 had used alcohol, more than half had tried marijuana

(more than a quarter reported using it in the past month), one in six had used cocaine, and one in eight had used hallucinogens, such as LSD. The great majority of drug-using children in the U.S. make their initial decision to try a drug between their 12th and 16th years — or between seventh and 10th grades.

When we consider that the metabolites of some commonly abused drugs, such as marijuana, remain active in the user's system for weeks, the implications for in-school behavior and performance grow ominous. In fact, in light of the figures for "recent heavy drinking" reported by the class of 1985 (45% of boys, 25% of girls), it seems statistically unlikely that on any given day there would be many American classrooms without *several* drug-altered students glassily meeting their teachers' expectant gazes.

Educationally and developmentally, this matters. It matters even more than whether students come to school underfed and underloved. For it is easier — much easier — to feed and to love and to teach a child than it is to reverse a pattern of drug abuse once it has begun. The most toxic effects of drug use have nothing to do with short-term stupefaction, nothing to do with "being high." The most toxic effects are not felt at all. The lodging of THC from marijuana in the fatty lining of a neuron is not felt by the user, nor is a teenager's passage from "ex-

perimental" drug use to "social" use, or from "social" use to chemical dependency.

Drugs are taken for the pleasurable feelings they produce — or are rumored to produce. A drug cannot create or alter feelings without chemically altering the functioning of the brain. Unfortunately, every external chemical known to produce changes in the nervous system also *damages* that system. There are no exceptions. There are no consequence-free drugs.

But while the brain is the principal organ affected by mind-altering drugs, it is an organ ill-equipped to register its own immediate impairment. The brain has no pain receptors: poke it, squeeze it, cut it, pound it, and it will not "hurt" (although the consequences will be otherwise dramatic). Because the brain doesn't hurt when it is injured, brain damage, whether caused by tumor growth, concussion, stroke, or drug abuse, often remains undetected until brain *function* is lost: speech, memory, movement, and so on. In the case of serious stroke, head trauma, or Alzheimer's disease, such losses are dramatic, but we should be no less attentive to losses caused by the use of alcohol and other drugs, even when those losses are subtler and are distributed over a longer period of time.

Most of us have observed a person in the process of getting drunk — a progres-

From *Phi Delta Kappan*, May 1987, pp. K1-K8. Reprinted by permission of the author.

sive pickling of the cortical functions. The subtlest and most elegant functions are the first to go: awareness of nuance, appraisal of consequences, responsiveness to time, place, and circumstance. A drink or two can reduce inhibitions. A few drinks in rapid succession knock out more basic functions: judgment, speech, motor coordination. Ultimately, consciousness itself is lost in the nervous system's last-ditch effort to preserve life. Occasionally, an impulsive or inexperienced drinker will take a fatal dose before losing consciousness. Yet, despite this progressive, easily observable impairment of brain function, the brain never once says ouch.

Herein, probably, lies the tenacity of the "drug problem." The impairment caused by many widely used drugs does not become obvious until an individual has become a confirmed user. Next to inhalable solvents, alcohol is probably the crudest of the nervous system depressants; its abuse is often followed by hangover — actually an indication of a healthy system working to expel poisons. But with more complex mind-altering drugs, such as marijuana, the hangover may be gradually distributed over days and weeks. The user may not link the uneasy, irritable feeling to marijuana at all, but rather to surrounding circumstances: family life, perhaps, or school.

Only when drug use has progressed to the point where a person's disposition and behavior are noticeably altered — to the "wasted" or "burned-out" condition — is it typically classified as a problem. And for more than a decade after the initial surge of illegal drug use in the Sixties, even the most dramatically and, as it happened, irreversibly "burned-out" individuals were often extolled for having *chosen* an alternative approach to life.

Tens of thousands of youthful chemical dependencies later, we know better — or we should know better. We should also know that, from an educational standpoint, the most abusive, dependent users are not the sole manifestation of the drug problem. The drug problem includes everything along the way. It includes the once-bright suburban pot-smoker who, in an under-challenging high school program, is "doing fine." I have met, spoken with, and observed hundreds of such students in such unchallenging programs. I have seen high school juniors showing "no academic deficit" due to occasional marijuana use, as long as nothing new — nothing beyond a healthy seventh-grader's range — is required of them.

THE DESTRUCTIVE effects of student drug use on learning and on the conduct of schooling in general are by no means limited to the users themselves. Even a few drug-enervated students in a classroom will change the learning climate for everyone. Drug-altered children are largely impervious to classroom business; teachers are apt to see them as unprepared, preoccupied, hostile. Such students — and again, it only takes a few — tend to shut teachers down and push them toward less-effective teaching. Teaching drugged children is like acting or singing in the presence of hecklers or hosting a party at which a few of the guests are bent on having a bad time.

A competent teacher who works hard trying to engage chemically impaired nervous systems is working against the grain. It is no coincidence that "teacher burnout" — the term itself is derived from the drug culture — should have surfaced as a national issue directly in the wake of epidemic student drug use. It is instructive that in the mid-Seventies, when the phenomenon of "teacher burnout" emerged so explosively, teachers' salaries (adjusted for inflation) were higher, class sizes and student loads were generally smaller, and school programs were overall less routinized and rigid than they were in the relatively drug-free years before the mid-Sixties.

Drugs change the people who use them, and when the users are students or teachers, drugs change schools. The use of drugs, including alcohol, is illegal for almost all school-age children. The use of drugs also violates school rules and most household policies. Drug use and exchange is therefore always a furtive business. As such, it is an inherently divisive force in school life. It divides straight groups from using groups, divides students from the faculty and the administration, divides strict from permissive faculty members. Especially in the aftermath of an embarrassing bust, a drunk-driving death, or the publication of poor scholastic performance, drug use causes people to point fingers of accusation. School boards find principals and faculty members lax. Teachers label whole classes

or whole generations hopeless. Students find the new school drug policy or newly formed parent network reactionary and repressive.

At the heart of such divisions is illegal drug use. A nearby public high school asked me to advise on a drug-related problem that had lowered student and faculty morale to the point that the continuation of the daily school program was in some doubt.

The basic problem in this school was as follows. Considerable community, school board, and administration concern had been raised about the extent of drug use and drug dealing taking place on school grounds during school hours. A student-conducted survey confirmed that more than 50% of the students used illegal drugs to some degree and that a majority of those who used drugs did so during school hours.

Administrators, counselors, and faculty members reflected on the problem and decided that the bulk of the drug traffic taking place during school hours was happening in unsupervised places, both on and off the school grounds. Thus it was decided that the school's relatively relaxed "open campus" policy, which allowed most students to study and socialize wherever they pleased — and even allowed some of them to leave campus during their unscheduled time — had to go. Supervised study halls were instituted, many of them housed in the student cafeteria and containing hundreds of students whose seats were assigned. Trips to the bathroom or to the library required a special pass. The students, as one might imagine, reacted angrily to what they perceived as "Gestapo" tactics. And the non-using students, who

TABLE 1.

Percentages of High School Seniors Saying They Had Ever Used Certain Drugs

| | Ever Used | | | | | | | | | | |
| | Class of | | | | | | | | | | |
	'75 %	'76 %	'77 %	'78 %	'79 %	'80 %	'81 %	'82 %	'83 %	'84 %	'85 %
Marijuana/Hashish	47	53	56	59	60	60	60	59	57	55	54
Inhalants	NA	NA	NA	NA	19	18	17	18	19	19	18
Amyl & Butyl Nitrites	NA	NA	NA	NA	11	11	10	10	8	8	8
Hallucinogens	NA	NA	NA	NA	19	16	16	15	15	13	12
LSD	11	11	10	10	10	9	10	10	9	8	8
PCP	NA	NA	NA	NA	10	10	8	6	6	5	5
Cocaine	9	10	11	13	15	16	17	16	16	16	17
Heroin	2	2	2	2	1	1	1	1	1	1	1
Other Opiates	9	10	10	10	10	10	10	10	9	10	10
Stimulants	NA	NA	NA	NA	NA	NA	NA	28	27	28	26
Sedatives	18	18	17	16	15	15	16	15	14	13	12
Barbiturates	17	16	16	14	12	11	11	10	10	10	9
Methaqualone	8	8	9	8	8	10	11	11	10	8	7
Tranquilizers	17	17	18	17	16	15	15	14	13	12	12
Alcohol	90	92	93	93	93	93	93	93	93	93	92
Cigarettes	74	75	76	75	74	71	71	70	71	70	69

Source: National Institute on Drug Abuse, Monitoring the Future Study, 1985.

had enjoyed their former liberties without breaking the rules, were the angriest. In this way the new policy united the "straights" and the "heads" in anti-authoritarian indignation.

With hindsight, it is easy to see what went wrong. The "blanket" solution of enforced study halls might have been improved had the student government or an open student forum been asked to propose a solution that would 1) stop illicit drug use *and* 2) preserve appropriate student liberty. The school administration could have taken this step without in any way compromising its resolve to eliminate drug use. The students needed help in seeing that student drug use, not their repressive elders, had caused the curtailment of their liberties. And while students were rather more comfortable reviling the administration than confronting one another about drug use, it was the latter, less comfortable process that eventually improved the climate of the school.

Apart from its general effects on a school's tone and quality, drug use has particularly demoralizing effects on particular organizations and activities. Quite recently I was asked to appraise a new athletic policy being tried out by a football coach at a prestigious independent school. The coach had read about drug-related effects on student performance,

had attended drug education conferences, had weighed his own recent experiences with drug-using students, and had decided that he would like to take the firmest possible stand against drugs. With approval from the administration and the athletic department, the coach explained his feelings to his players and announced the new policy: his players were to be drug-free. No compromises. Each player was to sign a pledge, indicating that he would not use alcohol or other drugs for the duration of the season and that he would remove himself, or consent to be removed, from the team if he did.

The policy sparked some controversy and also a good deal of interest and support. The coach was generally admired for his stand.

But by the time I visited the school and talked to the team, it was mid-season, and the players seemed troubled. When they were comfortable enough to speak confidentially, it was clear that the policy was not the problem, but what had happened to it. Because they liked the coach, the players had stuck to the pledge for the opening weeks of the season. Then parties and other tempting situations combined to break the resolve of some of the players. They waited to see what happened. And nothing happened. Before long, more than half of the team had

> **T**he long-term answer is to prevent drug abuse before it begins. This means placing programs in elementary schools.

broken the pledge. Students began calling the new policy a "farce." The coach himself suspected from his players' attitudes that they had broken the pledge, but he did not know for certain. Everyone was demoralized.

The coach's stand and the drug-free pledge were not the problems. The players' subsequent violations merely pointed up the real problem: the players drank and smoked pot. They either could not or would not stop — not for their coach, not for team solidarity, perhaps not for anything.

IN THE TWO decades that drug use has been a central factor in the lives of school-age children, the phenomenon has changed and "matured" in some particularly unattractive ways. Much wishful thinking and misguided editorial writing to the contrary, no healing "decline" in student drug use has taken place. But that statement needs some explaining.

Student use of illegal drugs increased steadily through the Sixties and Seventies and reached a peak for most categories of drugs in 1979-80. At that point, more than one in 10 high school students reported smoking marijuana *daily*. In the following five years, 1981 through 1985, the use of drugs by students gradually fell off — with the exception of cocaine, the use of which continues to rise.

But this recent decline should occasion only guarded optimism, at best. The real statistical story is that students in 1985 are using drugs (again, with the exception of cocaine) at about the same rate as in 1975. For example, 47% of the high school class of 1975 indicated that they had "ever used" pot; 54% of the class of 1985 indicated the same. The numbers reporting recent marijuana use (27% of

Building Drug-Free Schools

TO ADDRESS the need to bring together all the important elements of school-based drug prevention (policy, curriculum, and working with the community), the American Council for Drug Education has developed *Building Drug-Free Schools*. This four-part drug-prevention program for grades K-12 consists of three written guides and a film. It is designed to provide school administrators, teachers, counselors, parents, and other community members with detailed information and suggestions for developing a new school-based drug- and alcohol-prevention program or for augmenting an existing program. The four parts of the program are outlined below.

I. Policy. This part of the program details why drug and alcohol use is a serious detriment to education and spells out specifically which policies have proven effective in reducing drug use. It addresses curricular requirements, the role of law enforcement, and suspension, expulsion, and intervention procedures.

II. Curriculum. This part of the program provides a unique K-12 curriculum with easy-to-use and age-appropriate learning activities. It includes essential information for teachers, such as the effects of drugs on health, the "high-risk" child, and the developmental basis for a drug-prevention curriculum. The curriculum shows the

importance of avoiding dangerous "responsible use" messages, and it integrates the cognitive and affective dimensions of learning.

III. Community. This part of the program outlines specific techniques for enlisting the support of parents, businesses, religious groups, the media, medical professionals, fraternal organizations, and other community groups in reinforcing the drug-free message.

IV. Three Schools: Drug-Free. This part of the program is the film that accompanies the written guides. It features the principals of three schools, who describe how a clear and consistently enforced policy, an age-appropriate curriculum, and the involvement of the community have enabled them to significantly reduce drug and alcohol problems in their schools. The 29-minute film demonstrates for administrators, teachers, counselors, school board members, parents, and other community members that the goal of a drug-free school can be achieved.

The three guides that make up *Building Drug-Free Schools* are available for $50 a set. The film is available for purchase at $275 (16mm) or $225 (videotape) or for rental at $35. For more information or to place an order, contact the American Council for Drug Education, Department K, 5820 Hubbard Dr., Rockville, MD 20852. Ph. 301/984-5700.

the class of 1975, 26% of the class of 1985) have remained fairly constant over the past decade. It is hard to be encouraged by reported declines in drug use when the levels remain so high.

There are other general features of the drug epidemic that educators should note. One is a peculiar sort of Law of Unlimited Inclusion, according to which new drugs tend to be added to the illicit pharmacopoeia, but none is ever replaced. Thus pot and LSD, two of the most commonly used novelty drugs of the psychedelic Sixties, did not replace or even diminish the use of "established," legally available drugs, such as tobacco and alcohol. Nor has the more recent boom in the use of cocaine and "designer drugs" replaced pot or LSD.

This is not to say that, regionally and even nationally, the demand for particular drugs does not vary. It does. But the preference for individual drugs does not so much come and go, as it comes and goes and comes again. Two years ago streetwise kids in the city where I live were saying that "psychedelics" (read LSD) were out. But in the wake of a single sell-out Grateful Dead concert in the area, psychedelics have come back. This isn't a street rumor; this is the report of the families, schools, and treatment centers that have had to tend this newest crop of "Dead-heads."

None of this is meant to indict or belittle the efforts to fight drug abuse made by legislators, communities, schools, and parent organizations over the past decade. What declines have occurred in certain forms of drug use are almost certainly due to a growing consensus that drug use has no part to play in healthy child development. The consensus has expressed itself in a growing resolve to confront drug use, unpleasantness and all. The job, however, is barely begun.

II. HEALTHY CHILD DEVELOPMENT

TO THOSE with a vested interest in the physical, emotional, and intellectual development of children, the drug epidemic appears to have been designed with diabolical precision. Drugs block, retard, or distort the most crucial human capacities — perception, cognition, planning, physical coordination — and the loss of function is rewarded by surpassingly pleasurable sensations.

I noted above that American children are most likely to make their initial decision to try an intoxicating drug between the ages of 12 and 16: during the peak years of adolescent growth. During these years, every cell and tissue of the body is either altered or replaced altogether. Sexual potency, nearly all of one's adult skeletal stature, and the capacity for higher-order mental functions are produced during this developmental surge. The new mental attainments include the capacity to think abstractly, to interpret elaborate symbol systems (whether poetic or alge-

braic), and to deduce the present behavior needed to achieve a variety of future possibilities. With the exception of the first 18 months of life, adolescence is the most accelerated period of human growth. Unlike preverbal infants, however, adolescents are conscious — indeed, acutely and exquisitely *self*-conscious — of the changes they are undergoing.

Adolescents regard their new size, new sensations, and new capacities with a good deal of positive anticipation, but these same developments are also occasions for unexpected awkwardness, worry, and loss of personal control. Both the drama and the awkwardness of adolescence are developmentally necessary. Adolescents must define a new relationship to younger children and come to see themselves as former children. They must forge new relationships with their parents and with other adults in authority. There must also be an intensified relationship with the opposite sex.

So many changes would be challenging enough to manage if the onset and rate of adolescent development were uniform and predictable; in reality, though, adolescent growth is a capriciously uneven process. The appearance — seemingly always too early or too late — of adult stature, a croaking voice, a beard, breasts, or body hair can be the source of devastating self-doubt. All such changes are unbidden, and some seem revolting: new smells, regular eruptions of skin blemishes, oily hair, the onset of menstruation, the annoyance of irrelevant erections.

Developments that seem trivial from an adult perspective — for example, having the wrong kind of shoes — can imperil an adolescent's basic sense of well-being. Life itself has been known to hang on only slightly weightier issues: being in or out of the group, being on or off the team, being datable or not. Steering a survivable course through first love, first intimacy, finding oneself *adequate* — these are momentous challenges in adolescence. Each will arouse terrific stress, and the adaptive management of that stress *is* maturation. The only way out of adolescence is through it. Chemically anesthetizing oneself with drugs serves only to delay this maturation — or in some cases to replace it altogether — often with lifelong consequences.

ALONG WITH THE rapidly unfolding physical development in adolescence comes the capacity for new forms of thought. Measured on an electroencephalograph, an adolescent brain can put out faster, more "adult" brain waves than that of a preadolescent. Adolescents can perceive new gradations of color and musical pitch. They can see allegories in stories that were once understood only as literal narratives. Adolescents can understand whole systems (cellular systems, body systems, political systems, solar systems), make predictions about them, and draw inferences

from them. Adolescents are able to pursue higher mathematics, advanced physics, and other sciences that proceed deductively from their own axioms; these theoretical disciplines need not bear any demonstrable relationship to observable reality.

The most profound capacity for moral thinking can emerge during adolescence. Cognitively, this amounts to projecting oneself imaginatively forward and backward in time, plotting hypothetical actions and their potential outcomes, referring the outcomes to feeling centers for evaluation, formulating plans, and then executing reasoned, purposeful actions.

All this staggering complexity and elegance comes into play only if adolescent development is healthy, not polluted and impaired by drugs. If we step back and take a long look, we can see child development as a continuous process in which 1) simple mental structures are superseded by complex ones, 2) exclusively self-directed motivation and behavior becomes, at least in part, other-directed, and 3) utter dependence on nurturers develops into personal autonomy and one's own capacity for nurturing. Again, this is the direction of *healthy*, not necessarily typical, development.

Healthy maturation requires a capacity for managing pleasure. In other words, pleasure must be understood as a consequence of a good, not as an unqualified good in itself. The most reinforcing sensual pleasures — such as eating and sex — have evolved, I suspect, to promote such essential human purposes as survival, reproduction, and pair bonding. The non-sensual pleasures — such as pride, elation, and joy — have no doubt evolved to promote essential personal and social goods. But when pleasure is abstracted and pursued as an end in itself, people encounter such troubles of self-indulgence as obesity, promiscuity, emotional instability, and addiction.

Aristotle addressed the role of pleasure management in child development with remarkable clarity. His prescription has been revived intermittently through the centuries, most forcefully by Montessori and Dewey. Aristotle's point was that children must be "habituated" to desirable behavior — attending to tasks, sharing, telling the truth — before they can understand theoretically the benefit of doing so. By the time a developing child is able to understand why, theoretically, "honesty is the best policy," he or she may have internalized a pattern of truthfulness or deceit that is impervious to the more recently acquired, higher-order "theory." The standard educational rewards for desirable behavior are mastery, recognition, and praise. These rewards *follow* and thus reinforce the desired behavior.

Drug use inverts the healthy model. Complex thinking becomes simpler, distorted, even pathological — and not just while the user is high. Awareness of others and of the environment is replaced by euphoric, stupefied self-centeredness. Stress management is replaced by anesthetizing bad feelings or by chemically triggering good ones. Natural controls on pleasure are circumvented by chemicals that create rewarding sensations. In this way, essential developmental processes are not only reversed, but the *loss* is rewarded by indescribably compelling pleasure.

This is the real drug problem. It is also a disease and a sure sign of cultural deterioration. Because drug use runs so directly against the aims of education, school communities should not be reluctant to reestablish controls over the environment in which developing children make decisions. As current analysts have pointed out repeatedly, we are not enjoying a scholastic Golden Age.

III. HISTORICAL PERSPECTIVE

THE USE of alcohol and other intoxicating drugs in America extends back past the European settlement of the New World. Native Americans in the Southwest used naturally occurring hallucinogens in religious rites. The earliest dwellers in the high country of the Andes used coca leaves as a medicine and to achieve religious trances. The peoples of ancient China and India used cannabis (marijuana) for similar purposes. Down through the modern centuries, neither "white drugs" (those derived from opium) nor "brown drugs" (those derived from cannabis) made much of an impact on the culture of the West, where the preferred intoxicant was alcohol, in either distilled or fermented form.

The opiates, cannabis, and, after it was chemically extracted from the coca leaf in 1859, cocaine were contained in prescription and patent medicines in the 1800s. Cocaine was tried and found wanting as a local anesthetic. Freud initially used cocaine to relieve nervous disorders, but he later vilified the drug as a destroyer of health. It is also true that small amounts of cocaine were included in the original formula for Coca-Cola, but the drug was removed shortly after the turn of the century when cocaine was identified as a threat to health. The use of alcohol has also been intermittently accepted, regulated, deregulated, prohibited, and tolerated.

So drug use itself is not a late-20th-century novelty. The novelty is the *number* of people — especially young people — who are involved. There is no historical precedent for such phenomena as millions of school-age children using cannabis, cocaine, LSD, and other mind-altering drugs.

The reason the drug epidemic erupted in the mid-Sixties probably had less to do with the contemporary issues with which it is most often linked — protest over the Vietnam war, agitation for civil rights, and frustration with a repressively structured society — than it did with the fact that millions of baby-boomers were coming of age at the same time. As the Sixties turned uneasily into the Seventies, for the

---

Even the best programs can be subverted by the absence of strong, clear institutional policies forbidding drug use.

---

first time in American history there were more people under than over 25. An unprecedented proportion of them were clustered on college campuses, where adult presence was so minimal as to be unfelt, where a world of radical brotherhood and sisterhood was less rhetoric than daily reality.

A recurrent theme of the youth culture of the Sixties was a plea to sustain adolescence, not to complete the compromising passage into adulthood. In *Do It!*, his manifesto of the counter-culture, Jerry Rubin boldly stated the general aim: "When we're thirty-five, our ambition is to act like we're fifteen." In the Sixties, to act like a 15-year-old obliged one to defy standard conventions of dress, grooming, language, and public deportment. It also obliged one, perhaps most enduringly, to flout the conventional taboos against illicit drugs, especially pot and LSD. The older, pre-Sixties beats and hipsters became models for throngs of hippies, and within a year or two the long-standing barriers that had separated drug users from straight society had broken down.

From the standpoint of public health, the American drug epidemic has caused such severe problems because it had a decade's head start on any sustained, informed attempts to check it. Drugs were not merely used, they were extolled enthusiastically by the people and through music, the medium closest to the heart of the youth culture. The Beatles sang cheerily of "getting high with a little help from my friends," while the cast of *Hair* proclaimed the drug-lit profundity of "walking in space," explaining, "in this way we rediscover sensation."

Meanwhile, in 1965 a team of Israeli scientists investigating the 420-plus chemicals composing marijuana isolated the one, delta-9 tetrahydrocannabinol (THC), that is most responsible for making users

high. THC was further found to have some worrisome features. It lodged itself in fatty tissues all over the body, including the brain. It blocked healthy cell function and, over time, destroyed cells. It was a poison.

By the early Seventies, a federally funded project at the University of Mississippi was growing, under government supervision, a uniform grade of marijuana (about 2% THC) to be used in animal and human tests. With uniform marijuana available for tests, reliable, replicable studies could be made of the drug's effects on behavior and on cells, tissue, and vital human systems. Beginning in the mid-Seventies, improved and more persuasive studies were available, and important research is still under way.

But by the time the scientific and medical communities had begun to voice concerns about the health effects of marijuana and other drugs, patterns of drug use and supply were already deeply entrenched. Old, discredited research claiming the relative mildness or harmlessness of marijuana clashed with claims of its dangerous toxicity. Findings from casually conducted surveys were opposed to findings about cell metabolism. Small, dubious samples of ganja-smoking Jamaican cane farmers were used to suggest the relative safety of pot smoking among North American high school students. "Experts" appeared to disagree. Confusion reigned, and under the umbrella of so much confusion and controversy, drug use continued apace, reaching peak levels among high school students by 1980.

Slowly, however, a broadly based coalition of those opposed to illegal drug use began to make itself heard nationwide. The first people to organize and to articulate an anti-drug stand have been, appropriately, the ones among whom drug use has come inescapably to rest: families, schools, the staffs of drug treatment centers. National organizations, such as the Parents Resource Institute for Drug Education (PRIDE) and the National Federation of Parents (NFP), as well as regional movements, such as the Texans' War on Drugs, have made impressive progress in making freedom from drugs a goal for families, schools, and whole communities.

Yet even so agreeable-sounding a goal as "drug-free youth" is not as easy to sell as it may seem, particularly if "drug-free" is taken to mean "alcohol-free." There are handsomely printed books and curricular programs aimed not at "drug-free youth" but rather at the "responsible use" of drugs. Indeed, even as I write, the most widely distributed curricula for drug education in the country stress making considered responses to drugs. But these programs do not come out in favor of refusing to use drugs altogether.

LET ME PAUSE for a moment. For there is perhaps no greater indication of the inroads drug use has made on contemporary thinking than the fact that authoritative voices on the national education scene are endorsing *responsible levels* of criminal, not to mention health-endangering, activity. How does this reasoning translate into other areas of problem behavior for adolescents? Why not responsible levels of vandalism, assault, or reckless driving? Teenagers have problems with these behaviors, too, though they claim far fewer lives and sacrifice far fewer futures than drug abuse does.

Am I exaggerating? Readers who feel that I'm merely knocking down a straw man should consider the following. In Ruth Eng's 1979 book for teens, *Responsible Drug and Alcohol Use*, the chapter titled "Hints for the Responsible Use of Marijuana" cautions readers to smoke with friends, to sort the seeds out of their stash, to use clean smoking paraphernalia, and to avoid burning lips or carpets.

Andrew Weil, whose 1972 paean to drug-enhanced consciousness, *The Natural Mind*, was reissued last year, also collaborated with children's book author Winifred Rosen in 1983 to produce another drug book pitched to children: *Chocolate to Morphine: Understanding Mind-Active Drugs*. The first chapter, titled "Straight Talk," begins arrestingly, "Drugs are here to stay." The authors continue, "Drug education as it now exists is, at best, a thinly disguised attempt to scare people away from disapproved substances by greatly exaggerating the dangers of these substances." Young readers are advised to "question your parents about the drugs they use. Maybe they will agree to give up theirs if you will give up yours. If you can convince them that your drug use is responsible, you may be able to allay their anxiety."

Parents, too, are given counsel by Weil and Rosen. "Don't make your child feel it is wrong to get high," they argue, because "there are no bad drugs, only bad relationships with drugs." The authors look forward to the day when drug use will be woven comfortably and continuously into the fabric of ordinary life: "We have seen parents in good relationships with marijuana let their children take occasional puffs of joints in much the same way that some Jewish parents allow their children ceremonial sips of wine."

In 1986 Susan and David Cohen, another team of writers for teenagers, wrote an accessible guide to teen drinking called *A Six Pack and a Fake I.D.* The authors make some clear attempts at fair-mindedness, and they offer some informed cautions about alcohol abuse. But they couldn't quite bring themselves to advise their readers to obey drinking laws. Of drinking parties, they write:

> If you're planning a drinking party, and your parents accept the idea, then at least try to make your party a safe, pleasant, and interesting one, instead of a drunken bash. . . . Don't overdo the amount of alcohol in the punch and don't let anyone else add to it.

If the party doesn't run too long and if provisions are made to get drunken guests home, "so far so good. You have

behaved responsibly." In the book's final chapter, titled "Summing Up," there appears the incongruous caveat, "Adults who knowingly supply alcohol to minors may be liable to criminal penalties." (No doubt the publisher's legal counsel is responsible for this terse warning.)

There is a little craziness in these discussions of "responsible" law-breaking. I suspect that Weil would be both vocal and indignant if the teens (and their parents) in his neighborhood were exhorted to curtail his right of free speech or to threaten his person. Yet why, from the standpoint of those who genuinely feel that Weil is a social menace, should the laws respecting his welfare be taken more seriously than the drug laws he so energetically maligns?

It would be a mistake to dismiss the "do it anyway" drug message as a feeble cry of left-over voices from the Sixties. These books and similar school curricula continue to appear in the mid-Eighties. Nor are they the products of dingy underground presses. Macmillan brought out *Responsible Drug and Alcohol Use*, and Houghton Mifflin published both *The Natural Mind* and *Chocolate to Morphine*.

There is considerable optimism in drug education circles today about the anticipated gains to be made as a consequence of the Reagan Administration's Anti-Drug Abuse Act of 1986. If funded, this act is supposed to provide millions of dollars to schools for drug-related programs and materials.

But what materials? Very few comprehensive K-12 curricula come out clearly against the recreational use of drugs. Most of them aim to boost self-esteem and clarify values and decision making. Their stated goal is typically that students will learn to make informed, responsible choices about drugs. Most of them do not suggest that the informed, responsible thing for a child to do is to say no to drug use. In other words, there is nothing built into the new Anti-Drug Abuse Act to insure that existing patterns of drug use will not be reinforced by federal funds. It will take alert, informed school boards, principals, curriculum coordinators, and faculty members to prevent such a development.

IV. SCHOOL STRATEGIES THAT WORK

ONCE AGAIN I must stress that American education is not in the midst of a Golden Age. Schools are drug-ridden, and this is exacting an educational toll. Daunting though it may be, drug use by young people is a problem that can be beaten. Schools have been drug-free in the still-recollectable past; they can be again. Indeed, many have already begun.

Some prescriptions follow for changing the drug climate in the schools. Let me say at the outset that the policies I propose are my own passionate preferences, but they also happen to coincide

with the positions of the American Council for Drug Education, the National Federation of Parents, the Parents Resource Institute for Drug Education, and the Texans' War on Drugs, among other national and regional organizations.

• **The school's commitment must be to become drug-free.** This is a basic premise and a value-laden choice. It generates one kind of policy and program; other premises — to cut down on the levels of drug use or to help students make responsible drug choices — lead to different policies and programs. Robert DuPont, one of the clearest voices in the field of drug abuse prevention, likes to tell school faculties, "Every school will have precisely the amount of drug use that it tolerates."

It is only a sign of the times that the goal of maintaining drug-free schools is sometimes challenged as "unrealistic." The very mission of universal education requires a drug-free atmosphere for learning. Schools mobilize their energies and their money impressively to remove asbestos from the learning environment. And if the lives of a student or two were threatened by toxic shock, the suspected brand of tampons and the machines that vend them would be cleared out of the schools at once. But such threats will not take even a statistically measurable toll in student health and life. Drug use, by contrast, is taking a ghastly toll right now. Practically every reader of this article is acquainted personally with a casualty, if not a fatality, resulting from drug use. Allowing such a state of affairs to exist is inhumane — and "unrealistic."

• **Leaders must endorse, articulate, and stand by a school's commitment to be drug-free.** The responsibility for changing a school's drug climate should be widely shared, but it cannot be delegated. Especially in the early stages, a tough stand on drugs will involve confrontations, dispensing bad news, and taking criticism. If the "drug problem" becomes the special assignment of an assistant district superintendent or of a school's dean of students or of a special faculty task force, those people are likely to be seen as the district's or the school's drug fanatics, and school leaders will be asked to mitigate and temper drug policies that some may find uncomfortable. Maintaining a disinterested stance and keeping a reasonable distance from the problem by delegating the making of drug policy to others will seem the easier course to a school leader. But doing so is almost certain to impede the process of ridding the schools of drugs.

• **Preventing drug abuse is easier, more educational, and more fun than remediating drug problems once they exist.** Prevention, intervention, and treatment are all essential ingredients of anti-drug abuse policies, but prevention is by far the most promising approach. Unlike older, more stable drug abusers, adolescents pass from experimental drinking bouts to full-blown chemical dependencies in a matter of months. The news from the facilities that treat young drug dependents is frankly discouraging. The majority of those who have been treated lapse back into drug abuse. Even among those who persevere and remain drug-free, the reintegration into family, school, and community is not easy. Moreover, a newly described clinical syndrome, PDIS (Post-Dependence Impairment Syndrome), suggests that recovering dependents show abnormally high tendencies to chronic illness, injuries, learning difficulties, and depression.

The long-term answer is to prevent drug abuse before it begins. Schools are most likely to succeed in achieving this aim if they allot more and better instructional time to drug education *before* children confront the choice of whether or not to use a threshold drug. This means installing programs in elementary schools. Some exercises in such programs will be very basic and prescriptive: saying no. Some exercises will be affective: how to say no and how to avoid drug use and other harmful situations. Some lessons will be informational: what is safe and what is dangerous; what are the effects on the human system of various legal and illegal drugs. Special emphasis should be given to cigarettes, alcohol, marijuana, and inhalants, because these are the most prevalent threshold drugs.

However, even the best educational programs can be subverted by the absence of strong, clear institutional policies forbidding drug use. For the great majority of school-age children, adherence to the "rules" and observance of the law are the highest categories of ethical thought. Schools tend to stress the enforcement of those policies about which they care most strongly. Drug education must go hand in hand with an anti-drug policy.

Weary voices stating that "drug education" and "information" have proved ineffectual as ways of preventing drug abuse are misinformed and mistaken. A systematic, prevention-based program of drug education has barely begun nationwide. The drug epidemic arose in the absence of such educational measures, not despite them.

• **Changing the drug climate of a school begins with building a consensus among members of the faculty and staff.** School staffs whose members are divided among themselves cannot stand firm against student drug use. They will be divided in the same way inconsistent parents are divided. Building a durable consensus is apt to require some learning on the part of faculty members about the biomedical effects of drugs and about their special effects on developing children. This learning may require some high-

quality inservice training. The trainers and the materials they use should endorse the goal of a drug-free school. The entire faculty and staff (K-12) of a school system should be included in policy making and program building. Drug education is not the special business of health teachers and science teachers. The support of coaches and advisors is especially crucial to an effective school- or systemwide drug policy.

• **Faculty members and staff members must limit their own drug use to what is lawful and consistent with effective performance.** Employee Assistance Programs (EAPs) for faculty and staff members with drinking and other drug problems are increasingly common in both public and private schools. Adults who have been treated through EAPs and who have remained in their posts tend to bolster rather than undermine the overall morale of a school; at the same time, their presence underscores the school's commitment to be drug-free.

• **Drug-free means alcohol-free.** Alcohol is the principal drug of abuse among U.S. schoolchildren. It is the preferred drug of the majority of chemical dependents, and its use is more likely than any other disease, accident, or activity to lead to the violent death of young people. School faculty members must be educated to respond to the standard defenses for and denials of underage drinking: How much harm is there in a little? I don't want my son or daughter going off to college inexperienced. Well, if they're going to drink, I at least want them to do it here where I can watch them. Hell, I used to throw back a few myself. At least it's only alcohol. At least it's only beer.

Alcohol is the problem, not the form in which it is taken. A can of beer, a typical glass of wine, and a Scotch and soda served at a bar each contains about an ounce of alcohol. Two consecutive ounces of alcohol consumed by a 5-year-old can kill the child. The same dose is highly toxic to a middle-schooler. Growing children are in the process of developing controls that might allow them to drink moderately as adults; alcohol and other drugs *replace* these controls. The loss of performance, health, and life of young drinkers is well-documented and obvious. Against these losses, no positive benefits have been adduced. Camaraderie? Fellowship? Go *observe* the middle-schoolers in the basement rec room or the high school crowd at the rumored three-kegger at the home of a student whose parents are out of town. Observe, and perhaps clean up.

V. A PERSONAL NOTE

ALTHOUGH MY professional responsibilities are to direct a high school and my out-of-school preoccupations tend to be literary and musical, over the past 10 years I have done a good deal of writing, speaking, and conferring about drug-related issues. I never intended to do this, but, given my involvement with young people, I suppose an immersion in drug issues was inevitable. Sometimes I do wonder, though, whether I am coming to see the world through a drug-clouded lens. I have met some people who, it seems to me, have reduced all the world's problems to the drug abuse of American teenagers.

I don't want to become this way, and I try hard to maintain my balance. But I do read the paper. And on the morning that I wrote this paragraph these were the headline stories in the *Cleveland Plain Dealer*.

The leading national news was the revelation that the crew members of the Conrail train that collided disastrously with an Amtrak passenger train were under the influence of marijuana. Locally, the dominant story was the continuing investigation of a convicted drug dealer and police informant who apparently received protection from the Cleveland police force to sell cocaine in the inner city, provided he turned the profits over to the department, which then used the funds to pay for the biggest drug bust in the city's history. A curious sort of ethic at work here.

The sports coverage was replete with Brian Bosworth's indignation that his use of steroids had barred him from NCAA football competition. He claimed that pot-smoking athletes got away with murder because their positive drug tests could be interpreted as "passive inhalation" of other people's smoke.

As I said, I was pressed for time and had to get moving, but I glanced at one more story, one that was given less prominence. It summarized a survey of internationally prominent education experts who were asked to appraise the relative effectiveness of the teaching in six nations of math, science, social studies, foreign language, and each nation's own language. Japan and West Germany were rated highest; the U.S. fared poorly. In math and science we were ranked second to last, and in the teaching of our own language we ranked last.

Hmm. Television? Affluence? Poverty? Permissiveness? Restrictiveness? Outmoded pedagogy and curricula? Existential ennui? Angst? Ask on.

The Profession of Teaching Today

Today we are on the brink of a new era in the teaching profession. Preservice and inservice teachers are having to deal with changes in teacher certification guidelines and new systems of professional accountability. They are also gaining greater influence in public affairs relating to education because of effective national organizations and increased awareness on the part of teachers and the public regarding their social and economic status in North American society. The proposals outlined below and in this unit point to new ways in which teachers will be able to improve their social, professional, and economic circumstances. This is an exciting and promising time for those who are preparing to enter into the teaching profession as well as for those who are already there.

The American Association of Colleges for Teacher Education (AACTE) has called for and is implementing planning arrangements for the national certification of teachers. The National Education Association (NEA) and the American Federation of Teachers (AFT) have entered into dialogue over this matter. AACTE seems to be rallying for the medical model of national board certification in what would amount to the various teaching specialties for which persons would seek certification as teachers. The Carnegie Forum on Education has published *A Nation Prepared: Teachers for the 21st Century,* which calls for similar recommendations for the reform of teacher education. The Carnegie Forum on Education has powerful bipartisan economic and political support. In addition, the Holmes Group of deans, as well as other leaders in teacher education, has issued its own extensive report on reform of teacher education. The Holmes Group report, entitled *Tomorrow's Teachers,* has made recommendations for changing and improving the relationships between teacher education institutions and the elementary and secondary schools of the nation. All in all, almost thirty national reports relating in one way or another to dramatic change in North American teacher education have been published since 1983. Never before have there been such comprehensive and intensive reform recommendations for teacher education on this continent.

Though major changes have occurred in teacher education over the past fifteen years, recent developments indicate that even greater change can be expected in the next few years. The nation's teachers are confronting new proposals each year which directly affect their morale and security.

Difficult teaching conditions, created to a large extent by phenomena such as mainstreaming and competency testing, are intensifying pressures on teachers. They are being asked to do and know more while they receive less assistance in meeting the demands of nontraditional social and testing pressures in their classrooms.

In addition, teachers are deeply affected by economic frustrations caused by the fact that their real wages and purchasing power have declined in recent years. The President's Commission Report and others have called for higher pay and career ladders for teachers, as well as for merit pay to attract more academically talented young people into the profession. But, so far, little has been done by either the national or the state legislatures to fund such efforts, and most local communities are unable to do so.

How does a nation achieve a dramatic qualitative advance in the field of education if it is unwilling to pay for it? Blaming most of the problems in education on teacher incompetence is like blaming the victim. Several ways to improve the quality of teaching include the funding of inservice education for teachers, revising the funding of education so that teachers can earn wages adequate to their level of professional preparation, and implementing a way to demonstrate teacher competency in the profession.

According to the Rand Corporation and other research groups, critical shortages of teachers already exist in mathematics, the sciences, foreign languages, and in the education of children of linguistic minorities. Shortages are expected to develop in most, if not all, areas of teaching in the next ten years. Children will always need well-educated and competent teachers. However, the profession may not be able to provide them unless more academically talented people can be attracted to the field.

To give hope to the profession and to build both its competence and its self-confidence, teachers must be motivated to an even greater effort for professional growth. Teachers need support. Simply criticizing them and refusing to alter those social and economic conditions which affect the quality for their work will not solve national problems in education. Nor will it lead to excellence at the elementary or secondary school levels. There is no free lunch in educational reform. Not only must teachers work to improve the public's image of and confidence in them, but the public must confront its own misunderstanding of the level of commitment required to achieve excellence. If the American and Canadian peoples want quality schools, the working conditions and the means of funding elementary and secondary schooling must be examined by national, state, and provincial legislatures with wisdom, foresight, and compassion.

Children cannot learn well if they feel that no one believes in their ability to learn. The quality of teachers will not improve if they are not appreciated or respected. Teachers need to know that the public cares and respects them enough to fund their professional improvement and to recognize them for the important force they are in the life of the nation.

The articles in this unit consider the quality of education and the status of the teaching profession today.

Looking Ahead: Challenge Questions

List what you think are the five most important issues confronting the teaching profession today (with number one being the most important and number five the least important). What criteria did you use in ranking the issues? What is your position on each of them?

Does teaching have some problems that other professions don't seem to have? If so, what are they? What can be done about them?

What seem to be the major issues affecting teacher morale?

What are the best reasons for a person to choose a career in teaching?

What are the most critical social pressures on teachers? Why are teachers sometimes used as scapegoats?

What are the problems with some of the solutions offered for meeting the anticipated shortages of teachers? What are examples of "stir-and-serve" approaches to teacher education?

What are the advantages of peer review and observation processes in helping teachers improve their professional performance?

Our Profession, Our Schools: The Case for Fundamental Reform

ALBERT SHANKER

Albert Shanker is president of the American Federation of Teachers. This article is based on a series of speeches he delivered over several months.

ONCE IN a great while, and usually spurred by crisis, a combination of forces and ideas come together in a way that makes real change possible. In the field of education and in the lives of teachers and students, I believe that now is such a time. I would like to recount for you some of the events of the past few years, and particularly of the last few months, that have brought us to this point of both crisis and opportunity.

This year marks the three-year anniversary of the beginning of the education reform movement in this country. In the spring of 1983, the National Commission on Excellence in Education released its report, *A Nation at Risk*, which was soon followed by well over a dozen others. This union supported the basic thrust of those reports even while we had serious disagreement with some of their specifics. We did that for two reasons. First, we saw that the reports did not represent an attack by the enemies of public education. These were friends and potential allies talking, and they were powerful ones. Not a single report recommended tuition tax credits or vouchers. On the contrary, they accepted public education as the delivery system and said that what is needed is not to provide an alternative or destroy what we have, but rather to make it a high quality institution.

Second, many of the criticisms in the reports were accurate. While the schools had made admirable progress in some areas — particularly in reaching out to new populations that had been previously ignored, such as the handicapped — the overall picture was not encouraging. Standards had fallen. SAT scores had declined rapidly over two decades. Although there were isolated gains, significant numbers of our children were growing up without basic literacy and numeracy skills, and even larger numbers could not craft a well-structured sentence, explain basic concepts of science, or advance a logical argument. Discipline problems, particularly in urban settings, were draining and demoralizing teachers. High schools had too many electives, and too many of those were frivolous. In many places, student grades, promotions, and graduation certificates were becoming devalued currency.

The Gallup polls reflected the public's concern. Each year, a higher and higher percentage of the American people gave low or mediocre marks to the schools. Meanwhile, demographic changes — people having fewer kids, people living longer — meant that a smaller and smaller percentage of the adult population felt they had a direct stake in the public schools.

So, when the reform reports came, we welcomed them, both because we were deeply concerned about the problems they described and because they were authored by people who cared about public education and were in a position to do something about it. Throughout the period that followed, the AFT, its local affiliates, and its members engaged the debate fully. We led the fight for some of the changes that followed; we were strong supporters of others; equally important, we were able to beat back many of the dangerous and simple-minded proposals masquerading as education reform. Indeed, our receptivity to the reports enhanced our ability to be critical.

I don't think I have to tell all of you how successful our approach has been. Our open and welcome attitude toward school reform has evoked a tremendously positive response from governors, state legislatures, and the business community. People who once wanted to unilaterally impose their views on us now respect the positions that we have taken; generally, they no longer

Reprinted with permission from the Fall 1986 issue of the AMERICAN EDUCATOR, pp. 38-44, the quarterly journal of the American Federation of Teachers.

do what they once did as a matter of course, which is to act without talking to us first.

More often than not, we are now called in at the very beginning, and we are told, "You people took a responsible and courageous position three years ago. Without you, this entire reform effort would have been destroyed or seriously hampered. From now on we don't want to make any moves without bringing you in as partners."

What we did over these three years has been a tremendous success, and I think we should enjoy a round of self-congratulations for a good strategy.

I N THESE first years of the reform movement, not only has the voice of teachers been firmly established, but also, progress has been made in the schools. Course requirements have been stiffened. Teacher salary has gone up, in some cases significantly. Education budgets have gotten healthy new infusions of money — in South Carolina a 32 percent increase in just one year, teacher pay up 33 percent in Texas in a year, education spending up 12 percent in California in a year. In addition, important new alliances have been cemented. The business community, keenly aware that its own competitiveness rests on an educated workforce, has moved beyond token gestures to serious, long-term support for public education.

Yet, while the early reform reports were needed to get things started, they didn't go far enough. Not by a long shot. Their recommendations were compromised by a central flaw: They told us where to go but not how to get there. It is fine to call for three years of math and science. We're for that. But simply sounding the alarm will not produce the thousands and thousands of math and science teachers without whom those classes can't be taught. We don't have nearly enough math and science teachers to teach the classes now required. The National Science Teachers Association estimates that 30 percent of the teachers now assigned to teach science are doing so without the appropriate academic background.

The recommendations of the early reform reports were compromised by a central flaw: They told us where to go but not how to get there.

The same is true of the other recommendations. The reports called for children to write more — a paragraph a day, a paper a week, two papers a week, three papers a week, more writing all across the curriculum. We're for that. We know that writing is important not only as the development of a craft in its own right, but also because it is probably the best way to teach children to think clearly, cogently, critically. But for a teacher with five classes a day and thirty kids per class, where is the time going to come to really help a child learn to write? The marking and critiquing of a paper and the coaching of children — how to organize their thoughts, how to build an argument or create an image, how to know when to end — takes time. As Ted Sizer pointed out in his book *Horace's Compromise,* if a teacher with one hundred fifty students takes ten minutes for a marking and coaching session, each set of papers will take twenty-five hours to complete. Two sets would take fifty hours. Whom are we kidding? So we agreed with the reform reports on the necessity of more writing, but the much harder question of how to structure our schools to make that possible went unanswered, indeed, unasked.

Many of the other reform proposals were also only half-measures. They described the symptoms. They could even tell you what a healthy patient would look like: He would have so many years of English and math and science and history and foreign language. He would do his homework and listen attentively. His teachers would all be from the top of their class. They would engage him in Socratic discussion and he would develop his critical thinking abilities and be ready to take on the twenty-first century.

It is easy to agree on the final outcome. But how do we get there? How do we attract and retain the talented teachers? How do we create such a community of learning?

I F WE are serious about reform — and we are — we must be unmercifully honest about the problems we face. Otherwise, we are dealing only with slogans and wishes.

The first problem is that, given the way schools are currently organized, there is no conceivable way we can get the enormous numbers of talented teachers we need. The nation's talent pool isn't that big. There simply will not be enough high-caliber college graduates available to us. No single sector of the economy — not medicine, not industry, not transportation, not law and the judiciary, not the military — can successfully bid for 25 percent of the country's college graduates, which is what we need. The numbers just do not add up.

Secondly, even assuming we could capture one-quarter of the country's educated workforce, if we simply placed them into the existing structure of our schools and told them to do their best, their best would not be good enough. That structure, and the rigid, confining approach to teaching and learning that it imposes, never did work well for more than a minority of our students.

Let me first take up the problem of the limited talent pool.

The reality that casts its shadow over any discussion of education reform is the massive teacher shortage that we are now facing. I want you to walk through this with me, to add up the numbers, consider the alternatives, and grapple with the dilemma. After all, it is *our* profession; we are the ones who care most about what happens to it.

Over the next few years and at exactly the time that the public will be expecting results from the new monies they have voted for education, we will lose one-half of all current teachers. Just think of it. Within the next six years, through normal retirement and attrition, over 50 percent of all of you and of all your colleagues will no longer be teaching.

Who will replace you? The prospects are not good. Let me rephrase that, for some of you may have read reports saying that there will be no shortage. The prospects are fine if we don't care about quality. One can always fill a shortage by lowering standards. Shortages are always relative to standards, and if you have no standards, there is never a shortage.

> ### *The reality that casts its shadow over any discussion of education reform is the massive teacher shortage that we are now facing.*

Consider what happened last year in Baltimore, Maryland. The school district there instituted a new examination for all its prospective teachers. Although it was elementary, we should keep in mind that thousands of other districts don't even bother to test their applicants. The Baltimore exam was a simple writing test. But some of those who took it couldn't compose a simple note to a parent without making errors in grammar, spelling, and punctuation. Since they failed the test, they were not supposed to be hired. But on the opening day of school, they were given the jobs anyway because there were no better candidates available.

So that is one way to solve a shortage problem, but it spells disaster for our students, our profession, and the future of public education.

Teacher supply and demand are not within striking distance of each other because of an unfortunate confluence of demographics — a baby boomlet generation entering school while a baby bust generation graduates from college and an earlier baby boom generation retires from teaching. Let's look at the potential supply of teachers now moving through our colleges. Keep in mind that even with no reduction in class size or work load, we will need 1.1 million new teachers in the next seven years. That means 23 percent of each college graduating class must enter teaching if the demand is to be met — 23 percent this year, 23 percent next year, and so on into the 1990s. However, in 1983, only 4.5 percent of college students said they were planning to become teachers. Last year, things got a littler better, and now 6 percent say they will join our ranks. Even if more students eventually become teachers than say they will, the gap remains enormous. There will still be hundreds of thousands of missing teachers.

The gap becomes even more insurmountable if we want to recruit only from the top half of the college graduating class. Not an unreasonable standard, but it

means we would need to take 46 percent of that group. To add to the discouraging picture is the fact that — as we've all seen reported in the papers for a number of years now — a majority of those who say they are going into teaching are in the bottom quartile of all college students in the country.

There have been reports recently of former teachers re-entering the teaching force, but that surge is likely to be short-lived and certainly won't make much of a dent in the situation.

THE SECOND problem that any serious education reform effort must deal with is the limitations imposed by the current structure of our schools. Even at its best, that structure produces good schools for some of our children but not for all of them. It is hard to face up to this one, because it requires that we give up some of our nostalgia about the past. I know it took me awhile to do so.

Let's suppose that there were plenty of outstanding teachers available and that all of the commonly proposed reforms of the last few years were put into effect.

If this were the case, what would schools look like? Students would be required to learn reading, writing, and arithmetic in the early grades or they would not be promoted. Later they would learn science, math, literature, history. They would be tested on their knowledge before being passed on. Teachers would be tested in their subject areas before they were employed, and they would teach the mandated curriculum. There would be pressure on both students and teachers for greater achievement.

Does anyone recognize these schools? I do. They are very much like the schools I attended as a child in New York City, and I suspect, like many public schools across the country in the 1930s and 1940s. Is this what we want again? Weren't these schools good? They were certainly good for me and for many, many others. We were pushed and pressured; we were forced to learn things whether we liked them or not. There were many outstanding teachers. Some of them waited over five years to get their jobs during the Depression. The schools had their pick of the best and the brightest. And as students we did learn and later came to love and enjoy subjects that we hated at first.

Is this what the current reform movement is all about? Should we go back to the good old schools we used to have? That is exactly what we will do if we follow most of the reform reports. But, if we do, the results may be disastrous. According to statistics in the Spring 1986 issue of the *Teachers College Record*, in 1940 the high school dropout rate was 76 percent; it was not until the 1950s that the dropout rate fell below 50 percent! A traditional, tough academic program, even with outstanding teachers, did not benefit the majority of students. Therefore, if we simply return to the schools we once had, we can expect a huge dropout rate in the 1980s and 1990s, particularly among disadvantaged students, at a time when students will not have the benefit of the same family support system they had in 1940.

Furthermore, a dropout in 1986 is considerably worse off than he would have been forty years ago. In earlier periods, it was much more possible than it is today for a person to succeed on the basis of hard work even if he was not well educated. In contrast, our high-tech society will continue to demand an extremely sophisticated labor force; a person without basic skills will be defeated before he has begun.

These two problems — the demographic wall that we have now bumped up against and the limitations of the current structure even under the best of circumstances — must serve as the take-off point for any consideration of education reform proposals. If we don't come to grips with these problems or if we just make incremental change, we had better be prepared for the issuance of hundreds of thousands of emergency credentials to people who are not qualified to enter our profession. We will also have to live with the tragedy of millions of children ill equipped to take up a full life. We can't just sit this period out. If we do, we not only place in jeopardy an entire generation, but, in my opinion, we will irrevocably undermine the public's faith in our schools. This system that has played such a unique and noble role in this nation of immigrants could disappear or become unrecognizable.

WHAT DO we do? For over a year now, two groups of people have been grappling with that question. AFT leaders from around the country spent long days gathering the statistics, taking testimony from the experts, and, most importantly, reflecting upon the problems our members face in the classroom. Simultaneously, another group was taking up approximately the same agenda. This one was convened by the Carnegie Forum on Education and the Economy and was composed of governors, corporate executives, state legislative and university leaders, myself, and Mary Futrell, president of the NEA.

Late this spring, the Carnegie report, *A Nation Prepared: Teachers for the 21st Century,* was issued; in July, AFT delegates meeting in convention in Chicago endorsed the basic thrust of the Carnegie report and adopted one of their own: *The Revolution that Is Overdue: A Report of the AFT Task Force on the Future of Education.*

While the reports differ in some respects, they are kindred spirits. They both say that the time is past for marginal reforms that uphold the status quo. They both refuse to accept defeat, and they both dare to think of new ways of doing things. At their core are two ideas: First, we must seek the full professionalization of teaching. Second, and interwoven with the first, we must redesign our schools and rethink the way we approach teaching and learning. It is to these two interlocking ideas that I would now like to turn.

Professionalizing teaching means all the things this union has long stood for and worked for: higher salaries; smaller class size, a manageable work load, and relief from nonteaching chores. It means working conditions that other professions so take for granted that they often go unmentioned: an office, a desk, a telephone, a quiet place. It means enough textbooks to go around, equipment that doesn't fall apart, school buildings that are clean and safe. It also means time for preparation and new learning and for discussion and work with one's colleagues.

But true professionalism requires an even more basic

If there is one principle on which all the studies of effective schools — and effective businesses — agree, it is this: Top-down management does not work.

---

prerogative than these, and it is the recognition of this that distinguishes the AFT report and the Carnegie report from those that preceded them. The central recommendation of the new reports is to **empower** teachers, to give teachers control over the standards of their profession and the conduct of their work.

IF THERE is one principle on which all the studies of effective schools — and effective businesses — agree, it is this: Top-down management does not work. Neither does top-down reform. We cannot help Johnny overcome his reading problem by turning to page 234 of a state regulation. The people who wrote those regulations are not qualified teachers, nor have they spent six months in the classroom observing Johnny and trying out and discarding four different approaches to solving his particular difficulty. The fifth approach — the one that may work — is not to be found in a state law or a school district's administrative directive. It can only come from the mind and hands of a creative and sensitive teacher.

Teaching, like medicine, cannot operate by remote control. There is no formula that fits all children. The only treatment that works is one that is constantly adjusted and fitted and fine-tuned by the people on the scene. Intelligent change has its best hope in teachers because nobody knows better than teachers what is going on in schools.

This concept is not only honored in all the other professions, it is increasingly becoming the operating principle in blue-collar industries.

I had the privilege a couple of months ago of being at a conference where a group of labor leaders met with a group of university presidents under the sponsorship of the Labor/Higher Education Council. I was especially pleased to be present when the international secretary of the United Steelworkers of America, Edgar L. Ball, described some of the new work arrangements that are being tried in the steel industry. His remarks have now been published, and I would like to read one section from them, because it will show how far behind public education is compared to the innovations in private industry with blue-collar workers.

Earlier this year we finished a two-year plan to redesign labor/management relationships in an ALCOA plant in Arkansas. For forty-five years, a very strong, militant, adversarial relationship existed. The union faced the problem of changing the adversarial relationship and redesigning jobs and methods of doing work.

After two years, autonomous work crews went into effect in every department, almost eliminating the need for the shop floor management in the plant. Instead of eighteen job classifications, there are no more than three in any department. The crew in every department designed its own jobs based on what they felt would work and what they were willing to try to make work. The craftsmen also agreed to do away with pure crafts and go to multicrafts. They decided what the groupings would be and what the new jobs would be.

I talked to a group of employees in the first department that tried the new system. The first three months the plan was in effect, down-time was reduced by half, and within the next three months decreased by half again. I asked them, "Why? How did you do it?" and this is what they said: "What we used to do was come to work, punch time cards, go to our work station, and stand there until the foreman came by and told us what to do. If he didn't tell us to do something that needed to be done, we didn't do it. If he wasn't there enough, that was his fault, he was the boss. If he told us to do it wrong, we did it wrong even if we knew it was wrong, because we were subject to discharge if we didn't do what he told us to do.

"If something went wrong, after we knew it was going wrong with the equipment or process, we didn't say anything to anyone about it. If the foreman happened to come by and catch it, fine. If he didn't, we let it go. If equipment broke down, we shut the power off. We didn't call anybody. We stood there until someone from management came by and looked at it, and they had to decide to call maintenance. When maintenance got there, we didn't tell them what was going wrong with it and we didn't help them. If they knew how to fix it, fine, and if they fixed it wrong, too bad, that wasn't our concern. We weren't being paid to do those things. We were being paid to do the few little things that were in our job description and that's all we did."

I asked, "What are you doing now?" Their reply: "We know how to run the plant. We come to work; we start operating it. We are running maintenance even though it's not in our job description. We help each other. If one is having trouble, we help. If we think something is going to go wrong, we plan around that and we alert maintenance in advance and we have them there and we tell them what's wrong, and we show them and we help them fix it."

I have heard similar descriptions of auto plants, steel plants, and other companies all across the country that are starting to turn decisions over to the people who are closest to the work. These are companies that were going to close down or decide to take their operations overseas.

I would like to know why, if blue-collar workers can

be trusted to run their own plants and organize their own jobs, why can't teachers be trusted to do exactly the same thing?

P UTTING TEACHERS in charge of instructional decisions will lead to experimentation with new kinds of management in schools. Different models will emerge, but they will all be marked by a movement away from authoritarian, hierarchical structures. School management may look more like the professional partnerships of law firms. In some cases, teachers will want to hire administrators to carry out many of the noninstructional chores now assumed by the principal, much as a hospital hires a business manager. Whatever the particulars, the relationship between administrative functions and professional functions will be different from what it is now. Those not expert in the teaching field will not oversee those who are.

In discussing the empowerment of teachers, I want to be very clear on two points: First, we do not suggest that teachers should be the instructional leaders because we are a well-organized, powerful group that can commandeer that position. We are that, but that is not where the legitimacy for teacher authority lies. Doctors, too, are well organized and powerful, but their authority lies elsewhere: in their knowledge and expertise. It was not always so. Not until medicine had a substantial knowledge and clinical base underlying it, not until medical education was transformed from its once-scandalous state into a rigorous program, and not until the profession acted to establish high entry standards did authority, autonomy, and respect follow. And so it must be with our profession. The call for teachers to be the instructional leaders must rest on the demonstration of our expertise.

It must also rest upon our professional integrity. Let me return for a moment to the situation I described earlier where the school district in Baltimore, Maryland, hired clearly unqualified teacher applicants because, according to school officials, there were no better candidates available. The message that such a decision sends is that the school's custodial role takes precedence over its intellectual mission. If teachers were in charge of professional standards and instructional issues, we could not allow such a decision. We would have to make some hard choices and fashion some creative solutions. In doing so, we would make it clear that the overriding consideration is the protection of our professional standards and the safeguarding of the education of the children who are placed in our care.

Other professions frequently have shortages, but they find ways to serve their clients without sacrificing their standards. There often aren't enough doctors in rural areas or in certain specialties. Would anyone even consider issuing emergency or temporary medical credentials to ill-prepared "doctors"? Or accepting to the bar candidates who had flunked their law exams? To do so would be a betrayal of those professions, and to do so in our schools is a betrayal of the meaning of education.

As a profession, we would have to grapple with alternative solutions, none of them easy. For example, in the Baltimore situation, qualified teachers might be asked to volunteer to teach an additional period after school for extra pay, just as some now volunteer to coach. This

Would anyone even consider issuing emergency or temporary medical credentials to ill-prepared "doctors"? Or accepting to the bar candidates who had flunked their law exams?

The assessment process developed by the national board of teaching standards will stand in sharp contrast to the trivial, paper-and-pencil, multiple-choice, context-free questions that are all too typical of existing teacher tests.

would permit class-size limits to be maintained, but students would be divided in classes over a longer day. Or, teachers might be asked whether they would agree to an increase in class size for the year by one student per teacher, with the money saved on the salaries given to the teachers now in the system. Increasing class size or lengthening the school day are certainly not good, but is it more desirable to risk the education of hundreds of students? Spending a year with an unqualified teacher is not just a question of losing that year, as serious as that is. It could also permanently damage a child's desire to learn, undermining his confidence in himself and discoloring his whole outlook on school.

Another way to avoid hiring unqualified teachers would be to try to entice back former teachers who left the system five, seven, or ten years ago for jobs in industry by offering to place them at a step on the salary schedule that would give them credit for their outside experience. Likewise, appeals could be made to the thousands of people in the vicinity who were once licensed and qualified teachers in other states, offering to give them full salary credit for their work elsewhere.

None of these solutions is perfect, but they are better than letting our professional standards erode or jeopardizing a child's future. Making these difficult choices — some of which would involve real sacrifice on the part of teachers — would make it clear that our professional code of ethics has as its center a concern for what is best for our students. Once the resolve is made never to lower our standards, the discussion can then turn to how we can best deal with dilemmas like the one in Baltimore and the many others that we face on a daily basis.

What I'm saying, in effect, is that we cannot assume the prerogatives of a profession without also assuming the responsibilities. This brings me to one of the key recommendations of both the AFT and Carnegie reports: the creation of a national board of professional teaching standards. This will be a national, non-governmental board composed of a majority of outstanding teachers. It will set standards for what teachers ought to know and be able to do. Based on those, it will develop and administer a national certifying examination for teachers comparable to the bar and other professional exams.

The assessment process developed by the national board of teaching standards will stand in sharp contrast to the trivial, paper-and-pencil, multiple-choice, context-free questions that are all too typical of existing teacher tests.

The exam for basic certification would consist of three parts. First, there would be a stringent test of subject matter knowledge. The second part of the exam, which probably would be given on a different day, would test knowledge of pedagogy, educational issues, and the ability to apply educational principles to many different student needs and learning styles. Video presentations of actual classroom problems might be used, much as the medical boards are now utilizing computer simulations of real-life medical problems. Whatever the format, the tests would not be looking for a single "right" answer (there usually isn't one) so much as they would be assessing the candidate's thought processes and decision-making skills, based on known principles of effective practice. Finally, the third part of the assessment would be a clinical induction program of from one to three years in which teachers would be evaluated on the basis of how well they work with students and their colleagues. Rather than a sink-or-swim approach, staged induction would give novice teachers the time and opportunity to learn from and reflect on their practice with experienced teachers.

THE CERTIFICATION process will be a voluntary one. In addition to basic certification, those teachers who choose to do so will also have the option of pursuing advanced board certification, much as a doctor can become board certified in his specialty. Advanced certification will be a mark of superior quality. It will mean that teachers will finally have available to them a way of advancing in their profession without leaving it. No more phony merit pay schemes. No arbitrary limits on the number of teachers allowed to prove themselves. The standards will be visible and verifiable. Anyone who examines them will agree that anyone who meets them is an exemplar of the profession's highest reach.

A national board certification process would be a major leap toward the professional standards and status teachers have sought. Indeed, if the history of other professions, such as medicine and law, is a guide, such certification is one of the prerequisites of professionalization. Its potential is also great for breaking the grip of the present array of low-quality, low-cost, ill-conceived teacher tests and securing for teachers more rigorous and helpful training. Moreover, a fair assessment that candidates could prepare for and that minimizes the importance of test-taking skills would remove some of the obstacles that now stand in the way of our ability to replenish the ranks of minority teachers and thereby perpetuate their tradition of service to the nation's schools. As a powerful quality-assurance signal to the public, professional board certification also could spell an end to demeaning and bogus schemes to "improve" the teaching force.

The creation of such a national board would put teaching standards in the hands of the profession. After all, isn't that where they belong? Should commercial testing services — the developers of current teacher tests — determine our standards? Are state legislators or district administrators the appropriate people to say who is fit to enter and advance in our profession? The lay members of school boards? Do they know the research and practice base that underlies good teaching? Shouldn't it be to the best of our own ranks that we look? We will set our standards. They will be high ones and they will be fair ones.

MONUMENTAL AS these proposed changes are, they will not be enough unless they go hand in hand with a rethinking of the way we now approach teaching and learning. I go back to the basic dilemmas I raised before — the limited talent pool available to us and the need to design an approach to teaching and learning that can do a better job of reaching all our students.

Suppose medical care were structured so that everyone involved in patient testing, diagnosis, treatment, and care had to be a doctor? No nurses, no nurses' aides, no lab technicians, no operating room assistants, no pharmacists, no interns, no residents. What if everyone who operated a CAT scan, drew blood, took temperatures, handed out medication, made the early morning and middle of the night rounds, bathed patients, and kept their charts — that is, everyone who had anything to do with patient evaluation and care, from the most basic maintenance to the most sophisticated diagnosis — had to be a doctor? If that were the case, instead of having 520,000 doctors, as we now do, we would need 4.8 million.

They, of course, wouldn't be "doctors" as we now understand that term. If medicine were structured like education, with undifferentiated staffing — and it is hard to even imagine — each "doctor" would be assigned the near-total care of a certain number of patients.

Suppose medical care were structured so that everyone involved in patient testing, diagnosis, treatment, and care had to be a doctor?

In evaluating such a structure, one question outweighs all other considerations: Would medical care be improved? The answer is, it would be worse. Where would we find 4.8 million people capable of doing the broad range of work called for? Some patients would have very good "doctors," although they would be so busy running the X-ray machine and dispensing medication at the appropriate intervals, they would have very little time for what we now consider doctoring. Many of them would not want to stay in a "profession" where

they were not able to make the best use of their talents and where they were constantly frustrated by not having the support staff required to free them to concentrate their efforts on the more demanding aspects of their art and science.

The great majority of patients would not have "doctors" drawn from the top 10 percent or the top quartile or the top half of college graduates. Medicine would have to dip deeper and deeper into the talent pool. Salaries would be commensurately low, perhaps at about the average level of teacher salary, since the country — even one that values good medical care — could not afford to pay 4.8 million people $100,000 each. There would be calls for closer supervision of the less capable people; state legislatures would adopt rules and regulations governing the treatment of each disease. Talented young people would not be drawn to such a restricted, nonprofessional field, thus the downward spiral would continue.

Well, there are of course differences, but there is much food for thought in this analogy. We can't get 46 percent of the talented college graduates; no other profession and indeed no single sector of the economy can either. But we can get our fair share. And we can begin to think of new ways of organizing the way education services are delivered. The Carnegie report calls for teaching to be structured closer to the way other professions are:

> Professionals are a valuable resource in our society. It takes a lot of education and training to produce them and costs a lot of money to pay them. For that reason, most employers work hard at making the most of these professionals.
>
> That is why professionals are typically supported by many other people who do the work they would otherwise have to do. The services of these other people come at lower cost, so it is more efficient to use them to perform such tasks than to have them performed by the professionals. For the same reasons, professionals also have available to them a host of machines and services that improve their efficiency in countless ways, from computers and copying machines to telephones and adequate work space. These services are not perquisites for professionals. They are regarded by employers as necessary investments, enabling the professionals on their staffs to reach the highest possible levels of accomplishment.
>
> Not only do professionals typically have a range of support staff and services available, but they are usually organized so that the most able among them influence in many ways the work that others do, from broad policy direction to the development of staff members who might some day take on major responsibilities. This, too, is a matter of simple efficiency, making sure that the experience and skill embodied in these valuable people makes itself felt throughout the enterprise....
>
> America's schools can, without doubt, greatly improve their performance. They will not do so unless they prove to be an attractive employment opportunity to some of the most able college graduates in the country. But the schools cannot realistically expect that all 2.3 million teachers will be the best and brightest the country has to offer. Education, like other professions, will have to structure itself so that it can make the very best use of a distribution of talent. That means reorganization, because the current "eggcrate" organization does not permit efficient shared use of highly skilled people, support services, and equipment.

The Carnegie Task Force points out in its report that teacher salaries are not only extremely low but also extremely compressed compared to other occupations demanding a college degree. After ten to twelve years, most teachers have reached the top of the scale. The Carnegie report estimates that if teaching were restructured to be more like other professions, with different levels of teachers and corresponding levels of responsibility, starting salaries would be about what they are today, average teacher salary would be significantly higher, and a substantial number of people — those holding advanced certification — would be making $60,000 to $100,000, with local and regional variations determined by the same kinds of factors as they are today.

IN A RESTRUCTURED teaching profession, certified teachers could be assisted by interns and instructors and computer lab technicians, by paraprofessionals and clericals and administrative staff, by tutors and volunteers, and by an increasingly sophisticated and accessible selection of computer and video technology. Interns will be finishing their final stages of teacher preparation. Some instructors will be on loan from businesses for a year or two; others will be recent college graduates who have chosen to work in the schools as part of a tuition loan plan; still others may be drawn from the rapidly growing ranks of college-educated retirees who still have much to offer.

The professional teaching staff will be freed up to practice their profession. They will have more time to spend with their students — not setting up machinery, conducting routine drill sessions, or filling out forms, but teaching. They will have time to do what the earlier reform reports called for: to teach writing; to help children sort out fact from opinion; to lead discussions that take students beyond scattered names, dates, and places to real knowledge and understanding. They will have the time to develop new ways and new materials for conveying difficult concepts; and they will have time to work with the child whom no one else can reach.

With the aid of new technology and a diverse complement of teaching staff, new options of time, teaching method, and class arrangement will open up. While some students are analyzing ideas in a small seminar, others will be gathered around a computer station. While some are receiving intense assistance through one-on-one tutoring, others will be viewing historical footage in the video screening room. The effectiveness of our teaching will no longer be compromised by having to fit it into fifty-minute time slots. Nor will

The effectiveness of our teaching will no longer be compromised by having to fit it into fifty-minute time slots.

teachers be forced by an inflexible class schedule "to teach to the average."

Teachers will no longer be isolated all day long in a self-contained classroom. Like other professionals, they will have time during the school day to consult with their colleagues, to share ideas, and to brainstorm solutions to stubborn educational problems. Some teachers will want to divide their time between teaching and other professional responsibilities, such as the development of discipline policy and grading standards, the assignment of students, the allocation of their school's budget, the design of a staffing structure into which various categories of support staff would fit, and the evaluation of a mushrooming array of new software. Certified teachers will not only be on top of the latest research but will themselves be identifying the questions for which we do not yet have answers and will join with their colleagues at local universities in the development of classroom-based studies. In addition, they will do what every doctor in a teaching hospital does: perpetuate their profession by passing on the best of their science and art to the young interns who will eventually replace them.

Other instructional staff and support personnel, under the direction of certified teachers, will be available to conduct drill-and-practice sessions, lead small-section review classes much as teaching assistants do in graduate school, mark multiple-choice tests, coach multiplication tables, prepare a hands-on science lesson, read a story aloud, organize field trips, check a book review report, run the video equipment and monitor the viewing room, tinker with the mechanical problems that arise at computer work stations, persuade parents of the importance of providing time and space for homework, and so on.

The central function of the professional teaching staff will be to shape the climate and the structure of their school and its curriculum and to develop the best learning program for each individual child and see that it is executed.

I'VE BEEN talking about how a new structure would enable teachers to do their best teaching. Let me turn once again to our students, for the same system that has confined teachers has also confined children. As I mentioned earlier, even under the best of circumstances — when the supply of talented teachers was plentiful, when family structure was stronger than it now is, when homework time didn't have to compete with TV — even then, one-half to three-quarters of our young people did not complete high school. And is it any wonder? To again use a medical analogy, suppose that a doctor had to try to diagnose and treat patients in groups of thirty instead of individually. Ridiculous? Of course. But are the needs, the problems, the strengths, the achievement levels, the attention spans, or the learning styles of students any less diverse than the history and symptoms presented by patients?

How do children best learn? Is there any one of us who really thinks that it is by putting them together in groups of thirty, sitting at their desks for five or six hours a day? Do any of us believe that the lecture format — which numerous studies show constitutes approximately 85 percent of classroom time — is the desirable method for all subjects and all children? Is it any wonder that teachers, who on a daily basis are required to get thirty fidgety youngsters to master the same topic at the same pace and with the same instructional approach, are suffering from job stress?

Many critics have attacked teachers for the problems in our schools. But it is not teachers' fault, anymore than the problems of the auto industry are the autoworkers' fault. Our autoworkers are as good as the Japanese, but they are working in a defeating structure. What if you are a junior high school teacher and you get a student in your class who can't read? What do you do? You can't really help him. He needs a different setting. He needed a different setting six years earlier. He didn't get one because schools aren't structured to give him one.

> *In the end, it is we who must serve as the protectors of our students and our profession. We wouldn't want it any other way.*

But they could be. The new approaches to the staffing and design of schools that we have been discussing will do much more than enable us to cope with a teacher shortage, as important as that is. They will also allow us — finally — to begin to move in the direction of more individualized learning, fitting the structure to the child rather than the other way around.

Students learn at different paces and in different ways. Most students need more time in some subjects than in others, and most learn better through one method than through another. Some students learn best by reading a chapter in a book, others by watching a videotape, or by using programmed instruction on a computer. Some children can best master new material by teaching it to younger students, by reviewing it in a structured coaching session, or by analyzing it in a teacher-led seminar. Some students can master a concept the first time around. Others need two tries, or three, or more. Some students shine in large groups; others are too shy to participate. Some students can pace their efforts over a five-month semester; others need the sharper incentive of shorter time spans. The rigidity of the current structure forces us to try to fit these very different children into the same mold. The fit often isn't a good one.

Teachers know this better than anyone, but we've never had the flexibility or the personnel or the technology necessary to plan and oversee more individualized learning programs. We now have the possibility of bringing all those elements together for the first time. Teaching would be broadly defined as connecting students with the materials, experiences, and resources that will best help them learn. The teacher's job would be more like the doctor's: to diagnose and then to develop and execute a plan of educational action — like writing an educational prescription for each child.

Sometimes that program would be carried out by the certified teachers and sometimes by other instructional staff. And if the first prescription doesn't work, we will be able to try a second, or a third, or a fourth.

IN THINKING about the way things could be and should be, there is no blueprint before us. Our only sure principles are to hold to our standards and to give teachers the leeway to exercise their judgment and to start thinking about how to restructure and reshape our schools and our profession so that teaching and learning can flourish. We of course do not abandon what we have. We experiment; we refine; we try again. It will take time.

If we sit by and do nothing, or if we just make marginal repairs, we will see the quality of our teaching force rapidly decline. Emergency credentials will be issued in the hundreds of thousands. The country has built up great expectations. If things get only slightly better — or if they get worse — all the powers we can exercise at the bargaining table or in the legislative arena will not be enough to stop an angry public from getting even with the public school system.

But even if we could fool the public, we cannot fool ourselves. Nor would we want to. In the end, it is we who must serve as the protectors of our students and our profession. We wouldn't want it any other way.

We have before us the great possibility of forever transforming the lives of teachers and students in America. Many good people are on our side.

For students — especially those to whom life has not been so kind — it will be a new chance. And for teachers, it will mean the opportunity to give them that chance. It will mean a real profession and a real community of learning.

In closing, I want to acknowledge that many of the ideas I have been discussing will mean change, and change is always hard. Over the past couple of years, as these ideas have begun to take form, we have experienced two feelings in tension with each other. On the one hand, there are many things about our schools and our profession and our jobs that we do not like, so we project an image of hope, and hope gives us a picture of how things might be.

But at the same time, there is the fear of change. Is the change going to be in the direction we want it to be? Will things really get better, or will they get worse? So in the middle of our hopes, our fears take hold and we experience a kind of paralysis. Maybe, we say, it is better to hold onto things the way they are now; the terrain is familiar, and we have adjusted our dreams to fit the landscape.

I would hope that in this battle between hope and fear, we would be instructed by our experience over the past few years and indeed over the last seventy years. This union and its members have always been good for taking risks. We stood for unionism when no one else believed in it. With only a handful of members, and when others said it would be suicidal, we called for collective bargaining elections because we believed that when teachers had sketched before them a vision of what could be if they joined together, they would go with their hopes and not their fears. They did then, and I believe they will now.

On Stir-and-Serve Recipes for Teaching

Photos by David B. Sutton

Freeze-dried, ready-made teachers aren't the answer to the problems that face the teaching profession, says Ms. Ohanian. Children need real teachers, and real teachers must be trained.

Susan Ohanian

SUSAN OHANIAN, a third-grade teacher on leave of absence, is currently a senior editor for Learning: The Magazine for Creative Teaching.

THE NOTION that just about any Joe Blow can walk in off the street and take over a classroom is gaining ground. It makes me nervous. No, more than that: it infuriates me. We should squash once and for all the idea that schools can be adequately staffed by 32 bookkeepers and a plumber. The right teacher-proof curriculum is not sufficient; children need real teachers, and real teachers must be trained.

Nor am I charmed by the idea of signing up out-of-work computer programmers and retired professors to teach math and science. The mass media like to scoff that current certification requirements would keep Albert Einstein from teaching in the public schools. That news is not all bad. Is there any evidence that Einstein worked particularly well with young children? A Nobel Prize does not guarantee excellence in the classroom.

From *Phi Delta Kappan*, June 1985, pp. 696-701. Reprinted by permission of the author and Phi Delta Kappan.

207

We demand from our professors materials with immediate applicability. We are indignant when they try instead to offer ideas to grow on.

Having sat through more stupid education courses than I wish to recall, I am not altogether comfortable defending schools of education. But I suspect that the blame for worthless courses lies as much with the teachers who take them as with the professors who teach them. As a group, we teachers are intransigently anti-intellectual. We demand from our professors carry-out formulae, materials with the immediate applicability of scratch-and-sniff stickers. We are indignant when they try instead to offer ideas to grow on, seeds that we have to nurture in our own gardens.

We teachers frequently complain that education courses do not prepare us for the rigorous, confusing work ahead — that they do not show us how to run our classrooms. We refuse to admit that no course or manual can give us all the help we crave. We should not expect professors to set up our classroom systems, as though each of us were heading out to operate a fast-food franchise. There is no instant, stir-and-serve recipe for running a classroom.

Too often, teachers judge the success of education courses by the weight of the materials they cart away — cute cutouts or "story starters," all ready for immediate use. One popular journal for teachers promises 100 new ideas in every issue. "You can use them on Monday" is the promise. No one gets rich admitting that genuinely good ideas are hard to come by.

I understand only too well this yearning for the tangible, the usable. We are, after all, members of a profession ruled by pragmatism. People who sit in judgment on us don't ask about our students, "Are they happy? Are they creative? Are they helpful, sensitive, loving? Will they want to read a book next year?" Instead, these people demand, "What are their test scores?" — as if those numbers, though they passeth understanding, will somehow prove that we're doing a good job.

DURING MY FIRST 12 years of teaching I was desperate for new ideas, constantly foraging for schemes with which to engage the children. My frenetic activity was due, in part, to the fact that I was given a different teaching assignment every two years. I figured, "Different children require different methods, different materials." So I would race off to the library or to the arts-and-crafts store. I'd buy another filing cabinet and join another book club for teachers.

But even when I settled in with the same assignment for a six-year stretch, my frenzy did not abate. My classroom became a veritable curriculum warehouse, stuffed with every innovative whiz-bang gizmo I could buy, borrow, or invent. I spent hundreds of hours reading, constructing, laminating. My husband gave up reminding me that I had promised to put the cut-and-paste factory in our living room out of business, once I figured out what to teach. When I wasn't inventing projects, I was taking courses: cardboard carpentry, architectural awareness, science process, Cuisenaire rods, Chinese art, test construction and evaluation, curriculum development, and so on. I even took two courses in the computer language, BASIC. (I thought maybe I'd missed the point in the first course, so I took another — just to be sure.)

I didn't take those courses on whim, any more than I invented curriculum because I had nothing better to do. I chose my courses deliberately, trying to inform my work as a reading teacher. Although I now look back on much of my frenzied search for methods and media as rather

It is possible to have an inborn talent for teaching, but those teachers who endure and triumph are made — rigorously trained — and not born.

naive, I don't see it as time wasted. I learned a lot. Mostly I learned to simplify. And then to simplify some more.

But the path to simplicity is littered with complexities. And I suspect that it is hard to figure out how to simplify our lives if we haven't cluttered them in the first place. Sure, we teachers clutter up our classrooms with too much claptrap. The fribble is often alluring at first, and it is hard to recognize that the more gadgets we rely on, the poorer we are — at home as well as at school.

People probably always yearn for gadgets, especially if they haven't had much chance to fool around with them. A university research project makes this point rather nicely. The researcher decided to investigate the effects of computer-assisted instruction in English-as-a-second-language (ESL) classes. He set up a computer-taught group and a control group. Both were instructed in ESL for one year. And guess which group had the more positive attitude about computer-assisted instruction at the end of that year? The youngsters who *didn't* get to use the computers.

Not surprisingly, we teachers are compulsive pack rats. Fearing the vagaries of future school budgets, we hoard construction paper until it is old and brittle and unusable. We worry that we may need that paper more next year than we need it today. Have you ever known a teacher who could throw away a set of ditto masters? Or half a game of Scrabble? For years I had a gross of tiny, child-proof, left-handed scissors. Child-proof scissors are a horror in the first place. Those designed for left-handers are beyond description. Why did I keep them? Hey, they were mine, weren't they?

Most of us never use 80% of the materials jammed into our classrooms, but we cling to them "just in case." Because our job is hectic, pressured, stressful, we seldom have a reflective moment to clear our minds, let alone our cupboards. Maybe every teacher should change schools every three years and be allowed to take

along only what he or she can carry. However, I must add to this suggestion my own statement of full disclosure: the last time I changed classrooms, after 13 years in the district, it took six strong men and a truck to transfer my belongings. And that was *after* I had filled two dumpsters.

The good professors must stop yielding to our acquisitive pressures; they must refuse to hand out their 100 — or even 10 — snazzy new ideas for the well-stocked classroom. They must offer fewer methods, fewer recipes. We teachers need *less* practicality, not more. We need to have our lives informed by Tolstoy, Jane Addams, Suzanne Langer, Rudolf Arnheim, and their ilk — not by folks who promise the keys to classroom control and creative bulletin boards, along with 100 steps to reading success.

We need a sense of purpose from our professors, not a timetable. Better that they show us a way to find our own ways than that they hand out their own detailed maps of the territory. A map isn't of much use to people who don't know where they're headed. The only way to become familiar with the terrain is to explore a little. I nominate the professors to scout ahead, chart the waters, post the quicksand. I know that I still have to climb my own mountain, but I would welcome scholarly advice about the climbing conditions.

CRITICS OF schools of education insist that prospective teachers would profit more from observing good teachers at work than from taking impractical courses on pedagogy. Maybe so. But what are those novices going to see? Is one observation as good as another? After all, a person can look at "Guernica" and not see it, listen to the "Eroica" and not hear it. E.H. Gombrich says that every observation we make is the result of the questions we ask. And where do novices get the questions? How can they ask intelligent questions without knowing something about the subject? Can anyone really *see* a classroom without some theoretical, historical, developmental savvy?

No one enters a classroom as a *tabula rasa*, of course. We all know something about schools because we have, for better or for worse, been there. We know how schools are supposed to be. At least, we think we do. So we judge schools, as we judge anything, with a notion — or schema — of reality in our heads. Most of us don't just look *at* something; we look *for* something, because we have a hypothesis, a hidden agenda. We observe and evaluate with our minds, our memories, our experiences, our linguistic habits. Obviously, the more we know, the more we see.

But teachers cannot walk into classrooms and simply teach what they know. First, they don't know enough. Second, even this seemingly restrictive world — constrained by bells, desks, and textbooks — contains a rich stock of themes from which teachers must choose their own motifs. They must be flexible and inventive enough to modify the schema they carried into their classrooms.

I was one of those people almost literally picked up off a street corner and allowed to teach in New York City under an emergency credential. I walked into the middle of someone else's lesson plan, and, though it didn't take me 10 minutes to realize that a round-robin reading of "Paul Revere's Ride" was not going to work, it took me quite a while to come up with something much better.

All I could manage at first was to teach as I had been taught. But as I learned more about the students and about ways to get around the assigned curriculum, a more ideal classroom began to emerge in my head. It remains a shadowy image — one I glimpse and even touch occasionally, but one I have long since stopped trying to file neatly in my planbook. That's okay. The bird seen through the window is more provocative than the one in the cage.

Teaching, like art, is born of a schema. That's why we need the professors with their satchels of theory, as well as our own observations and practice. Those who hope to be effective teachers must recognize that teaching is a craft of careful artifice; the profession requires more than a spontaneous overflow of good intentions or the simple cataloguing and distribution of information. It is possible, I suppose, to have an inborn talent for teaching, but I am sure that those teachers who endure and triumph are *made* — rigorously trained — and not born.

Much of the training must be self-initiated. People who have some nagging notion of the ideal classroom tickling their psyches probably look more for patterns that appeal than for practices that are guaranteed to produce higher standardized test scores. Such teachers probably have a capacity for ambiguity; they look for snippets of familiarity but do not insist on sameness. Such teachers have a greater need for aesthetic and psychological satisfaction than for a neat and tidy cupboard. But they also have a willingness to practice the craft, to try out new brushstrokes, to discard dried-out palettes.

Most of us, children and adults alike, have a strong need to make sense of the disparate elements in our lives, to bring them together, to find patterns, to make meaning. This desire for meaning is so strong that some teachers, tired and defeated by the system, rely on ritual to get them through the day, the week, the year. External order and ritual are the only things they have left to give. And these things usually satisfy the casual observer, who believes that teachers who provide clean and orderly classrooms are providing enough.

This is one reason I want the professors in on the act — out of their ivory towers and into our dusty school corridors. Maybe well-informed people, good observers who are not bogged down by school minutiae, could convince us that a tidy desk is far from enough. The professors need to promote the search for a different order, a subtler pattern — one that lies not in behavioral checklists but rather, to use Chia Yi's words, in constant "combining, scattering, waning, waxing."

I T WAS MY OWN search for pattern that led me to try using science as a way to inform, enhance, and give order to my work as a reading teacher. The children and I were far too familiar with the rituals of remedial reading for those routines to fall much short of torture. I've never understood why students who have trouble with a certain sys-

tem of decoding should be made to rehearse that system over and over again. A few times over the course of a few years, maybe. But surely there comes a time to try a different approach. Reading had already been ruined for my students by the time they came to me. I needed to see how they approached pedagogic puzzlement, and such puzzlement would never occur if I persisted in making them circle blends on worksheets. That's why I learned how to mess around in science.

Tell a poor reader that it's time to read, and watch the impenetrable curtain of defeat and despair descend. So my students and I spent our time on science. All year. We made cottage cheese, explored surface tension, built bridges, figured out

optical illusions. And not once did my students associate experiment cards, books on the theory of sound, or my insistence that observations be recorded in writing with the onerous task that they knew reading to be. Children told me that my room was a good place. Too bad, they added, that I wasn't a real teacher.

That reading room, where children were busily measuring, making — and reading — received full parental support and had its moment in the limelight. There were a lot of visitors. The teachers among them invariably asked, "How did you get this job?" Clearly, they intended to apply for one like it.

Get the job? Only in the first year of my teaching career was I ever handed a

No job of any value can be given out, like a box of chalk. We get the jobs we deserve. Maybe that's why so many teachers are disappointed.

job. Ever after, I've made my own. No job of any value can be given out, like a box of chalk. We get the jobs we deserve. Maybe that's why so many teachers are disappointed. They believe all those promises that someone else can do the thinking for them.

I held seven different jobs in my school district, and I earned the right to love every one of them. That's not to say that I didn't have plenty of moments of anger, frustration, rage. But I also experienced deep satisfaction.

Because my seven jobs required some pretty dramatic shifts in grade level, people were always asking me, "Where is it better — high school or the primary grades?" It's a question I have never been able to answer, mainly because the more grade levels I taught, the more similarities I saw. Sure, high school dropouts enrolled in an alternative program are harder to tune in to the beauty of a poem than are seventh-graders. Third-graders cry more, talk more; seventh-graders scale more heights and sink into deeper pits. But a common thread runs throughout, and it was that thread I clung to.

Maybe I see this sameness because my teaching is dominated less by skill than by idea — the secret, elusive form. I have a hard time reading other people's prescriptions, let alone writing my own. I always figure that, if you can get the idea right, the specific skill will come. Teaching is too personal, even too metaphysical, to be charted like the daily temperature. Teaching is like a Chinese lyric painting, not a bus schedule.

We need to look very closely at just who is calling for "the upgrading of teacher skills," lest this turn out to be the clarion call of those folks with something to sell. The world does not come to us in neat little packages. Even if we could identify just what a *skill* is, does *more* definitely denote *better*? What profiteth a child whose teacher has gathered up an immense pile of pishposh? We must take care, lest the examiners who claim they can dissect and label the educational process leave us holding a bag of gizzards.

We teachers must recognize that we do not need the behaviorist-competency thugs to chart our course. For us, reality is a feeling state, details of daily routine fade, and what remains is atmosphere, tone, emotion. The ages and the talents of the children become irrelevant. What counts is attitude and endeavor. That's why, even when we try, we often can't pass on a terrific lesson plan to a friend; we probably can't even save it for ourselves to use again next year. It's virtually impossible to teach the same lesson twice.

I'M AFRAID that all of this sounds rather dim, maybe even dubious. But this is where the professors might step in. There are so many outrageous examples of bad pedagogy that it's easy to overlook the good — easy, but not excusable. The professors need to shape up their own schools of education first — getting rid of Papercutting 306, even if it's the most profitable course in the summer school catalogue. Then they need to get out in the field to work with student teachers, principals, and children.

Is it outrageous to think that the professors might even pop into the class-

> Teaching is too personal, too metaphysical, to be charted like the temperature. Teaching is like a Chinese lyric painting, not a bus schedule.

But aspiring teachers have a responsibility, too. They must heed the advice of Confucius:

> If a man won't try, I will not teach him; if a man makes no effort, I will not help him. I show one corner, and if a man cannot find the other three, I am not going to repeat myself.

We teachers must stop asking the education professors for the whole house. I know plenty of teachers who are disappointed, indignant, and eventually destroyed by the fact that nobody has handed them all four corners. But the best we can expect from any program of courses or training is the jagged edge of one corner. Then it is up to us to read the research and to collaborate with the children to find the other three corners. And, because teaching must be a renewable contract, if we don't keep seeking new understanding, we'll find that the corners we thought we knew very well will keep slipping away. There are constant, subtle shifts in the schoolroom. One can never be sure of knowing the floorplan forever and ever.

In trying to renew my faith in myself as a teacher, I find little help in the "how to" books, those nasty little tomes that define learning in 87 steps. I like to think of learning as a wave that washes over the learner, rather than as a series of incremental hurdles to be pre- and posttested. I reject *How to Teach Reading in 100 Lessons*, relying instead on *The Mustard Seed Garden Manual of Painting*, which advises that "neither complexity in itself nor simplicity is enough" — nor dexterity alone nor conscientiousness. "To be without method is worse."

What can we do? What is the solution? In painting, there is an answer: "Study 10,000 volumes and walk 10,000 miles." One more thing is required of teachers. We must also work with 10,000 children.

rooms of veteran teachers now and then? Wouldn't it be something if their research occasionally involved real children and real teachers (and if they had to face bells, mandated tests, bake sales, and field trips to mess up their carefully laid plans), instead of four children in a lab staffed by 63 graduate students? That's probably a scary thought for some professors.

I know of one school of education that relegates the observation and direction of student teachers to the local school district. The district, in turn, passes this responsibility on to an administrator who has never taught. In such a situation, pedagogy gets turned upside down and inside out. The outcome is empty platitudes, not effective classroom practice. The student teacher, who is paying for expert training, is being defrauded. The children are being cheated. The system is stupid and immoral. We need teacher trainers who know educational theory and who are savvy about children. Those professors who won't help us should be replaced by ones who will.

TEACHING KNOWLEDGE: HOW DO WE TEST IT?

*Not with Simplistic,
Multiple-Choice, Context-Free Exams*

LINDA DARLING-HAMMOND

Linda Darling-Hammond is director of the Rand Corporation's Education and Human Resources Program.

TESTING TEACHERS for certification is now the law in forty-four states. By 1990, virtually every state will require tests of basic skills, subject matter knowledge, or professional knowledge before a teacher can receive a standard license to teach. Although the tests being used make entry into teaching more selective, they do not, contrary to much of the current rhetoric, do very much to turn teaching into a profession. The tests are not developed or controlled by the profession, nor do they adequately represent what a teacher should know and be able to do.

If teacher tests are to serve the goal of professionalizing teaching, they must reflect what members of the profession believe is the fundamental knowledge required by teachers, and they must be professionally controlled. Recent proposals by teacher organizations and the Carnegie Task Force on Teaching as a Profession would lead to board certification by a professional teaching standards board, analogous to the certification awarded by the medical profession and other professional bodies. The testing involved in such certification would be voluntary, would represent a high standard of professional knowledge, and would be distinct and separate from state licensing and school district employment decisions. Teachers who decided to pursue board certification would be recognized by a body of their peers as having mastered the subject matter and professional knowledge needed for making appropriate teaching decisions.

Although such professional certification could be dismissed as overkill, given the other tests now in place,

there are important reasons why board certification would improve the status and substance of teaching. These reasons, and the limitations of current approaches to teacher testing, are explored herein.

THERE ARE two functions of professional tests. One is to sort and screen candidates. Many call this endeavor "raising standards." This function, which currently receives the most attention from test makers and test users, conjures up a vertical notion of standards. They go up or down; there are cut-off scores that may be raised or lowered to allow more or fewer people to pass. This function serves a symbolic purpose. It provides selectivity for entry, regardless of what the substance of the measure is. As long as a cut-off score is applied, some individuals will "pass" and others will not. The level of the standard can be changed simply by changing the pass rate on a test.

The second major function of testing — and the most important one for truly creating standards — is defining the professional knowledge base. Examinations are one means by which a profession makes an explicit statement about what is worth knowing and how it should be known and demonstrated. This statement can exert a powerful influence on training and practice independent from cut-off scores or pass rates.

When candidates prepare to take the bar examination, for example, they know they will have to study constitutional law, torts, contracts, tax law, criminal law, and so on. Regardless of the pass rate for that exam in a given year, candidates know that they will have to demonstrate their knowledge of those topics in particular ways. They will not only need to be able to identify facts about cases and legal rules, they will have to apply this knowledge in essays responding to case scenarios.

Reprinted with permission from the Fall 1986 issue of the AMERICAN EDUCATOR, pp. 18-21, 46, the quarterly journal of the American Federation of Teachers.

8. THE PROFESSION OF TEACHING TODAY

The examination provides an explicit standard of knowledge that influences legal training and practice in important ways, regardless of the "vertical" standards used to determine who will be licensed.

CURRENT TEACHER tests basically define the knowledge needed for teaching as (1) the recognition of facts within subject areas, (2) knowledge of school law and bureaucratic procedures, and (3) recognition of the "correct" teaching behavior in a situation described in a short scenario. The tests currently used do not allow for demonstrations of teacher knowledge, judgment, and skill in the kinds of complex settings that characterize real teaching. Furthermore, they may discourage the use of such knowledge by positing a unidimensional philosophy of teaching that the test taker must consistently apply if he/she is to find the "best" answers to poorly defined questions.

Less than 10 percent of over one hundred questions required knowledge of theory, research, or facts pertaining to teaching and learning.

My own content analysis of a sample test for one of the most frequently used tests of professional knowledge* revealed that less than 10 percent of over one hundred questions required knowledge of theory, research, or facts pertaining to teaching and learning. And most of these required only the identification of a single fact, for example, "Which of the following, if given to high school students at the beginning of a new course, is an example of an advance organizer?"

The remaining questions required knowledge about testing and assessment (10 percent), knowledge about school law and administrative procedures (25 percent), careful reading or knowledge of simple word definitions (15 percent), agreement with the test's teaching philosophy (25 percent), or agreement with the test's definition of socially or bureaucratically acceptable behavior (15 percent). About 40 percent of the questions, by my reckoning, did not have a "right" answer, either because the question contained insufficient information to allow a complete evaluation of the situation or because alternative answers would be correct depending on what research one relied upon.

The questions that rely on a simplistic view of teach-

---

* The sample test used for this analysis is the National Teacher Examination's Professional Knowledge Test. (A Guide to the NTE Core Battery Tests. Educational Testing Service, 1984.) The items published in this sample test are quite similar to the sample questions published by other testing firms; however, no other test publisher to my knowledge publishes an entire sample test allowing a full examination of content coverage. This discussion, therefore, uses the NTE exam as an illustration of the typical range of questions used in such tests.

214

ing are not only inadequate to assess what skilled and knowledgeable teachers know, they encourage a soft-headed approach to the preparation of teachers. In the area of educational research, consider the following question:

In general, which of the following factors has been shown in several studies to have the strongest relationship to variation in student achievement?

(a) Teacher experience;
(b) School size;
(c) Type of textbooks;
(d) Student/teacher ratio; or
(e) Community's average income.

Aside from the fact that many studies could be marshalled to support any one of the responses, the desired answer "e" is badly flawed, since most studies finding strong effects of income on achievement use measures of student family income, not general community income. Not surprisingly, only 19 percent of test takers chose the desired answer.

A question about statistical terms presents no right answer:

The mean, median, and mode may be best defined as:
(a) ranges of scores for a test;
(b) correlations of individual test questions with the total test;
(c) points about which scores on a test tend to cluster;
(d) minimal acceptable scores to be obtained on a test; or
(e) deviations of test scores from an expected value.

The desired answer, "c," is technically incorrect, since scores need not cluster about the mean or median when a normal distribution of scores does not occur. A teacher with statistical knowledge would find this question difficult to answer honestly.

Here is an example of a question intended to assess instructional knowledge:

Use of which of the following is most important in the beginning instruction of the young, visually impaired child?

(a) Machines with lighted screens to magnify print;
(b) A variety of large-print books;
(c) Extended periods of nondirected play;
(d) Many tactile and oral activities; or
(e) Large-print flash cards for learning sight vocabulary.

Since the question does not reveal how young the child is or how severe the visual impairment, the desired answer "d" is a safe guess, but it is not necessarily the course of action that would be appropriate for, say, teaching reading to a seven-year-old child who is at least partially sighted. Even a "correct" answer to the question does not reveal whether a teacher could design an appropriate learning experience for the child.

ALTHOUGH ONE might question why so large a portion (one-quarter) of a test of teaching knowledge is devoted to knowledge about school law and administrative procedures, these questions have the virtue at least of being mostly unambiguous, e.g. "The United States Supreme Court decision against permitting prayer in the public schools was based on which of the following?" Unfortunately, knowing the answer to such questions indicates very little about whether a candidate is likely to be a good teacher.

Similarly, the most straightforward instructional questions generally require only the ability to match words with their definitions. For example:

> Kinesthetic learners are likely to learn the letters of the alphabet best by doing which of the following?
> (a) Singing a song about the alphabet;
> (b) Playing an alphabet card game;
> (c) Manipulating large plastic letters;
> (d) Examining an alphabet book; or
> (e) Viewing "Sesame Street" regularly.

All one needs to know to answer the question correctly is that "kinesthetic" has something to do with physical, tactile activity. Knowing this definition does not reveal whether a candidate could identify different learning styles among children or develop suitable approaches for their classroom activities.

Some questions are designed to assess whether the teacher will embarrass school officials by handling sensitive situations in noninflammatory ways:

> A representative of a special interest group meets a teacher out of school and indicates that the group objects to a particular textbook being used in the teacher's classroom. Of the following, which is the best response for the teacher to give the representative in order to handle the situation in a nonthreatening manner?
> (a) "Such a response by parents would be appropriate, but not by groups such as yours that have no close connection with public schools."
> (b) "Your group should write a letter to me and to the principal specifying the passages that the group objects to and why."
> (c) "The Constitution protects a teacher's right to use any textbook that is appropriate for the purpose."
> (d) "Is your interest group able to propose an appropriate but less controversial textbook?"
> (e) "Since the textbook was adopted by the school board, any comments about it should be directed to the board."

The desired answer "d" keeps the burden off the principal and the school board for handling the situation, but it places the teacher squarely on a prickly professional thorn. As one teacher remarked when seeing this question, "What would I be expected to do when the group proposed a textbook that could not achieve the educational goals for the class?" Protecting the curriculum or establishing academic freedom in the schools are clear-

The most straightforward instructional questions generally require only the ability to match words with their definitions.

ly not part of the concerns suggested by this test's conception of "professional" behavior. "Professionalism" is keeping the public quiet and avoiding conflict at all costs.

Other questions are designed to evaluate whether the teacher subscribes to the kind of liberal, highly individualized philosophy of teaching underlying the test. Even when one agrees with the answer, it is nearly always possible to cite research or conventional wisdom that support an opposing point of view. For example:

> Research indicates that in classrooms where effective teaching and learning occur, the teacher is likely to be doing which of the following consistently?
> (a) Gearing instruction to the typical student at a given grade level;
> (b) Carefully grouping students at the beginning of the school year and making sure that these groups remain the same throughout the year;
> (c) Identifying the affective behaviors that students are likely to exhibit at a given level of development;
> (d) Working diligently with students to make sure that each learns all of the material planned for the class for the year; or
> (e) Pacing instruction so that students can move ahead when they are able to or receive extra help when they need it.

Although many teachers, like myself, would personally endorse the desired answer "e," there is a body of research (currently labelled as part of "teaching effectiveness" research) that suggests that whole-group instruction at a common pace is to be preferred to "individualized" instruction for increasing time on task and average achievement test scores. And there is a paradigm underlying most recent educational reforms that suggests that mastery of the year's material is the most important goal of classroom activities. So, selecting the right answer is more a matter of agreement with the test's philosophy of teaching than knowledge of the "research" that the question seeks to invoke.

The problem is not that the "right" answer is not right but that the question doesn't really allow for such a straightforward response. In fact, most of the knowledge and judgment involved in good teaching is not easily boiled down to a multiple-choice question with one simple answer.

IN THE FINAL analysis, the test defines the professional knowledge base for teaching primarily in terms of style and adherence to a particular approach to teaching. It quizzes knowledge of educational terms and laws. It does not encompass a rigorous and comprehensive understanding of educational theory and practice. It does not require much ability to apply knowledge and judgment in unique and complex situations.

Indeed, it is hard to argue that the knowledge required for scoring well on the test is of the sort that separates good teachers from teachers who are not as good. These questions are similar to those used on other tests of professional knowledge that publish sample questions. All of the tests I have seen are limited in their measurement by the scarcity of important teaching questions answerable in multiple-choice formats; the questions with clear, correct answers are not very important or profound.

The tests are sometimes tricky, but they are rarely difficult in terms of the level of knowledge required. It is not really difficult to identify an answer that suggests that Piaget's work had something to do with stages of development, for example. That is a different level of knowledge than the task of explaining what Piaget's work indicates for the teaching of number concepts to four- or seven- or nine-year-old children who exhibit the understandings common to various stages of development. An even greater level of knowledge would be required if the task were to evaluate alternative approaches to the teaching of number concepts for children with different learning styles.

We do not have a basis in current teacher tests with any of the latter kinds of questions. We test only factual recall or the ability to choose a teaching technique in response to short scenarios that give insufficient information to make a truly reasoned judgment. Although the desired answer can be found by eliminating the ridiculous answers or those that don't fit the topic of the question, a thoughtful, honest, and knowledgeable teacher would in most cases have to answer, "It depends." It is that understanding of the base for educational decisions that comprises the real knowledge base for teaching.

One of the things that is most striking about the current conception of professional knowledge in teaching is that it primarily emphasizes techniques, with little reference to the circumstances under which they might be appropriate and why they might be useful. This is true both in teacher education and in teacher testing. This conception of teaching knowledge not only ignores the fact that any technique has limited applications, it assumes that teachers don't need to have a basis for deciding what to teach, for what purposes, and when. They only need to have a battery of tactics at their disposal for implementing a curriculum that is prescribed for them.

Indeed this assumption pretty much matches the contemporary conception of the teacher's role in education. Until teachers are expected to understand the foundations of learning, and these foundations have been spelled out in concrete terms, there will be little ammunition for arguing that teachers should have a greater role in the design of education.

IN DEFINING the knowledge base for teaching, it might be useful to start by thinking about the building blocks for pedagogical knowledge. In medicine, the initial part of training and the first sections of the medical board examinations focus on knowledge of how the human body functions: knowledge of anatomy, physiology, endocrinology, pathology, and so on. It is assumed that making sound judgments about treatment depends on understanding the phenomenon one is about to treat.

In education, knowledge of how children (and adults) grow, develop, and learn is equally important for making judgments about what and how they might be taught effectively. This includes an understanding of cognitive, physical, and psychological development, as well as knowledge about how learning normally occurs and about deviations from the norm. Theories of teaching and learning posit relationships among various known attributes of learners and how they are activated in different learning situations. These theories inform judgments about the choice of techniques, suggesting alternatives and decision criteria, rather than simple choices.

Since all teachers, and even some researchers, know that effective teaching strategies vary depending on the goals of instruction, the subject being taught, the nature of the learners, and their stages of development, it is imperative that conceptions of teaching knowledge emphasize the importance of judgment in making teaching decisions in the face of uncertain and diverse situations. Although there is seldom a single right answer to a problem of teaching practice, there are bases for making a professionally appropriate judgment about how to proceed in a complex situation.

> *A **thoughtful, honest, and knowledgeable teacher** would in most cases have to answer, "It depends."*

Other professions that also require the application of knowledge in complex, nonroutine situations have developed methods for testing such abilities in a variety of ways. In law and accounting, for example, essay responses to case scenarios allow for multiple "right" answers. The test is designed to assess the candidate's understanding of important considerations and the ability to apply knowledge in a professionally acceptable manner to the case at hand.

The psychiatry boards use simulated interviews with real patients to assess a candidate's ability to apply appropriate considerations to the problem of diagnosis and initial treatment. Even though the jury of peers involved in the evaluation may not agree among themselves about a diagnosis, they can apply a common standard of practice to the assessment of the process.

The medical boards also use computer simulations to test a candidate's ability to follow through a course of diagnosis and treatment, to request and use new information appropriately, and to apply knowledge in the unique case presented by an individual patient.

All of these are ways of incorporating real-world uncertainties and judgment in a performance assessment that more nearly represents the knowledge needed to be a good practitioner. What is important is that these approaches conceive professional knowledge broadly and realistically, tolerating multiple approaches and perspectives while reinforcing a standard of professionally responsible practice.

When teacher tests can reflect such a view of the professional knowledge base, and when teacher education is designed to support such a view, teaching will become a profession with a claim to authority in the decisions that shape teaching work.

RELEARNING TO TEACH: PEER OBSERVATION AS A MEANS OF PROFESSIONAL DEVELOPMENT

ELIZABETH RORSCHACH AND ROBERT WHITNEY

Elizabeth Rorschach is assistant professor of English as a Second Language at City College in New York City. Her handbook on grammar, entitled The Right Handbook, *has been published by Boynton/Cook. Robert Whitney teaches rhetoric and composition at Milsaps College in Jackson, Mississippi, and has been invoved for some years with the National Writing Project. This condensed article is reprinted with permission from the October 1986 issue of* English Education, *the official journal of the Conference on English Education, National Council of Teachers of English. The authors would like to thank their colleagues at New York University, including Lil Brannon for her considerable help and encouragement in initiating this project and thinking about its implications as it progressed.*

IN GRADUATE school, and afterward in the college or university, a great deal of emphasis is placed on developing ourselves as scholars and very little on developing ourselves as teachers. There are probably many reasons for this, but one of them surely is the fact that the products of scholarship are tangible while the products of teaching are not. Two years ago, we were both preceptors in the Expository Writing Program at New York University, where we were Ph.D. candidates in English Education, a combination designed to encourage our interests in teaching. Among English Education students in this program, the conversation about teaching, learning, linguistics, and discourse theory and their application in the classroom tends to be quite intense. Yet even in such an intellectually rich and supportive environment the discussion of teaching has its limits: the talk was good as far as it went, but it didn't entirely satisfy our need to look closely at what was happening in our writing courses.

We were both, at that point, experienced teachers, having taught freshman writing in various colleges for ten years between us — experienced enough to know that the translation process from good idea to effective lesson is often unpredictable. We both enjoyed the talk, but we knew that something was missing: the phenomena themselves — the actual events of the classroom — remained sequestered behind closed doors. It is one thing to talk about what happens in our classes or to share ideas and lesson plans; it is quite another thing to be the one who is there when class is in session, trying to put those ideas into practice and meeting with the unexpected reactions of students. For example, many writing teachers have tried peer groups on the recommendation of colleagues only to be disappointed by the results. Why does this happen? Despite prodigious amounts of talking, we often remained baffled about why certain things worked and why other things didn't or why our classroom successes and failures so frequently contradicted the predictions of theory. Even when the talking did help us "understand" these events, our new understandings were seldom of use in getting something different to happen the next time. We needed a way to carry these discussions further; a way of connecting them more directly to the classroom experience itself. After considering a number of approaches, we decided to attend each other's freshman writing classes in the role of students — a version of the participant-observer method used in ethnographic research.

We expected that there would be two advantages to this approach. First, the project would be intensive and holistic. That is, we would not be just *observing* each other's teaching once or twice during the semester, getting bits and pieces of the courses, but *participating*

Reprinted with permission from the Winter 1987 issue of the AMERICAN EDUCATOR, pp. 38-44, the quarterly journal of the American Federation of Teachers.

in the courses as if we were members of the community, taking part in discussions and group work and even writing some of the assigned papers. This meant that we would be able to see each course as a whole, from the inside — to view each class meeting within a context that would gradually build throughout the semester. It also meant, we hoped, that we would get to experience what it was like to be a student in our courses — something we were aware that we really didn't know much about.

Second, having another pedagogically aware person to report on what happened in our classes brought us closer to a method that ethnographers call "triangulation" — analyzing events from multiple viewpoints. In practical terms, this meant that the other teacher would provide a check or test of our interpretations of events, giving us a means to build a more inclusive understanding of what had happened.

INITIAL METHODOLOGY

Our project's design turned out to be quite simple: For fifteen weeks, we attended each other's freshman writing course, which met twice a week for a total of three hours. The teacher in each class taught as she normally would, while the observer took the role of a student, participating in class discussions, writing drafts for most of the assignments, and sharing his writing in peer groups with the other students. We each kept a notebook on the experience, and we met once a week for about an hour to discuss what had been happening. In our earliest plans, we thought we might not tell the students, but we abandoned that idea as too risky, thinking that the students might find out and have genuine cause to feel betrayed. On the first day of classes the teacher simply introduced the observer, said something about what we were doing, and asked the students to treat the observer as they would any other student.

We were quite nervous about revealing our teaching to each other, but at our first weekly meeting we focused on the things we liked about each other's teaching, and the nervousness began to disappear. The care we took at the beginning to be supportive was probably crucial. Had we initially made comparisons — which could have had negative implications — the resulting increase in anxiety might have crippled our ability to work together in the open and trusting way that made this collaborative inquiry such a rich experience.

After a couple of weeks, and quite fortunately as it turned out, we decided that we could go no further without comparisons. This proved to be an important aspect of our method and led to some of our richest insights. We think what made the comparisons so powerful was the diversity of points of view, something that doesn't happen with solo teaching or even with team teaching of a single course when both teachers constantly share the leadership. Although we were never, of course, really in the roles of students either (among other things, we weren't being graded), our viewpoints were different enough to allow us to form divergent perceptions of the same events and then to compare those divergent perceptions with our perceptions of events in the other class, seen from reversed perspectives. It was this duality of viewpoints by the same observers reversing roles in parallel cultures that led us to the most important new learnings and insights and that allowed us, in the third week, to make a discovery that shaped our work for the rest of the semester.

INITIAL FINDINGS

From the beginning we had noticed two things. On a philosophical level, we were in almost complete agreement. Ideas of active learning, promoting the autonomy of students, forming a community in the classroom, and writing as the making of meaning, based on the works of Berthoff, Britton, Elbow, and Freire, among others, shaped most of our planning and provided a framework in which we interpreted classroom events. Central to this framework is the notion that writing is among the most authoritative and autonomous acts that human beings do. If this is true, and if becoming a writer means growing in one's ability to act on one's own authority, to think for oneself, then it seemed to us that in a writing class there needed to be a transfer of authority from the teacher to the students. The students needed to come to see themselves as making choices that shaped meaning for themselves and each other, instead of waiting for the teacher to make these choices for them by telling them exactly what to do. This, in turn, required a transition from a situation of singular authority vested in the discourse of the teacher to a situation of distributed authority — a community in which discourse is a shared creation.

On an experiential level, however, our classes proved to be very different. This was a surprise, but we initially avoided paying much attention to it. The difference had to do with what might be called an "atmosphere" of participation. This is not easy to describe in a way that conveys how striking it was to experience. We both felt markedly more comfortable in Betsy's class, and the students seemed to participate more. In Betsy's class, the students spoke a lot, actively and freely participating in the discussions she initiated. There were silences, but they had a thoughtful quality to them and did not make us feel anxious. It seemed to both of us that the students in her class had begun to recognize their own ability to carry on a discussion without the explicit leadership of the teacher. That is, students didn't wait to be called on by the teacher before speaking, they addressed each other as well as the teacher, and they asked a lot of their own questions rather than just answering the teacher's. In Bob's class, however, the students were uncomfortably quiet unless addressed directly by Bob. It was as if Bob remained much more in control over what was happening in the class, resulting in a conversation that revolved around him and stifled the students.

In our third weekly meeting we could no longer ignore this difference. Actually, the difference was so great it was hard to ignore, but when our avoidance of comparisons proved unsatisfactory we simply explained away this difference by attributing it to differences in our students. The fact was, our students *were* different. Betsy was teaching an out-of-sequence section of the first semester composition course, and over half of her students were upperclassmen. Bob was teaching all freshmen in a "natural science" section of the second semester course, where all the reading and writing topics were drawn from the natural sciences. These natural science sections had a reputation for attracting students least interested in writing. Those in Betsy's class were older (average age of about twenty-five) than those in Bob's class (average age of about eighteen), and some of the students in Betsy's class had returned to university after interrupting their schooling in order to begin careers or families. Bob's class had a higher percentage of premedical or predental students (whose concern for grades and aversion for the uncertainties of writing are well known at NYU). It was thus easy for us to account for the differences between our two classes by pointing to the types of students we had.

We felt there was a problem, however, with such an approach: If we blamed the students, however deserving they might be, we weren't going to learn anything much about teaching. So we decided to adopt what seemed to us at the time to be a personally risky hypothesis: that the differences in our classrooms resulted from differences in our behaviors as teachers rather than from differences in our students. Although threatening, such a hypothesis proved to be a lot more valuable.

Changes in Methodology

At this point, having identified a problem to solve — something we wanted to know more about — we decided to add several tools to our method of inquiry.

First, we began tape recording our classes so that we could look more closely at our classroom behavior. Although we shared a sense that we were probably behaving differently in our roles as teacher, it was not immediately apparent how, since neither of us really sought to create an authoritarian classroom and both of us went to great lengths to encourage participation, arranging the chairs in a circle and conducting our classes mostly as conversations of one kind or another. It would have, of course, been better to have recorded the initial classes, but we "reasoned" that whatever we had done in the early classes to set things up, we were probably still repeating in some form or other.

Second, we decided to look at our lesson plans for those first three weeks to see if any differences in the progression of each course would help us explain the experienced differences in the communities we had produced. Clearly the essential difference in our courses didn't lie in our goals. Consequently, we needed to look elsewhere, and the sketches of our lesson plans revealed some startling contrasts.

At first glance, our lesson plans didn't seem essentially different. Both involve whole-class discussions, small-group discussion, peer response to drafts, student-generated writing topics, reading and freewriting* in class. To us, as we went through the first three weeks with the students, the progression of events seemed merely like different arrangements of largely similar elements. However, when we compared these events on paper in the third week and began to talk about why we had arranged them in the ways we had, we saw one

crucial difference. This was not a difference of philosophy or of classroom method or execution, but of what might be called "strategy."

During the first three weeks, Betsy's strategy was focused on creating different classroom interactions to put into practice new rules and procedures for a course in which authority is shared. Betsy went to considerable lengths to demonstrate these new role expectations and set up her assignments with the intention of giving the class opportunities to think about them (for example, in the first week students freewrote about a previous writing class; in the second week they freewrote about and discussed the roles of the teachers and students in a writing class). She also had more small-group activities than Bob. Although it does not show up in the syllabus outline, she even went so far as to dramatize repeatedly the nonauthoritarian "culture" that she was developing. For example, at one point during a discussion, she left her seat and moved to a chair at the back of the room, outside the discussion circle. After listening for a while (and purposely neither speaking nor making eye contact with the students as they spoke) she interrupted to ask why everyone was craning his neck around to speak to the back of the room. She used this "drama" as a way of initiating a discussion of classroom roles and acknowledging each other's authority.

Bob's strategy during the first three weeks was focused on creating a different understanding for the activity of writing itself, having the students do a number of short, generative writing assignments to help them gain a sense of writing as a generative activity. Students wrote in class each day, discussing as a large group what had happened as they wrote. Throughout these discussions, Bob was the recognized leader, setting the tasks and asking the questions, and since the attention was on writing and its processes, the classroom roles remained largely unaffected.

Findings about the Role of the Teacher

As time went on, it was this issue of the role of the teacher in affecting the distribution of authority that became the central focus of our inquiry. The difference between the progression of events in our two classes was important, yet subtle. Betsy was no less a leader than Bob during those first three weeks, or for that matter during the rest of the semester. She also set the tasks for the students and was the primary agenda setter for the course as a whole, as was Bob. Nevertheless, her leadership had a different intention and purpose: to help the students discover their own autonomy and authority in and through the classroom conversation. Her idea was that once they began to experience this new relationship to themselves, each other, their teacher, and the educational process, it would transfer to their writing as well since their writing was part of the same conversation. Bob's idea was to have the students discover their autonomy and authority, their "voices" as writers in the experience and study of the writing process itself, without giving much attention to the classroom and its dynamics.

This difference had significant effects on the ways we employed the various elements of instruction. For example, the students in Betsy's class began working with

___
*Freewriting is writing quickly for five or ten minutes whatever is in the author's mind without judging or editing it.

each other in small groups at the second class session; those in Bob's class met in groups for the first time at the fourth class session. We felt that this delay, in combination with more frequent in-class writing assignments, allowed the students in Bob's class to maintain their conventional understandings of the classroom as composed mainly of one-way conversations with the teacher. While both of us had set out to build a community of writers, Betsy used the spoken conversation as the vehicle for the distribution of authority. Bob used the relationship of each writer to his writing as the vehicle, giving little attention to the form of the spoken conversation. Ironically, he ended up emphasizing writing as a solitary activity, despite his intentions to the contrary.

It is important to think of how all this affected the student's perceptions, a phenomenon we could at least speculate on from our positions as participant-observers. Take, for example, their perception of how the writing assignments were given. Both of us believed that the students should come up with their own topics as much as possible since choosing what to generate must be an integral part of any generative act. Both of us, in fact, offered this freedom, but we believe that only in Betsy's class did most of the students understand it and begin to make real use of it, choosing from their journals topics that they were personally interested in. In Bob's class, the students remained in an uncomfortable no-man's land between choosing their own topics and choosing what they thought Bob wanted them to choose. In spite of Bob's repeated entreaties to choose for themselves, this discomfort with autonomous choice remained throughout the semester. For the students, perceiving that Bob's actions belied his words, continued to act as though the real authority remained in his hands, and thus most of them never came to experience themselves as the authors of their own choices.

In our analysis of the transcripts of the tape recordings of our classes, we were especially interested in the beginnings, the ways discussions were initiated and conducted, and the ways our actions facilitated or interfered with autonomous activity by the students. In Betsy's class, the students were talking a great deal more than the teacher, and there was much more talk addressed by students to other students. Although it wasn't apparent on the audiotape, we also noted that Betsy made a point of not looking at the students when they were speaking, thus forcing them to look around the room at their other listeners. Perhaps the most important finding in the transcripts for Betsy's class was the pauses. Betsy would begin a discussion by asking a question and then would remain silent, waiting for a student to respond. Unlike Bob, who would usually say something himself if nobody responded, Betsy would wait until somebody spoke, even if the silence seemed interminable. We timed the silences in one discussion. Most of them were about five to seven seconds long, but one was fifteen seconds long, and another was twenty-three seconds long. We concluded that Besy's behavior and conscious actions had somehow set up the kind of classroom culture that encourages autonomous behavior within a community of writers. But we had to

wonder to what extent Betsy's students had made it easy for her to build the culture she wanted. Could the same community feeling be attained with a different group of students?

TESTING THE FINDINGS

Prior to our study, Bob had always been dissatisfied with the quality of classroom discussions in his courses, but since nothing he had done in his attempt to improve these discussions had made much difference, he had begun to wonder if he was wishing for something unattainable — maybe he was hoping for a quality of participation beyond the capabilities of college freshmen. Now he had reason to believe otherwise. What we needed was a way to test our hypothesis that the behavioral and strategic differences we had identified were indeed sufficient to create a different culture in Bob's classes.

Fortuitously, such an opportunity was available almost immediately because Bob was also teaching at a community college whose spring semester started four weeks later than NYU's. The students at the community college were very different from NYU's typical affluent students from suburban high schools. The students at the community college were among the least well prepared of college freshmen Bob had taught, mostly coming either from the inner city or from other countries. We felt, however, that in some ways this provided a better test than would a group of more similar students because such students generally have even greater expectations that teachers are supposed to act in authoritarian ways.

Bob revised his course outline in the light of what he and Betsy thought they had learned and included early freewritings and discussions on previous experiences in writing courses and teacher/student interaction, as well as several classroom dramas of the type Betsy had used, leaving the emphasis on writing and writing process to develop as the course progressed. He also worked consciously at changing his presence in the classroom. Together he and Betsy worked out ways that he could force himself to tolerate more silence and remove himself from the center of the discussion. One such plan was to make a point of sitting in some nonfocal position in the room. Another was to take notes during the discussion. This note taking served several purposes simultaneously — it kept him from talking, made it possible for him to endure the silences, and allowed him to break eye contact with the student who was speaking, forcing her to look elsewhere for someone to talk to.

Often Bob found that the change in his "normal" patterns of classroom behavior was so upsetting that he was unable to concentrate well enough even to take notes, so he just scribbled, freewrote, or drew lines on the page, but even this proved sufficient to break the cultural pattern and allow a new one to emerge. In fact, he was astonished by the effect these relatively superficial changes had on his behavior. In his new classes at the community college, and for the first time in his teaching career, he had discussions in the classroom that he enjoyed participating in and that didn't make him feel as though he were pulling them out of the students line by line. The students spoke back and forth as if they cared about what they were saying, and after a while he could join the discussions without taking them over.

IMPLICATIONS FOR PROFESSIONAL DEVELOPMENT

Does all this mean that as teachers we are now to take Betsy's approach as the final word on freshman composition? We don't believe so. The kind of experiential knowledge we generated in the course of our study is probably largely tacit and thus not generalizable beyond our own classrooms. It was not our intention to generate knowledge with wider application — all we wanted was to learn something about our own teaching and to construct a vehicle for carrying our development as teachers further. What can be shared, we feel, is our approach to method: collaboratively designed classroom research projects as a means of professional development for teachers and as a method of faculty development for institutions that train teachers or want to support the improvement of teaching. There are many ways such informal research could be done — peer observation is only one of them — but the need must arise from the teachers themselves so that they can work with peers on developing "research" methods appropriate to the kinds of pedagogical problems they want to investigate. We eventually found that the method we used was more elaborate than necessary — but then we started out not knowing what we were seeking so we needed to use a large net. For instance, if we were to do this again, it would probably be possible to make the necessary observations in only two or three weeks of participation, that is, if we knew ahead of time what we were looking for. We also feel that classroom visits are only one of several methods that are possible to gain more information about what is going on in our classrooms. Loren S. Barrett, an anthropologist at the University of Michigan, often advises teachers to find out more about what is going on in their classrooms by asking the students, a method that is notably absent from this study. Certainly, were we to study our teaching again we would spend more time conversing directly with our students about their various realities of the experience of the classroom.

Currently there is much talk — in writing projects, at conferences, and among colleagues — of classroom research. For some, the term "research" carries with it all the connotations of statistical methodology and experimental design that most teachers probably believe are beyond their abilities. When the goal of such "research" is to produce knowledge that has wider applicability — reliable knowledge for the larger community as a whole — carefully constructed methodology is necessary, and if we wanted to repeat our study for such purposes, we would have to set up the procedures and controls appropriate to the generation of such knowledge.

However, generalizable knowledge does not always have to be intended by an investigator. We set out to learn some things that would be useful in our own teaching, and we feel that we succeeded. For that, a casual and exploratory methodology was much more appropriate, perhaps even necessary. Indeed, a great deal of what we learned is not in this paper, nor even as yet consciously conceptualized in our own minds — it exists in the realm of what Michael Polanyi calls "tacit knowledge" and informs our decisions in the classroom without our even being aware of what it is.

One of the richest aspects of this project was the direct experience of another teacher's classroom over a period of time and a chance to think and talk about that experience with another teacher who was present. This is holistic learning of a kind that perhaps can never be fully understood in the abstract.

Such experience seems to wake up a kind of capacity for cultural awareness that we didn't know we had, and once awakened, that awareness applies even to participation in the familiar cultures in which we usually live and work. In fact, that was the primary benefit that Betsy felt she got from the study — a heightened awareness of what she was doing in her own classroom and an expanded ability to step back from and analyze her own behavior as a teacher. Prior to the study she had felt satisfied with her teaching, but she didn't know why, because she hadn't made concrete the connection between her conceptual system and what she actually did in the classroom. Our work afforded her that and enriched her experience of her own classroom as well.

The situation that we found ourselves in is not uncommon. Most teachers experience a yawning gap between the abstractions about education presented to them by university researchers and the pressing decisions about what to do in their classrooms tomorrow morning. Perhaps the fault for this gap lies neither with the researchers nor with the teachers but with the situation: the isolation of the one-teacher classroom, rigid scheduling patterns, limited or nonexistent opportunities for ongoing collaborative inquiry, and the lack of sufficient precedent and support for carrying out such inquiry even when the opportunities for it could be made. The great bulk of useful human knowledge, after all, is probably generated outside of laboratories and libraries by groups of people working to solve common problems, talking, and thinking together as they go. Through such collaborative inquiry, we teachers can become researchers in our classrooms and turn our valuable classroom experience into useful knowledge for ourselves and for one another.

WORKS CITED

Barrett, L. S. (1983). Practicing research by researching practice. In P. L. Stock (Ed.), *Fforum: Essays on Theory and Practice in the Teaching of Writing*. Montclair, NJ: Boynton/Cook.

Berthoff, A. E. (1981). *The Making of Meaning: Metaphors, Models, and Maxims for Writing Teachers*. Montclair, NJ: Boynton/Cook.

Britton, J. (1970). *Language and Learning*. Harmondsworth, England: Penguin.

Elbow, P. (1973). *Writing without Teachers*. London: Oxford.

Elbow, P. (1981). *Writing with Power*. London: Oxford.

Freire, P. (1973). *Pedagogy of the Oppressed*. New York: Seabury.

A Look to the Future

A great many articles in this edition have discussed change, reform, and excellence. These have been the educational watchwords of the final years of the 1980s in North American education. Individual, group, and organizational reports on the status of education in North America have generated a fundamental reconsideration of our past, present, and future in educational development. Although there were other periods of reassessment—rhetoric over using schools to recover from the Great Depression of the 1930s, attempts to relate schooling more directly to life in the 1940s and early 1950s, and criticism of the quality of American schooling following Sputnik in 1957—the level, depth, and intensity of the analysis of educational needs in North America since 1983 is in some ways historically unique. None of the earlier recommendations compare with recent suggestions for changing the way teachers are educated and for restructuring the entire teaching profession. The future is bright for education, provided a sufficient amount of national resources can be created or redirected to achieve the goals of the almost thirty formal group reports calling for reform. While many of the signals from the national commission reports are clear, some of the signals from state legislatures for revised state certification standards are ambiguous at best. Other state legislatures and teacher certification agencies are determined to support the many recent proposed reforms in teacher education and the conduct of schooling.

Given the tenor of all the reports and dialogue about increasing rates of technological development and social change in the nation, great changes in education can be expected as well. The future of education will be affected by many factors, such as the shifting social demographics of the population served by North American schools, and the revolution in the information sciences. The emergence of user-friendly software and the massive rate of growth in the popular use of personal computers ensures that schools of the future will rely on and use more and more of the new information technologies which facilitate high degrees of individualization in classrooms. In addition, major changes may be developing in how people become teachers and in the organizational structure of the profession itself.

The future of any system depends on the outcome of its past and present. The future of education will be determined by the current criticisms and proposals for change growing out of what is a significant dialectical debate. The focus of the debate concerns what constitutes a just, national response to human needs in a period of technological change. The reshaping of curricula at the elementary and secondary school levels as well as the reshaping of teacher education curricula will reflect the outcome of this debate. The history of technological change in all human societies since the beginning of industrial development in the late eighteenth century has clearly demonstrated that major advances in technological development and major breakthroughs in the basic sciences lead to more rapid rates of social change. Society is on the verge of discoveries which will lead to the creation of whole new technologies in the dawning years of the twenty-first century—hardly more than a dozen years from now. All of the social, economic, and educational institutions on earth will be affected by these scientific breakthroughs. A basic issue is not whether the schools can remain aloof from the needs of industry or the economic demands of society, but how to develop a just, humane, and compassionate expression of the noblest ideals of free persons in the face of inevitable technological and economic change. Another concern is how to let go of predetermined visions of the future which limit our possibilities as a free people. The schools, of course, will be called upon to face these issues. There is a need for the most enlightened, insightful, and compassionate teachers ever educated by North American universities in order to prepare the youth of the future in a manner which will humanize the high-tech world in which they live.

All of the articles included in this unit touch on some of the issues raised above. They can be related to any discussions on the aims of education, the future of education, or curriculum development. They also reflect highly divergent perspectives in philosophy of education.

Looking Ahead: Challenge Questions

What might be the shape of school curriculum by the year 2000?

What changes in society are most likely to affect educational change?

Unit 9

How can information about population demographics, potential discoveries in the basic sciences, and the rate and direction of technological change in Canada and the United States assist in planning for the educational future? What planning strategies are needed?

How can curriculum development today prepare students to work in an uncertain future? What knowledge bases are most important? What skills are most important?

Is a national consensus on educational values possible?

Based on all of the commission reports of recent years, is it possible to identify any clear directions in which teacher education in North America is headed?

What sort of a future do you see now for tomorrow's teachers? How can we build a better future for teachers?

How can educators better prepare the youth of today for managing social circumstances in the future?

Schools Must Provide for Lifelong Learning

Educating Children for the Coming Century

Edward Cornish

From *Curriculum Review*

Edward Cornish is Founder and President, World Future Society, Bethesda, Maryland, and editor of The Futurist.

CHILDREN entering first grade this year will graduate from college in the early twenty-first century and may still be actively working in the year 2050. They must acquire during their school years the skills and attitudes that will enable them to gain all kinds of new skills and understandings many years later. In the years ahead, people will have to do many difficult things in order to achieve success in their jobs, family life, and citizenship. Schools must indoctrinate youngsters with a clear understanding that hard work is required for success—and that hard work generally pays off.

We can anticipate some major shifts in education, based on certain identifiable trends:

• **Youngsters may begin their formal education at an earlier age, perhaps at three or four.** Children deprived during these years will suffer lifelong learning deficiencies. As adults, many may be unable to find jobs in our increasingly technological civilization.

Unfortunately, many parents—too poor, too uneducated, unmarried teenagers, persons too caught up in the stress of social changes to devote sufficient time to parenting—cannot give their children an adequate home learning environment. Sociologist Amitai Etzioni argues that society should shift some of its scarce educational resources from colleges and universities downward to meet the desperate needs of these very young children.

• **More youngsters will do school-work at home.** The educational system is now committed to providing an adequate education for all its charges, even if they are sick or handicapped. Working at home is the answer for these youngsters. Video, computer, and other new technologies will make it easier to provide those at home with rich educational experiences and test them on what they have learned. Learning at home also gives youngsters experience in learning when there is no teacher around—a skill that will be critically important after they leave school.

• **There will be a boom in new educational products.** Education is extremely expensive today because so much of it is provided as a service, and human labor is not cheap. One way to reduce the cost of a service is to convert it into goods.

Today, videotapes, videodiscs, computer programs, and other new educational goods are pouring onto the market. Prices will drop as the market grows; in a few years, we will very likely have video materials that provide hours of first-rate instruction at a very reasonable cost.

• **Teachers will pay more attention to students and less to their subjects.** The teacher will become the indispensable source of the human touch necessary to make learning real. A teacher will be needed to encourage students, to identify the difficulties they are having, and to make sure they are meeting their goals.

• **Class time will be increasingly devoted to group discussions rather** than lectures. A large-screen video-taped lecture, accompanied by relevant illustrations or motion picture segments, will provide students with a far better lecture than almost any human teacher can manage. But a human teacher will be needed to motivate, to guide discussions, and to produce the overall learning experience—tasks which have always comprised the real heart of the teaching experience.

• **"Experiential" education will grow in importance.** Field trips, demonstrations, investigative projects, and hands-on labs are now common experience for most school children. In the future, special trips will become increasingly common as the cost of travel diminishes.

• **Education will become more individualized.** New instructional materials will make it possible for slow students to proceed at their own pace while faster students race ahead. Students will have more time and resources to follow up on special interests. Teachers will have the task

> **A human teacher will be needed to produce the overall learning experience.**

of helping youngsters select individually appropriate courses and encouraging them to make the most of their time and talents.

• **Adults will resume their education periodically throughout their lives to acquire new skills—or to** function better as citizens, or simply

 From *The Education Digest*, October 1986, pp. 10-12. Originally appeared in *Curriculum Review*, March/April 1986, pp. 12-17. Reprinted with permission, *Curriculum Review*, Chicago.

to expand their cultural knowledge and general abilities. The potential of technology for time saving and individualization will make such interim learning possible.

● Education will occur increasingly in nontraditional settings. Courses are now being offered in hotels, vacation resorts, factories, office buildings, and the outdoors. Some courses are available on ships and trains.

A number of possible—but far from certain—developments in education include:

● **Schools may get smaller,** to combat alienation and violence. Students who want special instruction or facilities may be bused to a facility that has them, but new computerized and video courses may reduce the need to travel.

● **Schools may increasingly go private.** A proposed voucher system would allow parents more choice about where their youngsters went to school. A voucher system would also force poor schools to shape up or close their doors.

● **Educators may become more accountable for the quality of their products**—when, for example, former students fail to meet minimum standards, and parents feel they have endangered their children's profes-

---

More schools will insist that youngsters have the basic skills before moving them from grade to grade.

---

sional or intellectual lives. So far, schools have largely escaped legal accountability for their failures, but a general attitude of "consumer" toughness may demand more responsibility in the future.

● **There may be a new emphasis on discipline.** The call now is for maintaining order and discipline as a necessary precondition for learning. The solutions, however, are far from apparent at present.

● **There may be even more emphasis on fundamentals.** Reading and writing will receive new attention. The functional illiteracy of many high school graduates has now become a national scandal. One result is that more schools will insist that youngsters have the basic skills before moving them from grade to

grade. Another is that industry will refuse to hire graduates who cannot perform, or learn, on the job.

● **Schools will probably be open more of the time.** There is widespread concern that Japanese and European youth spend more time in school and consequently are better prepared for jobs and citizenship. Schools may consider year-round schooling, and may increasingly provide education for adults, many of whom can attend class only on evenings and weekends.

● **Videotapes should help many teachers** to improve their teaching and also make it easier to get objective evaluations of teacher performance. Students can also benefit from videotapes showing them interacting with their fellow students and teachers.

● **Well-to-do parents may buy computers and other educational equipment for their youngsters.** The result may be a widening gap between the educational haves and have-nots.

Educators must equip students with knowledge that will enable them to function successfully in a future world which we can know little about, but which will be drastically different from our world today. Learning how to learn will be the key to that future.

Marvin J. Cetron, Barbara Soriano, and Margaret Gayle

Schools of the Future

Education Approaches the Twenty-First Century

Surviving the current crisis in education requires major reforms. Schools must stay open longer, pay teachers better, and open their doors to a different kind of student—the adult worker in need of retraining.

Nearly 30 reports issued by commissions, task forces, and individuals have made it clear to the American people that their nation will be "at risk" unless they pay attention to their schools.

Most of these reports emphasize the need to better prepare students for entering college. Yet three-fourths of U.S. kids don't graduate from college.

A major responsibility of schools in the future will be to prepare students to enter a rapidly changing job market. If the United States is to continue to compete in the worldwide marketplace, American workers will need to be more highly trained than at present. This means a greater emphasis on high-tech vocational education will be needed—an issue most educational reformers have ignored.

Schools will be responsible for preparing students who are adaptable and able to respond quickly to the changing requirements of new technologies. In the near future, workers' jobs will change dramatically every 5 to 10 years. Schools will train both youth and adults; adult workers will need re-education and retraining whenever business and industry update their operations. In the future, workers will be displaced frequently and will be moving constantly from one occupation to another. They will need periodic retraining because each new job will be different from the previous one.

Schools of the Future

By 1990, most adults will be working a 32-hour week. During the time that they are not at work, many will be preparing for their next job. While the adult workweek is getting shorter, the student schoolweek will be getting longer.

Not only will the normal academic day be longer for children, but the buildings themselves will be open a minimum of 12 hours a day. Schools will be providing services to the community, to business, and to young students who will use the recreation facilities, computer labs, and job simulation stations—modules that combine computers, videodiscs, and instrumentation to duplicate job-work environments.

Many schools may be open 24 hours a day. They will be training centers for adults from 4 p.m. to midnight; some will also serve business through their computer and communication facilities from midnight until the next morning when young students arrive again.

Individual communities may conduct classes that include both adults and high-school students. But if for some reason this combination is unsuccessful, the groups can separate and work independently. In some communities, adults might take over portions of school buildings that have been closed because of declining school enrollments.

At present, most schools are in session for approximately 180 days a year. A number of the reform reports recommend an increase to 210 days a year or 240 days to match schools abroad, but many people have objected. Funds have not been available; some students and teachers feel they do not have the mental energy for a longer year; and families want free time to make summer plans. Also, school buildings generally are not air-conditioned.

Schools in the 1990s, however, increasingly will extend the time that buildings are in service. Air conditioning and modifications in the size and structure of classrooms will accommodate the changing purposes of school programs.

Some students will have the option of accelerating their progress through the school year in order to graduate and enter college or the job market earlier. Others may spend time at school in the summer to enrich their academic backgrounds through telecommunications coursework with another school district, state, or country.

Adults may find summer months a good time to train for a new phase of their careers. The core academic year will lengthen to 210 days, but students will not necessarily be in the school building at all times during this period.

Factors Affecting the Future of Schools

A number of current trends will affect work and schools in the twenty-first century:

• Minority populations will become the majority in most grade schools in the nation's large and middle-sized school districts.

• Computers will be available to students in prosperous districts on a 1:4 ratio. (The United States spent a total of $1 billion on textbooks in its entire 200-year history. In the next five to six years alone, the nation will spend $1 billion on computer-assisted education. Only one-third of this will be bought by and for schools; the remaining two-thirds will be provided by wealthier parents for their own children, thus creating an educational inequity far more debilitating than physical segregation. Society must do something to provide access to computers for all children.)

• Federal grants will provide a major portion of the funding for job training and equipment (including computers) in poor school districts.

• Total employment will rise by 17% to 25% as the workweek declines to 32 hours by 1990 and to 20-25 hours by 2000.

• Women, particularly married women, will enter the work force at a faster rate than any other group within the population.

• More businesses will be involved in schools, including apprenticeship training.

• Older citizens (over 55) increasingly will become students in public schools, job-training programs, and community source programs.

• A core, nine-month program will be offered in elementary and high schools, shifting electives to later in the lengthened day and to summer sessions.

• Teachers' salaries on an annual basis will be raised to within 10% of parity with other professionals requiring college degrees.

—Marvin J. Cetron, Barbara Soriano, and Margaret Gayle

Good-Bye, Little Red Schoolhouse?

Interactive cable television and computer communication links with the school may allow school districts to close down costly old buildings even if enrollments are increasing. As the workweek shortens from 32 hours a week in 1990 to 20-25 hours a week in the year 2000, families will want to make plans for the periods children would previously have been in school. Students will be able to time their study hours to fit these family schedules.

Computers will be used for the drill and practice of skills introduced by the teacher; they will also be used for helping students explore creative and problem-solving situations. Today's educational software, however, rarely does either job very well.

Teachers will effect some of the biggest changes in educational software. Their experience with computers in the classrooms during the late 1980s will give them insight into the ways such software will need to change. The teachers who are particularly good at making modifications may even leave the classroom and launch their own software-writing businesses.

Planning Individualized Education

Many teachers will operate in teaching teams, which will be able to use frequently updated information on their students to design individual education plans (IEPs). IEPs are simply plans for instruction. Each student will have a plan tailored to his or her own background, interests, and skills.

The IEPs in today's schools list skills in reading or math, for example, and suggest how the teacher should test the student to see if the skills have been mastered. IEPs in the future will also recommend whether students should learn each skill in a small or a large group, independently, one-on-one with a teacher, or a combination of these formats. They will suggest which senses the student should use more frequently to develop them further—for example, visual (reading books or computer screens) rather than aural (listening to tapes).

Once the quality of educational software improves, schools will be able to teach and drill students in basic skills more efficiently and also increase the percentage of students achieving certain minimum competencies.

Students who work relatively well without a great deal of supervision will be assigned to teachers who work well with large groups. Often, lessons will be introduced and skills developed through teacher-managed computer systems. Teachers will be responsible for setting up the instructional schedules, reviewing progress with the students, and seeing that students have opportunities to participate in a broad range of learning situations: problem-solving groups; independent information-gathering activities in the school or the community; music, art, or drama activities led by professionals from these disciplines; or computer-based drill routines.

For students who need to work in small groups, teachers skilled in handling and coordinating small-group experiences will move these students from teacher-student interaction to student-student interaction. Students will teach each other, not because the teacher does not have time and is trying to find a way to keep these student teams busy but because effective learning can take place in these teams.

Teachers will be assigned students based on the kind of teaching they do best. Students will be assigned to groups based on the way they learn best, according to what learning researchers feel they need to be successful. Students will not be assigned by grade level but by the developmental level they have reached in each area. Neither teachers nor parents will be concerned with pupil-teacher ratios.

No More Pencils, No More Books?

As software improves, computers will begin to replace some kinds of textbooks; they already can replace drillbooks. Software can be tailored to meet individual student needs and can be updated more quickly and inexpensively than textbooks. The writing and computing deficiencies that national educational reform groups have noted among today's students may often be remedied by simple practice—something computers do tirelessly.

Computers themselves could even provide income for the school: Parents might come to school to learn how to use computers in their businesses, and companies could use school computer facilities to run their data at night. And computers can be linked with videodiscs or with equipment that simulates the job environment.

Computers linked with videodiscs will provide sight, sound,

Adults may make up a large proportion of the future "student body" as they come back to classrooms to learn high-tech skills. To accommodate them, schools will be open longer—at night and during summers.

and movement. Some lessons in history, language, politics, psychology, math, word problems, and music, art, or dance could be taught or reinforced from one video-disc. Software, written by a member of a teaching team, will program sequences of visual images from a disc. The computer program will stop and start the disc every so often to ask the student questions.

Widespread use of computer-linked equipment will not be a major feature of schools until the twenty-first century, but certain schools will use computers in this way long before 1995. Computer simulations of certain job procedures have been used to train employees for 10 years in certain industries. Because sophisticated workplace simulation equipment is expensive, it will probably be placed only in regional centers where students will be sent for short periods of time to study and live in supervised dormitories attached to the public school system. Finally, individual high schools will begin to offer simulation as a means of job training.

Teachers and Business

Before the mid-1990s, teachers will receive higher pay—raised to at least 90% of comparable professionals' salaries. The current, popular concept of merit pay is not as relevant as the concept of pay equity, or parity. Teachers are the lowest paid of all professionals. In 40 out of the 50 states, a starting garbage collector earns more money than a starting teacher. Something must be done now.

Funding required to raise teachers' salaries will come in large part from businesses contracting with schools to retrain their workers; from private individuals studying skills for their next jobs; from selling computer time, day-care, and geriatric services to the community; and from other ways of using school buildings more efficiently.

As business becomes more closely connected with schools, it is possible that skilled teachers will join private business in even greater numbers than they do today. Teachers may choose to con-

Future Students

Students of the twenty-first century will probably include toddlers, children, youth, adults, and older citizens. A typical school district may provide learning experiences and training for students ages 3 to 21 and for adults ages 21 to 80-plus.

Students could have many options within the extended framework of the day and year:

● Attending school seven hours a day and 210 days or more a year, depending on their needs and ability to handle tasks.

● Selecting a variety of programs, both required and elec-

tive, in academic, vocational, or enrichment programs.

● Working from an interactive computer/videodisc learning station at home or school.

● Working on a job and going to school.

● Doing apprenticeships with master teachers.

● Having opportunities for expanded time in a science laboratory, music class, art class, or vocational class.

● Having opportunities to be tutored individually or in small groups.

—Marvin J. Cetron, Barbara Soriano, and Margaret Gayle

tinue their careers as trainers of employees for private businesses. Many times, however, businesses will find that teachers are valuable employees in other respects. Some of the services that teachers will be able to sell to businesses include communication skills, performance evaluation skills, group management abilities, and information management skills.

Schools that wish to keep their most skilled teachers will probably offer flexible work schedules so that teachers can participate in both worlds and will not be forced to make a choice. In this way, schools will not passively let businesses raid their personnel.

All Students Will Train for Jobs

Training for the job world does not keep people from going to college. One indication is that, from 1974 to 1979, part-time college enrollment increased by 25.8%. More students are now prolonging the period between when they graduate from high school and when they enter college. Some of that delay is caused by the fact that federal loans

and grants for college students have declined dramatically.

As schools provide more resources for teaching adults, they will be able to offer job training based on jobs that are actually available, not those that are becoming obsolete.

From the eighth grade on, many students may actually be placed in different businesses that use the skills they are learning. If businesses that might provide a wide range of experience are not immediately available to the school, students will be able to travel to a learning center staffed with instructors and containing the latest equipment suited to students' career fields.

In either location, students will have their work supervised and graded by employers' standards. A trainer will watch them at the work site or via television hookup. The trainer will be able to talk with the student. After this experience at the work site, students will return to the school to have their performance reviewed. The school will then judge whether the students

Future Teachers

It may not be necessary for all of a school's staff to be trained in education. Educators will be part of the career team and will be able to provide the guidance necessary to assure that experts from fields outside of education will present their materials effectively.

The educator of the future will have extensive experience with such topics as brain development chemistry, learning environment alternatives, cognitive and psychosomatic evaluation, and affective development.

The traditional teaching job will be divided into parts. After good computer-managed courseware has been installed in schools, the information gathered on teachers' performance in a variety of situations will determine which jobs will go to which teachers. School systems will encourage this specialization be-

cause they may make money from selling various services to business interests—or teachers may work part time and sell the services themselves. Some of the new jobs may be:
- Learning diagnostician.
- Information gatherer for software programs.
- Courseware writer.
- Curriculum designer.
- Mental-health diagnostician.
- Evaluator of learning performances.
- Evaluator of social skills.
- Small-group learning facilitator.
- Large-group learning facilitator.
- Media-instruction producer.
- Home-based instruction designer.
- Home-based instruction monitor.

—**Marvin J. Cetron, Barbara Soriano, and Margaret Gayle**

need additional attention, practice at a simulator, or study.

Taking the last two years of high school for job preparation does not mean that the advanced-course needs of students bound for college must be put aside. Schools will, however, be forced to become more effective in teaching English, mathematics, history, and science courses before the tenth grade. Students who plan to enter professions requiring intermediate or advanced skills in foreign languages, science, or math could sample jobs in related fields while studying those subjects.

Vocational education will no longer be a narrow field of study. Rather than the quickly legislated, quickly funded, inadequate remedy for a stalled economy that it has been in the past, vocational education will prepare students for careers of challenges and changes—not just for a first job.

Family purchases computer and software, enabling children to do much school work at home. Computer and communications technologies will allow some school districts to close down costly facilities despite increasing enrollments.

We can forecast a basically positive, progressive future for America's schools based on current international and national economic and social trends. These trends could change direction, however, thereby altering our predictions.

But nothing will alter these forecasts as greatly as inaction. If America's citizens ignore these warnings about their educational and industrial future, the nation's economic stability and preeminence will be jeopardized.

Marvin J. Cetron is president of Forecasting International, Ltd., 1001 N. Highland Street, Arlington, Virginia 22210. He is author of the best-seller *Encounters with the Future* (McGraw-Hill, 1982, 308 pages, paperback, $5.95) and *Jobs of the Future* (McGraw-Hill, 1984, 258 pages, $15.95).

Barbara Soriano is a Washington-based consultant and can be reached at Forecasting International, Ltd.

Margaret Gayle is an associate director of vocational education with the North Carolina State Department of Public Instruction, Raleigh, North Carolina 27611.

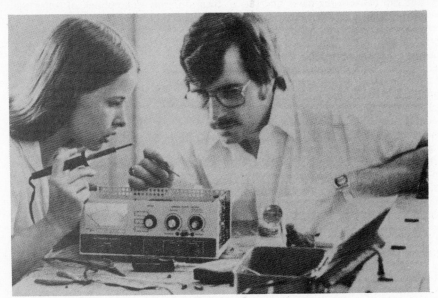

Students learn computer maintenance and electronics fabrication. High-tech vocational education will become a vital component of schools' curricula, say authors Cetron, Soriano, and Gayle.

CURRICULUM IN THE YEAR 2000: TENSIONS AND POSSIBILITIES

Michael W. Apple

MICHAEL W. APPLE is professor of curriculum and instruction and educational policy studies at the University of Wisconsin, Madison. He has written extensively on the relationship between curriculum and society. Among his books are Ideology and Curriculum *(1979) and* Education and Power *(1982). He thanks Shigeru Asanuma, Esteban De La Torre, David Hursh, Ki Seok Kim, Dan Liston, Yolanda Rojas, and Leslie Rothaus for their important contributions to this article.*

Predictions of the future, even in the best of times, are hazardous. So many unforeseen variables and unexpected circumstances can influence outcomes. If this is so in the best of times, it will be even more the case in the next few decades, for these are certainly not the best of times. Thus all of my claims in this article should be preceded by a single word: *if.*

Much of what I am predicting about U.S. education in general and the curriculum in particular depends on political and economic factors. For example, I am not very optimistic about the future for urban school districts. I see the curriculum in urban schools becoming more dated and less flexible in the next 10 to 20 years. I arrive at this prediction from a sense — backed by a decent amount of evidence — that our economy will continue to sputter, if not to stall, in the foreseeable future, thereby creating a serious dilemma for the hard-working teachers and administrators in numerous school districts across the U.S.[1] However, there are also hopeful signs, especially in attempts — even in the face of serious financial difficulties — to keep necessary programs alive and to make curricular content more representative and honestly reflective of a significant portion of the U.S. population.

Basically, though, I see the next two decades as a time of increasing conflict in curriculum. School programs will reflect the splintering of common interests and the polarization of the larger society, trends largely caused by pressures and conflicts over which the schools have little control. A significant amount of the blame will also lie in curricular decisions made as long ago as the early Sixties or as recently as today.

Before going further, I must review some important social and economic facts. It is unfortunate but true that 80% of the benefits of current social policies go to the top 20% of the population. Moreover, the gap between the haves and the have-nots is widening, due in part to the severe economic problems that the U.S. is now experiencing.[2] To their credit, most Americans feel uncomfortable about this situation. But this general discomfort will not prevent many interest groups from arguing that it is not "our" responsibility to alter economic disparities. Nor will it prevent economic inequities from creating serious tensions in U.S. education. If anything, the state of the economy and contradictory attitudes toward it will exacerbate the problems that educators now face. In the next two decades, the curriculum will reflect many of these tensions in the larger society. This should not surprise us. Only rarely has curricular content *not* reflected what is happening outside the school.[3]

I will focus here on three interrelated areas: the content of the curriculum, its form (or how it is organized), and the process of decision making that shapes it. Only by considering all three factors can we understand the forces, building today, that will set limits on and create possibilities for the curriculum in the year 2000.

One major issue that is brewing now and will continue to grow is the debate about "basics." This is not a simple problem. There are many competing conceptions of what everyone should be taught, of what knowledge will be the most valuable to students and to the society. The current controversy over bilingual programs in elementary schools and contemporary proposals to "upgrade" content and to reduce electives in the secondary schools are cases in point. Defining the basics will prove to be one of the most difficult issues that the schools will face, because schools will serve as arenas in which various groups will do battle for their differing conceptions of what the society should value.

It is clear, for instance, that the content of the curriculum has become a major political issue. The activism of conservative and extremist groups has increased measurably. This activism will continue to grow, feeding on past successes that result in increased funding. Mel and Norma Gabler of Longview, Texas, are prime examples; they speak for a larger movement that spends considerable time denouncing textbooks that are "unpatriotic," that reject "absolute values" and "free enterprise," that emphasize too strongly the contributions of minority groups, and so on. Armed with the notion that God is on their side, they are likely to scrutinize an ever-broader swath of curricular content, intent on purging it of any taint of "un-Americanism" and "secular humanism." The increase in book banning and the evolution/creation controversy document the growing willingness of such groups to enter into debates over what should be taught in the schools. Thus educators will have to give more attention to justifying *why* they teach what they do. And this task will be increasingly difficult, because

Reprinted from Phi Delta Kappan, January 1983. ©1983, Phi Delta Kappan, Inc.

teacher-training institutions are moving toward greater stress on *how* to teach, not on providing justifications for and skills in arguing about *why* educators teach particular information, skills, and attitudes. Unless this trend is reversed, teachers and administrators will be hard pressed to defend curricular decisions against well-organized and well-funded attacks.

Tension between business and organized labor will also manifest itself in conflict over curricular content. On the one hand, we are currently witnessing the emergence of industry as a powerful pressure group that seeks to influence education. Businesses across the U.S. have established departments whose goals are to distribute curricular materials to schools, to convince textbook publishers to tout the benefits of free enterprise, to lobby state legislators, and to provide summer internships for teachers that will help them develop a more positive perspective on business. I see no sign that this type of pressure will abate.[4] On the other hand, labor unions have begun to stress the importance of labor education. A movement is growing to teach labor history and to encourage students to examine critically the problems of the U.S. economy and the imbalance in economic planning. These conflicting goals — to teach content that will produce citizens who will meet the needs of industry and simultaneously to examine critically industrial models and power and the putative lack of concern of big business with the needs of workers — will create a good deal of friction over what should be taught.

This friction will be heightened by the growing cooperation between state departments of education and the business community. In times of economic difficulty, when tax revenues are lower and jobs are hard to find, it is not unusual for school programs to become more closely aligned to the needs of business. We can expect to see more emphasis on teaching job-related skills and on disciplining students according to the norms that guide the workplace. This shift will be difficult to accomplish, because the U.S. job market is clearly changing. New skills rapidly become obsolete, and new jobs are not being created quickly enough.[5] Furthermore, many individuals will object to this closer relationship between the schools and industry, arguing that business generally has its own profits, not the common good, at heart. Thus one more conflict over curriculum will arise.

These two "political" issues — defining the basics and determining the proper relationship of the school to business and to labor — will not be the only ones to surface. The basics will also be expanded to include academic areas that now seem to receive less attention than they deserve. Clearly, there will be attempts, largely positive, to strengthen the teaching of mathematics and science. Several states are already preparing to mandate more science and mathematics courses for high school graduation and the retraining of teachers at state expense, in an effort to reverse the current shortage of qualified math and science teachers. This increased emphasis on mathematics and science will be accompanied by a greater focus on computers in all areas of the curriculum, but especially in math and science. We must be exceptionally cautious and avoid jumping on yet another technological bandwagon. There is no quick fix for the difficult problems we face. Without higher salaries and greater prestige to attract and keep well-trained teachers in these curricular areas, the prospects for success are mixed.

An unfortunate trend will accompany this increased emphasis on mathematics, science, and technology: increased differentiation of the curriculum. Schools will try to identify "gifted" students much earlier. We will see a return to tracking systems and more ability grouping than is currently in evidence. When large amounts of financial, material, and human resources are available, such differentiation may make it easier for teachers and support personnel to meet individual needs by working intensively with students, taking each to the limit of his or her capabilities. But in a time of fiscal crisis, such resources will not be readily available; in such a time, the reinstitution of differentiated curricula and tracking systems will often have the opposite effect: to ratify the low socioeconomic position of many children.[6]

The fiscal crisis will have other profound effects. Since less money will mean fewer teachers and support services, we will see an accompanying steady decline in curricular alternatives as well. There will simply be fewer programs and options.

Moreover, fiscal constraints will hinder the replacement of existing instructional materials (which provide the foundation for nearly all curricula); the average age of textbooks used in the schools will increase and perhaps even double. This trend will be most evident in large urban areas, because they will suffer disproportionate declines in tax revenues and in state and federal support. As a result, the gap in the quality of curricular offerings and instructional materials will broaden between cities and their more affluent suburbs. Thus curricular content will differ by race and social class.

As I have already noted, we must consider curricular content, form, and the process of decision making simultaneously. There is no guarantee that President Reagan's New Federalism will go beyond rhetoric, but evidence suggests that decision making will shift to the state level. Oddly, this shift — though aimed at increasing the responsiveness of state authorities to local districts — will actually decrease curricular diversity. As decision-making power coalesces at the state level, publishers will tailor their textbooks increasingly to the values of those states that encourage statewide textbook adoptions — generally through reimbursements to local school districts for some portion of the cost if they select their instructional materials from an approved list. For publishers, getting materials placed on such lists is quite important, since it nearly guarantees high sales and profits. Given this economic fact, states such as Texas and California, which have state textbook adoption policies, will have disproportionate power to determine which textbooks and resources will be available throughout the U.S. Hence we will see even greater standardization of the curriculum. The curriculum will become "safer," less controversial, less likely to alienate any powerful interest group.

I have argued that curricular content will become both a political football and more homogenized (due to economic pressures on publishers and political and economic pressures on local and state education authorities). A third trend will also become apparent: The form or organization of the curriculum will become increasingly technical and management-oriented. And this will have a serious impact on teachers.

A fundamental change in the curriculum of the American school began in the early 1960s, especially at the elementary level. Sputnik inspired fear that the teaching of mathematics and science lacked sufficient rigor and that the academic disciplines were not central enough in the curriculum; in response, the U.S. government funded a large number of projects that focused on producing new curricular materials. A significant proportion of these materials turned out to be "teacher-proof." They specified everything that a teacher had to know, say, and do. Often, they even specified acceptable student responses. This approach — to specify *everything* and leave nothing to chance — was tacitly sexist, since it seemed to assume that elementary school teachers (most of whom were women) could not cope on their own with sophisticated mathematics and science.[7] To insure that these materials would be purchased and used, the government reimbursed school systems for the bulk of their costs.

Although many of these new materials were not used in the ways that their developers had envisioned,[8] they did signal an important modification in the curriculum — one that we will be living with for years to come. The curriculum became less a locally planned program and more a series of commercial "systems" (in reading, mathematics, and so on). These systems integrated diagnostic and achievement tests, teacher and student activities, and teaching materials. Such integration has its strengths, of course. It does make possible more efficient planning, for example. But its weaknesses may prove to outweigh its strengths.

What we have actually seen is the *deskilling* of our teaching force. Since so much of the curriculum is now conceived outside the schools, teachers often are asked to do little more than to execute someone else's goals and plans and to carry out someone else's suggested activities. A trend that has had a long history in industry — the separation of conception from execution — is now apparent as well in U.S. classrooms.[9]

This trend will have important consequences. When individuals cease to plan and control their own work, the skills essential to these tasks atrophy and are forgotten. Skills that teachers have built up over decades of hard work — setting curricular goals, establishing content, designing lessons and instructional strategies, individualizing instruction from an intimate knowledge of each student's desires and needs, and so on — are lost. In the process, the very things that make teaching a professional activity — the control of one's expertise and time — are also dissipated. There is no better formula for alienation and burnout than the loss of control of the job. Hence, the tendency of the curriculum to become totally standardized and systematized, totally focused on competencies measured by tests, and largely dependent on predesigned commercial materials may have consequences that are exactly the opposite of what we intend. Instead of professional teachers who care about what they do and why they do it, we may have only alienated executors of someone else's plans. Given the kinds of materials that now dominate many classrooms in such curricular areas as mathematics and reading, this danger seems likely to increase over time.

The economics of this process of deskilling is worth noting. In essence, we have established a capital-intensive curriculum in our classrooms. Simply to keep the program going, a large amount of money must be set aside for the ongoing purchase of consumable materials. School districts may soon find themselves burdened with expensive "white elephants," as school budgets are reduced and money is no longer available to purchase the requisite workbooks, tests, worksheets, revised editions of "modules," and so forth. School districts will then have to turn to their own staffs to create materials that are less expensive and more responsive to their students' needs — only to find that the necessary skills for doing this have been lost. This will be a very real predicament.

At the same time that teachers are being de-skilled, however, they are gaining greater control over which curricular materials and textbooks will be purchased for use in their classrooms. Curricular decision making is becoming more formally democratic; less power now resides in central curriculum offices or with select groups of administrators. Both teachers and parents are becoming more involved. Meanwhile, an increasing concern for accountability and for measurable achievement outcomes in a few "basic" areas will also bring a movement toward more standardized testing, more objectives, more focus on competencies, more centralized curricular control, and more teaching to the tests.

As this movement gains momentum, a vicious circle will develop. Publishers will further standardize content, basing it on competency tests and routinizing it as much as possible, so that their materials will produce measurable outcomes with little variability that will fit cost/control models.

Thus far, I have not been very optimistic about what will happen in the areas of curricular content, form, and decision making. I do not intend simply to be a nay-sayer. It is critically important to be realistic about the very difficult times that we educators will confront in the not-too-distant future. Only then can we begin to plan how to cope with what may happen. I would be remiss, however, if I did not point out some of the very beneficial tendencies that will become more visible by the year 2000.

Certain content areas — quite positive ones, in my opinion — will receive more emphasis than they do at present. Just as greater attention will be focused on mathematics and science (which, I hope, will be taught *not* as mere technical skills, but as creative and powerful ways of constructing meaning[10]), so, too, will teachers devote more time to the topics of ecology and peace. People from all walks of life, representing a variety of political persuasions, will coalesce around the topic of peace and urge that it be given more attention in the curriculum.

However, positive outcomes from additions to the curriculum will not be the dominant trend in a period of fiscal constraints. In fact, many school districts will be forced to save money by eliminating necessary programs. But this may prove beneficial, as well — especially in generating closer and more cooperative bonds between school personnel and the communities they serve. Teachers and parents will form coalitions to save programs that they see as essential. Difficult decisions will cause closer relationships to develop between community groups and the educators who must make those decisions. In a period of declining revenues and with the projected rise in enrollments, few outcomes will be more important. Funds will be needed to hire new teachers, to maintain and expand curricular offerings, to deal with students with special needs, and to carry on other essential tasks. Such funds can be generated only through greater cooperation with and increased support from the public. Even the scrutiny of the curriculum by conservative groups, to which I alluded earlier, should not be seen as merely a threat. The fact that parents — of whatever political persuasion — take a serious interest in their children's education suggests possible avenues for cooperation and fruitful discussion.

If we were freed from some of the tensions, conflicts, and pressures that will probably affect us as we strive to build or preserve a high-quality educational program for the children entrusted to us, what might we do about content, form, and decision making? Here I must be honest. A portion of what I will say has been recognized for years by knowledgeable educators. But such educators have seldom had the time, the resources, the support, or the freedom from contradictory pressures to act on this knowledge.

Let us look first at content. As attempts accelerate to redefine and to drastically limit what is taught to children, we should *broaden* our definitions of literacy and of the basics to include not only reading and writing — which are very important and must not be neglected — but also social, political, aesthetic, and technological literacy. Community action projects that provide curricular links between students and their local communities can help youngsters develop social and political responsibility and learn the necessary skills for active participation in the society.[11] At the same time, we should expose all students to beauty and form, aesthetics, and various ways of creating personal meanings — including research, poetry, dance, the visual arts, and film making. In other words, we should give equal weight to both "discursive" and "nondiscursive" subjects, so that each student has an opportunity to discover his or her talents and to develop the wide range of tools with which individuals control their own lives and their futures.[12] Thus we must define the "basics" very broadly.

Given the important role of technology in the future, *all* students — not just a select few who are "gifted and talented" — should be literate both in using computers and microcomputers *and* in analyzing their social implications. For example, computers and video-display equipment increase efficiency, but they may also cause untold thousands of workers (primarily women) to lose their jobs, become de-skilled, or work under stressful conditions. "Literacy" means the ability to analyze and deal with the social as well as the technical implications of this new technology.

In a recent column in the *New York Times*, Fred Hechinger noted that, if we approach computer literacy as a narrow vocational issue, we are bound merely to add one more relatively ineffective career education program to the many that already exist. As he put it:

> The visions of brave new electronic worlds of microchips and robots raise simultaneous demands for a schooling that looks to the future by learning from the past. Yes, the computer must be mastered by all, regardless of race, sex, or economic condition. But at the same time . . . the computer must be mastered by young people who are secure in a broad understanding of what used to be called general education — including language, history, economics, mathematics, science, the arts; in short, the human condition.[13]

To focus on a broad and general education requires that we be sensitive to the fact that the curriculum must represent us all. A "selective tradition" has operated in curriculum to date. This tradition may be more visible in some subjects than in others, but it is quite clear that the knowledge of some groups is not represented adequately in the curriculum.[14] For instance, we tend to teach military history or the history of U.S. Presidents; we teach less rigorously the history of the U.S. working class. Obviously, we have made advances here, just as we have made advances in teaching the real histories, contributions, and cultures of ethnic minorities and of women. Our progress in eliminating sexism and racism and in recapturing the lost past of U.S. labor is too important to allow these advances to slip away in the next decade or two. We must continue to pursue curricular balance. The content that we teach cannot be determined solely by the needs of any one group, even in times of severe economic difficulty. That would be short-sighted.

The curriculum must simultaneously be both conservative and critical. It must preserve the ideals that have guided discourse in the U.S. for centuries: a faith in the American people, a commitment to expanding equality, and a commitment to diversity and liberty. Yet it must also empower individuals to question the ethics of their institutions and to criticize them when they fail to meet these ideals. Curricular content should give people the ability to interpret social change and to reflect critically on what is happening in their daily lives. This is not a formula for an "easy" curriculum. It requires hard work and discipline on the part of both teachers and students.

Moreover, participation in such a curriculum is not merely an individual act; it is a profoundly social act as well. In an interdependent society, the curriculum should encourage cooperation and the testing of each individual's ideas against those of others. This requires countering — at least to some degree — the individualized instructional models now widely practiced in schools. All too many children sit isolated from one another in the elementary grades, completing worksheet after worksheet with little or no opportunity for serious discussion, deliberation, debate, or cooperation. Individualization is important; however, to be truly meaningful, it must be balanced by a sense of social responsibility.

The issue of time looms large here. Educators must have time to consider the curriculum carefully. Too many curricular decisions today focus on *how* to teach, not on *what* to teach. Teachers and other educators must have opportunities to discuss in detail what they want to do and why they want to do it. Creative scheduling is essential, in order to make time available for frequent, in-depth discussions of curricular content among local educators.

Obviously, teachers are not the only ones who are affected by what is taught. As much as possible, all individuals who are affected by a curricular decision should be involved in making it.[15] This includes parents, concerned citizens, organized labor and other interest groups, and, when possible, the students themselves. I recognize that such broad participation can lead to political conflict and to interminable meetings, but it can also lead to a greater sense of trust and cooperation on the part of all those involved. Indeed, broad participation may be one way to bolster flagging community (and financial) support of public education.

Educators who act on this suggestion must be willing to take risks and to work hard. School officials must aggressively present their curricular proposals and programs to the community — especially to the most disenfranchised groups. They must show their publics what they offer and communicate the justifications for these offerings. They must take criticisms seriously and respond to them honestly.

I have good reasons for making these suggestions. Available evidence suggests that, unless participation in curricular planning is widely shared among teachers, principals, central office staff members, students, and parents, the amount of support for any program is significantly reduced.[16]

In addition, direct parental involvement in the classroom tends to foster both more and longer-lasting changes in the daily activities of teachers. And evidence suggests that *how* a program is carried out is just as important as the specific content of a program.[17] The prospect of a continued decline in educational funding will give impetus to broad participation in the classroom. Parents will have to become more deeply involved, since schools will be hard pressed to afford many of the programs essential to high-quality education. As parents (and the elderly, I hope) volunteer to serve as tutors, as resource people, as counselors, and in other capacities, they will become more knowledgeable and more skillful at dealing with curricular issues. This is an important step toward a genuinely cooperative effort to guarantee high-quality programs for children.

If parental participation in decision making is important, teacher participation is even more important. There tends to be a very high correlation between the involvement of teachers in decisions related to changes in the curriculum and "effective implementation and continuation" of such changes.[18] When we consider going from what *is* to what *should be*, there are few things we know for certain. However, we do have some guidelines for strategies that seem to foster more effective and lasting changes in the curriculum, in what teachers do, and in what students learn. The findings of several studies have suggested that "what should be" will be enhanced to the extent that there is: 1) concrete, extended, and teacher-specific training related to the curricular change; 2) continuing classroom assistance from the district; 3) opportunities for teachers to observe similar projects in other classrooms, schools, or districts; 4) frequent meetings among the people involved that focus on practical problems; 5) local development of materials, insofar as this is possible; and 6) emphasis on teacher participation in curricular decision making.[19] As the financial crunch worsens, these guidelines will become even more important, especially in larger school districts.

So far, I have suggested certain attitudes and activities that should guide our policies on curriculum content, form, and decision making. However, this article would be both incomplete and deceptively simplistic if I did not add that, just as many of the tensions and conflicts over the curriculum arise outside the school, so too do many solutions to these problems require changes in the larger society. The issues of raising students' achievement levels and preventing dropouts are cases in point; solving these problems will require coordinated efforts by the larger society.

Educators have given a good deal of attention to reforming the secondary school curriculum to prevent dropouts. These reforms have had mixed results, in part because focusing solely on internal curricular changes is too limited a strategy. As Christopher Jencks has recently shown, the economic benefits for students who complete secondary school are still *twice* as great for whites as for blacks.[20] Moreover, completing secondary school provides relatively few benefits to students from economically disadvantaged backgrounds. Jencks and his colleagues have summarized their findings thus: "Apparently, high school graduation pays off primarily for men from advantaged backgrounds. Men from disadvantaged backgrounds must attend college to reap large occupational benefits from their education."[21] Clearly, those minority and economically disadvantaged students who stay in secondary school longer receive few economic rewards for their efforts — regardless of what common sense tells us about the benefits of increased schooling.

I am *not* arguing against making the curriculum more responsive to the needs of such youngsters. Rather, I am saying that, without a societal commitment to altering the structure of the economic marketplace so that these more responsive programs pay off for participants, such efforts may be doomed to failure. Why should such students wish to take part even in well-designed programs, if the statistical probability that these programs will improve their lives is very low? We *do* need better secondary programs, but these programs will be successful only to the extent that students feel that the school has something to offer — both now and for the future.

Improving the achievement of students poses similar problems. We have spent many years and huge sums of money attempting to raise achievement — especially scores on reading tests — through better instructional materials and curricula, more intensive teaching strategies, and so on. Yet these efforts, too, have had mixed results. We may have to take seriously the evidence that suggests a marked relationship between socioeconomic status and achievement in schools. The answers to many of the curriculum questions we face now and will certainly face in the next two decades — such as how best to increase the achievement of minority and poor

The future context of education must broaden the student's educational experience. Literacy should be defined to include social, political, aesthetic, and technological literacy.

students — may be found as much in social policies as in better teaching and curricula. As I mentioned earlier, doing well in elementary and secondary school does not guarantee economic success in later life.

The implications of this fact are striking. If we are really serious about increasing student mastery of content, especially among economically disadvantaged groups, then we might consider embarking on a serious analysis of the prevailing patterns of educational financing, of the possibility of redistributing income, and of ways to create jobs that would make possible a decent standard of living for the many families who will suffer the most if the economy continues its downturn. However, such analysis must not serve as an excuse for failing to do the important work of revising the curriculum and teaching practices. My point is that we must take seriously the complications that hinder the schools from reaching their goals. If we are to reach these goals by the year 2000, we will have to consider how our ability to do so is linked to the existing distribution of resources in our society.

I f our aim is a society in which all people are more equal in their opportunities to experience success and to exercise control over their own destinies, not a society in which the chasms between groups grow larger every day, then we must deal now with these larger social issues. Otherwise, the public will continue to blame the school and its curriculum, its teachers, and its administrators for something over which they have much less control than do other social agencies.

If I am correct that the success of the schools is very much tied to conditions in the larger society, then the training of curriculum specialists, teachers, and administrators for the year 2000 cannot be limited to such things as techniques of teaching, management approaches, and methods of financial planning. We must focus more rigorously — starting now — on the skills of democratic deliberation about such questions as social goals, the proper direction for schools to take, and what we should teach and why.[22] We will never have a curriculum free of tensions and conflicts. And it would probably not be good if we did, since such conflicts demonstrate the vitality of democracy. We must learn to work creatively with conflicts, seeing them not as hindrances but as possibilities for cooperative improvement of education.

The results of the decisions we make today about curriculum policies and classroom practices will be with us in the year 2000, which is just around the corner. It is crucial that we debate now the questions of what we should teach, how it should be organized, who should make the decisions, and what we as educators should and can do about (and in) a society marked by large and growing disparities in wealth and power. I hope that I have stimulated such debate, because that is the necessary first step to taking seriously the question of what the curriculum should be in the year 2000.

NOTES

1. I have discussed this in much greater detail in Michael W. Apple, *Education and Power* (Boston: Routledge and Kegan Paul, 1982). See also Manuel Castells, *The Economic Crisis and American Society* (Princeton, N.J.: Princeton University Press, 1980); and Lester Thurow, *The Zero-Sum Society* (New York: Basic Books, 1980).

2. For a detailed analysis, see Martin Carnoy and Derek Shearer, *Economic Democracy* (White Plains, N.Y.: M.E. Sharpe, 1980).

3. See Michael W. Apple, *Ideology and Curriculum* (Boston: Routledge and Kegan Paul, 1979).

4. See, for example, Sheila Harty, *Hucksters in the Classroom* (Washington, D.C.: Center for Responsive Law, 1979); and Apple, *Education and Power*, esp. Ch. 5.

5. Castells, pp. 161-85.

6. For a review of the literature on tracking and differentiation, see Caroline H. Persell, *Education and Inequality* (New York: Free Press, 1977); and Thomas Good and Jere Brophy, *Looking in Classrooms* (New York: Harper and Row, 1978).

7. Michael W. Apple, "Work, Gender, and Teaching," *Teachers College Record*, in press.

8. See, for example, Seymour Sarason, *The Culture of the School and the Problem of Change* (Boston: Allyn & Bacon, 1971).

9. For an empirical analysis of what is happening to some teachers in elementary schools because of this separation, see Andrew Gitlin, "School Structure and Teachers' Work," in Michael W. Apple and Lois Weis, eds., *Ideology and Practice in Schooling* (Philadelphia: Temple University Press, forthcoming). See also Apple, *Education and Power*.

10. For an interesting discussion of various forms of meaning and "representation," see Elliot Eisner, *Cognition and Curriculum: A Basis for Deciding What to Teach* (New York: Longman, 1982).

11. Fred Newmann, Thomas Bertocci, and Ruthanne Landsness, *Skills in Citizen Action* (Skokie, Ill.: National Textbook Co., 1977). See also Fred Newmann, "Reducing Student Alienation in High Schools," *Harvard Educational Review*, Winter 1981, pp. 546-64.

12. Elliot Eisner, *The Educational Imagination* (New York: Macmillan, 1979).

13. 10 August 1982, Sec. 3, p. 7.

14. Apple, *Ideology and Curriculum*, pp. 6-7.

15. Joseph Schwab, "The Practical: A Language for Curriculum," in Arno Bellack and Herbert Kliebard, eds., *Curriculum and Evaluation* (Berkeley, Calif.: McCutchan, 1977), pp. 26-44.

16. Paul Berman and Milbrey W. McLaughlin, *Federal Programs Supporting Educational Change, Vol. VIII: Implementing and Sustaining Innovations* (Santa Monica, Calif.: Rand Corporation, May 1978), p. 14.

17. Ibid., p. 24.

18. Ibid., p. 29.

19. Ibid., p. 34.

20. Christopher Jencks et al., *Who Gets Ahead?* (New York: Basic Books, 1979), pp. 174-75.

21. Ibid., p. 175. It is unfortunate that most of this research has dealt only with men.

22. Kenneth Zeichner is doing some of the best work on helping teachers to develop the skills of deliberation and reflection. See his "Reflective Teaching and Field-Based Experience in Teacher Education," *Interchange*, vol. 12, no. 4, 1981, pp. 1-22.

Will the Social Context Allow a Tomorrow for Tomorrow's Teachers?

Michael W. Apple

University of Wisconsin, Madison

First asking why schools and teachers should be called on to solve social and economically created structural problems in our society, Apple then raises related economic questions about how minorities and working-class students will pay for additional professional education and whether communities intent on keeping taxes low will maintain a lopsided temporary teacher workforce. He also warns of taking a scientific-technical view of teacher education.

There is a good deal to applaud in *Tomorrow's Teachers*. The report is quite insightful in a number of areas. For instance, in opposition to the very reductive proposals now surfacing in the media and elsewhere that blame the school for all of our social ills, the authors at least minimally recognize how closely tied the educational system is to social factors outside its doors. "Excellence" and responsiveness in schooling may require profound alterations in the unequal economic and political realms that dominate the larger society.

Second, the report shows its willingness to deal with complexity in its assertion (one that I believe is very well founded) that teaching is not reducible to "competencies" measured on paper-and-pencil tests. Rather, good teaching is a complex assemblage of knowledge "that," "how," and "to," none of which can be easily merged back into the others. Third, the author's recognition of the gendered specificities out of which many of the conditions of teaching were constructed is commendable. It is the case that whatever excellence our school system now has was built on the backs of the low-paid and committed labor of generations of teachers who were primarily women.[1] No other report of this type has dealt honestly with this critically important issue. I do not believe that the Holmes Group goes far enough with this recognition, but it is to the authors' credit that the question of *who* does the bulk of the teaching in the United States is at least raised. Any call for greater control over the teaching profession, any attempt to change teachers' work, is also a call to control the labor process of what is largely "women's work" and needs to be seen in the context of the frequent attempts to rationalize women's paid work in the past.[2]

Fourth, the wish to involve schools and especially teachers more directly in teacher education, to form more cooperative arrangements, is a clear sign of progress. It values the practical and political skills teachers have developed over decades of hard work. Further, and very importantly, such involvement could assist in the movement to resist the deskilling of teaching that has accelerated in the past few years.[3] The same could be said of the group's position on the necessity of more cooperative relations between faculties of education and the rest of the university.

Finally, *Tomorrow's Teachers* is clear about many of the dangers of short-term solutions to the problems confronting teaching. It rightly raises cautions about credential deregulation, a process that could have the same truly negative effects as other privatized and deregulated proposals such as voucher plans.[4] And it is self-reflective about some of the dangers of simple models of differentiated staffing. All of these points document why we should take the Holmes Group's recommendations seriously. Even though I have disagreements with a number of their specific proposals, the thoughtfulness and care that went into crafting their position is evident.

Even with the articulateness of these proposals, there are gaps and silences in the document. What I want to do here is raise a series of issues that need to be given further consideration. Obviously, these will by nature take the form of assertions that cannot be detailed in depth given space limitations. Interested readers who wish to pursue these claims will find further substantiation in the references that accompany these comments. I shall limit my attention to a few issues that may not usually surface in discussions of the document.

A number of points need to be made at the outset. The supposed crisis in teaching and in education in general is not an isolated phenomenon. It is related to a much more extensive structural crisis in the economy, in ideology, and in authority relations. As I have argued in considerably more detail elsewhere, we are witnessing an attempt to restructure nearly all of our major cultural, economic, and political institutions to bring them more closely into line with the needs of only a very limited segment of the American population.[5] Thus, we cannot fully understand why our formal institutions of education and the teachers and administrators who work so long and hard in them are being focused on so intently today unless we realize that economically powerful groups and the New Right have already been partly successful in refocusing attention away from the very real problems of inequality in the economy and in political representation and shifting most criticism to the health, welfare, legal, and especially educational systems. In technical terms, there has been a marked shift from a concern for "person rights" to those of "property rights" in our public discourse.[6]

In essence, dominant groups have been relatively successful in *exporting* the larger crisis away from themselves. When achievement is low among certain groups, when there are significant rates of negative intergenerational mobility, when workers have little enthusiasm for their jobs, and so forth, the public is asked to blame the school and the teachers. That is, rather than focusing directly on what may be the major sources of the problem—for instance, the immensely high under- and unemployment rates among working-class and especially minority youth who often see little future for themselves, an economy in which 80 percent of the benefits consistently go to the top 20 percent of the population, corporate decisions that cause millions of employees to work in low-paid, deskilled, and boring jobs (or to have no jobs at all), or an economic system that by its very nature needs to subvert traditional values, authority relations, self-discipline, and accepted conceptions of legitimate knowledge in order to create new "needs" and to stimulate the purchasing of commodities, and so forth[7]—the problem is placed on the educational system. If only teachers were better prepared, if only teaching and curricula were more tightly controlled and better managed, if only textbooks were more demanding and discipline and work skills were stressed, all of the above problems would be solved. The diagnosis and cure are actually a form of category error and would be easy to dismiss on empirical grounds if only they were not taken so seriously.

Tomorrow's Teachers, then, needs to be seen as something that follows in the footsteps of other documents such as *A Nation at Risk*. Its authors are considerably more aware of the larger structural situation in which schools and teachers exist and they are certainly not apologists for those people who wish to turn schools over to industrial and conservative needs and ideologies. The existing process of exporting the blame and bringing conservative ideologies into the heart of the educational enterprise helps, however, to construct the context in which the report of the Holmes Group will be *read* even though this may not be the authors' intention at all.

Obviously, *Tomorrow's Teachers* cannot solve all of these larger problems. No document about teachers and teaching could. But it is wise to keep the structural context in mind, since—while educators should direct their attention to what needs to be done in education—education itself must be wary of assuming that the answers to many of its very real dilemmas lie in preparing a more intellectually rigorous "profession." To do this may simply play into the hands of the attempt by dominant groups to export their crisis onto other areas. Thus, while I am in total agreement with the Holmes Group that some important things must be done in education and in teacher education, the latent

effects of limiting our attention to the internal issues need to be given a good deal of thought.

While I want to avoid being overly economistic here, let me use this larger social context as a backdrop to point to some of the economic problems that I believe will create serious difficulties in the way the report of the Holmes Group will be received. It may produce effects that its authors would not intend or approve.

There is one serious problem that needs to be given considerably more attention by those institutions and individuals that wish to take the report's recommendations seriously. Here I am speaking of the class and racial dynamics that could evolve in the elimination of an undergraduate education major. The Holmes report partly recognizes the fact that extending teacher training beyond the fourth year could present problems for some individuals. Hence, it calls for loan forgiveness for future teachers. Yet the problems go much deeper than this. Already, large numbers of students must work one and sometimes two jobs to make enough money to live on and pay college expenses during their four years of college. We are witnessing a severe downturn in minority and working-class college enrollments. Many universities have become bastions of the middle class and above. Extending professional training beyond the four years will simply have elitist effects unless large sums of money are made available not just in "forgiveable" tuition loans but in outright grants for living expenses, books, and so on. Absent this much more extensive financial commitment, the outcome of the Holmes Group recommendations will be to ultimately make it more difficult for less economically advantaged individuals to become teachers. Without such extensive financial support, movements to increase the amount of time spent in teacher education should be resisted, since their class- and race-stratifying effects could be massive.

The economic issues do not end here, however. Other elements of the report need further thought as well. The plan to have differentiated staffing patterns, for example, has major economic implications that may be hidden beneath the meritorious goals of the Holmes Group. In arguing for changes in the constitution of teaching we must realize that we live in the real world, a world of declining revenues, of anger over school budgets, of pressure to cut educational costs as much as possible. I do not like this situation, but it will not go away. These conditions—caused in large part by the fiscal crisis of the state[8]—are already creating immense pressures on local school districts to hire the least expensive teachers possible. With differentiated staffing, I would predict that many school systems will attempt to minimize costs by hiring as many Instructors as possible. These short-term, nontenured appointments would save districts a good deal of money. Pension costs would be minimal. There would be a continual large turnover of staff, even more than today. Thus, the bulk of the teaching force would be made up of those people who have less than five years seniority. The salary savings here would be enormous. The fiction of a reprofessionalized teaching force might be maintained, but there would be considerable pressure to minimize the number of Professional Teachers and to keep to a bare minimum the number of Career Professionals. The fiscal crisis is not a fiction, as anyone who works with school budgets knows. Any plan to differentiate teaching that does not include serious proposals to deal with the possible management offensive to cut costs that will undoubtedly arise from such plans is not as complete as it should be.

These economic points have important implications. The Holmes Group, as a group made up primarily of deans of major research institutions, needs to engage in intense and concerted lobbying and to put pressure on state legislatures and the federal government not only in support of its proposals, but just as importantly for considerable sums of money for students in these extended programs to live on. This can be accomplished only if organizations such as the Holmes Group join with others in questioning where financial resources are now going (i.e., into "defense," corporate tax "relief," etc.). Absent such alterations in our current "income transfer policies" (in which funding for human programs is transferred, say, to the military), the resources available to actually make a long-term difference will probably be insufficient. This may be hard for educators like ourselves to deal with, but we need to face up to how very complicated and far reaching the dilemmas we face actually are and what may actually be required to solve them.

Furthermore, guarantees need to be given by every school district that accepts models of differentiated staffing and career ladders similar to those proposed by the Holmes Group about the hiring ratios. This too will require money for financially crisis-ridden communities and will again require a significant reorientation of spending priorities at all levels, but especially at the national level. There are plans available for such changes both in spending priorities and in social goals, some of which are insightful and detailed. These take the common good, not only the needs of business, industry, and the Right, as their starting point, and integrate educational planning into proposals for more democratic planning in general.[9] These plans provide a platform on which we can stand and from which we can see the role of education in its larger context. I am afraid that without movement toward these kinds of more general changes, reports like that of the Holmes Group may play into the hands of the conservative restoration.

Let me raise one final caution. In a document produced by representatives of many of the major research institutions in education, it is not surprising that a faith in "science" as the primary road to pedagogic and curricular "progress" should be evident. I must admit, however, to having some serious reservations about the claim in *Tomorrow's Teachers* that the "promise of science of education is about to be fulfilled" (p. 52). The very metaphor of a science education is problematic. Education may not in fact "progress" in quite the same manner as even the most applied of the sciences.[10]

If by science we mean the more historical European idea of disciplined reason enlivened by a concern for value, that is one thing. If we mean a science in which the accumulation of atomistic facts that, when put together, will ultimately provide a strong empirical warrant for all we do in classrooms, that is another. Just as teaching itself is a complex assemblage of "thats," "hows," and "tos," so too is the study of pedagogy and curriculum. "Positive" science may provide a certain, actually rather limited, amount of insight into the process. Ultimately, however, decisions in and

about education are not technical, but ethical and political.[11] Whatever its glory, the history of the search for a science of education has also been the history of the transformation of educational discourse from a concern with *why* X should be taught to *how* to do it. The difficult and intensely valuative questions of content (of what knowledge is of most worth) and of teaching (of how to teach fairly and in an ethically responsive, not only efficient, manner) have been pushed to the background in our attempts to determine a set of technical procedures that will "solve" all of the problems we face.

Clearly, the report *does* recognize some of this dynamic, and in the struggle for respect and necessary resources, the notion of a science of education may be important rhetorically. After all, educators deserve respect and cannot fully succeed with the all too limited human and material resources now made available to them. However, we should not confuse the use of science as what might be called a rhetoric of justification with the much more complicated process of deliberation, conflict, and compromise that constitutes the real world of educational work.

Do not misinterpret me. There *is* a need for research. Much that goes on in classrooms *can* benefit from a closer "empirical" (interpreted as broadly as possible)[12] look and the quantitative and qualitative methods developed by social and educational researchers are essential, though not totally sufficient, tools in illuminating what is actually happening in schooling. Yet, so much of the weakest kind of educational theory and practice—overly competency based instruction, systems management, reductive accountability schemes, the construction of management systems that deskill teachers, and so on—has been justified by the claim to scientificity that I think we should be very careful of the latent effects of the current resurgence of "scientific approaches" to curriculum and teaching even when it is supported in such an articulate fashion as in *Tomorrow's Teachers*. Not only must we insist on the best of science—a commodity in rarer supply in education than we would like to admit given our propensity to borrow the reconstructed logic of science, not its logic in use[13]—but we need to avoid patterning all of education on science itself. Education is simply too ethically and politically complicated, too valuative, to be totally capturable by such a language system.

Let me repeat that even with all this said, I do have sympathy with many of the positions taken in the report. However, because of the social context in which it appears and because it has chosen to highlight certain elements in its arguments over others, its reception may signal something less than what its proponents hoped for. On a national level, the report may be used to largely justify mass testing of teachers of a very inflexible kind and a further move toward "scientific" curriculum making and competency-based teaching and teacher education. It can thereby actually depower, not empower, the very teachers the Holmes Group wishes to support.[14] At a state level, it may have the effect of reinforcing legislative intervention in the name of accountability and cost-cutting. On a local level, a number of its proposals may be used by financially troubled administrators and antagonists of teachers' unions to staff their schools with the cheapest teachers available.

These are all *possibilities*, not definites. Given the sensitivity and intelligence evident in so much of the report of the Holmes Group, and given the quality of the people involved in it, I trust that the next stages of their deliberations will take these issues into account. If they are not taken seriously, the Right, corporate America, and the efficiency experts who now pretend to be educators in the richest sense of that term will win. It will be the teachers and students who will suffer the loss. This will be at a cost that will be more than a little damaging not only to their futures but to all of ours as well.

Notes

1. For further discussion of the relationship between gender, class, and teaching, see Michael W. Apple, *Teachers and Texts; A Political Economy of Class and Gender Relations in Education* (New York: Routledge & Kegan Paul, 1987); and Sara Freedman, "Master Teacher/Merit Pay—Weeding Out Women from 'Women's True Profession,' " *Radical Teacher* 25 (November 1983): 24-28

2. Apple, *Teachers and Texts;* and Alice Kessler-Harris, *Out to Work* (New York: Oxford University Press, 1982).

3. See Michael W. Apple, *Education and Power* (Boston: Routledge & Kegan Paul, 1982); and Andrew Gitlin, "School Structure and Teachers' Work," in *Ideology and Practice in Schooling,* ed. Michael W. Apple and Lois Weis (Philadelphia: Temple University Press, 1983), pp. 193-212.

4. Apple, *Education and Power,* especially ch. 4.

5. Apple, *Teachers and Texts.* See also Ira Shor, *Culture Wars* (New York: Routledge & Kegan Paul, 1986).

6. See Francis Fox Piven and Richard A. Cloward, *The New Class War* (New York: Pantheon Books, 1982).

7. See, for example, Robert L. Heilbroner, *The Nature and Logic of Capitalism* (New York: Norton, 1985); Joshua Cohen and Joel Rogers, *On Democracy* (New York: Penguin Books, 1983); and Martin Carnoy, Derek Shearer, and Russell Rumberger, *A New Social Contract* (New York: Harper & Row, 1983).

8. See Manuel Castells, *The Economic Crisis and American Society* (Princeton: Princeton Universtiy Press, 1980); James O'Conner, *The Fiscal Crisis of the State* (New York: St. Martin's Press, 1973); and Apple, *Education and Power.*

9. Among the best is the masterful analysis and set of proposals in Marcus Raskin, *The Common Good* (New York: Routledge & Kegan Paul, 1987). I do not fully agree with all of Raskin's proposals for education, however.

10. Francis Schrag, "Knowing and Doing," *American Journal of Education* 89 (May 1981): 253-82.

11. This is discussed in more detail in Michael W. Apple, *Ideology and Curriculum* (Boston: Routledge & Kegan Paul, 1979). See also Dwayne Huebner, "Curricular Language and Classroom Meanings," in *Language and Meaning,* ed. James B. Macdonald and Robert R. Leeper (Washington: Association for Supervision and Curriculum Development, 1966), pp. 8-26.

12. See Eric Bredo and Walter Feinberg, eds. *Knowledge and Values in Social and Educational Research* (Philadelphia: Temple University Press, 1982).

13. Abraham Kaplan, *The Conduct of Inquiry* (San Francisco: Chandler Publishing Co., 1964).

14. See Michael W. Apple and Kenneth Teitelbaum, "Are Teachers Losing Control of Their Skills and Curriculum?," *Journal of Curriculum Studies* 18 (April-June 1986): 177-84.

Index

Abington v. Schempp, and prayer in schools, 146, 147

academic standards, public opinion on raising, 33

academic performance: and drugs, 129; relationship of, with good behavior, 129, 132, 133

Adler v. Board of Education, and teacher rights, 150

administration: vs. faculty, 7; *see also,* principal; superintendent

adolescent development, effect of drugs on, 192, 193

AFT, *see* American Federation of Teachers (AFT)

alcohol, and school children, 129, 130, 189, 190, 193

Americans United for the Separation of Church and State, 119

Anthony, Susan B., 18

applied ethics, 116, 117

appropriate public education, and handicapped children, 176–179

assaults, and crime in schools, 130, 131

basics, public opinion on importance of stressing, 35

behavior, relationship of, with academic performance, 129, 132

bilingual education, 158–164

Board of Education v. Allen, 145

Boston Safe Schools Commission, and crime in schools, 132

Black, Justice Hugo, and prayer in schools, 146

board certification, 213

books, censorship of, in school, 168, 169

boys, and classroom sexism, 165–167

brain, and effect of drugs on, 189, 190

Brown v. Board of Education, 8, 148–149, 151, 158

burnout, teacher, and crime in schools, 130

business, as ally of schools, 24, 31

busing, and U.S. Supreme Court, 148

"career education," 11

"career ladder," 30

Career Professionals, 88, 89, 92, 94

Carnegie Forum's Task Force on Education and the Economy, 92–97

censorship: and controversy over treatment of religion in school textbooks, 120, 121, 123; in schools, 168–173

certification: alternative paths to, 29; and need for reforms, 203; testing teachers for, 213–221

character education, 12, 36, 100–107

child abuse: characteristics of adults who commit, 186; indicators of, 185, 186; reporting of, 187, 188; role of teacher in preventing, 184–188

child-centeredness, vs. subject-centeredness, 9–11

child development, effect of drugs on, 192, 193

child guidance, 135–139

children: and drug abuse in school, 129, 130, 189–195; handicapped, and legally appropriate programs for, 176–179; identity needs of interracial, 152–157; and self-esteem, 180–183; status of, in U.S., 22–27; and teacher involvement

in preventing child abuse, 184–188; temper in, and learning self-control, 140–141

Children's Defense Fund, 26

China, education reform in, 68–73

church, and civic virtue, 103

citizenship, and excellence/character education, 101

civic virtue, 101–107

civil rights, 8

Cluster School, failure of, 114, 115

cocaine, and drug use by school children, 189–195

cognitive education, in teacher education, 29

cognitive moral development, 111, 112, 113

college: graduation requirements, 11–12; teachers' vs. liberal arts, 89, 93

combat neurosis, and crime in schools, 130

Commission on Excellence in Education, 78

Committee for Public Education and Liberty v. Nyquist, 145, 146

community: concept of, and civic virtue, 104, 105; and moral education, 114

computers: 13; and schools in future, 225, 227

crime, in schools, 128–134

cross-race marriages, 153

"culturally deprived," 10

curriculum: high school, 11, 57; parental input on, 34; and debate over religion in school, 119–125, 146–148; effects of social and economic factors on, in future, 232–236; reform of teacher education, 29–30

Davis v. Page, 169

de facto segregation, 148

de jure segregation, 148

desegregation, U.S. Supreme Court cases on, 148, 149

"developmental lesson," teaching style, 59

Dewey, John, 9

differentiated staffing, 87, 88

direct instruction: alternatives to, 59, 62–63; characteristics of, 61–62

disabled children, and educationally appropriate programs for, 178, 179

discipline: avoiding problems with, 136; and child guidance, 135–139; and relationship between good behavior and academic performance, 129, 132, 133; vs. punishment, 135; research on problem of, in United States, 128–134

dropout rate, 85

drugs/drug abuse, 129, 130, 189–195

economics, program to teach, to elementary school children, 49–54

economy: and education, 92–97; and education in China, 72, 73

education: in China, 70, 72, 73; and desegregation, 148–149; relationship of, with economy, 92–97; in future, 224–241; in Japan, 74, 75; lack of stated purpose of, 6–14; and prayer in schools, 119, 146–148; U.S. Supreme Court on, 144–151

educational change: changing attitudes toward, 78–83; *see also,* school reform

educationally appropriate special programs, and handicapped children, 176–179

education vs. liberal arts courses, for teacher preparation, 66–67

educators, *see* teachers

"effective schools," an example of, 55–60

Engle v. Vital, and prayer in schools, 146, 147

English as a Second Language (ESL), 163, 164

enrollments: future, 24; since World War II, 7

entrance exams, college, 11

entrepreneurship, and program to teach economics to elementary school children, 45–48

Epperson v. Arkansas, and religion in public schools, 147

equality of opportunity, 12

establishment clause: 144; of the First Amendment, and controversy over treatment of religion in school textbooks, 119–125

ethnic identity, and children of interracial marriages, 152–157

ethics, and moral education, 116, 117

ethics-without-virtue, 118

Everson v. Board of Education, 144, 145, 147, 151

excellence/character movement, 100, 101

expectations, for students, 60

experiential education, and schools of the future, 224

faculty vs. administration, 7

Falwell, Jerry, 119

family, and civic virtue, 103

federal government: role of, in education, 8; role of, in needs of children, 24–27; public opinion on role of, in education, 35–36; role of, in school reform, 25

feminization of teaching, 18

First Amendment: establishment clause of, and treatment of religion in school textbooks, 119–125; and issue of religion before U.S. Supreme Court, 144, 145; and teachers' rights, 149, 150

five-year teacher preparation program, pros and cons of, 66–67

Footnote Eleven, and separate but equal doctrine, 148

Fourteenth Amendment, and power of U.S. Supreme Court to overturn state law, 144

future, and trends in educating children, 224–236

Gallup Poll, of public's attitudes toward public schools, 32–41

girls, and sexism in classroom, 165–167

grade inflation, 57

Gramm-Rudman-Hollings legislation, 25

Great Awakening, 120

Green v. New Kent County, and desegregation, 148, 149

Grove v. Mead, and censorship in schools, 171

guidance, and discipline, 135

handicapped children: and legally appropriate programs for, 176–179; and minimum competency laws, 80

Head Start program, 26

hidden curriculum, 113
higher education, 71, 72, 74, 75
high school, example of an effective, 56–60
history: American and controversy over treatment of religion in school textbooks, 119–125; of teacher education, 15–21
Hobbs, Thomas, 101
Holmes Group Report, 84, 86–97
humanistic education, 110

identity, and needs of interracial marriages, 152–157
immersion, language and bilingual education, 161, 162
Individual Education Program (IEP), 80, 177, 227, 228
individualism, and Immanuel Kant, 101
individual responsibility, 118
interactive cable television, and schools of future, 227
interracial children, identity needs of, 152–157

Japan, education in, 74, 75
job training, and schools in future, 230
juku, 75
just community, 115

Keyishian v. Board of Regents: and religion in public schools, 147; and teacher rights, 150
key schools, and education in China, 71
Kohlberg, Lawrence, and moral development, 112–114
Kourilsky, Marilyn L., Mini-Society program of, 49–54

labeling, and interracial children, 156
lag time, for educational reform, 9, 10, 13
language immersion, and bilingual education, 161, 162
language learning, research on, 63
learning: effect of misbehavior on classroom, 130–133; research on language, 63
Lemon v. Kurtzman, 145
liberal arts education, and teacher training, 18, 39, 89, 93
liberal individualism, 101, 102
"life-adjustment education," 11
literature, in high school curriculum, 57
Locke, John, 101
low vs. high cognitive skills, need for multiple teaching strategies for, 62–64
loyalty oath law, 150

mainstreaming, 80
Marbury v. Madison, and desegregation of schools, 48
marijuana, and school children, 189–195
Marland, Sidney, Jr., 11
marriages, and identity needs of children of interracial, 152–157
medical education, teacher education compared to, 95, 96
methodology, as priority in teacher education, 20
middle schools, in China, 70
military personnel, and interracial marriages, 153
mind sex, and sexism in the classroom, 166
minimum competency laws, 79, 80

Mini-Society, program to teach economics to elementary children, 49–54
misbehavior: relationship of, with academic behavior, 129; relationship of, with effective teaching, 130, 131, 132, 133
mistaken behavior, three levels of, 136, 137
moral agnosticism, 116
moral consensus, 103, 104
moral education, 108–118, 122
morality, and controversy over treatment of religion in school textbooks, 119–125
Moral Majority, 119
Mozert v. Hawkins County Public Schools, 17, 172
Mueller v. Allen, 145, 146
Murray v. Curlett, and prayer in schools, 146
Murrow High School of Brooklyn, New York, as example of an effective school, 56–60

National Children's Center, 26
National Coalition of Advocates for Students (NCAS), 26
National Council for the Social Studies (NCSS), and religion in textbooks, 124
National Education Association (NEA), 7
National Education Commission, powers of, in China, 69, 70
National Institute of Education (NIE), and discipline in schools, 129, 130, 131
Nation at Risk, A, 78, 84–86
Nation Prepared, A, and evaluation of Holmes Group Report, 92–97
NEA, see National Education Association (NEA)
nineteenth century, teaching in, 16

parents, and child abuse, 184–188
peer evaluation, for teacher education, 30
Pickering v. Board of Education, and teacher rights, 150
Plessy v. Ferguson, and segregation, 148
pluralism, concept of, and school curriculum, 122, 123
politics, and issue of textbook treatment of religion, 122
poor, children of, 22–27
positive group management, and child guidance, 135, 136, 137
poverty, of children in America, 22–27
prayer in schools: 119, 146–148; see also, school prayer
precensorship, 170
Presidential Responsibility System, 72
primary education: in China, 70; in Japan, 74
principal, role of, 45–48
professional development schools, and teacher training, 67, 90
professional education: and teacher training, 89; see also, schools of education; teacher college; teacher education; teacher training
professional teachers, and Holmes Group Report, 88, 89, 92, 94, 95, 96
progressive education, 9–10
Proposition 13, impact of, on children's services, 25
Proposition 2½, impact of, on children's services, 25
Prosser, Charles, 11

public aid to nonpublic schools, and U.S. Supreme Court cases involving, 144–146
Public Education Research Studies Center (PERSC), 124
public good, concept of, and civic virtue, 104
Public Law 94-142, and controversy over legally appropriate programs, 176–179
public opinion, on public schools, 32–41
public roles, of teachers, 16, 17, 18
public schools: Gallup Poll of public's attitudes toward, 32–41; see also, schools
publishers, and controversy over treatment of religion in textbooks, 122, 123
punishment, distinction of, from discipline, 135–139
Puritanism, and controversy over treatment of religion in school textbooks, 120

reading instruction, research on, 62–63
Reagan, President, effects of budget cuts by, on children, 23, 25–26
Rehnquist, Justice William, 145
religion, controversy over treatment of, in school textbooks, 119–125
remedial instruction, and bilingual education, 161
Republicans, indifference of, to needs of today's children, 21
research: on language learning, 63; on reading instruction, 62–63; on teacher effectiveness, 62
robbery, and schools, 129

"Safe School Study," and discipline in schools, 129, 130, 131
salaries, of teachers, 17
school prayer: public opinion on, 37; see also, prayer in school
school reform: difficulty instituting, 45–48; influence of "A Nation at Risk" report on, 84, 85; see also, educational change
school reform movement, 25
schools: administrators view of, 44–48; and bilingual education, 158–164; censorship in, 168–173; in China, 68–73; and civic virtue, 103; criticism of public, 6–14; and desegregation, 148, 149; and discipline problems 128–134; and use of drugs by children, 189–195; "effective," 56–60 and education in the future, 224–236; and moral education, 108–110; prayer in, 37, 119, 146–148; professional development, for teachers, 90; responsibility of, 12; sexism in, 165–167; see also, public schools
schools of education: and need for better teacher training, 207–212; see also, professional education; teacher college; teacher education; teacher training
secular humanism, and controversy over treatment of religion in school textbooks, 119–125
secular vs. sectarian, and debate over aid to nonpublic schools, 145
self-concept, and child guidance theory, 135–139

self-control: and discipline vs. punishment, 135; helping students to learn, 140–141

self-esteem: and child guidance, 135–139; and controlling a hot-tempered child, 140, 141

self-image, 180–183

separate but equal doctrine, 148

sex education, public support for, in schools, 40

sexism, in classroom, 165–167

Shelton v. Tucker, and religion in public schools, 147; and teacher rights, 149, 150

"socialized recitation," teaching style, 59

social needs, of today's children, 23

social promotion, 57

social studies, in high school curriculum, 58

solution orientation, and discipline problems, 138, 139

staff development, 48

stereotyping, of children, 10

Stewart, Justice Potter, 146

stress: and child abuse, 186; and crime in schools, 130

students: and censorship, 172; as crime victims in schools, 129–131

student teaching, criticism of, 89, 90

Supreme Court, *see* U.S. Supreme Court

Swann v. Charlotte-Mecklenburg Board of Education, 149

tax credits, 83

teacher college: vs. liberal arts college, and teacher preparation, 18, 39, 89, 93; *see also,* professional education; schools of education; teacher education; teacher training

teacher education: linking, to community resources, 31; five-year requirement for, 66–67; history of, 15–21; vs. liberal arts education, 30; reform of, 15, 28–30, and Holmes Group report, 86–97; and other university disciplines, 30–31; *see also,* professional education; schools of education; teacher college; teacher training

teachers: loss of authority of, 59–60; and bilingual education, 160; and censorship in schools, 168–173; and certification testing, 213–221; effect of change on, 81; role of, in child abuse prevention, 184–188; as crime victims in schools, 129–131; and differentiated staffing, 87, 88; firing tenured, 59; and education in the future, 224, 226–231; 238–241; and handicapped children, 80; and hot-tempered children, 140, 141; role of, in identity needs of interracial children, 154, 155; importance of, to program success, 51; and approaches to deal with misbehavior, 135–139; in nineteenth century, 17–19; and helping students with self-esteem, 180–183; and sexism in classroom, 166, 167

teacher shortages, 15, 24

teachers' rights, and U.S. Supreme Court decisions concerning, 149, 150

teacher strikes, 7

teacher training: reform of, 86–97, 207–212; and teaching effective use of research findings, 64; undergraduate, 66–67; *see also,* professional education; schools of education; teacher college; teacher education

teaching; need to use multiple methods of, 62–64; in nineteenth century, 16–17; reforms in, 198–206; "socialized recitation" style of, 59

technology, and schools in the future, 225–231

telos, 102, 103, 104

temper, learning to control, by children, 140–141

tenure, grounds for firing teachers with, 59

testing, of teachers for certification, 213–221

textbooks, controversy over treatment of religion in school, 119–125

theft, and crime in schools, 130, 131

theocracy, 122

Tinker v. Des Moines, 150

Tomorrow's Teachers, and Holmes Group Report, 86–97

tracking, academic, 56

tradition, 105

transcendence, 105, 106

tuition tax credits, 121

undergraduate education, pros and cons of, for teacher training, 66, 67

U.S. Supreme Court: and bilingual education, 163; and censorship in schools, 168, 170; and education cases before, 144–151; and religion in schools, 119; *see also,* specific cases and issues

values clarification, and moral education, 111, 113

values education, and treatment of religion in school textbooks, 122

vandalism, 129

victimization, and crime in schools, 131

violence, in schools, 128–134

virtue: civic, 101–107; teaching of, 112, 113, 114, 115

Vitz, Paul, and controversy over treatment of religion in school textbooks, 120–123

vocational education: 9, 10; in China, 71

volunteers, school, 31

vouchers, 34, 83, 121

Widmar v. Vincent, and aid to nonpublic schools, 146

women, in teaching, 18

Credits/ Acknowledgments

Cover design by Charles Vitelli

1. Perceptions of Education in America
Facing overview—The Dushkin Publishing Group, Inc.

2. Continuity and Change in Education
Facing overview—Apple Computer, Inc. 68—Illustration by Harvey Chan.

3. The Struggle for Excellence
Facing overview—United Nations/Milton Grant.

4. Morality and Values in Education
Facing overview—United Nations/photo by F.B. Grunzweig. 109—Anna Kaufman Moon.

5. Discipline and Schooling
Facing overview—UNICEF photo.

6. Equal Opportunity and American Education
Facing overview—Apple Computer, Inc.

7. Serving Special Needs and Humanizing Instruction
Facing overview—United Nations/photo by S. Dimartini.

8. The Profession of Teaching Today
Facing overview—United Nations/photo by Marta Pintar. 207–212—Photos by David B. Sutton.

9. A Look to the Future
Facing overview—United Nations/photo by Y. Nagata. 226, 228-231—From "Informational Technology and Its Impact on American Education" (Washington, D.C.: U.S. Congress, Office of Technology Assessment, OTA-CIT-187, November 1982). 236—Mattel Toys.

We Want Your Advice

ANNUAL EDITIONS: EDUCATION 88/89
Article Rating Form

Here is an opportunity for you to have direct input into the next revision of this volume. We would like you to rate each of the 40 articles listed below, using the following scale:

1. **Excellent: should definitely be retained**
2. **Above average: should probably be retained**
3. **Below average: should probably be deleted**
4. **Poor: should definitely be deleted**

Your ratings will play a vital part in the next revision. So please mail this prepaid form to us just as soon as you complete it.
Thanks for your help!

Annual Editions revisions depend on two major opinion sources: one is our Advisory Board, listed in the front of this volume, which works with us in scanning the thousands of articles published in the public press each year; the other is you—the person actually using the book. Please help us and the users of the next edition by completing the prepaid article rating form on this page and returning it to us. Thank you.

Rating	Article	Rating	Article
	1. Schools: Cacophony About Practice, Silence About Purpose		20. The Treatment of Religion in School Textbooks: A Political Analysis and a Modest Proposal
	2. Learning from Experience: History and Teacher Education		21. Research Evidence of a School Discipline Problem
	3. The Prospect for Children in the United States		22. Punishment or Guidance?
	4. Professional Credibility Through Wider Links		23. Help for the Hot-Tempered Kid
	5. The 19th Annual Gallup Poll of the Public's Attitudes Toward the Public Schools		24. The Courts and Education
			25. Are You Sensitive to Interracial Children's Special Identity Needs?
	6. An Inside View of Change in Schools		26. The Bilingual Education Battle
	7. The Business of Talentville		27. Sexism in the Schoolroom of the '80s
	8. A Good School		28. Censorship in the Public Schools
	9. Helping Preservice Teachers Learn to Use Teacher Effectiveness Research		29. "Appropriate" School Programs: Legal vs. Educational Approaches
	10. Should Four-Year Education Major Be Ended?		30. Self-Esteem Success Stories
	11. Education Reform in China		31. Child Abuse and Neglect: Prevention and Reporting
	12. Learning About Education from Fifth Graders in Japan		32. Schoolchildren and Drugs: The Fancy That Has Not Passed
	13. Changing Our Thinking About Educational Change		33. Our Profession, Our Schools: The Case for Fundamental Reform
	14. School Reform: Recent Influences		34. On Stir-and-Serve Recipes for Teaching
	15. Tomorrow's Teachers: The Essential Arguments of the Holmes Group Report		35. Teaching Knowledge: How Do We Test It?
	16. The Holmes Group Report and the Professionalization of Teaching		36. Relearning to Teach: Peer Observation as a Means of Professional Development
	17. Repairing the Public-Private Split: Excellence, Character, and Civic Virtue		37. Educating Children for the Coming Century
	18. Moral Education in the United States		38. Schools of the Future
	19. Ethics Without Virtue: Moral Education in America		39. Curriculum in the Year 2000: Tensions and Possibilities
			40. Will the Social Context Allow a Tomorrow for Tomorrow's Teachers?

(cont. on next page)

ABOUT YOU

Name_____ Date_____

Are you a teacher? ☐ Or student? ☐

Your School Name _____

Department _____

Address _____

City _____ State _____ Zip _____

School Telephone # _____

YOUR COMMENTS ARE IMPORTANT TO US!

Please fill in the following information:

For which course did you use this book? _____

Did you use a text with this Annual Edition? ☐ yes ☐ no

The title of the text? _____

What are your general reactions to the Annual Editions concept?

Have you read any particular articles recently that you think should be included in the next edition?

Are there any articles you feel should be replaced in the next edition? Why?

Are there other areas that you feel would utilize an Annual Edition?

May we contact you for editorial input?

May we quote you from above?

EDUCATION 88/89

BUSINESS REPLY MAIL

First Class   Permit No. 84   Guilford, CT

Postage will be paid by addressee

**The Dushkin Publishing Group, Inc.
Sluice Dock
Guilford, Connecticut 06437**